THE JOHANNINE CORPUS IN THE EARLY CHURCH

The Johannine Corpus
in the Early Church

Charles E. Hill

OXFORD
UNIVERSITY PRESS

OXFORD
UNIVERSITY PRESS

Great Clarendon Street, Oxford ox2 6DP

Oxford University Press is a department of the University of Oxford.
It furthers the University's objective of excellence in research, scholarship,
and education by publishing worldwide in

Oxford New York

Auckland Bangkok Buenos Aires Cape Town Chennai
Dar es Salaam Delhi Hong Kong Istanbul Karachi Kolkata
Kuala Lumpur Madrid Melbourne Mexico City Mumbai Nairobi
São Paulo Shanghai Taipei Tokyo Toronto

Oxford is a registered trade mark of Oxford University Press
in the UK and in certain other countries

Published in the United States
by Oxford University Press Inc., New York

British Library Cataloguing in Publication Data
Data available

Library of Congress Cataloging in Publication Data
Data available
ISBN 0-19-926458-9

1 3 5 7 9 10 8 6 4 2

Typeset by Kolam Information Services Pvt. Ltd, Pondicherry
Printed in Great Britain
on acid-free paper by
Biddles Ltd,
King's Lynn.

ACKNOWLEDGEMENTS

The translation of the Bible customarily cited in this book is the Revised Standard Version. Much of the research for this book was done during the tenure of a Lilly Faculty Fellowship for the year 2000–1, administered through the Association of Theological Schools. I want to express my profound thanks to Maurice Wiles, Brian Daley, and Everett Ferguson, who supported my candidacy, to the administrators of this Fellowship, and to the board of Reformed Theological Seminary for granting me leave to accept it. Thanks also go to Dan Wright, Kevin Nelson, and Jennifer Redd for interlibrary loan help, to Jon Thompson and to Joyce Sisler for various forms of efficient clerical assistance, and to John and Kathy Muether for agreeing to compile an index. I wish to thank Lucy Qureshi at OUP for her advice and help at many points; June Brooks for her prayers; my beloved wife, Marcy, for the many sacrifices she has made over the years in support of this work; and my children, Sean, Charity, and Jamie, for putting up with 'the laptop'.

CONTENTS

LIST OF FIGURES AND TABLE

ABBREVIATIONS

Abbreviations of biblical books follow established usage.

AB	The Anchor Bible
ACW	Ancient Christian Writers
Adv. omn. haer.	Pseudo-Tertullian, *Adversus omnes haereses*
AJ	*Acts of John*
ANF	*Ante-Nicene Fathers*, ed. A. Roberts and J. Donaldson, 10 vols., rev. A. C. Coxe (repr. Grand Rapids, Mich., 1950–)
ANRW	*Aufsteig und Niedergang der romischen Welt: Geschichte und Kultur Roms in Spiegel der neueren Forschung*, ed. H. Temporini and W. Haase (Berlin, 1972–).
ANT	*The Apocryphal New Testament: A Collection of Apocryphal Christian Literature in an English Translation* (Oxford, 1993)
Ap. Jas.	*Apocryphon of James*
Ap. Jn.	*Apocryphon of John*
Apost. Const.	*Apostolic Constitutions*
ATANT	Abhandlungen zur Theologie des Alten und Neuen Testaments
Athenagoras	Athenagorus
—— *Plea*	—— *A Plea for the Christians*
Barl.	*Life of Barlaam and Joasaph*
BETL	Bibliotheca ephemeridum theologicarum lovaniensium
BHTh.	Beiträge zur historischen Theologie
BJRL	*Bulletin of the John Rylands University Library of Manchester*
BP	*Biblia Patristica: Index des citations et allusions bibliques dans la literature patristique. *Des origins à Clément d'Alexandrie et Tertullien* (Paris, 1986)
BZNW	Beihefte zur Zeitschrift für die neutestamentliche Wissenschaft
CBQ	*Catholic Biblical Quarterly*
Clement of Alexandria, *Ecl. Proph.*	Clement of Alexandria, *Eclogae propheticae*
—— *Fr. Cass.*	—— *Latin Fragments of Cassiodorus*

—— *Hypot.*	—— *Hypotyposeis*
—— *Paed.*	—— *Paedagogus*
—— *Protr.*	—— *Protreptikos*
—— *Qds*	—— *Quis diues salvetur*
—— *Strom.*	—— *Stromateis*
—— *Theod.*	—— *Excerpts from Theodotus*
Clement of Rome, *1 Clem.*	Clement of Rome, *1 Clement*
CSCO	Corpus scriptorum christianorum orientalium
CSEL	Corpus scriptorum ecclesiasticorum latinorum
Cyprian of Carthage, *Demetr.*	Cyprian of Carthage, *Ad Demetrianum*
—— *Ep.*	—— *Epistula*
Cyril of Jerusalem, *Catech. Lects.*	Cyril of Jerusalem, *Catechetical Lectures*
DB	*Dictionnaire de la Bible*
DCB	*Dictionary of Christian Biography*, ed. W. Smith and H. Wace, 4 vols. (London, 1877–87)
Diogn.	*Ad Diognetum*
Ep. Apost.	*Epistula Apostolorum*
ET	English translation
ETL	*Ephemerides theologicae lovanienses*
Eusebius, *Dem. Evang.*	Eusebius, *Demonstratio evangelica*
—— *HE*	—— *Historic Ecclesiastica*
FRLANT	Forschungen zur Religion und Literatur des alten und Neuen Testaments
GCS	Die griechische christliche Schriftsteller der ersten drei Jahhunderte
GP	*Gospel of Peter*
GT	*Gospel of Thomas*
GTr.	*Gospel of Truth*
Hippolytus, *Antichr.*	Hippolytus, *Treatise on Christ and Antichrist*
—— *Apost. Trad.*	—— *Apostolic Tradition*
—— *Noet.*	—— *Against Noetus*
—— *Ref.*	—— *Refutation of All Heresies*
HTR	*Harvard Theological Review*
HTS	Harvard Theological Studies
ID	The Interpreters Dictionary of the Bible
Ignatius, *IEph.*	Ignatius, *To the Ephesians*
IMagn.	—— *To the Magnesians*
IPhilad.	—— *To the Philadelphians*
IPolyc.	—— *To Polycarp*
Irenaeus, *AH*	Irenaeus, *Adversus Haereses*

—— *Dem.*   —— *Demonstration of the Apostolic Preaching*
—— *Ep. Flor.*   —— *Epistle to Florinus*
—— *Ep. Vict.*   —— *Epistle to Victor*
—— *Fr.*   —— *Fragment*
Ignatius
IRom.   —— *To the Romans*
ISmyrn.   —— *To the Smyrnaeans*
ITr.   —— *To the Trallians*
JBL   *Journal of Biblical Literature*
JECS   *Journal of Early Christian Studies*
JEH   *Journal of Ecclesiastical History*
Jerome, *De vir. Illust.*   Jerome, *De viris illustribus*
—— *Ep.*   —— *Epistle*
JSNT Sup.   Journal for the Study of the New Testament: Supplement Series
JSP   *Journal for the Study of the Pseudepigrapha*
JTS   *Journal of Theological Studies*
Justin, *1Apol.*   Justin, *1 Apology*
—— *2Apol.*   —— *2 Apology*
—— *Dial.*   —— *Dialogue with Trypho the Jew*
Lactantius, *D. Inst.*   Lactantius, *Divine Institutes*
LCC   Library of Christian Classics (Philadelphia, 1953–   )
LCL   Loeb Classical Library
LE   Longer Ending of Mark
LHH   *The Apostolic Fathers: Greek Texts and English Translations*, updated edn. of *The Apostolic Fathers: Greek Texts and English Translations of their Writings*, 2nd edn., ed. and tr. J. B. Lightfoot and J. R. Harmer, ed. and revised Michael W. Holmes (Grand Rapids, Mich., 1999)
LSJ   *A Greek–English Lexicon*, compiled by Henry George Liddell and Robert Scott, revised and augmented by Henry Stuart Jones *et al.*, 9th edn. (Oxford, 1968)
Mand.   Mandates
Mart. Polyc.   *Martyrdom of Polycarp*
MF   *Muratorian Fragment* (or *Canon*)
NA²⁷   Nestle-Aland, *Novum Testamentum Graece*, ed. Barbara Aland *et al.*, 27th edn. (Stuttgart, 1993).
NHC   Nag Hammadi Codices

NHS	Nag Hammadi Studies
NHLE³	*Nag Hammadi Library in English*, ed. J. M. Robinson, 3rd rev. edn. (San Francisco, 1990)
Nov. T.	*Novum Testamentum*
Nov. T. Suppl.	Supplement to *Novum Testamentum*
NPNF	*A Select Library of Nicene and Post-Nicene Fathers of the Christian Church*, 2nd series, 14 vols., ed. Philip Schaff and Henry Wace (New York, 1890–1900)
NT	New Testament
NTA²	*New Testament Apocrypha*, rev. edn., 2 vols., ed. Wilhelm Schneemelcher, ET ed. Robert McLachlan Wilson (Cambridge, 1991)
NTAF	*The New Testament in the Apostolic Fathers* (Oxford, 1905)
NTS	*New Testament Studies*
NTTS	New Testament Tools and Studies
Odes Sol.	*Odes of Solomon*
OECT	Oxford Early Christian Texts, ed. H. Chadwick (Oxford, 1970)
OJP	the orthodox Johannophobia paradigm
Origen, *C. Cels.*	Origen, *Contra Celsum*
—— *C. John*	—— *Commentary on John*
—— *C. Matt.*	—— *Commentary on Matthew*
—— *C. Rom.*	—— *Commentary on Romans*
—— *De orat.*	—— *De oratione*
—— *Hom. Luke*	—— *Homilies on Luke*
OT	Old Testament
OTP	*Old Testament Pseudepigrapha*, ed. J. H. Charlesworth, 2 vols. (New York, 1983)
Panar.	*Panarion*
PGL	*A Patristic Greek Lexicon, with Addenda et Corrigenda*, ed. G. W. H. Lampe (Oxford, 1987)
Photius, *Bibl.*	Photius, *Bibliotheca*
Polycarp, *Phil.*	Polycarp, *To the Philippians*
P. Pasch.	Melito of Sardis, *Peri Pascha*
Ps. Barn.	*Epistle of Pseudo Barnabas*
Pseudo-Clement, *Hom.*	Pseudo-Clement, *Homilies*
—— *Recogn.*	—— *Recognitions*
Ptolemy, *Flor.*	Ptolemy, *Letter to Flora*
PTS	Patristische Texte und Studien

RB	*Revue biblique*
RE	*Realencyklopadie*
SBL	Society of Biblical Literature
SC	Sources chrétiennes (Paris, 1943–)
Sec. Apoc. Jas.	*Second Apocalypse of James*
SGM	*Secret Gospel of Mark*
Sib. Or.	*Sibylline Oracles*
Sim.	Similitudes
Tatian, *Diatess.*	Tatian, *Diatessaron*
—— *Or.*	—— *Oratio*
Tertullian, *An.*	Tertullian, *De anima*
—— *Apol.*	—— *Apologeticum*
—— *Bapt.*	—— *De baptismo*
—— *Carne*	—— *De carne Christi*
—— *Fuga*	—— *De fuga in persecutione*
—— *Herm.*	—— *Adversus Hermogenem*
—— *Marc.*	—— *Adversus Marcionem*
—— *Monog.*	—— *De monogamia*
—— *Praescr.*	—— *De praescriptione haereticorum*
—— *Prax.*	—— *Adversus Praxeam*
—— *Pud.*	—— *De pudicitia*
—— *Scap.*	—— *Ad Scapulam*
—— *Val.*	—— *Adversus Valentinianos*
TLZ	*Theologische Literaturzeitung*
TP	*Trimorphic Protennoia*
TRE	*Theologische Realenzyklopadie*, ed. G. Krause and G. Muller (Berlin, 1977–)
TU	*Texte und Untersuchungen*
TZ	*Theologische Zeitschrift*
VC	*Vigilae christianae*
VC Suppl.	Supplement to *Vigilae christianae*
Victorinus of Pettau, *CA*	Victorinus of Pettau, *Commentary on the Apocalypse*
Vis.	Visions
WBC	Word Biblical Commentary
WMANT	Wissenschaftliche Monographien zum Alten und Neuen Testaments
WTJ	*Westminster Theological Journal*
WUNT	Wissenschaftliche Untersuchungen zum Neuen Testament
ZAC	*Zeitschrift für Antikes Christentum/Journal of Ancient Christianity*
ZNW	*Zeitschrift für die neutestamentliche Wissenschaft und die Kunde der älteren Kirche*

Introduction

The subject of the formation of the New Testament canon is of perennial interest among both students and practitioners of Christianity. While the idea of canon is a theological idea, and the postulation of a canon is not fully supportable from purely historical study, clear and profitable thinking on it does require a lot of toilsome—but for some, fascinating—historical work. The early Christian sources can tell us much about how the idea of a collection of Christian scripture took hold in the Church, and much about the process of canon forming. The motivation behind the present project is the wish to shed light on the origin of one very significant portion of the New Testament canon, the Johannine corpus, and the process by which these books were recognized as scripture within the Church at large.

Anyone very familiar with Christianity will also have some impression of how influential in this religion are those books which have traditionally gone under the name of John the son of Zebedee, the apostle of Jesus: the Gospel according to John, the First, Second, and Third Epistles of John, and the Revelation of John. Yet despite their profound and far-reaching impact upon Christian theology, piety, art, and even upon modern, secular culture, nearly every aspect of the origins and early reception of these books is obscure and has been under dispute for quite some time. The model which for decades has been dominant in Johannine studies has often been criticized as highly conjectural but has retained its supremacy in the absence of a more thorough and convincing alternative. Though there are important differences among scholars holding to this basic model, several characteristics are commonly agreed upon today. One is the tendency to recognize multiple stages of writing within the Fourth Gospel, and within the entire corpus, corresponding roughly to describable stages in the history of the 'Johannine community'. Usually from four to seven distinct individuals, including a 'beloved disciple', an 'evangelist', one or more Gospel redactors, at least one 'elder' and a seer named John, are thought to have been involved in the production of the Johannine corpus, and this is not counting the 'elders' which are often said to stand behind the plural 'we' in John 21: 24.

A passing acquaintance with Christian sources of the second century shows that this kind of sophistication was utterly lost upon them. It appears that only one, or at most two, persons by the name of John were known as the authors of the entire corpus, and the geographical setting of the Apocalypse in Asia Minor is, as far as we can tell, accepted as the backdrop for the other books as well. There is certainly an ample amount of legend in the remaining second-century depictions of 'John' and his alleged writings, and in anyone's estimation the evidence presents quite a mixed bag. But even the most sober and 'documented' reports are often dismissed simply for their departures from the current scholarly consensus. This points to another characteristic of the model under discussion, and that is its predominantly negative evaluation of the extent and the quality of the second-century evidence pertaining to the origins of the Johannine works. The recent work of Martin Hengel is an outstanding exception to this trend, but his work is itself largely outside and opposed to this model.[1] Whether or not one agrees with Hengel's answer to 'the Johannine Question', his alternative is clearly rooted in and characterized by a greater respect for the second-century materials in their own terms.

It is not, however, that Johannine scholarship in general has ignored the second century altogether or has considered it inconsequential. While the witnesses, by and large, are not taken to be particularly credible in their claims about Johannine origins, what they disclose of the respective reactions to the Johannine Gospel on the part of orthodox and heterodox[2] writers of the period is considered of prime importance. In a word, the reception of this Gospel by heterodox groups is said to have been swift and enthusiastic, while among the orthodox it endured a long and mighty struggle for acceptance, until about the time of Irenaeus.

For some time the inadequacies of certain elements of the common model have been apparent to some (myself included), but, as was already noted, there has been no broad, well-researched, and convincing alternative available. The present project on the rise of the Johannine corpus, of which this volume is the first planned instalment,[3] is an attempt to lay foundations for a model of the origin and reception of this corpus in the Church which is less speculative and more thoroughly grounded in both the internal and the early, external evidence. This volume, *The Johannine Corpus in the Early Church*, is a study of the emergence of the 'Johannine corpus' as Christian scripture in the nascent orthodox and heterodox communities of the second century.

As was said, it is widely believed that John's Gospel was used first, more regularly, and with a greater sense of its scriptural authority by those outside the mainstream of the Church. As far as we know, it found its first commentator in a man named Heracleon, an influential Valentinian teacher of the late second century. That the (orthodox) Church of the

---

[1] Martin Hengel, *The Johannine Question* (London, 1989); *idem*, *Die johanneische Frage. Ein Lösungsversuch*, with a contribution on the Apocalypse by Jörg Frey, WUNT 67 (Tübingen, 1993).

[2] For reflection on my use of the terms 'orthodox' and 'heterodox', see below.

[3] Some indication of the envisaged, future volumes is here in order. A second volume intends to examine the controversy which lies behind the rupture reported in 1 John 2: 18–19 and echoed elsewhere, and the part it played in the origin and reception of these books. A third volume will centre on the question of the authorship and authorial setting for each of these books.

second century was quite reluctant to use the Gospel of John, not only because of its differences with the Synoptic Gospels, but chiefly because of its widespread use, and possible origin, in gnostic or heterodox circles, has become a scholarly commonplace. So deep was the affinity for this Gospel among Valentinians and gnostics, and so close was its identification with these groups in the popular Christian mind, that many Church leaders suspected it or opposed it. This is the phenomenon we shall be calling 'orthodox Johannophobia'. Before the Fourth Gospel could find general acceptance it had to be 'rescued' by Irenaeus of Lyons and others, who were able to promote its use by capitalizing on its associations with the apostle John and by showing how it could actually be used against the heretics themselves.

This understanding of the second-century Church's regard for the Fourth Gospel has been a force in the academic study of early Christianity for a long time, and its effects are sometimes seen in the Church as well. With many in Church leadership having been trained under this model it is perhaps no wonder that John's Gospel (particularly in its Christology) is sometimes thought to be more than a little tinged with gnosticism. The legitimacy of this Gospel's place in the Church's canon of scripture is thus, for some, under a shroud. The study of the original character and early reception of the Gospel of John, then, has potentially significant implications both for present-day theologizing and preaching, and for the understanding of Christian origins as it is portrayed in the academy and therefore in other public media as well.

While major studies devoted to the early reception of the Fourth Gospel have been surprisingly rare enough, none in recent decades has attempted in any intentional way to address the fortunes of all five members of the Johannine corpus. This is understandable simply from a consideration of the scope of the task involved, but it may also be said that the predominant model, with its assumptions about diverse origins and sometimes clashing roles for the books in the course of Johannine community history, has not encouraged a unified approach. Though the focus of the present study will be on the Fourth Gospel, not only shall attention be paid to the other Johannine books, as making up part of a recognizable unit of the eventual NT canon, but it will become clear that there are sound contextual reasons for doing so. After a certain point in the second century an awareness of a Johannine literary corpus is a real factor in considering even the fortunes of the Fourth Gospel alone.

A Note on the Terminology of 'Orthodox' and 'Heterodox'

There are problems with naming the competing parties within Christendom in the second century. The use of the words 'orthodox' and 'catholic', or 'heterodox', 'sectarian' and 'heretical', for the second century is subject to criticism, not only as being anachronistic, as such terms are sometimes taken to be importations of fourth-century standards into the second, but also as being partisan, as using the terms in their traditional sense may seem to take the side of the 'winning' faction in the controversies. Some scholars therefore prefer to use the terms 'proto-orthodox' or 'proto-catholic' to describe people or churches in the second century. But while this may alleviate the impression of anachronism, it does not necessarily eliminate the charge of favouring the terminology of the winning side. Moreover, it also carries the disadvantage of defining a thing in terms of what it will (or presumably will) become, not by what it is. Its point of reference is even more explicitly the fourth century rather than the second, and it assumes a continuity between the second and fourth centuries which could in some cases be open to challenge itself.

The charge of anachronism, however, should not be made more serious than it is. For, even in the absence of any official definitions promulgated by Church councils or imperial decrees, it is not as if there were no fairly clear and widely agreed-upon lines of demarcation in the second century (even when conscious attempts were made to blur the lines). We have all come to appreciate the variety of the forms of Christianity in the early centuries of its existence. And at least since the publication of Walter Bauer's *Rechtgläubigkeit und Ketzerei im ältesten Christentum* in 1934,[4] many have considered a wonderfully boisterous diversity to have been the norm throughout the first and second centuries, with no single network—certainly no recognizably 'orthodox' network—on hand which held at the same time a cohesive set of beliefs and a numerical majority among the churches. It is sometimes held that whatever unity might seem to characterize a number of the surviving sources is due more than anything else to the stark and simple fact that these were the documents selected to be preserved by the side that eventually won. 'It is the winners who write the histories' and who preserve the documents. My own experience with the second-century data has made me sceptical of this approach. Amid the many diversities which existed among earlier writers who are usually regarded as playing for the side which eventually won, certain theological[5] commonalities are clearly visible, many of which also served as boundaries between them and many of the 'losers'. These included critical aspects of the Christian views of God, creation, Christ, humanity, and salvation. If, for instance, one affirmed the existence of a Supreme Being above the Creator of the physical universe, if one believed that the misguided Creator's creation was inherently flawed and irredeemable, that likewise only that aspect of humanity which origin-

---

[4] Walter Bauer, *Rechtgläubigkeit und Ketzerei im ältesten Christentum* (Tübingen, 1934), ET, *Orthodoxy and Heresy in Earliest Christianity* (Philadelphia, 1971).

[5] This is not to deny that there were sociological dimensions to the formation of 'orthodoxy' and 'heresy'.

ated from a supercelestial source could return to its own essence and be saved, if one embraced a Christology which eschewed a real union of the divine and the human, and which downplayed the reality or redemptive significance of the death of Jesus, and if one were open and honest about these affirmations,[6] more than likely one would not be admitted to any position of authority in a church known as 'catholic'.

To some extent, even the terminology in question was present and evolving in the second century. Ignatius uses the adjective καθολική to describe ἡ ἐκκλησία in the early years of the second century (*ISmyrn.* 8. 2). Though it is debatable just what weight is borne by the term in this context, it at least includes the notion of universality, a universality that was threatened by elements Ignatius perceived to be present at that time in Smyrna.[7] And even if we cannot know for certain whether he was using the term in order to exclude the docetic elements in Smyrna and elsewhere, to judge from the perspective of his letters, he could have done so. By the time the author of the *Epistula Apostolorum* wrote, still in the first half of the second century, 'the Catholics' (1. 1) was a title evidently meant to exclude the factions against which he wrote, which promoted a docetic Christology. The author of the *Martyrdom of Polycarp* in the 150s used the term ἡ καθολικὴ ἐκκλησία four times (*praef.*; 8. 1; 16. 2; 19. 2) in describing the Church in which Polycarp had served as bishop. The catholic Church in the *Muratorian Fragment* (lines 61–2, 66)[8] is said to receive certain writings and to reject others. The language of 'orthodoxy' is not as well-attested, but it too is developing. The author of the *Ad Diognetum* speaks of the disciple who has been 'rightly taught' (ὀρθῶς διδαχθείς). His use may or may not have any reference to the ecclesiastical debates that we are speaking about, but it does indicate the currency of the terminology and implies a contrast with those who are not rightly taught. Justin, who elsewhere commends 'right reason' (ὀρθός λόγος, *Dial.* 3. 3; *2Apol.* 9. 4), acknowledges that there are some 'called Christians' who blaspheme the God of Abraham, Isaac, and Jacob, and thinks they have no right to that title. He distinguishes himself and others from them with the phrase 'those who are right-minded (ὀρθογνώμονες) Christians on all points' (*Dial.* 80. 5).[9] Irenaeus too speaks of those who have 'rightly believed' (*recte credidisse*—the Greek was probably

[6] If we may believe Irenaeus, it was sometimes a problem that those who held views like these were able to confess one thing publicly and teach another privately (*AH* 3. 16. 8; 4. 32. 1; 33. 3).

[7] W. R. Schoedel, *Ignatius of Antioch*, Hermeneia (Philadelphia, 1985), 243, 'Opposition to division plays some role in Ignatius' reference to the catholic church, for the sentence is immediately preceded and immediately followed by statements attacking the problem of unauthorized assemblies'.

[8] The word used in l. 69 probably refers to 'the catholic (epistle)', i.e. 1 John.

[9] The 'on all points' (κατὰ πάντα) may have specific reference to otherwise acceptable Christians who differ with Justin on the matter of the earthly, millennial reign, but it is clear that the major contrast intended by the phrase 'right-minded Christians' here is between those who honour the God of Abraham, Isaac, and Jacob, and those who blaspheme him.

ὀρθῶς πεπιστευκέναι—*AH* 5. 31. 1), in contrast to Valentinians and others who do not acknowledge the salvation of the flesh and the material world. There was thus not only a concept of what belonged to 'right' or 'orthodox' teaching and what was characteristic of the 'catholic' Church in the second century, but also an evolving use of these very terms.

The objection that the use of these terms for the second century is anachronistic, then, has very little force. It is only anachronistic if one reads into them the fuller and more precise definitions of the fourth century. The charge that the continued use of these categories, or some form of them prefixed by 'proto-', is to frame things prejudicially in the terms of the winners of the debate seems perhaps harder to shake, particularly if 'What later came to be known as orthodoxy was simply *one* among a number of competing interpretations of Christianity in the early period'.[10] Should we then privilege this one interpretation by adopting its labels? We could, of course, adopt the terminology of the losing interpretations. We know that Valentinians referred to themselves as 'the spiritual ones', to non-Valentinian Christians as 'psychics', and to Jews and other non-Christians as 'carnal' (Irenaeus, *AH* 1. 6. 1–4; Origen, *C. Cels.* 5. 61). Tertullian tells us they also used the terms 'innocents' and 'wise' for common Christians and themselves, respectively (*Val.* 2). But to adopt this terminology would be to play favourites with the other side, and would only be accurate if applied strictly to Valentinians. For other groups, our poverty of sources often makes it difficult or impossible to tell what their preferred designations for themselves and for their opponents might have been. Irenaeus informs us that there were a few groups who actually used the term 'gnostic' for themselves (like the Carpocratians), so, this term, at least if it is used in a historically defensible way (see below), cannot fall under the indictment of partisanship. Those who belonged to eponymous groups such as Cerinthians, Basilideans, Carpocratians, Marcionites, doubtless did not prefer these modes of reference, but no one today alleges bias for the continued use of these names.

Some scholars have used the words 'Great Church' to designate the side that eventually won. This is another phrase which has second-century precedent. It comes from one of the century's bitterest critics of Christianity, but one who was relatively impartial as regards the debates with which we are concerned,[11] Celsus, the pagan philosopher. 'It is certain, indeed, that

---

[10] Bart Ehrman, *The Orthodox Corruption of Scripture: The Effect of Early Christological Controversies on the Text of the New Testament* (New York, 1993), 9. He continues, 'Indeed, as far back as New Testament times, Christianity was remarkably varied in its theological expressions, with the diversity of the New Testament becoming manifest yet more clearly in the diversity of the second and third centuries, when competing groups embraced a wide range of conflicting theologies, and fixed lines of demarcation were in scarce supply.'

[11] The importance of Celsus' testimony on the subject was recognized by Gary T. Burke, 'Walter Bauer and Celsus: The Shape of Late Second-Century Christianity', *The Second Century*, 4 (1984), 1–7, who criticized Bauer's use of Celsus.

the members of the great Church (τῶν ἀπὸ μεγάλης ἐκκλησίας) admit this [i.e. that Jews and Christians have the same God],[12] and adopt as true the accounts regarding the creation of the world which are current among the Jews' (Origen, *C. Cels.* 5. 59). Adherence to the 'Jewish' God and acceptance of the account of the creation of the world by this God contained in the Jewish scriptures certainly marked one line which separated the 'orthodox' from a great many of the 'heterodox' in Celsus' day. Celsus, who we know had gained familiarity with Valentinian and Ophite sources (among many others), knew that groups like these viewed the God of the Jews in quite a different light, and held to cosmogonies of the material world which, while they may have tried to incorporate some reinterpreted elements of Genesis, were quite inimical to its presentation of a 'good' creation by the sovereign God. Besides describing this church as 'Great', Celsus also refers to its members as 'those of the multitude' (ἀπὸ τοῦ πλήθους)' (*C. Cels.* 5. 61).[13]

It appears then to have been Celsus' disinterested observation that this Church, which believed in the Jewish God as supreme and adopted as true the Genesis account of creation by this God, was simply the Church of the majority, 'the multitude', and no doubt therefore the Church of greater influence. Bauer argued that Celsus did his research about Christianity in Rome and wrote in Rome,[14] and therefore implied that Celsus' judgement

---

[12] This point of distinction was reiterated by Celsus, Origen informs us, when he declared that 'some of them will concede that their God is the same as that of the Jews, while others will maintain that he is a different one, to whom the latter is in opposition, and that it was from the former that the Son came' (*C. Cels.* 5. 61). Here Celsus appears to speak of Marcionites. He is also aware of those 'who call certain persons "carnal," and others "spiritual"', by which Origen took him to be referring to Valentinians (*C. Cels.* 5. 61).

[13] From these and the following chapters Origen makes clear that Celsus knew of Simonians, Marcionites, Valentinians, 'Harpocratians' (Carpocratians), followers of Marcellina (who Irenaeus says was a Carpocratian who came to Rome), 'and others who derive their name from Mariamne, and others again from Martha' (*C. Cels.* 5. 62). On Mariamne, cf. Hippolytus, *Ref.* 5. 7. 1, who says the Naassenes claimed a tradition from Jesus through James to Mariamme.

[14] There is some doubt about where Celsus lived; it is usually thought to have been Rome, though Alexandria has been defended (see the section on Celsus below). Bauer, *Orthodoxy and Heresy*, 216 n. 36, claims that Celsus 'could hardly have gained his insight that orthodoxy represented the "great" church over against the heretics ... anywhere but in Rome'. Burke, 'Bauer and Celsus', 3, in fact, points out that nothing definitely places Celsus in Rome, and that Celsus speaks of travelling throughout Phoenicia and Palestine (*C. Cels.* 7. 3–11), and that if anything, this places him in the East. If indeed Celsus wrote from Alexandria (or just about anywhere besides Rome), it would pose enormous problems for Bauer's construction of the evidence. About the situation reflected in Celsus' testimony Bauer also says (237 n. 13), 'the overriding impression remains one of extreme diversity. In a bewildering way, the lines cross one another ... Is there anything that did not have its place alongside everything else in primitive Christianity!' Burke, 'Bauer and Celsus', 4–5, takes Bauer to task for, on the one hand, saying that Celsus' statement about the numerical superiority of the Great Church pertains only to Rome, and on the other for using the same passage in Celsus to magnify the supposed diversity and blurred distinctions, which elsewhere Bauer says characterized every place but Rome! Burke, while noting with Bauer that Celsus sometimes uses the term Χριστιανοί indiscriminately for all sects, says that 'Celsus does not, however, support Bauer's overall position on the blurred distinction between orthodoxy and heresy. Celsus was able to perceive the differences between rival Christian groups with remarkable clarity for a pagan outsider,

could only apply to Rome. But even if Celsus wrote his *True Discourse* in Rome, he himself seems to have intended his judgement to be general and not restricted to any one city or region. Certainly the focus of Celsus' attack throughout the bulk of his treatise indicates that he perceived this 'Great Church' to be the chief representative of Christianity.[15] As Burke says, 'for Celsus Christianity was predominantly of the orthodox type, which he recognized as theologically closer to its origins and numerically stronger than the other forms'.[16] While it may be, and has been, debated whether this numerical superiority pertained in any other region throughout the period, it is entirely a historical judgement on our part to say that the leading form of Christianity at least in Rome, Asia Minor, and western Syria/Palestine,[17] probably North Africa and even Egypt/Alexandria (if not the majority there, a large and influential minority) appears to have been one which answered to Celsus' description of the 'Great Church'.[18] It is not to be ignored that Origen recognizes Celsus' 'Great Church' to be his own; for him this body is simply 'the Church'. This suggests a substantial unity between the majority church in Rome in the period *c*.160–80 (the time frame for Celsus' work) and the church in Alexandria which had a pedigree down to at least that time through Origen, Clement, and Pantaenus.

As to the theological content of the faith of the 'Great Church', we recognize, as most do, that Celsus' description, brief and fragmentary though it is, fits also the majority of our remaining Christian sources from the second century, including Justin in Rome, Theophilus in Antioch, Irenaeus in Gaul, Tertullian in North Africa, and the Alexandrians named above. It may of course be alleged that the greater bulk of 'proto-orthodox' witnesses is only due to a later orthodox 'weeding process'. This is a question which cannot be entered into here. But regardless of what was lost

---

and those instances where he mixes up conflicting theological elements can usually be accounted for by a consistent principle' (p. 5).

[15] Burke, 'Bauer and Celsus', 6, 'the order or arrangement of the material in the *TD* suggests that Celsus regarded the orthodox as the main enemy. The form of Christianity at which virtually every attack in the first five books of the *TD* is aimed bears an orthodox stamp. Only late in book V does he begin to distinguish other competing groups, and even there the orthodox are regarded as numerically superior (V.61)'. Burke (pp. 5–6) also notes the stunning way in which Celsus would confirm a view of the origins of Christian 'diversity' advocated by Irenaeus (*AH* 3. 28. 1) but rejected by Bauer and many others, 'When they were beginning they were few and were of one mind; but since they have spread to become a multitude, they are divided and rent asunder, and each wants to have his own party. For they wanted this from the beginning' (*C. Cels.* 3. 10)

[16] Burke, 'Bauer and Celsus', 7.

[17] It does appear that in portions of east Syria it was a form of Marcionism which first gained a foothold, and which for a long time was the majority form of Christianity there. See H. J. W. Drijvers 'Marcionism in Syria: Principles, Problems, Polemics', *The Second Century*, 6 (1987–8), 153–72, at 153–4.

[18] Irenaeus, *AH* 1. 10. 2, claims that the churches established (ἱδρυμέναι) in Germany, Spain, Gaul, the East, Egypt, Libya, and those in the 'central regions' of the world all teach the same faith. Without accepting his blanket statement at face value, it may be wondered whether he did not have at least some credible information from all of these regions.

or destroyed from that period, the writers customarily identified as precursors to the fourth-century orthodox did hold in common several central tenets, tenets which set them apart from other groups, even though no central authority, such as a pope or a council, had laid down these boundaries for them.[19] And those who held to these tenets appear to have been in the majority, not in every locality, to be sure, but at least in many major areas throughout the empire.

The designation 'Great Church', then, would seem to provide for us a fairly neutral and unobjectionable designation,[20] one also based on a primary source. The term is used by many scholars, even by those who are quite sympathetic to Bauer's position. But the acceptance of this name and its implications, in turn, seems to decide for the legitimacy of the others mentioned above. For 'orthodox' and 'catholic' are both terms which ordinarily stem from the sense of a majority or wide consensus. It is usually the majority, conventional, or 'standard' position to which, in an objective and non-partisan way, is ceded the right to define an 'orthodoxy'. And such terms, once accepted, define dissent in a natural way as heterodox or sectarian/heretical. While it is recognized that the use of terms such as 'heterodox', 'heretical', and 'gnostic' might seem discourteous or even abusive to many today, it should not be forgotten that there were worse epithets in use in the period under discussion (e.g. 'atheists, impious, unrighteous, and sinful, and confessors of Jesus in name only', Justin, *Dial.* 35).

A special note is required for the terms 'gnostic', 'gnosis' and 'gnosticism'. I am in general agreement with critics who say that these words have been greatly misused. 'Gnosticism' as it has commonly been used in modern scholarship is an artificial construct. Clement of Alexandria uses the adjective 'gnostic' freely and without embarrassment to describe his ideal, orthodox believer. Irenaeus applies the terms 'gnostic' and 'gnosis' actually quite discriminatingly to a limited number of groups or individuals who evidently used the terms for themselves, though he sarcastically relates these to 1 Timothy 6: 20 (*AH* 2, *praef.*). The category of 'gnostic' did not properly include the Valentinians, though Irenaeus believed the latter were parasitic off of the former. My own desire is to reserve these terms for those groups who either used them for themselves or, secondarily, were so designated by second-century writers. In a book like the present one, however, in which I am interacting with the statements of so many other scholars with different views and practices, it has proved impossible to follow my preferences very

---

[19] That the Valentinians and others were able to go undetected for a long time in many congregations does not have to do with the 'absence of clear boundary lines' between them and the orthodox (*pace* Ehrman, *Corruption*, 10) so much as with their ability to 'hide' and to be less than straightforward about their actual tenets. See n. 6 above.

[20] This is true though one senses that among recent scholars it has tended to be used with the pejorative connotation of 'powerful' or 'oppressive'. This itself is anachronistic, as if the Great Church had at this time the kind of political, imperial clout that it had through much of the 4th cent.

consistently. 'Gnostic' will sometimes, therefore, be used in a common, rather broad but not strictly accurate way to designate religious ideas which tend towards belief in a Supreme Being (or beings) above the Creator, an inherently flawed material creation, a docetic Christology, and a salvation limited to the non-material aspects of man and the world.

Thus in the following pages I shall refer to certain entities as the 'Great Church', or the 'mainstream Church', and will not feel a need to avoid the traditional terminology of 'orthodox' and 'catholic', along with 'heterodox', 'heretical', or 'sectarian' to describe other, dissenting groups or views. I simply wish to assure readers that when referring to 'orthodoxy' in the second century, I have second-century orthodoxy, not fourth-century orthodoxy, in mind.

I

The Orthodox Johannophobia Theory

That there existed a close connection between the gnostics and the Gospel according to John, or between 'gnosticism' and Johannine Christianity, is axiomatic in the modern study of ancient Christianity. The interpretation of this relationship has supplied a major building block in many presentations of the rise of the Christian movement. As I noted in the Introduction, the second-century evidence of a relationship between John and the early Christian gnostics and Valentinians is also profoundly linked with common views of the reception of that Gospel among the non-gnostic or orthodox churches in the second century. A major aspect of this is the view that gnostic use of and affinity for John precipitated or perpetuated a long-standing attitude of suspicion or antagonism towards that Gospel, a phenomenon we may, for convenience, call 'orthodox Johannophobia'. In many sections of the academy this way of viewing the evidence has practically become, in Kuhnian terms, 'normal science'. In order to understand the rise of this commonplace and its authority in recent scholarship, I catalogue here some important contributions on the subject by a number of prominent scholars of the past seventy years or so, the main architects and builders of the consensus, as well as its main critics.

1

The Making of a Consensus

The history of the current consensus in Johannine scholarship could be viewed in a number of ways. One way which makes sense is to see it as evolving in three phases: foundations—Bauer to Braun (1934–59); heyday—Schnackenburg to Koester (1959–90); and uneasy supremacy—Hengel to Nagel (1989–2000).

Foundations: Bauer to Braun (1934–1955)

WALTER BAUER

The current consensus surely owes much to the labours and the authority of Walter Bauer. He is not the first to have espoused each element of the consensus, nor has his work been the single most influential on this subject. But, as we shall see, the major conclusions about the early development of Christianity set out in his epoch-making book, *Rechtgläubigkeit und Ketzerei im ältesten Christentum*,[1] provided the fertile field from which a consensus could grow. Against what he perceived to be the common assumption of scholarship at the time, Bauer contended that in the second century orthodoxy and heresy were by and large very loosely defined, that the primitive expression of Christianity in many regions was a form which would later be branded heretical, and that in fact 'the heretics considerably outnumbered the orthodox'.[2] 'Orthodoxy' in the period was defined and promulgated almost single-handedly by the Roman hierarchy and by its satellites in other parts of the empire. Bauer's thesis has certainly been challenged by later scholars, and even his heirs today would not accept his theories without significant modifications. Nevertheless, as a grand, organizing principle for understanding the spread of Christianity in the second century, his approach has retained much of its force among scholars, particularly since the appearance of the English translation of the book decades later in 1971. In a section

---

[1] ET, *Orthodoxy and Heresy in Earliest Christianity* (Philadelphia, 1971), from which my citations will be taken. One recent writer has called this book 'possibly the most significant book on early Christianity written in modern times' (B. Ehrman, *The Orthodox Corruption of Scripture* (New York, 1993), 7). A preliminary outline of his views of the Fourth Gospel in the 2nd cent. may be seen in the introduction to his 1912 commentary, W. Bauer, *Johannes*, Handbuch zum Neuen Testament, 2, Die Evangelien, 2 (Tübingen, 1912), 3–5.

[2] Bauer, *Orthodoxy and Heresy*, 194.

devoted to the role of written authorities Bauer had much to say about the Fourth Gospel. Speaking of Justin Martyr, he wrote,

The least that we can say is that the gospel of John has left no noticeable impression on Justin. But in this respect, Justin represents the position of ecclesiastically oriented Rome in the middle of the second century.[3]

Can it be a coincidence that immediately after Justin, the enemy of heretics who also took aim at the Valentinians (*Dial.* 35. 6), we note the appearance in Italy-Rome of two representatives of this latter school who especially treasure the Fourth Gospel—namely Ptolemy and Heracleon (Hippolytus *Ref.* 6. 35)? To be sure, Justin's disciple Tatian placed the gospel of John on the same level as the synoptics, but he also broke with the church on account of profound differences in faith—poisoned, so Irenaeus thought, by the Valentinians and Marcion (AH 1. 28. 1 [= 1. 26. 1])—and he left the world capital to move once again toward the East. Thus Tatian cannot provide us with a satisfactory testimony concerning the moods and conditions within the 'church' at Rome...When an ecclesiastically oriented Roman again expressed himself with respect to our problem, it is for the purpose of vigorously rejecting the Fourth Gospel.[4]

Bauer is speaking in the last sentence of Gaius of Rome, who in about the year 200 is said to have claimed that the Gospel and Apocalypse of John were written not by the apostle but by the heretic Cerinthus. Of Gaius and those later called 'the Alogi' by Epiphanius, Bauer writes further,

Their view concerning the Fourth Gospel is already present by the year 175, as the opposition of Irenaeus indicates...; and even if Gaius had not been active before the end of the century, he nevertheless appropriated for himself many of the views of that group. But he did not thereby fall under the charge of heresy on the part of his catholic opponents...It was thus permissible for a Roman Christian from these circles, and an officeholder as well, to consider not only the Apocalypse but even the gospel of John as a forgery of the gnostic Cerinthus. He reproaches it for its contradictions with the other gospels, plays Mark off against John (Epiphanius *Her.* 51. 6), and betrays in general an extraordinary sympathy for the earthly life of Jesus as presented by the synoptics. Of course, the reasons thus advanced are not the true cause for his rejection of John. Rather, he sensed in the gospel of John a spirit of heresy with which his Roman-ecclesiastical attitude could not be reconciled.[5]

---

[3] Bauer, *Orthodoxy and Heresy* 206.

[4] Ibid. 206–7.

[5] Ibid. 207–8. Bauer's interpretation of the evidence surrounding Gaius was, as has been pointed out by J. D. Smith, jun., 'Gaius and the Controversy over the Johannine Literature' (Ph.D. dissertation, Yale University), 107, strongly influenced by the construction given many years earlier by Adolf von Harnack, *Das Neue Testament um das Jahr 200* (Freiburg, 1889), 58–70. Harnack believed that the attribution to Cerinthus, a docetic gnostic heretic, and the rejection of the Fourth Gospel and its Logos doctrine showed that the Alogi considered that Gospel to be docetic and gnostic. Harnack also deduced that the attack from the Alogi, in his view a group of orthodox in Asia Minor, meant that the position of the Fourth Gospel in the Church, and its claim to apostolic authorship, were weak. Harnack, however, did not connect Gaius closely with the Alogi, as Bauer did. According to Harnack, Gaius did not reject the Fourth Gospel or ascribe it to Cerinthus. See Smith, 'Gaius', 30–4.

If we listen to the sources without prejudice, it seems to me that this is the result: a current of caution with regard to the gospel of John runs continuously through *ecclesiastical* Rome, that center of orthodoxy, right up to almost the end of the second century—a mood that manifests itself through silence and through explicit rejection. Even the silence becomes eloquent if one notices that people such as Ptolemy, Heracleon and Tatian, who are sharply attacked by the church, can treasure the gospel for similar reasons. Gaius in his own way gives expression to a feeling which dominated Roman orthodoxy ever since the Fourth Gospel appeared on its horizon and which doubtless accounts for Justin's attitude when he consciously appeals to the synoptics for support, just as do the alogoi. Apparently the gospel of John was introduced into the world capital by personalities whose recommendation could not be accepted by the 'church' there. Up until the end of the epoch with which we are dealing, it had still not overcome such reservations.[6]

Bauer was convinced that none of the Apostolic Fathers had relied on the authority of the Fourth Gospel. It was the gnostics, the Marcionites, and the Montanists who first used it and introduced it to the Christian community in Rome. Tatian indeed accepted it, but only after he had stepped into the embrace of 'heresy'; the Valentinians Ptolemy and Heracleon 'treasured' it. Understandably then, 'a current of caution' prevailed among the orthodox in Rome, 'a mood that manifests itself through silence and through explicit rejection': Justin did not know or did not like it; Gaius sensed in it 'a spirit of heresy' and vigorously rejected it. Even at the end of the second century it had not overcome this orthodox suspicion, this orthodox Johannophobia.

J. N. SANDERS

It is fair to say that the chief architect of the current paradigm on orthodox Johannophobia is J. N. Sanders, for many years Fellow of Peterhouse in Cambridge. In 1939 Sanders was awarded the Kaye Prize at Cambridge for research which was later embodied in his book, *The Fourth Gospel in the Early Church*, published in 1943. This book of 87 pages has had an influence quite disproportionate to its size.[7] With carefully chosen selections and concise but apposite commentary, Sanders put together a picture of the second century and the place of the Fourth Gospel in it, which for sixty years since its publication has been a mainstay in Johannine scholarship. Sanders began by examining the alleged parallels with John in Ignatius, Polycarp, 'Barnabas', and the *Epistle to Diognetus*, and concluded that there were no certain traces of the Fourth Gospel's influence among any of the Apostolic Fathers.[8] 'The first really indisputable traces of the use of the

[6] Bauer, *Orthodoxy and Heresy*, 208.
[7] J. N. Sanders, *The Fourth Gospel in the Early Church: Its Origin and Influence on Christian Theology up to Irenaeus* (Cambridge, 1943).
[8] In a strange twist, though Sanders was followed in this conclusion by many later writers, he later modified his views somewhat, particularly with regard to Ignatius of Antioch. Writing in the introduction to his posthumously published commentary on John, he said that while Ignatius did

Fourth Gospel' among 'orthodox' writers were instead to be found in the work of the apologists.[9] But Justin, Tatian, Athenagoras, and Theophilus used this Gospel only sparingly and cautiously, and with confidence increasing only as time went on.[10] On the other hand, 'The Gospel appears to have been used first of all by the Gnostics, and particularly by the Alexandrians . . . It was the Valentinians who first ascribed it to "John"'.[11]

Sanders saw the copious evidence for gnostic, particularly Valentinian, use as pointing also to an Alexandrian origin for the Fourth Gospel itself. The author of this Gospel probably 'wrote for people influenced by Proto-Gnostic speculation, and used the language of this speculation, and was accordingly mistrusted by conservative Christians'.[12] Sanders had read Walter Bauer's *Rechtgläubigkeit und Ketzerei* and was convinced by the German scholar's proposals about the nature of earliest Christianity in Egypt. 'There would be an adequate reason for the reluctance of the early Church to accept the Fourth Gospel if it came from Alexandria, since it is probable', Sanders wrote, referring to Bauer's book, 'that the early church of Alexandria was not, by later standards, orthodox. This would explain why the Gospel was at first popular among the Gnostics and opposed by the conservative, orthodox, anti-Gnostic *Alogi* . . .'[13] All of these facts also show why 'Irenaeus is of great importance . . . because he was the first Catholic writer to overcome the prejudice which appears to have been felt against the Fourth Gospel, at least in Rome, in the latter half of the second century, and to make it a weapon in the controversy *adversus haereses* . . .'[14] It is, in fact, 'highly probable that it was through the influence of Irenaeus that the Fourth Gospel was eventually accepted as Canonical Scripture by the universal consent of the Catholic Church, when he had shown beyond a shadow of doubt that it was in fact the corner-stone of orthodoxy'.[15]

---

not quote John, there were so many passages in Ignatius which showed 'resemblance of thought and language to the FG . . . that is seems reasonable to suppose that he knew the FG' (J. N. Sanders, *A Commentary on the Gospel According to St John*, ed. and completed by B. A. Mastin (New York, 1968), 33. In his article, 'John, Gospel of', in *IDB* (Nashville, Tenn., 1962), ii. 932–46, at 944, he states that 'the first clear traces of fairly systematic use of John are in the epistles of Ignatius of Antioch (*ca.* A.D. 110) and in the writings of Justin Martyr, a generation later'. Despite this, Sanders maintained his position on gnostic use of John and on the existence of widespread Johannophobia among the orthodox (*St John*, 25, 37–44).

[9] Sanders, *Fourth Gospel*, 20; see pp. 20–36.

[10] Ibid. 20, 'The traces in Justin are clearer than those in the Epistle to Diognetus, in Tatian than in Justin, and in Theophilus than in Tatian. With Theophilus certainty is reached.'

[11] Ibid. 86 (his treatment of the gnostics covers pp. 47–66, almost a third of the book). The heretical origin of the apostolic attribution was reiterated in *St John*, 44, 50, etc.

[12] Sanders, *Fourth Gospel*, 86.

[13] Ibid. 41.

[14] Ibid. 66. His treatment of Irenaeus, pp. 66–84, takes up nearly as much space as his treatment of the Gnostics.

[15] Ibid. 84. Despite the tone of much of his book, Sanders in the end does believe that Irenaeus' interpretation of John was 'incomparably superior' to that of the Valentinians (86) and that he was justified in using it to refute them (though not in taking over from them the attribution to John the son of Zebedee).

Sanders's book, which, unlike Bauer's, was dedicated to the Fourth Gospel, did much to define the terms of the orthodox Johannophobia consensus. While his theory of an Alexandrine origin for the Fourth Gospel is held by a small minority of scholars today (Sanders himself later retreated from it),[16] the outlines of his treatment have held up astonishingly well amid the papyrological discoveries and the onward march of scholarship during the past sixty years or so. As we shall see, each of the major elements of his construction—the relative silence of the earliest 'orthodox' sources, the contrastingly free use among 'gnostics', the turning of the tables by Irenaeus and others, the adverse reaction of staunch, orthodox theologians like Gaius in Rome, has found general support by scholars right up to the present.

C. K. BARRETT, 1955

In 1955 Charles Kingsley Barrett published an important and influential commentary on the Gospel according to John which went through several printings and was revised in a second edition in 1978. His treatment of the place of the Gospel in the development of theology and in the Church is strongly coloured by J. N. Sanders's research in *The Fourth Gospel in the Early Church*, to which he refers explicitly and repeatedly. Relying on Sanders, he writes of the Johannine parallels in Ignatius: 'There is nothing in these (or any other) passages to prove that Ignatius had read John';[17] and of Justin's parallels, 'There are undoubted similarities, but no convincing evidence of literary dependence'.[18] Melito of Sardis 'was familiar with gospel material peculiar to John',[19] and from the time of Melito 'there is little difficulty in finding references to the gospel' in Theophilus, Tatian's *Diatessaron*, and in Irenaeus himself.[20] It is indeed only 'in the second half of the century, and chiefly through Irenaeus', that the Fourth Gospel 'took its place as the sheet-anchor of orthodoxy'.[21] On the other hand, 'It is the gnostic heretics themselves who are the first to show certain traces of knowledge of John'.[22]

---

[16] J. N. Sanders, *The Foundations of the Christian Faith: A Study of the Teaching of the New Testament in the Light of Historical Criticism* (London, 1951), 162, saying that Syria was more likely.

[17] C. K. Barrett, *The Gospel According to John: An Introduction with Commentary and Notes on the Greek Text* (London, 1955), 93. This statement, and most of what I cite here, is repeated in Barrett's 2nd edn. (1978 edn., 111).

[18] Barrett, *John* (1955), 93 (1978 edn., 111); on p. 94 Barrett cites Sanders's opinion about Justin's writings illustrating the first tentative use of the Fourth Gospel by an orthodox writer; Sanders is cited on the other apologists as well (p. 54).

[19] Barrett, *John* (1955), 94 (1978 edn., 112).

[20] Barrett, *John* (1955), 94–5 (1978 edn., 112).

[21] Barrett, *John* (1955), 116 (1978 edn., 141).

[22] Barrett, *John* (1955), 95 (1978 edn., 113), for which he again refers the reader to Sanders (and in the 1978 edn. to Elaine Pagels's *The Johannine Gospel in Gnostic Exegesis: Heracleon's Commentary on John* (Nashville, Tenn., 1973)). He then quotes a paragraph from Sanders's conclusion with regard to Ptolemy's exegesis of John from Irenaeus, *AH* 1. 8. 5.

While he does mention Valentinus, Ptolemy, and Heracleon, Barrett is not specific as to who the first gnostic users of the Gospel were. The contrasting attitudes, however, of orthodox and gnostic are reiterated several times in Barrett's introductory material, and one can sense a serious wrestling with the data.

Orthodox Christian writers seem unaware, or scarcely aware, of the existence of the gospel, perhaps even suspicious of it...Even Polycarp...shows no knowledge of the gospel...It is among gnostic heretics that John can first be proved to have been used. Only in the last third of the second century (perhaps from Tatian's use of it in the *Diatessaron*) does John come into clearer and less ambiguous light...and it remains quite uncertain whether Rylands Papyrus 457 was in orthodox or gnostic hands, and in what relation Egerton Papyrus 2 stood to the gospel.[23]

Without accepting the theory of an Alexandrian origin for the Fourth Gospel, Barrett still accepts Sanders's logic: 'since it seems that the church of Alexandria was not in its earliest days strictly orthodox, it is easy to understand that a gospel proceeding from such a source should at first be looked upon with suspicion by orthodox Christians'.[24] On the first use and reception of the Fourth Gospel:

There is no evidence that John was used by other than heretical Christians before the middle of the second century, and its ultimate acceptance recalls the inclusion of the fuller form of the heretic Marcion's gospel (Luke). The fourfold canon, when it was made (perhaps principally as a counterstroke to Marcion), was an inclusive canon. Whatever was suitable of the heretics' own literature was taken over and used against them; thus Luke and John were added to Matthew and Mark, for which we have the earlier authority of Papias...its early disuse by orthodox writers and use by gnostics show that it originated in circles that were either gnostic or obscure. There need be no hesitation in affirming that the gospel, though it uses gnostic terminology, is not gnostic in a heretical sense...it arose in quarters away from the main stream of the Church's life and activity, and did not at once become widely known.[25]

We may say that Barrett seems to have established the orthodox Johanno-phobia paradigm further. The Fourth Gospel originated outside the main stream of the Church in gnostic or obscure circles, was first used by gnos-tics, while the orthodox remained for a long time suspicious of it. It was only taken over as plunder from 'the heretics' own literature', as Luke was taken from Marcion. The inference is that the suspicion arose both from the relative obscurity of the Gospel and more so from the eager and equit-able reception of it by Gnostics. For Barrett, however, Irenaeus and others, though mistaken about the apostolic origins of the Gospel, were not ultim-ately mistaken in using it to forge an answer to heresy.

[23] Barrett, *John* (1955), 106 (cf. 1978 edn., 125, and my comments below).
[24] Barrett, *John* (1955), 109 (1978 edn., 129).
[25] Barrett, *John* (1955), 111–12 (1978 edn. 131–2).

It was first seized upon by gnostic speculators, who saw the superficial contact which existed between it and their own work; they at least could recognize the language John spoke. Only gradually did the main body of the church come to perceive that, while John used (at times) the language of gnosticism, his work was in fact the strongest possible reply to the gnostic challenge; that he had beaten the gnostics with their own weapons, and vindicated the permanent validity of the primitive Gospel.[26]

F.-M. BRAUN

In 1959 there appeared in a major French work by F.-M. Braun, one of the few, substantial attempts at refuting the elements of the paradigm.[27] Braun was disturbed by the popularity of a view which he specially attributed to the two British scholars just treated. The 'intéressante problématique', which saw the late second-century reception of the Fourth Gospel in the Church as a relatively late achievement by the apologists, resulting from their efforts to find *ad hominem* arguments against the gnostics, is attributed to Sanders's 1943 book and its revival some fifteen years later is credited to Barrett's commentary.[28] Braun devoted over 200 pages to showing why he could not accept their solution. He criticized it first for being constructed on too narrow a basis. It centred on gnostic writings and the writings of the Apostolic Fathers and apologists while neglecting other evidence. The discovery of $\mathfrak{P}^{52}$ (P. Rylands Gk. 457) and P. Egerton 2 from the first half of the second century suggests that the Fourth Gospel was known in Egypt before the foundation of the gnostic schools.[29] Also, the iconographic themes from the Roman catacombs, which include scenes drawn evidently from the Fourth Gospel, can be supposed to give expression to a more ancient acceptance of those scenes and their source. Braun criticized Sanders's 'sévérité' in treating ancient authors, holding them to the standard of explicit or literal citation before allowing that they could have known the Fourth Gospel.[30] After a lengthy study of the relevant sources, treated according to their geographical origin, Braun offered his conclusions about the pertinence of a number of documents prior to Irenaeus:

A.   Certain dependence: P. Rylands 457 (i.e., $\mathfrak{P}^{52}$) and P. Egerton 2, Ignatius of Antioch, Justin, Tatian, Theophilus of Antioch, Ptolemy, Heracleon, Theodotus, *Epistula Apostolorum*, P. Bodmer II (i.e., $\mathfrak{P}^{66}$).

B.   Very probable dependence: Marcion, *Gospel of Truth*, *Gospel of Peter*, the epistle *ad Diognetum*.

---

[26]   Barrett, *John* (1978), 134.
[27]   F.-M. Braun, *Jean le Théologien et son Évangile dans l'église ancienne* (Paris, 1959).
[28]   Ibid. 290.
[29]   Ibid.
[30]   Ibid. 291.

C.   Probable dependence: Polycarp, the *Didache*, the *Acts of John*, the *Odes of Solomon*.

D.   Possible dependence: 'Barnabas', Saturninus, Basilides.[31]

Braun concluded that the Fourth Gospel was received first in Egypt, where the early papyri were found, where the Valentinians flourished, where the epistle of Ps.-Barnabas and the *ad Diognetum* were presumably written, and in Syria, where Ignatius at the beginning of the second century and Theophilus later on ministered, and where, Braun thought, the Gospel must have originated.[32] As to gnostic use, Braun pointed out that neither Simon nor Menander, the earliest of this type of Christian thought, used the Fourth Gospel. The same is probably true of Saturninus. The composer of the *Odes of Solomon* is all but alone among Asian or Syrian gnostic authors (Braun considered him closely related to the Valentinians) in using John, but by the time he wrote—according to Braun near the end of the second century—the authority of the Fourth Gospel in the churches was well established.[33] Yes, it was used by the docetists, like the authors of the *Acts of John*, and the *Gospel of Peter*, but docetism could develop apart from gnosticism proper. Irenaeus, in Braun's view, showed how the innovative followers of Valentinus had tortured the text of the Fourth Gospel. Braun also denied that we have any evidence that by about 140, when Valentinus arrived in Rome, the Johannine Gospel was held in suspicion by representatives of official orthodoxy. This is the case particularly with regard to Syria and with the churches in Asia to which Ignatius wrote.[34] Moreover, Braun suggested that Valentinus' use of the Fourth Gospel ought to be seen as implying that it was already received without contest among the orthodox communities he courted.

Sanders wrote before the discovery of the Nag Hammadi codices; Braun wrote after, but in the early stages of their investigation, and treated only the *Gospel of Truth* at any length.[35] Each writer also held some views about the dating and the character of certain documents which would be widely dismissed today. The main lines of their investigations and their conclusions, however, marked out obvious and clearly diverging approaches to the evidence. Though from our present vantage point there is no question which scholar's approach has enjoyed the most success among the succeeding generation of scholars, on the international scene shortly after Braun's book was published the future course of scholarship may have appeared unclear. The next phase of our story would witness the virtual conquest of one outlook by the other.

---

[31] Ibid. One will notice that Braun disagrees with Sanders on several authors, affirming that Ignatius, Justin, and *Diogn.* knew or very probably knew John's Gospel, that Polycarp probably did, and adding the *Ep. Apost.*

[32] Braun, *Jean le Théologien*, 293.

[33] Ibid. 295.

[34] Ibid. 296.

[35] Ibid. 112–33.

Heyday: Schnackenburg to Koester (1959–90)

RUDOLF SCHNACKENBURG

One of the first important commentaries on the Gospel to appear after the publication of Braun's book was that of Rudolf Schnackenburg, who published the first volume of a massive, three-volume commentary on the Fourth Gospel in 1965. Its significance was recognized by an English translation in 1968.[36] Schnackenburg sought that his commentary should 'make its contribution to the present state of studies, without abandoning Catholic tradition or the scientific method used by New Testament scholars of all confessions'.[37] He was thus well aware of the questions surrounding the fortunes of the Fourth Gospel in the second century.[38] He began his review of the data with 'the Gnostics, who undoubtedly came very soon to regard John as their own domain', something which becomes 'most noticeable in the Valentinian school, for which we can now draw on the texts from Nag-Hammadi'.[39] He drew then from the *Gospel of Truth* and the *Gospel of Philip* in particular, both dependent upon John, before mentioning Heracleon, probably the first to write a commentary on John.[40] With regard to the relationship between these works and John, Schnackenburg noted both the 'affinities', which 'may have been one of the reasons why the Gnostics were so quick to take up John',[41] and the 'content of Gnostic thought', which is 'completely different, with an understanding of existence and a doctrine of salvation utterly alien to the fourth Gospel'.[42]

When he came to examine the question of the use of the Fourth Gospel among 'admittedly orthodox "ecclesiastical" writers', he referred to the work of F.-M. Braun, whose 'very favourable verdict on John is, in fact, based on a positive approach to possible allusions, which will not commend itself to all critics'. Parallels in the Apostolic Fathers, with the Synoptics as well as with John, are vague or otherwise problematic.[43] The one possible

---

[36] Rudolf Schnackenburg, *Das Johannesevangelium*, Herders Theologischer Kommentar zum Neuen Testament, 1 (Freiburg, 1965); tr. Kevin Smyth, *The Gospel According to St John*, i (London, 1968).

[37] Schnackenburg, *St John*, i. 3.

[38] Ibid. 192, 'Was it mainly adopted by Gnostics to start with and made to serve their opinions, or was it quickly acknowledged by the whole Church? Did the Apostolic Fathers know and use the fourth Gospel, and in particular Ignatius of Antioch? How does the Logos doctrine of the early Christian apologists . . . stand to that of John?'

[39] Ibid. 193. Schnackenburg also writes that 'it is certain that especially in Egypt, the Gnostics took over John. The origins of Christianity in Egypt are wrapped in obscurity, and it has been suggested that they were Gnostic and heretical', at this point relying upon Bauer's thesis in *Rechtgläubigkeit und Orthodoxie* (195).

[40] Schnackenburg, *St John*, i. 194–5.

[41] Ibid. 194.

[42] Ibid. 195.

[43] Ibid. 197–9. Schnackenburg observes the 'interesting contrast between the opinions of Massaux, *Influence de l'Évangile de s. Matthieu sur la littérature chrétienne avant s. Irénée*, who sees a direct literary dependence, and of Köster, *Synoptische Überlieferung bei den Apostolischen Vätern*, who denies it' (197 n.

exception is Ignatius of Antioch, whose knowledge of John had been affirmed in some recent studies, though even here Schnackenburg seemed to place on equal footing the possibilities that Ignatius knew a form of the written Gospel of John, an oral Johannine kerygma, or 'may simply be in a similar tradition with regard to doctrine'.[44] Unlike Bauer and Sanders, Schnackenburg was confident, however, that Justin knew the Fourth Gospel, and he believed we have 'certain proof of the high estimation in which John was held from the *Diatessaron of Tatian*', while not mentioning Tatian's eventual slide into heresy. From here we have an appeal to the 'inspired' John by Theophilus of Antioch, a 'great use of John in the struggle with the Gnostics' by the *Epistula Apostolorum*, and then the examples of Melito of Sardis and Polycrates of Ephesus.[45] This, for Schnackenburg, was enough to prove

> that it was not Irenaeus who discovered John in his refutation of Gnosticism and caused it to be adopted by the Church. It had already been held in high theological esteem. It is true that there are not irrefutable proofs for the use of John in the Church in the first decades of the second century, but there are still enough traces to enable us to recognize its growing influence. Along with the literary evidence from the second century, the pictures in the catacombs bear eloquent and reliable testimony to how the fourth Gospel, with its language and imagery, made its way into the life and piety of the Church.[46]

Schnackenburg then considered the opposition to the Johannine writings in the anti-Montanist group mentioned by Irenaeus (*AH* 3. 11. 9), in Gaius, a 'learned man in Rome', who was also 'mainly interested in refuting the Montanists' and who in his rejection of John and Revelation 'obviously meant to deprive the Montanists of a weapon', and in the nameless and insignificant group which Epiphanius called the Alogi.[47] Schnackenburg freely acknowledged the catholicity of the theological beliefs of these opponents of John, but stressed none the less the restricted influence which they had. 'John soon became, along with Matthew, the most highly treasured of the Gospels'.[48]

Thus Schnackenburg was much more hesitant about, even perhaps mildly resistant towards, the affirmation of what we are calling Johannophobia; we might say that the approaches of Sanders on the one hand and Braun on the other were still struggling for dominance. He noted all the

---

14). His assessment of Köster's work is to be seen in his comment about the Apostolic Fathers: 'that they attest an older, pre-canonical tradition cannot be proved, and is unlikely, to judge by the way they use Scripture, where their allusions are vague and hard to trace' (197).

[44] Schnackenburg, *St John*, i. 198.

[45] Ibid. 199–200.

[46] Ibid. 200.

[47] Ibid. 201. It is interesting that Schnackenburg makes no mention of an ecclesiastical office for Gaius.

[48] Ibid. 202.

elements of the paradigm: the affinity between John and 'the Gnostics' and their making it 'their own domain', the lack of clear attestation of John among the orthodox writers in the first half of the second century, and the decided opposition to John at the end of the second century by some within the Church. But in each area his presentation is more 'temperate', or perhaps some would say 'minimizing', than that of many other scholars. He in fact never drew the explicit conclusion from these phenomena that the orthodox in any significant numbers were suspicious about John due to the affinities it had with the gnostics. John, he thought, was being used by the non-gnostic Church well before Irenaeus. But it was for Schnackenburg no less true 'that Irenaeus saw the value of the fourth Gospel in the struggle against Gnosticism and that it is due to him above all that John was launched on its triumphal march in the Church'.[49]

Melvyn R. Hillmer

The fortunes of the consensus were to receive a significant boost in 1966. Despite the fact that Melvyn Hillmer's Harvard dissertation of that year, 'The Gospel of John in the Second Century'[50] was never published, it has had a momentous influence on Johannine scholarship in the area of the reception of the Fourth Gospel in the early Church. It has been cited by Harry Y. Gamble and by D. Moody Smith as providing a corrective to the work of F.-M. Braun, and it continues to be cited in recent studies of the matter. Hillmer in fact did not interact with Braun's work in any detail, offering only a very brief but devastating critique. He criticized Braun for jumping too quickly to the conclusion of literary dependence on the part of several early Christian writers while discounting the possibility that these writers might instead be indebted to common traditions.[51] He faulted Braun for not seeing that some parallels are closer to other NT passages than to John; for alleging dependence based on 'very indistinct parallels as in his discussion of Ignatius, Mag. 8. 2, and the Gospel of Peter'; for failing to give clear criteria for quotations and allusions; for being 'obviously biased in his intention to show at any cost that orthodox Christians used John at an early date'; and for failing to consider the *Excerpta ex Theodoto*, the Naassene Fragment in Hippolytus, or the exegetical work of Ptolemy and Heracleon.[52]

By contrast, Hillmer stated the criteria which he sought to apply to the texts studied.

---

[49] Ibid. 192.

[50] Melvyn Raymond Hillmer, 'The Gospel of John in the Second Century' (Th.D. dissertation, Harvard University, Apr. 1966).

[51] Ibid. 4.

[52] Ibid. 4. Even so, Braun considered more texts than Hillmer did.

Most obviously explicit quotation formulae accompanied by a citation or definite allusion to the Fourth Gospel, and especially references to John as the author, make certain the use of this gospel. In the case of parallels other than these it is necessary to determine whether the writer shows knowledge of material or characteristics which are peculiar to the evangelist. If a writer has parallels only with material contained in John's sources or the traditional material in the gospel then there is no proof that he has used the Fourth Gospel. This means that there is some doubt in a number of instances and we must admit that no firm conclusions can be made.[53]

The phrase 'John's sources' here refers to a core of traditional material John is assumed to have reworked, and which, it is again assumed, may be segregated from the present text of the Fourth Gospel by the application of source- and redaction-critical methods. An example would be the pre-Johannine hymn still thought to be visible in the Prologue of the Fourth Gospel. This means that in order to be sure that a second-century author borrowed from John, one must be able to establish that the 'Johannine' material came from 'the evangelist' or from the final redactor of the Fourth Gospel himself, and not from some source which John and the second-century author might have had in common (even when this source is un-attested and only inferred by Bultmannian principles). Thus, even an obvi-ous use of certain portions of the Johannine Prologue is not necessarily proof that the author knew the Johannine Gospel, for the Prologue in a pre-Johannine form can be assumed to have circulated independently both prior to and after the publication of the Fourth Gospel. This method had been pioneered for Hillmer by Helmut Koester (who was teaching at Har-vard at the time) in his 1957 book, *Synoptische Überlieferung bei den apostolischen Vätern*.[54] This book has had its own profound influence upon scholarship, essentially setting forth the thesis that the Synoptic-like material one reads in the Apostolic Fathers is in almost every case to be attributed not to a knowledge of the written Gospels which we possess today, but to common tradition, mostly unwritten, which was reworked by the Evangelists them-selves. Hillmer's dissertation can in a real sense be seen as the completion of the project begun by Koester's *Synoptische Überlieferung*, doing for John what Koester had done for the Synoptic Gospels—except that the project for John was carried further into the second century.

As to the substance of the dissertation, Hillmer focused on Ignatius of Antioch, the *Epistula Apostolorum*, and then on the apologists Justin, Tatian, Athenagoras, and Theophilus among the orthodox, on six gnostic works, and on Ptolemy and Heracleon. The reason that, apart from Ignatius of Antioch,

---

[53] Melvyn Raymond Hillmer, 'The Gospel of John in the Second Century' (Th.D. dissertation, Harvard University, Apr. 1966) 6. In his introductory summary the criteria are stated a bit differ-ently: 'In order to establish definitely that the written gospel has been used it is necessary to have either explicit quotation formulae or some indication that the written gospel is being cited, or else it is necessary to prove that parallels are with material in the gospel which has been written by the author himself or which reflects characteristics of his work.'

[54] Helmut Köster, *Synoptische Überlieferung bei den apostolischen Vätern*, TU 65 (Berlin, 1957).

Hillmer did not deal with the Apostolic Fathers is that 'the conclusions of von Loewenich and Sanders that the use of John is not reflected in these writings may be regarded as final'.[55] Hillmer found it significant that Ignatius never referred explicitly to the Fourth Gospel or to John the apostle, and that 'no alleged parallel with the gospel is introduced as a quotation'.[56] He concluded that 'any similarities are of a general nature and can best be explained as part of the church tradition known both to John and Ignatius'.[57] The author of the *Epistula Apostolorum*, however, 'has made use of the Gospel of John to a degree which is highly unusual previous to Irenaeus';[58] this writer 'found the Fourth Gospel most congenial to his thought and valuable in his polemic against certain forms of docetic gnosticism'.[59] Hillmer tentatively placed this work in the second half of the second century.

Hillmer took issue with Sanders's conclusion about Justin Martyr and was able to find no evidence of a relationship between Justin and the Fourth Gospel. He instead explained the parallels 'on the basis of traditions which contain similar elements', concluding, as with Ignatius, in favour of the existence of 'a continuing independent tradition which has correspondences with traditional materials in the Fourth Gospel'.[60] He does not at this point speculate as to the cause of the lack of knowledge of John by Justin.[61] But at a later point we read the following:

The lack of references to the Fourth Gospel in the writings of Justin and the use of it by Tatian raises an interesting question considering their relationship as teacher and pupil. The best explanation is probably that Justin refused to use John because it was popular among the Valentinians in Rome at the time of Justin (cf. the Excerpta ex Theodoto and the Commentaries of Ptolemaeus and Heracleon), while Tatian, who shows much more sympathy for the teachings of these Gnostics, could readily accept and use this gospel.[62]

Here Tatian's different attitude is tied to his sympathy towards gnosticism. Hillmer also denies that Athenagoras used the Fourth Gospel, though because this author also 'reflects very sparing use of other New Testament writings . . . there is little significance in his failure to use John'.[63] Theophilus of Antioch definitely made use of the Fourth Gospel, but not extensively, even though he attributes the words of John 1. 1–3 to an 'inspired man'.

Hillmer was unable to be sure that the *Apocryphon of James* from Nag Hammadi was directly dependent upon John, though there was 'considerable

[55] Hillmer, 'Second Century', 2, cf. also 6.
[56] Ibid. 26.
[57] Ibid.
[58] Ibid. 49.
[59] Ibid. 50.
[60] Ibid. 72.
[61] Ibid. 72–3, 'We cannot be certain of the reason that Justin did not use John, whether he knew it and refused to use it or simply did not know it.'
[62] Ibid. 79–80. On the dates of these Roman Valentinians I shall have more to say later.
[63] Ibid. 81–2.

correspondence between them'.[64] Nor, because it lacked sufficient exactitude in its corresponding features, could Hillmer affirm that *The Gospel of
Truth* was familiar with John as a literary work. But it was much different
for Ptolemy, Heracleon, and Theodotus, as the latter is known from the
Excerpta ex Theodoto. In all three of these Valentinian writers we have actual
quotation with verbal fidelity, and in each a definite attribution to John the
apostle of Jesus. Not only this, but these writers are the first to attest to a
recognition of John's Gospel as having scriptural authority.

At a time in history when the Apologists were using John very sparingly, with only
incidental citations, these gnostic writers were writing commentaries on the text.
This seems to be clear indication that John was first fully accepted and used as
authoritative in gnostic circles; not until Irenaeus does it have the same kind of
position in other than gnostic writers.[65]

The Commentaries of Ptolemaeus and Heracleon from the second generation of
Valentinianism, give the earliest clear indication of the acceptance of the Gospel of
John as canonical and worthy of verse by verse comment. The interpretation in
these commentaries is in terms of Valentinian gnosticism but nevertheless demon-
strates a final stage in the recognition of the gospel as a writing which has scriptural
authority. It is significant that this position is first accorded to John in the work of
Valentinian teachers, who were able with relative ease to interpret the Fourth
Gospel in terms of their own theological system.[66]

With the acceptance of it by Irenaeus there comes to an end an interesting but
perplexing period in the history of the use of the Fourth Gospel when it was sparingly
used and infrequently quoted and in which it only gradually gained acceptance as an
authoritative and scriptural writing written by John the disciple of the Lord.[67]

Apart from the example of Justin, Hillmer did not expand much on the
actual existence of Johannophobia among the orthodox, though it is the
obvious inference from his work. He was more interested in establishing
that a scriptural respect for the Gospel of John developed with the Valentinians while the orthodox were either unaware of it or avoiding it.

Hans Von Campenhausen

In 1968 Hans Von Campenhausen published a magisterial and very influential study of the formation of the Christian Bible which was translated
into English in 1972.[68] In it he wrote in a now familiar vein about the
Fourth Gospel—'a gospel particularly valued by the Valentinians'.[69] In

---

[64] Hillmer, 'Second Century', 96.

[65] Ibid. 169.

[66] Ibid. 172.

[67] Ibid.

[68] H. Von Campenhousen, *The Formation of the Christian Bible*, tr. J. A. Baker (Philadelphia, 1972;
German original, 1968).

[69] Ibid. 168, cf. 141.

Rome 'the Gospel of John, which the Valentinians had promoted, is not only ignored by Justin, but even a generation later could be attacked by the orthodox theologian Caius as a forgery'.[70] Irenaeus too knew of 'a rejection of the Gospel of John by orthodox Christians' in anti-Montanist circles.[71] Promoted by the Valentinians, ignored by Justin, and attacked by an ortho- dox theologian: that about sums up the fortunes of the Fourth Gospel in the second century, at least in Rome, in the eyes of this historian. Whatever else may be said about it, such a presentation certainly leaves the reception and recognition of the Fourth Gospel in other parts of the Church by the end of the second century deep in the realms of the mysterious.

T. E. POLLARD

In 1970 T. E. Pollard published an important monograph on Johannine Christology and its effects and development in the early Church,[72] and in 1982 his article on John's Gospel appeared in the *Dizionario patristico e di antichità cristiane*.[73] In his chapter on the second century in the 1970 book he reviewed the debate about the place of the Fourth Gospel in that century and offered his own analysis. While he admitted that Braun's exhaustive study had scored decisive points against Sanders's more negative conclu- sions, it left us, Pollard thought, with certain questions.

[F]or all the weight of evidence which Braun adduces, the fact that in no extant 'orthodox' writing from before A.D. 170 is there any explicit quotation from the Gospel and First Letter of St John still remains a problem. Did early second-century writers know the Johannine writings or were they acquainted only with a Johannine type of theology?[74]...Why, then, did ecclesiastical writers not quote from them, especially when quotation could have added considerable force to their argu- ments?[75]

---

[70] Ibid. 172. Justin's avoidance of John is mentioned again on p. 169, where von Campenhausen refers to the studies of Bauer, *Orthodoxy*, 205, among others. He indicates that 'Further Johannine "echoes" will be found' in Braun, *Jean le Théologien*, 136–9. He does not refer to Sanders in this regard.

[71] Campenhousen, *Formation*, 238.

[72] T. E. Pollard, *Johannine Christology and the Early Church* (Cambridge, 1970). In the same year J. C. Fenton would write in his commentary on John, 'it seems that the book was not at first accepted by orthodox Christian writers...in the first half of the second century, John's Gospel made more appeal to the Gnostics than to the orthodox, and seemed to favour their point of view rather than that of their opponents. From the time of Irenaeus, however, the Gospel was used by the orthodox against the heretics...' (J. C. Fenton, *The Gospel according to John in the Revised Standard Version with Introduction and Commentary* (Oxford, 1970), 25).

[73] ET, 'John the Evangelist, Gospel of', in Angelo di Berardino (ed.), *Encyclopedia of the Early Church*, tr. Adrian Walford (New York, 1992), i. 448–9.

[74] Pollard did not speculate on how a Johannine type of theology could have, apart from the written Gospel, inspired 'the frescoes of the Roman catacombs which give ample proof of the popularity of Johannine symbolism in second-century Roman Christian art' (*Johannine Christology*, 24). I shall have more to say on this below.

[75] Ibid. 24–5.

Pollard then says there are two pieces of evidence which

support the view developed by J. N. Sanders that gnostic use of the Johannine writings made 'orthodox' writers hesitate to use them openly. Early gnostic use of them has been confirmed by the discovery of *The Gospel of Truth* and the fragment of an unknown gospel (Papyrus Egerton 2).[76] It is known that the first commentary on the Gospel was written by the gnostic Heracleon, while Epiphanius records the existence of a group in Rome,[77] whom he calls *Alogoi*, who rejected the Gospel because they believed it had been written by Cerinthus the gnostic. It would not be unusual for theologians to be hesitant about writings which popular piety was prepared to use without hesitation.[78]

Pollard clearly assumed that the significance of a writing, at least the Fourth Gospel, must be indicated by actual quotations or commentary (though it is not stated that this is found either in the *Gospel of Truth* or in Papyrus Egerton 2; indeed neither contains direct quotation or commentary). The roles of Heracleon and the Alogi are again singled out as crucial. Pollard could not understand why in Justin's writings we find no 'indisputable quotation from St John's Gospel', especially 'in view of the fact that there are verbal reminiscences at numerous points and that quotation from the Gospel could often have added weight to his arguments'.[79] He concluded with Sanders that Justin therefore did not regard 'the Fourth Gospel as Scripture, or as the work of an Apostle'.[80] In his dictionary article Pollard attributed to Irenaeus 'the removal of suspicion and the recognition of the fourth gospel as orthodox, both by his affirmation of its apostolic authorship and parity with the synoptics and, above all, by his using it as his main weapon in refuting the heretical teaching of the gnostics'.[81] Despite the gnostic preference for John, Pollard also argued that Bultmann's proposal of a gnostic origin for the book cannot be accepted. In this context he offers us a fine description of what we are calling orthodox Johannophobia, 'that second-century writers hesitated to use St John's Gospel because gnostic use of it made them either suspicious of its orthodoxy or afraid that to use it might give the impression that they were allying themselves with gnosticism'.[82]

ERNST HAENCHEN

Before his death in 1974 Ernst Haenchen had spent decades researching and writing what has become a very well-used commentary on John. This

---

[76] This list of gnostic works which use John is expanded in his dictionary article to include *Apocryphon of John, Gospel of Thomas, Gospel of Philip, Treatise on the Resurrection, Tripartite Tractate*, all of which show that John 'enjoyed a particular popularity in 2nd- and 3rd-c. gnostic circles' ('John', 448).

[77] In fact, Epiphanius does not specify where this group lived.

[78] Pollard, *Johannine Christology*, 25.

[79] Ibid. 39.

[80] Ibid.

[81] Pollard, 'John', 448.

[82] Pollard, *Johannine Christology*, 25.

commentary, which appeared posthumously in 1980 in German and in 1984 in an English translation for the *Hermeneia* series, also embodied the fruit of many years of study on the relationship between the Fourth Gospel and gnosticism. Of this relationship Haenchen wrote the following:

we know that the Gnostic Heracleon, who was a disciple of the Gnostic Valentinus, wrote the first allegorical commentary on the Gospel of John...This early appropriation of the Gospel of John by Gnosticism precipitated the durable suspicion that the Gospel taught Gnosticism. Only when it was recognized that the Gospel could really be used against Gnosticism did it find its approbation in the 'great' church in spite of its differences from the Synoptics. Since it had already been brought into connection with John by the Gnostics, the 'great' church was able to build on this tradition. The form of the beloved disciple was now brought under the cover of the form of the son of Zebedee, who had transmitted the genuine Jesus tradition in superior rivalry with Peter.[83]

In *Adv. Haer.* 3. 11. 9, Irenaeus fought a group that went so far in their antithesis to Montanism (and Gnosticism) that they rejected the Gospel of John and the Apocalypse as works of the heretic Cerinthus. Epiphanius gave these people a name of opprobrium, Ἄλογοι ('without reason, without the logos'). The Roman bishop Gaius, whose orthodoxy is beyond dispute, also rejects the Fourth Gospel and the Apocalypse as gnostic-Montanist writings, as Eusebius reports.[84]

Heracleon is the only named example of gnostic appropriation of John, though Haenchen certainly meant to imply that there existed a much wider interest in John among gnostics.[85] Johannophobia is indicated here by the notice of a 'durable suspicion that the Gospel taught Gnosticism', which is said to have followed upon the publication of Heracleon's commentary (later, Haenchen indicates that this Gospel also 'fell into discredit because of its references to the paraclete' which were seized upon by Montanus from about the middle of the second century to its close).[86]

We see that in presenting the picture of a long-standing, united opposition to John among the orthodox, Haenchen found it necessary to associate gnosticism closely with Montanism in order to state a link between the former and John's Gospel. Like Sanders, Haenchen too concluded from his researches that the attribution to John the apostle, though it soon became

---

[83] Ernst Haenchen, *John 1: A Commentary on the Gospel of John Chapters 1–6*, tr. R. W. Funk (Philadelphia, 1984), 18–19.

[84] Ibid. 23–4. Eusebius, in fact, reports no such thing! Haenchen goes on to claim that the story of John and Cerinthus at the Ephesian bath-house recorded by Irenaeus (*AH* 3. 3. 4) was 'intended to show that John regarded Cerinthus as a heretic. Therefore Cerinthus could not have been the author of the Gospel of John.' This means that Irenaeus is refuting a position which, if authentic, only becomes known to us some 15 or 20 years later. The layers of misunderstanding here are too deep to enter at this point. See the discussion of the Gaian controversy below.

[85] As James M. Robinson says, 'Haenchen...recognized in the Gnostic Gospels from Nag Hammadi the opportunity to trace the outcome of the Gnosticizing trajectory in which the Gospel of John is in some way involved, as a new way of casting light on John itself' ('Foreword', in Haenchen, *John 1*, p. xi).

[86] Haenchen, *John 1*, 23.

'the early Christian tradition regarding the Fourth Gospel', was first made by the gnostics. Its takeover by their opposition in the Great Church is reported (varyingly) to have taken place 'very quickly' at about 180 CE,[87] but also 'suddenly' at about 200 CE.[88] In any case, somehow the orthodox were able to engineer a surprisingly swift takeover of a book they had previously opposed and to make it a canonical Gospel, accepted throughout the Church. Also like Sanders, Haenchen saw Great Church approbation of this Gospel as tied to the dawning recognition that it could actually be used polemically against Gnosticism.

C. K. BARRETT, 1978

In 1978 C. K. Barrett published a revised edition of his commentary on John. One subject which received more attention in Barrett's new introduction was the relation of John to gnosticism. The greater exploration of the Nag Hammadi texts between the first and second editions made this possible and perhaps necessary. It may seem surprising that in his essay Barrett took absolutely no notice of F.-M. Braun's volume on the Fourth Gospel in the ancient Church, which had credited Barrett himself with such influence, and which had developed a lengthy reply to the theory Barrett had propounded on this subject.[89] Perhaps the neglect is one indication of the abandonment Braun's study had suffered in the nearly twenty years which had elapsed since its appearance.

In any case, in 1978 Barrett was able to write in greater awareness of the significance of the Nag Hammadi finds and to state that these new discoveries 'confirm the use of the gospel in gnostic circles', represented particularly by the *Gospel of Truth* and the *Gospel of Thomas*.[90] Barrett stood by what he had written in 1955: 'it remains substantially true that the Gnostics used John because out of it, by exegesis sound or unsound, they were able to win support and enrichment for preconceived theories and mythologies'.[91] He

---

[87] Haenchen, *John 1*, 6. 'about 180 CE there spread abroad, and very quickly, what one may call the early Christian tradition regarding the Fourth Gospel: the Apostle John wrote the Fourth Gospel in his old age'; ibid. 23, 'about 180 CE Christendom appeared to be of one mind regarding the Gospel of John. John the son of Zebedee and beloved disciple of Jesus had written it. It was accordingly taken into the circle of canonical gospels.'

[88] Ibid. 14, 'About 200 CE the situation is suddenly altered: all at once the "ecclesiastical tradition" of the son of Zebedee as the author of the Gospel of John appears. This tradition is present on a broad front: the Muratorian Canon, Irenaeus, Theophilus of Antioch, Polycrates of Ephesus, and somewhat later, Clement of Alexandria.' On the same page, however, he mutes the Muratorian Canon's witness to this tradition and eventually denies that Polycrates attributed the Fourth Gospel to John the apostle.

[89] He referred once in the 2nd edn., 64, to a 1958 article by Braun which investigated the Fourth Gospel's influence on *Ps. Barnabas*, only to disagree with it. He also referred to one of Braun's later volumes.

[90] One will find, according to the index, 25 references to logia of *Thomas* in the 2nd edn., though, interestingly, several times the relevance of a particular logion is denied.

[91] Barrett, *John* (1978), 66.

continued, 'We should not be justified in speaking of second-century gnosticism as in any sense a creation of John', but at this point in the second edition he added, 'John must be seen as one stage in the development of full-blown gnosticism... Their proportions and blendings were not, in John, such as to produce a truly gnostic result, but when other writers used the same ingredients genuine gnosticism—in the sense of a Christian heresy—was sure sooner or later to emerge'.[92] This is just one of several indications that by the time he published the second edition Barrett felt that the cords which bound John to developing gnosticism were even stronger than he had realized before.[93] John was now seen as 'one stage in the development of full-blown gnosticism'; in performing its theological task it 'entered the realm of gnosticism and contributed to its evolution. If it is true... that Paul did not hellenize Christianity but put it into a form in which it could be hellenized, it is perhaps equally true that John was not a heretic (as Dr Käsemann says...), but put Christianity into a form in which it could easily be turned into a heresy'.[94] The Johanno-gnostic paradigm and the theory of orthodox Johannophobia appeared to be even better substantiated in 1978 than they had in 1955.

RAYMOND BROWN

Perhaps the single most influential scholar of the second half of the twentieth century in matters of Johannine history and interpretation is Raymond Brown—and with good reason. His two-volume commentary on the Fourth Gospel published in 1966 and 1970 and his large volume on the Johannine Epistles in 1982 in the *Anchor Bible*[95] series set new standards for critical commentaries in several ways. Brown's elaboration of a grand and detailed theory of the history of the Johannine community has had a profound and lasting effect on Johannine and New Testament scholarship. This theory was developed in his first volume of the John commentary in 1966 with respect to the pre-history and composition of the Johannine Gospel but not

---

[92] Ibid. (cf. 1955 edn., 55).

[93] The following examples will suffice. To his comment on the *Diatessaron* from the 1st edn. (cited above) Barrett adds, 'even here it must be remembered that the origins of the *Diatessaron* are shrouded in some obscurity, and that Tatian was not orthodox', and in the same paragraph Egerton Papyrus 2, is now said to be 'a mildly gnostic work' (125); to his original statement that John had 'vindicated the permanent validity of the primitive Gospel', he added 'by expressing it in new—and partly gnostic—terms' (134); the words in the 1st edn., 'There need be no hesitation in affirming that the gospel, though it uses gnostic terminology, is not gnostic in a heretical sense', were replaced in the 2nd edn. by 'It was gnostic, not in that it was docetic, but in that its author took seriously the new movements of thought that agitated his intellectual environment, and obscure in that he stood apart from the ecclesiastical developments in which Ignatius, for example played so combative a part' (131–2).

[94] Barrett, *John* (1978), 127.

[95] Raymond E. Brown, *The Gospel According to John (i–xii)*, AB 29 (Garden City, NY, 1966); idem, *The Gospel According to John (xiii–xxi)*, AB 29A (Garden City, NY, 1970); idem, *The Epistles of John*, AB 30 (New York, 1982).

with respect to the continuation of the Johannine community in the second century. In his attempt to determine the date of the Gospel Brown did, however, consider the question of its first use, and here he had to acknowledge the contrasting estimates of Sanders and Barrett on the one hand and of F.-M. Braun on the other, noting that 'there remains much difference of opinion among competent scholars'.[96] He voiced his own attraction, at that time, to what he regarded as the carefully qualified work of Braun.[97] Though some, including von Loewenich, Sanders, and Barrett, had argued the Gospel had been used and received first in gnostic circles, Brown opposed to their work the conclusions of Braun, that 'orthodox use of the Gospel was both earlier and more faithful to the Gospel than Gnostic use'.[98] He then brought in the finds at Chenoboskion, and stated that 'John has little in common with works like the *Gospel of Truth* and the *Gospel of Thomas*... Thus, it seems clear that 2nd-century Gnosticism as is known to us from Chenoboskion is post-Johannine'.[99]

Though Brown's 1966 statements on this subject are short and amount to a very minor part of his large commentary, they are significant, more especially because of the rather drastic change they would undergo in his 1979 book, *The Community of the Beloved Disciple*.[100] It is in this book, written as he was engaged in the preparation of his commentary on the Johannine Epistles,[101] that Brown developed further his views about the history of the Johannine community. Here we read statements like the following:

The Great Church, which had accepted elements of the Johannine tradition when it accepted the Johannine Christians who shared the author's views, was at first wary of the Fourth Gospel because it had given rise to error and was being used to support error.

...the Fourth Gospel...is cited earlier and more frequently by heterodox writers than by orthodox writers.[102]

All our evidence points to the fact that a wide acceptance of the Fourth Gospel came earlier among heterodox rather than among orthodox Christians. Our oldest known commentary on the Gospel is that of the gnostic Heracleon (A.D. 160–180). The Gospel was greatly appreciated by the Valentinian gnostics...[103]

---

[96] Brown, *John (i–xii)*, p. lxxxi.

[97] Ibid.

[98] Ibid. p. lxxxii.

[99] Ibid.

[100] Raymond E. Brown, *The Community of the Beloved Disciple* (New York, 1979). In this book he also reversed himself on the question of the identity of the Beloved Disciple, moving away from his earlier position that he was John the son of Zebedee to the view that he was an otherwise unknown Jerusalem disciple of Jesus.

[101] Ibid. 5; the book was an expansion of his 1977 presidential address to the Society of Biblical Literature and his 1978 Shaffer Lectures at Yale University.

[102] Ibid. 24.

[103] Ibid. 146–7.

Because the secessionists and their heterodox descendants misused the Fourth Gospel, it was not cited as Scripture by orthodox writers in the first part of the second century. However, the use of the Epistles as a correct guide to interpreting the Gospel finally won for John a place in the canon of the church.[104]

... because a majority of those who claimed the Gospel as their own had become heterodox, there would have been a reluctance among the orthodox to cite the Gospel as Scripture.[105]

Despite once being impressed with Braun's study of Ignatius, which had determined that Ignatius likely used John,[106] Brown now stressed that 'There is no specific citation of John in Ignatius of Antioch', and that Braun himself had admitted that 'there is no verbatim citation'.[107] Instead of mentioning the contrast with Nag Hammadi documents and the post-Johannine character of second-century gnosticism, as he had done in his 1966 commentary, Brown observed that 'There is abundant evidence of familiarity with Johannine ideas in the recently published gnostic library from Nag Hammadi', and then went on to mention Christological affinities between John and the *Tripartite Tractate*, the *Second Apocalypse of James*, *The Thunder, the Perfect Mind*, and the *Trimorphic Protennoia*.[108] Instead of supporting Braun's conclusions about the 'earlier and more faithful' use of the Gospel by the orthodox, 'all our evidence', Brown now said, supports the earlier acceptance of the Fourth Gospel among the heterodox. This certainly gives the impression of a consistent and monolithic message from the evidence. Now, like Sanders, who spoke of a 'prejudice', and Barrett, who spoke of a 'suspicion', Brown spoke freely of a 'wariness' and a 'reluctance among the orthodox' due to the prevalent use of the Fourth Gospel by the heterodox—'because it had given rise to error and was being used to support error'. This is orthodox Johannophobia.

What caused the change in Brown's evaluation of 'all our evidence'? Whether it was due to a more rigorous investigation of the second-century sources on Brown's part I cannot say, but we do know that by the late 1970s Brown had crafted a theory which could accommodate the Sanders–Barrett position. Brown never found himself able to follow the German scholars who had theorized that the Fourth Gospel itself was gnostic, or had its origin among genuine gnostics.[109] But for him the schism reflected in 1 John held the key. Brown believed that the majority in the Johannine community must have sided with the seceders of 1 John 2:18–19; this, he

---

[104] Ibid. 24.   [105] Ibid. 149.   [106] Brown, *John (i–xii)*, p. lxxxi.

[107] Brown, *Community*, 148, with n. 282, where he points out that both Sanders and Barrett denied Ignatius' knowledge of the Fourth Gospel. See his further thoughts on Ignatius and John, ibid. 155–9.

[108] Ibid. 147–8.

[109] Ibid. 180–2. Brown also parts company with some when he maintains that 'the Gospel was not a heterodox work being made orthodox for the first time at the end of the second century—even though it had been misused by gnostics throughout the second century. It had a pedigree of orthodoxy going back to "apostolic" times' (150).

thought, could account for the earlier and greater use of John among the heterodox in the second century. The seceders, then, brought the Fourth Gospel with them[110] on their various journeys towards docetism, gnosticism, Cerinthianism, and Montanism,[111] thus offering these groups 'a new basis on which to construct a theology—indeed, [the Fourth Gospel] served as a catalyst in the growth of Christian gnostic thought'.[112] The author of 1 John, on the other hand, wrote for the beleaguered minority in the community who tried to maintain what they regarded as the central truths of the Fourth Gospel. This author showed

> that there was an orthodox way to read the Gospel, and the Epistle's campaign against the secessionists ultimately encouraged writers like Irenaeus to employ the Gospel in a war against Gnostics who were spiritual descendants of the secessionists. Thus the ultimate contribution of the author of I John to Johannine history may have been that of saving the Fourth Gospel for the church.[113]

Those familiar with Johannine studies of the last twenty years will know how influential Brown's thesis has been.

D.   MOODY SMITH

One of the present generation's most respected and prolific Johannine scholars, called 'in some sense, the dean of U.S. Johannine specialists',[114] is D. Moody Smith, who taught many future Johannine scholars at Duke Divinity School. In an essay written for his 1984 book, *Johannine Christianity*,[115] he reviewed briefly the state of the question at that time and then offered his own considered reflections. Smith began with Sanders's book and its picture of John among the gnostics and the orthodox, then spoke of Braun's attempt 'to demonstrate the widespread use of the Gospel among the earliest orthodox fathers', and then of Hillmer's dissertation, which in the main tended to vindicate Sanders and concurred with the conclusions of Walter Bauer from much earlier in the century.[116] In Smith's view, Hillmer had 'rather successfully disputed Braun's position, bringing into consider-

---

[110] Brown, *Community*, 107, 'The adversaries were not detectably outsiders to the Johannine community but the offspring of Johannine thought itself, justifying their positions by the Johannine Gospel and its implications.'

[111] Ibid. 24, 149.

[112] Ibid. 146. This is reminiscent of Barrett's statement that John is 'one stage in the development of full-blown gnosticism'.

[113] Ibid. 149–50.

[114] G. Sloyan, *What are they Saying about John?* (New York 1991), 38. For an assessment of Smith's Johannine scholarship, see Robert Kysar, 'The Contribution of D. Moody Smith to Johannine Scholarship', in R. Alan Culpepper and C. Clifton Black (eds.), *Exploring the Gospel of John: In Honor of D. Moody Smith* (Louisville, Ky., 1996), 3–17, which volume also contains a selected bibliography of Smith's publications up to 1995 (pp. xvi–xxxvii).

[115] D. Moody Smith, 'Johannine Christianity', in D. Moody Smith, *Johannine Christianity: Essays on its Setting, Sources, and Theology* (Columbia, SC, 1984).

[116] Smith, *Johannine Christianity*, 5.

ation the recently discovered Coptic Gnostic texts of Nag Hammadi'.[117] Smith's main concern in this essay, however, was with the origin of the Fourth Gospel. And somewhat like Barrett in 1955, he resisted the conclusion that the predominance of gnostic use in the second century necessarily pointed to a 'heretical' original situation for the book itself, and yet, somewhat like Barrett in 1978, he also acknowledged that the Fourth Gospel may have represented 'an early stage in the emergence of motifs that had a later flowering in Gnosticism'.[118] 'The heretical use of the Gospel in the second century may reflect its own genuinely heretical tendencies, yet Irenaeus' efforts to claim the Gospel for the catholic church and thus to oppose both the heretics and, possibly, the opponents of the Gospel surely had basis and justification in the text itself.'[119]

But while it did not prove a gnostic origin, the place of the Fourth Gospel in the second century was clear enough to support another thesis regarding the Gospel's origins. 'If the Johannine Gospel or tradition actually originated in a rather remote corner of the Christian map, its distinctive character as well as its difficulty in finding acceptance in the emerging catholic church become more intelligible. Nor is such an origin incompatible with John's Gospel's having rather early made friends among Christians later branded heretical'.[120] From Sanders in the 1940s,[121] to Barrett in the 1950s and 1970s,[122] to Smith in the 1980s, the disparity in orthodox and heterodox use of John in the second century has been seen as requiring or supporting either a somewhat heretical or at least an obscure origin for this Gospel, away from the mainstream of the Church.

In two essays which appeared in 1992, Smith seems to have resolved some of the tensions which were evident in his 1984 essay.

The fact that the Valentinian Heracleon had written in Rome a commentary on John doubtless raised questions in orthodox circles... Irenaeus' arguments for the necessity of four gospels may amount to a covert defense of the Gospel of John.[123]

Perhaps some conservative Christians were uneasy about John precisely because it was popular and widely used among gnostic Christians and others deemed heretical.[124]

---

[117] Ibid. 4–5. He later (21 n. 43) indicated that he regarded Hillmer's arguments against Ignatius' direct literary dependence upon the Johannine Gospel and Epistles as persuasive.

[118] Ibid. 25.

[119] Ibid. 5.

[120] Ibid. 22.

[121] Sanders, *Fourth Gospel*, 41.

[122] Barrett, *John* (1955), 111–12; (1978), 131–2, 133–4.

[123] D. M. Smith, 'The Problem of John and the Synoptics in Light of the Relation between Apocryphal and Canonical Gospels', in A. Denaux (ed.), *John and the Synoptics*, BETL 101 (Leuven, 1992), 147–62, at 157.

[124] D. M. Smith, *John Among the Gospels: The Relationship in Twentieth-Century Research* (Minneapolis, 1992), 7.

Smith thus also credited Heracleon for Johannophobic effects among the
orthodox, and echoed the sentiment that Irenaeus' defence of John had to
be covert because of a general Johannophobia. Still, he stated the existence
of Johannophobia with more caution than some, and one senses in some of
Smith's remarks the suspicion that perhaps the last word had not been
given on the subject.[125]

HARRY Y. GAMBLE

The labours of J. N. Sanders and Melvyn Hillmer on the use of John in the
second century are also visible in Harry Y. Gamble's relatively short but
widely used book on the history of the NT canon published in 1985:[126]

> The Gospel of John seems not to have been known or used by most second-century
> Christian writers, and to all appearances was first employed among gnostic Chris-
> tians. Basilides, a gnostic teacher in Alexandria (ca. 130) may well have cited it, and
> the Valentinian gnostic teachers Ptolemaeus and Heracleon (160–170) both wrote
> expositions of this Gospel . . . and the fact that they considered it worthy of such
> detailed study shows that John had acquired considerable standing in gnostic Chris-
> tianity by the middle of the second century. By contrast, outside gnostic circles there
> was scant knowledge of or interest in John, and prior to the late second century no
> broad recognition of its authority. It is possible that the almost exclusively gnostic
> provenance of this Gospel through most of the second century militated against its
> more general acceptance.

The evidence for this summary is said to have been 'fully canvassed' by
Sanders and Hillmer.[127] Gamble cites these two writers again for the conclusion that Justin's use of the Fourth Gospel is 'on the whole unlikely'.[128]
The actual assertion of orthodox Johannophobia in the passage cited above
is a bit muted ('it is possible . . . '), but what is asserted with more certainty
by Gamble is the 'scant knowledge of or interest in John' outside gnostic
circles and, contrastingly, the 'almost exclusively gnostic provenance of this
Gospel through most of the second century'. Gamble agrees with the
scholars cited above that this Gospel was apparently employed first and
with more authority by gnostic Christians. Besides mentioning Ptolemy and
Heracleon, Gamble agrees with Sanders in suggesting an earlier use by
Basilides as early as 130.

In an article published in 2000 Gamble reiterated his conclusions, still
basing his summary of the second century use of John on the works of

---

[125] Most tellingly, 'If we have lost track of the connecting links between the evidences of the use
of the Fourth Gospel in the second century and its earlier origins, we are not necessarily left without
a clue. If knowledge is not augmented by future manuscript discoveries, it may be advanced by
further assessment and clarification of data already known' (*Johannine Christianity*, 6).

[126] Harry Y. Gamble, *The New Testament Canon* (Philadelphia, 1985), 33.

[127] Ibid. 33, n. 27.

[128] Ibid. 28, with n. 15.

Sanders and Hillmer, with no reference to the work of Braun, Hengel, or Röhl (see below).

It is uncertain whether Justin knew the Gospel of John, but he seems not to have used it (Sanders; Hillmer).[129] The Gospel of John was especially favored in the second century by gnostic Christians and Montanists, which may have inhibited its use by others. But reservations about this Gospel must have rested mainly on its far-reaching differences from other, more popular Gospels, and it was easier to neglect or reject it than to account for the discrepancies.[130]

Here the reservations about the Fourth Gospel are seen as due more to its discrepancies with the 'more popular Gospels'[131] than to orthodox Johannophobia, though the latter was a factor, due the special favour this Gospel enjoyed among gnostics and Montanists.

F. F. Bruce

In 1988 the versatile New Testament scholar F. F. Bruce published a book on the canon, in many ways quite different from those of Gamble and von Campenhausen.[132] In general Bruce's book is more favourable towards what other scholars would call the 'winning' side in the church-political battles of Christianity's first few centuries. But this does not prevent him stating that,

Of the four gospels, John's took longer to win universal acceptance among catholic Christians than the others because (almost from its first publication) some gnostic schools treated it as though it supported their positions. The earliest known quotation from John comes in the gnostic writer Basilides (c 130); the earliest known commentary on John was written by the gnostic Heracleon (c 180).[133] But those, like Justin Martyr, who read it more carefully found that it supplied more effective anti-gnostic ammunition than any other New Testament book.[134]

This goes a bit further than Bruce's analysis published just five years earlier in his commentary on John, where he had summarized, 'In the earlier part of the second century the Fourth Gospel was recognized and quoted by gnostic writers at least as much as by those whose teaching came

---

[129] In an even more recent article Gamble reaffirms the difficulty of establishing that Justin knew John, 'The New Testament Canon: Recent Research and the status Quaestionis', in Lee Martin McDonald and James A. Sanders (eds.), *The Canon Debate* (Peabody, Mass., 2002), 267–94, at 279, 281.

[130] H. Y. Gamble, 'Canonical Formulation of the New Testament', in C. A. Evans and S. E. Porter (eds.), *Dictionary of New Testament Background* (Downers Grove, Ill., 2000), 183–95, at 185.

[131] Besides the Gospel of Matthew, it is hard to find a Gospel known to us which appears to have been as popular in the 2nd cent. as the Gospel of John. Certainly Mark cannot be demonstrated to have been 'more popular'.

[132] F. F. Bruce, *The Canon of Scripture* (Downers Grove, Ill., 1988).

[133] Bruce also repeats Brown's suggestion 'that 1 Jn. took issue with people who were perverting the teaching of the Fourth Gospel in this way' (128 n. 40).

[134] Ibid. 128.

to be acknowledged as more in line with the apostolic tradition'.[135] And, while one may or may not agree with Bruce that Justin knew this Gospel, few will agree with the implication from his words that John was used by Justin in an anti-gnostic polemic. Bruce's book on the canon gives little more on the Fourth Gospel in the second century (more is to be found in his commentary). His work is cited here mainly to signify the popularity and acceptability of the basic paradigm under discussion.

HELMUT KOESTER

Helmut Koester, for many years professor at Harvard, established himself as one of the late twentieth century's most prominent, though sometimes controversial, scholars of early Christianity, on either side of the Atlantic. His long and productive writing career has contributed much to the questions surrounding the rise of the Gospels, beginning with his landmark study, already mentioned, of the Synoptic tradition in the Apostolic Fathers in 1957,[136] a work which was instrumental for that of Hillmer. Koester's fundamental approach to early Christian gospel or gospel-like texts is through a nuanced form-critical and redaction-critical method which tends to result in non-canonical 'gospel' texts embodying material that is earlier or more original in form than that contained in the canonical Gospels. In cases such as these the question of a text's possible knowledge of John is often turned around, or otherwise complicated. We shall see how this works out in several instances later in this study. Yet despite the peculiar intricacies which result from his distinctive approach, Koester still writes in general conformity to the pattern already observed. In his 1982 book on New Testament history and literature he stated that 'Uncertainty with respect to the Fourth Gospel prevailed in the west for some time, while in the east the Revelation of John remained under suspicion for centuries'.[137] He wrote of Justin in particular. 'It is not impossible that Justin rejected that gospel [i.e. John] because it was particularly popular among his gnostic opponents.'[138] Though there is ambiguity here concerning the role of Johannophobia in Justin's thinking, a great deal of confidence obviously undergirds Koester's assertions both that Justin rejected the Fourth Gospel and that this Gospel was of special importance to the gnostics. Speaking of Egypt in particular, he writes in his 1990 book, *Ancient Christian Gospels*,

The early distribution and usage of the Gospel of John in Egypt is confirmed by external evidence. Several Gnostic writings from Egypt used it, and the first commentaries ever written on any gospel are commentaries on the Gospel of John which

---

[135] F. F. Bruce, *The Gospel of John: Introduction, Exposition and Notes* (Grand Rapids, Mich., 1983), 7.

[136] Helmut Köster, *Synoptische Überlieferung bei den apostolischen Vätern*, TU 65 (Berlin, 1957).

[137] Helmut Koester, *Introduction to the New Testament*, ii. *History and Literature of Early Christianity* (Berlin, 1982), 11.

[138] Ibid. 9.

derived from Egypt. On the other hand, John's Gospel is not well known elsewhere. Ignatius of Antioch, although his theological language is closely related to that of John, does not seem to know this writing. Nor is the Gospel of John known in Asia Minor before the middle of the 2d century: Polycarp of Smyrna, Papias of Hierapolis, and the Pastoral Epistles (written in Ephesus after the year 100) never refer to it. In Rome, neither 1 Peter nor *1 Clement* nor Justin Martyr reveal any knowledge of the Fourth Gospel. However, later in the 2d century, this Gospel begins to be used also in Asia Minor and Rome. Justin's student Tatian includes it in his four-gospel harmony, the *Diatessaron*; Irenaeus knows a tradition about the disciple John, a tradition according to which this disciple became established in Ephesus; and the Montanist movement, which arose in Phrygia of Asia Minor after the middle of the 2d century, understands its prophecy as the return of the Johannine Paraclete.[139]

Besides the first commentaries written on the Fourth Gospel, Koester names for us some other Egyptian gnostic writings which used the Gospel of John, namely the Valentinian texts cited in Clement of Alexandria's *Excerpta ex Theodoto* and the Naassene Fragment quoted by Hippolytus, *Refutation of All Heresies* 5. 7. 2–9. He observes as well that, 'Some of the earlier writings from Nag Hammadi also display usage of the Fourth Gospel, e.g., the *Gospel of Philip*...the *Testimony of Truth*. In other instances, dependence upon the Gospel of John is not clear (*Gospel of Truth*) or unlikely (*Apocryphon of James, Dialogue of the Savior, Gospel of Thomas*...)'[140]

One will notice that, unlike Barrett and others, Koester does not believe the *Gospel of Thomas* used John. He believes instead that this work is independent of all four canonical Gospels. Koester's approach is now taken by a number of other scholars as well, as we shall see.

Uneasy Supremacy: Hengel to Nagel (1989–2000)

MARTIN HENGEL

So far, with the exception of the out-of-step F.-M. Braun, we have observed the nearly uniform march of Johannine and early Christian scholarship to the cadences of the orthodox Johannophobia paradigm. Braun's work was effectively neutralized by the researches of Hillmer and the widely respected voices of C. K. Barrett and Raymond Brown in particular, and then virtually ignored by the great majority of scholars of all types. The publication of Martin Hengel's immensely learned study, *The Johannine Question*, in 1989, followed by an even more extensively documented German edition in 1993,[141] however, signalled the potential for a major disruption in the

---

[139] Helmut Koester, *Ancient Christian Gospels: Their History and Development* (Philadelphia, 1990), 245–6.

[140] Ibid. 245–6 n. 6.

[141] Martin Hengel, *The Johannine Question* (London, 1989); idem, *Die johanneische Frage: Ein Lösungsversuch*, with a contribution on the Apocalypse by Jörg Frey, WUNT 67 (Tübingen, 1993).

ranks. The central contribution of this work is its bold revival of the thesis
that the single authority behind the Johannine corpus is the enigmatic John
the Elder mentioned by Papias and Eusebius. But what is most pertinent to
our study is Hengel's compendious treatment (expanded in the German
edition) of the second-century evidence, wherein the author displays an
attitude and approach quite uncharacteristic of much of contemporary
scholarship. Nor is Hengel shy about calling attention to this difference. He
charges, for instance, 'The criticism usual today, which is abstract and
historically barren, far removed from real life in history, is only possible
because it dismisses all too lightly what is clearly stated in the tradition of
the church'.[142] He is entirely unsympathetic towards the scepticism which
characterizes the work of many critical scholars, including, by name,
Haenchen and Koester.[143] Undeniably, Hengel himself shows a great respect for the tradition of the Church, though of course he is well aware of
its inconsistencies and has to make choices himself about what is reliable
and what is not. He not only knows the early evidence, and its secondary
literature, intimately but is able to take readers off the beaten path and
show them new sights and new perspectives on old ones. Tatian's late drift
into heresy is not held against him when Hengel observes that by around
170 Tatian 'had already used the framework of the Fourth Gospel and thus
John's chronology, in opposition to that of the Synoptics, as the basis of his
Diatessaron',[144] and this '"unification" of the four Gospels directed against
the threat by the Marcionite "Gospel of unity" presupposes the recognized
use of all of them in church worship'.[145] A few years earlier Appolinarius of
Hierapolis had used 'the Johannine chronology of Jesus' passion quite naturally' and 'Das 4. Evangelium ist für ihn unbestrittene Autorität und so
wichtig wie die ältern Evangelien'.[146] Hengel finds that 'Melito of Sardis,
too, made abundant use of the Fourth Gospel in his Paschal homily' written
between 160 and 170;[147] and that Irenaeus' attribution (*AH* 5. 36. 1–2) of a
harmonization of Matthew 13: 3 with John 14: 2, 'in my Father's house are
many mansions', to 'the elders' and 'disciples of the apostles' is plausibly
assigned to a passage in Papias' work, or else to another early Asian
source.[148] He mentions the oft-neglected *Epistle to Vienne and Lyons* from the

---

[142] Hengel, *Question*, 144 n. 30.
[143] *Passim.* On Haenchen's knowledge and use of the 2nd-century materials, see esp. *Frage*, 75, 78 n. 236. Nor is the Tübingen professor afraid, as he says, to 'speak out against' one prominent Johannine scholar's '"progress" towards an ahistorical nirvana' (*Frage*, 137 n. 3). The German version replaces this with, 'Hier verbinden sich Naivität und Unwissenheit auf modisch-fortschrit-tliche Weise' (*Frage*, 12 n. 8).
[144] Hengel, *Question*, 4.
[145] Ibid. 140 n. 14.
[146] Ibid. 4; *Frage*, 23.
[147] Hengel, *Question*, 4. J. N. Sanders, *Fourth Gospel*, on the other hand, denied that this work bore any firm evidence of the use of John
[148] Hengel, *Question*, 4–5.

year 177, in which 'we find hints of the Fourth Gospel'.[149] He cites the role
of the Fourth Gospel in the quartodeciman controversy and in the Montanist movement.[150] He finds 'some allusions to the Johannine passion narrative' in the *Martyrdom of Polycarp*, allusions 'which prove that its usage in
Smyrna was a matter of course between 160 (150?) and 170 CE'.[151] In later
sections Hengel gives extended treatments, particularly in the German edition, of Polycrates, bishop of Ephesus in the 190s, the early Johannine
apocrypha and the apocryphal Gospels, then Justin, Ignatius, Polycarp, and
Papias, concluding usually that the use of the Fourth Gospel in these writers
is greater or clearer than is often allowed by critical scholarship, or that this
Gospel and its author fare not much differently than the other Gospels and
their authors.[152] As to the remaining Apostolic Fathers, 'The *argumentum e
silentio*, which is so often misused, is no proof that an author did not know a
particular text. It only shows that he did not use it explicitly. Unequivocal
quotations of any of the Gospels in the Apostolic Fathers are very rare.'[153]

Besides pointing to works which are customarily overlooked, which seem
to provide more attestation for the Fourth Gospel, Hengel insists that the
'silence' of certain other authors does not need to be read to the disadvantage of the Fourth Gospel. And what about the opposition to the Fourth
Gospel in the mainstream Church which has been highlighted by so many?
'It is understandable', Hengel says, 'that this enthusiastic over-estimation of
the Johannine writings in Montanist (and other, e.g. Valentinian . . .) circles
should also provoke opposition. However, we know of open criticism of the
Fourth Gospel only in the period between Irenaeus and Hippolytus (between 180 and 220).'[154] Here Hengel mentions the opponents of the Fourth
Gospel in *AH* 3. 11. 9; cf. *Epideixis* 99, and the Roman presbyter Gaius. But
once again his reading of the situation is markedly different from that of
Sanders, von Campenhausen, Haenchen, and others. He asserts that Gaius
and his circle were not a large or influential group even in Rome, and that
outside Rome their effectiveness is not visible.[155] Hengel's acquaintance
with the history of scholarship is impressive, and he goes back at this point to
Theodore Zahn, who observed that Gaius, 'in declaring that the Johannine

---

[149] Ibid. 5.

[150] Ibid.; pp. 141–2, rightly taking J. J. Gunther to task for proposing that 'the creation of a
Johannine Asian myth started with Montanism' (J. J. Gunther, 'Early Identifications of Authorship
of the Johannine Writings', *JEH* 31 (1980) 407–27, at 410).

[151] Hengel, *Question*, 5.

[152] In some of Justin's echoes of Johannine material, 'the dependence is quite clear' (*Question*, 12);
'mit Händen zu greifen' (*Frage*, 63). He only claims for Ignatius a 'kindred theological milieu' and
no literary dependence 'in the strict sense', and he does not think Ignatius ascribed this Gospel to
an apostle (*Question*, 15).

[153] Ibid. 14.

[154] Ibid. 5. It is interesting, however, that Hengel entitles this section, 'The last attacks on the
Johannine corpus . . .' (*Die letzten Angriffe gegen das Corpus Johanneum*), implying that there were earlier
ones.

[155] Hengel, *Frage*, 27.

writings were unworthy to be in the church, acknowledged that they were in fact recognized in the church, and in attributing their authorship to Cerinthus, a contemporary of John, acknowledged that they were written during John's lifetime'.[156] The protest of Gaius and the Alogi is only the exception which proves the rule.[157] By this time, Hengel thinks, the recognition of the Johannine corpus 'had long been a matter of fact'.[158] He claims that 'About 170/180 it was as well known from West to East as the Synoptics. Its attribution to the apostle John in Ephesus and inclusion in the collection of four Gospels is certainly not a *Diktat* on the part of Irenaeus, but extends far into the second century.'[159]

Hengel's view on the heterodox use of the Fourth Gospel also goes against the grain. 'One main argument' for J. N. Sanders's theory of an Alexandrian origin of the Fourth Gospel, writes Hengel, 'is the alleged early use of the Gospel among the Gnostics. In reality this preference was restricted to the Valentinians.'[160] 'The Fourth Gospel played no major role in Gnosticism before the school of Valentinus, i.e. 140/150.'[161] If this is indeed the case, it alone takes a good deal of wind out of the sails of the orthodox Johannophobia theory. Hengel therefore does not invoke the gnostic monopoly on John as a cause for the book's relatively weak attestation in Justin's writings, though he too resorts to some degree of speculation: 'Possibly also in his time, as the latest of four, it was still not generally acknowledged in the Roman community. For Roman Christians it seemed to be a bit too speculative and "spiritual".'[162]

It would be a few years before we see efforts to come to grips with Hengel's attempt to shift the paradigm; indeed, one may wonder if anyone has yet come to grips with it. Time will tell whether his trek off the beaten path will end much as Braun's did, as a curious but derelict side road, or will become a major alternative route to a more popular destination.

JEAN-DANIEL KAESTLI, JEAN-MICHEL POFFET, AND JEAN ZUMSTEIN

Since Braun's work in 1959 there has been no work by a single author in French on our subject on the same scale. But a multi-author volume appeared in 1990 in the series '*Le monde de la Bible*'[163] which contained

---

[156] Hengel, *Question*, 6, citing T. Zahn, art. 'Aloger', *RE*³ (1896), i. 386–8 at 387.

[157] Hengel, *Frage*, 30.

[158] Hengel, *Question*, 6.

[159] Ibid.

[160] Ibid. 145 n. 37.

[161] Ibid. 9. Also, 'In Irenaeus, who evidently does not know the works of Valentinus but only those of his disciples (*Adv. haer.*, Prol. §2), only Valentinian Gnostics refer to the Fourth Gospel, and he complains bitterly about this (3. 11. 7)...Only in Hippolytus do quotations from John also appear in non-Valentinian Gnostic texts' (*Question*, 146 n. 42).

[162] Ibid. 13.

[163] J.-D. Kaestli, J.-M. Poffet, and J. Zumstein (eds.), *La Communauté johannique et son histoire: La Trajectoire de l'évangile de Jean aux deux premiers siècles* (Paris, 1990).

important articles by Jean-Michel Poffet on the reception of John in the second century, by Jean-Daniel Kaestli on Valentinian exegesis of John, and by Jean Zumstein on the history of the Johannine community, which together present a fairly unified treatment of our topic.[164] Kaestli summarizes two of the conclusions which both he and Poffet had reached in their separate contributions in this way:

1) On one side, we have underscored the lack of clear attestation of a use of the fourth gospel in the texts and with the authors who have been considered afterwards as the representatives of 'orthodox' Christianity. One must await the last quarter of the second century, with Irenaeus and Theophilus of Antioch, to find the first sure witnesses attesting to the full acceptance of John in the 'canon' of the Great Church.

2) On the other side, contrasting with this absence of attestation, we have recovered the place of choice which the gospel of John held with the gnostics of the Valentinian School, with Heracleon in particular.[165]

Poffet lays great stress on the criterion of citation, as opposed to mere allusion, which is always more difficult to judge. And he finds that citation of John 'est constant' among the Valentinians and virtually absent from the representatives of the Great Church before the Valentinians.[166] In fact, with the Valentinians one is confronted 'non seulement à des citations ou évocation évidentes, mais encore à un véritable commentaire suivi du quatrième évangile de la part d'un maître gnostique'.[167] Both Kaestli and Poffet refer to Sanders's explanation of the difference as due to gnostic promotion of the Fourth Gospel which led to a negative reaction towards it in 'la Grande Église'.[168] Both writers hesitate either to endorse or to deny this view, while simply affirming two of the legs on which it stands: orthodox neglect and wide gnostic patronage.

The contribution of Jean Zumstein in this volume, and in a reprise of the subject which appeared in 1997,[169] is a good example of how the understanding of the second-century reception of the Fourth Gospel can and has affected larger theories about Johannine literary and community origins. Zumstein observes that by the end of the second century the Gospel according to John is accepted 'for example in Roman and Gallic Christianity and that its dogmatic rectitude is affirmed'.[170] But prior to the *Muratorian*

---

[164] J.-M. Poffet, 'Indices de réception de L'Évangile de Jean au IIe siècle, avant Irénée', 305–21; J.-D. Kaestli, 'L'Exégèse valentinienne du quatrième évangile', 323–50; J. Zumstein, 'La Communauté johannique et son histoire', 359–74.

[165] J.-D. Kaestli, 'Remarques sur le rapport du quatrième évangile avec la gnose et sa réception au IIe siècle', in Kaestli, Poffet, and Zumstein (eds.), *La Communauté johannique*, 351–6, at 352–3, referring to the two articles just mentioned.

[166] Poffet, 'Indices', 313–14.

[167] Ibid. 316.

[168] Kaestli, 'L'Exégèse valentinenne', 237; Poffet, 'Indices', 321.

[169] J. Zumstein, 'Zur Geschichte de johanneischen Christentums', *TLZ* 122 (1997), cols. 417–28.

[170] Zumstein, 'Communauté', 360.

Canon, Irenaeus, and Theophilus (the first proto-catholic to cite the Gospel),[171] the situation was different. Zumstein speaks of a 'silence relatif des cercles proto-catholiques', which contrasts with the recovery and exegesis of the book by the Valentinian school and by Heracleon in particular.[172] It is interesting to note that in his 1997 article the 'silence relatif' becomes 'the astonishing silence of proto-Catholic circles of the second century concerning the Gospel'.[173] Here he speaks of 'a certain attitude of reserve (Zurückhaltung) of the Great Church with respect to the Johannine work', a 'Zurückhaltung' which is understandable when we recall that the first known exegete of this Gospel was the Gnostic Heracleon.[174] Relying on the work of Poffet and Kaestli on the second-century evidence, Zumstein concludes that (*a*) the early Johannine communities must have ceased to exist and that the Johannine literature was transmitted and interpreted (as scripture) by other groups, and (*b*) that the (eventual) reception of the Johannine literature among diverse groups of Christians corresponds to a conflict of interpretations: essentially, the conflict poses the question, should the Gospel be read as a document of Christian gnosis, or does it refute such gnosis?[175] The Gospel itself was ambivalent, and had been interpreted in a gnosticizing way within the community. The Second and Third Epistles show that their author, representing the proto-catholic interests in the community, soon found himself in the minority; people like Diotrephes had succeeded in obtaining ecclesiastical power. The salvation of the Johannine Gospel for the Great Church was accomplished by means of a late redaction, which featured primarily the addition of John 21[176] to an earlier form of the book, and by the supplement known to us as 1 John, which Zumstein, agreeing with Brown, calls 'the orthodox commentary on the Gospel'.[177]

Details of the exegesis of the Fourth Gospel, which Zumstein and others believe show a connection with early gnosticism, cannot be entered into now. I only note at this point how the gnostic appropriation of the Fourth Gospel serves, and indeed provides a historical foundation for, certain theories regarding the origins of the Johannine literature and the crucial periods of Johannine community history.

---

[171] The reference to Theophilus is added in his 1997 article, 'Geschichte', 419. I note that Zumstein speaks specifically of 'citation' or 'clear citation' of the Gospel as his test for orthodox reception.

[172] Zumstein, 'Communauté', 360.

[173] Zumstein, 'Geschichte', 419.

[174] Ibid. He later says that in gnostic circles this Gospel was 'hoch geschätzt' (420).

[175] Zumstein, 'Communauté', 361; 'Geschichte', 420.

[176] Cf. Zumstein's other contribution to the 1990 volume, 'La Rédaction finale de l'évangile selon Jean (à l'exemple du chapitre 21)', 207–30.

[177] Zumstein, 'Geschichte', 421. The Gospel 'benötigt offenbar einen hermeneutischen Kanon, dessen Ausdruck der erste Johannesbrief sein möchte' (ibid.).

WOLFGANG RÖHL

In 1991 Wolfgang Röhl published an examination of the reception of the Fourth Gospel in five Nag Hammadi texts, the *Apocryphon of James*, the *Gospel of Truth*, the *Gospel of Philip*, the *Letter of Peter to Philip*, and the *Testimony of the Truth*.[178] His conclusions, echoing and substantiating some of Hengel's, have potentially disturbing implications for the consensus. I have already observed that Hillmer's ideal criterion of exact citation could not be met by the *Gospel of Truth*, and so he had concluded that its use of the Fourth Gospel was probable but not certain. In treating the question of 'reception', Röhl does not bind himself to this same standard. Rather he is interested in any verbal or theological parallels which would seem to demonstrate a real congruency of thought with the Johannine passage or verses in question. His unexpected conclusion is that the Fourth Gospel was in no way a 'special Gospel' for the authors of these five documents, and in many cases even their knowledge of John is not easy to affirm.[179] In the case of the *Gospel of Philip*, for instance, Röhl determines that any allusions to the Fourth Gospel are 'eher akzidentiell'.[180]

It is noteworthy that Röhl draws from the negative results of his study an inference about the character and origin of the Fourth Gospel itself: 'Thus has the non-gnostic character of the Johannine Gospel been shown in the mirror of the Nag Hammadi Writings'.[181] This may seem too sweeping a generalization to make from these five works; there are certainly other Nag Hammadi texts, such as *Trimorphic Protennoia* and others, which the consensus of scholarship would deem important to consider, not to mention the Valentinian works of Ptolemy, Heracleon, and Theodotus. But two aspects of his work are of special interest to us at this point. First, in drawing conclusions about the character of the Fourth Gospel from the degree and manner of use in the second century, Röhl simply mirrors the practice of other scholars, though his conclusions are diametrically opposed to some of theirs. This underscores the potential importance of a clearer understanding of developments in the second century and their connection to the Johannine writings themselves. Second, even if his findings are limited in their validity to the five works mentioned, it is significant that these works, at least, fail to demonstrate a gnostic preference for the Fourth Gospel. His work, even in its somewhat limited scope, tends to support Hengel's assertion that such a preference is not visible outside Valentinian circles.

---

[178] Wolfgang G. Röhl, *Die Rezeption des Johannesevangeliums in christlich-gnostischen Schriften aus Nag Hammadi*, Europäische Hochschulschriften. Publications Universitaires Européennes, 23, Theologie, 428 (Frankfurt am Main, 1991).

[179] Ibid. 206–10.

[180] Ibid. 186.

[181] Ibid. 207. He believes that his results refute the idea that there was ever an enduring group of Johannine gnostics (208). The faith of the authors of these five works was founded on

RENÉ KIEFFER

Two years after the studies of Poffet, Kaestli, and Zumstein came another article on the early reception of John in a multi-author work in French which criticized their work and arrived at very different conclusions.[182] In his study René Kieffer draws heavily upon the nearly forgotten work of Braun and, despite noting a tendency of the earlier writer to see influence from John too easily, essentially reaffirmed Braun's conclusions.[183] Kieffer also acknowledges the work of Hengel. After traversing most of the second century in summary fashion, Kieffer concludes from the existence of Papyrus Rylands Gr 457 ($\mathfrak{P}^{52}$), Papyrus Egerton 2, and the Nag Hammadi library that the Gospel of John must have been known in Egypt some time between about 110 and 120, and from other evidence that it was known in Rome, Syria, and Asia Minor certainly in *c.*150 and probably *c.*130.[184] The focus of Kieffer's article then moves to Ignatius of Antioch. Kieffer thinks that at least six passages in Ignatius' letters demonstrate the bishop's certain knowledge of the Fourth Gospel, possibly in an earlier form but most probably in essentially the same form in which it has come down to us.[185] This would mean that by around *c.*110 this Gospel was known not only in Egypt but also in Asia Minor. Kieffer speaks throughout about 'knowledge' of John's Gospel, both among gnostics and catholics, without much discussion of its religious authority. Nevertheless, if he is correct, a conclusion follows which would still be quite important for our interests, 'Nous aurions donc chez Ignace une preuve supplémentaire du fait que l'évangile de Jean était connu en Asie Mineure, avant que les gnostiques ne s'en emparent.'[186] And yet the next few entries in this survey will show just how far outside the mainstream of scholarship Kieffer's conclusions are.

R. ALAN CULPEPPER

In 1994 R. Alan Culpepper, one of North America's leading Johannine scholars, published a remarkably learned and absorbing account of the life of John the son of Zebedee and the traditions, legends, and artistic representations which have been attached to his name. In this volume Culpepper

individual spiritual experience, not on a historical gospel message, such as the Gospel of John was (209).

[182] René Kieffer, 'Les Premiers Indices d'une réception de l'évangile de saint Jean', in F. Van Segbroeck, C. M. Tuckett, G. Van Belle, and J. Verheyden (eds.), *The Four Gospels 1992: Festschrift Franz Neirynck*, 3 vols. (Leuven, 1992), iii. 2225–38.

[183] Ibid. 2225, 2232–4. Kieffer would add Melito of Sardis to Braun's list of those 'very probably dependent' on John, and the *Gospel of Thomas* and the *Trimorphic Protennoia* to his list of those 'possibly dependent' on John, while he would demote Polycarp's epistle, the *Didache*, the *Odes of Solomon*, and Hermas into the category of only 'possibly dependent' on John.

[184] Kieffer, 'Les Premiers Indices', 2232.

[185] These are *IPhilad.* 7. 1; *IEph.* 5. 2; *IRom.* 7. 2; *IRom.* 3; *ISmyrn.* 7. 1; *IPhilad.* 2. 1 (9. 1); *IMagn.* 8. 2.

[186] Kieffer, 'Les Premiers Indices', 2238.

sifts through and summarizes in a balanced way the results of contemporary scholarship. Though well aware of Hengel's treatment of the Johannine question, even its German edition, Culpepper is able to write the following.

The nearly complete absence of any explicit reference to the apostle or to the Gospel of John in the first half of the second century is surprising.[187]

One of the remarkable items in the history of the traditions about John is the nearly complete silence of the record during the crucial decades of the early second century. If one or more of the Johannine writings was authored by the apostle, or if they emerged from an influential school associated with a cluster of communities in Asia Minor, then why is there such a gap in the record so soon after the composition of these works?[188]

The figure of Gaius...shows us that the authority of the Gospel of John was still quite tenuous up to the time of Irenaeus.[189]

There can be little doubt, however, that these words [i.e. of Ptolemy on John's Prologue cited in Irenaeus, *AH* 1. 8. 5] are the earliest attribution of the Gospel to the apostle John.[190]

Prior to Irenaeus, therefore, the Gospel of John was quoted and used extensively by the Valentinians. Valentinus himself probably knew the Gospel. Ptolemy wrote a commentary on the prologue to the Gospel which attributes the Gospel to 'John, the disciple of the Lord.' Heracleon apparently wrote a commentary on the entire Gospel...a fact which suggests that Heracleon regarded the Gospel as scripture. Excerpts from Theodotus attribute verses from the Gospel to 'the Apostle,' and the *Apocryphon of John* shows that the figure of the apostle had already assumed a place of great importance among the Gnostics.[191]

Is it an accident of history that the evidence for the knowledge and use of the Johannine writings is so scarce among the Apologists and 'orthodox' Christian writers through the middle of the second century, while John's place among the Valentinian Gnostics is secured by quotations, allusions, commentaries, and an apocryphon bearing the name of John? Perhaps. Nevertheless, while the Johannine writings were used only tentatively by the church fathers before Irenaeus, the Gospel was treated as an authoritative writing by the Valentinian school in Rome. The contrast with Justin, who was in Rome about the same time, after having come from Ephesus, is particularly striking. Did Justin treat the Gospel with caution because of its popularity among the Valentinians? Unfortunately, Justin does not provide an answer to this question, but it is reasonable to assume that his reticence about using the Gospel was influenced by its popularity among the Gnostics.[192]

Who indeed can deny the reasonableness of assuming that Justin's reticence to use the Fourth Gospel was due to its popularity among the

[187] R. Alan Culpepper, *John, the Son of Zebedee: The Life of a Legend* (Columbia, SC, 1994), 108.
[188] Ibid. 131.
[189] Ibid. 122.
[190] Ibid. 116.
[191] Ibid. 118.
[192] Ibid. 118–19.

gnostics?[193] Culpepper generally does not say how the Fourth Gospel was used by these writers, except (following Hillmer) to say that Heracleon's writing of a commentary suggests that he regarded as scripture, and there is no reflection on what it might mean for a Valentinian to acknowledge something as 'scripture'. Nor does he speak so much of pre-Valentinian, heterodox use, perhaps because of his reading of Hengel. But under the circumstances, the simple fact that the Valentinians used John appears to speak volumes in the light of the contrasting desuetude which characterized the non-Valentinian Church. Culpepper's rather thorough treatment shows the reasonableness of the orthodox Johannophobia theory: the Valentinians in Rome were the first to use the Fourth Gospel extensively and the first to attribute it to John the apostle; it was scarcely if at all known before the middle of the second century and was avoided or opposed by the orthodox; and these reactions are at least mainly due to the recognized esteem in which this 'apostolic' Gospel was held among the Valentinians.

Michael Lattke

So far, this study has shown the nearly unanimous judgement of scholars that a strong affinity existed between the Fourth Gospel and various early expressions of docetic or 'gnostic' or at least Valentinian theology. Yet many of these, from J. N. Sanders to D. Moody Smith, have none the less signi-fied their belief that the orthodox at least had solid footing for some of their fundamental ideas in John, once they figured out how to read it.[194] But alongside the approach of these scholars, there has existed a school of thought derived mainly from Rudolf Bultmann and his followers, which has maintained an even closer connection between the Fourth Gospel and gnosticism. These scholars explain the attractiveness of the Fourth Gospel to gnostics as due to an inherent 'gnostic' quality to the Gospel itself, developed by an author or redactor either in critical reaction, or in a more congenial, further development. One of the best-known representatives of this approach was Ernst Käsemann, who famously stated that the Fourth Gospel's Christology was naïvely docetic.[195] For Louise Schottroff, writing in 1970, the Fourth Gospel, 'ist die gnostische Heilslehre in den Kanon

---

[193] Though Culpepper had earlier (114) stated that 'even in the second-and early third-century Gnostic literature, however, common use of the Gospel of John is limited to the students of Valentinus'.

[194] e. g. Barrett, *John* (1978), 133–4, repeating with only minimal modification what he had written in 1955, 'It was too original and daring a work for official backing. It was first seized upon by gnostic speculators, who saw the superficial contact which existed between it and their own work; they at least could recognize the language John spoke. Only gradually did the main body of the church come to perceive that, while John used (at times) the language of gnosticism, his work was in fact the strongest possible reply to the gnostic challenge; that he had beaten the gnostics with their own weapons, and vindicated the permanent validity of the primitive Gospel by expressing it in new—and partly gnostic—terms.'

[195] E. Käsemann, *The Testament of Jesus: A Study of the Gospel of John in the Light of Chapter 17* (ET: Philadelphia, 1968).

gelangt'.[196] In 1994, even after the publication of Hengel's English and German editions, Michael Lattke wrote not so much of Johannophobia itself (which may be assumed as a natural consequence of the Gospel's origins), but of the way in which the Fourth Gospel had to be reclaimed from the gnostics by the orthodox.

The process of canonising early Christian writings was at the same time a process of arguing about the 'right' ecclesiastical interpretation of 'New Testament' writings...This is particularly true for the Fourth Gospel, the product of a Christian–Gnostic–Jewish syncretism within the late Hellenistic era and Roman empire. The early Catholic church snatched John away from the growing Gnostic movement and canonized it by redaction and the formation of Ephesian legends. For the time being this concealed the strange ambivalence of John...I rather think that the Christian canonization of John resulted in the breaking off of the gnosticising trajectory in which the Gospel had its *religionsgeschichtlich* origin.[197]

The early use of John on the part of gnostics, then, was to be expected as this Gospel was itself 'the product of a Christian–Gnostic–Jewish syncretism'. Its takeover by the catholics had to be effected by redacting the Gospel and by fabricating stories which connected it to the safe authority of the Ephesian church.

JAMES H. CHARLESWORTH

In 1995 James H. Charlesworth, George Collord Professor at Princeton, published a lengthy volume on the Fourth Gospel's origins.[198] His major thesis is that the famous Beloved Disciple whose witness lies behind the 'proto-gnostic'[199] Gospel of John is none other than the apostle Thomas. A very small portion of this large book is devoted to the situation of the Fourth Gospel in the second-century Church, but the summary statements provided are certainly delivered with an air of learned conviction.

The GosJn was not considered authoritative or 'canonical' by the early scholars of the church because its apostolic origins were disputed and especially because the gnostics adopted it as their special gospel. For example, Irenaeus was disturbed that the 'heretics'—that is the Gnostics—had chosen the GosJn as their own because of their metaphysical theology. As is common knowledge, the earliest commentary on the GosJn was by the Valentinian gnostic Heracleon (c. 160–180). Were the so-called church fathers not blinded by the brilliance of gnostic speculation on the GosJn that was often, but not always, aberrant? [200]

[196] L. Schottroff, *Der Glaubende und die feindliche Welt*, WMANT 37 (1970), 295.

[197] M. Lattke, in M. Franzmann and M. Lattke, 'Gnostic Jesuses and the Gnostic Jesus of John', 'Part II', in H. Preißler and H. Seiwert (eds.), *Gnosisforschung und Religionsgeschichte: Festschrift für Kurt Rudolph zum 65. Geburtstag* (Marburg, 1994), 143–54 at 151.

[198] J. H. Charlesworth, *The Beloved Disciple. Whose Witness Validates the Gospel of John?* (Valley Forge, Pa., 1995).

[199] Ibid. 366.

[200] Ibid. 382.

Many pre-Nicene critics did not consider it reliable and authentic; it was tainted by the interpretations found in Heracleon's Ὑπομνέματα [*sic*]. Other Valentinians and numerous gnostics almost caused the GosJn to be cast into the rubbish heaps of condemned literature.[201]

Charlesworth thus reports a definite rejection of the Gospel's authority by (speaking inclusively) 'the early scholars of the church', and a denial of its authenticity and reliability by 'many pre-Nicene critics'. He appears to have found two causes: disputes over its authorship, and 'especially because the gnostics adopted it as their special gospel', the cause of which adoption was presumably the affinities in 'metaphysical theology'. Charlesworth too credits Heracleon with tainting the Gospel by his interpretations, but also cites the influence of 'other Valentinians and numerous gnostics' whose effect upon the orthodox was so powerful as nearly to cause the book to be burnt as heretical.

GERARD SLOYAN

Among Gerard Sloyan's publications on John's Gospel are his 1988 commentary on John in the Interpretation series and his 1991 *What are they Saying about John?*, in the popular series by Paulist Press.[202] In 1996 Sloyan published an article entitled, 'The Gnostic Adoption of John's Gospel and its Canonization by the Church Catholic' in which he develops his own analysis of the matter.[203] He begins by observing the early work on John by Heracleon, Ptolemy, and 'even earlier, it seems, the Naassenes', who 're-ferred to the Fourth Gospel to the virtual exclusion of the Synoptic authors'.[204] 'What seems clear', wrote Sloyan, 'is that John's Gospel had certain difficulties getting accepted into the Christian canon of Scriptures because of its adoption by a movement that ended outside the Church: namely, Gnosticism.'[205] This presupposes the phenomenon of orthodox Johannophobia. Sloyan set out to investigate, among other things, why John's Gospel 'was so attractive to those whom we might have thought the last people in the world to accept the peculiar mythology of Gnosticism', and to explore 'what a "near miss" it was for the whole Church which

---

[201] J. H. Charlesworth, *The Beloved Disciple*, 407.

[202] Gerard S. Sloyan, *John*, Interpretation: A Bible Commentary for Teaching and Preaching (Atlanta, Ga., 1988); *idem*, *What are they Saying About John?* (New York, 1991). In the latter volume (49–50) there is a short review of Hengel's *The Johannine Question*, which includes the sentence, 'Especially important in [*sic*: is] his marshaling of the second century evidence on Johannine authorship and on the non-espousal of Jn by any gnostic group except the Valentinian Christians' (50).

[203] G. S. Sloyan, 'The Gnostic Adoption of John's Gospel and Its Canonization by the Church Catholic', *Biblical Theology Bulletin*, 26 (1996), 125–32.

[204] Ibid. 125.

[205] Ibid.

providentially did not go Gnostic, and how the once suspect Fourth Gospel ended up as the backbone of Catholic Christology'.[206]

After quoting a long passage from the *Apocryphon of John*, Sloyan reflects on its author's methods.

The author of the tractate possesses a few names from the first three Gospels (John's Gospel never mentions the disciple John); he knows the vocabulary at least and the general outline of the first 18 verses of John 1. He draws on the words John most favors—eternal life, light, only-begotten, foreknowledge, thought, spirit—and uses them to flesh out (if the expression is not out of place) his preexistent myth.[207]

This, the reader might observe, seems to indicate that the use of John in this document was rather secondary and does not necessarily explain why John was attractive to its author. Despite seeming at one point to question whether the gnostics used the canonical Gospels,[208] Sloyan does give one reason for the gnostic attraction to John: dualism.

John's Gospel in its prologue and in many soliloquies both of Jesus and of the evangelist himself were ready-made for the Christian Gnostics' project. There is undoubtedly a dualism between spirit and flesh in John, the world above and the world below, a society that is 'of this world' but another that derives 'from above': namely, the community of the Johannine Christians.[209]

At the end of a remarkably brief, two-paragraph summary of non-gnostic use of John in the second century,[210] in which he acknowledges that Justin 'seems to be quoting John's Gospel' in *1 Apology* 3. 3. 5, that an anti-Marcionite prologue to John was written in about 180, that the *Muratorian Fragment*, Irenaeus, Clement, and Origen accepted John's Gospel, and that Eusebius hints that Papias knew it, Sloyan writes, 'So much for the evidence that led up to its appearance as an authentic apostolic writing. But it did not make it into the canon without a struggle.'[211] As signs of this struggle he gives two apparent examples. First, he cites Heracleon's exegesis of John 4, the encounter with the Samaritan woman, from Origen's commentary and points out that, despite Origen's own commitment to allegorical interpretation, 'that performance by Heracleon was too much for him'.[212]

---

[206] Ibid. 126.

[207] Ibid. 128.

[208] 'Did Gnostic Christianity possess any of the canonical Gospels? This is likely not to have been the case; but its creative minds undoubtedly had fragments of the reminiscences and reflections on the God–Christ relation that went into the making of the Gospels and may even have had some gospel texts' (ibid. 129).

[209] Ibid. Sloyan cites the 'gnostic' interpretations of John by Bultmann and particularly by Käsemann, whom he only implicitly criticizes for exaggeration.

[210] This is particularly puzzling after Sloyan's statement concerning Hengel's research on the 2nd cent, cited in n. 202.

[211] Ibid. 130.

[212] Ibid. This may raise the immediate question, if Origen had trouble with Heracleon's exegesis, how can we imagine that multitudes of other Christians thought it was so compelling?

Second, 'Telling seriously against the immediate acceptance of John into the canon', says Sloyan, 'was the attribution of authorship of this Gospel to a heretic named Cerinthus. A group called the *álogi*, some time between 160 and 170, named that late first-century Gnostic as the one who had composed it.'[213] The dates given for this group are undocumented, and even if Sloyan is identifying them with the group Irenaeus mentions in about 180 in *AH* 3. 11 (very questionable, as we shall see), there is no cause for specifying such an early date.

Sloyan eventually turns to ask whether there was any response to gnostic inroads coming from 'the Johannine circle that had produced this Gospel'—and indirectly, one might surmise, whether there is a way to answer the gnostic claims on John. He finds the most promising answer in 1 John, which is 'a marvel of down-to-earth application of both the doctrine and the ethical teaching of the Gospel. It may have done much to keep devotees of the Gospel within the Catholic camp.'[214] While '1 John is not clearly identifiable as an anti-Gnostic tract', it does 'discourage any flights of fancy that John's Gospel might have been patient of, if not anxious for'.[215] 'No one can know how influential the Johannine letters were in curbing a second-century exodus from the Catholic Church. One can say only that they imposed a clearly understandable reading on that marvel of mystical reflection, the Fourth Gospel—a reading that it badly needed.'[216] In this assessment of the original purpose of 1 John and of the actual role it played in the second century in the interests of an orthodox appropriation of John, we see that Sloyan agrees with Brown. Ultimately Sloyan believes that 1 John got it right: 'John's Gospel means what 1 John says it means for the benefit of those in the third group—ordinary Christian believers— which is most of us', and this should be an anchor for us to our 'earthiness' in the face of various Gnostic orientations of Christianity which are confronting the Church today.[217]

Titus Nagel

Late in the year 2000 Titus Nagel published a very large and systematic study of the reception of the Fourth Gospel in Christian literature prior to Irenaeus.[218] This is a work which I secured only after the research for this

---

[213] Sloyan, Gnostic Adoption, 130.

[214] Ibid. 131.

[215] Ibid. It does this by emphasizing the earthy, the material, what 'we have heard, seen with our own eyes, looked upon and touched with our hands' (1 John 1:1), and even the blood of Jesus which cleanses from sin, things no gnostic tractate would dare to emphasize.

[216] Sloyan, 'Gnostic Adoption', 131.

[217] Ibid.

[218] Titus Nagel, *Die Rezeption des Johannesevangeliums im 2. Jahrhundert: Studien zur vorirenäischen Auslegung des vierten Evangeliums in christlicher und christlich-gnostischer Literatur*, Arbeiten zur Bibel und ihrer Geschichte, 2 (Leipzig, 2000).

book was virtually finished, too late for it to figure integrally in the book. I have been able, however, to incorporate some of Nagel's conclusions in later sections and present a summary here. Though he does not treat Irenaeus or later writers, Nagel treats the earlier literature in great detail. Significantly, this most recent and most substantial contribution to our subject does not conform to the consensus under discussion. Nagel speaks of the debate about gnostic use of John[219] mainly in terms of its importance for the question of the Gospel's gnostic or non-gnostic character.[220] He concludes that there is strong evidence for a susceptibility of John to gnostic interpretation, but not for a gnostic origin.[221] He also gives closer attention to the criteria for 'recognition' than any other writer I have mentioned.

Due to the chronological limitations he has set for his study, Nagel does not treat the opposition to the Fourth Gospel which is said to have arisen from the 'Alogi', and others, near the end of the second century. But his results do, in effect, challenge the basis for assuming widespread Johannophobia among the orthodox in the earlier part of the second century. Agreeing with only a few of the authors we have observed (namely, Braun, Hengel, and Kieffer), Nagel allows that Ignatius of Antioch knew the Fourth Gospel, and that his use of it in his letters to churches in Asia implies that it was known to these churches too.[222] If these letters are authentic, this shows a use in the first or second decade of the second century by a non-gnostic writer. Like Hengel, Nagel too argues that Papias offers indirect evidence for the use of John in his brief discussion of the τάξις of Matthew and Mark in Eusebius, *HE* 3. 39. 15.[223] Evidence for the use of the Fourth Gospel in Syria is implied by Ignatius, and is ratified by the *Odes of Solomon*, by Theophilus of Antioch, and possibly by other works whose provenance is, however, hard to confirm.[224] Justin, Nagel concludes, does show sufficient signs of a use of the Fourth Gospel, and he is 'das früheste römische Zeugnis für die Rezeption des JohEv liefern'. Ptolemy's *Epistle to Flora* and his exegesis of John's Prologue, also belong to Rome at around the midpoint of the century, and from some time between 160 and 180 we have Heracleon's commentary, possibly written in Rome, possibly in Alexandria. Rome is also conceivably the place where Tatian composed his *Oratio*. As to Egypt, besides the early papyri finds, there are many works, such as the *Epistula Apostolorum*, possibly Heracleon's

---

[219] For the opposing view he goes back to the work of G. Heinrici, *Die Valentinianische Gnosis und die Heilige Schrift: Eine Studie* (Berlin, 1971), who regarded the work of Heracleon as demonstrating the distance between Heracleon and John and the secondary character of the gnostic reception of John (32). He cites the work of C. Barth, *Die Interpretation des Neuen Testaments in der valentinianischen Gnosis*, TU 37/3 (Leipzig, 1911), as an early representative of the view that gnostic use of John demonstrated that John was paving the way for Christian Gnosis (32).

[220] Nagel, *Rezeption*, 24–35, etc.

[221] Ibid. 34.

[222] Ibid. 473–4.

[223] Ibid. 474.

[224] Ibid.

commentary, the *Acts of John*, as well as some Nag Hammadi texts, which may be Egyptian, and together argue for a reception of John from around the middle of the second century. The widespread reception in east and west around 150 is consistent with an origin of around 100–110 for the Gospel, but the lack of definite attestation in Rome and Egypt before mid-century rules them out as places of origin, leaving Syria and Asia Minor.[225] Nagel maintains that John's Gospel plays an important role in the theological arguments of Appolinarius of Hierapolis, in Tatian's *Oratio*, and in the homily of Melito.[226]

Nagel observes that in pre-Irenaean literature John is seldom used with literal exactness, and even more seldom with express reference to the source: 'das einzige gekennzeichnete Wortlautzitat aus dem vierten Evangelium findet sich bei Theophilus von Antiochien'.[227] But this changes strikingly in the writings of the Christian Gnostics who are cited or excerpted in the Church Fathers.[228] In Heracleon's commentary we find the majority of all literal citations from the Fourth Gospel in the pre-Irenaean literature. Next to this is the Valentinian exegesis of the Prologue (usually attributed to Ptolemy) found in Irenaeus, *AH* 1. 8. 5, Ptolemy's *Letter to Flora*, the excerpts of Theodotus and Hippolytus' report of the Naassenes. The text of the Gospel is here either the object of exegesis or the ground for an argument, and often the author is named, something which only happens elsewhere with the Pauline corpus.[229] Like so many others, Nagel finds it remarkable that the earliest attribution of the Fourth Gospel to the apostle John occurs on the Christian gnostic side.[230]

Nagel then observes that it is only in the (Valentinian) sources cited by patristic authors that the Fourth Gospel is cited literally and exactly and appears as the preferred object of gnostic reception,[231] that the primary sources themselves, like the *Acts of John* and the Nag Hammadi texts, show a reception pattern comparable to that of the rest of the Christian literature of the period, without literal citation but with some kind of modification of the text. Is there a reason for this? Nagel proposes that the difference has to do with the type of writing, that is, exegetical writing, to which the secondary, Christian gnostic sources belong. Among the apologists, only Theophilus of Antioch, in his more exegetically oriented writing to Autolycus, comes close to this.[232] This is a potentially important suggestion for determining attitudes towards John's scriptural status.

---

[225] Nagel, *Rezeption*, 475–6.

[226] Ibid. 476.

[227] Ibid. 477.

[228] Ibid.

[229] Ibid.

[230] Ibid. 477–8. Nagel had not read my 1998 article, 'What Papias Said about John (and Luke): A "New" Papian Fragment', *JTS* NS 49 (1998), 582–629.

[231] Nagel, *Rezeption*, 479.

[232] Ibid. Nagel notes a similar phenomenon with the way the Gospel of Matthew is used.

Nagel ends his book with another important conclusion.

At the same time, examples may be shown that gnostic reception of Gospel of John worked itself out not only in terms of (partly unfounded) claims, but also in rejection (Abweisung) of Johannine positions. To the first named type of gnostic reception most of the cases explained above...may be reckoned. The polemic of the EpJac (NHC I. 2) against the hope of the Paraclete, and probably also the polemical reference to the incarnation Christology of John 1:14 through the Christian-gnostic handling of the Prot (NHC XIII. 1) show that the second example just discussed is no solitary one, but in fact belongs to its own type of gnostic reception. That the Gospel of John was not only the object of gnostic claims, but also the object of gnostic rejection (*Abweisung*) and polemic, makes clear once more, with the help of the texts of Nag Hammadi, that the popularity of the Gospel of John with the Valentinians represents only one aspect of the gnostic reception of John. The Valentinians, in accordance with their self understanding as pneumatics, estimated the Gospel of John as a spirit-Gospel and formed thereby a way of viewing it, which in a modified understanding the Great Church also adopted: a little later the church father Clement of Alexandria gave his high estimation of the Fourth Gospel expression with the name πνευματικὸν εὐαγγέλιον.[233]

Thus, in a way, Nagel has solidified the contention of Hengel that the 'special' use of John among the heterodox sects seems to be virtually restricted to the Valentinians. The 'tradition' from Sanders, Hillmer, and others has generally been to interpret the Nag Hammadi findings in light of the Valentinian exegetical works by Ptolemy, Heracleon, and Theodotus, and to assume that evidence for the knowledge of John in these texts is evidence for the early gnostic reception of John, an earlier reception by the gnostics than by the orthodox. Nagel has also enhanced the conclusions of Röhl about the nature of the 'reception' of the Fourth Gospel in some of the Nag Hammadi texts. Not only is the 'reception' minimal in many cases, there are some texts, in particular the *Apocryphon of James* and the *Trimorphic Protennoia*, which contain what can fairly be called polemic against certain aspects of the Fourth Gospel. This phenomenon has yet to be seen in its full extent, nor, as we shall see below, has its full relevance been realized. None the less, it is hard to overstate the importance of Nagel's detailed study for the reception of the Fourth Gospel in the pre-Irenaean Christian literature.

---

[233] Nagel, *Rezeption*, 491.

2

The State of the Question and Plan of this Book

Reception of the Consensus

As is apparent from this review, the phenomenon of orthodox Johannophobia has been for several decades a generally recognized principle among
scholars working in Johannine studies, and in New Testament and early
Christian history. It has been endorsed by most of the trusted names in
Johannine studies, one of whom declares it to be supported by 'all our
evidence'. Many of these scholars shaped Johannine studies, and New Testament studies in general, in the last half of the twentieth century. Others
are highly qualified and respected historians of early Christianity. Their
work is quite naturally relied upon by other Johannine scholars and by
specialists in related fields. When one scholar wrote that 'It is well known
that the orthodox were unwilling to quote the Fourth Gospel in the second
century, for it was much the preserve of heretics',[1] she was stating what is,
in the mainstream of the academic community, utterly non-controversial.

There has been, as we have seen, some significant resistance to the
consensus, particularly since 1989, but the theory has generated surprisingly
little controversy on explicitly theological grounds even among scholars
loyal to the Roman Catholic Church, such as Raymond Brown, or among
conservative Protestants, such as F. F. Bruce and at least two authors in the
Dictionary of the Later New Testament and its Developments, published in 1997.[2]
One of these, Gary Burge, follows Brown in pointing to the role of 1 John
in 'redeeming' the Fourth Gospel from the Gnostics.

Hippolytus (c. 170–c. 236) describes how Johannine language was used by his
gnostic opponents. This may explain why the orthodox church (the 'Great Church'
as some label it) embraced the Fourth Gospel reluctantly. In fact there is a surprising lack of interest in the Johannine writings among the leading second-century
writers. The church's gnostic opponents were using the Fourth Gospel or a form of

---

[1] C. Trevett, *A Study of Ignatius of Antioch in Syria and Asia*, Studies in the Bible and Early Christianity, 29 (Lewiston, NY, 1992), 197. In the next year the summary statement, 'The Fourth Gospel
was opposed as heretical in the early church', appeared in a book whose authors announced that
they had been 'trained in the best universities in North America and Europe' (*The Five Gospels. The
Search for the Authentic Words of Jesus. New Translation and Commentary by Robert W. Funk, Roy W. Hoover,
and the Jesus Seminar* (Toronto, 1993), pp. ix, 20.
[2] G. Burge, 'John, Letters of', in R. P. Martin and P. H. Davids (eds.), *Dictionary of the Later New
Testament and its Developments* (Downers Grove, Ill., 1997), 587–99; J. D. G. Dunn, 'Pseudepigraphy',
DLNTD, 977–84.

it. As many scholars believe, it was the epistles of John—1 John in particular—that redeemed the Fourth Gospel for the NT we possess today.[3]

The prolific New Testament scholar and exegete J. D. G. Dunn has recently written of the eccentricity of the Johannine Gospel and has cited the salvaging efforts of Irenaeus:

we must acknowledge also that John's developed *content* validates . . . even a dangerous use as 'Gospel,' since that same portrayal seems to have given scope to those who pushed Christology in a docetic direction.[4]

Indeed, we may deduce from the infrequency of reference to John's Gospel in the early Fathers and from the copious use of it by the Valentinians,[5] that John's Gospel was in some danger of being taken over by the Gnostics and thus lost to the emerging Great Church. Here again it was probably Irenaeus who stemmed the tide and demonstrated John's authenticity as a statement of the one gospel.[6]

In John's case the degree of elaboration of the Jesus tradition brought it close to the boundary of what was and was not counted acceptable. It was Irenaeus's advocacy of John as part of the fourfold Gospel witness, despite its attractiveness to the Gnostic sects, that made its place within the emerging orthodox canon secure.[7]

Though Dunn had access to Hengel's *The Johannine Question* when he wrote at least one of the essays cited above, he was obviously not moved by it away from the Sanders line on orthodox Johannophobia and Valentinian Johannophilia. It is interesting to note the inferences Dunn has drawn with the help of this analysis. Using this Gospel in the second century was 'dangerous' because it was also being used by docetists, thus implying a susceptibility to docetic interpretation. While denying that John's *religions-geschichtilich* context is gnosticism of any intelligible kind, Dunn finds that the gnostic appropriation of John, at least by Valentinians, was serious enough to have greatly endangered its survival among the Church's Gospels. The Church's reluctance towards John is also taken as a reflection on the acceptability of John's distinctive 'elaboration of the Jesus tradition'. The eventual acceptance of this 'dangerous' Gospel also shows for Dunn the acceptable limits of pseudonymity in the New Testament documents.

In the presentations of many experts, the evidence for the theory of orthodox Johannophobia appears to be so thoroughgoing and monolithic that the theory might seem to be amenable to only minor adjustments or

---

[3] Burge, 'John, Letters of', 590.

[4] J. D. G. Dunn, 'John and the Synoptics as a Theological Question', in R. Alan Culpepper and C. Clifton Black (eds.), *Exploring the Gospel of John: In Honor of D. Moody Smith* (Louisville, Ky., 1996), 301–13, at 307. For this Dunn cites the support of Brown, *Community*, 110–20.

[5] At this point Dunn refers to J. N. Sanders's *The Fourth Gospel in the Early Church*, 55–66, and to D. M. Smith's 1984 essay which briefly updated Sanders.

[6] Dunn, 'Theological Question', 308.

[7] Dunn, 'Pseudepigraphy', 981.

corrections of detail. Did the orthodox, one might ask, always use 'rubbish heaps', as Charlesworth assumes, when discarding copies of the Fourth Gospel they came across, or were there other customary ways of disposing of dangerous gnostic or proto-gnostic texts? We know for a fact that several copies of the Fourth Gospel ended up in the rubbish heap at Oxyrhynchus in Egypt (nine, at last count, though the number may yet rise higher). But then, so did copies of the First Gospel and the Letters of Paul, and even an early copy of Irenaeus' anti-gnostic *Against Heresies*, thus raising another topic for study, 'Did the orthodox and the heterodox use the same rubbish heaps?'[8]

Resistance to the Consensus

It is fair to say that F.-M. Braun's substantial 1959 study, while it sometimes received a respectful nod from later scholars, has commanded relatively little of their attention and less of their assent. In influence it was virtually buried by the much shorter, but ostensibly more convincing, studies of Sanders and Hillmer—despite the fact that Hillmer's was never published! The monographs of Sanders and Hillmer had the support of Koester, Barrett, Brown, Culpepper, and Johannine scholars generally until the appearance of Martin Hengel's 1989 and 1993 books. Hengel seemed intent on demolishing many of the household idols of contemporary scholarship regarding several aspects of Johannine studies. Yet despite predictions of a violent response to Hengel's criticisms,[9] much of scholarship, so far, seems to have received its spanking quite gingerly, and to have gone on almost unaffected. Culpepper's 1994 book may certainly be credited with acknowledging some use of the Fourth Gospel among the orthodox prior to about 150. He mentions some of the sources cited by Hengel but usually neglected. But if anything, Charlesworth's 1995 book goes beyond the pre-Hengel consensus in its penchant for dogmatic generalizations. The articles by Lattke in 1994, Sloyan in 1996, Zumstein in 1997, and Gamble in 2000 take no visible steps away from Sanders and Hillmer. And so, right up until the year 2000, most scholars who have touched on the subject since Hengel, even while mentioning the Tübingen professor and giving him much praise, do not seem dissuaded from the orthodox Johannophobia paradigm.

[8] In his study of intentional book-burning in antiquity, 'Books for the Burning', *Transactions and Proceedings of the American Philological Association*, 67 (1936), 114–25, Clarence A. Forbes lists no instance of Christians deliberately burning heretical books before Christianity became the official religion of the Roman Empire. He even says, 'The surprising thing is not that some books got burned in the conflict between moribund paganism and nascent Christianity, but that the burned books were so few. When early Christianity had to fight for its life and when it found obnoxious matter in so much of the pagan literature, it really exercised great tolerance in destroying few books except those that contained heresies or frontal attacks upon itself' (125).

[9] e.g. Ruth B. Edwards, *The Expository Times*, 102 (1990), 88, 'I have little doubt that this work will provoke a strong reaction'; Randall D. Chestnutt, *Restoration Quarterly*, 34 (1992), 121, 'the book is certain to evoke extreme reactions'.

It may be asked whether, since Hengel's 1989 book, the counter-evidence is not mounting to the point where it will have to demand more critical attention. There is a willingness on the part of Kieffer, Röhl, and now Nagel to take another look at the question of the 'silence' of the earliest ecclesiastical authors, and to examine not only the extent but also the nature of gnostic use of John. These scholars, at least, have found reason for thinking that the Fourth Gospel left more traces of its use among the orthodox than has usually been admitted, and each has challenged in some way the alleged hegemony of heterodox use. Nagel's recent study in particular deserves attention for its careful scrutiny of the sources and for its departure from the norm on the question of the extent of orthodox use.

The present volume will show further grounds for a shift in the paradigm which has for so long guided, and in some cases, I fear, controlled investigation. There is scope, I believe, for a study larger and more encompassing than Hengel's or Kieffer's and focused differently from Röhl's or Nagel's. There is a need to address the consensus directly at each major point and to place the question of the reception of the Johannine Gospel in the context of the reception of the entire Johannine corpus.

Consequences of the Question

The place of the Johannine literature in the Church of the second century is a topic worthy of protracted study in its own right, given the important role this literature has played in the life of the Church, and in Western culture, ever since. As such, the consensus about orthodox Johannophobia has several important implications or consequences which scholars have not hesitated to draw. These include the following.

FOR THE RECEPTION OF THE FOURTH GOSPEL AS SCRIPTURE

It is common for scholars to state that the Fourth Gospel had 'certain difficulties getting accepted into the Christian canon of Scriptures', difficulties which are related at least to a great extent to its 'adoption by a movement that ended outside the Church: namely, Gnosticism'.[10] This Gospel was in real danger of being permanently co-opted by gnostics and Valentinians, and so the orthodox were reluctant to use it. A key role is usually assigned to Irenaeus in either snatching back or snatching away a Gospel which had formerly been the recognized property of heretics. And yet, even if the paradigm is correct at this point, it is very questionable whether the turnabout said to have been effected by Irenaeus and others has ever been adequately accounted for. The circumstances of the reception of the Fourth

---

[10] Sloyan, 'Gnostic Adoption', 125.

Gospel as scripture by the Church in the second half, even the third quarter, of the second century, remain largely a mystery.

FOR THE PHENOMENON OF A JOHANNINE CORPUS

Another consequence of the paradigm is the entrenchment of the separation between the several members of the Johannine corpus. The tendency of scholarship to assign each member of the corpus not only to different authors but to quite different socio-religious situations is only strengthened by the idea, promoted particularly by Brown and many since, that 1 John was written in great part to 'redeem' the Fourth Gospel for but one faction of the splintered Johannine community, at a time when that Gospel was being claimed as the legitimation for other factions. The relation of the two remaining Johannine epistles is left unclear, and the distance between the 'proto-gnostic' Gospel and the apocalyptic Revelation is certainly great. Here the paradigm leaves a gaping hole to be filled, for somehow all five (or possibly four, for 3 John has left little trace) of these by the time of Irenaeus were so closely related in the minds of at least some orthodox Christians that they were confidently used as products of the same author. Part of our concern then will be to ask when a consciousness of a Johannine corpus emerged and what it meant for the Church of the second century to conceive of these works as a corpus.

FOR JOHANNINE ORIGINS

J. N. Sanders concluded that the Fourth Gospel was used first by gnostics and Valentinians before it caught on in the mainstream Church. What does this have to say about the Gospel's origins? Based upon the record of the second century, and relying upon Bauer's conclusion that there was no such thing as 'orthodoxy' in early, Christian Alexandria, Sanders proposed that the Fourth Gospel itself arose in this open, free-thinking, Alexandrian environment. Barrett could not endorse Alexandria, but still reasoned that the Fourth Gospel must have had its origin 'in circles either gnostic or obscure . . . away from the main stream of the Church's life and activity'.[11] Barrett, as observed above, ultimately rejected the first possibility (a gnostic origin) but affirmed the second. His conclusion was echoed by D. M. Smith, who deduced that the Johannine Gospel 'originated in a rather remote corner of the Christian map'.[12] The traditional connection with Ephesus, acknowledged by all to be secure from about the time of Irenaeus, is thus all but excluded by many scholars, as it was hardly a Christian backwater even by the end of the first century.

---

[11] Barrett, *John* (1955), 111–12 (1978 edn., 131–2).
[12] Smith, *Johannine Christianity*, 22.

This evidence might also have direct implications for the question of authorial origins. Culpepper puts it provocatively, 'If one or more of the Johannine writings was authored by the apostle, or if they emerged from an influential school associated with a cluster of communities in Asia Minor, then why is there such a gap in the record so soon after the composition of these works?'[13] That is, for Culpepper, as for Sanders, Haenchen, and many others, the apparent absence of influence in the early second-century Church is prohibitive of an apostolic origin for this Gospel;[14] it challenges just as forcefully the notion that this Gospel could have emerged from an influential school in Asia Minor. Certainly scholars have other reasons for rejecting the tradition of apostolic authorship, but it cannot be denied that the second-century evidence has played an important role.

Hand in hand with questions of geographical and authorial origin go questions of intellectual/religious milieu. Since the days of Bultmann and Dodd there has been a noticeable shift in preference away from Hellenism towards a more Jewish context for the Fourth Gospel among scholars. But while Qumran exercises a pull towards Palestinian Judaism, Nag Hammadi tugs in the direction of popular Greek philosophy and religious syncretism. The Fourth Gospel is also embroiled in the ongoing debate about the Jewishness or otherwise of the earliest gnostics. But it is fair to say that advocates of a gnostic or gnosticizing Fourth Gospel, though they represent only a minority of current scholarship, have only been helped by the consensus of thought which, following Sanders, has recognized an early reception of that Gospel among heterodox groups. Thus both Röhl and Nagel, who have found that use to be somewhat less pervasive and enthusiastic than advertised, see their research as undermining the argument for a gnostic origin of the Fourth Gospel.

These then are some of the implications for our historical understanding of the early fortunes of the Johannine corpus which arise directly or indirectly from the dominant paradigm. There are possible practical effects for the Church which might be mentioned as well.

FOR THE CONTEMPORARY CHURCH

Only a minority of scholars have argued for a very thoroughly gnostic context for the Gospel itself. But its early use by 'heterodox' elements in Christianity, indicating its susceptibility to docetic and gnostic interpretation, and the possible support of some of these tendencies by the original author(s), has been strongly endorsed by the majority. It is legitimate then to ponder the ramifications this might have if allowed to penetrate the believing communities of Christians abroad.

---

[13] Culpepper, *John*, 131.

[14] Presumably this should also hold for Charlesworth's identification of the Beloved Disciple as the apostle Thomas.

It is possible, first of all, that there need be no ramifications at all for the Church. The use of the Fourth Gospel by early heterodox groups may have been essentially illegitimate, or, it may have been mainly for the purposes of seducing simple believers in the orthodox congregations. This was certainly the position of Irenaeus by about AD 180 and it is a possible position today.[15] Some, however, might charge that this position turns a blind eye to the facts. If there was a real affinity, even a consanguinity, between this Gospel and the heterodox groups which used it throughout the second century, should this not be interpreted as indicating the need for the Church to be ever welcoming of theological diversity (to say nothing, for the moment, of other forms of diversity)? Various forms of (what have been seen as) gnostic impulses have been advocated in the Church of Jesus Christ in recent times,[16] and the susceptibility of one of the Church's foundational documents to a 'gnostic' interpretation in the early Church could be regarded as a justification for accepting and encouraging such impulses.

On the other hand, some might consider that the gnostic reading of the Fourth Gospel, whether it is considered historically legitimate as, for instance, by Lattke, or even as understood by Brown, is undesirable for the Church. In this case, as in the case of the allegations of anti-Semitism in the Fourth Gospel, one might advocate a circumscribed or limited authority for this Gospel in the Church. If the Church is to continue according the Fourth Gospel a place in its canon of scripture, if preaching and teaching based on this early Christian source is to go forward for Christian communities of faith, an implicit or explicit criticism of some views of the evangelist might be thought necessary to accompany the use of his work.

What direction the discussion should go in is of course a matter for the scholars, leaders, and the laity of the churches to consider, and my study will not enter further into this discussion. But there is one thing which I take to be at least theoretically agreeable to those on every side, to those at least who have not completely abandoned the idea of inherent meaning in texts and in history. And that is that the responses of the Church should be formed in the light of the most accurate historical conclusions possible.

The Three Empirical Bases for the Consensus

From the writings of the scholars quoted above, it is apparent that three major planks, three major empirical bases, are thought to support the con-

---

[15] e.g. Barnabas Lindars, *The Gospel of John*, New Century Bible (London, 1972), 63, 'the fact that Gnostics, holding Docetic views, were the first to value the Fourth Gospel only shows that it is possible to interpret it in this way, given their presuppositions, and it does not prove that John would have agreed with them'.

[16] As noted by Sloyan, 'Gnostic Adoption', 131,

clusion of a widespread orthodox Johannophobia throughout most of the second century. They are as follows.

JOHANNOPHOBIA PROPER

First, 'Johannophobia', as I am using it here, properly refers to an actual state of mind thought to have existed widely among the orthodox, that is, a mental state of suspicion, prejudice, fear, or opposition as regards the Fourth Gospel. We might expect that actual statements expressing such attitudes of mind would be available in some abundance from the second century. And yet, surprisingly, the only orthodox specifically named by the scholars above as exhibiting explicit animosity towards this Gospel are (1) Gaius of Rome, (2) those mysterious people whom Epiphanius later dubs 'the Alogi', and (3) an equally mysterious group mentioned some years earlier by Irenaeus in the third book of *Against Heresies*. As we shall see, many scholars believe that Epiphanius' Alogi are simply Gaius and Gaius alone.[17] This would reduce the 'many pre-Nicene critics' of the Fourth Gospel to a party of one individual and one group, neither of whom is very well understood. We have seen that Hengel claims that real opposition to the Gospel does not appear until between 180 and 200 (though we might allow that the group known to Irenaeus may have been active a bit earlier, say, 175).[18] Are these then the only known orthodox, or possibly orthodox, sources which manifest animosity towards the Fourth Gospel? This question will have to be part of our investigation. But in any case, the two or three sources mentioned constitute the prime extent of the positive, evidentiary basis for the existence of widespread orthodox Johannophobia.

THE SILENCE OF THE EARLY ORTHODOX SOURCES

But of course this positive evidence, such as it is, is not the sole basis for the claim of orthodox Johannophobia in the second century. Johannophobia can also refer to a suspicion, a wariness towards the Fourth Gospel, which did not express itself in explicit statements of rejection. This is assumed to describe much of the attitude of the orthodox towards John up to Irenaeus. Thus, whatever clear-cut statements of Johannophobia we might chance to find are regarded by scholars as simply the confirming complement of the very remarkable failure of orthodox writers in the first half or three-quarters of the second century to 'quote' or make constructive use of the Fourth Gospel in their writings.[19] This Gospel was either unknown to the orthodox

---

[17] Culpepper, *John*, 122, in fact has remarked that 'Recent scholarship has therefore dismissed the Alogoi from the stage of history. We have no evidence of such a group.'

[18] This is the year specified, for some reason, by Bauer, *Orthodoxy and Heresy*, 207–8.

[19] '[T]he nearly complete silence of the record during the crucial decades of the early second century', as Culpepper, *John*, 131, says.

or avoided by them. But, of course, to say that such a silence was due to a perceived gnostic contamination of the Fourth Gospel (or that it was due to anything else, for that matter) is to argue from silence; the sources themselves, being silent, do not supply a motive. Searching the orthodox literature of the second century for the knowledge and 'reception' of the Fourth Gospel (along with the rest of the Johannine literature), particularly prior to Irenaeus, will be a major part of the investigation below.

THE GNOSTIC PREFERENCE FOR JOHN

Some arguments from silence, of course, are weightier than others, depending on the import of the positive data surrounding the silence. And the pertinent evidence surrounding this reported orthodox silence, in fact the real, positive, evidence cited to support the conclusion of a widespread orthodox Johannophobia, is found in what is by contrast the relatively abundant and free use of the Fourth Gospel on the part of 'gnostics' and other heterodox teachers in the same period. As J.-M. Poffet says, there is seen to be 'a fundamental difference between the writings of the Great Church and those of the Valentinians. From the one side, an absence of clear Johannine citations, and this even when the thought is very close, for example in Ignatius of Antioch; from the other side, an omnipresence (*omniprésence*) of the texts of the Fourth Gospel'.[20]

This 'omniprésence' of the Fourth Gospel among the Valentinians, if not among other heterodox groups, is the bedrock upon which all proponents have erected the theory. But, as we have seen, at this point there exists a continuum of thought on the precise relationship between the Fourth Gospel and heterodoxy. It is possible, while perhaps recognizing certain commonalities between Johannine and 'gnostic' thought, to believe that the heterodox use of the second century was essentially adventitious or illegitimate, that Irenaeus had every right to react against the Valentinians as he did. F.-M. Braun and probably Martin Hengel would be near this point. A step away are those who recognize deeper affinities with heterodox thought while still holding that John's use of 'gnostic' terminology and modes of thought was essentially apologetic or missionizing, so that Irenaeus was still being faithful to the spirit of John in seeking to use it, in certain important theological areas at least, against the heretics. One might see J. N. Sanders and the 1955 Barrett, and perhaps D. Moody Smith, at this juncture. A step or two further along the continuum would find us perhaps in the company of the 1978 Barrett or the post-1979 Brown, in recognizing a greater legitimacy in the heterodox use, going back all the way to the seceders of 1 John themselves, who, it is thought, had some real and valid claim to the Johannine inheritance. Even here, however, there is an allow-

---

[20] Poffet, 'Indices de réception', 320.

ance that some of the 'common ground' may have been unintended by the author or redactor of the Gospel, and that Irenaeus and the orthodox are ultimately to be considered the more trustworthy exegetes of the original Johannine legacy. Beyond this point in the continuum we have probably crossed the line which separates John as an orthodox or proto-orthodox work from John as the product of the heterodox or, as Charlesworth puts it, 'proto-gnostic' trajectory in early Christianity. Here we might distinguish the view of Bultmann, who saw John operating within a gnostic framework but reacting against it, from the views of scholars like Schottroff, Käsemann, Lattke, Gesine Schenke Robinson, and others, who regard John, at least at a primary redactional stage, as fully within the early gnostic trajectory. In the latter case, use of John was always more natural and legitimate for the heterodox than for the representatives of the Great Church. And for scholars on this end of the spectrum, and perhaps for some of the others as well, the eventual orthodox takeover of John was essentially political, and very likely accomplished by the conscious employment of underhanded means.[21]

Nearly all of the scholars we have mentioned, however, recognize at least a real 'affinity' between the Fourth Gospel and gnostic thought, though they differ on the extent of that affinity. And for a great majority the story of the 'reception' of the Fourth Gospel by the Great Church in the last two or three decades of the second century is essentially the story of the orthodox either 'recovering' or 'snatching away' a Gospel which had never before had any secure home among them.

The Orientation of the Following Study

We must acknowledge then that the existence of a widespread orthodox Johannophobia seems a very plausible conclusion— perhaps the inevitable conclusion—from these three perceived phenomena: extensive gnostic use; virtual orthodox disuse; and occasional, express orthodox hostility,[22] the latter assumed to have been more frequent than our sources now show. Yet I have chosen to call these perceptions because I believe that all three are inadequate representations of the facts and all three are due to be challenged.

The sections which immediately follow, then, are oriented towards these three empirical bases for the Orthodox Johannophobia Paradigm (OJP).

---

[21] e.g. Lattke, 'Gnostic Jesus', 151, 'The early Catholic church snatched John away from the growing Gnostic movement and canonized it by redaction and the formation of Ephesian legends.'

[22] Sanders stated the three planks concisely in his 1950 book, *The Foundations of the Christian Faith*, 158, 'The tardy acceptance of the Fourth Gospel as the work of John by orthodox writers, in contrast to the welcome which it received from the Gnostics, and a certain amount of active opposition to it on the part of otherwise orthodox Roman Christians.'

Since the period from about 170 or 175 to about 200 is said even by the proponents of the paradigm to be the time in which the Fourth Gospel was quickly gaining the ascendancy among the orthodox, just about everywhere but in Rome, I shall attempt in Chapter 3 a sketch of the situation with regard to the Fourth Gospel among the orthodox churches, starting in the 170s, leading up to the time of Gaius and 'the Alogi' probably shortly after the year 200. The concern here will be (1) not only to see how each author in this period treats the Fourth Gospel and to consider its place in that author's Christian community, but also to look for (2) signs of controversy, signs of awareness that these orthodox writers were taking over, or taking back, a Gospel from 'gnostics' or Valentinians. (3) The role played by Irenaeus will be of particular interest, (4) as will any reaction which might be detected from Rome. (5) The examination seeks to discover what the authors of this period might tell us about any previous use of this Gospel, whether among orthodox or heterodox, for the OJP dictates that use of it was scant among the orthodox but plentiful among the heterodox of earlier periods. (6) In addition, attention will be drawn to the relationship between members of the Johannine corpus in the writings of each person or document treated.

Chapter 4 is devoted to Gaius of Rome and the alleged controversy over the Johannine Gospel and Apocalypse. Should this protest be seen as the expression of a long-standing, conservative attitude which wanted to protect the Church from a Gospel tainted by heresy? Or is it perhaps an interesting but essentially anomalous reaction to the status quo? Are we in fact sure of the nature of Gaius' position with regard to the Johannine writings?

Chapter 5 investigates the chief empirical basis for the OJP, the abundant use of the Fourth Gospel (with an eye also upon the Letters and Apocalypse) among heterodox, particularly Valentinian, authors and groups, which can be plausibly dated to the second century. The purpose will be to gain an accurate picture not only of the extent of that use, but also of the attitudes displayed towards that Gospel, and the likelihood that heterodox use and attitudes generated orthodox Johannophobia. At the end of this discussion it will be asked what it was about the Fourth Gospel which, scholars have determined, attracted these groups, in the light of the evidence found in the sources.

At this point attention returns to the orthodox, to consider the remaining empirical basis for the OJP, the paucity or absence of orthodox use of the Johannine Gospel before about the time of Irenaeus. Beginning then from about 170 and working backwards from there to 150 (Chapter 6), and then into the period prior to 150 (Chapter 7), the investigation seeks evidence of the use of the Fourth Gospel primarily, and of the rest of the Johannine corpus as well, among Irenaeus' orthodox predecessors. Since the role of Justin is accentuated by many proponents of the OJP as representing the position of the orthodox in Rome with regard to the Fourth Gospel, special attention will be given to his writings.

An Observation about Method: The Quotation Standard

Before proceeding, and while on the topic of the bases for the consensus view, I must observe a methodological question of great significance regarding the standards for determining literary borrowing. It will have been noticed even from the excerpts above (and will be seen at several points below) how often advocates of the consensus speak of the 'silence' of the orthodox with regard to the Johannine Gospel, and how often this silence is couched in terms of a failure to provide 'clear' or 'explicit quotations'[23] of the Fourth Gospel, or to name its (assumed) author. 'Explicit quotation' usually means a quotation introduced by a citation formula,[24] and which corresponds to its alleged exemplar with exact or near-exact verbal precision. And even an exact correspondence with Johannine material might not always suffice to show an author's knowledge of John, if the possibility exists that the material in question might be attributable to 'the tradition' and not exclusively to John.[25] In this matter of explicit quotation and attribution the gnostics, particularly the Valentinians,[26] are thought to have greatly surpassed the orthodox, and this is taken to signify that it was the former who first received the Fourth Gospel as an authoritative or scriptural document.

Some scholars, it is true, have objected to the standard of exact or near-exact verbal correspondence as unjustified (particularly, it seems, with regard to Ignatius of Antioch),[27] but for whatever reason, most scholars have accepted it as a matter of course. Yet it is more than ripe for scrutiny. In his recent work Nagel defends a much looser, but arguably much more realistic, standard for recognizing literary dependence or 'reception'.[28]

The assumption among most Johannine scholars and scholars of early Christianity right up to the present seems to have been that literary quota-

---

[23] e.g. Pollard, *Johannine Christology*, 24–5; Zumstein, 'Communauté', 360.

[24] 'In order to establish definitely that the written gospel has been used it is necessary to have either explicit quotation formulae or some indication that the written gospel is being cited, or else it is necessary to prove that parallels are with material in the gospel which has been written by the author himself or which reflects characteristics of his work' (Hillmer, 'Second Century', introductory summary).

[25] 'If a writer has parallels only with material contained in John's sources or the traditional material in the gospel then there is no proof that he has used the Fourth Gospel' (ibid. 6).

[26] Nagel, *Rezeption*, 479, has made the acute observation that it is only in the 'exegetical' works of the Valentinians where one can see a greater concern for accurate quotation of the Johannine material, not in the Nag Hammadi treatises or in Ptolemy's *Letter to Flora*.

[27] See e.g. the history of research on Ignatius up to 1940 given by Walter J. Burghardt, 'Did Saint Ignatius of Antioch Know the Fourth Gospel', *Theological Studies*, 1 (1940), 1–26; 130–56, who cites the repeated objections of scholars like Camerlynck to von der Goltz's 'unwarranted insistence on the norm of perfect identity of form' (11).

[28] Nagel, *Rezeption*, 34–40.

tions in antiquity were customarily made with the source open in front of the writer, or, if the writer was quoting from memory, that memorized material was always reproduced nearly flawlessly, but that in either case, that the unwavering ideal of the secondary author was to replicate the words of the original with perfect verbal precision and with as much contextual fidelity as possible (much as it is today among Western scholars). In this case, any but the most minor deviations may be read as indicating that the secondary author did not know the Fourth Gospel but was indebted to a similar tradition, perhaps even a source relied upon by the Fourth Gospel itself. But how appropriate is this standard for determining borrowed material? Does it accurately reflect the literary customs of antiquity, or is it based more on modern notions and practices?

A very helpful study has been made by John Whittaker of what turns out to be a quite widespread, and at least in some circles a well-recognized,[29] tendency of ancient writers to introduce deliberate changes into the texts they quote. As a result of his extensive work in editing ancient texts, mainly in the philosophical tradition, Whittaker takes for granted that many *bona-fide* textual borrowings reproduce their sources very inexactly. He writes concerning the causes of the phenomenon.

That faulty memory in the case of short quotations, and carelessness in the case of longer passages, do play their role in the garbling of indirectly transmitted portions of text, I do not, of course, intend to contest. What I do emphasize is that in the indirect transmission[30] of philosophical texts (and, I suspect, of many others) an equally frequent and fertile source of corruption (if this be the appropriate term) can be found in the persistent inclination of the scholars and writers of the ancient world to introduce into their quotations deliberate alteration.[31]

That is, authors often consciously adapted the material they quoted or borrowed, for varying reasons.

Whittaker takes as one prime example a text which he has edited, the *Didaskalikos* or *Epitome* of Platonic doctrines, a 'handbook of Platonic philosophy', written by Alcinous in the first or second century. This book contained an 'enormous profusion of quotations and reminiscences of Plato in particular', in which 'many of these quotations and reminiscences were not

---

[29] Annewies van den Hoek, 'Techniques of Quotation in Clement of Alexandria: A View of Ancient Literary Working Methods', *VC* 50 (1996), 223–43, at 228, speaking of Clement of Alexandria's practice, 'not all material taken from other writers is a clear-cut quotation. This problem is well-known to anyone who works with quotations in authors of almost any period of the past.' She also later observes, 'It has often been said that in ancient rhetorical traditions, citing by name was not customary or even polite, because the educated audience was supposed to know their classics' (229). See also Nagel, *Rezeption*, 36–7.

[30] That is, transmission not directly, though editions of entire works, but indirectly, through second-hand quotation or borrowing.

[31] John Whittaker, 'The Value of Indirect Tradition in the Establishment of Greek Philosophical Texts or the Art of Misquotation', in John N. Grant (ed.), *Editing Greek and Latin Texts: Papers Given at the Twenty-Third Annual Conference on Editorial Problems, University of Toronto 6–7 November 1987* (New York, 1989), 63–95, at 64.

only brief but also out of context . . . and . . . the vast majority of these borrow-ings diverged to a greater or lesser degree from the wording of their original'.[32] Whittaker observes that this author's 'technique of manipulating the text of Plato and others is not peculiar to himself but at the very least characteristic of his epoch, and in large measure of Greek literature generally' (citing Philo, Plutarch, Galen, and the Stoicizing Arius Didymus).[33] He documents the common disturbances of word-order,[34] addition, subtraction, and substitu-tion[35] of different words or different forms of the same words, all in 'quoted' or clearly borrowed material, in cases wherein it certainly cannot be argued that Alcinous 'was not acquainted at first hand with the text of Plato'.[36]

Another example treated by Whittaker, Porphyry's collection of *Oracles*, shows that these same techniques can be found in Greek literature even in the quotation of 'sacred' materials. In his introduction to the *Oracles*[37] Por-phyry claims that he has 'added nothing to nor subtracted anything from' the *sentiments* (νοημάτων) of the divine oracles he has cited (Eusebius, *Praep. Evang.* 4. 7. 1). Yet he also informs the reader that he has indeed at times altered the wording of the texts themselves, and not merely to correct what he regarded as erroneous readings. 'What does provoke a shudder is Por-phyry's ready admission that he has willfully rephrased the text in the interest of clarity, and that he has deliberately omitted material which he considered irrelevant to his own end . . . even in the case of a text such as the *Oracles*, which the editor claimed to be divinely inspired!'[38] Such an attitude towards the alteration of texts in quotations or expositions (one presumes, when the substance of a source was not considered violated), evidently drew little objection.[39] Porphyry's case could become particularly

---

[32] Ibid. 66.

[33] Ibid. 68.

[34] 'Modification of word-order is the most elementary of the four categories of textual change. To modify the word-order is, in a sense, to make no change at all. Every word still stands intact. They simply follow each other in a new order, the very novelty of which, by flouting the expect-ation of the reader, strikes him more forcibly than would the familiar original' (ibid. 73); 'Nor are these techniques confined to philosophical literature. I mention for what it may be worth that modifications of word-order and logical order are among the major means employed by St Luke to distinguish his own gospel from the rest of the synoptic tradition. We may conclude that such modifications were not considered improper, even where, in the case of alteration of the logical sequence, they might necessitate changes in the grammatical forms of words' (74–5).

[35] Ibid. 85–6, 'The evidence indicates that substitutions were an integral and intentional con-stituent of commentary and exposition . . . a further dominant motive, I suspect, was, as in the case of other phenomena we have considered, the desire to put a personal mark upon the material one comments, expounds, or otherwise appropriates.'

[36] Ibid. 73.

[37] Unfortunately, we no longer have the *Oracles* itself, only Porphyry's introduction to it preserved by Eusebius.

[38] Whittaker, 'Indirect Tradition', 70.

[39] Ibid. He observes, 'Nor does Eusebius offer any criticism of Porphyry's editorial principles—with good reason, one might say, considering Eusebius' own reputation in modern times for editor-ial practice . . . Theodoret has no word of criticism . . . for Porphyry's editorial procedure, which by his own standards he presumably found unexceptionable' (70).

relevant, for example, when assessing the question of Justin's knowledge of the Fourth Gospel.

We have then to reckon with the fact that, in the second century, literary customs of borrowing or citation demanded neither the exact reproduction of texts, nor the explicit acknowledgement of the author of the borrowed texts.[40] It was evidently little or no different with regard to religious texts. It is certainly true, of course, that exact citation and acknowledgement of sources did occur and was also consistent with a high admiration for the source. But it is worth observing that such carefulness did not always convey such admiration. Annewies van den Hoek remarks concerning Clement of Alexandria, 'It is particularly striking that Clement acknowledges the works of his gnostic adversaries in such an accurate way, naming author and book. This scrupulousness stands in sharp contrast to his practice in borrowing from authors to whom he apparently felt a kinship, such as Philo, Tatian, and Pantaenus.'[41] She reports on Clement's leaving 'strange gaps in the credits to authors that seem to have been dear to his heart'.[42] This shows that it is even possible for an author to be most scrupulous about sources precisely when he might want to take issue with them. This of course is not to say (in advance of study) that any exact quotations or explicit acknowledgement of John, whether by Valentinian or by Great Church writers, should be thought to signify a critical attitude towards it. It should only caution us about making automatic assumptions without close examination of a number of situational factors.

What is the consequence of this brief reflection on the standards of literary borrowing in antiquity? Obviously, there comes a point at which the 'inexactness' of a proposed reference is so pronounced as to call the identity of the source into question or to rule out a given source altogether. I do not believe it is possible to specify in advance precise quotas or standards in this matter; much will depend upon factors such as the length or level of detail of the parallel material, the secondary author's use of elements characteristic of or unique to the proposed source, the presence of other reminiscences from the same source, contextual references or allusions to the (presumed) author of the source, a comparison with the author's use of OT or other NT sources, and other contextual features which might reflect on the probability of the secondary author's knowledge of the proposed source. The question of possible alternative sources, whether oral or written, must also frequently come into play. I only wish to emphasize at this point that a relatively greater precision in literary borrowing and a relatively more frequent explicit naming of the author of the Fourth Gospel

---

[40] I have not addressed directly the matter of citation formulas, but, in the light of what we have seen, who is to say that the use of such formulas always denotes a higher respect for a text than does the incorporation of words and phrases from that text into one's own thought?

[41] Van den Hoek, 'Techniques', 233.

[42] Ibid. 237.

on the part of gnostic or Valentinian writers as compared with orthodox (if indeed this proves to be the case) should not be exclusively relied upon to decide the matter of who first treasured the Fourth Gospel and accorded it a scriptural status. We may find that the standards which have often been applied in the question of literary borrowing from the Fourth Gospel on the part of Great Church writers have not always been in keeping with the standards of the day, nor with a given author's own method and intentions.

II

The Johannine Writings in the Second Century

3

John among the Orthodox, *c.* AD 170–200

Scholars who support the OJP differ somewhat over the question of exactly who first introduced the Fourth Gospel to orthodox audiences and initiated the orthodox retrieval of John, and over exactly when this occurred. The name most frequently associated with the recovery is that of Irenaeus, whose use of this Gospel is the most accessible of any orthodox writer to his time, and whose influence as an author is widely recognized. Yet some scholars will allow for a bit of tentative, antecedent use. Koester thinks that before Irenaeus quoted from it in Gaul in the 180s he must have become acquainted with it in Asia Minor, though he does not speculate on whether Irenaeus ultimately got it from Church leaders or from heretics.[1] Haenchen concedes that 'John 1: 5 is quoted in *Oratio ad Graecos* 13. 1 as scripture' by Tatian. But he adds, 'that takes us approximately to the year 176 CE, and thus very close to the time of Irenaeus; it would thus not be a fundamentally new piece of evidence'.[2] Walter Bauer and Raymond Brown also cite Tatian, but only his *Diatessaron*, which used all four of the canonical Gospels. And both of these writers promptly remove Tatian from the orthodox witness stand and make him a witness for the heterodox. Tatian broke with the Church in Rome 'on account of profound differences in faith',[3] by becoming 'an encratite who played down the value of the flesh, and so he should be reckoned on the heterodox side of the usage of John'.[4] Brown goes on to propose that 'The earliest indisputable orthodox use of the Fourth Gospel is by Theophilus of Antioch in his *Apology to Autolycus (ca.* A.D. 180)'.[5] Brown discovers the first indisputable orthodox use in about 180; Haenchen will come down as far as 176, each finding but one slightly earlier precursor to the practice of Irenaeus in the 180s.

Culpepper, perhaps owing to the researches of Hengel, is willing to see orthodox use of John beginning somewhat earlier. He begins his examination of 'the Church's acceptance of the Johannine writings' with the anti-heretical apocryphon, the *Epistula Apostolorum*, which he dates to *c.*160–70.

---

[1] H. Koester, 'Ephesos in Early Christian Literature', in H. Koester (ed.), *Ephesos: Metropolis of Asia Minor*, Harvard Theological Studies (Valley Forge, Pa., 1995), 119–40, at 138.

[2] E. Haenchen, *John 1* (Philadelphia, 1984), 14.

[3] W. Bauer, *Orthodoxy and Heresy in Earliest Christianity* (Philadelphia, 1971), 206–7.

[4] R. E. Brown, *The Community of the Beloved Disciple* (New York, 1979), 148.

[5] Ibid. 149. J. D. Kaestli, 'Remarques sur le rapport du quatrième evangile avec la gnose', in Kaestli *et al.* (eds.), *La Communauté Johannique et son histoire* (Paris, 1990), 352, agrees, so does J. Zumstein, 'Zur Geschichte de Johanneischen Christentums', *TLZ* 122 (1997), 419.

This document certainly knows the Fourth Gospel, but its witness for the orthodox is not without problems, for Culpepper, relying on several observations made by Hillmer, stresses that the *Epistula* has both orthodox and gnostic features. For one thing, it uses 'the genre of post-resurrection revelatory discourses that are found frequently in Gnostic materials' and this feature itself, in the gnostic discourses, 'may have been influenced by the Gospel of John'.[6] Also, the fact that the *Epistula* names John first in its list of disciples of Jesus is paralleled by the Gospel according to the Ebionites, according to Epiphanius (*Panar.* 30. 13. 10). Thus, it appears that the earliest witness for the orthodox is somewhat compromised.

Culpepper then mentions the quartodecimans of Asia Minor, whose number included Melito of Sardis. 'Melito of Sardis, whose writings can be dated between 169 and 177,[7] makes extensive allusions to the Gospel of John in his Paschal homily.'[8] Culpepper mentions no more actual use of the Fourth Gospel by other quartodecimans, though he may imply such when he states that Polycarp's Easter observance as early as 154–5 followed 'the chronology of the Gospel of John', and maintained 'that Easter should be celebrated on the 14th day of the Jewish month of Nisan, the same day as the Passover'.[9] Culpepper then goes on to detail the role of the Fourth Gospel among the Montanists, 'whose origins also predate Irenaeus or are contemporary with him' at 'around 170 or slightly earlier',[10] and with Gaius of Rome. The Montanists relied on John for their claims about possessing the Paraclete, and upon John's Revelation for their millennial views. The upshot of Culpepper's discussion of the Montanists is that this relatively early use of the Fourth Gospel is ascribed, not to gnostics, to be sure, but still to a group quite at the margins of the Church. The greater emphasis in his discussion, however, falls upon their opponent, Gaius of Rome, who was 'a presbyter and noted orthodox scholar', who carefully chronicled John's 'historical discrepancies and its contradictions of the syn-

---

[6] R. A. Culpepper, *John the Son of Zebelee* (Columbia, SC, 1994), 119.

[7] For this date he cites Stuart G. Hall, *Melito of Sardis: On Pascha and Fragments* (Oxford, 1979), p. xii. But here Hall is writing about Melito's *Apology*. For the *Peri Pascha* Hall (p. xxii) gives a date between 160 and 170.

[8] Culpepper, *John*, 120.

[9] If he is serious about this it would mean that Polycarp, whom everyone considers orthodox, and presumably Asia Minor generally, was reading John and accepting its chronology at around the midpoint of the second century—and possibly much earlier, as Polycarp, according to Irenaeus, claimed he had held the same practice with John himself. This is actually a bit problematic, however, since by 'the chronology of the Gospel of John', I take it Culpepper is referring to the common view that John's chronology of the passion contradicts that of the Synoptics, and that this contradiction was at the root of the quartodeciman controversy: Asia Minor followed John, but Rome and the rest of the world followed the Synoptics (see e.g. V. Loi, 'Quartodeciman', *EEChurch*, ii. 728). But the actual day on which Jesus died, whether it was the 13th, the 14th, or the 15th of Nisan, evidently had little if anything to do with the quartodeciman controversy (see e.g. S. G. Hall, 'The Origins of Easter', *Studia Patristica*, 15 (1984), 554–67; cf. also C. K. Barrett, *The Gospel according to John*, 2nd edn. (Philadelphia, 1978), 131).

[10] Culpepper, *John*, 120.

optic Gospels'.[11] And 'Gaius's standing as a leader of the church at Rome shows that the authority of John and its apostolic authorship were not so firmly established (at least in Rome, from which we have the most evidence for the use of the Gospel in the mid-second century) that it could not be challenged by one of the scholars of the church'.[12] 'The figure of Gaius... shows us that the authority of the Gospel of John was still quite tenuous up to the time of Irenaeus.'[13]

Culpepper treats Tatian, but somewhat more positively than do Haenchen and Brown. Writing sometime after the death of Justin and in Syria, Tatian used John 1: 5 in his *Oration* 13. 1 and used John along with the three other Gospels in his *Diatessaron*. 'The contrast between Justin's silence and Tatian's acceptance of John can be explained on the assumption that Justin was reluctant to use the Gospel because of its popularity among the Valentinians, while Tatian, whether because of the influence of the Valentinians or the growing acceptance of the Gospel, had no such reservations.'[14] Thus without diminishing the possible role played by the Valentinian use of John, Culpepper does cite a 'growing acceptance' of the Fourth Gospel in the Church at large. Also like Haenchen and Brown, Culpepper briefly treats Theophilus, who, in 168–81, or 188, became 'the first orthodox writer to identify John as the author of the Gospel of John',[15] and as 'inspired'.

Brown and Haenchen, then, allowed for a budding orthodox use of John just on the eve of Irenaeus' writing career. Culpepper allows for the possibility of a bit more pre-Irenaean use, but stresses the tentativeness of that use, questions its orthodoxy, points to its opposition by an influential, orthodox presbyter, and contrasts this situation with that of the Valentinians, who throughout this period used John's Gospel as an authoritative writing.[16] Like scholars generally, though, Culpepper notes a swift change from about the time of Irenaeus. 'After Irenaeus, neither the authority of the Gospel as scripture nor its apostolic authorship were debated until modern scholarship began to challenge the latter.'[17] Lattke's take on this is that, 'The early Catholic church snatched John away from the growing Gnostic movement and canonized it by redaction and the formation of

---

[11] Ibid. 121. Irenaeus in fact 'did not mention Gaius by name, however—probably because of Gaius's reputation in the church'. Culpepper assumes that Irenaeus is responding specifically to Gaius in about 185 when he criticizes those who reject John's Gospel in *AH* 3. 11. 1. The *Dialogue with Proclus*, to which Eusebius refers as written in the times of Zephyrinus, bishop of Rome (199–217), Culpepper thinks, was written years after (about twenty years after) the actual debate.

[12] Culpepper, *John*, 121.

[13] Ibid. 122.

[14] Ibid. For this he is indebted to M. R. Hillmer, 'The Gospel of John in the Second Century' (Th. D. diss., Harvard University, Apr. 1966), 79–80.

[15] Culpepper, *John*, 122.

[16] Ibid. 119.

[17] Ibid. 123. He is of course assuming that Gaius was dealt with by Irenaeus in *AH* 3. 11. 9, forgetting momentarily that this controversy resurfaced in the early 3rd cent.

Ephesian legends'.[18] If this is anywhere close to being true, it should make for a fascinating sidelight, as we examine the authors of this period, to inquire into the methods and mechanics of the turnabout. How did orthodox leaders pull off what was certainly the literary *coup* of the century? First of all, can we tell why so many of them agreed to pull it off? What sort of apology did they offer for this dangerous Gospel which effectively hoisted it to respectability among a group of Church leaders who were growing increasingly hostile towards heretics and their writings? How did they deal with the suspicions and objections which must have come hard and fast from some quarters for introducing the gnostics' 'special gospel' into the anti-gnostic Church? In short, how did Irenaeus and his allies succeed in overturning what by this time must have been the standard and traditional way of interpreting the Fourth Gospel and replacing it with another approach still acceptable to the mainstream Church?

I shall take as the first object of study, in this chapter, the period from about 170 to 200, when this Gospel was quickly achieving a status alongside Matthew, Mark, and Luke, and up to the time of the Gaian controversy. Since I regard the relevant works of Tatian as somewhat earlier than does Brown, and that of Melito slightly earlier than does Culpepper, I shall have to exclude them from study here and come back to them at a later point. Even so room will be found for a few other sources not treated by Brown, Haenchen, or Culpepper, or by the proponents of the OJP generally, which in all probability should be dated with Theophilus in the 170s, just before Irenaeus wrote. I shall then examine the way Irenaeus uses the Fourth Gospel before seeking to round out the second century with several other authors, including Clement of Alexandria and Tertullian, before culminating in Chapter 4 with the case of Gaius.

Theophilus of Antioch

Theophilus of Antioch was a fairly prolific writer. Jerome (*De vir. illustr.* 25), agreeing with Eusebius (*HE* 4. 24), tells us that Theophilus wrote apologetic works against Marcion and against Hermogenes, in addition to his apology *ad Autolycum*, the only one of his works which survives. Jerome also notes that commentaries 'on the Gospel' and on the Proverbs went under his name, though these were written in a less elegant style. In the preface to his own *Commentary on Matthew* (AD 398) Jerome refers again to a commentary of Theophilus on Matthew as genuine. Thus Theophilus' commentary on Matthew would certainly rival Heracleon's as the earliest Christian commentary on a New Testament book. According to Jerome, Theophilus also

---

[18] Lattke, 'Gnostic Jesuses', in H. Preißler and H. Seiwert (eds.), *Grosisforschung und Religionsgeschichte* (Marburg, 1994), 151.

produced a book in which he 'combined the words of the four Evangelists in one' (*Ep.* 121. 6. 15).[19] It is not clear whether this is the same work as his commentary or a separate 'harmony'.

As to his dates, Eusebius' *Chronicle* places Theophilus' death under the reign of Marcus Aurelius. Jerome agrees, telling us that Theophilus composed his works in the reign of Marcus Aurelius (that is, prior to 17 March 180). When Theophilus of Antioch wrote the third book of his *Ad Autolycum* (3. 28), however, Marcus Aurelius was already dead. R. M. Grant's view that Theophilus wrote the first two books of his treatise against Autolycus probably before 177, and the third book after 180,[20] is a reasonable solution. It will be likely that the rest of Theophilus' works were written sometime prior to 180.

Theophilus' surviving reference to John comes in the second book of his defence to Autolycus. 'Hence the Holy Scriptures and all the inspired (οἱ πνευματοφόροι) [writers] teach us [as] one of these, John, says, "in the beginning was the Word..."' (*Ad Autolycum* 2. 22).[21] There are precious few other traces of the knowledge of John in this apology, and if he had not specifically mentioned John and cited his writing here, we would not have concluded it necessary that he knew the Fourth Gospel. Yet we can supplement our knowledge of Theophilus' view of this John, author of the Fourth Gospel, by noting his conception of an 'inspired' person, detailed earlier in his treatise. This had emerged in 2. 9, where he had said, 'But men of God carrying in them a holy spirit and becoming prophets, being inspired and made wise by God, became God-taught, and holy, and righteous.' Later he speaks of utterances which confirm 'the law' and are to be found 'both with the prophets and in the Gospels, because they all spoke inspired by one Spirit of God' (3. 12). Here he explicitly equates the prophets and the Gospels as instruments of the Spirit. It is fairly obvious then that Theophilus knew the source of his Johannine quotation as a 'Gospel'. It is significant then that when he comes to quote from the Gospels in the next two chapters, he introduces them with 'the holy word teaches us...' (3. 13); 'the voice of the Gospel teaches still more urgently...' (3. 13); 'And the Gospel says' (3. 14)—each time referring to a saying of Jesus himself. He later refers to 'the divine word', which he cites from Paul in 1 Timothy 2: 2; Romans 13. 7–8 (3. 14).

---

[19] 'Theophilus Antiochenae ecclesiae...qui quattuor evangelistarum in unum opus dicta compingens ingenii sui nobis monumenta dimisit' (cited from H. von Campenhausen, *The Formation of the Christian Bible* (Philadelphia, 1972), 174 n. 132). See J. Quasten, *Patrology*, 3 vols. (Westminster, Md., 1984; repr. of 1950 orig.), i. 238.

[20] R. M. Grant, *Greek Apologists of the Second Century* (Philadelphia, 1988), 143.

[21] Hillmer says, 'It is not quite clear whether Theophilus intends a distinction between scriptures (αἱ ἅγιαι γράφαι) and the inspired men (οἱ πνευματοφόροι), or whether these expressions are to be taken as more or less identical' (Hillmer, 'Second Century', 83). Culpepper, *John*, 123, says this 'forces a nuance that is not called for by Theophilus'.

Theophilus shows no awareness that his use of the Prologue to the Fourth Gospel was in any way controversial. He makes no apology for it and is not embarrassed to cite its author by name and attribute to him the status of one inspired. He cites this Gospel as he does the other Gospels, and indeed, from what we can see of his view of inspiration, as he would cite one of the prophets. There is no attempt to address any gnostic monopoly or to appease any possible orthodox objection to the use of this book.

Moreover, from Theophilus' fortuitous reference to John 1: 1 and its author we can tell that he considered the man John to be inspired, on a par with the prophets in this regard, author of a Gospel, and no doubt, an author of 'Holy Scripture'. Theophilus certainly had a notion of New Testament scripture, and John's Gospel must have been included among the contents of this scripture, with other Gospels and at least a collection of letters by Paul.

In all likelihood John's Apocalypse was included as well. Eusebius had read Theophilus' now lost work against Hermogenes, and he reports (*HE* 4. 24. 1) that in it Theophilus 'used testimonies' from the Apocalypse of John. The main position of Hermogenes which drew attack from other Christian theologians was his assertion that God created the world from pre-existing matter. Some twenty to thirty years later, Tertullian would also take up his pen against Hermogenes, who had by then retired to Carthage. In his treatise against Hermogenes Tertullian also used the Apocalypse. Waszink writes, 'in this connection it may be observed that the *Adversus Hermogenem* contains six quotations from the Apocalypse of St. John and that these are found in no other work of Tertullian. Thus the possibility suggests itself that Tertullian borrowed them from, or owed them to, Theophilus, as is certainly the case in regard to a number of ideas occurring in this author.'[22] These quotations are from Revelation 6: 13 (*Herm.* 34. 2); 20: 3 (*Herm.* 11. 3); 20: 11 (*Herm.* 34. 2); 21: 1 (*Herm.* 34. 2, twice); 22. 18 ff. (*Herm.* 22. 3). One of these passages, Revelation 20: 3, seems to be alluded to by Theophilus in the *Ad Autolycum* 2. 28, at a point where Theophilus tells the reader that he has explained elsewhere that the dragon, or devil, was originally an angel.[23] We may be reasonably confident, then, that the 'elsewhere' is his work against Hermogenes. Thus it would seem that Theophilus used the Apocalypse of John in his treatment of the problem of the devil and evil (a problem thrown up by Hermogenes against the inference that if God created all things out of nothing, he must also have created evil), and judging from Tertullian's treatise, it is probable that Theophilus also used it

---

[22] J. H. Waszink, *Tertullian: The Treatise* Against Hermogenes, ACW 24 (New York, 1956), 89 n. 1.

[23] The connection is noted by P. Nautin in his article on Theophilus in *EEChurch*, ii. 831–2, who also deduces that this is a reference to the work against Hermogenes. Theophilus' treatment may have been quite similar to what was contained in the contemporary work of Melito of Sardis, *On the Devil and the Apocalypse of John*.

for its revelations about the end of the world, as they helped resolve the question of the eternality of matter.[24]

It appears then that, well before Irenaeus wrote, Theophilus in Antioch was using the Apocalypse of John as a textual, religious authority. This certainly implies that he regarded this John too as a real and inspired prophet. His definite ascription of the Fourth Gospel to an inspired man named John naturally raises the question whether he, like Irenaeus, believed this was the same John as wrote the Apocalypse. From the evidence which remains of Theophilus' works we cannot answer this question, but if we take into account the testimonies of his contemporaries we would have to consider an affirmative answer to be virtually certain.

Though Irenaeus, in his works addressed to Christians, uses the Fourth Gospel much more profusely than Theophilus does in his work addressed to a pagan, the latter's testimony already indicates that Irenaeus was not an innovator in his treatment of the Fourth Gospel as Christian scripture.

Athenagoras of Athens

Theophilus' contemporary, Athenagoras, wrote an apology, *Plea for the Christians*, addressed to Marcus Aurelius and Commodus in 176 or 177,[25] probably on the occasion of their visit to Athens.[26] Very little is known of him outside what is revealed in this apology and possibly in another work often reckoned to him, a treatise *On the Resurrection*. In the tenth chapter of the *Plea* we read the following.[27]

10. 2 For we think there is also a Son of God. Now let no one think that this talk of God having a Son is ridiculous. For we have not come to our views on either God the Father or his Son as do the poets, who create myths in which they present the gods as no better than men. On the contrary, the Son of God is the Word of the Father in Ideal Form and Energizing Power; for in his likeness and through him all things came into existence (δι' αὐτοῦ πάντα ἐγένετο), which presupposes that the Father and the Son are one (ἑνὸς ὄντος τοῦ πατρὸς καὶ τοῦ υἱοῦ). Now since the Son is in the Father and the Father in the Son (τοῦ υἱοῦ ἐν πατρὶ καὶ πατρὸς ἐν υἱῷ) by a powerful unity of spirit, the Son of God is the mind and reason of the Father.

---

[24] Tertullian, *Herm.* 34. 1, 'The fact that everything sprang from nothing will ultimately be made plausible by the dispensation of God which is to return all things to nothing. For "the heaven shall be rolled together as a scroll..."' (Rev. 6: 14). At this point there are three quotations from Revelation, including one which is introduced by 'Scripture says...'.

[25] William R. Schoedel, *Athenagoras. Legatio and De Resurrectione*, OECT (Oxford, 1972), p. xi; T. D. Barnes, 'The Embassy of Athenagoras', *JTS* ns 26 (1975), 111–14; Grant, *Greek Apologists*, 100; Anthony R. Birley, *Marcus Aurelius: A Biography*, rev. edn. (London, 1987), 194, 'the imperial titles [in the address] clearly belong after the summer of 175. Further, since he refers to the whole world enjoying profound peace, he could hardly have written later than mid-178.'

[26] Birley, *Marcus Aurelius*, 194, 259, who puts the event in 176.

[27] Text and translation from Schoedel, *Athenagoras*.

It is clear that Athenagoras has borrowed terms and concepts from the philosophers,[28] but just as clear that his philosophizing with regard to the Son of God as the Word is based on the revelation of the Fourth Gospel. Athenagoras' δι' αὐτοῦ πάντα ἐγένετο mirrors the words of the Evangelist in John 1: 3, πάντα δι' αὐτοῦ ἐγένετο; his statement that ἑνὸς ὄντος τοῦ πατρὸς καὶ τοῦ υἱοῦ reflects Jesus' self-assertion in John 10: 30, ἐγὼ καὶ ὁ πατὴρ ἕν ἐσμεν; and his statement of the mutual indwelling of the Father and the Son, τοῦ υἱοῦ ἐν πατρὶ καὶ πατρὸς ἐν υἱῷ, draws upon words of Jesus spoken in John 10: 38, ἐν ἐμοὶ ὁ πατὴρ κἀγὼ ἐν τῷ πατρί; John 14: 10, 11, ἐγὼ ἐν τῷ πατρὶ καὶ ὁ πατὴρ ἐν ἐμοί ἐστιν . . . ἐγὼ ἐν τῷ πατρὶ καὶ ὁ πατὴρ ἐν ἐμοί; and John 17: 21, σύ, πάτερ, ἐν ἐμοὶ κἀγὼ ἐν σοι. This apparently shows knowledge of the Johannine Prologue and Johannine sayings of Jesus which portray the Son's relationship to the Father. He goes on in chapter 10 to elaborate on Christology, describing the eternal generation of the Son.

10.3 . . . he is the first begotten of the Father. The term is used not because he came into existence (for God, who is eternal mind, had in himself his Word or Reason from the beginning, since he was eternally rational) but because he came forth to serve as Ideal Form and Energizing Power for everything material . . .

Here the Johannine Prologue probably also stands behind 'the first begotten of the Father' (πρῶτον γέννημα; cf. John 1: 14, ὡς μονογενοῦς παρὰ πατρός), though Colossians 1: 15, 18 (ὅς ἐστιν εἰκὼν τοῦ θεοῦ ἀοράτου, πρωτότοκος πάσης κτισεως . . . ὅς ἐστιν ἀρχή πρωτότοκος ἐκ τῶν νεκρῶν)[29] may be more immediately present, and in the statement that God had his Λόγος in himself ἐξ ἀρχῆς (cf. John 1: 1, ἐν ἀρχῇ ἦν ὁ λόγος). He finds agreement with this Logos doctrine in 'the prophetic Spirit' who said, 'For the Lord made me the beginning of his ways for his works', citing Proverbs 8: 22, much as Justin had done in *Dial.* 61. 3; 129. Athenagoras goes on to relate the Christian view of the Holy Spirit, rounding out his picture of the Godhead with mention of the host of angels too. He does not cite any literary sources for these doctrines[30] but he asserts confidently that they are 'not man-made but ordained and taught by God (θεοδιδάκτοις)' (11. 1; also in 32. 4). This parallels what he had earlier said about the prophets, who spoke out 'by a divinely inspired Spirit (πνεύματι ἐνθέῳ ἐκπεφωνήκασι) about God and the things of God' (7. 3),[31] in contrast to the poets and philosophers, who spoke of these

---

[28] Schoedel, *Athenagoras*, 21 n. 2, 'It appears that a Platonic term (Form, Idea) is linked with one that is Aristotelian (Energizing Power, Act). The phrase as a whole, however, is probably modeled on the Stoic–Philonic distinction between the (cosmic) *logos endiathetos* (containing all the Forms) and the *logos prophorikos* (as agent in creation). Cf. Theophilus, *Ad Autol.* 2. 10, 22'.

[29] See my comments below on the compatibility of Col. 1: 15 with John 1: 1–3, 14 in Tatian and Justin.

[30] Though he never cites a NT author by name it is clear that he knows at least Matthew (possibly Mark; cf. 33. 5), Luke, John, and a collection of Pauline letters which included Romans, 1 Corinthians, Galatians, and 1 Timothy.

[31] The prophets who spoke by the divine Spirit include Moses, Isaiah, and Jeremiah (9. 1). But the prophetic Spirit also spoke by the writer(s) of Proverbs (10: 1;18: 2).

matters by guesswork (7. 2), and who 'would not stoop to learn about God from God' (7. 2).

Thus, while it is possible that Athenagoras was influenced by Justin in his adoption and development of the Logos idea,[32] it appears that his statements reflect his own reading of the Fourth Gospel, bearing the mark of passages that do not show up in Justin. It is notable that the two Christian philosopher/apologists we have examined so far, Theophilus and Athenagoras, use the Gospel according to John to construct their Christology. Without formally quoting this Gospel, Athenagoras uses its teaching in setting forth to his secular sovereigns the Christian understanding of the Logos, expressed here as part of the 'God-taught', Christian doctrine of God.[33] The Fourth Gospel's 'high Christology', its teaching of the full deity of the Logos, is obviously not regarded by him as a problematic, much less as a dangerous or heretical, feature. Quite to the contrary, John's portrayal of Jesus as the Logos, at the same time united with and distinct from the Father, was quite fundamental to his Christology and, for this reason, constitutive of his Trinitarianism (see 10. 2–5; 13. 3; 18. 2; 24. 2; 30. 6).[34]

The Epistle of Vienne and Lyons

The year 177 must have been a particularly disturbing one for many Christians. In that year Smyrna in Asia Minor was destroyed by a great earthquake. Smyrna had been the boyhood home of Irenaeus and of course was the place where Polycarp had fulfilled a long and remarkable ministry. But by this time Irenaeus had long since emigrated from Smyrna. He had spent some time in Rome and was now an elder of the church of Lyons in Gaul, a church made up of many Asian émigrés. As perilous as things were in Smyrna that year, the immigrant Christian population of Gaul could not have been more racked by hardship if they had been back home. For a cruel bloodletting was being carried out in Vienne and Lyons[35] on the region's Christians, who for a time were not allowed to be seen in public

---

[32] It appears certain that Athenagoras knew at least Justin's two *Apologies* (see Schoedel, *Athenagoras*, p. xiii).

[33] For ethical teaching Athenagoras cites from the synoptic Gospels, and Paul. Had Athenagoras chosen to draw attention to the more controversial doctrine of the incarnation (Schoedel, *Athenagoras*, p. xviii), with little doubt we would have seen more of the Fourth Gospel in the *Plea*. There is an apparent allusion to John 11: 25, 'the resurrection and the life', in the treatise *On the Resurrection* (8. 4).

[34] Both his Christology and his conception of the Godhead are foundational to his entire thought. Though a relatively small portion of the *Plea* is devoted to this, an indication of how intrinsically important it is to Athenagoras and his companions is seen in 13. 3: 'For we are men who consider life here below of very little worth. We are attended only by the knowledge of him who is truly God and of the Word that issues from him—a knowledge as to what is the unity of the Son with the Father, what is the communion of the Father with the Son, and what is the Spirit, what is the unity of these powers—the Spirit, the Son, and the Father—and their diversity when thus united'.

[35] There has been debate about which year this is. Eusebius places it in 177 (*HE* 5. *praef.* 1), though in his *Chronicle* he had placed it under Marcus and Lucius (161–9). The mention of the

places without an uproar and possible arrest. Most of a long letter which was sent out by the Church leaders in Vienne and Lyons is preserved, thanks to Eusebius. Apart from its importance for documenting the experience of the Christians in the persecution, this work is quite valuable for our purposes also. In the tense and excited atmosphere of persecution, but removed from concerns of the controversy with heresy, this letter tells us much about the status of the Johannine corpus among its communities. As William Frend has remarked, 'Clearly the Fourth Gospel and the Apocalypse were two of the main sources of inspiration to the writer.'[36]

Referring to one of the disciples, Vettius Epagathus, this author wrote,

he was called the 'Comforter of Christians', but had the Comforter in himself, the spirit of Zacharias which he had shown by the fullness of his love when he chose to lay down even his own life for the defence of the brethren, for he was and he is a true disciple of Christ, and he follows the Lamb wheresoever he goes. (5. 1. 10)[37]

This remarkable sentence incorporates allusions to the Fourth Gospel, the First Johannine Epistle, and the Revelation (along with Luke 1: 67). Vettius (earlier compared to Zacharias, father of John the Baptist (5. 1. 9; Luke 1: 6)) is called the παράκλητος of the Christians because he had 'τὸν παράκλητον in himself, the Spirit of Zacharias'. This use of the term for the Holy Spirit invokes the promise of Jesus in John 14: 16–17, 26; 16: 7; to send ὁ παράκλητος to his disciples. In accord with the words of 1 John 3: 16, which the author has clearly adapted for this purpose, Vettius showed the fullness of his love by choosing to 'lay down even his own life for the defence of the brethren'.[38] And the 'Johannine' tribute to Vettius extends to the appraisal of his position in the afterlife, as it is said, in the words of Revelation 14: 4, that he 'follows the Lamb wheresoever he goes'.[39] He is thus placed in the company of the 144,000 chaste and spotless ones redeemed from the earth, who now worship before the throne (cf. *Mart. Polyc.* 14. 1–2; *5 Ezra* 2. 38–40). It appears that the author and his community, for it is the community who dubbed Vettius 'the Advocate', are steeped in the Johannine literature.

emperor in the singular (5. 1. 44, 47), and the letter of the martyrs to Eleutherus of Rome (who entered office in 175) would seem to show that in the *Chronicle* Eusebius was mistaken and that he corrected the error in the *HE*. T. D. Barnes, 'Pre-Decian *Acta Martyrum*', *JTS* 19 (1968), 509–31; 'Eusebius and the Date of the Martyrdoms', in *Les martyrs de Lyon* (Paris, 1978), 137–41, has suggested a date some years after 177. See Birley, *Marcus Aurelius*, 261.

[36] W. H. C. Frend, *Martyrdom and Persecution in the Early Church: A Study of a Conflict from the Maccabees to Donatus* (Oxford, 1965; repr. Grand Rapids, Mich., 1981), 19. See his summary.

[37] Translations are those of Kirsopp Lake, in Kirsopp Lake, J. E. L. Oulton, and H. J Lawlor, *Eusebius: The Ecclesiastical History*, 2 vols., LCL; i, ed. and tr. Kirsopp Lake (Cambridge, Mass., 1925), from which the Greek text is also taken.

[38] ὁ διὰ τοῦ πληρώματος τῆς ἀγάπης ἐνεδείξατο, εὐδοκήσας ὑπὲρ τῆς ἀδελφῶν ἀπολογίας καὶ τὴν ἑαυτοῦ θεῖναι ψυχήν; 1 John 3: 16, ἐν τούτῳ ἐγνώκαμεν τὴν αγάπην, ὅτι ἐκεῖνος ὑπὲρ ἡμῶν τὴ ψυχὴν αὐτοῦ ἔθηκεν· καὶ ἡμεῖς ὀφείλομεν ὑπὲρ τῶ ἀδελφῶν τὰς ψυχὰς θεῖναι.

[39] See Hill, *Regnum Caelorum: Patterns of Millennial Thought in Early Christianity*, 2nd edn. (Grand Rapids Mich., 2001), 138.

The community saw in their own experience an explicit fulfilment of Jesus' prediction in John 16: 2.

When this rumour spread all men turned like beasts against us, so that even if any had formerly been lenient for friendship's sake they then became furious and raged against us, and there was fulfilled that which was spoken by our Lord, that the time will come when 'whosoever killeth you will think that he doeth God service'. (5. 1. 15)[40]

The author, hardly 'tentative' in his appropriation of this saying, obviously accepts it as a real prediction of the historical Jesus, and his use of it is consistent with a very high regard for the written source of this prediction.[41] He seems to assume that recipients of the letter will recognize the prediction and, presumably, its written source. Later in the account he speaks of those who denied Christ and did not repent as οἱ υἱοὶ τῆς ἀπωλείας (5. 1. 48). A contextual exegesis of John 17: 12, where Judas, the archtypical denier of Jesus, is named ὁ υἱὸς τῆς ἀπωλείας, seems to lie behind this use.[42]

We have observed one clear allusion to 1 John 3: 16 above (in 5. 1. 10). There appears to be another allusion to 1 John in 5. 2. 6, where the author writes of the great contest of the martyrs in praying for those who had fallen, those the beast 'had at first thought to have swallowed down. For they did not boast over the fallen, but from their own abundance supplied with a mother's love those that needed, and shedding many tears for them to the Father, they prayed for life, and he gave it to them' (ζωὴν ᾐτήσαντο, καὶ ἔδωκεν αὐτοῖς). Surely the author knows 1 John 5. 16, 'If any one sees his brother committing what is not a mortal sin, he will ask, and God will give him life (αἰτήσει καὶ δώσει αὐτῷ ζωήν) for those whose sin is not mortal.'

Besides his application of Revelation 14: 4 to Vettius Apagathus in 5. 1. 10, the author invokes Revelation 22: 11 as 'the scripture' which offered a prediction which was also fulfilled in their midst: 'The governor and the people showed the like unrighteous hatred against us that the scripture might be fulfilled, "Let him that is unlawful be unlawful still, and he that is righteous be righteous still"' (5. 1. 58). Though the wording has been adapted, or perhaps cited from memory,[43] there is no doubt that this is a reference to Revelation 22: 11. In 5. 2. 3 he reports that the martyrs, before

---

[40] Ἐλεύσεται καιρὸς ἐν ᾧ πᾶς ὁ ἀποκτείνας ὑμᾶς δόξει λατρείαν προσφέρειν τῷ θεῷ; cf. John 16: 2, ἔρχεται ὥρα ἵνα πᾶς ὁ ἀποκτείνας ὑμᾶς δόξῃ λατρείαν προσφέρειν τῷ θεῷ.

[41] The endurance of a Christian named Sanctus is praised, who held 'firm in his confession, refreshed and strengthened by the heavenly spring of water of life which proceeds forth from the body of Christ' (5. 1. 22). This seems to draw on the idea, if not the exact wording, of John 7: 38, possibly combined with a reminiscence of John 19: 34. Cf. Irenaeus, *AH* 3. 24. 1.

[42] Cf. Eph. 2: 2 where Paul uses υἱοὶ τῆς ἀπειθείας generically.

[43] The author abbreviates, leaving out one clause (καὶ ὁ ῥυπαρὸς ῥυπανθήτω ἔτι, which, however, is also absent from codex A and some later MSS), and substitutes ὁ ἄνομος ἀνομησάτω for ὁ ἀδικῶν ἀδικησάτω. He reproduces καὶ ὁ δίκαιος δικαιωθήτω ἔτι (the early Greek texts have δικαιοσύνην ποιησάτω for δικαιωθήτω, but the latter is presumed by some early Latin MSS and the Bohairic).

they were executed, refused the title of martyr, but 'gladly conceded the title of martyrdom to Christ, the faithful and true martyr and first-born from the dead (τῷ πιστῷ καὶ ἀληθινῷ μάρτυρι καὶ πρωτοτόκῳ τῶν νεκρῶν) and author of the life of God'. This surely means they knew the titles given to the risen Christ in Revelation 1: 5 (ὁ μάρτυς, ὁ πιστός, ὁ πρωτότοκος τῶν νεκρῶν) and 3: 14 (ὁ μάρτυς, ὁ πιστός καὶ ἀληθιν ός, cf. 19: 11). The author apparently connects the state-sponsored persecution (it involved the Governor and the instructions of the Emperor himself) with one or the other of the Beasts of Revelation 13 (5. 1. 57; Revelation 2: 6). Further, his notion of the saints conquering their adversaries by remaining faithful unto death (5. 2. 58, etc.) is that of the book of Revelation (2: 7, 11, 17, 26; 3: 5, 12, 21; 5: 5; 12: 11; 15: 2; 21: 7, cf. 1 John 4: 4).

The author regards the Revelation of John as fully scriptural; it is transparent that he must have held the same view of the Fourth Gospel, and very probably of 1 John as well. Did these Christian communities learn their appreciation for the Fourth Gospel from the gnostics in the region? If so, from where did they get their appreciation for the First Epistle and the Revelation? On the contrary, there is no reason to think that the communities among whom Irenaeus served as presbyter in the 170s made any such distinctions between these books of the Johannine corpus as are wont to be made by modern scholars. If it is true that Heracleon the Valentinian was writing or had written his commentary on the Fourth Gospel by this time (I shall inquire about the date at a later point), it is also true that the Valentinians were not writing any accounts of martyrdom which applied the Fourth Gospel, along with other Old and New Testament writings, to the life-and-death struggles of Valentinian Christians. Who is to say that Heracleon's commentary depicts a greater appreciation for the divine quality of the words of that Gospel than does this account of the persecution of the non-Valentinian Christians of Gaul?

Irenaeus, the churches in Gaul, and the churches in Asia Minor

This early account of persecution assures us at least that Irenaeus' estimate of the Johannine literature (not just the Fourth Gospel but the Revelation and the Epistles as well) in his *Against Heresies* written in the 180s was entirely in line with his own Christian community's esteem for them in the 170s. It was Irenaeus who was the courier of the letter to the outside world. Several scholars have posited that Irenaeus was also its author.[44] This is quite plausible, though it cannot be proved conclusively. But in either case,

---

[44] P. Nautin, *Lettres et éscrivains chrétiens des IIe et IIIe siècles*, Patristica, 2 (Paris, 1961), 54–61; R. M. Grant, *Eusebius as Church Historian* (Oxford, 1980), 118–19, who traces the theory to Oecumenius in his *Commentary on 1 Peter*.

the letter went out under the auspices of the Church leaders and was implicitly endorsed by its martyrs (5. 4. 1–2), who wrote in commendation of Irenaeus. In their words of commendation, the martyrs themselves call Irenaeus their 'brother and companion' (τὸν ἀδελθὸν ἡμῶν καὶ κοινωνόν) (5. 4. 2), perhaps borrowing a phrase used by an earlier Asian 'martyr', John, in Revelation 1: 9 (ὁ ἀδελφὸς καὶ συνκοινωνός). The clear allusions to and sometimes quotations of the Johannine literature imply the community's knowledge and reception of the Fourth Gospel, the First Epistle, and the Revelation as scripture. We may hesitate to say that this community was conscious of a Johannine corpus only because we have no attributions of authorship expressed. But recall in particular the encomium on Vettius Epagathus in 5. 1. 10, which remarkably incorporates allusions to passages in all three documents. We may be confident that this author's use of each member of the Johannine corpus would have been familiar and quite conventional to the congregations in Gaul, judging from this work. The letter was sent to the churches of Asia and Phrygia, from whence many in the Gallican congregations, like Irenaeus, had emigrated[45] (perhaps in the wake of Polycarp's martyrdom?). Presumably these Asian and Phrygian churches would have recognized the allusions to and citations of the Johannine books and received them without controversy.

THE LETTER IN ROME

This letter was sent to the churches of Asia and Phrygia, but it was taken there by way of Rome, where a copy was also presented by the presbyter Irenaeus to the Roman bishop, Eleutherus. If the present consensus about the Fourth Gospel is true, this surely involved some risk, invoking, as this letter does, a contaminated, proto-gnostic Gospel and the rest of the Johannine corpus right alongside the safer and more familiar Lukan Gospel, Acts, a Pauline corpus, and 1 Peter, and sending these notices into the heart of orthodox, Johannophobic suspicion in Rome. Along with reporting, for the edification of the churches, the atrocities they suffered and the heroism of the martyrs, did these churches also have the agenda of surreptitiously gaining admission for a rehabilitated Gospel? If so, they had Theophilus in Antioch and Athenagoras in Athens as their simultaneous co-conspirators. Or could it be that the 'canon' of the Gallican churches was simply the one they had used before they left Asia Minor, which would have been recognizable among Christians in almost any portion of the empire? Could it be that such a use of the Fourth Gospel created as few waves in Rome as it apparently did in Asia, Antioch, and Athens? I turn now to the only Roman Christian writer we have from this period.

---

[45] Frend, *Martyrdom*, 2–5; Lawlor, *Eusebius*, ii. 154–5.

Hegesippus

Although his work has not survived to our day except in small fragments, Hegesippus was quite an important second-century source for Eusebius. Whether or not he was of Semitic stock as Eusebius says, he travelled from Palestine to Rome in about AD 155 when Anicetus was bishop (*HE* 4. 22. 2–3). Probably sometime between 175 and 180 (during Eleutherus' episcopate, *HE* 4. 11. 7; 4. 22. 3), Hegesippus published five books of 'notes' (ὑπομνήματα) described by Lawlor as 'an Apology for the Faith against unbelievers, for orthodoxy against misbelievers'.[46] Although we find no explicit citations of the Fourth Gospel in the surviving fragments, most of which are of a historical character, Hegesippus is not insignificant for our quest, thanks largely to Hugh Lawlor's painstaking research. Lawlor attempts to reconstruct as much of the work of Hegesippus as is possible from the various quotations and paraphrases of Eusebius, Epiphanius, and others. He determines that Eusebius cited details from Hegesippus' account in several places where he does not acknowledge him by name. Two of these have to do with the John who wrote the Apocalypse. They are found in *HE* 3. 18. 1; 20. 9; and are supported by an ancient and independent summary of the corresponding section of Hegesippus' book found in two manuscripts.[47] The two accounts are set out here side by side.

EUSEBIUS

HE 3. 18. 1 Ἐν τούτῳ κατέχει λόγος[48] τὸν ἀπόστολον ἅμα καὶ εὐαγγελιστὴν Ἰωάννην ἔτι τῷ βίῳ ἐνδιατρίβοντα, τῆς εἰς τὸν θεῖον λόγον ἕνεκεν μαρτυρίας Πάτμον οἰκεῖν καταδικασθῆναι τὴν νῆσον…

At this time, the story goes, the Apostle and Evangelist John was still alive, and was condemned to live in the island of Patmos for his witness to the divine word.

SUMMARY OF HEGESIPPUS

καθ ὃν καὶ τὸν ἀπόστολον καὶ εὐαγγελιστὴν Ἰωάννην ἐν Πάτμῳ περιώρισεν.

According to which [persecution] also he [i. e. Domitian] confined the apostle and evangelist John on Patmos.

---

[46] Lawlor, *Eusebiana: Essays on* The Ecclesiastical History *of Eusebius Pamphili, ca 264–349 A.D. Bishop of Caesarea* (Oxford, 1912; repr. Amsterdam, 1973), 3. Kirsopp Lake, LCL, i. 320–1, n. 1, says 'The word ὑπομνηνήματα, which was translated in Latin by *commentarii*, means a report made by an official to the emperor or other authority, and so came to be used of an historical work which had not yet been put into literary form.'

[47] Paris MS. 1555 A in J. A. Cramer, *Anecdota Graeca e codd. manusriptis Bibliotheca Regiae Parisiensis* (Oxford, 1839), ii. 88 and the Bodleian MS. Barocc. 142 ed. by C. de Boor, 'Neue Fragmente des Papias, Hegesippus und Pierius in bisher unbekannten Excerpten aus der Kirchengeschichte des Philippus Sidetes', TU 5/2 (1888), 165–84, at 169.

[48] As Lawlor demonstrates, this expression normally indicates a written source in Eusebius.

3. 20. 9   Τότε δὴ οὖν καὶ τὸν ἀπόστολον
Ἰωάννην ἀπὸ τῆς κατὰ τὴν
νῆσον φυγῆς τὴν ἐπὶ τῆς Ἐφέσου
διατριβὴν ἀπειληφέναι ὁ τῶν
παρ᾽ ἡμῖν ἀρχαίων παραδίδωσι λόγος.

At that time, too [i.e. under Nerva],
the story of the ancient Christians hands
down that the Apostle John, after his
banishment to the island, took up his
abode in Ephesus.

Lawlor's already persuasive demonstration[49] could be further enhanced by referring to Origen's words on Matthew 20: 23 (*C. Matt.* 16. 6), where he discusses the fortunes of the two sons of Zebedee.

The sons of Zebedee did certainly drink the cup and were baptized with the baptism, since Herod killed James, the brother of John, with the sword, and the Emperor of the Romans, as tradition teaches (ὡς ἡ παράδοσις διδάσκει), condemned (κατεδίκασε) John to the island of Patmos for testifying to the word of truth. John himself hands down in the Apocalypse the circumstances of his martyrdom (μαρτύριον), passing over the name of him by whom he was condemned.

John also passed over in Revelation 1: 9 that he was 'condemned' to Patmos by a Roman emperor. Origen thus did not get this information from the Apocalypse but from his παράδοσις. Could it have been Hegesippus, directly or indirectly? Eusebius' paraphrase of Hegesippus uses the word καταδικάζω, as does Origen's. Hegesippus attributes the banishment to Domitian, and though Origen does not name the emperor, he knows it was an emperor and not some local official.[50]

At any rate, the unattributed excerpts from Eusebius combined with the attributed summary, allow us to attribute to Hegesippus the testimony, 'that St John the Apostle was banished to Patmos under Domitian, and resided at Ephesus under Nerva. That is to say, he must be added to the small band of early witnesses to the late date and apostolic authorship of the Apocalypse'[51]—and not only to this, but also to the common apostolic authorship of the Apocalypse and the Fourth Gospel, for Hegesippus clearly calls him 'the evangelist'.[52] In these points he agrees with the tradition of Irenaeus.

---

[49] See particularly pp. 40–56.

[50] Irenaeus says John saw the apocalypse at the end of Domitian's reign (*AH* 5. 30. 3). Clement called the banisher a tyrant, without naming him (*Qds* 42). Victorinus, *CA* 10. 11, knows he is Domitian.

[51] Lawlor, *Eusebiana*, 95; cf. 53.

[52] Both sources contain the words, τὸ ἀπόστολον καὶ εὐαγγελιστὴν Ἰωάννην. Lawlor, *Eusebiana*, 47, is able to infer that the wording of *HE* 3. 18. 1 'adheres pretty closely to Hegeisippus. And we may, at any rate, feel confident that the expressions which are common to *E* xvii. xviii, 1 and *C* 1, 2 [that is of *HE* 3. 17–18. 1 and the summary cited above] were also used by him'.

There is no basis in what is left to us, though admittedly Eusebius does little to help us in this regard, for imagining that Hegesippus regarded the Fourth Gospel as in any way a dangerous or controversial document. We know on the other hand that Hegesippus was actively engaged in the effort to disprove the legitimacy of the heretical sects. Yet he connects the apostle John as straightforwardly to a Gospel, as 'evangelist', as he does to the Apocalypse.

Hegesippus published his works probably some time between 170 and 180. But there is no telling how far back his information about John went. He may have obtained it from traditions of Asia, through which he passed on his journey to Rome, which Lawlor thinks took place about 155. In Rome he would have had access to Asian tradition through the many immigrants who took up their abode in the capital city. It is even possible that Hegesippus may have gained some of his information from the work of Papias which must go back to about 130 or before. But in any case Hegesippus reveals the attribution of the Gospel and Apocalypse to John the apostle, and its acceptability to an orthodox controversialist in Rome who had travelled widely and had many contacts in various churches around the empire. Though neglected in studies of this kind, Hegesippus is an important witness to the favourable reception of these two members of the Johannine corpus before Irenaeus' *Against Heresies*. And his long residence in Rome is worthy of note. For it is here that a hostile sentiment towards this Gospel is often said to have prevailed throughout the second century. And yet the few fragments left of Hegesippus' witness only tend to confirm that when the *Epistle of Vienne and Lyons* arrived at the Church in Rome in the hands of the presbyter Irenaeus in 177 or 178, its use of the Fourth Gospel (and the Apocalypse) would not have stirred any controversy. On the contrary, it seems the appeal to these works in the *Epistle* would have been welcomed, at least among some circles in Rome very concerned to maintain orthodoxy in the face of gnostic heresy. Along with Theophilus, Hegesippus effectively demonstrates that the tradition of apostolic authorship of the Gospel of John was not a fiction of Irenaeus.[53]

Sibylline Oracles 1. 324–400; 8. 217–500[54]

Before we come to Irenaeus, there is another source, or two, which may well date from some time prior to 180 and should be mentioned. These are the Christian additions to books 1 and 8 of the *Sibylline Oracles*. The present book 8 of the *Sibylline Oracles* divides itself rather clearly into two parts,

---

[53] *Pace* Koester, 'Ephesos', 138.

[54] Greek text from J. Geffcken, *Die Oracula Sibyllina*, GCS 8 (Leipzig, 1902); translations are those of J. J. Collins, 'Sibylline Oracles (Second Century B.C.—Seventh Century A.D.): A New Translation and Introduction', in *OTP* i. 317–472.

8. 1–216, which appears to be a Jewish composition, and 217–500, which is quite obviously Christian. *Sibylline Oracles* 8. 1–216 was written during the reign of Marcus Aurelius, as is clear from predictions made in 8. 65.[55] There is no definite indication of the date of the Christian stratum of book 8, though we know that it was considered an integral part of the traditional text of the *Oracles* at least by the time Lactantius wrote, probably in the second decade of the fourth century. Geffcken and Collins suggest that there is 'no great lapse of time between the various parts',[56] and this stratum may well also predate 180. Another important factor, however, is the existence of another Christian interpolation in *Sibylline Oracles* 1. 324–400. Here material similar to the Christian section of book 8 requires some kind of literary relationship. Geffcken thought that books 1 and 2 were dependent upon book 8, but Collins says this is 'open to question', and agrees rather with Kurfess, who saw the dependence moving in the other direction, and who dated the Christian sections of books 1 and 2 to some-time before AD 150.[57] While we cannot be sure about this, the literary parallels I shall observe below are certainly consistent with a setting near the middle of the second century.[58] It is even possible that the author of both Christian sections is the same. Here I shall accept as a working hypothesis Collins's view of the differentiation of the authors and of the dependence of 8. 217–500 on 1. 324–400, and I shall not insist that the author of 1. 324–400 is writing any earlier than the reign of Marcus Aur-elius, though he may well be.

Belonging to the genre of 'prophetic' writing, the kind of literature to be found in the *Sibylline Oracles* is not the kind which tends to identify its sources explicitly or to reproduce them word for word, particularly for the sources which may have come into being after the time of the fictitious setting of the *Oracles*. This does not, however, mean that these 'prophets', Jewish or Christian, regarded no written religious works as divine author-ities. This seems obvious when we consider the Jewish *Oracles*, but is easily forgotten when we consider the Christian ones. Interestingly, the Christian book of Revelation appears to have been known even to the author of the 'Jewish' section of *Sibylline Oracles* 8. 194–216 (8. 196–7).[59] The Christian

---

[55] In the section on the Emperor Hadrian the author says, 'After him, three will rule who have the last day of all...' (l. 65), and goes on to predict the return of Nero and the destruction of Rome. The 'three' here are Lucius Verus, Antoninus Pius, and Marcus Aurelius (161–80).

[56] J. Geffcken, *Komposition und Entstehungszeit der Oracula Sibylla*, TU NF 8/1 (Leipzig, 1902), 44; Collins, *OTP* i. 416–17.

[57] Collins, *OTP* i. 331, citing Geffcken, *Komposition und Entstehungszeit*, 49, and A. Kurfess, 'Ora-cula Sibyllina I/II', *ZNW* 40 (1941), 151–65, at 165.

[58] I may also mention that the notions of the 'seven days of ages' given for human repentance (2. 311–12; 8. 357–8; *Ps. Barn.* 14. 4–8), and of the 'two ways, of life and death' (8. 399; *Ps. Barn.* 18), and the reference to Moses' prefiguring the cross by 'stretching out his holy arms, conquering Amalek by faith' (Exod. 17: 11 in *Sib. Or.* 8. 251–2 ; *Ps. Barn.* 12. 2) perhaps argue for a knowledge of *Ps. Barnabas*, at least on the part of the author of 8. 217–500.

[59] Collins, *OTP* i. 416.

author of 8. 217–500 knows the Christological application of Psalm 2: 9 in Revelation 2: 27; 12: 5; 19: 15. This author knows not only Revelation, but also the Fourth Gospel (and much of the rest of the NT), as the following instances show.

> ... having washed off their former vices with the waters
> of an immortal spring, so that, born from above (ἵνα γεννηθέντες ἄνωθεν)
> they may no longer serve the lawless customs of the world.
> First, then, the Lord was seen clearly by his own,
> incarnate (σάρκινος) as he was before, and he will show in hands and feet
> four marks fixed in his own limbs,
> east and west and south and north.   (8. 315–21)

The immediate source for the 'born from above' image here may well be its occurrence in *Sibylline Oracles* 1. 340:

> ... and that every human person
> be illumined by waters, so that, being born from above (ἵνα γεννηθέντες ἄνωθεν)
> they may no longer in any respect at all transgress justice ...   (1. 339–41)

But the source for 1. 340 is with little doubt the distinctive words of Jesus in John 3: 3, ἀμὴν ἀμὴν λέγω σοι, ἐὰν μή τις γεννηθῇ ἄνωθεν, οὐ δύναται ἰδεῖν τὴν βασιλείαν τοῦ θεοῦ. Each author places the reference to being born from above in a different context: in book 1 it is part of a description of the ultimate issue of the baptism of John; in book 8 it is a result of Jesus' resurrection. But other points of contact with the Fourth Gospel show that each author must be somewhat familiar with that Gospel firsthand. In the same context the author of 8. 217–500 goes on to speak of Christ's appearance to his disciples 'in the flesh' after the resurrection, and mentions the nail marks in his limbs. Since John's is the only Gospel, among the four canonical Gospels at least, to mention the nailing of Jesus to the cross and the only one to 'show' the 'marks' they made on his body, it is likely that this information also has come to the author by means of John's Gospel, either directly or indirectly.

Sibylline Oracles 8. 255 announces that 'The one who has believed in him will have eternal life' (εἰς ὃν ὁ πιστεύσας ζωὴ αἰώνιον ἕξει), which is taken almost verbatim from the Evangelist's words in John 3: 36 (ὁ πιστεύων εἰς τὸν υἱὸν ἔχει ζωὴν αἰώνιον).[60]

These two Sibylline authors also share a description of the sufferings of Christ which must be ultimately dependent upon John.

> But when he will stretch out his hands and measure all,
> and bear the crown of thorns—and they will stab
> his side with reeds (πλευράν νύξωσιν καλάμοισιν)—on account of this,
>   for three hours
> there will be monstrous dark night in midday. (1. 372–5)

---

[60] Cf. also 8. 292–3, μή τις ἐπιγνῷ ... πόθεν ἦλθεν; John 7: 27, 28; 8: 14; 9: 29; 19: 9.

... and he will wear the crown of thorns. For, made of thorns,
the crown of chosen men is an eternal delight.
They will stab his side(s)[61] with a reed on account of their law
(πλευρὰς νύξουσιν καλάμῳ διὰ τὸν νόμον αὐτῶν) (8. 294–6).

Only John refers to a stabbing (John 19: 34, ἔνυξεν; *Sib. Or.* 1. 374, νύξωσιν; 8. 295, νύξουσιν) of Jesus side on the cross,[62] though John uses the word λόγχη, spear, instead of καλάμος, reed, as here. The substitution of καλάμος here by the first Sibyllist may be an innocent slip based on a reminiscence of the accounts of Matthew and Mark, which refer to the soldiers beating Jesus' head with a reed (καλάμος) before the crucifixion (Matthew 27: 30; Mark 15: 19). *Sibylline Oracles* 1 has the stabbing take place on the cross, as in John; *Sibylline Oracles* 8 is somewhat vague about the timing of the stabbing, but this association of John's stabbing in the side with the spear and Matthew's or Mark's beating of his head with the reed seems to be further confused by the author of *Gospel of Peter* 3. 9, 'And others who stood by spat on his face, and others buffeted him on the cheeks, others nudged [or stabbed, ἔνυσσον] him with a reed (καλάμῳ)' (Matthew 27: 30 and Mark 15: 19 both have ἔτυπτον). Here the author seems to be thinking of the pre-crucifixion abuse of Jesus and the only remnant of John's account is in the transfer of his word νύσσω for the Synoptic τύπτω. (This author does not say the stabbing was made in Jesus' side or sides.) The *Acts of John* also knows this 'traditional' confusion, but restores the 'lance' of John 19: 34 in its account. Here 'Jesus', while his *alter ego* was hanging on the cross, tells John, 'John, for the people below in Jerusalem I am being crucified and pierced with lances and reeds (καὶ λόγχαις νύσσομαι καὶ καλάμοις) and given vinegar and gall to drink' (*AJ* 97). I shall not try to sort out the possible literary relationships of these four sources (*Or. Sib.* 1 and 8, *GP*, and *AJ*), a task rendered more difficult by the fact that all seem to have had independent access to the earlier Gospels, including John.[63] But a further indication of the ultimate source for this information about Jesus' stabbing is apparently given in *Sibylline Oracles* 8. 296. The reference here to the stabbing taking place 'on account of their law' (διὰ τὸν νόμον αὐτων) is probably an inclusive reference to the scriptural passages, taken to be predictions in the Fourth Gospel, which follow the account of the stabbing in John 19: 36–7, 'For these things took place that the scripture might be fulfilled, "Not a bone of him shall be broken." And again another scripture says, "They shall look on him whom they have pierced"'.

---

[61] Collins's translation gives the plural, which follows Geffcken's text. But Geffcken's apparatus notes that several MSS have the singular. Also, the parallel text in *Sib. Or.* 1. 373 has the singular.
[62] From at least the 4th cent. there are MSS which show an interpolation of John 19: 34 into the text of Matt. 27: 49: ℵ B C L U Γ and some MSS of the Vulgate.
[63] See P. J. Lalleman, *The Acts of John: A Two-Stage Initiation into Johannine Gnosticism*, Studies on the Apocryphal Acts of the Apostles, 4 (Leuven, 1998), 129–31. See the treatments of *GP* and *AJ* below.

Finally, in an account of the incarnation in 8. 456–79 (not paralleled in book 1) we read of Mary's encounter with the angel Gabriel (Luke 1: 26–56). Here the author writes,

> A word (ἔπος) flew to her womb.
> In time it was made flesh (σαρκωθέν) and came to life in the womb,
> and was fashioned in mortal form and became a boy
> by virgin birth (παρθενικοῖς τοκετοῖς). (8. 69–72)

This account of the 'Word' being 'made flesh' (σαρκωθέν) seems based on John 1: 14, καὶ ὁ λόγος σὰρξ ἐγένετο, though the word ἔπος is used instead of λόγος. Indeed the whole sentence seems to come from an attempt to harmonize the Fourth Gospel's account of the incarnation with the Lukan account of the annunciation. We see something similar in the *Epistula Apostolorum*, a work from the 140s or earlier (see below), which also amalgamates the Lukan and Johannine accounts (citing from the Coptic):

> Then he answered and said to us, 'On that day, when I took the form of the angel Gabriel, I appeared to Mary and spoke with her. Her heart received me and she believed; I formed myself and entered into her womb; I became flesh [*Ethiopic*: and I, the Word, went into her and became flesh]. For I alone was servant to myself with respect to Mary in an appearance of the form of an angel'. (14. 5).[64]

It must be noted that here Jesus, the Word, is said to have taken the form of the angel Gabriel. But in both accounts the Word is said to have entered Mary at that time and to have 'become flesh' in her womb. It is possible that the Christian Sibyllist is not completely independent of the *Epistula* at this point, at any rate both attest to the attempt to combine John 1: 1–14 with Luke 1: 26–56 in an amalgamation of the two accounts of the incarnation. But the number of Johannine elements used by both Christian Sibyllists argues strongly for an independent knowledge of the text of the Fourth Gospel and a high value placed upon that text.

Unfortunately, it is not possible to be certain about the provenance of the Christian Sibyllists. The Jewish substratum of book 1 is known to have come from Phrygia.[65] This may be prima-facie evidence for the interpolator of book 1 coming from Asia Minor, though it is no more than that. The links cited above with the *Epistula Apostolorum* in book 8 might point to Asia Minor, and the same might be said about the links to the *Gospel of Peter* and the *Acts of John*, both arguably, though not certainly, Asian works.

One might question just what sort of relationship these Christians who took it upon themselves to add to the Jewish Sibylline literature maintained with the Great Church. Whatever their affiliations were, and whatever

---

[64] Though this conception is the result of an attempt to combine the accounts of Luke and John, it is an 'orthodox' attempt, and contrasts with the Valentinian notion of the heavenly Christ 'passing through Mary, as water passes through a tube'.

[65] Collins, *OTP* i. 332, citing 1. 196–98, 261–2.

notions they had of authoritative scriptures, neither of these authors is gnostic or Valentinian but each shows every sign of adhering to the major doctrines of the mainstream Church. They used several of the NT writings along with books such as *Ps. Barnabas* and perhaps the *Gospel of Peter* (though it is somewhat more likely that this work knew *Sib. Or.* 1 than vice versa). They were Christians who were interested in the Jewish Sibylline writings, and were thus likely familiar with other Jewish pseudonymous or apocryphal writings as well. They may well be related to the Jewish Christianity with which Papias was intimate, which recorded a traditional Jewish saying about the fruitfulness of the earth in the times of the kingdom, and attributed it to Jesus via the disciple John.

We may in any case be confident that the Christian authors of *Sibylline Oracles* 1. 324–400 and of 8. 217–500 each knew special Johannine material and used it as reliable information about the life and words of Jesus, alongside the Synoptics. In the case of the author of 1. 324–400, this may be as early as some time prior to 150. For the author of 8. 217–500, who shows a greater use of the Fourth Gospel, it probably pertains to the period 161–80. At least the second author, and probably the first, also knew the book of Revelation. Such as it is, *Sibylline Oracles* 8. 217–500 attest the views of a non-gnostic Christian writer during or just after the reign of Marcus Aurelius who knows and uses both the Fourth Gospel and the Apocalypse of John.

Irenaeus of Lyons

We come now to Irenaeus of Lyons, who became through his writings a major figure in the Church during this period. He is certainly a central figure in the OJP. It is with Irenaeus that most scholars mark a sea change in the fortunes of the Fourth Gospel among the orthodox. As we have seen, the first effective attempt at taking over (or taking back) the Fourth Gospel for the orthodox is customarily credited to him. J. N. Sanders thought, 'he was the first Catholic writer to overcome the prejudice which appears to have been felt against the Fourth Gospel, at least in Rome, in the latter half of the second century, and to make it a weapon in the controversy *adversus haereses*',[66] a judgement which has been echoed by many others.[67]

We have already gained an idea of how poorly this popular scholarly opinion stands up to the evidence. Seen in the context of the immediately preceding decade, Irenaeus seems utterly conventional in his use of the Fourth Gospel; he differs from his predecessors mainly in the extent of his

---

[66] J. N. Sanders, *The Fourth Gospel in the Early Church* (Cambridge, 1943), 66.

[67] A. H. B. Logan, 'John and the Gnostics: The Significance of the Apocryphon of John for the Debate about the Origins of the Johannine Literature', *JSNT* 43 (1991), 41–69, at 41; Culpepper, *John*, 123; Lee Martin McDonald and Stanley E. Porter, *Early Christianity and its Sacred Literature* (Peabody, Mass., 2000), 615.

use, and that may be partly because we have more of his writings addressed to fellow Christians than we do of the writers already treated. In any case, Irenaeus' great work, *Against Heresies*, does mark a watershed in our available traditions about the Fourth Gospel. What he gives us, both in the variety and extent of his use of that Gospel and in the traditions surrounding it and its supposed author, is by far the most voluminous we have up to that date. And beginning about the time of Irenaeus though, as we have seen, before his writing career began, the evidence of orthodox use of John becomes much more plentiful. The importance of Irenaeus in the story of the Johannine literature in the second century is hard to overestimate.

Irenaeus' use of the Johannine corpus

To examine all the instances of Irenaeus' use of John, of the Johannine Epistles, or the Revelation would make for a very long study. The index in the *ANF* edition shows references to all but three chapters of the Fourth Gospel (10, 18, 21), and *BP* shows references to these chapters as well. The extent of his use of all of the Johannine corpus, with the possible exception of 3 John, is not at all under dispute. This extensive use is not only admitted by the proponents of the OJP but is showcased both as contrasting to the dearth of previous orthodox use and as exhibiting Irenaeus' attempt to recoup this Gospel from the heretics and use it against them. The present study then shall be more focused on what Irenaeus' works can tell us about the existence of a Johannine corpus, and particularly about the status and use of the Fourth Gospel in the Church in his day, and about the previous history of that use. It will be of interest to observe how he uses these works and his attitude towards them; what he says about their origins and previous use in the Church, both by heretics and by his orthodox predecessors; and any indications of controversy concerning them. It will be most critical to uncover any signs that Irenaeus is introducing a new Gospel to orthodox audiences, or that he is defending a Gospel that was known but had been under attack or was held in suspicion by other orthodox Christians.

Irenaeus' own attitude towards this Gospel is not hard to gather. From his first treatment of the Fourth Gospel he calls it scripture (1. 8. 2, cf. 1. 9. 1; 1. 22. 1, see below). It is an apostolic (3. 21. 3; cf. 4, *praef.* 3)[68] and eyewitness account by John 'the disciple of the Lord' (2. 2. 5; 3. 1. 1; 3. 16. 2, 5; 3. 22. 2; *Dem.* 43, 94), the disciple who reclined at Jesus' side at the supper (3. 1. 1; 4. 20. 11). This identification means that Irenaeus also knew John 21, where this link is explicitly made. He quotes the Fourth Gospel sometimes by invoking John's name (2. 2. 5; 3. 8. 3; 3. 11. 1, 2, 4; 3. 22. 2;

---

[68] That Irenaeus believed the author to be John the son of Zebedee is generally admitted, though it has been challenged by Richard J. Bauckham, 'Papias and Polycrates on the Origin of the Fourth Gospel', *JTS* ns 44 (1993), 24–69. I hope to treat this matter in another volume.

4. 2. 3; 4. 10. 1; 5. 18. 2; *Dem.* 43, 94), sometimes by citing 'the Gospel' (3. 11. 2; 4. 20. 6; 4. 33. 1), sometimes without formal introductions at all (3. 9. 3; 3. 10. 2). Its words of Jesus he cites as such, without qualification (2. 22. 6; 3. 8. 1; 3. 17. 2; 3. 19. 1; 4. 2. 3; 4. 5. 2; 4. 13. 4; 4. 14. 1; 4. 18. 3; 4. 23. 1; 4. 36. 6; 5. 6. 2; 5. 13. 1; 5. 15. 2; 5. 18. 1; 5. 22. 2; 5. 25. 4; 5. 27. 2)[69]—even occasionally citing the theological declarations of the author himself as words of the Lord (4. 20. 11, twice). This forms a parallel to what he says about the words of Moses and the prophets being also Jesus' words (4. 2. 4) and belonging to the Church. In what follows it will be imperative to see how Irenaeus reacts to the use of this Gospel by heretics, but as to his own positive use, it is evident that he regards (or, if one prefers, he pretends to regard) this Gospel as scripture and presents it to the reader ostensibly as part of the Church's inheritance from the apostles, like the other three Gospels. And one thing which most proponents of the OJP seem to ignore is that Irenaeus' 'reader', his 'dear friend' whom he addresses personally in many asides in the *Against Heresies*, is very likely a friend in the Roman church. At any rate, we may be sure that the majority of his intended audience were members of the church at Rome.[70]

There can be no doubt that Irenaeus sees the Gospel according to John as a bulwark for the Church's faith and theology in the face of heresy.[71] He uses this Gospel in theology proper to prove the doctrine of God's creation of the physical world (John 1: 3 in 1. 22. 1; 2. 2. 5); the greatness of the Father (John 14: 28 in 2. 28. 8); the unity of the God of Old and New Testaments (John 14: 6–7 in 4. 7. 3). The Gospel according to John is rich in teaching about the person of Jesus Christ. It proclaims the Father's glorification of the Son before the world was (John 17: 5 in 4. 14. 1); the agency of the Word in the creation of all things (John 1: 3 in 3. 11. 1, 2; 3. 21. 10; *Dem.* 43); the true incarnation of the Word (John 1: 13, 14 in 3. 11. 3; 3. 19. 1; *Dem.* 94) and his true manhood (John 4: 6; 11: 35; and 19: 34 in *AH* 3. 22. 2); the unity of the one person, Jesus Christ (John 1: 13–14 in 3. 16. 2; John 20: 31 in 3. 16. 5); that the Lord is himself the resurrection (John 11: 25 in 3. 5. 2); Jesus' priority to Abraham (John 8: 58 in 4. 13. 4); Abraham's knowledge of Jesus (John 8: 56 in 4. 5. 3, 5; 4. 7. 1); that the words of Moses and the prophets are Jesus' words (John 5: 46–7 in 4. 2. 4); that the Old Testament speaks of Jesus (John 5: 46 in 4. 10. 1); and for various facets of the life of the Lord, cited for various purposes (2. 22. 6; 3. 11. 5; 4. 2. 7; 4. 9. 2; 4. 18. 3; 4. 22. 1; 4. 23. 1). That the bulk of these

---

[69] Likewise with speeches assigned to others in the Gospel (John the Baptist, 3. 10. 2; the Jews, 2. 22. 6; Nathanael, 3. 11. 6).

[70] See Unger's discussion of Irenaeus' readers, *St Irenaeus of Lyons: Against the Heresies*, ACW 55, tr. D. J. Unger, rev. J. J. Dillon (New York, 1992), 4–6. That Irenaeus had a readership in Rome in the late 180s is also shown by his two treatises written against problem presbyters in that city, *To Florinus, On the Sole Sovereignty*, and *To Blastius, On Schism* (Eusebius, *HE* 5. 15; 5. 20, 1, 4–8).

[71] As W. von Loewenich says, *Das Johannes-Verständnis im zweiten Jahrhundert* (Giessen, 1932), 118, as *regula veritatis*.

occur in polemical contexts is of course only natural in a work which is
explicitly polemical in character.[72] And one can readily see how useful and
versatile the Gospel according to John was to Irenaeus in the struggle
against the heretical sects.[73] But not all of Irenaeus' theologizing is polemically oriented, and the edificatory value of what he sees in John's Gospel
stands and has stood over the centuries, long since the time when the
second-century sects faded away.[74]

It is often stated as a matter of course that Irenaeus 'defended' this
Gospel.[75] Looking at his use of this Gospel as a whole, however, we fail to
see the signs of this. Irenaeus does not defend the Fourth Gospel, he merely
uses it. He uses this Gospel unselfconsciously and authoritatively, as he does
the other three; much more often than Mark, though not quite as often as
either Luke or Matthew. He uses it as he does the rest of the scriptures.
Proponents of the OJP often point to 3. 11. 8–9, where it is said that
'Irenaeus' arguments for the necessity of four gospels may amount to a
covert defense of the Gospel of John'.[76] The flaw in this argument is that it
works just as well against Matthew, Mark, and Luke, as against John. Why
should John be singled out? In this context Irenaeus mentions one heretical
group which used Matthew but rejected Mark, Luke, and John; another
which used Luke but rejected Matthew, Mark, and John; another which
preferred Mark to the others; another which used the Prologue of John
copiously; and one which rejected John. And even in 3. 11. 9, where he
speaks of this obscure group which rejected John, where we might most

---

[72] On the polemical aspects see von Loewenich, *Das Johannes-Verständnis*, 118–30, who uses the
headings, 'Gegen die ptolemäische Prologauslegung'; 'Die polemische Verwertung von Joh 1. 3';
'Gegen den Dualismus zwischen AT und NT'; Gegen die valentinianische Chronologie des Lebens
Jesu'; 'Gegen die häretische Christologie'; 'Verschiedene Polemik'.

[73] In fact, one might well wonder how it would be possible for someone to use this Gospel to
argue for the views Irenaeus opposes. Could one, for instance, argue from John 1 that God and the
Word had no part in the creation of this world? We shall have occasion later to see what in this
Gospel appealed to the 'gnostics'.

[74] See von Loewenich, *Das Johannes-Verständnis*, 130–7, who describes Irenaeus' use of John
without direct polemical motives under the headings, 'Gott und Christus'; 'Schöpfung und Rekapi-
tulation'; 'Heiliger Geist, Kirche und Ketzer'.

[75] e.g. Culpepper, *John*, 123, 'Irenaeus is the first writer to offer a defense of the apostolic
authorship of the Gospel and Epistles'; 127, 'If not entirely original with Irenaeus, therefore, the
coalescing of the traditional view...owes a great deal to Irenaeus's interpretation of the tradition he
used in his defense of the Gospel of John as an orthodox, apostolic writing'; Logan, 'John and the
Gnostics', 41, 'Irenaeus...is perhaps the first mainstream Christian writer to defend the orthodoxy
of the Fourth Gospel over against its extensive use by Valentinians and other Gnostics'.

[76] D. M. Smith, 'The Problem of John and the Synoptics', 157. See also Culpepper, *John*, 131,
'Irenaeus defended the fourfold Gospel and the apostolic authorship of the Gospel, 1 and 2 John,
and Revelation as well'; McDonald and Porter, *Sacred Literature*, 615, speaking of *AH* 3. 11. 8, 9, say
that Irenaeus' 'unconvincing arguments (by today's standards) appear to have been a means of
including recognition of the Gospel of John, which was under suspicion in many second-century
churches. Why else would he give such a fanciful and forceful argument if everyone was already in
full agreement on the matter (see *Haer.* 3. 11. 8, 9)'. Considering some of the fanciful arguments
used by the opponents of these Gospels, the one used by Irenaeus may have been better 'context-
ualized' than we now are given to think.

expect that he should defend this Gospel, his response hardly qualifies as a 'defence'. Neither here nor anywhere else does he 'argue' for the identity of its author, against some denial of it or against some alternative proposal; neither here nor anywhere else does he insist that it (in distinction from the other apostolic documents) had been handed down from the apostles through the Church's presbyters or bishops. Instead of focusing on any claims he might want to make about the Fourth Gospel he simply exposes the sin of these people in rejecting the Spirit which John's Gospel had promised in the person of the Paraclete. The closest he comes to a defence is to say that if these people reject John's Gospel they also ought to reject Paul too, for he too taught about the prophetical gifts in the Church. If Irenaeus 'defends' any Gospel, it is the Gospel according to Luke, on which he writes at length against the Ebionites who rejected it (3. 14. 3) and the Marcionites and Valentinians who rejected parts of it (3. 14. 4).

Irenaeus uses the rest of the Johannine corpus in much the same way. He considers both 1 and 2 John to be 'letters'[77] by the same disciple who wrote the Gospel according to John (3. 16. 5, 8). He uses 1 John for its statements on the unity of the person of Jesus Christ against the adoptionist docetists, like Cerinthus and the Valentinians (1 John 2. 18 in 3. 16. 5; 1 John 4: 1–2; 5: 1 in 3. 16. 8).[78] Irenaeus first uses 2 John in 1. 16. 3 when discussing the teachings of the Marcosians, 'And John, the disciple of the Lord, has intensified their condemnation, when he desires us not even to address to them the salutation of "good-speed;" for, says he, "He that bids them be of good-speed is a partaker with their evil deeds"' (2 John 10, 11). 2 John 7–8 is cited in 3. 16. 8 in the context of proving the unity of the person of Christ. It is questionable whether Irenaeus used 3 John in his writings. Most say he did not, but there seems to be an allusion to 3 John 9 in *AH* 4. 26. 3, when Irenaeus refers to presbyters who 'conduct themselves with contempt towards others, and are puffed up with pride of holding the chief seat'.

He uses the entire book of Revelation (citations from all but chapters 10, 14–16, 18 are listed in *BP*). Not surprisingly, Irenaeus uses Revelation most often for information about the future coming of Christ in glory and what will ensue at that time. He cites the prophecy of Revelation 12: 14 about the dragon 'who will with his tail cause a third part of the stars to fall from their place, and will cast them down to the earth' (2. 31. 3); Revelation 17: 8 for the coming and final destruction of the Antichrist (5. 30. 4); Revelation 13: 18 for the number of his name (5. 30. 1–4); Revelation 20: 6 for the first resurrection which will inaugurate the millennium (5. 34. 2); Revelation 20: 11–14 for the general resurrection and great judgement (5. 35. 2); Revelation

---

[77] His reference to 'his Epistle' for both 1 John (3. 16. 5) and 2 John (3. 16. 8) may sound like his reference to 1 Corinthians as 'the Epistle to the Corinthians' in 3. 13. 1.

[78] His citation of 1 John 4: 1–2 in 3. 16. 8 takes the controversial variant 'every spirit which separates' instead of 'every spirit which does not confess' (unless this is an alteration by the Latin translator). This may have started as a marginal gloss, as it still survives in 1739 mg.

21: 2, 10 for the descent of New Jerusalem to earth after the millennial kingdom (5. 35. 2); Revelation 21: 2 for the future tabernacling of God with man (4. 18. 6). A recurring string of references, introduced as the words of 'John in the Apocalypse', is found in book 4 (4. 14. 2; 4. 17. 6; 4. 18. 6; 4. 20. 11; 4. 21. 3). Concepts and images from Revelation 3 and 5 appear in 4. 20. 2. But Irenaeus also uses the Revelation to speak of present realities (the Spirit, 4. 14. 2; incense as the prayers of the saints, 4. 17. 6; the heavenly temple where God receives the prayers and oblations, 4. 18. 6). This book speaks of past aspects of Christ's redemption as well. These include Christ's resurrection (3. 22. 4) and, interestingly, given Irenaeus' later arguments for a future millennium, for Satan's past binding (Rev. 20: 2) in 3. 23. 8. In his regard for John's Apocalypse he is entirely in line with the *Epistle of Vienne and Lyons*, which, as we have seen, used the Revelation of John as scripture.

Irenaeus is very comfortable using each one (with the possible exception of 3 John) of the Johannine writings. He is confident of their acceptability among his readers. But we would be giving a skewed picture of the Johannine corpus in the works of Irenaeus if we simply treated his use of each member of that corpus separately and failed to observe the profound unity which Irenaeus assumes between the entire corpus. Not only does Irenaeus identify at least the Gospel, 1 and 2 John, and the book of Revelation as the products of the same disciple (3. 16. 5, 8; 4. 20. 11), but on this basis he sometimes cites portions of two or more Johannine documents together, as from the same source.

The Gospel, therefore, knew no other son of man but him who was of Mary, who also suffered; and no Christ who flew away from Jesus before the passion; but Him who was born it knew as Jesus Christ the Son of God, and that this same suffered and rose again, as John, the disciple of the Lord, verifies, saying: 'But these are written, that ye might believe that Jesus is the Christ, the Son of God, and that believing ye might have eternal life in His name (Jn. 20. 31),'—foreseeing these blasphemous systems which divide the Lord, as far as lies in their power, saying that He was formed of two different substances. For this reason also he has thus testified to us in his Epistle: 'Little children, it is the last time . . . Who is a liar, but he that denieth that Jesus is the Christ' (1 Jn. 2. 18 ff.). (*AH* 3. 16. 5)

Here Irenaeus links together John 20: 35 and 1 John 2: 18–22 as forming aspects of a single thought of one person, a thought which tells against the Valentinians. Three paragraphs later (3. 16. 8), he uses four texts from three Johannine works (2 John 7–8; 1 John 4: 1–2; John 1: 14; and 1 John 5: 1), all attributed to 'John, His disciple', to establish further that Jesus Christ was one person. This ability to fuse similar passages from the Gospel and two Johannine Epistles is familiar to many readers today but is at odds with prevailing theories of Johannine origins which hold each member of the corpus apart and assign each to distinct periods of Johannine history and to diverse authors. The unity of the Johannine works in the mind of Irenaeus is demonstrated most strikingly in 4. 20. 11, where he exegetes John's experience in the Apocalypse by referring to his experience recorded in the Gospel. After citing John's vision of the risen Jesus Christ in Revelation 1: 12–17, Irenaeus says,

But when John could not endure the sight (for he says, 'I fell at his feet as dead;' that what was written might come to pass: 'No man sees God, and shall live' [Exod. 33: 20]), and the Word reviving him, and reminding him that it was He upon whose bosom he had leaned at supper, when he put the question as to who should betray Him, declared: 'I am the first and the last, and He who liveth, and was dead, and behold I am alive for evermore, and have the keys of death and of hell' [Rev. 1: 18].

So implicitly does Irenaeus assume the unity of authorship of Gospel and Apocalypse. He makes no apology and gives no explanation for using the Johannine works in this way. His unaffected manner certainly suggests that he expected his readers would not regard it as unusual or problematic. And many or most of his first readers were surely in Rome, the alleged nerve centre of orthodox Johannophobia.

IRENAEUS ON THE ORIGIN OF THE FOURTH GOSPEL

Irenaeus, as noted, is quite definite on the identity of the man who wrote the 'Gospel according to John'. If this identification is part of a fiction created by him, as some have held,[79] the fiction grows to the point of inventing details about John's life and about the origin of the Gospel and passing it off as tradition. The Apocalypse which John the disciple of the Lord received during his exile on the island of Patmos was seen toward the end of the reign of Domitian (5. 30. 4). After his release John came to live in Ephesus, where, according to eyewitness testimony, he remained until the times of Trajan (2. 22. 5; 3. 3. 4).[80] It was also at Ephesus, whether before or after his captivity on Patmos, that John published the Gospel (3. 1. 1).[81] Irenaeus never says anything about the circumstances of John's death.

Irenaeus even has something to say about the circumstances of writing. Irenaeus claims there was a polemical motive for John in writing his Gospel and Letters (and perhaps the Revelation too).

John, the disciple of the Lord, preaches this faith, and seeks, by the proclamation of the Gospel, to remove that error which by Cerinthus had been disseminated among

---

[79] Koester, 'Ephesos', 138. Charlesworth, *Beloved Disciple*, 410, seems to approach almost everything Irenaeus says with grave suspicion.

[80] '... even as the Gospel and all the elders testify; those who were conversant in Asia with John, the disciple of the Lord, [affirming] that John conveyed to them that information. And he remained among them up to the times of Trajan. Some of them, moreover, saw not only John, but the other apostles also, and heard the very same account from them, and bear testimony as to the [validity of] the statement' (2. 22. 5); 'Then, again, the Church in Ephesus, founded by Paul, and having John remaining among them permanently until the times of Trajan, is a true witness of the tradition of the apostles' (3. 3. 4).

[81] 'Afterwards, John, the disciple of the Lord, who also had leaned upon His breast, did himself publish a Gospel during his residence at Ephesus in Asia' (3. 1. 1).

men, and a long time previously by those termed Nicolaitans, who are an offset of that 'knowledge' falsely so called, that he might confound them, and persuade them... The disciple of the Lord therefore desiring to put an end to all such doctrines, and to establish the rule of truth in the Church, that there is one Almighty God, who made all things by His Word, both visible and invisible; showing at the same time, that by the Word, through whom God made the creation, He also bestowed salvation on the men included in the creation; thus commenced His teaching in the Gospel: 'In the beginning was the Word...' (3. 11. 1)

Thus he links John's interests in the Gospel directly to the controversy with Cerinthus.[82] It is true that he also mentions the Nicolaitans in 3. 11. 1 as among those John wished to refute, and then includes the views of unnamed others, who must be Valentinians.[83] But the references to the Valentinian version of adoptionism are simply expansions upon the basic structure of Cerinthus' teaching as recorded in 1. 26. 1, added for the sake of showing that John wrote to put an end to all such ideas. He mentions only Cerinthus and the Nicolaitans by name, the latter already known to have been opposed by John from his Apocalypse, the former not named in John's writings but known from tradition received from Polycarp. An enmity between John and Cerinthus had been brought before the reader's eyes already in 3. 3. 4 in the story about John and Cerinthus at the Ephesian baths. This enmity is thus of a piece with what Irenaeus now tells the reader in 3. 11. 1 about John's motivation in writing the Gospel. We may also note in passing that the *Epistula Apostolorum*, which is an anti-docetic tract, knows the Fourth Gospel and claims to have been written against Cerinthus and Simon. This is significant because other early notices of the origin of the Fourth Gospel, which seem to be dependent upon Papias, namely those of Clement of Alexandria and the *Muratorian Fragment*, say nothing of this.[84]

IRENAEUS ON THE PREVIOUS USE OF THE FOURTH GOSPEL

From this summary of Irenaeus' use of the Fourth Gospel and the rest of the Johannine corpus, we might surely conclude that he, and those whom he thought would read his writing in the 180s, considered the Fourth Gospel to be scripture and to be part of a corpus written by a disciple of the Lord. It will now be of interest to see what Irenaeus' writings can show us about the use of this Gospel before he wrote. Irenaeus is aware of other individuals and groups who had come into contact with this Gospel. These

---

[82] R. M. Grant, 'The Origin of the Fourth Gospel', *JBL* 69 (1950), 304–22; M. A. Donovan, *One Right Reading? A Guide to Irenaeus* (Collegeville, Minn., 1997), 74, 'Surely he here contributes what must be one of the earliest opinions about the authorial intent of any gospel (*AH* III. 11, 1)'.

[83] '...and flew back again into His Pleroma; and that Monogenes was the beginning, but Logos was the true son of Monogenes' is a reference to Ptolemaian Valentinianism, from 1. 8. 5.

[84] The connection with Cerinthus does not show up again until Victorinus, who seems to combine this account of Irenaeus with that of Clement or the *Muratorian Fragment*.

include Ptolemy and other unnamed Valentinians, but they evidently also include Polycarp, Papias, and some unnamed elders of a previous generation.

Valentinians and the Fourth Gospel

We find, of course, that Irenaeus is well acquainted with some previous Valentinian attempts to claim support for their doctrines from the Fourth Gospel. If he knew of Heracleon's now famous commentary on that Gospel, it is strange that he never mentions the book, nor evidently does he cite anything from it.[85] But he does know and reproduce in *AH* 1. 8. 5 extended comments made regarding the Johannine Prologue by a Valentinian writer, traditionally thought to have been Ptolemy, though there is now some dispute about the attribution. But for my purposes in this section, it is not crucial to establish whether it was Ptolemy or another, later Valentinian writer. Nor am I so much interested here in analysing this example of Valentinian exegesis *per se* (I shall have more to say about that later). At this point I am primarily interested in how Irenaeus presents and reacts to previous, heterodox use of the Fourth Gospel and what this might tell us about its place in the Church in Irenaeus' time and before.

Having described in the preceding chapters the system of the Valentinians, Irenaeus begins a section in 1. 8 intended to show how they try to support that system by an illegitimate appeal to 'the parables of the Lord, the sayings of the prophets, and the words of the apostles, in order that their scheme may not seem altogether without support'. Irenaeus then demonstrates this with regard to four areas of Valentinian teaching.[86] First, in 1. 8. 2 he writes, 'as to those things outside of their Pleroma, the following are some specimens of what they attempt to accommodate out of the Scriptures to their opinions'. These specimens include texts from Matthew, Luke, Paul, and one modified text[87] from John 12: 27, all accommodated to elements of the Valentinian myth. Second, in 1. 8. 3 he gives their scriptural support for the 'three kinds of men', material (hylic), animal (psychic), and spiritual (pneumatic), using texts from Luke, 1 Corinthians, and Romans. Third, in

---

[85] It is true that in 1, *praef.* 2 he says he had read 'some of the Commentaries, as they call them, of the disciples of Valentinus'. But the word used, ὑπομνήματα, is often translated 'notes' or 'reminiscences' and was common as a reference to other types of literature (the full title of Clement of Alexandria's *Stromateis* is *Miscellanies of Notes* (ὑπομνήματα) *of Revealed Knowledge in Accordance with the True Philosophy*, and Clement uses it often in referring to his *Stromateis*; it was the title given to Hegesippus' historical and anti-heretical work). And even if given the meaning 'commentary' here it probably does not refer to commentaries on scriptural books. On the Valentinian school's commentaries on the hymns or writings of Valentinus himself, see Christoph Markschies, 'Valentinian Gnosticism: Toward the Anatomy of a School', in J. D. Turner and A. McGuire (eds.), *The Nag Hammadi Library after Fifty Years: Proceedings of the 1995 Society of Biblical Literature Commemoration*, Nag Hammadi and Manichaean Studies, 44 (Leiden, 1997), 401–38, at 423–5. Identifying 1, *praef.* 2 as a reference to such works would strengthen Markschies's thesis at this point.

[86] Donovan, *One Right Reading*, 35, 40–1, nn. 1–4.

[87] Καὶ τί εἴπω οὐκ οἶδα, in place of simply καὶ τί εἴπω, the reading of all the MSS.

1. 8. 4 he reports how they use three passages from Luke and one each from 1 Corinthians and Ephesians to relate to the situation of Achamoth in her wanderings outside the pleroma. Finally, in 1. 8. 5 he sets out to give the Valentinian scriptural support for 'the first Ogdoad, expressing themselves in these words', and at this point produces a long quotation, interrupted perhaps only once, which, in the Latin text, ends with the words, 'Such are the views of Ptolemaeus' (*et Ptolomaeus quidem ita*). Here is where some controversy currently exists, as these words in the Latin text find no correspondence in the Greek text preserved by Epiphanius in *Panarion* 31.[88] Though the quotation in 1. 8. 5 undoubtedly comes from some written source, whether Ptolemy or not, it is contextually quite probable that the material in the immediately preceding sections, in which Irenaeus does not quote but merely paraphrases his source, has come from the same work. This is because he frames his entire section here with references to Valentinians (plural) and keeps with the plural all the way through, even in introducing his citation of the written source, until the (apparent) attribution to Ptolemy at the end of 1. 8. 5.

Several relevant points emerge from this notice of a previous use of the Fourth Gospel by the Valentinians. First, if Irenaeus had known that the Gospel according to John was an acknowledged Valentinian or heretical work, it would have been easy and natural for him simply to ignore this inflammatory 'exegesis' of its Prologue. Why would he need to bother refuting Valentinian exegesis of another Valentinian or gnostic tract? This in itself suggests that the Fourth Gospel held among Irenaeus' potential readers in the Church a status alongside Matthew and Luke (Mark is not specifically cited in 1. 8).

Second, Irenaeus' first open citation of the Fourth Gospel in *Against Heresies* comes precisely here, in material which is quoted from a Valentinian writer (1. 8. 5). If Irenaeus is out to gain support for a Gospel which was unknown or had been under a cloud of gnostic suspicion, it is passing strange that he should introduce it to his readers in a quotation from a Valentinian. He appears on the other hand to be totally oblivious to the dangers involved in placing this already dubious Gospel in such hands. But as it is, his citation of Valentinian use of John is no different from his citation of Valentinian use of Matthew, Luke, and the Pauline Epistles in the immediately preceding context (1. 8. 2–4). Each, so he charges, is a perversion.[89]

---

[88] See Christoph Markschies, 'New Research on Ptolemaeus Gnosticus', *ZAC* 4 (2000), 225–54, at 249–50, who also cites G. Lüdemann, 'Zur Geschichte des ältesten Christentums in Rom. I. Valentin und Marcion II. Ptolemäus und Justin', *ZNW* 70 (1979), 86–114, at 99, and C. Barth, *Die Interpretation*, 19. I shall reserve comment on this matter until the section on Ptolemy in Ch. 5 below.

[89] The Valentinians in general were not like the Marcionites, who accepted only a version of Paul and Luke. Rather, says Irenaeus, they 'do certainly recognize the Scriptures; but they pervert the interpretations, as I have shown in the first book' (3. 12. 12). Or, paraphrasing what Tertullian would later say, the Marcionites took a knife to the scriptures, the Valentinians a pen.

Third, we see plainly from his treatment of this Valentinian text that Irenaeus himself conceives of the Fourth Gospel as fully scriptural, just as much as the other three Gospels, the letters of Paul, indeed, as much as the Old Testament. He both introduces and concludes this section, in which he cites and deals with a Valentinian's pleromatic exegesis of John 1, by referring to Valentinian attempts to support their fictions from 'scripture'.[90] He repeats both the writer's exposition of John 1 and his exposition of parts of Matthew, Luke, and 1 Corinthians, Romans, and Ephesians. He follows his refutation of this Valentinian exegesis of John with this conclusion:

For since Logos, and Monogenes, and Zoe, and Phos, and Soter, and Christus, and the Son of God, and He who became incarnate for us, have been proved to be one and the same, the Ogdoad which they have built up at once falls to pieces. And when this is destroyed, their whole system sinks into ruin,—a system which they falsely dream into existence, and thus inflict injury on the Scriptures (τῶν γραφῶν), while they build up their own hypothesis. (1. 9. 3)

Fourth, the tone of Irenaeus' evident displeasure at this Valentinian maiming of the Fourth Gospel is revealing. As the preceding passage, among others, shows, Irenaeus takes great umbrage at this Valentinian's 'deceitful' procedure in misusing this scriptural text (1. 9. 1), 'wresting from the truth every one of the expressions which have been cited' (1. 9. 2). It is surprising that Irenaeus could be so offended by the Valentinians simply using their own 'special gospel'. It is surprising unless, of course, this response is being carefully staged by Irenaeus as part of what Koester calls his 'fiction' about the Fourth Gospel. But this gets a bit complicated. Irenaeus not only seems to think his readers will agree with him in his regard for Matthew, Luke, John, and the Pauline Epistles as scripture, but he explicitly appeals to them (at least to his addressee, but through him to all readers) in this very matter: 'You see, my friend, the method which these men employ to deceive themselves, while they abuse the Scriptures by endeavouring to support their own system out of them. For this reason I have brought forward their modes of expressing themselves, that thus thou mightest understand the deceitfulness of their procedure, and the wickedness of their error' (*AH* 1. 9. 1). He seems fully to expect from his readers—even his readers in Rome—the same sort of reaction he has had, an instinctive, visceral sensation that the Valentinians are abusing scripture when they abuse the Gospel according to John. Could this too be part of his act, part of an increasingly elaborate ruse to fool readers into thinking that a recent gnostic apocryphon had long enjoyed scriptural standing in the Church?

---

[90] The entire section 1. 8. 2–5 is introduced by Irenaeus thus: 'the following are some specimens of what they attempt to accommodate out of the Scriptures to their opinions' (1. 8. 2). At the end of this section, and speaking specifically about Ptolemy's exposition of John 1, Irenaeus exclaims, 'You see, my friend, the method which these men employ to deceive themselves, while they abuse the Scriptures by endeavouring to support their own system out of them' (*AH* 1. 9. 1).

The level of sophistication, and risk, not to mention the level of dishonesty, necessary for such a psychological charade should surely place this line of explanation where it belongs. There is no reason to believe that Irenaeus is anything but sincere.

And here is where a review of the immediately preceding decade becomes so helpful. Irenaeus' respect for the Fourth Gospel and his frustration with the Valentinians who misused it are entirely consistent with even the limited scope of works from the previous decade which have already been examined. Even before coming to the writings of Irenaeus there has been enough to assure us that catholic Christians in various parts of the empire were treating this Gospel as the inspired work of an apostle of Jesus. In other words, there was no need for Irenaeus to concoct an elaborate hoax in an attempt to drum up sympathy for the Fourth Gospel.

A final observation with regard to the Valentinian writer himself is appropriate here. While we can obviously tell from Irenaeus' notice here and elsewhere[91] that Valentinians like this one had used the Fourth Gospel before he wrote, we cannot yet tell that it held any special fascination for them over a number of other New Testament books. As I pointed out above, it is most likely that the same author, whether Ptolemy or not, is the source for the exegetical material in 1. 8. 2–4 as well as for the material quoted in 1. 8. 5. If it is not Ptolemy himself, then it is another Valentinian writer of the so-called Italian school. We observe then that he expounds Matthew, Luke, and the Pauline letters with as much as conviction, and with the same method, as he does John. Even in the midst of the 'exposition' of John 1 this writer also invokes Ephesians 5: 13. Thus, despite the singular attention to selected words and phrases from John 1: 1–14, we already see from Irenaeus' notice in *AH* 1. 8. 2–5 that the Valentinians made copious use of the other Gospels and of Paul. Irenaeus had charged earlier,

And it is not only from the writings of the evangelists and the apostles that they endeavor to derive proofs for their opinions by means of perverse interpretations and deceitful expositions: they deal in the same way with the law and the prophets, which contain many parables and allegories that can frequently be drawn into various senses, according to the kind of exegesis to which they are subjected. (1. 3. 6)

Certainly up to this point Irenaeus does not seem aware of John's Gospel being a favourite target of Valentinian exegesis;[92] their manipulation of the Church's scriptures was without prejudice.

---

[91] In 2. 17. 9 Irenaeus alludes to Valentinians who refer to the man born blind in John 9 to illustrate the blindness and ignorance of 'the Word' as to his paternity. This may have come from some published work or from personal conversations with Valentinians to which he refers earlier in this paragraph.

[92] One place where the Valentinians did not use the Fourth Gospel was in their assertion that Jesus' ministry lasted only one twelve-month period (based on a literal interpretation of Isa. 61: 2)

But then there is *AH* 3. 11. 7. It is here that Irenaeus makes his well-known statement about the Valentinians' copious use of the Gospel according to John. It is important here not only to see what he actually says, but also to see it in its context. Irenaeus is making a point about the authority of the Church's four Gospels.

So firm is the ground upon which these Gospels rest, that the very heretics them-selves bear witness to them, and, starting from these [documents], each one of them endeavours to establish his own peculiar doctrine. For the Ebionites, who use Matthew's Gospel only, are confuted out of this very same, making false suppos-itions with regard to the Lord. But Marcion, mutilating that according to Luke, is proved to be a blasphemer of the only existing God, from those [passages] which he still retains. Those, again, who separate Jesus from Christ, alleging that Christ remained impassible, but that it was Jesus who suffered, preferring the Gospel by Mark, if they read it with a love of truth, may have their errors rectified. Those, moreover, who follow Valentinus, making copious use of that according to John, to illustrate their conjunctions, shall be proved to be totally in error by means of this very Gospel, as I have shown in the first book.

Irenaeus thus associates each heterodox group with a Gospel, though *not* in the same way in each case. The Ebionites' and the Marcionites' use of the Church's four is restricted to one Gospel each—in Marcion's case, a muti-lated form of one Gospel. For the unnamed docetic group, he says simply that they 'prefer' (*praeferentes*) the Gospel by Mark, without denying their use of any of the others. With the Valentinians he says only that they make copious use of John 'to illustrate their conjunctions',[93] and does not allege that they did not use the other Gospels in other areas of their teaching. In the case of each heresy Irenaeus asserts that their errors could be refuted even by that portion of the fourfold Gospel that they either retain or 'prefer'.

The first thing that stands out in his statement about the Valentinians and John is that Irenaeus makes the connection only with regard to the Valentinians among all the heresies, not with regard to 'gnostics', like the Basilideans, Carpocratians, and Barbeloites, in general. Second, he does not suggest the Valentinians had anything like a monopoly on the book. He neither implies that the orthodox avoided the book nor that the Valentinians

---

after his baptism before being crucified (*AH* 2. 22. 1). This they said in hopes of demonstrating 'that passion which, they say, happened in the case of the twelfth Aeon, from this fact, that the passion of the Saviour was brought about by the twelfth apostle, and happened in the twelfth month' (2. 22. 1). On this point Irenaeus castigates them for their ignorance of the Gospels: 'But it is greatly to be wondered at, how it has come to pass that, while affirming that they have found out the mysteries of God, they have not examined the Gospels to ascertain how often after His baptism the Lord went up, at the time of the passover, to Jerusalem' (2. 22. 3). From here Irenaeus takes the reader to the only Gospel which can demonstrate that Jesus observed more than one Passover after his baptism, the Gospel according to John. It appears that this analogy is to be attributed to Ptolemy himself (2. 22. 5). This does not support the idea that Ptolemy and the Valentinians were experts in this Gospel.

[93] *Plenissime utentes ad ostensionem 'coniugationum' suam.*

used it above all others.[94] In fact, two paragraphs later he remarks on
Valentinian recklessness in putting forth their own compositions, and this
agrees with what he had said earlier about the Marcosian Valentinians, who
use 'an unspeakable number of apocryphal and spurious writings, which
they themselves have forged, to bewilder the minds of foolish men, and of
such as are ignorant of the Scriptures of truth' (1. 20. 1). He certainly does
not connect the Valentinians to the origins or early history of the Fourth
Gospel concerning which, as we have seen, he has quite another tradition.

Third, and most importantly, he in fact is quite specific about the scope
of the Valentinians' use, saying that they use it copiously to illustrate their
'conjunctions', that is, the conjunctions of aeonic syzygies in the pleroma.
Here he has the pleromatic exegesis of the Johannine Prologue in 1. 8. 5
directly in view, for he refers the reader to his demonstration of the error of
such exegesis in his first book![95] That means he considers his relatively short
refutation of the Valentinian distortion of John 1: 1–14 in *AH* 1. 9. 1–3 to
be a sufficient answer to the 'copious use' of John by the Valentinians.
Beyond this he reports no more extensive connection between the Valentinians and what has been called their 'special gospel'. This is surprising,
given the paradigm under discussion.

Polycarp

Irenaeus claims to know quite a bit about John from Polycarp. Most of this
concerns not John the Gospel, however, but John the man, the apostle and
disciple of the Lord. Irenaeus claims that Polycarp was ordained by the
hand of John and at least one other apostle (3. 3. 4). Though the reference
to John is often thought to be a case of mistaken identity, Irenaeus is at least
maintaining consistency with his tradition about John surviving till the time
of Trajan (2. 22. 5; 3. 3. 4).[96] If this is true, the lives of John and Polycarp
must have overlapped by a good thirty years or so. Irenaeus tells the
Roman Bishop Victor that Polycarp had appealed to his observance of the
quartodeciman Easter with John and other apostles (*HE* 5. 24. 16). He
attests to Florinus that he could remember much of what Polycarp handed
down from the oral teaching of John himself, and other 'eyewitnesses of
the word of life' (Eusebius, *HE* 5. 20. 6; cf. 5. 24. 16). Irenaeus' use of the

---

[94] Valentinian use of nearly all the books of the NT is easily documented. At one point Irenaeus
comments specifically on their selective use of Luke, while they take from that Gospel 'many
occasions for their own speculations'. 'If, on the other hand, they feel compelled to receive the
remaining portions also, then, by studying the perfect Gospel, and the doctrine of the apostles, they
will find it necessary to repent, that they may be saved from the danger [to which they are
exposed]' (3. 14. 4).

[95] Where he says, 'But that the apostle [i.e. John] did not speak concerning their conjunctions,
but concerning our Lord Jesus Christ . . . he himself has made evident' (1. 9. 2).

[96] Bauckham, 'Origin', 61, believes that this latter was merely the independent deduction of
Irenaeus, who believed that John's Apocalypse was written near the end of Domitian's reign (*AH*
3. 1. 1). But if this is so, why does he choose Trajan's reign and not simply Nerva's, who came
between Domitian and Trajan?

phrase, 'eyewitnesses of the word of life', obviously adapted from 1 John 1: 1, surely means to identify this John with the author of 1 John. This implies that Polycarp too used and referred to 1 John, something we can confirm from his letter to the Philippians. Then there is the Ephesian bath-house story, and the 'apostolic tradition' of disassociating oneself from the enemies of the truth (*AH* 3. 3. 4; 4. 2; Eusebius, *HE* 5. 20. 7), which probably implies a use of 2 John 10. These matters will be explored at a later point. Therefore the link between John and the church at Ephesus, emphasized in 3. 1. 1, where his publication of the Gospel is said to have been done from that city, and in 3. 3. 4, where he is made part of that church's apostolic foundation,[97] is supported by his tradition from Polycarp, though no doubt from other sources as well. In fact, in 3. 3. 4 he says that the entire Ephesian church is a witness to the apostolic tradition. He means by this primarily that that church is established in apostolic doctrine, but also presumably that the Ephesian church in his day attested to these very same apostolic foundations by Paul and John as Irenaeus reports.

From the bath-house story we know not only that Polycarp associated John with the Ephesian church but that he also taught about John's opposition to 'Cerinthus, the enemy of the truth'. Later in book 3 Irenaeus connects the motive for John's writing of his Gospel to his desire to oppose Cerinthus (*AH* 3. 11. 1).[98] I have observed elsewhere that it is likely that this too came from Polycarp.[99] Such a connection also fits with what Irenaeus reports about Polycarp's appeal to John and the other apostles in arguments against heresy.[100] Irenaeus mentions in connection with John's antagonism to Cerinthus also his antagonism to the Nicolaitans, which obviously comes from Revelation 2. 6, 15. This text and others (*AH* 4. 20. 11; 30. 4) show that Irenaeus believed in the common authorship of the Gospel and Apocalypse. It is not unlikely that Polycarp was one source for this connection as well.

In most of his references to the Johannine books Irenaeus mentions no prior source for his exegesis. This does not mean that he had none, given his stress on following the exegetical traditions of the presbyters in book 4 of *Against Heresies*, only that he does not directly attribute them. For instance, there are certain places where he echoes the exegesis of Justin, without attribution. In fact, there is the probability of a use of John 5: 24 and 8: 56 on the part of an earlier, unnamed presbyter in 4. 31. 1. Almost certainly, this was Polycarp, but this will have to be argued for elsewhere.

---

[97] 'Asia' as his residence is mentioned also in 2. 22. 5.

[98] Robert M. Grant, 'The Origin of the Fourth Gospel', *JBL* 69 (1950), 304–22.

[99] C. E. Hill, 'Cerinthus, Gnostic or Chiliast? A New Solution to an Old Problem', *JECS* 8 (2000), 135–72, at 155–8.

[100] Note the special relationship in the *Ep. Apost.* to John the author of the Gospel and its concern to refute Cerinthus.

I shall postpone any further discussion of these reports by Irenaeus. I am simply interested in them now as ostensible evidence from his writings of a prior use of the Johannine literature among the orthodox. It is likely that many of his ideas about that literature may be linked to Polycarp, though no doubt he has other sources as well. What is clear is that Polycarp put him in touch with early tradition about the man who was thought to have written the Fourth Gospel, Letters, and Apocalypse, a corpus of writings which Irenaeus and the church of his contemporaries regarded as scripture. Tradition about this man is tradition about an apostle, a disciple of the Lord, *the* disciple of the Lord who leaned on the Lord's breast at the Supper.

Papias and his elders

According to Irenaeus, Polycarp was not the only one of the hearers of John to have left behind some record of the experience. He states once that Papias himself was a hearer of John (*AH* 5. 33. 4), though in this case, much more so than in the case of Polycarp, it is most likely that Irenaeus made a mistake. Because Eusebius says he traversed the work of Papias with the latter's possible relationship to the apostle John in mind, we must probably allow his testimony more weight when he says that Irenaeus must have been misled at this point (*HE* 3. 39. 2–7). It was perhaps an easy mistake because Irenaeus knew that Papias and Polycarp had been contemporaries in Asia, and it is possible that a few of Papias' references to 'John', meaning John the Elder were too quickly assumed to refer to John the apostle.

Even so, the conclusion is warranted that some that Papias knew in the generation before him had used the Fourth Gospel and the Revelation of John. Near the conclusion of *Against Heresies* Irenaeus reports a tradition of the elders which includes a reference to John 14: 2.

And as the presbyters say, 'Then those who are deemed worthy of an abode in heaven shall go there, others shall enjoy the delights of paradise, and others shall possess the splendour of the city; for everywhere the Saviour shall be seen according as they who see Him shall be worthy'. 2. [They say moreover], that there is this distinction between the habitation of those who produce an hundred-fold...and that it was on this account the Lord declared, 'In My Father's house are many mansions', each according to his worthiness...The presbyters, the disciples of the apostles, affirm that this is the gradation and arrangement of those who are saved, and that they advance through steps of this nature...(5. 34. 2)

Most agree that Irenaeus got this report of the presbyters' words from Papias. If so, this is evidence that the Fourth Gospel had been used among the orthodox from a time well before Papias wrote, and this would put it in perhaps the first or second decade of the second century, in Papias' time, and of course in Polycarp's time. This, needless to say, is earlier than Valentinus. Irenaeus' use of this tradition is in the context of supporting his teaching about the eschaton. It is not in an effort to bolster the Fourth

Gospel or to defend its use in the Church. Instead it assumes once again that that Gospel needed no defence with his readers.

Irenaeus does not say that these elders knew John, only that they were disciples of the apostles. There are three references in Irenaeus to 'elders' or presbyters (besides Polycarp) who knew John. He mentions in 5. 30. 1 that certain men 'who saw John face to face' bore witness to the correctness of the number 666 for the name of the Beast (Rev. 13: 18) in copies of the Apocalypse of John which were then extant. This means at least that they used the book of Revelation. These may or may not be the same elders who testified to the age of the Lord while he held the office of teacher in 2. 22. 5, who are said there to have been conversant with John in Asia. They may or may not be 'the elders who saw John, the disciple of the Lord' who 'related that they had heard from him how the Lord used to teach in regard to these times', teaching them about the ten-thousandfold exuberance of plant life in the kingdom, as recorded by Papias (5. 33. 3, 4). All these passages will be taken up later, when I revisit the testimony of Papias and these elders. But while it is far from clear just what the facts are which underlie these statements, with little doubt Irenaeus derived all of them from the books of Papias, as he tells us in one instance (5. 33. 4). And they offer ostensible proof that both the Fourth Gospel and the Revelation were used not only by Papias, but by elders of the generation before him. Again, in none of these passages is Irenaeus trying to defend the Fourth Gospel.

Taken together, Irenaeus' reports from Polycarp, from Papias, and possibly from other sources appear to demonstrate a much earlier use of the Fourth Gospel, the Revelation, and the First Epistle among the orthodox, at least in Asia Minor. They argue in fact for a continuous use of these Johannine works among the 'apostolic' churches from a time very early in the second century on through to Irenaeus' day. The testimony is explicitly set in terms of sources which are supposed to have had direct contact with John or other apostles. These are important data which are frequently ignored by advocates of the OJP. Whether and to what extent Irenaeus' testimony about previous use of the Fourth Gospel can be believed, whether he might be innocently passing along erroneous tradition or deliberately fabricating a web of untruths, is something that we shall be better able to assess after examining the earlier period itself.

Those who Oppose the Fourth Gospel in AH 3. 11. 9

Up until now there has been no indication from Irenaeus that the Fourth Gospel had ever had anything but a universally warm reception among catholic Christians. We have found no reason to think that either orthodox teachers or simple believers avoided or rejected it because of suspicions that it taught heresy, as the OJP states. But there is a reference made by Irenaeus to an earlier opposition to John's Gospel which many have linked to the protest of Gaius, which seems to have occurred some fifteen to twenty years later. This reference has thus been used to construct a hoary line of orthodox opposition to the Fourth Gospel at least in Rome, if not else-where.[101] In book 3 of his *Against Heresies* Irenaeus mentions some who,

> to nullify the gift of the Spirit which has been poured out on the human race in accordance with the Father's good pleasure in the last times, do not receive that form [of the gospel] which is the Gospel according to John, in which the Lord promised to send the Paraclete. These reject, at the same time, the Gospel and the prophetic Spirit. They are miserable indeed, since they certainly do not wish that there be false prophets,[102] but they remove the prophetic gift from the Church. (*AH* 3. 11. 9, Heine's translation)

Here at last is a group which, Irenaeus alleges, is vocal in its opposition to the Fourth Gospel, a group of true Johannophobes. What is the nature of their antagonism? The motive given by Irenaeus is that by rejecting the Gospel according to John they would thus be rid of the promise of a coming Para-clete, presumably the justification for the New Prophecy. They want to cur-tail 'false prophets' and what Irenaeus designates the 'prophetic Spirit'. Irenaeus too is against false prophecy (4. 33. 6)[103] but he is not for removing the prophetic gift altogether. That is, he believes the promise of the Paraclete from the Gospel according to John has already been realized in the pouring out of the Holy Spirit upon the whole Church. Some years earlier the *Epistle of Vienne and Lyons* had alluded to that promise and had proclaimed that the Spirit dwelt in the worthy Vettius Apagathus, not because he prophesied but because he courageously acted as the advocate for the Christians.

In the light of modern interpretation, it is important to point out what is absent from this notice. First of all, Irenaeus does not mention any contro-versy over the authorship of the Fourth Gospel.[104] That is, these rejecters of the Fourth Gospel do not allege, so far as we can tell, any author besides the apostle John. Secondly, it is of great interest to observe that one can find no trace here of an allegation of docetism, ditheism, or pleromatic teaching in the Fourth Gospel. The only criticism named by Irenaeus is completely tied to the promise of the Paraclete and the gift of prophecy. Finally, there is no indication of a concurrent opposition to the book of Revelation,[105] or any of the rest of the Johannine literature.

---

[101] e.g. Bauer, *Orthodoxy and Heresy*, 207–8; Haenchen, *John 1*, 23–4; Culpepper, *John*, 121–2.

[102] Accepting, with most scholars, the proposed *nolunt* for *volunt*, which is in the text. It should be noted, however, that Smith, 'Gaius', 151–3 proposes a way of reading the extant text which results in virtually the same meaning but with an ironical twist. The consequence of these people's position is that they in effect show themselves to wish to be false prophets, even though they deny the current existence of prophecy in the Church.

[103] Here he speaks of 'false prophets, who, without having received the gift of prophecy from God, and not possessed of the fear of God, but either for the sake of vainglory, or with a view to some personal advantage, or acting in some other way under the influence of a wicked spirit, pretend to utter prophecies, while all the time they lie against God'. This probably was aimed at the New Prophets; it compares very well to the account of Eusebius' anonymous anti-Montanist source, 5. 16–17.

[104] Noted also by Smith, 'Gaius', 143.

[105] A complaint against the Revelation of John is not explicit here, though it could be compre-hended in their rejection of 'the prophetic Spirit' (cf. Rev. 19: 10; 22: 6).

Who then are these opponents of the Fourth Gospel? They are certainly not Valentinians, whom Irenaeus mentions separately in this very context, and who had their own way of interpreting the sending of the Johannine Paraclete (*AH* 1. 4. 5). On the surface it seems that they are critics of the early Montanist movement. Since the authority of John's writings is assumed to have been better established at this time in Asia Minor, many would locate these critics outside that province. Heine for this reason locates them in Rome,[106] where they could then legitimately be seen as forerunners to the Roman Gaius.[107] J. D. Smith concluded that they represent not another earlier, orthodox group but none other than Gaius himself at an earlier stage of his teaching.[108] The supposed orthodoxy of this group is often stressed by scholars.[109] But, to the contrary, there is nothing in Irenaeus' report which can be said to support the idea that these critics were recognized by anybody as 'orthodox', and apart from the desire to connect them with Gaius and to find a unified opposition to the Fourth Gospel, it is doubtful that this would ever have been maintained.

Whoever they were, it cannot be missed (and yet it routinely is) that Irenaeus classes them with heretics in 3. 11. 9, listing them between Marcionites and Valentinians. And later in the same paragraph he goes so far as to accuse them of the unforgivable sin against the Holy Spirit—a charge he does not even make against Marcion or Valentinus! In chapters 99 and 100 of the *Demonstration of the Apostolic Preaching*, written probably soon afterwards, he refers to this group once again.

And others do not admit the gifts of the Holy Spirit, and reject from themselves the charism of prophecy, being watered whereby, man bears fruit of life to God. And those are the ones spoken of by Isaias; 'for they shall be', he says, 'as a leafless terebinth, and as a garden without water'. And such men are of no use to God, in that they can bear no fruit. (99)[110]

He concludes the *Demonstration* with the following paragraph:

---

[106] R. Heine, 'The Role of the Gospel of John in the Montanist Controversy', *The Second Century*, 6/1 (1987–8), 1–19, thinks that Irenaeus learnt of this group as early as his trip to Rome in AD 177 just after the pogroms in Gaul.

[107] Heine, 'Role of the Gospel of John', 16, 'Against such claims by the Roman Montanists based on the Gospel of John, the group to which Irenaeus refers, and with which Gaius was later associated, rejected the authority of the Gospel of John. It was in Rome, then, that the Paraclete passages in John first assumed a central position in the Montanist controversy.' Heine thinks that 'the Asian debate over Montanism centered on the question of true and false prophets, not on whether there could be contemporary prophets' (11). But the position that legitimate prophecy ceased with the Apostles and the prophecies approved by them is more than hinted at by the unidentified source of Epiphanius. Further, Eusebius' anonymous source indirectly chides the New Prophets for adding to scripture. These are both probably Asian sources, demonstrating that 'canonical' concerns were important to these early Asian critics as well as to their partners in Rome.

[108] Smith, 'Gaius', 207–8, 259–60. He is followed in this by Culpepper, *John*, 121.

[109] e.g. Bauer, *Orthodoxy and Heresy*, 141; Sanders, *Fourth Gospel*, 38; von Campenhausen, *Formation*, 238–9. See also Gunther, 'Early Identifications', 411.

[110] Translation is that of J. P. Smith, *St Irenaeus: Proof of the Apostolic Preaching*, ACW 16 (New York, 1952), 108–9.

So error with respect to the three articles of our seal has brought about much wandering away from the truth. For either they despise the Father, or they do not accept the Son, they speak against the dispensation of His incarnation, or they do not accept the Spirit, that is, they reject prophecy. And we must beware of all such men, and flee their ways, if we really desire to be well-pleasing to God and receive from Him salvation. (100)

Here Irenaeus does not mention their rejection of John's Gospel but only their opposition to the Spirit, for which sin he places them alongside those who blaspheme the Creator and Father, and those who despise the incarnation of the Son of God, for they 'do not accept the Spirit, that is, they reject prophecy'. Clearly, whoever these people are, Irenaeus does not treat them as he does the non-millennialists or the quartodecimans, that is, as fellow orthodox believers who take an erroneous but tolerable position,[111] but as seriously deluded heretics who deny one of the very foundational 'three articles of our seal', of whom believers must 'beware' and 'flee their ways' (*Dem.* 100).[112] Particularly given Irenaeus' strong connections with and respect for the church in Rome, it is inconceivable that such a group could represent any official or standard position of that church. At the time that he wrote book 3 of *Against Heresies*, Irenaeus had the highest estimation of this church's transmission of the 'one and the same vivifying faith, which has been preserved in the Church from the apostles until now, and handed down in truth' (3. 3. 3). Whatever else can be said of the Johannophobes of 3. 11. 9, we may rule out the theory that they were a contingent of orthodox believers in good standing with the hierarchy in Rome,[113] whether they had any connection to Gaius or not.

Further confirming the heterodox character of these opponents of John is the larger context of Irenaeus' comments. *Against Heresies* 3. 11. 9 is actually the continuation of an argument that began in 3. 11. 7. There, as we have seen, Irenaeus had alleged a tendency of certain heretical forms of Christianity to want to establish their doctrine from only one of the Church's four Gospels, and had argued that each heresy could be refuted from the very Gospel it chose. He mentions the Ebionites who use only Matthew;

---

[111] It is frankly astonishing that Smith, 'Gaius,' 164–5, can say, after acknowledging that these are the same people Irenaeus reprehends in *Dem.* 99–100, that they are not admonished for false teachings and that they still could have been considered 'catholic' by him. That Irenaeus does not mention them by name is no indication that they are still in good ecclesiastical standing. He often identifies heretics not by name but by doctrine. Smith wishes to identify the opponents of the Fourth Gospel in *AH* 3. 11. 9 as Gaius himself, whose position would then have been known to Irenaeus before the publication of the *Dialogue with Proclus*. Unfortunately, Smith's conclusions here have, I believe, misled other writers.

[112] It may not be insignificant, in the light of what will now follow, that Irenaeus more than once urges 'fleeing' from heretics, following the examples of Polycarp in his treatment of Marcion and of John in his treatment of Cerinthus (*AH* 3. 3. 4; cf. 1. 16. 3).

[113] J. J. Gunther, 'Early Identifications', 411, says that 'Irenaeus suggests nothing unorthodox about their tradition'. Apart from their destroying the form of the Gospel, rejecting the Holy Spirit, and committing the unpardonable sin, this may be correct!

Marcion, who uses a mutilated form of Luke; some unnamed docetists, who 'prefer' Mark; and the Valentinians, who make copious use of John to establish their conjunctions. After his famous expostulation on the necessity of there being four and only four ecclesiastical Gospels, Irenaeus returns in 3. 11. 9 to the heretics who 'destroy the form of the Gospel', either by adding to or by subtracting from their number. And just as in 3. 11. 7, he mentions here (3. 11. 9), in order, the Marcionites, who whittle the Gospels down to some fractions of Luke, an unnamed group that rejects John's Gospel and its Paraclete Spirit outright, and then the Valentinians, who now are castigated not for 'subtracting from' but for 'adding to'—for putting forth their own compositions and in effect increasing the closed number of Gospels. If the group sandwiched between the Marcionites and the Valentinians in 3. 11. 9 is the same one he had sandwiched between these same sects in 3. 11. 7, it would be a group of adoptionistic heretics who 'separate Jesus from Christ, alleging that Christ remained impassible, but that it was Jesus who suffered'. These people, in other words, followed the heresy pioneered by the infamous Cerinthus (*AH* 1. 26. 1), nemesis of John (3. 3. 4; 11. 1). If this connection is valid, it establishes beyond doubt that these people are not orthodox opponents of the Fourth Gospel in the bosom of the catholic Church, in Rome or anywhere else, but docetists in the tradition of Cerinthus himself, against whom Irenaeus has already claimed earlier in this very chapter that John wrote his Gospel (3. 11. 1). Thus their opposition to John's Gospel is entirely to be expected (at least in Irenaeus' mind), as it coheres with Irenaeus' overall portrayal of the circumstances which led to the production of the Johannine Gospel and Letters. As it happens, this understanding of the anti-Johannine group in 3. 11. 9, which combines a docetic Christology, a deviation on the Holy Spirit and prophecy, and even evidently an opposition to John, can now be illustrated from an outside source.

One of the intriguing tracts in the Nag Hammadi collection which has eluded classification is the work called *The Apocryphon of James*. This work will be treated later, in Chapter 5, but I draw attention to it here because of its unnoticed but important correspondences with the group mentioned by Irenaeus. Scholars have placed this writing in Asia, Syria, or Egypt and anywhere from the early second to early third century. It has certain ties with the *Epistula Apostolorum* and is best placed perhaps just prior to that writing and probably in Asia, or if in Egypt it soon made its way to Asia. This author speaks for a docetic understanding of the Saviour, thus at least approximating the view of the heretics mentioned by Irenaeus in 3. 11. 7. This is easily recognizable and is not, of course, unusual among the Nag Hammadi texts. What is unusual is the *Ap. Jas.*'s radical understanding of prophecy ceasing with John the Baptist. 'James' reports a conversation with the risen Jesus: 'Then I asked him, "Lord, how shall we be able to prophesy to those who request us to prophesy to them? For there are many who ask us, and look to us to hear an oracle from us." The Lord answered and said,

"Do you not know that the head of prophecy was cut off with John?" ' (6. 21–31). As van der Vliet observes, 'The general tendency of Jesus' answer is quite clear: no more prophecy is possible, as it came to an end with the death of John the Baptist.'[114] This means not only that the gift is not available to Montanists or any of the faithful in the author's own time,[115] but that it is also denied to the apostles! Significantly, this author knows of a Paraclete (11. 11–12), but identifies it with Jesus, as in 1 John 2: 2, not with the Holy Spirit, as in John 14: 16, 26. It must be recalled that in the Gospel of John the Paraclete Spirit is claimed first and foremost as the one sent to the apostles, and it is He who 'will teach you all things, and bring to your remembrance all that I have said to you' (John 14: 26), that is, He is to be a guarantor of the truth of their later teaching (John 16: 13).[116] The position of the author of the *Ap. Jas.*, therefore, means that he probably would not have contested apostolic authorship of the Church's scriptures; he would not have needed to. Instead he would have contested divine authority as being guaranteed to the apostles by the Spirit-Paraclete, who was given to them, as John's Gospel says, that He might 'declare to you the things that are to come' (John 16: 13).

The connections between the views of this author and the views of those Irenaeus opposes in *AH* 3. 11. 7, 9, are obvious. There does, however, seem to be a difference in emphasis between the restriction of prophecy by the author of the *Ap. Jas.* and by the Johannine opponents in *AH* 3. 11. 9. The latter's antagonism to the Spirit seems generalized while that of the former seems concentrated on the apostles and designed to diminish apostolic authority. But the ideas are compatible, and a group which started with the denial of divine speech and authority to the apostles could hardly have reacted any differently to the advent of the Montanist claims than did the opponents mentioned by Irenaeus.[117] And they have in common an opposition to the Paraclete revelation in the Fourth Gospel.

Our correlation of the *Ap. Jas.* and the opponents of John mentioned by Irenaeus might also be questioned on the basis that the *Ap. Jas.* uses not only many of the New Testament documents, but also the Fourth Gospel and 1 John, which in fact figure somewhat prominently. But while I would certainly not claim that Irenaeus was responding specifically to this document, there is an important observation that must be made which will bring

---

[114] J. van der Vliet, 'Spirit and Prophecy in the Epistula Iacobi Apocrypha (NHC I, 2)', *VC* 44 (1990), 25–53, at 35, which see for a fuller discussion of the passage. Van der Vliet points out that *Ap. Jas.* contrasts with another Nag Hammadi tractate, *Interpretation of Knowledge* (NHC XI, 1), which encourages prophecy.

[115] Van der Vliet connects this to the Montanist crisis.

[116] Cf. Tertullian, *Praescr.* 8. 14, 15 on this.

[117] In fact, if the views represented by the *Ap. Jas.* were present and circulating in Asia Minor or Phrygia before the rise of Montanism, one might easily imagine that their stifling approach, which shut off prophecy from the apostles and from the Church at large, could have been a factor in provoking the reaction in Phrygia which was Montanist prophetism.

the group Irenaeus mentions into closer proximity to the apocryphon. While the *Ap. Jas.* certainly uses the Fourth Gospel and First Epistle of John, the use it makes of them is overall a disparaging one, even bringing its critical eye at times to the author, or reputed author, of these documents.[118] For instance, this apocryphon claims superior teaching revealed not to the apostles as a group, but only to James and Peter. There is some question whether this James is the half-brother of Jesus or the son of Zebedee. But in either case, the exclusion of one man from his place in the triumvirate which included Peter and James the son of Zebedee in the synoptic Gospels, or from that which included Peter and James the Just in Acts and Galatians, is conspicuous. Another interesting point comes from Irenaeus' testimony that the Johannophobes of *AH* 3. 11. 9 (if they are indeed the same one mentioned in 3. 11. 7) preferred the Gospel according to Mark to support its docetic views. A preference for Mark meant in this environment also a preference for Peter, whose interpreter Mark was.

One more thing unites Irenaeus' group with the *Ap. Jas.* and separates both from the usual picture of Gaius of Rome. As I have pointed out, Irenaeus gives no indication that the group in question contested the apostolic authorship of the Fourth Gospel. Nor does the *Ap. Jas.* contest apostolic authorship of the Church's Gospels, but simply seeks to supersede them. This conforms to a tendency outlined by Irenaeus of heterodox groups who claimed that they were wiser than the apostles, and that the apostles 'intermingled the things of the law with the words of the Saviour' (3. 2. 2), or that the apostles wrote before they had perfect knowledge (3. 12. 7), or that their group had secret traditions not made known by the public apostolic documents (3. 2. 1). To anticipate for a moment the more thorough discussion below, this explains the interesting fact that heterodox groups of the second century as a rule did not seek to deny apostolic authorship of the Church's documents. This is because they sought to supersede apostolic authority. They could then either with Marcion pare down the number and form of the literature used by the Church, or with Valentinus reinterpret them, and add more. Such an approach operates from a fundamentally different frame of mind from that which seeks to attribute the Gospel and Apocalypse to a heretic who allegedly forged them in his name. I shall examine this subject at greater length in Chapter 4 on Gaius below.

Can we then say that the group mentioned by Irenaeus in 3. 11. 7, 9 who rejected the Fourth Gospel, is the same group, perhaps at a later point in their development, for which the author of *Ap. Jas.* wrote? Not with any

---

[118] Pheme Perkins, demonstrates the extensive knowledge of the Fourth Gospel by the author of this work (P. Perkins, 'Johannine Traditions in *Ap. Jas.* (NHC I, 2)', *JBL* 101 (1982), 403–14, but fails to note that his use of this Gospel and the related 1 John is critical and sometimes antagonistic. We shall examine this point further in Ch. 5.

certainty, though some kind of relationship is quite possible. What these correspondences do show, I believe, is that the profile of the group of Johannophobes mentioned by Irenaeus bears a much greater resemblance to tendencies we see in the heretical sectors than in the mainstream, orthodox sectors of the Church. And in any case, this only supports what has already been seen from Irenaeus' account itself, that he describes and treats this group of Johannine antagonists as being well outside the bounds of right belief.

Have we found any good reason for thinking that Irenaeus was either introducing an unknown Gospel, or defending a contested one, in his bountiful use of the Gospel according to John? Quite the contrary. We have instead uncovered numerous signs, both in Irenaeus' method and in the sources he cites, for believing that this Gospel, along with at least the Apocalypse and First Epistle of John, were treasured as scripture by his contemporaries, even, by inference, his contemporaries in Rome, and had been well-known and used in the previous generations, practically since they had appeared. In order to contest these data, some interpreters are willing to charge Irenaeus with fabrication and deception on a grand scale. If they are correct, his mendacity takes him to the point of playing psychological games with his unsuspecting readers. The store of exegetical and theological fruit he has pulled out of the Fourth Gospel in support of anti-heretical orthodoxy, single-handedly, and without the aid of any previous tradition, would then only serve to draw attention to the soaring heights of his evil genius. But all this is too complicated and fanciful to be true. And it conflicts with what we have seen merely from 170 to 180 in the mainstream Church, a Church which, from Antioch to Athens and on to Rome and to Gaul, prized the Fourth Gospel as inspired scripture.

Polycrates of Ephesus and Victor of Rome

Polycrates was bishop of the church in Ephesus at the time of the quartodeciman controversy in the early to mid-190s. In *HE* 5. 24. 2–7 Eusebius, who had access to a collection of documents relating to this controversy, cites a brief excerpt from a letter which Polycrates wrote to Victor of Rome in protest at the Roman bishop's desire to impose upon all the Church a uniform mode of Easter observance. This letter refers at least once to John. Polycrates' words about John in their full context in *HE* 5. 24. 2–7 are as follows:

As for us, then, we keep the day without tampering with it, neither adding, nor subtracting. For indeed in Asia great luminaries have fallen asleep, such as shall rise again on the day of the Lord's appearing, when he comes with glory from heaven to seek out all his saints: to wit, Philip, one of the twelve apostles, who has fallen asleep in Hierapolis, [as have] also his two daughters who grew old in virginity, and

his other daughter who lived in the Holy Spirit and rests at Ephesus; and, more-
over, [there is] John too, he who leant back on the Lord's breast, who was a priest
wearing the sacerdotal plate, both martyr and teacher. He has fallen asleep at
Ephesus.[119] Moreover, Polycarp too, at Smyrna, both bishop and martyr; and
Thraseas, both bishop and martyr, of Eumenia, who has fallen asleep at Smyrna.
And why need I mention Sagaris, both bishop and martyr, who has fallen asleep at
Laodicea? or the blessed Papirius, or Melito the eunuch who in all things lived in
the Holy Spirit, who lies at Sardis, awaiting the visitation from heaven when he
shall rise from the dead? These all observed the fourteenth day for the Pascha
according to the Gospel, in no way deviating therefrom, but following the rule of
faith. And moreover I also, Polycrates, the least of you all, [do] according to the
tradition of my kinsmen, some of whom were bishops, and I am the eighth. And
my kinsmen always kept the day when the people put away the leaven. Therefore I
for my part, brethren, who number sixty-five years in the Lord and have conversed
with the brethren from all parts of the world and traversed the entire range of holy
Scripture, am not affrighted by threats... [120]

The identification of John as the one who 'leaned on the Lord's breast'
clearly identifies him as the Beloved Disciple and the author of the Fourth
Gospel. The claim is sometimes made that this could not be the apostle
John, for he is not called an apostle here,[121] and because Philip is mentioned first.[122] But for a well-known apostle, another distinctive characteristic—and what could be more distinctive than his having leaned on the
Lord's breast at the Supper?—would have served quite as well as the title
'apostle' as a description; indeed Bauckham thinks that this description gave
him greater authority.[123] And as Lawlor and Oulton point out, 'the names
which follow are apparently in chronological sequence', so Philip may well be
mentioned first because he died first.[124] Surely Polycrates and Irenaeus had
the same man in mind when each refers to a John who reclined on the
Lord's breast at the Last Supper (*AH* 3. 1. 1; 4. 20. 11). This man was
buried in Polycrates' own city of Ephesus.

[119] The Greek of the section concerning John is ἔτι δὲ καὶ Ἰωάννης, ὁ ἐπὶ τὸ στῆθος τοῦ
κυρίου ἀναπεσών, ὃς ἐγενήθη ἱερεὺς τὸ πέταλον πεφορεκὼς καὶ μάρτυς καὶ διδάσκαλος,
οὗτος ἐν Ἐφέσῳ κεκοίμηται.
[120] The translation of H. J. Lawlor and J. E. L. Oulton, *Eusebius, Bishop of Caesarea: The Ecclesiastical History and the Martyrs of Palestine, Translated with Introduction and Notes*, 2 vols. (London, 1954,
repr. of 1927 ed.), i. 169.
[121] Hengel, *Frage*, 35–6.
[122] Hengel, *Question*, 7, 'It is striking that he does not mention him first, since in all the lists of
apostles in the New Testament John the son of Zebedee is listed before Philip; moreover, he is not
given the title apostle.'
[123] Bauckham, 'Origin', 33, 'it could be replied that, if it were generally believed that the John
who wrote the Gospel was one of the twelve apostles, Polycrates could take this for granted, while
using instead a description (ὁ ἐπὶ τὸ στῆθος τοῦ κυρίου ἀναπεσών) which gave him even greater
authority: not just one of the twelve, but that member of the twelve who was most intimate with the
Lord'. I will deal elsewhere with Bauckham's theory that this John was John the Elder not John the
apostle.
[124] Lawlor and Oulton, *Eusebius*, 186.

This reference to John's experience in John 13: 23, 25, etc., shows that Polycrates is familiar with the Fourth Gospel (including the controverted chapter 21, where the identification of the author is made) and accepts the attribution to John, the man who was buried in Ephesus. As bishop of the Church in that city, Polycrates presumably speaks for the community in his high regard for this disciple and his Gospel. Even from this short fragment of a single letter we can tell that Polycrates had access to a collection of 'Holy Scripture', which he had searched carefully for guidance in the quartodeciman controversy. Since he also mentions in this context 'the Gospel', to which he claims the quartodeciman practice fully conformed, it is unlikely that for him 'Holy Scripture' would have been confined to the Old Testament, and there should be little doubt that for him, as for Irenaeus, the Gospel written by John, who leaned on his Master's breast at the Supper, was included in that designation. It may well have been, in fact, this Gospel which he had specially in mind when claiming support for the practice.

It is significant that Polycrates needs to make no introduction, nor any apology, for the man John, 'who leaned on the Lord's breast, who was a priest wearing the sacerdotal plate, both martyr and teacher'. His identification of John in terms of a unique experience he had with Jesus himself, even in terms of a unique role he played in such a crucial event in Jesus' life as the Last Supper, must have been made on the assumption that Victor would have recognized John from this description. That is, he assumes that Victor knows the Fourth Gospel. Not only did the event mentioned have ongoing importance for the entire Church, it was quite at the centre of the debate which was the cause for Polycrates' letter to the Roman bishop. That is, this very John, who had reclined next to Jesus on that night on which he was betrayed, used to begin the commemoration of the Lord's passion and resurrection, so Polycrates claims, on the 14th of Nissan, regardless of the day of the week on which it fell, and regardless of whether resurrection day fell on a Sunday. Polycrates in Ephesus can assume that Victor in Rome knew of this Gospel and its portrayal of the Beloved Disciple, and can assume that the witness of this disciple would carry weight with Victor.

This is also supported by the later correspondence between Irenaeus and Victor. After Victor had proceeded to the drastic measure of cutting off from communion with the church at Rome 'the dioceses of all Asia, together with the adjacent churches' (Eusebius, *HE* 5. 24. 9), Irenaeus was among other bishops who wrote to him in protest. In his letter he appeals to the tolerance which characterized the approach of Victor's predecessors in office, even during the time of Anicetus (155–66) 'when the blessed Polycarp was staying in Rome' (*HE* 5. 24. 16). The matter of differing paschal practice had come up during that visit and Polycarp and Anicetus remained amicable despite being unable to persuade each other of their respective views. Irenaeus says that Polycarp could not surrender his custom 'inasmuch as he had always done so in company with John the disciple of our Lord and the other apostles with whom he had associated' (*HE* 3. 24. 16). Thus Irenaeus appeals again to two of the venerable men who appeared in Polycrates' list, this time bringing them into direct contact with an episode in Victor's own city and with one of his predecessors. Though no direct link is made here to the Fourth Gospel, it is assumed that Victor will know both Polycarp and John, the same John to whom Polycrates had appealed as the intimate of the Lord at the Last Supper and by implication the author of the Gospel according to John.

In this way the witness of Polycrates also indirectly implicates Victor. Not that we know, of course, what Victor himself thought of the Fourth Gospel and its reputed author. We only know that Polycrates and Irenaeus could assume the Roman bishop's knowledge of this Gospel and the tradition of its authorship with no embarrassment, neither writer feeling any necessity to defend this Gospel or to correct any misconceptions which might have attended a reference to its author. In this it is much like Irenaeus' *Against Heresies*, which surely had an intended readership in Rome. The assumption, on the contrary, is that a reference to the man who wrote the Fourth Gospel will actually carry some weight with the Roman bishop. The correspondence of Polycrates and Irenaeus with Victor then not only adds weight and substance to Irenaeus' Asian tradition about John but also, along with the fact that Irenaeus' books were being read in the capital city, and the tradition of Hegesippus published some fifteen to twenty years earlier, speaks against the notion that the Fourth Gospel was rejected, avoided, or feared in the orthodox church at Rome at this time.

Clement of Alexandria

The witness of Clement of Alexandria is often rather vaguely set in the third century, but much of his work has to be placed well before the year 200. In the first book of the *Stromateis* Clement brings his chronology up to the death of Commodus, which occurred on 31 December 192. Eusebius, *HE* 6. 6. 1, concludes that the work was written during the reign of Severus, 193–211, and for some, perhaps most, of the seven (Eusebius says there were eight) books he is no doubt correct. But Clement's chronology does not include Publius Helvius Pertinax, who reigned for about three months of the year 193, nor Didius Iulianus, who succeeded him and was beheaded after a reign of only sixty-six days.[125] Since Clement brings the chronology to the death of Commodus and not Pertinax or Iulianus, it is likely that he finished at least this first book of the *Stromateis*, if not others as well, in

---

[125] Lawlor and Oulton, *Eusebius*, ii. 188.

193.[126] We know Clement did not avoid cataloguing emperors whose reigns lasted only a period of months, for in this same chronological section he includes Galba, Otho, and Vitellius. It is likely then that the next books of the *Stromateis* succeeded the first in short order, though some have thought that last few books were only completed after Clement fled Alexandria in 202. The *Stromateis* is not the earliest work we have from him. In *Stromateis* 6 Clement refers to his *Paedagogos* as a finished work. And his *Protreptikos* preceded this one. Eusebius cites an anonymous writer of the early third century who mentions Clement as one who wrote before the time of Bishop Victor of Rome and treated Christ 'as God' (*HE* 5. 28. 4). This is likely referring to *Protreptikos* 1, 'This Word, who alone is both God and man...' If this author is correct, it would place *Protreptikos* before Victor's election in 189,[127] making it practically contemporary with the later books of Irenaeus' *Against Heresies*. The other works of Clement are more difficult to place chronologically. Clement fled the persecution in Alexandria in about 202, and went probably to Cappodocia where he died probably around 215. The *Quis dives salvetur* was probably addressed to the rich Christians in Alexandria and would predate his departure from there. He also wrote a treatise on the Passover, in which he interacted with the work of Melito and of Irenaeus (*HE* 6. 13. 9), which is most likely to have come from the 190s, while the quartodeciman controversy was fresh. We have two fragments from this work, preserved in the *Chronicon Paschale*, in which Clement explicitly relies upon John and harmonizes his account of the last days of Jesus with that of Matthew.[128] Eusebius also mentions a work entitled *Hypotyposeis*, of unknown date, which he quotes several times. According to Eusebius, this work contained 'concise explanations of all the canonical scriptures' (πάσης τῆς ἐνδιαθήκου γραφῆς ἐπιτετμημένας πεποίηται διηγήσεις), including the disputed ones. Some of these explanations have evidently been preserved in a Latin translation by Cassiodorus from the sixth century. These notes are not extensive but are fairly said to be some of the earliest 'commentaries' on the NT books ever written.

CLEMENT'S USE OF THE JOHANNINE CORPUS

From his earliest writings on, Clement perceives the Fourth Gospel to be part of his Christian scriptures. In *Paedagogos* 7, for instance, he introduces a clause from John 1: 17 with the words, 'Wherefore also the scripture says...', and then again, 'Mark the expressions of scripture'. This is consist-

---

[126] W. Wilson, translator of the *ANF* edn., placed the first part of the work in 194 (i. 168).

[127] Cf. Simon Wood, *Clement of Alexandria: Christ the Educator*, The Fathers of the Church (New York, 1954), pp. xi–xii. Westcott, in his article, 'Clement of Alexandria', in *DCB* i. 559–67, indicated that these three works were composed in order, *Ptroteptikos* in about AD 190, *Paedagogos*, about 190–5, and the *Stromateis* thereafter.

[128] There is an English translation in *ANF* ii. 581.

ent with his authoritative use of John from the first chapter of what is probably his first work, the *Protreptikos* (citing John 1: 1) written in *c*.189, and throughout his career (cf. *Strom*. 1. 21 (135. 2); 5. 13). Although he used other gospel-like sources, there were only four ecclesiastical Gospels regarded as scripture, and the Gospel 'according to John' was among them (*Hypot*. in Eusebius, *HE* 6. 14. 7; *Strom*. 3. 93. 1, 'the four Gospels handed down to us').[129] Clement uses the Fourth Gospel as scripture, much as does Irenaeus, sometimes citing it formally, many more times simply alluding to or incorporating phrases or ideas from this Gospel. From tradition Clement has received the view that John, 'divinely moved by the Spirit, composed a spiritual Gospel' (Eus. *HE* 6. 14. 7). Citing John 1: 16, he includes John the Evangelist among the prophets (*Strom*. 1. 17 (87. 5)). To Clement, John's Gospel is an integral part of the 'New Testament' (*Strom*. 5. 13).[130]

Of the First Epistle of John he also says, 'Following the Gospel according to John, and in accordance with it, this Epistle also contains the spiritual principle' (*Fr. Cass.* 3). The 'spiritual principle' apparently refers to the same quality which was perceived in the 'spiritual Gospel' (*HE* 6. 14. 7). This is echoed again in *Qds* 37, where we read, 'Divine indeed and inspired (θείως γε καὶ ἐπιπνόως) is the saying of John: "He that loveth not his brother is a murderer" (1 John 3: 15), a seed of Cain, a nursling of the devil'. He knows 1 John 5: 16, 17, as written by John 'in his larger Epistle' (*Strom*. 2. 15 (66. 4)), showing his knowledge of at least one more epistle. The Latin translation of Cassiodorus includes Clement's comments on 1 and 2 John. He quite transparently receives the Revelation of John as authentic and prophetic. In *Stromateis* 6. 16 Clement blends clauses from Revelation 21: 6 and John 1: 3, as if they were parts of the same sentence.

CLEMENT ON THE ORIGINS OF THE JOHANNINE WRITINGS

Clement knows and uses the common second-century title for the Fourth Gospel, 'The Gospel according to John' (*Paed*. 6; *Fr. Cass.* 3). For him, as for Irenaeus, this was John the apostle, the same man who also wrote the Apocalypse of John and the Johannine Epistles. This may be seen from the following examples. There are two references in *Qds* 42 to the author of the Apocalypse, who 'removed from the island of Patmos to Ephesus' after the death of the tyrant, as John 'the apostle'. Earlier in the

---

[129] Scripture, as the voice of God, has the highest epistemological value for Clement. 'If a person has faith in the divine Scriptures and a firm judgment, then he receives as an irrefutable demonstration the voice of the God who has granted him those Scriptures. The faith no longer requires the confirmation of a demonstration. "Blessed are those who without seeing have believed" (Jn. 20. 29)' (*Strom*. 2. 2 (9. 6) (J. Ferguson's translation, *Clement of Alexandria. Stromateis. Books One to Three*, The Fathers of the Church (Washington, DC, 1991).

[130] The textual tradition of John known to Clement had already diverged in minor but textually significant ways from that which Irenaeus was using. In *Strom*. 2. 13 (58. 2), he quotes John 1: 13 as speaking of the believer, and seems not to know of the Christological form of this verse. His text of John 1: 18 has 'only begotten God' not 'only begotten Son' (*Qds* 37; *Strom*. 5. 12 and in *Excerpta*).

same work (ch. 8) Clement had also clearly ascribed the words of John 1: 17 to 'the apostle'. Also in the same work he identifies the author of 1 John as 'John' (ch. 37), as he does in *Paed.* 12. In *Strom.* 6. 15 he includes John 1: 3 with Matthew 13: 34 as statements made by 'the apostles'. In the fragments from Cassiodorus on 1 and 2 John he calls the author of these letters both 'John', and 'the presbyter', following 2 John 1 and 3 John 1, but also identifies him as the author of the Fourth Gospel. This shows that, for Clement, 'the presbyter' of 2 and 3 John was John the apostle and author of the rest of the Johannine literature of the NT. Of any other 'Presbyter John' he shows no knowledge. It is therefore appropriate to speak of a Johannine corpus with regard to Clement, for to him, as to Irenaeus, all these writings are products of the same man, John the apostle.

Clement knows from older tradition that the Fourth Gospel was the last of the four to be written (Eusebius, *HE* 6. 14. 7). He knows from tradition that after John was released from Patmos he based his ministry in Ephesus (*Qds* 42). Irenaeus places the publication of the Gospel in Ephesus, though Clement is silent on this point.[131] Clement also says that John was aware of the other Gospels when he wrote. Two motivations for the writing of the Gospel are mentioned: an evident desire to supplement the 'outward facts (τὰ σωματικά)' represented by the other Evangelists in their Gospels, and the desire to satisfy a request by his disciples (τῶν γνωρίμων) (Eusebius, *HE* 6. 14. 7). His words, 'Following the Gospel according to John, and in accordance with it, this Epistle [i.e. the First Epistle] also contains the spiritual principle' (*Fr. Cass.* 3), probably indicate a belief that the Gospel was written before the Epistles.

CLEMENT ON THE PREVIOUS USE OF THE FOURTH GOSPEL

Clement uses the Fourth Gospel and the rest of the Johannine corpus as scripture. Like Irenaeus, Clement signals the acceptance of a four-Gospel canon in the Church at large. Nowhere does he indicate that there was any controversy about his or the Church's use of the Fourth Gospel. Does all this implicate him, as many think Irenaeus is implicated, in an attempt to suppress or overcome the truth about this gnostic Gospel and claim it for the Church? What do the writings of Clement tell us about previous use of this Gospel either in the Church or outside it?

Clement certainly knew that the Fourth Gospel had been used by Valentinians. He once calls Heracleon 'the most distinguished of the school of Valentinians' (*Strom.* 4. 10), though he never mentions Heracleon's comments on the Fourth Gospel. Nor does he mention Ptolemy's exegesis of the Fourth

---

[131] In one place Clement speaks of the time of the apostles ending with Nero (*Strom.* 7. 17 *ANF*; 7. 106. 4 Stählin). This is in the context of pointing out the lateness of the heresies, which, he says, arose not until the age of Hadrian. It is possible he has simply slipped, momentarily forgetting about John, or he may be speaking in general terms.

Gospel, though, as we shall see, he probably made use of it. We do know, however, from notes he took on some writings of Theodotus, a Valentinian teacher in Alexandria, that Theodotus too used the Fourth Gospel. These notes, along with others taken on other Valentinian works, with some of Clement's exegetical and theological reflections interspersed, survive in Clement's *Excerpts from Theodotus*, an unfinished work probably never intended for publication. It is not known just when Clement wrote this work or when Theodotus wrote.[132] We may only say that Theodotus was a second- or third-generation Valentinian teacher who wrote in the late second or early third century.

In this work there are epitomies of Valentinian references to the Johannine Prologue (*Theod.* 6–7), relating some of the nouns in that passage to the Valentinian aeons, much as in the work of Ptolemy (or the Ptolemaeans) as we have seen above. Clement does not give the source for these references, but Casey is probably correct in denying that it was Theodotus, and in identifying it instead with the source used by Irenaeus in *Against Heresies* 1. 1. 1; 1. 8. 5[133]—that is, either Ptolemy himself or perhaps one of his followers. Other portions of the Gospel were used by Theodotus and unnamed Valentinians,[134] all in the cause of expounding the Valentinian myth of the pleroma and the salvation of the seed of Sophia. Yet more significant, at this point, than the use of the Fourth Gospel by Theodotus and the Valentinians (they also used the Synoptics and Paul, not to mention several OT books), is the fact that this did not affect Clement's assessment of this Gospel in the least. He obviously continued to use it authoritatively, along with the other scriptures which the Valentinians used. Most of the time Clement simply records Valentinian excerpts without responding. Sometimes he cannot help responding briefly to a Valentinian interpretation with one of his own (verses from John 1 in 8. 1–4; Theodotian's interpretation of the Paraclete in 24. 2).[135] Elsewhere he counters Valentinian teaching by using other

---

[132] In the MS tradition these occur after the seventh book of Clement's *Stromateis*, along with *Eclogue ex Propheticae* and what appear to be notes or partial drafts for a promised eighth book. This position itself, along with the obviously unfinished character of the work, suggest that these notes belonged to a project which was never completed and therefore that they were among the last things written by him. But this cannot be said for certain, for scholars have noted parallels between the *Excerpta* and Clement's earlier works.

[133] R. P. Casey, *The Excerpta ex Theodoto of Clement of Alexandria* (London, 1934), 8–9. He cites O. Dibelius, 'Studien zur Geschichte der Valentinianer', *ZNW* 9 (1908), 230–47, who also held that Irenaeus, *AH* 1. 1–8 and *Excerpta* 43–65 had a common source. This must be Ptolemy or some product of the Ptolemaean school.

[134] Use of the term Paraclete from John 14: 16, 26; 15: 26 or 16: 7 in *Theod.* 23. 1–2; John 10: 7 in *Theod.* 27. 2–3; John 1: 9 in *Theod.* 41. 3; John 1: 3 in *Theod.* 45. 3; John 14: 6 and 10: 30 in *Theod.* 61. 1; John 19: 34 in *Theod.* 61. 3; John 19: 36, 37 in *Theod.* 62. 2; allusions to John 2: 9 and 3: 29 in *Theod.* 65. 1; John 10: 1, 11–13 in *Theod.* 72. 2–73. 1. Of these, only the references to the Paraclete in *Theod.* 23. 1–2 and to John 1: 9 in *Theod.* 41. 3 come from material which can be attributed to Theodotus himself, according to Casey, *The Excerpta*, 5.

[135] See discussion by Everett Procter, *Christian Controversy in Alexandria: Clement's Polemic against the Basilideans and Valentinians*, American University Studies, 7, Theology and Religion, 172 (New York, 1995), 70–2, and notes.

passages of John (and other scripture) not treated by them (citing John 6: 32, 49, 51 in ch. 13; John 4: 24; 3. 8; in 17. 3–4).

The *Excerpta ex Theodoto* contains the unguarded expressions of a researcher, not his finished work. If a closet Johannophobe were ever to slip up, and reveal the otherwise hidden traces of orthodox Johannophobia, it might well be here. But Clement's attitude towards the Fourth Gospel in these notes is entirely consistent with what we have seen in the rest of his writings. Though the level of his expressed indignation may not match that of Irenaeus,[136] there is no doubt that he resents Valentinian attempts to adapt the scriptures to their own 'chirpings and chatterings' (*Strom.* 2. 37. 1). Clement had inherited his respect for the Fourth Gospel from his non-Valentinians forebears in the faith, and all the Valentinian exegesis which came his way had evidently done nothing to alter it.

Clement had inherited more than a respect for this Gospel. When Clement reports that 'John, last of all, conscious that the outward facts had been set forth in the Gospels, was urged on by his disciples, and, divinely moved by the Spirit, composed a spiritual Gospel' (Eusebius, *HE* 6. 14. 7), he is repeating (and probably adapting) something which he had received as 'a tradition of the primitive elders' (τῶν ἀνέκαθεν πρεσβυτέρων). This certainly goes further back than Irenaeus. The statement that John was 'divinely moved by the Spirit' when he wrote is comparable to the conception of Theophilus of Antioch, who some years earlier cited John 1: 1 as from John, an 'inspired' writer. But the 'primitive elders' are certainly older than Theophilus. As we shall see later, it is likely that this testimony from the primitive elders has come ultimately from the books of Papias.[137] Clement's view of the antiquity of the four Gospels is reflected again when he speaks in *Stromateis* 3. 93. 1 of the normative authority of 'the four Gospels handed down to us'. All this means that, while it is likely that he had read the great work of Irenaeus, he did not simply get the idea of using this Gospel from Irenaeus. It had evidently been used in the Alexandrian church for a long time, had been 'handed down', and its origins had been vouched for by 'primitive elders'.

Like Irenaeus, Clement also had an edifying story about the author of the Fourth Gospel, a story he got from oral tradition. This one was not a story about an apostle and a heretic, a story with a polemical, anti-heretical moral. It is a story about a compassionate pastor and one of his wayward charges. It is the story of a young convert who turned aside and became a vicious outlaw, and of the apostle's self-sacrificial love which pursued the

---

[136] For at least two reasons: (1) the *Excerpta* is a mere notebook and not a full treatment; (2) due to what Casey, *The Excerpta*, 25, calls, 'the eclectic character of his mind and his capacity to study sympathetically systems with which he did not agree and to assimilate their material to the full measure of consistency', Clement's temperament was not as easily given to such forms of expression.

[137] Hill, 'What Papias Said about John'; see also Bauckham 'Origin', 62.

sinner to extreme lengths and restored him to life in Christ and in the Church (*Qds* 42). This story did not come from Irenaeus; it was received *viva voce* and learnt by heart. But it shares a broad agreement with the tradition of Irenaeus in attributing the Apocalypse to John the apostle, in holding that the apostle did not die on Patmos but was eventually released and then came to dwell in Ephesus,[138] and in acknowledging that he was at that time an old man. We do not know just when Clement learnt this story, or from whom, but it is quite possible he received it as early as the 170s.

One more group is known from Clement's writings to have used the Fourth Gospel. In *Stromateis* 1. 17 (81. 1) Clement reports the views of some Christians who disapprove of the way he uses philosophy and the works of the philosophers. 'But, say they, it is written, "All who were before the Lord's advent are thieves and robbers"' (John 10: 8). As 'thieves and robbers' the pagan philosophers have no claim on the Christian's attention, and should rather be avoided.[139] At length Clement allows that the objection is true, that the Greek philosophers have stolen fragments of the truth from the true Hebrew prophets, or that some of the truth was revealed to them directly from angels who had stolen the truth but had grasped it only partially and imperfectly. But for Clement, this does not invalidate the study of their writings by the Christian. The theft on the part of the philosophers meant that they at least had stolen some truth, and were therefore not completely unworthy of attention. The Christians who raised this objection are not heterodox Christians; theirs is a sentiment which is not likely to have belonged to Valentinians. Irenaeus, in fact, had used this same Johannine passage in much the same way, though applying it not to pagan philosophers but to Christian heretics.[140] Clement thinks these objectors are petty, but not heretical; he obviously cares what they think and takes their scriptural objection seriously (see chapters 2, 9, as well; surely they are among 'those who are called orthodox' at the end of chapter 9). These were instead ordinary, less philosophically minded Christians known to Clement, probably in Alexandria, who would introduce this saying of Jesus from the Fourth Gospel with 'it is written'. Probably they were his

---

[138] 'When after the death of the tyrant he removed from the island of Patmos to Ephesus' (*Qds* 42, Butterworth's translation in *Clement of Alexandria*, LCL (Cambridge, Mass., 1982). Eusebius, *HE* 3. 23. 1–2, 5, perceives the continuity in the two writers.

[139] Clement seems to indicate that some might have applied the words to the prophets of old, an interpretation he has no trouble dispensing with. According to Hippolytus, *Ref.* 6. 35. 1, Valentinus, or the Valentinians, had applied the same verse to the OT prophets and the law, which 'spoke by means of the Demiurge'.

[140] *AH* 3. 4. 1, 'Since therefore we have such proofs, it is not necessary to seek the truth among others which it is easy to obtain from the Church; since the apostles, like a rich man [depositing his money] in a bank, lodged in her hands most copiously all things pertaining to the truth: so that every man, whosoever will, can draw from her the water of life. For she is the entrance to life; all others are thieves and robbers. On this account we are bound to avoid *them*, but to make choice of the things pertaining to the Church with utmost diligence, and to lay hold of the tradition of the truth'.

contemporaries, and do not antedate his writing of the *Stromateis* (*c*.193) by much. But Clement's reference to them is none the less extremely valuable, for it allows us a glimpse at the attitudes and practice of 'simple' Christians, probably in Alexandria. Not only does it demonstrate that the use of this Gospel among the orthodox was not restricted to Christian intellectuals like Theophilus, Athenagoras, Irenaeus, and Clement. It tells us that, while ordinary Christians like the ones mentioned here might be put off by the thought of importing philosophy into Christianity, they were not at all put off by the Fourth Gospel. To the contrary, far from showing us a defensive attitude against this Gospel, as against some foreign intruder, it shows instead how they used this Gospel to ward off the intrusion of foreign influences from a purer Christianity. They show much the same instinctive attitude as was seen already in Irenaeus, who used the Fourth Gospel as a weapon against heresy. Clement's high regard for this Gospel seems to be matched by the common orthodox believers in Alexandria, whom we cannot imagine would have adopted this Gospel only recently.

When Clement wrote, from the late 180s probably into the second decade of the third century, all signs point to the wide recognition of the divine authority of the Gospel according to John. It was used authoritatively by the orthodox and by Valentinians, and was acknowledged on the one hand as part of a corpus of four Gospels, and on the other as belonging to a corpus of at least four but more probably five writings attributed to the apostle John. And there is no reason to think that this Gospel was either a newcomer among the catholics in Clement's universe of discourse or that it had suffered among them by contamination from heretics. On the contrary, the Fourth Gospel appears in the work of Clement as the inspired work of an apostle, handed down through the authorized channels of the Church, functioning in its rightful place among the books of the New Testament, and fully possessed of the authority of scripture, not only among intellectuals but generally in the Church.

The *Muratorian Fragment*

It is generally acknowledged that, by the end of the second century, the Fourth Gospel had found a home among the orthodox, though many hold that this was still not the case in Rome. This is a natural point, then, at which consider the witness of the *Muratorian Fragment*, which preserves what appears to be the first New Testament 'canon list' of its kind now known. It is natural, that is, if we accept what has been the traditional dating of the fragment, to the end of the second or beginning of the third century. But there has been strong criticism of this dating of the fragment from Albert C. Sundberg and Geoffrey Mark Hahneman, who have argued at length that it is a fourth-century, Eastern production and fits better alongside several other canon lists from the second half of the fourth century and later.[141] For detailed arguments against this redating and in support of the traditional date I shall refer the reader to other places.[142] Yet due to the very recent appearance of a restatement of the case for a late date by Hahneman, the division of scholars on the question, and its relevance to the present study, some attention must be given to this matter.

PROVENANCE

That the author of the fragment says that Hermas wrote the *Shepherd* 'quite recently in our times (*nuperrime temporibus nostris*) in the city of Rome, while his brother, Pius, the bishop, occupied the [episcopal] seat of the city of Rome', is still the most obvious and straightforward indication (though by no means the only one) that the work of which the *MF* is a fragment is early rather than late. Hahneman has recently given a succinct summary of the arguments for the opposite conclusion, in four main points.[143] First, the information the fragmentist gives about Hermas, that he was the brother of Pius, bishop of Rome *c.*140–54, is extremely unlikely. Second, the fragmentist's assumption that the *Shepherd* could have been written so late is also mistaken, as other evidence suggests a date of some forty to fifty years earlier. Third, the fragment's position on the *Shepherd*, that it may be read privately but not publicly, fits fourth-century custom, but does not fit the late second century. Fourth, given these inaccuracies, the statement which seems to date the document to the late second century (linking the *Shepherd* to 'our time') must also be confused or mistaken. To defend the early date of the *MF*, Hahneman argues, one must defend all of the fragment's other inaccuracies about Hermas and the *Shepherd*.[144] It is not clear to me why this last conclusion follows. Even if the writer is mistaken about the date and author of the *Shepherd*, this does not require that he lived long after the end of the second century. He could have been wrong in the late second century just as well as in the late fourth. Many scholars, to cite just one example, believe Irenaeus was quite mistaken in his identification of the

---

[141] A. C. Sundberg, 'Towards a Revised History of the New Testament Canon', *Studia Evangelica*, 4/1 (1968), 452–61; *idem*, 'Canon Muratori: A Fourth-Century List', *HTR* 66 (1973), 1–41; G. M. Hahneman, *The Muratorian Fragment and the Development of the Canon*, Oxford Theological Monographs (Oxford, 1992); most recently in 'The Muratorian Fragment and the Origins of the New Testament Canon', in Lee Martin McDonald and James A. Sanders (eds.), *The Canon Debate* (Peabody, Mass., 2002), 405–15.

[142] E. Ferguson, 'Canon Muratori: Date and Provenance', *Studia Patristica*, 17/2 (Oxford, 1982), 677–83; *idem*, 'Review of Geoffrey Mark Hahneman, *The Muratorian Fragment and the Development of the Canon*', *JTS* NS 44 (1993), 696; P. Henne, 'La Datation du *canon de Muratori*', *RB* 100 (1993), 54–75; W. Horbury, 'The Wisdom of Solomon in the Muratorian Fragment', *JTS* NS 45 (1994), 149–59; C. E. Hill, 'The Debate over the Muratorian Fragment and the Development of the Canon', *WTJ* 57 (1995), 437–52.

[143] Hahneman, 'Origin'.

[144] Ibid. 411–12.

author of the Johannine books and in his report of the circumstances of their writing, even though the span of time between the publication of these books and Irenaeus' testimony is roughly the same as or less than that posited between an early *Shepherd* and an early *MF*. Having said this, it is widely agreed today that the *Shepherd* was composed (perhaps published) in stages, and many scholars who have studied the matter do not in fact find it implausible that Hermas might have been Pius' brother or that a final edition, at least, of his book might have appeared as late as the 140s.[145]

If, on the other hand, the author of the *MF* is claiming that the *Shepherd* was written in the days of Pius of Rome (*c*.140–54), and that these both occurred 'in our times', and if this author is writing in the fourth century, then he is projecting himself back in time and the work he is writing would have to be considered a hoax.[146] This is indeed not the scenario Hahneman envisions, but it seems that the only way to avoid affirming it is either to posit a textual corruption at this point (no plausible emendation has, to my knowledge been suggested) or to accept the proposal made by Sundberg and advanced by Hahneman that the phrase *nuperrime temporibus nostris*, instead of meaning 'most recently, in our time' means 'most recently (of all the books mentioned), in our post-apostolic time' (in contrast to 'apostolic time').[147] Without the concept of 'our time' = 'non-apostolic time' being introduced, however, this would certainly not be the 'plain sense' of the passage.[148] On the other hand, relating the date of certain events, even the writing of a book, to the speaker's own lifetime (not to 'apostolic time'), was apparently not an uncommon practice in the second century, as at least four examples testify: (1) In a treatise addressed to Hadrian, the early apologist Quadratus spoke of some who had been cured by the Lord as surviving 'even till our own time (εἰς τοὺς ἡμετέρους χρόνους)' (Eusebius, *HE* 4. 3. 2). (2) According to Eusebius, Hegesippus (*c*.175–80) discussed 'the so-called apocrypha', relating that some of them had been 'fabricated by certain heretics in his own time (ἐπὶ τῶν αὐτοῦ χρόνων)' (*HE* 4. 22. 9). Though this is put into the third person by Eusebius, it must correspond to something Hegesippus said in the first person. It is to be noted that Hegesippus' indictment of certain 'apocrypha', as being written 'in our own time', forms a very close parallel to the statement of the *MF*. (3) Irenaeus, also writing at about this time, says the Apocalypse of John was seen 'not a very long time ago, but almost in our own generation (οὐδὲ γὰρ πρὸ πολλοῦ

---

[145] e.g. Carol Osiek, *The Shepherd of Hermas: A Commentary* (Minneapolis, 1999), 19–21; Michael W. Holmes (ed. and reviser), *The Apostolic Fathers: Greek Texts and English Translations*, updated edn. of *The Apostolic Fathers: Greek Texts and English Translations of Their Writings*, 2nd edn., ed. and tr. J. B. Lightfoot and J. R. Harmer; ed. and revised by Michael W. Holmes (1999) (hereafter LHH), 331. Others have supposed that Pius had a brother named Hermas, with whom the author of *The Shepherd* was confused by the fragmentist. See the discussion of Hermas in Ch. 7.

[146] See Ferguson, 'Review', 692; Hill, 'Debate', 439.

[147] Hahneman, 'Origin', 409.

[148] Cf. Hahneman, *Muratorian Fragment*, 30.

χρόνου...ἀλλὰ σχεδὸν ἐπὶ τῆς ἡμετέρας γενεᾶς) towards the end of the reign of Domitian' (*AH* 5. 30. 3; *HE* 5. 8. 6). Despite the claim by Sundberg and Hahneman that Irenaeus' phrase supports their interpretation of *temporibus nostris*, it is plain from the context that Irenaeus is by no means contrasting 'apostolic' and 'non-apostolic' time, but is in fact linking 'our generation' closely with the time of writing of Revelation by the apostle.[149] (4) An anonymous writer in the early third century speaks of an incident concerning 'a certain confessor, Natalius, not long ago but in our own time (οὐ πάλαι, ἀλλ᾽ ἐπι τῶν ἡμετέρων γενόμενος καιρῶν)' (Eusebius, *HE* 5. 28. 8). Here the contrast is explicitly not with 'apostolic time' but with 'long ago'. The statement of the *MF* that *The Shepherd* was written 'most recently, in our time', that is, within, so he believed, the lifetime of the author, thus fits quite well within this second-century context.

Hahneman's third argument concerns the fragmentist's attitude towards Hermas' work. The *Shepherd* 'should indeed be read, but it cannot be published for the Church, neither among the Prophets, since their number is complete, nor among the Apostles for it is after their time'. Hahneman argues that this 'mediating' position on the *Shepherd*, allowing it to be read but not to be considered with the prophets or apostles, fits the late fourth century but is out of place near the end of the second. Irenaeus cites it as scripture, Clement of Alexandria uses it authoritatively, and this seems to parallel the attitude of the early Tertullian, before he turned to Montanism and to a rigorism which caused him to reject the *Shepherd* as 'the book that loves adulterers'. But Irenaeus' position may just parallel that of the *MF* after all. Many[150] have accepted the conclusion that Irenaeus cited the *Shepherd* as scripture. It is possible to read *Against Heresies* 4. 20. 2 in that way ('Truly, then, the Scripture (or writing) declared which says...'). But Adelin Rousseau, Irenaeus' learned editor, thinks, and other Irenaean scholars have agreed with him, that his reference should not be to the *Shepherd* as scripture but as a 'writing'.[151] Robert Grant explains, 'At Rome Irenaeus found two other early Christian writings treated as authoritative. He probably does not refer to them as "scripture" when he calls each *graphé*. In each instance the word may simply mean "writing" (3. 3. 3; 4. 20. 2).'[152] The other *graphé* is *1 Clement*. That is, Hermas's writing, like that of Clement, was valued and used by Irenaeus but did not belong with the writings of the apostles (Clement is cited by Irenaeus in *AH* 3. 3. 3 as an eyewitness to the apostles). It is probable that Irenaeus viewed the man Hermas, who refers to Clement himself in the *Shepherd* (*Vis.* 2. 4. 3), much as he viewed Clement, as someone who knew or had seen apostles. This means Irenaeus may

---

[149] Hill, 'Debate', 439.
[150] Including Hahneman, *Muratorian Fragment*, 61, and even, formerly, myself, Hill, 'Debate', 439.
[151] SC 100, i. 248–50.
[152] Robert M. Grant, *Irenaeus of Lyons* (London, 1997), 38. Grant's translation of the passage is 'The writing well says...'.

have been familiar with the view, mentioned by Origen, that Hermas was the man Paul referred to in Romans 16: 14[153] (cf. his linking of Linus of Rome with 2 Tim. 4: 21 in *AH* 3. 3. 3). This understanding of Irenaeus' regard for the *Shepherd* is more consistent with the fact that, though it is a very long work, even longer than the collected corpus of Paul's Epistles,[154] Irenaeus only alludes to the *Shepherd*'s teaching twice (1. 22. 1; 4. 20. 2), and nowhere names it. Even his use of the term γραφή forms a parallel to the usage of Tertullian in the very place (*Pud.* 10) where the latter explicitly rejects the *Shepherd*'s claim to a place in the 'canon' (*si scriptura Pastoris, quae sola moechos amat, diuino instrumento meruisset incidi*). Thus the proper 'category' for both Hermas and *1 Clement* in the writings of Irenaeus is probably that of valuable works of those who had known the apostles, cited for their testimony to the rule of truth (*AH* 3. 3. 3). As such, Irenaeus' attitude towards the *Shepherd* forms a very close likeness to that of the *MF*, which would have the work read, but not publicly in the churches.

One criticism of an early date is the apparent lack of a context for the appearance of such a list of authoritative writings, particularly when compared with the fifteen or so catalogues which appear in the fourth century and are claimed to be the natural context for the *MF*.[155] While no comparable lists from the early period have survived, some must have existed.[156] One context for the generation of such lists is the councils mentioned by Tertullian, which must have taken place before about 210, when he wrote *De pudicitia*. These councils, while we do not know their number or even their locale, are of supreme importance here, as Tertullian indicates that at least some of them represented the 'catholic' Church in Carthage (or

---

[153] *C. Rom.*, in Rufinus' Latin translation. Hahneman believes this identification is presupposed by the *MF*, though regarded as false by the author. This, Hahneman thinks, shows that the fragment is Eastern and later than Origen. For, first of all, it is thought that Paul's Letter to the Romans only circulated, at least in the West, in a recension that lacked chapters 15 and 16, and that those chapters were unknown in the West until much later (*Muratorian Fragment*, 48–50). Hence the connection with the author of the *Shepherd* (and the mention of Paul's planned journey to Spain from Rom. 15: 24, mentioned in l. 39) could not have been made in the West so early. Secondly, it is assumed that this identification of Hermas was not made before Origen. But that Rom. 15–16 was known in Rome before the end of the 1st cent. may be signified already in 1 Clem. 5. 7, where Clement seems to know of Paul's planned trip to Spain mentioned in Rom. 15: 24. And it is likely that the identification of Hermas with Paul's associate in Rom. 16: 14 was made much earlier than Origen. It appears that Tertullian is aware of it when he charges that the work is 'apocryphal and false' in *Pud.* 10. This implies the judgement that it went under a false name, that the name of Hermas is a pseudonym. Tertullian also indicates that this was the judgement of more than one council before he wrote. Cf. Serapion of Antioch (*HE* 6. 12. 3–6), 'we receive Peter and the other apostles as Christ, but the writings which falsely bear their names (τὰ δὲ ὀνόματι αὐτῶν ψευδεπίγραφα) we reject'.
[154] In the stichometry of Codex Claromontanus, the corpus of Paul's thirteen letters totals 3,723 lines, *The Shepherd* 4,000.
[155] There are important problems for this view, however, in both the order and the exact list of books in the *MF* as compared with these catalogues. This is a matter, however, which cannot be entered into here.
[156] Hill, 'Debate', 447–52.

Rome), and as he says that they explicitly rejected the *Shepherd*, 'But I would yield my ground to you, if the scripture of "the Shepherd," which is the only one which favours adulterers, had deserved to find a place in the divine canon (*divino instrumento meruisset incidi*); if it had not been habitually judged by every council of Churches (even of your own) among apocryphal and false (*falsa*) writings' (*Pud.* 10). This matter deserves more attention than we can give it here, but a few salient factors, beyond its rejection of the *Shepherd*, call for mention. First, the writer of the *MF* does presume to speak on behalf of the catholic Church, which is a quality we might expect from a council document of the type mentioned by Tertullian. Second, its form seems to correspond to that of other joint letters drafted by councils from the period, in which one bishop writes a letter or report in the first person singular (*HE* 5. 19. 1–2) or plural (*HE* 5. 25), with others signing their names at the end (*HE* 5. 19. 3, cf. 5. 25). We cannot, of course, claim more than a realistic possibility here. But Tertullian's knowledge of councils which rejected the *Shepherd*[157] may take on added importance when correlated with a neglected passage written at about the same time as *De pudicitia*, which bears a certain resemblance to a portion of the *MF*. When he wrote the fourth book of *Adversus Marcionem*, Tertullian spoke of the four Gospels in this way:

These all start with the same principles of the faith, so far as relates to the one only God the Creator and His Christ, how that He was born of the Virgin, and came to fulfil the law and the prophets. Never mind if there does occur some variation in the order of their narratives, provided that there be agreement in the essential matter of the faith (*dummodo de capite fidei conueniat*), in which there is disagreement with Marcion. (4. 2. 2)[158]

This compares well to the approach to the differences among the Gospels which we read in the *MF*,

And so, although different beginnings might be taught in the separate books of the Gospels, nevertheless it makes no difference to the faith of believers, since all things in all [of them] are declared by the one sovereign Spirit—concerning his nativity, concerning [His] passion, concerning [His] resurrection, concerning [His] walk with His disciples, and concerning His double advent: the first in humility when He was despised, which has been; the second in royal power, glorious, which is to be. (ll. 16–26)

---

[157] The *MF*'s rejection of *The Shepherd* from public reading does not seem to match the rhetoric of Tertullian's assertion that these councils rejected the work 'as apocryphal and false'. And yet, this could well be Tertullian's conclusion from such statements as are in the *MF*, taken to indicate that the work was pseudonymous, that is, not written by a companion of one of the apostles and (perhaps) not even a companion of Clement of Rome.

[158] The *MF*, l. 83, is also concerned with Marcionism (ll. 65, 83). In fact, as Ferguson, 'Canon Muratori', 677–83, has pointed out, consistent with the early date is that the fragment mentions, as far as we know, only 2nd-cent. heresies (Marcion, 'Arsinoeites', Valentinians, Mitiades, Basilides, and the Cataphrygians).

While we cannot speak of proof, the correspondence in thought between these two passages, combined with Tertullian's profession to know the results of certain councils which had deliberated at least to some extent upon the identity of the books of the divine covenant (*diuino instrumento*), is extremely suggestive. At any rate, the councils he mentions do seem to form a plausible context for a document like the *Muratorian Fragment*.

As we shall see below, at least one scholar thinks it possible that one of the *MF*'s comments about the Fourth Gospel is a partial response to the criticism of Gaius of Rome. But, apart from the question of Gaius' relation to the Fourth Gospel,[159] there is no response to any corresponding criticism of the Apocalypse, which Gaius is thought to have attacked just as stridently.[160] If the original author of the *MF* wrote in Rome, this is all the more puzzling. All things considered, it seems more likely that the author of the *MF* wrote without knowledge of the specific criticisms associated with Gaius. But in any case, there are factors which suggest the two are not far removed from one another in time. In particular they have in common the concern to specify the limits of the New Testament in general (small fragments from Gaius' dialogue preserved by Eusebius indicate that he seems to have had the idea that the NT 'canon' was closed).[161] The fact that both authors omit Hebrews from their Pauline corpus also links them, and speaks for a Western, perhaps Roman, provenance for the *MF*, for, when Eusebius informs us of Gaius' position on this matter, he says that 'even to this day among the Romans there are some who do not consider it to be the Apostle's' (*HE* 6. 20. 3).[162]

RECEPTION OF A JOHANNINE CORPUS

The author of the *MF* knows the Fourth Gospel as that of John, one of the disciples, whose fellow disciple was the apostle Andrew. He relates a story about the origin of this Gospel, one which was apparently based on tradition recorded by Papias (see Chapter 7), having elements in common with statements by Clement of Alexandria, Origen, and Victorinus, but embellished with details found nowhere else.

[159] Which is now not as clear as it was once thought to be. See Ch. 4.

[160] Though it is possible that its position in the list is in that of the disputed books, which would indicate that questions had been raised (Horbury, 'Wisdom of Solomon', 155, 159; Henne, 'La Datation', 60). See below.

[161] Gaius is critical of the Montanists for their 'recklessness and audacity...in composing new scriptures' (Eusebius, *HE* 6. 20. 3); he reproves Cerinthus for being 'an enemy of the scriptures of God' (*HE* 3. 28. 2); and Eusebius says Gaius enumerated thirteen epistles of Paul, either omitting or rejecting Hebrews as Pauline.

[162] Many have thought that there is some material missing from the original in this mistake-prone transcription, and that James, 1 Peter, and Hebrews were originally included (cf. Hahneman, *Muratorian Fragment*, 25–6). This may well be; at least it is difficult to imagine a rejection of 1 Peter (1 Peter may well have been mentioned as well in the missing material on Mark's Gospel). But even if the original contained a notice of the reception of Hebrews, what is left shows that Hebrews was

The fourth [book] of the Gospels is that of John [one] of the disciples. When his fellow-disciples and bishops urged [him], he said: 'Fast together with me today for three days and, what shall be revealed to each, let us tell [it] to each other'. On the same night it was revealed to Andrew, [one] of the Apostles, that, with all of them reviewing (*recognoscentibus*) [it], John should describe all things in his own name. And so, although different beginnings (*varia . . . principia*) might be taught in the separate books of the Gospels, nevertheless it makes no difference to the faith of believers, since all things in all [of them] are declared by the one sovereign Spirit—concerning his nativity, concerning [His] passion, concerning [His] resurrection, concerning [His] walk with His disciples, and concerning His double advent: the first in humility when He was despised, which has been; the second in royal power, glorious, which is to be. What marvel, then, if John so constantly brings forward particular [matters] (*singula*) also in his Epistles, saying of himself: 'What we have seen with our eyes and have heard with [our] ears and our hands have handled, these things we have written to you.' For thus he declares that he was not only an eyewitness and hearer, but also a writer of all the wonderful things of the Lord in order (*Per ordinem*).[163] (*Muratorian Fragment*, ll. 9–34)

Many things could be said about this testimony, some of which will be taken up in Chapter 7 below. Here it should be noted that the author obviously has a closed Gospel 'canon' of four Gospels, of which Luke's is third and John's is fourth. John was one of Jesus' disciples, 'an eyewitness and hearer but also a writer of all the wonderful things of the Lord in order'. Though he wrote this Gospel in his own name, everything in his Gospel, like the contents of the other three, is 'declared by the one sovereign Spirit'. It may be that the author is aware of some objection to this Gospel—or to one or more of the others—based on differences in their contents, specifically due to their different beginnings (this is probably signified too in the first lines of the fragment, which mention that Luke began his story 'from the nativity of John'). But he gives no place to such criticisms, for believers, he says, are not troubled by this because all four Gospels speak with the voice of the sovereign Spirit and agree on the major events in the first and second comings of the Lord. It is possible that this reflects the controversy associated with Gaius, though charges based on discrepancies between John and the Synoptics had surfaced earlier in the second century.[164] In either case, it is to be noted that there is no hint of any underlying criticism of the Fourth Gospel's Christology and no defence against any charge of gnosticism, Montanism, or any questionable alliances.

Not only does the author of the *MF* indicate the Church's acceptance of the Fourth Gospel, he attests that the Church receives (*recepimus*) the whole

---

not considered a letter of Paul. This is enough to support a Western (probably Roman) and probably early provenance. The epistle to the Hebrews was generally accepted even in the West by the 4th cent.

[163] I am using the translation and the restored Latin text in D. J. Theron, *Evidence of Tradition* (Grand Rapids, Mich., 1957).

[164] At least since the time of Papias. See Ch. 7.

Johannine corpus. John's Epistles are mentioned first in line 28, where the author gives a selective and paraphrastic quotation of 1 John 1: 1–4. There is some question about whether his later mention of 'the two' Epistles 'with the superscription, "Of John"', which are accepted by the catholic Church (ll. 68–9), designate 1 and 2 John, or 2 and 3 John. Since the author has already mentioned 1 John and quoted from it, he probably means to speak of two more epistles which went under the superscription 'Of John' (*Ioannis*; Ἰωαννου, as is preserved in the MSS א, A, and B).[165] P. Katz added more weight to this argument, pointing to the use of the word 'catholic' here, used normally of 1 John alone and not of 2 and 3 John, and pointing to a possible mistranslation of the Greek by the Latin translator (δύο σὺν καθολικῇ, translated *dua(e) sin catholica*).[166] He suggested the original Greek might have been translated, 'Certainly the epistle of Jude and two [epistles] of the afore-mentioned John are held in addition to the catholic [epistle]'.[167] It is also unlikely that the author of the fragment would have known 2 John and not 3 John, for by this time it is unlikely that they would have customarily circulated separately (see the discussion of this matter in Chapter 9).

The author explicitly accepts the Revelation of John. William Horbury has argued that the position occupied by the Revelation, near the end of the 'list', is indicative of its disputed status, as it comes after the *Wisdom of Solomon*, and along with the *Apocalypse of Peter*, the *Shepherd* of Hermas, and before the rejected books.[168] This too might possibly indicate that Revelation had already been called into question by Gaius or others, though nothing of Gaius' specific criticisms is mentioned or addressed. But it is not clear, on the other hand, that the author is indeed arranging books into the categories of accepted, disputed, and rejected.[169] And in any case, the place of the Revelation in the author's own ecclesiastical circles appears to be quite solid indeed. The book is first alluded to, interestingly enough, in the context of the author's discussion of the Pauline letters: 'since the blessed Apostle Paul himself, imitating the example of his predecessor, John, wrote to seven churches only by name [and] in this order' (ll. 47–50); 'For John also, though he wrote in the Apocalypse to seven churches, nevertheless he speaks to them all' (ll. 57–9).[170] That he actually uses the Johannine

---

[165] This contextual argument was made by B. F. Westcott, *A Survey of the History of the Canon of the New Testament*, 6th edn. (Grand Rapids, Mich., 1980 repr. of 1889 edn.), 219 n. 1; S. P. Tregelles, *Canon Muratorianus* (Oxford, 1867), 49–50 (see Hahneman, *Muratorian Fragment*, 14).

[166] P. Katz, 'The Johannine Epistles in the Muratorian Canon', *JTS* NS 8 (1957), 273–4.

[167] Cf. Hahneman, *Muratorian Fragment*, 16, who seems to agree.

[168] Horbury, 'Wisdom of Solomon'.

[169] It must be said that the author mentions two rejected books out of place, at the end of his catalogue of Pauline letters (to the Laodiceans and to the Alexandrians) and before mention of the catholic epistles. The Wisdom of Solomon may have been mentioned for no other reason than that it came to the author's mind at this point

[170] This particular intercanonical cross-referencing, here validating Paul's letters by appeal to John in the Revelation, is attributed to 'Hippolytus' by Dionysius bar Salibi, *in Apocalypsim* 1. 4 (I.

Apocalypse to explain Paul, to some degree as a legitimization of Paul's practice and showing the ground for considering Paul's seven letters to churches to have universal application in the Church, shows his routine acceptance of the former. The book of Revelation is then mentioned towards the end of the fragment, either in its 'canonical' place at the very end of the New Testament, or as among disputed works: 'We accept (*recipimus*) only the Apocalypses of John and of Peter, although some of us do not want it [presumably the Apocalypse of Peter] to be read in the Church' (ll. 71–3).

The author regards the apostle John as author of the entire Johannine corpus. He knows the man who wrote the Johannine Apocalypse, who wrote to all the churches by writing to the seven, as a 'predecessor' of the apostle Paul. This certainly means that he regards him as the apostle, the one who was 'an eyewitness and hearer' of all the wonderful things of the Lord (ll. 32, 33). The Gospel and First Epistle are linked together in a special way:

What marvel, therefore, if John so constantly brings forward particular [matters] also in his Epistles, saying of himself: 'What we have seen with our eyes and have heard with [our] ears and our hands have handled, these things we have written to you'. For thus he declares that he was not only an eyewitness and hearer, but also a writer of all the wonderful things of the Lord in order.

The personal testimonium of 1 John 1: 1–4, then, is regarded as a documentary attestation, testifying not that he had written the Epistle, but that he had written the Gospel![171] That is, the author of the *MF* regards 1 John 1: 1–4 as John's own self-verification of the Gospel. With little doubt this is the sort of 'testimony' from the First Epistle which Papias must have given in his 'quotations' from it, as reported all too briefly by Eusebius (*HE* 3. 39. 17; cf. 3. 15. 2). It also reminds us of the sort of thing we observed in Irenaeus, *AH* 4. 20. 11, where he interprets a text in Revelation by referring to the experience of the author of the Gospel according to John.

Though we cannot be sure, it is most likely that the original document was written in Rome, or perhaps North Africa. It is quite possibly related to one of the councils mentioned by Tertullian which must have deliberated to some degree on the authenticity and acceptability of certain New Testament documents. Its temporal proximity to the time of Gaius must also be close. If Gaius, or anyone at this time, raised strong objections against the use of the Fourth Gospel, the *MF* helps indicate the *status quo* against which such

Sedlacek, *Dionysius bar Salibi in Apocalypsim, Actus et Epistulas catholicas*, CSCO, Scriptores syri, 2, CI (1909, text) (1910, Latin version), 2–3), and is found in two 3rd-cent. Latin writers. In ch. 11 of his *Ad Fortunatum*— Cyprian of Carthage mentions Paul's writing to 'the seven churches. And in the Apocalypse the Lord directs His divine and heavenly precepts to the seven churches and their angels'; Victorinus of Pettau also knows the limitation of seven churches to which Paul wrote letters, and this is signified by the seven stars in Jesus' hand (named in 1. 16). He also assumes that beyond this Paul wrote to individuals, 'so as not to exceed the number of seven churches'.

[171] So also Westcott, *Canon of the New Testament*, 215 n. 2.

objections had to contend. It attests once again the awareness and recognition of a Johannine corpus and uses intertextual self-referencing.

Epiphanius' Asian Source

Since the work of Voigt and Lipsius in the nineteenth century, it has been recognized that Epiphanius in *Panarion* 48 utilized and reproduced virtually untouched an earlier source in a portion of his refutation of the Montanists.[172] This person wrote probably from Asia Minor and in the late second or early third century.[173] Epiphanius, *Panarion* 48. 10. 1–2 mentions 'the holy John in the Apocalypse' and in 48. 11. 7, 'the holy John in the Gospel'. These references do not specify whether John was the apostle or some other, but they do signify the authority and sanctity of both the Fourth Gospel and the Apocalypse and their obvious attribution to the same John. There is no reason to think that this author had any other John in mind than the John so identified by his fellow Asians, Irenaeus and Polycrates. This anti-Montanist author then naturally adds his voice to their witness to (*a*) the unity of authorship of Gospel and Revelation, (*b*) that each was written by 'the holy John', (*c*) consideration of these books as scripture.

Apollonius of Ephesus

Another prominent, Asian, anti-Montanist writer of the period was Apollonius of Ephesus (Eusebius *HE* 5. 18. 14). Apollonius tells us that he wrote forty years after the beginnings of Montanus' prophesying. This places his work in all probability at about AD 200,[174] very close to the time of Gaius' debate with Proclus the Montanist in Rome. Eusebius tells us that Apollonius reported, 'as though from tradition, that the Saviour ordered his apostles not to leave Jerusalem for twelve years.[175] He also makes quotations from the Apocalypse of John and tells how by divine power a dead man was raised by John himself at Ephesus.' Apollonius also complains about a Montanist named Themiso, who 'dared, in imitation of the apostle, to compose an epistle general, to instruct those whose faith was better than his' (*HE* 5. 18. 5). In all probability the apostolic 'epistle general' in view is 1 John, and may be related to the expression in the *Muratorian Fragment* (ll.

---

[172] See R. Heine, *The Montanist Oracles and Testimonia* (Macon, Ga., 1989), pp. x, 28–51.

[173] R. Heine, 'The Role of the Gospel of John in the Montanist Controversy', *The Second Century*, 6 1 (1987–8), 1–19.

[174] Eusebius himself dated the rise of Montanism to the year 172, but this is certainly too late. Most scholars today accept the date given by Epiphanius, *c.*160, as much more accurate.

[175] Cf. the *Kerugma Petri*, as recorded by Clement of Alexandria, *Strom.* 6. 5. 43, 'If now any one of Israel wishes to repent and through my name to believe in God, his sins will be forgiven him. And after 12 years go ye out into the world that no one may say, "We have not heard it"'.

57–9) noted above.[176] Eusebius does not tell us about the other scriptures Apollonius used; it was not his purpose to record the usage of the undisputed books, of which Eusebius considered the Gospel according to John to be one. Given that he used quotations from the Apocalypse and apparently spoke of 1 John as a general epistle of an apostle, it is hard to believe he did not also have the same high regard for the Johannine Gospel, but we cannot tell this for certain simply from the fragments left us.

Apollonius' treatise quickly gained a high reputation. Not many years later Tertullian in Carthage would devote the seventh book of his *On Ecstasy* to the refutation of Apollonius.[177] These tiny fragments from his work, despite their size, still attest the common view about the author of the Apocalypse being John the apostle and about his residence in Ephesus. Like Epiphanius' anonymous source, Apollonius must also have appealed to the Apocalypse of John in his work against the Montanists. These are both significant, then, in the light of the criticism of that book and the Fourth Gospel which is usually associated with Gaius of Rome.

The Early Works of Tertullian

As we reach the end of the second century we must also take note of the testimony of Tertullian to the Church's tradition about the Fourth Gospel, and the rest of the Johannine corpus. I shall focus attention here on those early works of Tertullian's which it is commonly agreed were written before his Montanist period, and between about 197 and 203, in other words, up until about the time of Gaius' *Dialogue with Proclus*, namely (according to the list in Corpus Christianorum, Series Latina II, 1627–8), *Ad martyres, Ad nationes, Apologeticum, De testimonio animae, De praescriptione haereticorum, De spectaculis, De baptismo, De patientia, De paenitentia, De cultu feminarum, Ad uxorem, Adversus Hermogenem*.[178] It will come as no surprise that Tertullian's views on the Johannine literature were essentially those of Irenaeus. But there is still much to be gained by an examination of these early works.

In the early apologetic works, *Ad nationes, Apologeticum*, and *De testimonio animae*, there are scarcely any allusions to scripture at all, let alone to the Johannine corpus. The main reason for this is probably revealed in a passing

---

[176] Katz, 'Johannine Epistles', 273; A. F. Walls, 'The Montanist "Catholic Epistle" and its New Testament Prototype', in F. L. Cross (ed.), *Studia Evangelica*, 3/2, The New Testament Message (Berlin, 1964), 437–46, at 440, though at 441 Walls also suggests 1 Peter as a possibility.

[177] Jerome, *De vir. illust.* 40.

[178] Timothy D. Barnes, *Tertullian: A Historical and Literary Study* (Oxford, 1971; with corrections and a postscript, 1985), 30–56, has offered a somewhat provocative redating of the works of Tertullian which has not been universally accepted. With the exception of the first book of *De cultu feminarum* (205–6) and the *Adversus Hermogenem* (204–5), however, he too places all these works between 196 and 203. David Rankin, *Tertullian and the Church* (Cambridge, 1995), pp. xiv–xvii, accepts these proposals.

comment in the first chapter of *De testimonio animae*, where Tertullian notes the method of many Christian writers in seeking to convict 'the rivals and persecutors of Christian truth, from their own authorities', from philosophers, poets, 'or other masters of this world's learning and wisdom'; he notes as a matter of course that 'far less do men assent to our writings, to which no one comes for guidance unless he is already a Christian'. These words provide an important warning about judging an author's 'canon' from only a portion of his or her own writings, particularly from openly apologetic writings (something which will return to our attention when we come to Justin). Even in the *Ad martyres* there is not much explicit advertance to scripture. If we had only these four works from the hand of Tertullian we might perhaps have concluded that Tertullian had no concept of Christian scripture, or that it weighed little with him. But such a conclusion would have been seriously mistaken.

In some of Tertullian's moral treatises, where there is more indication of his New Testament authorities, the Johannine writings play only a very minor role. The *Ad uxorum* contains, at best, no more than a few possible allusions to the Johannine literature. In *De patientia* we find an allusion to 1 John 1: 1 (in 3. 1), but in this moral treatise there is perhaps no allusion to the Fourth Gospel, while Tertullian does refer to passages from Matthew (mostly the Sermon on the Mount). It is likewise with *De paenitentia*, where we apparently have only a brief citation, 'God is light', from 1 John 1: 5 (6. 10), though in one section, on the willingness of God to forgive, Tertullian runs through five of the seven churches of Revelation, those who are upbraided by the Lord but charged to repent (8. 1–2). The importance of the book of Revelation, and the suitability of its images to this context, comes into view in *De cultu feminorum*, where he refers to Babylon the great, mother of harlots, and her royal session on the seven hills from Revelation 17. Tertullian refers to this allegory as coming from the Lord and as being scripture (2. 12. 2). The general scarcity of references to the Fourth Gospel in the moral works of Tertullian is also noteworthy, and suggests that this Gospel was not the first place to which he, and probably other Christian teachers, would turn for lessons on Christian ethics—and this is surely not out of accord with the emphases of the Gospel itself. This too is a phenomenon which may prove instructive to us later.

The Gospel, the First Letter, and the Revelation of John, however, are all used in one of his first books, *De spectaculis*,[179] Tertullian's criticism of the shows. Here Tertullian cites Jesus from John 16: 20 in 28. 2; alludes to John's vision of 'the city New Jerusalem' of Revelation 21 and 22 in 30. 1; and seems to allude to 1 John 2: 15–17 when he speaks of divine instruction to reject the *concupiscentiae saeculi* in 14. 2.

---

[179] Barnes, *Tertullian*, 55, placed this among Tertullian's earliest works, from 196 or early 197, but later (in his postscript, 325) conceded that it followed the *Apologeticum*, which he placed in 197 or later.

In *Adversus Hermogenem*[180] more is revealed of Tertullian's regard for two of the Johannine books. Along with a few allusions to other portions of these books,[181] Tertullian repeatedly takes up the exegesis of John 1: 1–3 in chapters 18, 20, 22, and 45 against Hermogenes' notion of creation from pre-existing matter, referring to these verses as being in 'the Gospel'. Tertullian attests that 'I revere (*adoro*) the fulness of His Scripture', meaning that he adored not just the Old Testament but also the New,[182] and that 'In the Gospel, moreover, I discover a Minister and Witness of the Creator, even His Word (Jn. 1. 3)' (22. 5). He then warns Hermogenes in the words of Revelation 22: 18–19, not to add to or take away from what is 'written' by maintaining that God created out of existing matter. There are several more borrowings from Revelation in this treatise,[183] most or all of which, as we have seen, were probably suggested to him by the earlier work of Theophilus against Hermogenes. Clearly, however, to Tertullian both the Gospel and the Revelation of John are recognized portions of scripture.

De baptismo, also from this early period,[184] contains many clear allusions to and citations of the Fourth Gospel. In a section where Tertullian reviews the incidents in Christ's life in which water figured, he includes references to the water at the wedding feast in Cana (John 2: 1–11); Christ's invitation to the thirsty (John 4: 14 or 7: 37–8); his stopping for refreshment at a well (John 4: 6); his ministry of water to the feet of his disciples (John 13: 1–12); and the water which burst forth from his side due to the soldier's lance (John 19: 34) (9. 4). In the next chapter he cites words of Jesus and John the Baptist from John 16: 6–7 and John 3: 30–1.

The treatise *De baptismo* had been called forth by the unsettling teaching of a female representative of the Cainite heresy who had lately arrived in Carthage and had 'carried away a great number with her most venomous doctrine, making it her first aim to destroy baptism' (1. 2).[185] This had the effect on many Christians in Carthage of 'taking them away from the water'

---

[180] Barnes, *Tertullian*, 55, places this work after the *De praescriptione* in about 204/5

[181] In the words of John 4: 24, Tertullian declares that 'God is a Spirit' in 32. 3. To demonstrate God's future destruction of the material creation, Tertullian cites words from Rev. 21: 1, 11 in 34. 1 and Rev. 6: 13 in 34. 2.

[182] 'In conclusion, I will apply the Gospel as a supplementary testimony to the Old Testament (*instrumenti veteris*)...inasmuch as it is therein plainly revealed by whom He made all things. "In the beginning was the Word" (Jn. 1. 1)—that is, the same beginning, of course, in which God made the heaven and the earth (Gen. 1. 1),—"and the Word was with God, and the Word was God. All things were made by Him, and without Him nothing was made"...What, therefore, did not exist, the Scripture was unable to mention; and by not mentioning it, it has given us a clear proof that there was not such thing: for if there had been, the Scripture would have mentioned it' (20. 4–5).

[183] Rev. 6: 13 (*Herm.* 34. 2); 20: 3 (*Herm.* 11. 3); 20: 11 (*Herm.* 34. 2); 21: 1 (*Herm.* 34. 2, twice); 22: 18:20 (*Herm.* 22. 3).

[184] Quasten, *Patrology*, ii. 280, placed it between 198 and 200; Barnes, *Tertullian*, 55, between 198 and 203.

[185] Probably Tertullian has the Cainites directly in his sights when he says in 13. 1, 'Here, then, those miscreants provoke questions. And so they say, "Baptism is not necessary for them to whom faith is sufficient; for withal, Abraham pleased God by sacrament of no water, but of faith"'.

(1. 3). In chapter 11 we see how this played out among some of the faithful. Tertullian now has to answer the objection, ' "But behold", say some, "the Lord came, and baptized not; for we read, 'And yet He used not to baptize, but His disciples! (Jn. 4. 2)' " '.[186] Tertullian of course does not dispute the factuality of the Gospel statement which underlies the objection, simply its interpretation. His answer is that the disciples were baptizing into John's baptism and that real, Christian baptism awaited the passion and resurrection of Jesus and the descent of the Holy Spirit (alluding no doubt to John 7: 39). But the interesting thing here is that this objection provides another window on the status of John's Gospel among the 'common' Christians of his day (cf. my comments above on Clement). These had been led to doubt the necessity of baptism, and they had seen in John 4: 2 a fact from the Lord's life which would seem to downplay its importance. These struggling Christians and Tertullian obviously share the same esteem for the authority of this Gospel and its portrayal of the life of Jesus. In the very next chapter Tertullian will indicate that the Church's insistence upon the necessity of baptism is based 'chiefly on the ground of that declaration of the Lord, who says, "Unless one be born of water, he hath not life" ' (John 3: 5, loosely cited).[187] At another point he finds it useful to emphasize Jesus' words to Peter in John 13: 9–10, 'He who hath once bathed hath no necessity to wash a second time' (12. 3). Referring later to the source of this saying, Tertullian calls it, 'the Lord's Gospel' (*ex domini euangelio*), and lays it alongside material from 'the apostle's letters' (15. 1). The man who wrote that Jesus came 'by means of water and blood' (1 John 5: 6) Tertullian knows as 'John' (16. 1). He links these elements to the water and the blood which flowed from Jesus' pierced side (John 19: 34 again) (16. 2).

It is clear that both Tertullian and the rank-and-file Christians in Carthage at the end of the second century value the Fourth Gospel as they value the other three, undoubtedly as scripture. They also hold the Apocalypse of John and at least the First Epistle in equal esteem. But among his early works it is in Tertullian's *Prescription against Heretics*, assigned by Quasten to the year 200 and by Barnes to the year 203,[188] where the often unspoken rationale for using New Testament writings authoritatively as scripture emerges and where the place of the Gospel according to John and the rest of the Johannine corpus in the Church of Tertullian's day comes even more clearly into view.

---

[186] Tertullian is evidently answering a problem put by Christians who had been enticed by the Cainite arguments. It is of course possible that the Cainites themselves used the example of Jesus from John 4: 2. It is clearly the Cainites, whom he calls 'miscreants', who also used the example of Abraham, who had faith without baptism, probably from Galatians 3 (13. 1), and who cited Paul's words from 1 Cor. 1: 7 that he was not sent to baptize (12. 1).

[187] Paraphrased a bit differently again in 13. 3.

[188] Quasten, *Patrology*, ii. 270; Barnes, *Tertullian*, 55.

In *De praescriptione haereticorum* we see that, like Irenaeus and Clement, Tertullian also explicitly treats the Fourth Gospel as the work of John the apostle, and as one of the Church's four Gospels. As in the works cited above, so here, he uses it instinctively as a reliable source for the life and sayings of Christ (*Praescr.* 3. 10; 8. 6, 14–15), interweaving its words with those of the other Gospels. We also see more clearly displayed his assumption of the common authorship of at least the Gospel, the First Letter, and the Revelation: in *Praescr.* 33. 10–11 he assumes that the John who wrote the Apocalypse and chastized the Nicolaitans is the same man who wrote in his epistle against those he called 'antichrists' (1 John 4. 3; he cites 1 John 2: 19 elsewhere). This John clearly is the apostle of that name (33. 1; 34. 1; 36. 3). Throughout this treatise Tertullian mentions Marcionites and Valentinians. But though he once affirms that Valentinus, as opposed to Marcion, 'seems to use the entire volume (*integro instrumento*)' (38. 8),[189] there is no sign of awareness that the Valentinians, or any of the heretics, had a 'special gospel' among the four, or any particular relationship to the Fourth Gospel. This goes equally for his later treatise *Adversus Valentinianos* from around 213, where no special attachment to John is noted.

'In the Lord's apostles we possess our authority; for even they did not of themselves choose to introduce anything, but faithfully delivered to the nations (of mankind) the doctrine which they had received from Christ. If, therefore, even "an angel from heaven should preach any other gospel" (Gal. 1. 8), he would be called accursed by us.' So Tertullian affirms, setting out the Church's position against the heretics in *De praescriptione* 6. 4. This apostolic authority[190] is established in part through the Johannine Gospel, where the apostles are set to receive 'the Holy Ghost, the Comforter, who, the Lord said, would guide them into all the truth' (John 16: 13); they were indeed 'ordained (*destinati*) to be teachers to the Gentiles' and 'were themselves to have the Comforter for their teacher' (8. 14, 15).

There is a problem, however, with using scripture, even apostolic scripture, in confrontations with heretics. The heretics themselves 'actually treat of the Scriptures and recommend (their opinions) out of the Scriptures! To be sure they do. From what other source could they derive arguments concerning the things of the faith, except from the records of the faith (*ex litteris fidei*)?' (*Praescr.* 14. 14). 'They put forward the Scriptures, and by this insolence (*audacia*) of theirs they at once influence some. In the encounter itself, however, they weary the strong, they catch the weak, and dismiss waverers with a doubt' (15. 2). The heretics too, then, use the scriptures

---

[189] Though he also charges Valentinus with 'different expositions and acknowledged (*sin dubio*) emendations' (*Praescr.* 30. 11).

[190] Cf. his words from *Marc.* 4. 2. 1, 'We lay it down as our first position, that the evangelical Testament (*instrumentum*) has apostles for its authors (*auctores*), to whom was assigned by the Lord Himself this office of publishing (*promulgandi*) the gospel. Since, however, there are apostolic men also, they are yet not alone, but appear with apostles and after apostles.'

(though not in their entirety, and though what they receive they pervert, 19. 1). He comes then to his 'prescription': 'Accordingly, we oppose to them this step above all others, of not admitting them to any discussion of the Scriptures'. 'If in these lie their resources, before they can use them, it ought to be clearly seen to whom belongs the possession of the Scriptures, that none may be admitted to the use thereof who has no title at all to the privilege' (15. 4). The heretics, then, have no title to the scriptures which they use to advance their views. In this Tertullian seems to be articulating words for which Irenaeus had been searching when he too accused the Valentinians of 'adapting' the scriptures to their own inventions. Not wanting to place the scriptures at the centre of the fray, because, when arguing with heretics, 'a controversy over the Scriptures can, clearly, produce no other effect than help to upset either the stomach or the brain' (16. 2), Tertullian wants to ask instead 'with whom lies that very faith to which the Scriptures belong?...For wherever it shall be manifest that the true Christian rule and faith shall be, there will likewise be the true Scriptures and expositions thereof, and all the Christian traditions' (19. 2). And so he wants to apply another test, another and a more personal way, of establishing the truth from the apostles. The truth may be established through 'those very churches which the apostles founded in person, both *viva voce*, as the phrase is,[191] and subsequently by their epistles' (21. 3). It is to these living churches that we must go to find the doctrines of the truth, 'whereas all doctrine must be prejudged as false which savours of contrariety to the truth of the churches and apostles of Christ and God' (21. 3, 5).

But here Tertullian sees more reprehensible tactics of the heretics in that, when confronted with apostolic teaching, 'they usually tell us that the apostles did not know all things' (22. 2; 27. 1 cf. Irenaeus, *AH* 3. 1. 1; 3. 12. 5, 7), or else 'they turn round to the very opposite point, and declare that the apostles certainly knew all things, but did not deliver all things to all persons'. But who can assert that the Lord kept anything from Peter, 'the rock on which the church should be built'? (22. 4). Or, 'was anything...concealed from John, the Lord's most beloved disciple, who used to lean on His breast (Jn. 21. 20) to whom alone the Lord pointed Judas out as the traitor (Jn. 13. 25), whom He commended to Mary as a son in His own stead (Jn. 19. 26)?' (22. 5). Besides, Jesus promised the Spirit of truth, the Paraclete, to the apostles (John 16: 12–13; *Praescr.* 22. 8–9). From this we can see both how Tertullian knows the beloved disciple and author of the Fourth Gospel as the apostle John, and how the promise of the Paraclete made by Jesus in this Gospel is a foundation stone for his understanding of

---

[191] *Viva, quod aiunt, voce.* Tertullian probably has *AH* 3. 2. 1 in view, where Irenaeus repeats the heretical allegation 'that the truth was not delivered by means of written documents, but *viva voce* (*per vivam vocem*)'. Tertullian's assertion that the apostles did indeed deliver the truth 'subsequently by their epistles' is then a reaffirmation of the ecclesiastical position of the authority of the apostolic epistles in the face of such arguments.

apostolic authority, the authority upon which the Church stands or falls (6. 4; 8. 14, 15).

Chapter 22 of *De praescriptione* has disclosed to us, then, Tertullian's view of the authorship and authority of the Gospel according to John. He identifies John as the disciple and apostle who was most beloved by the Lord and who was to take the role of son to Jesus' own mother, based upon statements made in that Gospel. At length Tertullian tells us more about this man which has not come from the Gospel but from Irenaeus. He reprises Irenaeus' tradition about Polycarp, here making explicit what Irenaeus had left implicit in *AH* 3. 3. 4, that one of the apostles who ordained Polycarp was John, and maintaining that this fact was transmitted in the registers (*fastos*) of the Smyrnaean church;[192] while claiming the same kind of succession for Clement of Rome from Peter (32. 2, cf. *AH* 3. 3. 3). When Tertullian later turns to review the heresies which were confronted by the apostles in their own day, seedlings of the current crop, he mentions John again, who was charged to chastize the Nicolaitans in his Apocalypse (2. 14), and who designated false teachers as 'Antichrists' in his epistle (33. 10–11).

We have seen then how the Gospel according to John is used as scripture by Tertullian, how its promise of the Paraclete authenticateed the knowledge and authority of the apostles, and how the historical activity of John himself in ordaining Polycarp served to show the apostolic foundation of the church in Smyrna. Already from Tertullian's closeness to the Roman church at this time, his claim to being of the same faith with it (21. 7; 36. 4), and his express acknowledgement that Christianity in Carthage was derived from Rome (36. 2, 4), we would have ample reason to suspect that his views about this apostle and his writings would not be at odds with views widely held in that church. But one more reference to John takes on a special significance in this regard. Like Irenaeus and Clement, Tertullian knows of another tradition about the apostle John.[193] This one concerns John as prisoner, who, he reports, 'was first plunged, unhurt, into boiling oil, and thence remitted to his island-exile' (36. 3, cf. Jerome, *Against Jovinian* 1. 26). This torture took place, he says, in Rome. The story has of course been challenged on more than one ground.[194] To say nothing of the mir-

---

[192] In *Marc.* 4. 5 he speaks of 'John's foster churches', speaking of the seven churches of the Apocalypse, and claims that the successions of their bishops go back to John.

[193] His later statement in *De monogamia* 17 about John being 'a noted voluntary celibate of Christ's' may be a reference to John the apostle or to John the Baptist.

[194] Culpepper, *John*, 179 n. 2, refers to Eric Junod and Jean-Daniel Kaestli, *Acta Iohannis*, Corpus Christianorum Series Apocryphorum, 2 (Turnhout, 1983), 775–80, for discussion. The latter point out that Jerome refers to this passage in Tertullian and amplifies the story (*Against Jovinian* 1. 26; *Commentary on Matthew* 3. 20, 23), stating once that it took place under Nero. The later *Virtutes Iohannis* places the incident in the time of Domitian, but says that it took place in Ephesus by order of the Proconsul. In all these sources this attempted execution precedes the exile to Patmos (Junod and Kaestli, *Acta Iohannis*, ii. 773–4).

acle of emerging unscathed from a vat of boiling oil, we have no confirmation that the apostle John was ever in Rome (unless it be Hippolytus,
Antichr. 36, where Hippolytus says that Babylon (read Rome) sent John into
banishment). The possibility that the exiled author of the Apocalypse had in
fact been brought to Rome for trial perhaps cannot be dismissed out of
hand. But whether Tertullian's report is entirely legendary or has been built
upon the memory of a historical trial in Rome, what is important for us to
observe is that Tertullian is citing it here in order to support a particular
church's authority or honour. And that church is not in Carthage, but in
Rome, 'How happy is its church, on which apostles poured forth all their
doctrine along with their blood! Where Peter endures a passion like his
Lord's! where Paul wins his crown in a death like John's [i.e. the Baptist's]'.
It is not likely that Tertullian, in Carthage, came up with a story about the
apostle John's presence in Rome which was unheard of in Rome itself. No
doubt the story was current in at least some ecclesiastical circles in Rome at
the time and was seen as adding to Rome's apostolic legacy; at any rate it
was eventually immortalized architecturally in the Church of San Giovanni
in Olio. And what also must be observed is that the story does not simply
invoke the name of the apostle John, known from the synoptic Gospels. It
invokes the apostle John who was author of the Revelation, who from
Rome was 'thence remitted to his island-exile', and to whom Tertullian in
this same work attributes also an apostolic Gospel and Letter. In chapter 22
Tertullian had pointed to John the Beloved Disciple, author of the Gospel,
to establish the truth of the Church's teaching. Here in chapter 36 he points
to John as author of the Apocalypse to establish the true apostolic credentials of the church at Rome.

Tertullian is important for his tacit recognition of the authority of the
Johannine writings, as well as for his explicit statements about the assumed
apostolic author of these books, and for his concept of a canon of the New
Testament (esp. *Praescr.* 36–8). His esteem for these writings was a purely
literary one, taken from Irenaeus. His response to the troubles over baptism
raised by the Cainites unwittingly provides for us a reflection of the esteem
in which the Fourth Gospel was held by the rank-and-file Christians in
Carthage at the end of the second century. Tertullian's witness is not only
important for Carthage but also holds certain implications for Rome. This
is not only because of his connections to Rome and, at this point at least,
his willingness to defer to the Roman church as the apostolic fount which
brought the waters of Christianity to Carthage. Tertullian's register of the
Roman church's apostolic foundations strongly suggests that the church in
Rome was glad to appeal to the authority of John the apostle and the Seer
of the Patmos visions. He thus adds one more piece of circumstantial evidence for the use of the Fourth Gospel and the Apocalypse among the
orthodox in Rome and their common attribution to John the apostle by the
time Gaius wrote.

The Passion of Perpetua and Felicitas

Closely connected with this early period of Tertullian's writing career is the account of the sufferings and deaths of several Christians in Carthage in 202–3. Many have thought that Tertullian himself authored at least the final, published version of their martyrdom. This remains only a possibility.

Chapter 6. 2 contains a quotation of John 16: 24 by the author, 'But he who had said, "Ask, and ye shall receive," gave to them when they asked, that death which each one had wished for'. The words of Christ from John 16 are accepted as authentic and the firm basis of a promise. The author and one of the martyrs also apparently know the Revelation of John. In 4. 2 Saturus tells of his vision of ascending to heaven.

And being clothed, we entered and saw the boundless light, and heard the united voice of some who said without ceasing, 'Holy! Holy! Holy!' And in the midst of that place we saw as it were a hoary man sitting, having snow-white hair, and with a youthful countenance; and his feet we saw not. And on his right hand and on his left were four-and-twenty elders, and behind them a great many others were standing.

This does not tell us who these North Africans thought wrote these Johannine works. It does tell us that they used them and that the book of Revelation played a role in forming their concepts of the other world. It tells us that the narrator considered the words of Jesus recorded in the Fourth Gospel to be genuine. Its witness conforms to that of Tertullian and to the general picture of the Church empire-wide in its day.

Proclus and the Montanists

It is widely believed that both the Fourth Gospel and the Revelation of John played important roles in second-century Montanism. Even if Ronald Heine is correct that we cannot prove that 'the earliest Montanists in Phrygia made any use of the Paraclete passages in John',[195] this would no longer be the case by the end of the second century, as we may see from the account in Hippolytus, *Refutation* 8. 12, and from several works of Tertullian. Heine thinks the criticism of Montanism typical in Rome[196] was that the New Prophecy could not be accepted because there was no legitimate prophecy after the

[195] Heine, 'The Role of the Gospel of John', 19. He argues that it was not early on in Asia Minor but later 'in Rome, then, that the Paraclete passages in John first assumed a central position in the Montanist controversy' (16).

[196] Heine thinks that 'the Asian debate over Montanism centered on the question of true and false prophets, not on whether there could be contemporary prophets' (ibid. 11). But the position that legitimate prophecy ceased with the apostles and the prophecies approved by them is more than hinted at by the source of Epiphanius. Further, Eusebius' anonymous source indirectly chides the New Prophets for adding to scripture (5. 16. 3). These are both probably Asian sources, demonstrating that 'canonical' concerns were important to these early Asian critics as well as to their partners in Rome.

apostles. 'The Montanists, therefore, had to justify the validity of post-apos-tolic prophecy. The Paraclete passages in John offered such a justification.'[197] Justification may also have been sought in the example of John, the seer of the Apocalypse, though this is more conjectural. The group mentioned by Irenaeus 3. 11. 9 was particularly animated by what appears to have been the reliance of the Montanists on the Paraclete passages of John. This would indicate that at least by about 175 or 180 the Montanists were using these passages. It also seems that Gaius of Rome may have made some remarks about the Apocalypse of John in his *Dialogue with Proclus*,[198] which associated it with Cerinthus the heretic, and many have concluded that he disparaged the Fourth Gospel as well. This, as we shall later see, is much more dubious. In any case, Montanist use of the Fourth Gospel and the Apocalypse[199] in the last two or three decades of the second century can be taken as assured, though, apart from the specific claim of the Johannine Paraclete, this use is probably no more significant than their use of the rest of the Bible.

Manuscripts of the Fourth Gospel

Evidence for the orthodox use of John

At the time of writing, manuscript fragments have been found from the beginning of the fourth century or earlier representing fifteen separate codi-ces which once contained the Fourth Gospel. This represents a rather healthy percentage of the total number of such manuscripts (fifteen out of sixty-nine).[200] Such representation is particularly impressive for a Gospel which is said by the majority of Johannine scholars to have been so un-popular among the Great Churches in the second century. Three of these fragments, $\mathfrak{P}^{52}$, $\mathfrak{P}^{66}$, and $\mathfrak{P}^{90}$, are regarded by most experts as coming from the second century itself (six more, $\mathfrak{P}^{75}$, $\mathfrak{P}^{45}$, $\mathfrak{P}^{5}$, $\mathfrak{P}^{22}$, $\mathfrak{P}^{28}$, $\mathfrak{P}^{80}$, as coming from the third). This too is quite impressive, and has led Kurt Aland to remark that 'This triple attestation of a New Testament text from the second century is unique, as the early tradition of the Gospel of John generally is unique.'[201] Because nearly all of these texts have come to us courtesy of the dry sands of Egypt, which indeed have yielded nearly all the

---

[197] Heine, 'The Role of the Gospel of John', 15.

[198] See Ch. 4, on Gaius, below.

[199] Cf. Hill, *Regnum Caelorum*[2], 148–9.

[200] According to P. W. Comfort and D. P. Barrett, *The Text of the Earliest New Testament Greek Manuscripts: A Corrected, Enlarged Edition of The Complete Text of the Earliest New Testament Manuscripts* (Wheaton, Ill., 2001), 17. Comfort and Barrett have selected the manuscripts which they believe predate the persecution under Diocletian (303–5).

[201] 'Der Text des Johannesevangeliums im 2. Jahrhundert', in W. Schrage (ed.), *Studien zum Text und zur Ethik des Neuen Testaments: Festscrift zum 80. Geburtstag von Heinrich Greeven*, BZNW 47 (Berlin, 1986), 1–10, at 1 (ET, in Hengel, *Question*, 144 n. 27).

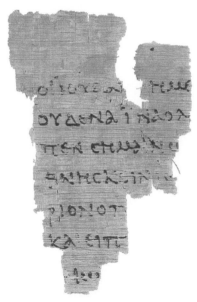

Figure 1. $\mathfrak{P}^{52}$ (Ryland 457), recto, fragment of a second-century codex which contained John's Gospel. Photo shows John 18: 31–3. Courtesy of the Director and University Librarian, the John Rylands University Library of Manchester.

Figure 2. $\mathfrak{P}^{66}$ (P. Bodmer II + Inv. Nr. 427/4298), 156 page codex from the second century containing John's Gospel alone. Photo shows John 1: 1–14. Courtesy of Fondation Martin Bodmer, Cologny-Genève.

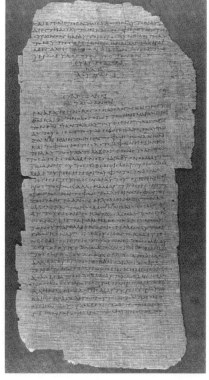

Figure 3. $\mathfrak{P}^{90}$ (P. Oxy. 3523), verso, fragment of a second-century codex which contained John's Gospel. Photo shows John 19: 2–7. Courtesy of the Egypt Exploration Society.

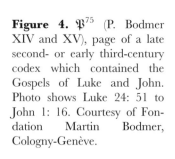

Figure 4. $\mathfrak{P}^{75}$ (P. Bodmer XIV and XV), page of a late second- or early third-century codex which contained the Gospels of Luke and John. Photo shows Luke 24: 51 to John 1: 16. Courtesy of Fondation Martin Bodmer, Cologny-Genève.

rest of the NT papyri as well, these proportions might be thought capable of more than one reading, as we shall see shortly. But one of the few challenges I have seen to the reigning consensus on orthodox Johannophobia, and this done only indirectly, has been made from this papyri evidence.[202]

S. R. Llewelyn has addressed specifically the still influential view of Walter Bauer that gnosticism and what we now call heterodoxy was the original form of Christianity in Egypt and remained dominant there until near the end of the second century. As we have seen above, part of Bauer's argument for this conclusion was that the Fourth Gospel, which seems to have been unusually popular in Egypt, was regarded with caution elsewhere because of its divergence from the Synoptics, and because of its association with heterodox groups. Bauer had written just before the publication of $\mathfrak{P}^{52}$ and Egerton Papyrus 2, and before the discoveries of early papyri in the twentieth century began to accumulate. But Kurt Aland, the great textual critic, was instrumental in bringing many of these to light, and he interpreted the 'unique', relative abundance of papyrus manuscripts of the Fourth Gospel which gradually emerged from the Egyptian sands in the light of Bauer's thesis. For Aland the discovery of these many fragments of John in Egypt, combined with the (alleged) silence on John by orthodox writers, supported Bauer's theory that the early Church in Egypt was gnostic. 'There is, however, a difficulty in Aland's argument', writes Llewelyn. 'The data show no significant difference between the proportions of papyri of John in the two periods, i.e. between 12 in 55 in the earlier period and 10 in 39 in the later period ... The result is similar if one compares the data for New Testament texts on parchment which are predominantly (85%) assigned to the later period.'[203] Llewelyn goes on to ask, 'If gnosticism accounts for the number of papyri of John in the earlier period, what accounts for the sustained frequency of the same gospel in the later period?' And instead of proceeding with a theory to explain how the orthodox, in Egypt and elsewhere, were able to engineer such a clinically clean takeover of the Fourth Gospel from the heterodox, Llewelyn continues with a question and an observation: 'Indeed, may the data not show a simple but persistent preference for the Gospel of John among the speakers of Greek in Egypt? The question which is raised concerning their orthodoxy may prove to be an altogether irrelevant and unnecessary complication.'[204]

---

[202] S. R. Llewelyn, 'A Fragment of the Gospel of John', in S. R. Llewelyn and R. A. Kearsly, *New Documents Illustrating Early Christianity, vii. A Review of the Greek Inscriptions and Papyri Published in 1982–83*, The Ancient History Documentary Research Centre Macquarie University, (Sydney, 1994), 242–8.

[203] Llewelyn, 'A Fragment', 246. See his charts indicating the distribution of NT papyrus and parchment MSS by book on pp. 257, 258. His count of twelve papyri of John from the 4th cent. or earlier, out of fifty-five total NT papyri of the same period, can now be expanded. According to Comfort and Barrett, *Text*, 17, there are now sixty-nine such NT papyri or vellum MSS, of which fifteen are portions of John.

[204] Llewelyn, 'A Fragment', 246.

Much the same point could probably be made from the 'non-continuous' New Testament papyri, that is, from papyri which contain portions of the NT in extracts, quotations, and allusions in other works, in which the Fourth Gospel is well represented (though no comprehensive catalogue has been made).[205]

Bearing on this question, Llewelyn also points to the contrasting paucity of gnostic works found among the papyri: 'Only one of the fourteen Christian texts of the second century may be regarded as gnostic according to Roberts'.[206] This seems to confirm that most of the texts found at places like Oxyrhynchus, Antinoöpolis, Arsinoe, and elsewhere, did not belong to heterodox owners. Besides this, there are a few other factors which may be relevant to our study.

EVIDENCE FOR SACRED USE

Binding into a fourfold Gospel codex

All of our texts of John are from codices, even the fragment known as $\mathfrak{P}^{52}$, in all probability our earliest NT fragment.[207] John's Gospel may have existed alone in this codex, or may have been bound with other works. But from at least the latter part of the second century or early part of the third we do have manuscript evidence of the Fourth Gospel being bound together with the other three into a four-Gospel canon. Our earliest surviving codex which contains parts of all four Gospels is $\mathfrak{P}^{45}$, from the early or middle third century, which, most experts believe, originally had them in the so-called Western order (Matthew, John, Luke, Mark), followed by Acts. The important codex $\mathfrak{P}^{75}$ was copied in the late second or early third century and now contains substantial portions of the Gospels of Luke and John, in that order. While the size and construction make it doubtful that the original codex contained any other Gospels, the attachment of John to Luke in a continuous codex may well imply that it originally had a companion codex containing Matthew and Mark. T. C. Skeat has confirmed the opinion expressed some years earlier by C. H. Roberts[208] that the papyrus fragments $\mathfrak{P}^{4}$, $\mathfrak{P}^{64}$, $\mathfrak{P}^{67}$, containing parts of Matthew and Luke, were once part of the same codex. Skeat has also concluded that this must have been a four-Gospel codex with the order Matthew, Mark, Luke, John.[209] He has also determined that this

---

[205] See S. R. Pickering, 'The Significance of Non-Continuous New Testament Textual Materials in Papyri', in D. G. K. Taylor (ed.), *Studies in the Early Texts of the Gospels and Acts* (Birmingham, 1999), 121–41, who lists twenty-one examples of papyri containing non-continuous texts of John.

[206] Llewelyn, 'A Fragment', 247, citing C. H. Roberts, *Manuscript, Society and Belief in Early Christian Egypt* (Oxford, 1979), 52.

[207] Until recently it had consistently been dated to *c*.125. On the recent redating of $\mathfrak{P}^{52}$ to a later point in the 2nd cent., see Koester, *ACG.* 205–7; Andreas Schmidt, 'Zwei Anmerkungen zu P.Ryl. III 457', *Archiv für Papyrusforschung*, 35 (1989), 11–12.

[208] Roberts, *Manuscript, Society and Belief*, 13.

[209] T. C. Skeat, 'The Oldest Manuscript of the Four Gospels?', *NTS* 43 (1997), 1–34, esp. 15. See also G. N. Stanton, 'The Fourfold Gospel', *NTS* 43 (1997), 317–46, at 327–8.

codex was written in the late second century and that it must have had an exemplar reaching back to an earlier time. Another conclusion he draws is more inferential: that 'the Four-Gospel Canon and the Four-Gospel codex are inextricably linked, and that each presupposes the other'.[210] Skeat believes 'the reason why the Christians, perhaps about AD 100, soon after the publication of the Gospel of John, decided to adopt the codex was that only a codex could contain all four Gospels'.[211] It must be observed, however, that there are as yet no surviving codices from this early which are large enough to have accommodated this much material. At any rate, the binding of the Gospel according to John with one ($\mathfrak{P}^{75}$) and with the three Synoptics (possibly by the end of the second century in $\mathfrak{P}^{4, \ 64, \ 67}$ and certainly in the third century in $\mathfrak{P}^{45}$), is evidence of an esteem for this Gospel which is entirely commensurate with our literary evidence explored so far. In no early codex is it bound together with a non-canonical Gospel.

'Pulpit Bibles'?

Kim Haines-Eitzen has demonstrated from the fund of literary papyri of all kinds that most copies of books in antiquity were made for private purposes and were copied one at a time, as need arose.[212] This may hold as well for the NT papyri; at least it is a factor which should be taken into account in studies of textual transmission, though it rarely has been. There are indications in some early copies of NT books, however, that they were prepared for public reading in a church setting. This has been seen in the size and formation of the letters, the use of columns, and in the way certain texts were marked into subdivisions. $\mathfrak{P}^{45}$, the third-century codex containing the four Gospels and Acts, for instance, has no such markings, and this and other factors are consistent with the conclusion that this codex was a private copy made for private use. But Philip Comfort writes about $\mathfrak{P}^{75}$ that its 'large typeface indicates that the manuscript was composed to be read aloud to a Christian congregation. The scribe even added a system of sectional divisions to aid any would-be lector.'[213] We also find such markings in $\mathfrak{P}^{66}$, a codex of the middle second or perhaps as late as the early third century containing John only.[214] $\mathfrak{P}^{5}$, a third-century copy of the

---

[210] T. C. Skeat, 'Irenaeus and the Four-Gospel Canon', *Nov. T.* 34 (1992), 194–9.

[211] Skeat, 'The Oldest Manuscript', 31; cf. idem, 'The Origin of the Christian Codex', *Zeitschrift für Papyrologie und Epigraphik*, 102 (1994), 263–8.

[212] Kim Haines-Eitzen, *Guardians of Letters: Literacy, Power, and the Transmitters of Early Christian Literature* (Oxford, 2000), particularly chs. 1, 4, and 5. '(O)ur evidence points quite uniformly to the norm of private copying and transmission of literature', 83; 'what remains constantly before us are circles of readers and scribes who transmitted Christian literature individually and privately', 84. One of her theses is 'that social networks among early Christians provided the framework by which Christian literature was transcribed, transmitted, and disseminated … that the scribes who copied early Christian literature did so from within private scribal networks', 78.

[213] Comfort and Barrett, *Text*, 503.

[214] J. van Haelst, *Catalogue des papyrus littéraires juifs et chrétiens* (Paris, 1976), 148; Eric G. Turner, *The Typology of the Early Codex* (Philadelphia, 1977), 84–6; Comfort and Barrett, *Text*, 381.

Fourth Gospel found at Oxyrhynchus, has 'espaces blancs pour indiquer les divisions du text'.[215] This means that such indications of probable ecclesiastical usage are found in three of the four earliest fragments of the Fourth Gospel which preserve a substantial amount of text. There is also $\mathfrak{P}^{4, \ 64, \ 67}$, mentioned above, fragments of the Gospels of Matthew and Luke which scholars now believe are from the same codex, a codex written towards the end of the second century and which originally contained all four Gospels. Graham Stanton writes that its two-column format 'is very probably an indication of a high-class codex, a splendid "pulpit edition" intended for liturgical use'.[216]

This means that at least from some time in the latter half of the second century, if not before, copies of the Fourth Gospel were being produced which would be suitable for public reading in the churches. We thus have manuscript evidence from only a little later than Justin which suggests the practice he attests of the reading of the 'memoirs of the Apostles' in the worship services of orthodox Christians in Rome (*1Apol.* 67. 3). This early liturgical use supports the picture of the Johannine corpus which is emerging from our study but directly contradicts the usual contention about orthodox Johannophobia.[217]

Excursus: Revelation

While attention here is focused primarily on the Fourth Gospel, one of the best attested portions of the New Testament, I must say something about the manuscripts of the book of Revelation. Five of the sixty-nine earliest NT manuscripts are fragments of Revelation.[218] We have evidence that by some time before the middle of the third century the book of Revelation too had been divided into chapters as it was copied. Victorinus of Pettau, around the middle of the third century, refers to material 'in this chapter' (*in hoc capitulo*) of the book in his *Commentary on the Apocalypse* 11. 4. Also, at about this time, Dionysius of Alexandria speaks of some before his time examining the book 'chapter by chapter' (καθ᾽ ἕκαστον κεφάλιον) (Eus. *HE* 7. 25).

---

[215] Van Haelst, *Catalogue*, 157. $\mathfrak{P}^5$ was almost certainly a codex containing only the Fourth Gospel, because it contains probably the second and next to last sheets of what van Haelst *Catalogue*, 157, says was likely to have been a single codex containing twenty-five double leaves. Comfort, *Text*, 74, dates it to the early 3rd cent.

[216] Stanton, 'Fourfold Gospel', 327.

[217] There may be something to gain from reflection on the state of the text transmitted, as we now have it. The transmission of the Gospel according to John is not only very well-attested, but relatively stable. 'In the Gospels...Mark has the largest amount of variation per page of text, while John has the least', G. D. Fee, 'The Myth of Early Textual Recension in Alexandria', in E. J. Epp and G. D. Fee, *Studies in the Theory and Method of New Testament Textual Criticism* (Grand Rapids, Mich., 1993), 247–73 at 249, originally published in R. N. Longenecker and M. C. Tenney, *New Dimensions in New Testament Study* (Grand Rapids, Mich., 1974). This may be an indication, among other things, of the relatively late date of John's production, but also of the relatively better equipped and more highly developed industry of Christian publishing available at that time.

[218] $\mathfrak{P}^{18}$, $\mathfrak{P}^{24}$, $\mathfrak{P}^{47}$, $\mathfrak{P}^{98}$, $\mathfrak{P}^{115}$. The earliest of these is $\mathfrak{P}^{98}$, from the late 2nd cent.

For Victorinus in Pettau and Dionysius in Alexandria both to speak of chapters in their copies of Revelation must mean that this form of standardization in copying goes back at least to the early third century.[219] And Dionysius' statement that his dubious predecessors examined the book 'chapter by chapter' suggests that chapter divisions were present already in texts used near the beginning of the third century when these predecessors presumably wrote. This is indicative of the high regard in which Revelation was evidently held among catholics in East and West (Dionysius' predecessors notwithstanding).[220] This is entirely consistent with the status it held with Irenaeus in the 180s and the *Epistle of Vienne and Lyons* in the 170s. I shall later observe that it probably was regarded similarly by Justin in the early 150s, and possibly a good deal earlier.

Early Christian Iconography

In his 1959 volume *Jean le théologien*, F.-M. Braun criticized other scholars, J. N. Sanders and C. K. Barrett in particular, for neglecting a good deal of evidence from the second century in their studies of the reception of the Fourth Gospel. A case in point was the Roman catacomb paintings, which, Braun argued, demonstrated that the Church in Rome valued the Fourth Gospel in the second century, even in the *early* part of the second century. Indeed, one of the great pioneers of the study of the catacombs, Giuseppe Wilpert, dated the scenes of the raising of Lazarus and of the Samaritan woman at the well from the Crypt of the Passion in the Catacomb of Praetextatus to the first half of the second century,[221] and a representation of the raising of Lazarus in the Greek Chapel of the Catacomb of Priscilla to the beginning of the second century![222] It must be immediately pointed out that scholars have generally abandoned these early dates as mistaken.[223]

---

[219] M. Dulaey, *Victorin de Poetovio, Sur l'apocalypse, suivi du* Fragment chronologique *et de* La construction du monde, introduction, texte critique, traduction, commentaire et index (Paris, 1997), 189.

[220] Hippolytus, in *c.*202 or 203, speaks casually of the book of Revelation as scripture (*On Christ and Antichrist* 5).

[221] G. Wilpert, *Le pitture delle Catacombe Romane* (Rome, 1903), i. 207, 286, pl. 19 (the plates are in vol. ii).

[222] Wilpert, *Le pitture*, i. 286. See pp. 286–7 for descriptions of the paintings of Lazarus from the Chapel of the Sacraments A2 and A6 in the Catacomb of Callistus; pls. 39. 1, 46. 2. Another painting of the woman at the well is mentioned (18) from the Chapel of the Sacraments A3 from the same period. From the Catacomb of Peter and Marcellinus there is a fine depiction of the miracle of the changing of water into wine at Cana, dated to the first half of the 3rd cent. (278; pl. 57).

[223] Umberto Fasola, 'Cemetery', in *EEChurch*, i. 155–8, at 155; Vincenzo Fiocchi Nicolai, 'Painting', in *EEChurch*, ii. 629–32, at 629; P. C. Finney, 'Art', *EEChry* (1990), 97–103 at 99, who says, 'The oldest paintings overall come from two regions within the Callistus catacombs...but there are fragments in Domitilla, and it is possible, although unlikely, that other early fragments survive in the Praetextatus and Priscilla catacombs as well'. Finney places these *c.*200.

The earliest of these artistic portrayals in all probability go back no further than the last years of the second century or the first years of the third.[224] But even at this date, such depictions surely would seem to indicate that certain incidents from the life of Jesus recorded only in the Fourth Gospel must have been favourites for quite some time among groups of Christians in Rome. In these circumstances it is surprising that, despite the fairly routine dismissals of Braun's volume over the years, few if any have attempted to refute or really even contest this evidence from Roman iconography.[225] Here I shall remark on a few of the most significant, early images found in the ancient catacombs and elsewhere which to a significant degree appear to owe their existence to the Fourth Gospel.

THE RAISING OF LAZARUS

One of the most popular of all the subjects of catacomb paintings is the raising of Lazarus from John 11, portrayed no less than fifty-three times.[226] Not all of these, of course, are in the earliest portions of the catacombs, but a few are, namely, one in the catacombs of Callistus (A2 east wall, centre of register; level 2, area I, cubiculum A6, south wall, west side),[227] one in the 'Greek Chapel'[228] of the catacombs of Priscilla, and one in the 'cubicle of the coronation' in Praetextatus.

The importance of the Lazarus story among groups of Christians is reflected to some degree from contemporary literary sources. Tertullian referred to it in his refutation of Praxeas in about 213 (*Prax.* 23. 1, 4). Clement of Alexandria quoted Jesus' call to Lazarus from John 11: 43 (*Paed.* 1. 2). Some years earlier Irenaeus used the raising of Lazarus as a proof of the future resurrection of the body (*AH* 5. 13. 1), and quoted Jesus' words to Lazarus' sister, 'I am the resurrection and the life' (John 11: 25; *AH* 4. 5. 2, cf. also 2. 22. 3). Before Irenaeus, Melito had referred to Jesus

---

[224] From the beginning of the 3rd cent. we have literary sources attesting the management of Christian cemeteries by the churches in Rome and North Africa (implying that this must have commenced some years earlier). See Tertullian, *Scap.* 3; *Apol.* 39. 5–6; Hippolytus, *Apost. Trad.* 34; *Ref.* 9. 12. 14. In the latter passage, 'Hippolytus' implies that Callistus was appointed by Zephyrinus over the cemetery in Rome shortly after the death of Bishop Victor, which took place in 199.

[225] Of the scholars mentioned in Ch. 1 above, the only one who has brought attention to this in any significant way is R. Kieffer, in 1992, who simply repeated the data mentioned by Braun (including the unrevised dates) and drew much the same conclusions from it.

[226] According to A. G. Martimort, 'L'Iconographie des catacombes et la catéchèse romain', *Rivista di archeologia cristiana*, 25 (1949), 107. See his chart on pp. 106–7. See also the article by Giuliana Santagata, 'Lazarus: Iconography', in *EEChurch*, i. 477, for a brief indication of the wide variety of media in which Lazarus' raising was depicted in the first six centuries AD.

[227] Wilpert's pl. 46.

[228] This area was dated to *c.*170–180 by L. De Bruyne, 'La "Capella greca" di Priscilla', *Rivista di archeologia cristiana*, 46 (1970), 291–330, but to after 268 by A. Recio, 'La "Capella Greca" vist y diseñada entre los años 1783 y 1786 por Seroux d'Agincourt', *Rivista di archeologia cristiana*, 56 (1980), 49–94.

raising 'a corpse...from a tomb already four days old', an obvious reference to John 11: 39 (*P. Pasch.* ll. 552, 656).

The story of Lazarus, with its revelation of Jesus as 'the resurrection and the life' (Jn. 11. 25), held an obvious meaning for Christians in the face of death.[229] That it appears so early and so frequently among the catacomb frescoes must say something about the acceptability of the Fourth Gospel, the only Gospel to contain the story, in Rome at least in the latter part of the second century.

THE SAMARITAN WOMAN AT THE WELL

The ancient Christian cemeteries in Rome contain four representations of the Samaritan woman at the well,[230] another figure who appears only in the Johannine Gospel (John 4). Probably the earliest of these is in the Callistus catacomb (level 2, area I, cubiculum A3, south wall, east end), dating from near the beginning of the third century.[231] It also appears juxtaposed with a scene of the raising of Lazarus in a contemporary fresco in the catacomb of Praetextatus.[232] The revelation of Jesus in this story as the giver of the 'living water' (John 4: 10) which springs up to eternal life (John 4: 14), like the story of Lazarus, held the precious promise of life beyond the grave, and also commended itself to Christian funerary settings. It apparently had sacramental connotations as well, as Tertullian tells us (*Bapt.* 9), and as is confirmed by a painting of the scene found in the baptistery of the house church at Dura Europos, a fortress city on the banks of the Euphrates in Eastern Syria, dating from the 240s. Elements from this passage in the Fourth Gospel were alluded to several times in the second century, by Irenaeus (*AH* 2. 22. 3; 3. 22. 2; 4. 36. 4; Nitrian Fragments, *ANF*, no. 52), by Heracleon (Origen, *C. John*), by Clement (*Paed.* 1. 45. 2; 83. 3), and in the early writings of Tertullian (*Bapt.* 9. 4).[233]

---

[229] Generalizing from the depictions of the raising of Lazarus in early Christian art, an image frequently found on sarcophagi as well as in catacombs, Robin Margaret Jensen, *Understanding Early Christian Art* (London, 2000), 170, says, 'The sepulchral location of most of these Lazarus compositions suggests that the scene conveys a message of reassurance of resurrection, or life beyond death. Lazarus, returned to this life, is a prototypical figure symbolizing the recently dead one's resurrection to the next life'. See also Graydon F. Snyder, *Ante Pacem: Archaeological Evidence of Church Life before Constantine* (Macon, Ga., 1985), 60–1.

[230] According to Martimort, 'L'Iconographie', 107.

[231] Fiocchi Nicolai, 'Painting', 629; Wilpert's pl. 29.

[232] The cubicle of the coronation; Wilpert's pl. 19; dated to the early decades of the 3rd cent. by Fiocchi Nicolai, 'Painting', 629.

[233] This continued in his works written in the early 3rd cent., e.g. *Monog.* 8. 7; *Fuga* 11. 1; *Marc.* 4. 35. 9–10; *Prax.* 21. 8; 27. 11; *Carne.* 9. 7. In each of the last two texts Tertullian cites back to back the two examples of Jesus' encounter with the Samaritan woman and his arrival at the tomb of Lazarus as proofs of the reality of Jesus' human nature, thirsting in the one case and weeping in the other; in *Bapt.* 9. 4 he had connected the water of the well to the water of baptism.

Figure 5. The Raising of Lazarus, Catacomb of Callistus. Photo courtesy of Pontificio Istituto di Archeologia Cristiana.

Figure 6. The Samaritan Woman, Catacomb of Callistus. Photo courtesy of Pontificio Istituto di Archeologia Cristiana.

THE HEALING OF THE PARALYTIC

Depictions of a man carrying a pallet appear twenty times in the Roman catacombs,[234] including an early instance[235] in Callistus (level 2, area I, cubiculum A3, west wall, middle register), as well as on the baptistery wall at Dura Europos. The early iconography is simple and the figure could also represent the man healed by Jesus in Mark 2: 1–12 (parallels).[236] But many art historians believe that the figure is indebted to a greater extent, if not indeed completely, to the paralytic healed by Jesus in John 5: 1–9, by the Sheep Gate pool. This makes sense because of the associations with water both in the Callistus painting[237] and in the Dura Europos baptistery. Also, if there is iconographic continuity with the later, so-called Bethesdà type sarcophagi mentioned by Marinone, which include details of 'many of the elements of John's text',[238] this strengthens the impression that the Johannine story was the leading textual influence.

THE GOOD SHEPHERD

The widely popular image (114 times in the Roman catacombs[239] and often in other media[240]) of the so-called 'good shepherd' occurs among the earliest of the catacomb paintings, on the ceiling in Area 2 the crypt of Lucina,[241] and adjacent to the tomb of Cornelius in the catacomb of Callistus, as well as on the baptistery walls at Dura Europos. It is clear that this image is a Christian adaptation of a pre-existing pagan image of the κριοφόρος, or 'ram bearer', often used to represent Hermes, or as a symbol of bucolic peace or of the virtue of *humanitas*. The image in Greco-Roman art has a shepherd figure carrying a ram (sometimes a sheep) on his shoulders,

---

[234] According to Martimort, 'L'Iconographie', 107.

[235] Mariangela Marinone, 'Paralytic, Healing of the: Iconography', *EECh.* ii. 650, dates it to the second quarter of the 3rd cent.

[236] Marinone, 'Paralytic', 650, cites the lack of indication in the earliest examples of which miracle, the Synoptic or the Johannine, is intended.

[237] Jensen, *Understanding Early Christian Art*, 48, 'Chamber 21 of the Catacomb of Callistus ... contains two parallel combinations of scenes that include Moses striking the rock, a man fishing, the paralytic carrying his bed (referring to the Johannine story which mentions an angel stirring up water for a healing purpose), a baptism, and a banquet scene'. Tertullian also refers to the incident in his treatise on baptism (*Bapt.* 5).

[238] Marinone, 'Paralytic', 650.

[239] Martimort, 'L'Iconographie', 107.

[240] The shepherd image is found on the earliest of Christian sarcophagi, dating from the mid-3rd century (Manuel Satomayer, 'Sarcophagi, Early Christian', *EEChurch*, ii. 755–6; see fig. 277).

[241] Among the seven painted ceilings which Paul Corby Finney says come from 'the earliest period of occupation in these two burial nuclei', *The Invisible God: The Earliest Christians on Art* (New York, 1994), 160. The crypt of Lucina is often acknowledged to be earlier than the rest of the Callistus catacombs (Jensen, *Understanding Early Christian Art*, 84), and its art is dated to the last decades of the 2nd cent. by L. De Bruyne, see Louis Reekmans, 'La Chronologie de la peinture paléochrétienne: Notes et réflections', *Rivista di archeologia cristiana*, 49 (1973), 271–91, at 284.

Figure 7. The Paralytic, Catacomb of Callistus. © The International Catacomb Society. Photo: Estelle S. Brettman.

Figure 8. The Good Shepherd, Catacomb of Callistus. © The International Catacomb Society. Photo: Estelle S. Brettman.

sometimes also carrying a purse, a set of pipes, or a bucket of milk.[242] It would therefore have been easy for Christians to have seen in it a representation of Jesus,[243] who goes after the lost sheep (Matt. 18: 10–14; Luke 15: 3–7, cf. Heb. 13: 20; 1 Pet. 2: 25; 5: 4; Rev. 7: 17). We know that the figure of Christ as a shepherd was popular in second-century Christian literature (e.g. Hermas' *Shepherd* Vis. 5. 1; *Mart. Polyc.* 19. 2; Clement Al., *Paed.* 1. 7 (53. 2–3)) and hymnody (Clement's 'Hymn to Christ the Saviour', at the end of *Paed.* 3. 12), as well as in the plastic arts.[244] Shortly we shall see evidence that John 10: 1–19 was also regarded as a key source for this popular symbol.

Detailing an interesting parallel to the catacomb paintings, Paul Corby Finney has written about a corpus of over 100 'shepherd lamps' unearthed in central Italy, dating from 'the late Antonine to late Severan period, approximately 175–225'.[245] That is, these oil lamps were produced in the same region and in the same period as the earliest catacomb paintings. These lamps, manufactured by six or seven different potters (known from their stamps), are distinguished by their scenes illustrating 'the shepherd-*kriophoros*'. Finney explains the likelihood of the purchase and use of such lamps by Christians.

But on the twin presumptions of invisibility and adaptation, the shepherd-*kriophoros* figure was an ideal device. It was an image Christians could easily adopt and adapt to their own universe of private meanings. Christians who bought Annius' lamps[246] (and surely some did) would have simply been continuing their own material anonymity—nothing objectively new in the iconographic realm would have come into existence by their act of purchasing Annius' product. They would have been exercising their right of selection, as Clement said conscientious Christians should do.[247] For their own private reasons, they would have been adopting a ready-made Greco-Roman pictorial cliché and thereby adapting to the already-existing pictorial tradition. But if there were enough of these clients, and if nine times out of ten they chose shepherds over *hetairai*, Annius and his fellow potters might have begun to rethink their strategy for selling lamps. In short, with numbers on their side, the new religionists might have begun to exercise an influence on the supply side of the

---

[242] Jensen, *Understanding Early Christian Art*, 37. See her discussion of the good shepherd in early Christian art, pp. 37–41. Anna Maria Giuntella, 'Shepherd, The Good. II. Iconography', *EEChurch*, ii. 776–8, writes that it 'should not be considered as a portrayal of Christ, but as an ideogram...The pagan repertoire thus suggested scenes to Christian art and responded to the need of Christian artists and clients to introduce symbolic elements agreeable to popular spirituality and in tune with the literary traditions of the sacred texts' (777).

[243] Some art historians have seen it not as a representation of Christ but only as the personification of an abstract idea such as philanthropy or *humanitas* (e.g. Snyder, *Ante Pacem*, 22–4). For a more convincing treatment, see Jensen, *Understanding Early Christian Art*, 37–41.

[244] In his famous inscription, dated to *c.*200, Abercius of Hieropolis calls himself 'a disciple of the pure Shepherd (ποιμένος ἁγνοῦ), who feedeth His flocks of sheep on mountains and plains'.

[245] Finney, *Invisible God*, 116.

[246] Annius was one of the manufacturers of shepherd lamps of the period, according to known surviving examples the most prolific (Finney, *Invisible God*, 118–19).

[247] The reference is to *Paed.* 3. 59. 1–60. 1, where Clement advises Christians that they should select from the shops only such signet rings which bear images which can be accommodated to Christian meanings, such as a dove, a fish, a ship, a lyre, or an anchor.

Roman ceramic industry. This would explain the dramatic growth in the manufacture and distribution of shepherd lamps in the early third century.[248]

One of the factors in indicating Christian use of these lamps, says Finney, is that 'some Severan-Roman Christians were beginning to commission paintings in their underground funerary chambers, and it is clear that one of the most conspicuous iconographic features of these burial paintings was the image of the shepherd-*kriophoros*'.[249] I pause to observe as well that fossors (diggers) and painters who laboured in these underground chambers in this period would naturally have needed large numbers of oil lamps for their work. It may well be that this partly accounts for the 'dramatic growth in the manufacture and distribution' of these lamps, to which Finney points.

Intriguingly, we also know from a couple of *ad hoc* comments made by Tertullian that, contemporary with the earliest catacomb paintings and the manufacture of shepherd lamps, Christians at least in Carthage were also using another form of distinctively Christian art—or art adapted to distinctively Christian interpretation—namely, communion chalices decorated with painted images. These images depicted a shepherd with his sheep. Unlike the shepherd lamps but like the catacomb paintings, these cups denote not simply Christian patronization of art made by non-Christians, but the commissioning of art by Christians, and specifically for religious purposes. The context for Tertullian's mention of the eucharistic cups is his argument for a stricter church discipline than had recently characterized the mainstream Christian Church in Carthage. Representatives of that more tolerant approach had argued that Jesus left them an example in the parable of the man who went after the sheep that strayed (Luke 15: 3–7; cf. Matt. 18: 10–14). Tertullian attempts to show that the sheep in Jesus' parable represents not a wayward Christian but the lost pagan, whom the Saviour wins to himself. In making his case, Tertullian cites the material example of the eucharistic cups commonly in use in Carthage—and if commonly in Carthage, very likely somewhere like Rome as well. The justification for the paintings on the chalices is what demonstrates the link with John 10. Putting words into the mouths of his opponents, Tertullian gives what would be their explanation of the artwork: 'But a "sheep" properly means a Christian, and the Lord's "flock" is the people of the Church, and the "good shepherd" (*pastor bonus*) is Christ; and hence in the "sheep" we must understand a Christian who has erred from the Church's "flock"' (*Pud.* 7.4). Whether the iconography of these paintings differed in any considerable way from the typology of the catacomb paintings or the shepherd lamps of

---

[248] Finney, *Invisible God*, 126. Finney examines (126–31) a unique example, known as Wulf 1224, which has besides the 'good shepherd' as the central figure, depictions of Jonah being cast up from the belly of the fish, Jonah resting under the colocynth bush (Jonah 4: 5–6), Noah's ark, and Noah's dove. This lamp decoration, unlike most of the standard shepherd lamp decorations, is explicitly Christian, and its iconography parallels some of the favourite images in the catacombs.

[249] Finney, *Invisible God*, 125.

Figure 9. The Good Shepherd, Crypt of Lucina, Catacomb of Callistus. © The International Catacomb Society. Photo: Estelle S. Brettman.

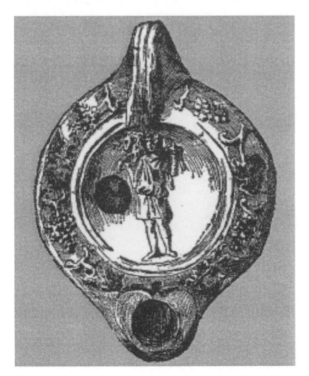

Figure 10. Shepherd lamp of Annius. Reproduced from Rodolfo Lanciani, *Pagan and Christian Rome* (Boston, 1892).

central Italy we do not know. What is significant here is the name given to the Christ figure—not κριοφόρος (the ram-bearer), not 'the man who goes after the lost sheep' from Luke 15: 3–7 or Matthew 18: 10–14 (neither of which uses the word 'shepherd'), not even 'the great shepherd of the sheep' of Hebrews 12. 20, nor 'the chief shepherd (ἀρχιποίμενος)' of 1 Peter 5. 4, but 'the good shepherd', a title for Jesus used by himself, which occurs only in John 10: 11 and 14.[250] Tertullian uses the same title elsewhere when clearly alluding to John 10. 11:[251] Naming the figure 'the good shepherd' surely shows a dependence upon Jesus' self-designation in the text of John 10: 11, 14 and would seem to demonstrate that the Christian adoption of the shepherd 'ideogram' was in part motivated by this evocative Johannine passage.[252] The rare literary comment on a piece of early Christian art by Tertullian, coinciding as it does with the contemporary use of shepherd iconography in the early catacomb paintings and in shepherd lamps, is instructive.

The representations of the raising of Lazarus and of Jesus and the Samaritan woman from the cubicles A3 and A6 of the sacraments in the catacomb of Callistus[253] appear, in the words of Fiocchi Nicolai, in 'icono-graphical formulations which have no exact parallels in later paintings... and which are evidence of what we may call the initial or formative phase of the Christian iconographical repertoire, a phase characterized by the elaboration of figurative formulae not yet codified into those fixed schemes which, typical of subsequent eras, would make their subjects easily recogniz-able and comprehensible to all'.[254] Scenes depicting the raising of Lazarus, the Samaritan woman, along with the healing of the paralytic and Christ the good shepherd, all deriving either wholly or in large part from the Fourth Gospel, occur among the very first pictorial depictions of biblical scenes among the catacomb paintings,[255] indeed, among all of Christian art. They are found amid depictions of scenes from the Old Testament[256]

---

[250] The Greek of John 10: 11, 14 is ὁ ποιμὴν ὁ καλός. ὁ ποιμὴν ὁ καλὸς ... ὁ ποιμὴν ὁ καλός. The Vulgate (Wordsworth and White) reads *pastor bonus. Bonus pastor...pastor bonus.*

[251] 'His soul...which the good shepherd (*bonus pastor*) himself lays down for his sheep', *An.* 13. 3; 'Most assuredly a good shepherd (*bonus pastor*) lays down his life for the sheep', *Fuga* 11. 1.

[252] In the 190s Clement of Alexandria referred to John 10: 11 several times, using the title 'good shepherd' (*Paed.* 1. 6 (347. 3); 1. 7 (53. 2); 1. 8 (84. 1; 85. 2); 11 (97. 3); *Strom.* 1. 26 (169. 1). The same kind of interplay between the good shepherd discourse of John 10 and Jesus' parable of the lost sheep in Luke 15: 3–7 is seen in Clement of Alexandria, *Strom.* 1. 26 (169. 1), writing in *c.*193. We recall that Clement reported the views of some Christians who criticized his use of the philoso-phers with Jesus' words from John 10. 8 about 'thieves and robbers' (*Strom.* 1. 17 (81. 1)). Jesus as the good shepherd was also known to the Valentinian Theodotus (*Theod.* 73. 2).

[253] Wilpert's pls. 29. 2; 39. 1; 46. 2.

[254] Fiocchi Nicolai, 'Painting', 630.

[255] Wilpert, *Le pitture*, i. 17–18, 36–7.

[256] Fiocchi Nicolai, 'Painting', 629. Braun, *Jean le théologien*, 150, points out that the frequently reproduced OT image of the water flowing from the rock in the wilderness (Exod. 17. 1–7), pictured the water of the Spirit and was probably 'une allusion à la parole de Jésus: *Comme le dit l'Écriture, de son sein couleront des fleuves d'eau vive* (*Jo.* VII, 38); pour le quatrième évangéliste, cette

in the early period, a period known for its numerically circumscribed corpus of themes.[257] Other scenes from the life of Christ represented in the paintings, such as his baptism and the multiplication of the loaves and fishes, might also be indebted to John, though they are also connected to the Synoptic Gospels, and other Johannine scenes, such as the wedding at Cana, appear but are not among the earliest examples.

Historians of Christian art, such as Robin Jensen, have written of the 'exegetical' aspect of early Christian iconography: 'Since the artistic themes are mostly drawn from biblical stories, we must assume that they serve an exegetical function—that is, they are commentaries on the texts as well as references to them.'[258] We have seen that each of the images referred to above as being derived from the Fourth Gospel also had literary attestation in the second and early third centuries, some fairly extensive. It therefore cannot be argued that these Johannine images were merely 'floating' religious images, unanchored to any well-known or received texts. Whatever other functions these paintings might also have been designed to serve,[259] their presence in Roman catacombs near the turn of the third century poses a significant problem for the usual theory of orthodox Johannophobia, which tends to generalize for Rome and the Roman hierarchy from the (dubious, as we shall see) examples of Gaius and the Alogi. And the problem for this theory deepens when we consider an aspect of the socio-ecclesiastical situation. Braun spoke of the popularity of the Fourth Gospel on the part of the Christian artists who executed the paintings.[260] But it is very doubtful how much liberty the painters themselves had in selecting the subject matter. They must have worked at the request of families, in private cemeteries like those of Domitilla and Praetextatus, and with church leaders in church-owned ones, like the catacomb of Callistus.[261] In fact, as Finney writes, the latter 'were church property, and what went on in them should be viewed as public and communitarian rather than private and individ-

---

parole prophétique avait été accomplie au Calvaire lorsque le corps du Sauveur fut percé par la lance (*Jo.* XIX, 34–35)'. The connection between the water-giving rock and the body of Jesus, from which flows the water of life, and which was signified by the effusion from the lance wound, is made explicitly by Cyprian, *Ep.* 63. 8 (G. Hartel, *S. Thasci Caecili Cypriani Opera Omnia*, CSEL 3 (Vienna, 1871), ii. 706). Braun finds echoes of John 7: 38 in Hippolytus and in Justin, which may well also be connected with the rock in the wilderness (151–2).

[257] Jensen, *Understanding Early Christian Art*, 9–10.

[258] Ibid. 77. Wilpert, *Le pitture*, i. 37, wrote that the paintings make 'un commentario figurato della Sacra Scrittura'.

[259] Martimort, 'L'Iconographie', emphasized what he saw as the catechetical intent of the images, so many of which find textual parallels in catechetical literature. The liturgical aspect of many of the paintings is also well recognized. See Jensen, *Understanding Early Christian Art*, 84–8.

[260] Braun, *Jean le Théologien*, 149.

[261] It may be observed that two of the earliest literary references to the Church's management of involvement in burials refer to the practice, in both Rome and Carthage, as a ministry to the poor (Tertullian, *Apol.* 39. 5–6; Hippolytus, *Apost. Trad.* 34), who presumably would not be able to pay for such decorations themselves.

ual'.[262] Jensen agrees: 'the establishment of a Christian iconographic language should not be seen as the work of individuals, but rather as a part of the gradually emerging public "face" of a religion that was developing its identity—and making it visible...the art's content reflected the faith and values of the whole Christian community'.[263] The prominence of scenes from the Fourth Gospel in these church-owned and operated burial sites implies church approval, and even church commissioning, of these scenes, and church approval of their textual source. This is grossly inconsistent with the hypothesis that the Fourth Gospel was a newcomer in Roman ecclesiastical circles at that time, and an embattled newcomer at that.

The iconography of the early catacombs, along with the slightly later wall paintings at Dura Europos,[264] combined with the apparent Christian patronization of 'shepherd lamps' and Christian adaptation of the κριοφόρος image to represent Christ the 'good shepherd' on communion chalices, all point to the same conclusion to which the literary evidence has been steadily leading us so far, namely, that the Fourth Gospel was not only known but was very highly valued for its presentations of the life and teaching of Jesus among the orthodox churches, even at Rome, at least by the latter portion of the second century. Together with the papyri evidence, the evidence from early Christian art provides from material culture extremely valuable sociological authentication of the literary sources. All three funds of evidence are consistent with, one might say they require, an even earlier appreciation of the Fourth Gospel being behind the burgeoning record of the late second century. From every corner it appears that if Gaius of Rome indeed criticized and rejected the Fourth Gospel at the beginning of the third century, he was grossly out of step with the mainstream of the church(es) in Rome and elsewhere. Besides throwing into greater relief the apparent anomaly of the approach usually attributed to Gaius and the 'Alogi', the evidence of early Christian iconography whets the appetite to consider the situation in Rome in Justin's day as well.

---

[262] P. C. Finney, 'Catacombs', *EEChry* (1990), 182–4 at 184.

[263] Jensen, *Understanding Early Christian Art*, 22.

[264] The paintings at Dura, though dating from slightly later, in the 230s to the 250s (M. Rostovtzeff, *Dura-Europos and its Art* (Oxford, 1938), 101, believes the early 3rd-cent. house was transformed into a Christian meeting place in about 232; Dura was destroyed in 256), are very important. Three of the four Johannine images reviewed here (the Samaritan woman, the paralytic, and the good shepherd) are represented on the baptistery walls. Though Roman influence on the Christianity in Dura is likely, 'it would not be accurate to presume that all data from outside Rome were little more than local adaptations of Roman models. Evidence of early Christian artistic activity in other parts of the Roman empire, from Spain to Syria and the Tigris–Euphrates region, and from the British Isles to North Africa, refutes such assumptions' (Jensen, *Understanding Early Christian Art*, 20). Not far from the Christian house a fragment of what was apparently a Gospel harmony (until recently believed to be from the *Diatessaron*) was discovered on 5 Mar. 1933. The small fragment contained a paraphrase of John 19: 38 (see the account in Clark Hopkins, *The Discovery of Dura-Europos*, ed. Bernard Goldman (New Haven, 1979), 106–9; p. 111 is a large photo of the painting of the Samaritan woman).

Summary

POSITIVE USE OF THE GOSPEL AND THE JOHANNINE CORPUS

This chapter has surveyed the period identified by many scholars as the time when the Fourth Gospel began to be claimed by the orthodox and used against the gnostic sects. One would have to say that the situation from about 170 to the time of Gaius' *Dialogue with Proclus* in the first years of the third century, shows a remarkable cohesiveness. Catholic writers of this period are using the Fourth Gospel with ease and regularity, in an authoritative manner, and often explicitly as scripture. This Gospel is used like the other three and explicitly linked with them in a canon of four by Irenaeus, Clement of Alexandria, Tertullian, and the *Muratorian Fragment*. Among surviving manuscripts, it is already found bound together with Luke ($\mathfrak{P}^{75}$) and will soon be attested in a codex with Matthew, Mark, Luke, and Acts ($\mathfrak{P}^{45}$). Its impressive showing among the number of early NT papryi, including its unique 'triple attestation' in the second century, seems strikingly paralleled by its disproportionately high representation among images painted on the walls and ceilings of the ealiest Roman catacombs. It is called scripture, its author is called holy, inspired, an apostle, is named John, and is assumed to have reposed on his Master's breast at the last supper. The only indication of opposition to this cherished Gospel has come from an unspecified group mentioned by Irenaeus who, despite the popular contention that they were orthodox, are presented by him as blasphemers against the Holy Spirit and thus beyond the pale of the true Church. Moreover, of any consciousness that the orthodox were taking over a previously unused or suspected or rejected Gospel we have no valid evidence. Of any suggestion that this Gospel was tainted with gnosticism or tagged with a docetic Christology we have no evidence whatsoever.

THE FOURTH GOSPEL IN ROME

Particular interest belongs to the situation in Rome. Walter Baur said that, after Justin, the next time we hear from an ecclesiastically minded Roman, it is Gaius, who 'sensed in the gospel of John a spirit of heresy', and that in his opposition Gaius expressed 'a feeling which dominated Roman orthodoxy ever since the Fourth Gospel appeared on its horizon'.[265] With somewhat more moderation, this general picture has been upheld by many scholars since Baur. The period between Justin and Gaius happens to be woefully underrepresented in the Christian literary record. We have only the few, scattered fragments of Hegesippus, and the mostly fragmentary works of two authors whose provenance in Rome is probable but not

---

[265] Bauer, *Orthodoxy and Heresy*, 208.

certain, namely, Tatian (who, at any rate, we know lived for a time in Rome), and the author of the *Muratorian Fragment*. Tatian will be treated at a later point. But Hegesippus in the period 160–80, we now know, apparently accepted the Fourth Gospel and the Revelation of John as scripture; at any rate he attributed both of these writings to John the apostle. The author of the *Muratorian Fragment*, probably in Rome in this period, accepted this Gospel as canonical and apostolic, as one of the four, and along with the rest of the Johannine literature. For the rest of our knowledge of Rome in this period we rely on non-literary or indirect, circumstantial evidence. But as far as it goes, this evidence too is consistent, and it too stacks up against the OJP. The paintings in some of the earliest portions of the Roman catacombs, *c*.AD 200, depict scenes or ideas taken from the Fourth Gospel, and these must presuppose a favourable attitude towards this Gospel in the second half of the second century, if indeed not before, when that Gospel's narratives of the life of Jesus, particularly its scenes relating to the sacraments and to eternal life, were well-known and treasured by the Church leadership and by the laity.

The *Epistle of Vienne and Lyons*, which relies upon the Gospel, First Letter, and Revelation, and treats them as scripture (Revelation explicitly so), was carried to Rome and delivered to the bishop there in person by the presbyter Irenaeus in 177 or 178. This was a natural choice, for Irenaeus had lived in Rome for a period and certainly had a relationship with the church there. When he wrote his five books *Against Heresies* in the 180s, he could count on finding a major portion of his readership in the capital city. In these books he too uses the Johannine Gospel, Letters, and Apocalypse as a corpus of inspired scripture written by one of Jesus' apostles. He betrays no hint of an awareness that he might be using a questionable or dangerous Gospel when he uses John. On the contrary, he expects his readers will share his revulsion at the Valentinians' abuse of 'scripture' when he points out their abuse of John's Gospel. During the quartodeciman crisis both Polycrates and Irenaeus cited the example of John, who had lain on Jesus' breast, in defending Asian practice or in appealing for tolerance of it to Victor. Thus both letters presume that they shared with the hierarchy in Rome an appreciation for the authority of a man named John, whom Polycrates identified as the Beloved Disciple of the Fourth Gospel, who lived to a great age in Asia Minor. Irenaeus could not have known that such an appeal would be unappreciated in Rome, or his repetition of Polycrates' error would have been foolish and counterproductive to his cause.

And finally, we have every reason to assume that the treatment of the Gospel, the First Letter, and the Revelation all as products of the stylus of the apostle John and as scripture in the early work of Tertullian would not have conflicted with conventional Roman attitudes. Even the story of John the seer and the boiling oil in Rome, no matter how legendary, hardly leaves room for thinking that the works commonly attributed to the apostle John were not highly regarded in the capital city.

THE QUESTION OF PREVIOUS USE

We remind ourselves here of the view of Haenchen and others that the Church's takeover of the Fourth Gospel happened suddenly and was practically without precedent. Koester has concluded that the attribution of this Gospel to John and the placing of it in Asia Minor is a fiction created and popularized by Irenaeus which quickly spread far and wide. This much at least, we may say with full assurance, is false. If it is a fiction, it is a much older one. Long ago William Sanday wrote of the evidence for the distribution of the Fourfold Gospel in this period in words which apply perforce to the distribution of the Gospel according to John.

> ... Irenaeus and the Letter of the Churches of Vienne and Lyons in Gaul, Heracleon in Italy, Tertullian at Carthage, Polycrates at Ephesus, Theophilus at Antioch, Tatian at Rome and in Syria, Clement at Alexandria. The strategical positions are occupied, one might say, all over the Empire. In the great majority of cases there is not a hint of dissent. On the contrary the fourfold Gospel is regarded for the most part as one and indivisible.[266]

If we were speaking about the attestation of the Fourth Gospel we should have to add many more names to this list. Be that as it may, I cite Sanday here for a particular illustration which he went on to make and which poses a question for those who advocate the theory of orthodox Johannophobia.

> Let us for the moment treat these great outstanding testimonies as we should treat the reading of a group of MSS. The common archetype of authorities so wide apart and so independent of each other must go back very far indeed. If we were to construct a *stemma*, and draw lines from each of the authorities to a point *x*, representing the archetype, the lines would be long and their meeting-point would be near the date at which according to the tradition the Gospel must have been composed.[267]

Should we believe, then, that in 170–200 we are seeing, as Sanday's analogy would suggest, the flowering buds of long branches, the natural outgrowth of a mature tree? Or are we witnessing instead an abrupt and fateful change in the practice of the orthodox across the empire, so that their use of the Fourth Gospel is perhaps more like the movements of adept stagehands working quickly and in concert between the scenes to garnish the set with colourful but artificial foliage? A full answer to this dilemma must of course be postponed until the study of the very imperfect record of the earlier part of the second century is completed. But already from our

---

[266] W. Sanday, *The Criticism of the Fourth Gospel* (Oxford, 1905), 238.
[267] Ibid. 239.

examination above we can see the outlines that such an answer will most likely take. For not only have there appeared no signs of defensiveness, no awareness that the Johannine Gospel was in need of 'redemption' from gnostics or Valentinians. Not only has it become clear that the use of the Fourth Gospel by these authors as scriptural or inspired is uncontrived and natural. Not only does the geographical distance between the authors render absurd a theory of collusion or conspiracy. It is also the case that many of these authors refer implicitly or explicitly to a previous use of this Gospel by their orthodox predecessors. To what extent this may be either confirmed or refuted by the evidence, both from heterodoxy and from orthodoxy, of previous periods will be the subject of later sections of this study. But considering only the thirty or so years immediately preceding the emergence of Gaius' alleged criticism, it would have to be said that it is Gaius, not Irenaeus, who appears to be the innovator.

THE EXISTENCE OF A JOHANNINE CORPUS

Finally notice must be taken here of the propensity of writers in this period to use all three portions (Gospel, Letters, Apocalypse) of the five-member Johannine corpus. The studies of recent decades have tended to consider the attribution of these five books to the same author as a fairly late phenomenon and to treat the early history of each book separately and on its own merits. The tendency of catholic writers in our period, however, is to use all of these books (with the possible exception of 3 John), in virtually the same manner, and to attribute them to the same author. While they may not address the subject of the authority of their sources explicitly, it seems from an examination of their usage that to acknowledge one of these books as 'inspired' or scriptural or 'canonical' meant to acknowledge them all. This is illustrated most clearly in Irenaeus of Lyons, Clement of Alexandria, and Tertullian of Carthage—in terms of their writings which have survived, the three most voluminous authors of the period—and in the *Muratorian Fragment*, the only remaining New Testament 'canon list' of the period. But it also follows from the *Epistle of Vienne and Lyons*, which, though it does not give any attribution, uses the Gospel, the Apocalypse, and the First Epistle as scripture, and the Apocalypse explicitly so. And it might also follow from Theophilus' designation of John as an 'inspired' (πνευματοφόρος) writer, like the prophets, a designation which pertained to the person and could therefore quite conceivably be applied to all the writings of that person. In all likelihood Theophilus connected the same inspired John to the Apocalypse, a book we know he used in refuting the teachings of Hermogenes. Hegesippus' designation of the author of the Apocalypse as evangelist and apostle points in the same direction, as does the designation of both the author of the Gospel and the author of the Apocalypse as 'the holy John' by Epiphanius' Asian source. All of these show that the three portions of the Johannine writings are commonly received as scripture by the Church in their time. And they combine to justify speaking of an ecumenical recognition of a Johannine corpus at least in this period, *c.*170–200.

4

Gaius of Rome and the Johannine Controversy

Exactly where do we find examples of 'the durable suspicion that the Gospel taught Gnosticism' of which Haenchen speaks, or evidence that the Great Church was wary or suspicious of this 'tainted' Gospel, or that it came close to discarding this Gospel altogether because of its association with gnostic error? If Charlesworth and others are correct it should not be difficult to form a long and eminent list of the 'many pre-Nicene critics' who 'did not consider it reliable and authentic' because of its use by heretics like Heracleon and the rest. And yet, despite the sweeping and dogmatic statements of some scholars, seldom are any of the host of orthodox Johannophobes ever named besides Gaius of Rome and those Sanders calls the 'conservative, orthodox, anti-Gnostic *Alogi*'. We certainly cannot say that we have encountered any of their number in our survey of the last thirty years of the second century, up to the emergence of Gaius himself. Tradition-bound Rome is said to have been the bastion of orthodox anti-Johannine sentiment, yet so far we have observed from the very limited remains of Roman Christianity of this period only a quite positive engagement with the Fourth Gospel. The church there wanted scenes from this Gospel to adorn the subterranean caverns where it buried its faithful; Hegesippus in Rome evidently connected the Fourth Gospel and the Revelation with the apostle John; Polycrates could assume the Roman Bishop Victor would know about John the disciple of Jesus who reclined next to the Lord at his Last Supper; both Polycrates and Irenaeus could assume that this Roman bishop would respect the apostolic authority of this figure; the author of the *Muratorian Fragment* accepted this Gospel as canonical and apostolic, as one of the four, and along with the rest of the Johannine literature; Tertullian in Carthage, in putting forth the apostolic connections of the church at Rome, links that church not only to Paul and Peter but also to John, the author of the Apocalypse, who is the same apostle who wrote the Gospel and the First Letter. At this point, then, instead of looking like a late manifestation of a long-standing, principled, orthodox opposition to the Fourth Gospel, the criticisms of which have been attributed to Gaius would seem to be an interesting but essentially anomalous deviation from the *opinio communis* of the churches throughout the empire, including Rome, at the time.

The Sources and the Common Reading

It will be necessary now to find out what we can about the circumstances and character of Gaius' campaign against the Johannine writings. When someone says,

In *Adv. Haer.* 3. 11. 9, Irenaeus fought a group that went so far in their antithesis to Montanism (and Gnosticism) that they rejected the Gospel of John and the Apocalypse as works of the heretic Cerinthus. Epiphanius gave these people a name of opprobrium, Ἄλογοι ('without reason, without the logos'). The Roman bishop Gaius, whose orthodoxy is beyond dispute, also rejects the Fourth Gospel and the Apocalypse as gnostic-Montanist writings, as Eusebius reports.[1]

such a straightforward statement actually masks an elaborate configuration of a very complex set of data. It may be a plausible configuration, but it is a configuration none the less. In entering into the question of its correctness we now face a situation with regard to the sources which is even knottier than it was just a few years ago. This is largely because of the researches of Alan Brent,[2] who, as we shall see in due time, has challenged the usual construction of the evidence by challenging customary readings and the authenticity of some of the witnesses. The puzzle involves analysing and coordinating evidence from, besides several other minor characters, a group of principals including the people mentioned by Irenaeus in *AH* 3. 11. 9 in the second century; Gaius of Rome, a mysterious group later dubbed the 'Alogi', an alleged lost work of Hippolytus, and Dionysius of Alexandria and some unnamed predecessors mentioned by him in the third century; Eusebius and Epiphanius in the fourth century; Photius of Constantinople in the ninth century; Dionysius bar Salibi in the twelfth century; and Ebed-Jesu in about 1300 (not to mention a sterling cast of nineteenth-and twentieth-century scholars who played roles in formulating the configuration). In order to assess the validity of statements of scholars from Bauer to Culpepper we must have some idea of the sources involved.

1. Irenaeus, as we have seen, describes a group who rejected the Fourth Gospel, primarily, according to his presentation, because of its teaching about the Holy Spirit in the Church. This group must have been active sometime before *c*.180–85. It has become customary to tie this group to Gaius in some way, as precursors, or as a group to which he himself belonged, or as a cipher for Gaius himself. This is despite the facts that, as I have observed, (*a*) we have no evidence that they attributed the Fourth Gospel to Cerinthus, (*b*) no evidence that they attacked the Johannine Apocalypse, and (*c*) common assertions to the contrary notwithstanding

---

[1] E. Haenchen, *John 1* (Philadelphia, 1984), 23–4.

[2] A. Brent, *Hippolytus and the Roman Church in the Third Century: Communities in Tension before the Emergence of a Monarch-Bishop*, VCSuppl. 31 (Leiden, 1995), esp. 131–84.

Irenaeus considered them to be not fellow orthodox believers but heretics, on a level with the Marcionites and Valentinians.

2. In the Jerusalem library (*HE* 6. 20. 1–3) Eusebius had come across a copy of work entitled *Dialogue with Proclus*, a Montanist, by a certain Gaius, which Eusebius placed in Rome during the episcopacy of Zephyrinus (199–217, *HE* 2. 25. 7; 3. 31. 4). Though Eusebius does not seem to know much about Gaius,[3] he does call him a churchman (ἐκκλησιαστικὸς ἀνήρ, *HE* 2. 25. 6) and judged from his *Dialogue* that Gaius was a 'very learned person' (λογιωτάτου, *HE* 6. 20. 3). He does not ascribe a Church office to him. Eusebius cited this work several times for the interesting titbits it contained, both from Gaius and from Proclus. Among these is Gaius' description of Cerinthus' heresy and the charge that Cerinthus wrote some revelations which he attributed to a great apostle.

Moreover, Cerinthus, who through revelations attributed to the writing of a great apostle, lyingly introduces portents to us as though shown him by angels, and says that after the resurrection the kingdom of Christ will be on earth and that humanity living in Jerusalem will again be the slave of lust and pleasure. He is the enemy of the scriptures of God and in his desire to deceive says that the marriage feast will last a thousand years. (Eusebius, *HE* 3. 28. 2)

No connection with the Apocalypse of John is explicitly made in this quotation, nor does Eusebius here or elsewhere explicitly make the connection,[4] though it would not take much reading between the lines to make one. Scholars have found various ways of viewing this report as not affirming that Gaius believed Cerinthus to have authored the Johannine Revelation. It would be possible to hold that Gaius knew of an apocalypse composed by Cerinthus but under the name of an apostle, which detailed the expectation of a carnal, earthly kingdom lasting a thousand years, or that Gaius is saying that Cerinthus claimed support for his sensual millennium from the Johannine Apocalypse. Nevertheless, many have concluded that the apocalypse Gaius speaks of here is indeed the Apocalypse of John, which he attributed to Cerinthus. This may be supported from the next source.

3. Later, in book 7, Eusebius reports on a controversy which arose over the Apocalypse of John in Egypt, in which Dionysius of Alexandria participated shortly after the midpoint of the third century. The controversy involved the teaching of a future kingdom of Christ on earth. A local bishop

---

[3] He apparently did not find a copy of Gaius' book in the Caesarean library but came upon it at the library at Jerusalem (6. 20. 1–3), and reveals nothing about him from other sources. Later statements which ascribe an ecclesiastical office to Gaius do not come from Eusebius. I shall return to this matter later.

[4] R. M. Grant, 'Ancient and Modern Questions about Authenticity', in B. H. McLean (ed.), *Origins and Method: Towards a New Understanding of Judaism and Christianity. Essays in Honour of John C. Hurd*, JSNT Sup. 86 (Sheffield, 1993), 295–301, at 297, thinks Eusebius does not mention Gaius' rejection of Revelation because 'he fails to understand that Gaius was writing not about "Cerinthus" but about Revelation (3. 28. 2) and was the source of Dionysius (7. 25. 1–3; cf. 3. 28. 4)'.

named Nepos, lately deceased, had written a book promoting a chiliastic reading of the book of Revelation, and Dionysius travelled to the area and met with his defenders. Here Eusebius quotes Dionysius, who speaks of an earlier criticism of the Johannine Apocalypse.

Some indeed of those before our time (πρὸ ἡμῶν) rejected and altogether impugned the book, examining it chapter by chapter and declaring it to be unintelligible and illogical, and its title false. For they say that it is not John's, no, nor yet an apocalypse (unveiling), since it is veiled by its heavy, thick curtain of unintelligibility; and that the author of this book was not only not one of the apostles, nor even one of the saints or those belonging to the Church, but Cerinthus, the same who created the sect called 'Cerinthian' after him, since he desired to affix to his own forgery a name worthy of credit. (Dionysius of Alexandria, in Eusebius, *HE* 7. 25. 2)[5]

The resemblance is so close between this report and the words of Gaius that it is easy to conclude that the 'some before us' of whom Dionysius speaks were, or included, Gaius of Rome. It must be said, however, that this is not the only possible conclusion. Dionysius goes on to give certain details about Cerinthus' teaching that are not contained in the excerpt preserved by Eusebius from Gaius' *Dialogue*. And Dionysius is not forthcoming about the identity of these predecessors. It is conceivable that he is referring to another group, perhaps to earlier participants in the debate in Egypt over the Apocalypse of John, who themselves might have had access to Gaius' *Dialogue*, or some other record of Cerinthus' beliefs, and who might have made the leap from Cerinthus' 'revelations' to the Revelation of John. At any rate, we may be sure that, before Dionysius wrote, someone had taken the step of attributing the Apocalypse of John to Cerinthus, particularly with reference to its teaching about the thousand years. We note that in everything which concerns Gaius, Dionysius, and Eusebius, the antagonism recorded is aimed solely at the Apocalypse; there is no mention yet of an attribution of the Fourth Gospel to Cerinthus.

4. We come now to Epiphanius of Salamis on Cyprus, writing in *c.*375–7.[6] He devotes a long chapter of his anti-heretical *Panarion* to a sect he calls the 'Alogi' and to concerns raised from their views.

51. 3. 1   Now these Alogi say—this is what I call them. They shall be so called from now on, and let us give them this name, beloved, Alogi. (2) For they believed in the heresy for which \<that\> name \<was a good one\>, since it rejects the books by John. As they do not accept the Word which John preaches, they shall be called Dumb (Ἄλογοι). (3) As complete strangers to the truth's message they deny its purity, and accept neither John's Gospel nor his Revelation.
(4) And if they accepted the Gospel but rejected the Revelation, I would say they might be doing it from scrupulousness, and refusing to accept an 'apocryphon'

---

[5] Oulton's translation in LCL II.

[6] J. F. Dechow, *Dogma and Mysticism in Early Christianity: Epiphanius of Cyprus and the Legacy of Origen*, Patristic Monograph Series, 13 (Macon, Ga., 1988), 66, determines that *Panarion* 48–66 was written in 376.

because of the deep and difficult sayings in the Revelation. (5) But since they do not accept the books in which St John actually proclaimed his Gospel, it must be plain to everyone that they and their kind are the ones of whom St John said in his General Epistles, 'It is the last hour and ye have heard that Antichrist cometh; even now, lo, there are many Antichrists'. (6) For they offer excuses [for their behaviour]. Knowing, as they do, that St John was an apostle and the Lord's beloved, that the Lord rightly revealed the mysteries to him, and <that he> leaned upon his breast, they are ashamed to contradict him and try to object to these mysteries for a different reason. For they say that they are not John's composition but Cerinthus', and have no right to a place in the church.[7] (51. 3. 1–6)

He deals with three interrelated objections to the Fourth Gospel on the part of the Alogi, and with three objections to different parts of the Revelation. I here briefly summarize the contradictions with scripture alleged by the 'Alogi', according to the presentation of Epiphanius, three against John, three against the Apocalypse:

I*a* [John gives a chronology after Jesus' baptism which differs from that of the other Gospels.] 'And what did he say?' they argue, 'In the beginning was the Word . . .' [then, after citing several verses from John 1 and 2, moving quickly from the baptism to the wedding in Cana] But the other evangelists say that he spent forty days in the wilderness tempted by the devil, and then came back and chose his disciples. (51. 4. 5–10; cf. 21. 15–16).

I*b* Not understanding the meaning of the Gospels they say, 'Why have the other evangelists said that Jesus fled to Egypt from Herod, came back after his flight and remained at Nazareth, and then, after receiving the baptism, went into the wilderness, and returned after that, and after his return began to preach? But the Gospel which was issued under John's name lies,' they say. 'After "The Word was made flesh and dwelt among us" and a few other things, it says at once that there was a wedding in Cana of Galilee'. (17. 11–18. 1).[8]

But these people say that the Gospel according to John is non-canonical (ἀδιάθετον) because it did not mention these events—I mean the events of the forty-day temptation—and they do not see fit to accept it, since they are misguided about everything, and mentally blind. (51. 18. 6)

II Again, they also accuse the holy evangelist—or rather, they accuse the Gospel itself—because, they say, 'John said that the Savior kept two Passovers over a two-year period, but the other evangelists describe one Passover.' (51. 22. 1; cf. 28. 6; 30. 14)

III But again, these people are not ashamed to take arms against the things St John has said, supposing that they can overthrow the truth, but unaware that they are attacking themselves rather than the sound doctrine. For they derisively say against

---

[7] The translation is that of F. Williams, *The Panarion of Epiphanius of Salamis*, books 2 and 3 (Leiden, 1994).

[8] Cf. 51. 21. 15–16, 'For even though they say that the evangelists Matthew, Mark and Luke reported that the Savior was brought to the wilderness after his baptism, and that he spent forty days in temptation, and after the temptation heard of John's imprisonment and went to live at Capernaum by the sea—but [then go on to say] that John is lying because he did not speak of this but straight off of the Savior's visit to John [the Baptist], and all the other things John says he did— [even if this is their argument], their entire ignorance of the Gospels' exact words will be evident.'

Revelation, 'What good does John's Revelation do me[9] by telling me about seven angels and seven trumpets'. (Rev. 8: 2; *Panar.* 51. 32. 1–2)

IV Then again, some of them seize on the following text in Revelation, and say in contradiction of it, 'He said, in turn, "Write to the angel of the church in Thyatira [Rev. 2: 18]," and there is no church of Christians in Thyatira. How could he write to a non-existent church?' . . . For since these Phrygians settled there, snatched the simple believers' minds like wolves, and converted the whole town to their sect, those who reject Revelation[10] attacked this text at that time in an effort to discredit it. (51. 33. 1, 3)[11]

V Again, in their endless hunt for texts to give the appearance of discrediting the holy apostle's books—I mean John's Gospel and Revelation and perhaps the Epistles as well, for they too agree with the Gospel and Revelation—these people get excited and quote, 'I saw, and he said to the angel, Loose the four angels which are upon the Euphrates. And I heard the number of the hosts, ten thousand times ten thousand and thousands of thousands, and they were clad in breastplates of fire and sulfur and hyacinth [Rev. 9: 14–15]'. (51. 34. 1–2)

This is what Epiphanius records of the objections of the Alogi. Numbers I*a* and I*b* are really two parts of the same objection, that John leaves out several important incidents from the early life and ministry of Jesus, particularly the forty-day temptation in the wilderness, and seems to contradict the other Evangelists by teaching that Jesus went straight from his baptism to attend a wedding at Cana in Galilee. I shall not give here Epiphanius' replies to these objections. It is notable, however, that for the first time in our sources a single group is mentioned who is said to have opposed both the Gospel and the Apocalypse. It will be noticed that Epiphanius never names any members of this group of 'Alogi', and we cannot tell if he connected the name of Gaius with the predecessors Dionysius mentioned, who had assigned the Apocalypse of John to Cerinthus. Also, though Epiphanius charges that this group rejected both the Gospel and the Apocalypse and assigned them both to Cerinthus, neither Cerinthus nor his views are mentioned in their specific objections to the Johannine books.

5. The next key player is Photius of Constantinople writing in about AD 850, in his book about books, *Bibliotheca*. Photius reports that a note in the margin (ἐν παραγραφαῖς)[12] of a book entitled *On the Essence of the Universe*

---

[9] The use of the first person singular here is one reason some have concluded that Epiphanius' 'Alogi' are a group of one: Gaius. See J. D. Smith, 'Gaius and the Controversy over the Johannine Literature' (Ph.D. diss., Yale University, 1979), 238–9.

[10] 'Those who reject Revelation' is Williams's gloss; the text simply says 'they' and is ambiguous as to whether the Alogi or the Phrygians are the subject.

[11] This objection tells us something about the time and character of the 'Alogian' argument. Epiphanius says 'at that time' there was no church then there, after it was taken over by the Phrygians. But later the non-Montanist church was restored there. Epiphanius saw John's words then as a proof that Revelation was real prophecy, for it predicted the false prophetess Jezebel in Thyatira, a prediction fulfilled in the prophetesses Priscilla, Maximilla, and Quintilla.

[12] Text reprinted in J. B. Lightfoot, *The Apostolic Fathers: Clement, Ignatius, and Polycarp. Revised Texts with Introductions, Notes, Dissertations, and Translations*, 2nd edn., 2 parts in 5 vols. (Grand Rapids, Mich., 1981 repr. of the 1889–90 edn.), i 2. 347–8.

ascribed this book, along with three others, *The Labyrinth, Against the Heresy of Artemon*, and a *Dialogue with Proclus* the Montanist, to Gaius, a certain presbyter who lived in Rome. Photius tells us then that the note went on to say 'that this Gaius was made presbyter of the church in the time of the high-priesthoods (ἀρχιερέων) of Victor and Zephyrinus, but was ordained also bishop of the nations (ἐθνῶν ἐπίσκοπον)' (*Bibl.* 48). This is the first, and the only, notice which gives Gaius an ecclesiastical title.

Apart from a few minor notices, which simply summarized what was known from Eusebius, this was just about the extent of our knowledge of Gaius and the controversy over the Johannine literature prior to 1888. Until that time the majority of scholars did not interpret the fragment from Gaius in Eusebius *HE* 3. 28 to mean that Gaius had rejected the Apocalypse, but concluded instead that Gaius was speaking of another, lost, work actually written by Cerinthus. Indeed, up until this time there was no direct evidence to connect Gaius with Epiphanius' Alogi, certainly not to their rejection of the Fourth Gospel. This was not only the position of scholarship, it was the uniform position of Christian historians at least since the time of Eusebius. That is, prior to the twelfth century, there is no notice that Gaius of Rome, the author of the *Dialogue with Proclus*, was ever an opponent of John's Gospel; all the sources who know of him, such as Jerome, Theodoret, and Photius, seem to know him only through the account of Eusebius, and laud him for his stance against Montanism.

6. This all changed, however, in 1888 when John Gwynn, a Syriac scholar at Dublin, published some fragments from the twelfth-century commentary of Dionysius bar Salibi, Jacobite bishop of Amid (d. 1171), on the Apocalypse.[13] It is from this commentary of bar Salibi that we finally learn of a work by 'Hippolytus of Rome' in which he refuted 'the heretic Gaius', an opponent of the Johannine literature. Bar Salibi employs five citations from such a work, in each of which an objection is lodged by Gaius and then refuted by Hippolytus. Here I reproduce Gwynn's translation of those objections (omitting the responses of Hippolytus).

A [Concerning the prediction of Rev. 8: 8 that a great mountain will be cast into the sea and a third of the sea turn to blood.] On this, Caius the heretic objected to this revelation, and said that it is not possible that these things should be, inasmuch as *a thief* that *cometh in the night*, so is the coming of the Lord [1 Thess. 5: 2].[14]

B [Concerning the third part of sun, moon, and stars being darkened, according to Rev. 8: 12.] On this Caius said that, just as in the Flood the heavenly bodies were not taken away and suddenly submerged, thus also is it to be in the end, as it is written [Matt. 24: 37]; and Paul says, *When they shall say, Peace and safety, destruction shall come upon them* [1 Thess. 5: 3].[15]

[13] John Gwynn, 'Hippolytus and his "Heads against Caius"', *Hermathena*, 6 (1888), 397–418.
[14] Ibid. 399.   [15] Ibid. 400.

C [Concerning the locust plague predicted in Rev. 9: 2–3.] On this Caius objects, that according to this, the unrighteous are consumed by the locusts; whereas Scripture has said that *sinners prosper* and the righteous are persecuted, *in the world* [Ps. 73: 12]; and Paul, that the faithful *shall be persecuted and the evil shall flourish, deceiving and being deceived* [2 Tim. 3: 12, 13].

D [Concerning the notice of Rev. 9: 15 that angels are to be released to slay the third part of mankind.] On this Caius says: It is not written that angels are to make war, nor that a third part of men is to perish; but that *nation shall rise against nation* [Matt. 24: 7].

E [Concerning the binding of Satan for a thousand years in Rev. 20: 2–3.] On this Caius the heretic objected: that Satan is bound here, according to that which is written, that Christ *went up into the strong man's house and bound him, and spoiled his goods* for us [Matt. 12: 29].

It is immediately obvious that one of these objections (D) is comparable to that of the Alogi in Epiphanius in *Panarion* 51. 34. 2–8, cited above. The respective replies to these objections also have in common, (*a*) that the four angels at the Euphrates indicate the nations who lived in that vicinity, the Assyrians, Babylonians, Medes, and Persians, and (*b*) that this is supported by Deuteronomy 32: 7–9 which assigned nations to angels. This implies that there must be some link between the sources of Epiphanius and bar Salibi. Either Epiphanius too had Hippolytus' work, and thus the 'Alogi' may in fact be identified with Gaius himself, or, could bar Salibi simply have adapted this from Epiphanius' work? Gwynn concluded that Epiphanius must have used the same Hippolytan source which bar Salibi had, simply without acknowledgement. Special interest attaches to the last objection, as it has to do with the millennium. It seems to presuppose that Gaius interpreted Revelation 20 literally and futuristically (as Justin and Irenaeus had). We know from Eusebius' citation of Gaius from his *Dialogue with Proclus* that Gaius opposed a chiliasm which he attributed to Cerinthus, though this was a chiliasm which featured an earthly cornucopia of sensual delights, which is nowhere visible in the text of the Johannine Apocalypse. There is no charge of a sensual millennium in the bar Salibi extracts, either in the objections nor in the replies, a charge which, if Gaius had made it, both Hippolytus and bar Salibi surely would have included and refuted. Gwynn saw this problem as prohibiting the conclusion that Gaius, in the passage cited by Eusebius, or here, had attributed the Johannine Apocalypse to Cerinthus.[16] There is one more curiosity which pertains to this objection. Gwynn pointed out, in a supplementary note, that a discrepancy exists between Hippolytus' response to this objection and his understanding of the binding of Satan as expressed in the *Commentary on Daniel*.[17]

---

[16] See his discussion, ibid. 405–6.

[17] Ibid. 418. Nor does it comport with the *On Christ and Antichrist* of Hippolytus. See Hill, *Regnum Caelorum*[2], 160–5. It is conceivable then either that this last extract, at least, was taken from a

Gwynn himself believed that these excerpts preserved by bar Salibi from the earlier debate were not literal citations, 'they have the air rather of brief summaries of the arguments on either side: those of Caius ... being stated in the barest possible form, while those of Hippolytus are given in more detail, yet highly compressed'.[18] Gwynn considered that the Hippolytan work in question must have been the *Heads* or *Chapters against Gaius*, a work mentioned for the first time in a catalogue of Hippolytan works compiled by Ebed-Jesu in c.1300. That catalogue also included a work entitled *Defense of the Gospel and Apocalypse according to John*, which is also a close approximation of a title found engraved upon what has traditionally been regarded as a statue of Hippolytus of Rome found on the via Tiburtina in the sixteenth century.[19] Gwynn's discovery seemed clearly to demonstrate that Gaius had indeed opposed the book of Revelation, making a secure link between Gaius and the predecessors of Dionysius of Alexandria, who had rejected Revelation and ascribed it to Cerinthus. But Gwynn had to observe that in the excerpts he published there was no charge that Revelation was written by Cerinthus. He also noted that in one of the responses Hippolytus cited the Fourth Gospel, 'evidently as an authority admitted by his opponent',[20] and this hardly supports the idea that this opponent rejected that Gospel. Gwynn concluded that Gaius had not rejected it, and therefore also that Gaius could not be identified in any way with Epiphanius' Alogi.

It did not take long for scholars such as J. B. Lightfoot, Theodore Zahn, and Adolf von Harnack to respond to the exciting new findings, though they still produced quite varying estimates of Gaius and his relation to the group mentioned by Irenaeus and Epiphanius, to the Johannine books, and to the charge of Cerinthian authorship.[21] Another advance, however, came in 1895, when Rendel Harris reported the existence of another fragment from bar Salibi, this one in a Latin translation made by Dudley Loftus in the seventeenth century (*Bodleian Fell* 6 and 7) from a now lost Syriac manuscript of bar Salibi's *Commentary on the Gospel of John*. In this work Gaius is recorded as criticizing the author of the Fourth Gospel with one of the same objections which Epiphanius had attributed to the Alogi.[22] 'A certain

non-Hippolytan source or, that the Hippolytus who wrote the *Heads against Gaius* was not the same person who wrote the above mentioned works. (On the theory of two Hippolyti, see V. Loi, 'L'identità letteraria di Ippolito di Roma', in V. Loi et al. (eds.), *Ricerche su Ippolito*, Studia Ephemeridis 'Augustinianum', 13 (Rome, 1977), 67–88.)

[18] Gwynn, 'Heads', 404–5.
[19] That inscribed title is [τ]ὰ ὑπὲρ τοῦ κατὰ Ἰωάννου εὐαγγελίου καὶ ἀποκαλύψεως.
[20] Gwynn, 'Heads', 406.
[21] For the history of scholarship see Smith, 'Gaius', 13–115. The most interesting from this period, from our perspective, is that of Harnack, who thought the attribution to Cerinthus was on the basis of his docetism and that the Alogi rejected John as a gnostic document with a docetic Christology (Harnack, *Das Neue Testament*, 63–5; see Smith, 'Gaius', 31–3). Harnack did not, however, believe that Gaius himself either rejected John or ascribed it to Cerinthus, only that he may have used some of the Alogi's arguments against Revelation.
[22] J. R. Harris, *Hermas in Arcadia and Other Essays* (Cambridge, 1896), 48–9.

heretic Gaius criticized John because he did not agree with his fellow evangelists who say [emend to: in that he says] that after the baptism he went to Galilee and performed the miracle of the wine at Cana' (John 2: 1–11)[23]

This, at last, appeared to establish that Gaius had also opposed the Fourth Gospel—though doubts were still possible for the sceptic, for Loftus's translation of the name of Gaius was evidently based on a Syriac text which included it only as 'added in the margin by a later hand'![24] Another Syriac copy of the text discovered later (*British Museum Add.* 12,143) in fact did not include the name of the heretic.[25] The objection is followed in the commentary, however, by a reply from Hippolytus, as in the extracts from the *Commentary on Revelation*. In any case, Harris's discovery was corroborated when T. H. Robinson in 1906 discovered and published a manuscript of bar Salibi's *Commentary on Revelation* which contained its prologue (missing in the manuscript used by Gwynn), in which bar Salibi explicitly named Gaius as one who attributed both Johannine works to Cerinthus.[26] 'Hippolytus of Rome states that a man named Gaius had appeared, who said that neither the Gospel nor yet the Revelation was John's; but that they were the work of Cerinthus the heretic. And the blessed Hippolytus opposed this Gaius, and showed that the teaching of John in the Gospel and Revelation was different from that of Cerinthus.[27]

Bar Salibi's collected extracts have now enabled Gaius of Rome to become a linchpin in an argument concerning the reception of the Fourth Gospel which dominated twentieth-century Johannine scholarship and studies of the history of the New Testament canon. But even within this paradigm, many of the dots lie unconnected, and scholars' attempts to connect them have produced varying outlines. By far the most thorough study of the entire problem was made by Daniel Joseph Smith, jun., in his 1979 Yale dissertation, upon which several later scholars have relied.[28] Smith's conclusions included: (*a*) that Gaius and the Alogi are one and the same: '*The name "Alogi" is entirely a fictitious fabrication by Epiphanius himself and in no way does it represent an historical group.* There is *only one known so called "Alogi"* who rejected the Gospel of John and Revelation and denied that John the Disciple was the author, and *he is the historical Gaius of Rome*';[29] (*b*) that Irenaeus too was

---

[23] Text from an unpublished Syriac MS, *Cod. Paris. syr.* 67, fol. 270, r°, col. 2, contained in the Bibiothèque Nationale in Paris, tr. by Smith, 'Gaius', 200–1, 591.

[24] Smith, 'Gaius', 201. That MS is *Cod. Mus. Britt. Add.* 7184, fo. 2432.

[25] Cf. Brent, *Hippolytus*, 145.

[26] T. H. Robinson, 'The Authorship of the Muratorian Canon', *The Expositor*, 7/1 (1906), 481–95.

[27] Ibid. 487. Dionysius' commentary was finally published in full in 1909 (I. Sedlacek).

[28] Culpepper, *John*, 137 n. 86, calls it 'definitive'.

[29] Smith, 'Gaius', 427; see also ibid. 137, 265–6, etc. Smith had been preceded in this judgement by a number of scholars, including G. Salmon, 'The Commentary of Hippolytus on Daniel', *Hermathena*, 8(1893), 161–90, at 185 n. 11; E. Schwartz, 'Über den Tod der Söhne Zebedaei: Ein Beitrag zur Geschichte des Johannesevangelium', *Abhandlungen der Kgl. Gesellschaft der Wissensch. zu Göttingen*, 7/5 (1904), repr. in K. A. Rengstorf (ed.), *Johannes und Sein Evangelium* (Darmstudt, 1973),

responding to Gaius in *AH* 3. 11. 9, but did not name him because of Gaius' rank and reputation in the Church[30]—Smith conjectures that Gaius' views were thus known before Irenaeus wrote, but that Gaius did not publish his views on the Johannine works until some fifteen or twenty years later when he wrote his *Dialogue with Proclus*[31]—(*c*) that Gaius indeed criticized and rejected both the Johannine Gospel and Apocalypse as non-apostolic and as in conflict with scripture, though this was 'merely incidental or secondary to his primary intense opposition to the recent Montanist influx and influence in Rome',[32] but also (*d*) that Gaius never charged that these Johannine works were written by Cerinthus. He charged only that Cerinthus had used the Apocalypse of John to support his chiliasm. It was instead Hippolytus who, in his *Defense of the Gospel of John and Revelation*, laid this rather outlandish position on Gaius in his acrimonious and overzealous rebuttal.[33] If we accept Smith's interpretation, we shall have to support the conclusion that Gaius was in fact a Roman church leader who opposed the Fourth Gospel and the Apocalypse on critical grounds, but we shall have to modify common views in at least two ways. First we shall have to concentrate this anti-Johannine movement from three sources (Gaius, Irenaeus' Johannophobes, and the Alogi) into one, the presbyter Gaius.[34] Culpepper believes this has been done definitively, 'Recent scholarship has therefore dismissed the Alogoi from the stage of history. We have no evidence of such a group.'[35] The opposition was therefore real and forceful, but quite isolated, and even localized to Rome.[36] Second, we shall have to drop the contention that Gaius, or any possible sympathizers, seriously attributed either the Fourth Gospel or the Apocalypse to Cerinthus the heretic. Culpepper thus acknowledges, in a departure from most earlier advocates of the consensus, that Gaius 'did not challenge [the Fourth Gospel] on theological grounds'.[37] This would include the grounds that it taught gnosticism or docetism. It still remains unclear, however, even on Smith's reading, how or to what extent the following conclusions can be justified:

202–72; P. Ladeuze, *Caius de Rome, le seul Aloge connu*, in *Mélanges Godefroid Kurth* (Liege, 1908); Dom J. Chapman, *John the Presbyter and the Fourth Gospel* (Oxford, 1911), 53 n. 1.

[30] Smith, 'Gaius', 168; Culpepper, *John*, 121.

[31] Smith, 'Gaius', 167, etc.

[32] Ibid. 429; cf. 265.

[33] Ibid. 324–2. 'With regard to the fourth Gospel there is absolutely no evidence to support the summary statements reproduced by Epiphanius and Dionysius bar Salibi. These summary statements have too often provided the point of departure for the studies and arguments of modern scholars and have shaped the interpretations of the only statement of Gaius about Cerinthus which Eusebius preserves from the *Dialogue with Proclus* (*E.H.* iii, 28, 1–2) who had direct access to the *Dialogue* in the library at Aelia' (327).

[34] Smith, 'Gaius', 427, '*All evidence* of criticisms against the Gospel of John and Revelation, their rejection, and denial of apostolic authorship can be traced back to Gaius of Rome and to no other person or group'.

[35] Culpepper, *John*, 122.

[36] Smith, 265, 'Gaius', 'the entire controversy was limited to Rome'.

[37] Culpepper, *John*, 121.

Gaius's standing as a leader of the church at Rome shows that the authority of John and its apostolic authorship were not so firmly established (at least in Rome, from which we have the most evidence for the use of the Gospel in the mid-second century) that it could not be challenged by one of the scholars of the church;[38]

The figure of Gaius . . . shows us that the authority of the Gospel of John was still quite tenuous up to the time of Irenaeus.[39]

The Current Challenge

The perpetual thrill of scholarship is that 'definitive' studies and 'permanent' results do not always last very long. Along came a study in 1995 which threatens to upset the fine balance on the Gaian Controversy thought to have been achieved.

Before talking about Allen Brent, however, one should mention that in 1972–4 Pierre Prigent presented a series of detailed studies of the Hippolytan material in bar Salibi's commentary.[40] Bar Salibi happens to cite Hippolytus fairly often, and in only a portion of these instances does Gaius, or a controversy, figure; most of the Hippolytan excerpts are simply exegetical fragments which bar Salibi cites for their inherent value. Prigent noticed that many of these Hippolytan fragments corresponded to exegesis contained in the exegetical works of Hippolytus, namely the *On Christ and Antichrist* and the *Commentary on Daniel.* Yet other fragments were close to Irenaeus, and others had no parallel in any known work of Hippolytus or any of his contemporaries, and in fact, some seemed to contradict known Hippolytan exegesis. Prigent concluded that bar Salibi did not have direct access to Hippolytus' exegetical treatises but instead used a florilegium of Hippolytan extracts which had been culled from various works. He still assumed, however, that the *Heads against Gaius* was not a part of this florilegium but that bar Salibi had it as a separate work.

The potentially devastating development came in the form of Allen Brent's book on Hippolytus published in 1995. Brent chides Prigent for continuing to assume without good reason that bar Salibi possessed a copy of the κεφάλια and argues that the anti-Gaian material too was part of the catena tradition. Not only this, but Brent argues that the bar Salibi material allegedly stemming from a debate between Hippolytus and Gaius is fictional, the result of Hippolytan pseudepigrapha such as is seen elsewhere in other Eastern literary works.

[38] Ibid. 121; cf. Smith, 'Gaius', 429, 431.
[39] Culpepper, *John*, 122.
[40] Pierre Prigent, 'Hippolyte, Commentateur de l'Apocalypse', *TZ* 28 (1972), 391–412; 'Les Fragments du De Apocalypse d'Hippolyte', *TZ* 29 (1973), 313–33; Prigent and R. Stehly, 'Citations d'Hippolyte trouvée dans le ms. Bodl. Syr 140', *TZ* 30 (1974), 82–5.

That Hippolytus was used as a character in such a dialogue in the East by Barsalîbî should not strike us as surprising. Hippolytus' name was used there to create a number of pseudonymous works, amongst which were κατὰ Βήρωνος καὶ Ἥλικος and περὶ τῆς συντελείας τοῦ κόσμου and the *In Sancta Theophania*. The former represents a rough parallel with Barsalîbî's dialogue since it consists of a number of extracts allegedly from Hippolytus directed against a heresy. Κατὰ Βήρωνος is found as part of a *florilegium* entitled *Doctrina Patrum*, whose original dates from c.A.D. 650, and is preserved in a Latin translation of Anastasius Bibliothecarius.[41]

Brent points to another example of Hippolytan pseudepigrapha in an Arabic manuscript tradition, wherein Hippolytus is cited as *Hippolytus expositor Targumista* or *Hippolytus expositor Syrus Targum*.[42] He also catalogues several Eastern writers from the fifth to seventh centuries who in one way or another identify Hippolytus anachronistically with an earlier age, even the apostolic age, in some kind of 'legend construction'.[43] Of the κεφάλαια against Gaius he says, 'both external and internal considerations preclude it from being anything else than a general exegetical tradition dressed up pseudepigraphically under the cipher-names of "Hippolytus" and "Gaius"'.[44]

What about the Hippolytan works, *Heads or Points against Gaius* and *Defense of the Apocalypse of John and the Gospel* mentioned by Ebed-Jesu in around 1300? Does not Ebed-Jesu attest to the independent existence of these two works, or to the κεφάλαια as a section of the ἀπολογία? Ebed-Jesu, Brent reasons, did not know of either a κεφάλαια or an ἀπολογία apart from what he deduced must lie behind bar Salibi's commentary.[45] The work on the Gospel and Apocalypse of John mentioned on the statue of Hippolytus cannot really support the existence of such a Hippolytan work known to Ebed-Jesu, for the statue reads [τ]ὰ ὑπὲρ τοῦ κατὰ Ἰωάννου εὐαγγελίου καὶ ἀποκαλύψεως, *Matters concerning the Gospel and Apocalypse according to John*.[46] The treatise mentioned in Ebed-Jesu's catalogue has a polemical title, ἀπολογία, and mentions the Apocalypse first, ἀπολογία ὑπὲρ τῆς ἀποκαλύψεως καὶ τοῦ εὐαγγελίου Ἰωάννου. Ebed-Jesu, then, is unaware of the work mentioned on the statue and is instead 'heir to the tradition of

---

[41]   Brent, *Hippolytus*, 178. He refers to Manlio Simonetti, 'Un falso Ippolito nella polemica monotelita', *Vetera Christianorum*, 24 (1987), 113–46, esp. 114–21, in which the author demonstrates that Anastasius Apocrisarius composed 'eight testimonies of St. Hippolytus, bishop of Portus of Rome and martyr of God Christ'.

[42]   Brent, *Hippolytus*, 178–9.

[43]   Ibid. 182–3. These are Theodoret (c.AD 446); Palladius c.AD 421); Andreas of Caesarea (c.AD 500); Cyrillus of Scythopolis (c.AD 555); Leontius of Byzantium (c.AD 620); Pseudo-Chrysostom (no date given).

[44]   Brent, *Hippolytus*, 184.

[45]   Ibid. 170–4.

[46]   Ibid. 172. Brent observes that De Rossi's original transcription of the title on the statue had it beginning with ὑπέρ, but that 'Guarducci has detected a [τ]ά before the ὑπὲρ that means that ἀπολογία was not part of the original title'. He suggests that this treatise might have concerned 'the Johannine dating of the Crucifixion on Passover Day'.

Epiphanius that succeeded in uniting a disparate group of objectors and objections into a composite heresy called the Ἄλογοι. That tradition was later to combine Gaius' objections to Cerinthus' visions recorded in Eusebius with those of other groups who attacked both the *Apocalypse* and the Gospel more directly, and whom Dionysius of Alexandria originally addressed'.[47] Thus,

> Barsalîbî emerges at the end of the production of such a literary legend in which the diversity of attacks on the Johannine Literature, some of which only contained the association with Cerinthus are first reduced by Epiphanius to the views of a particular group, the Ἄλογοι, for whom he constructs a heresy, and then the amorphous group is finally by Barsalîbî given a leader, namely Gaius who in Eusebius attacked Cerinthus' personal visions, and not the *Apocalypse* itself as did the nameless opponents of Dionysius of Alexandria.[48]

> Barsalîbî is arguably dramatizing that tradition in terms of a dialogue between his characters...[49]

As already intimated above, Brent's researches concern Epiphanius as well. Brent rather perceptively argues that Epiphanius was not representing the views of a single individual, Gaius, or even a single group, in his report of the Alogi but was amalgamating various criticisms of the Johannine literature from earlier times and presenting them as if from a single heretical sect.

> Epiphanius...makes it clear that he is constructing a heresy. The Ἄλογοι clearly are not a group of people who define themselves in this way. He makes it clear that this is a title that he is giving to any who reject the 'books of John'. Clearly he is therefore grouping under this one term disparate groups of people not necessarily doctrinally united, such as the Montanists alone.[50]

He is right to observe an

> absence of a specific anti-Montanist polemic on the part of the Ἄλογοι... There is no discussion of the Paraclete passages nor of *Jn.* 21, and the relationship between charisma and Order. Instead the argument for the authenticity of the Fourth Gospel proceeds by Epiphanius reconciling the synoptic chronology with the Johan-

---

[47] Ibid. 173.

[48] Ibid. 176.

[49] Ibid. 178. Because bar Salibi is dealing with a 'literary and historical problem', Brent believes we are 'justified in claiming that Barsalîbî has in his preface gone beyond what the text before him will actually justify and entered the realm of reconstructive speculation encouraged by the Eusebian fragments' (147).

[50] Ibid. 140. He thinks 51. 3. 3–4 shows that Epiphanius has at least two groups in mind, one which rejected both Johannine works, one which rejected only the Apocalypse. He thinks Epiphanius is talking about Montanists in 51. 33. 1–3 who criticized Revelation because of its prophecy about Thyatira (142–3). This is more difficult to agree with. What about the use of the singular in the citation in 51. 32. 2, which Schwartz, Smith, and others have seen as pointing to a single individual? 'The phrase τί με φασίν occurs only in 51,32 to introduce an objection and not generally' (Brent, *Hippolytus*, 140 n. 95). On Brent's view, some of the objections could have come from individuals, just not always the same individual.

nine over the date of the Passover, justifying the omission of synoptic incidents whilst showing that there is chronological space to allow for what is omitted to have happened, etc. Moreover, the association of these kinds of chronological objections to the Fourth Gospel with a group denying the gifts of the Spirit is peculiar to Epiphanius...which further evidences our claim that he is constructing a quite composite heresy. (143)[51]

Brent even suggests that some of the criticisms might come from 'Porphyry, Celsus, and Philosabbatius', who are named by Epiphanius as enemies of the Gospel accounts in 51. 8. 1.[52]

If Brent is correct, the entire edifice of opposition to the Fourth Gospel based around Gaius of Rome completely implodes, leaving scarcely a trace. But is he correct? The evaluation of some of the evidence requires an expertise far beyond that of the present writer. The input of other orientalists on the history of Hippolytan legends and traditions in the East leading up to bar Salibi is much to be desired. But, while in several instances I honestly cannot agree with (or necessarily even follow), his specific arguments, I do have to say that Brent scores some very important points and may be correct overall. He may well be correct that Epiphanius was amalgamating different sources in his portrait of the Alogi. And there are some factors, only touched on or not mentioned at all by Brent, which I think support his case.

Whether Epiphanius had a treatise by Hippolytus is debatable. But we can be sure that he had a copy of Irenaeus' *Against Heresies* and was quite familiar with Eusebius' *Historia Ecclesiastica*. From these two sources alone he could have put together quite a bit. Unmentioned until now is the section in *HE* 3. 24. 5–17 in which Eusebius records an early tradition about the origin of John's Gospel. I have argued elsewhere and shall argue below that Eusebius' source is Papias of Hierapolis. Epiphanius would not have known the ultimate source, but there are telltale signs in chapter 51 that Epiphanius was well aware of this section of the *HE*.[53] It contains the tradition that John wrote his Gospel partly to pass on what the other Evangelists had omitted concerning the beginning of Jesus' ministry, namely, what Jesus had done after his baptism but before John the Baptist was cast into prison (John 3: 24; *HE* 3. 24. 11–12). Eusebius observes that 'If this be understood the gospels no longer appear to disagree, because that according to John contains the first of the acts of Christ and the others the narrative of what he did at the end of the period' (*HE* 3. 24. 11–12). In *HE* 3. 28 Epiphanius would have read the association of Cerinthus with certain 'revelations as from a great apostle', and from 7. 25 he would have known that 'some before us', as Dionysius put it, had actually attributed the Apocalypse of

---

[51] Ibid. 143.
[52] Ibid. 143–4.
[53] Cf. 51. 4. 10; 6. 5; 12. 2; 21. 1; 21. 18, 24.

John the apostle to Cerinthus. He also knew there existed at some time a group which had rejected the Fourth Gospel, as they had been mentioned by Irenaeus, *AH* 3. 11. 9. Epiphanius' knowledge of this passage in Irenaeus, either first or secondhand, is plain from the concluding paragraphs of his chapter on the Alogi.

But since these people have not received the Holy Spirit they are spiritually condemned for not understanding the things of the Spirit, and choosing to speak against the words of the Spirit. This is because they do not know the gifts of grace in the holy church, which the Holy Spirit, the holy apostles, and the holy prophets have expounded truly and soundly, with understanding and a sound mind. One of the apostles and prophets, St John, has shared his sacred gift with the holy church, through the Gospel, the Epistles and the Revelation. But these people are liable to the scriptural penalty, 'Whoso blasphemeth against the Holy Spirit it will not be forgiven him, neither in this world nor in the world to come' (Matt. 12: 32). For they have gone to war against the words the Spirit has spoken.

Epiphanius' ultimate dependence upon *AH* 3. 11. 9 is patent. These people do not accept the Holy Spirit and His gifts, and in particular the gift given to John as manifested in his writings (though Irenaeus mentions only the Gospel). Both accounts accuse the offenders of sinning against the Spirit, the sin which has no forgiveness. Thus Irenaeus' notice of these opponents of the Fourth Gospel and Dionysius' report of those who ascribed the Johannine Apocalypse to Cerinthus could easily have been combined, quite apart from dependence upon a lost work by Hippolytus. Many have speculated about whether Epiphanius got his name for this group from Hippolytus.[54] In fact, it may be that he was inspired in his naming by the charges against the Apocalypse reported by Dionysius. Dionysius says that some had rejected the apocalypse, 'declaring it to be unintelligible and illogical (ἄγνωστόν τε καὶ ἀσυλλόγιστον), and its title false' (*HE* 7. 25. 1). Based on the idea that these people were the same group mentioned by Irenaeus, the alpha-privative adjectives they used to slander John's Apocalypse could have given Epiphanius the idea for his pejorative Ἄλογοι, aptly taken from John 1: 1, 14.

Epiphanius shows his awareness of two or three other relevant portions of Irenaeus' *AH* in this chapter. On the question of the number of Passovers recorded in the Gospels, Irenaeus had recorded in *AH* 2. 22. 3 an earlier controversy with the Valentinians, mentioned above.[55] Epiphanius knows and even refers to this controversy (without mentioning Irenaeus)[56] in 51.

---

[54] Lightfoot, *AF* i/2. 394; Harris, *Hermas in Arcadia*, 43–57 at 52. Smith, 'Gaius', 217–21, however, holds that it was Epiphanius' own invention.

[55] Epiphanius argues there are three (2. 13; 6. 4; 11. 55, etc.—John 5: 1 being another feast, not the Passover). 'The acceptable year of the Lord' was for the Valentinians the alleged single year of Jesus' ministry; for Irenaeus it was the whole period of Gospel preaching; for Epiphanius it is 'a year without opposition', i.e. the first year of Jesus' ministry (51. 25. 1).

[56] The omission is probably because he disagreed with Irenaeus' interpretation, which saw the four Passovers (Irenaeus included John 5: 1), and potentially more, of Jesus' ministry as implying that the Lord lived past 40.

23. 3–4, 'This is the downfall of the earlier Valentinian sect and certain others, with their fictitious record of the thirty aeons they thought they could compare with the years of the Savior's life, making it possible for them to write the story of their aeons and first principles, if you please. (4) For in fact, it was in the *thirty-third* year of his incarnation that the Only-begotten suffered for us...' After some intervening chronological study, Epiphanius returns to this episode, 'Valentinus, first of all, is at once <exposed> as a schemer, since he expects <to prove> to us, from the years of the Savior's rearing and coming to manhood, that there are thirty aeons. He does not realize that the Savior did not live for only thirty years' (51. 28. 1). Jesus in fact was 32 years and 74 days old when he was cruci-fied, so 'Valentinus stands refuted, and the many who are just as foolish. The ones who reject John's Gospel have also been refuted' (51. 28. 3–4). Thus he regards the Valentinian controversy as a precursor to that of those who reject John's Gospel, partly because of bad chronology.

Now we come to Origen. The problem of John's omission of the forty-day temptation after Jesus' baptism is not addressed in Irenaeus or Euse-bius. But Origen had mentioned it in book 10 of his *Commentary on John* and had given a different answer, one which, we might imagine, may not have satisfied Epiphanius.[57]

Those who accept the four Gospels, and who do not consider that their apparent discrepancy is to be solved anagogically (by mystical interpretation), will have to clear up the difficulty, raised above, about the forty days of the temptation, a period for which no room can be found in any way in John's narrative; and they will also have to tell us when it was that the Lord came to Capernaum...Now, if we ask when Christ was first in Capernaum, our respondents, if they follow the words of Matthew, and of the other two, will say, After the temptation, when, 'leaving Nazareth, He came and dwelt in Capernaum by the sea.' But how can they show both the statements to be true, that of Matthew and Mark, that it was because He heard that John was delivered up that He departed into Galilee, and that of John, found there, after a number of other transactions, subsequent to His stay at Caper-naum, after His going to Jerusalem, and His journey from there to Judaea, that John was not yet cast into prison, but was baptizing in Aenon near Salim?

If the discrepancy between the Gospels is not solved, we must give up our trust in the Gospels, as being true and written by a divine spirit, or as records worthy of credence, for both these characters are held to belong to these works...The stu-dent, staggered at the consideration of these things, will either renounce the attempt to find all the Gospels true, and not venturing to conclude that all our information about our Lord is untrustworthy, will choose at random one of them to be his

---

[57] We know that Origen and his methods were generally despised by Epiphanius, as is mani-fested at great length in *Panarion* 64. Dechow, *Dogma and Mysticism*, 13, regards Origen as the focal point of Epiphanius' *Panarion*; 'Epiphanius was sure that Origen was the epitome and exemplar of all heresies from the beginning of time'; 'All heresies, in Epiphanius' mind, are ultimately related to the mode or content of Origen's thought'. There is little doubt that Epiphanius was at least familiar with Origen's great commentary on John.

guide; or he will accept the four, and will consider that their truth is not to be sought for in the outward and material letter. (*C. John.* 10. 2).[58]

It has been argued by Schwartz and by Smith that this shows that Origen knew of the criticisms of Gaius against the Fourth Gospel.[59] This is possible (or he could have known a refutation by Hippolytus), but it is interesting that Origen never hints that this problem of Gospel disharmony reflects more negatively on John's Gospel than on the others. The troubled student, he says, will either randomly choose to follow the account of one Gospel, or will accept the four and try to find their truth outside the material letter. Epiphanius, on the other hand, found his truth within the material letter, so to speak, and the proof of his discovery takes up a great deal of space. Interestingly, one may fairly recognize other points in common, treated by Epiphanius and by Origen in the tenth book of his commentary on John,[60] with Origen generally taking an anagogical approach to the problems and Epiphanius a historical/literal one.[61] Most significant is the fact, which neither Schwartz nor Smith noted, that Origen mentions a discrepancy between John and the other Gospels on the number of Passovers, and trips of Jesus to Jerusalem, recorded in each.

In *Commentary on John* 10. 14 Origen begins, 'We must not, however, fail to enquire into the statement that the Passover of the Jews was at hand, when the Lord was at Capernaum with His mother and His brothers and His disciples' (John 2: 13). Then he points out that in the other Gospels 'after the stay at Capernaum it is long till we come to any mention of the Passover'. In John, Jesus' trip to Jerusalem for this Passover is the occasion for his cleansing of the Temple, and this is, after the miracle at Cana, his second sign, 'while the other Evangelists narrate a similar incident almost at the end and in connection with the story of the passion' (10. 15). Origen then writes out long sections from the other Gospels

in order to exhibit the discrepancy at this part of our Gospel. Three of the Gospels place these incidents, which we supposed to be the same as those narrated by John, in connection with one visit of the Lord to Jerusalem. While John, on the other hand, places them in connection with two visits which are widely separated from each other and between which were various journeys of the Lord to other places. I consider it impossible for those who admit nothing more than the history in their interpretation to show that these discrepant statements are in harmony with each other. If any one considers that we have not given a sound exposition, let him write a reasoned rejoinder to his declaration of ours.

[58] The translation of Alan Menzies, *ANF*, p. x.

[59] Schwartz, 'Über den Tod', 44–5; Smith, 'Gaius', 195–6.

[60] Such as the apparent discrepancy between Jesus calling Andrew and Peter in Judea after the baptism in John 1: 40–2 and his calling of them in Galilee by the Lake in Matt. 4: 18–22 (*C. John* 10. 6; *Panar* 51. 15. 7–12; 17. 4, 9).

[61] Origen's allegorical method of interpretation is repeatedly cited against him in *Panar.* 64; it had been the object of anti-Origenists like Eustathius of Antioch, one of Epiphanius' predecessors, in his *On the Ventriloquist against Origen* 22 (see Dechow, *Dogma and Mysticism*, 117–18).

What Epiphanius writes in *Panarion* 51 could practically be seen as just such a 'reasoned rejoinder'! Epiphanius shows from a detailed 'history' of Gospel events how 'everything is said truthfully and in agreement by the four evangelists' (51. 21. 18).[62] When Epiphanius cites the second objection of the Alogi against John, we seem to hear echoes of Origen's voice.

> Again they also accuse the holy evangelist—or rather, they accuse the Gospel itself—because, they say, 'John said that the Savior kept two Passovers over a two-year period, but the other evangelists describe one Passover.' (2) In their boorishness they fail to realize that the Gospels not only acknowledge that there are two Passovers as I have fully shown, but that they speak of two earlier Passovers, and of that other Passover on which the Savior suffered, so that there are three Passovers, over three years, from the time of Christ's baptism and first preaching until the cross. (51. 22. 1–2)

It is almost as if Epiphanius found his historical clue for answering Origen in Eusebius' *Historia Ecclesiastica*, 3. 24, where he read an ancient tradition discovered by Eusebius that said that John's purpose was to record what the Lord did at the beginning of the Gospel, before the Baptist had been thrown in prison.

Does this prove that Epiphanius had no 'Alogi' at all, and that he simply put together past criticisms of the Johannine Gospel and Apocalypse, possibly based on the suspicion that there must have been, behind all these disparate criticisms, some single, heretical source? In any case, one might posit that a supposed work of Johannine criticism by Gaius, or by Hippolytus, would add little to what we can be confident Epiphanius already knew from two sources he certainly knew quite well (Irenaeus and Eusebius) and one which he must have known to some degree (Origen's *C. John*). In other words, one could hold that Epiphanius has done what many modern scholars have done with the evidence available to them from Irenaeus and Eusebius, that is, to link together a group who opposed John's Gospel largely because they opposed its view of the Spirit, a comment made by Gaius about Cerinthus's adherence to a carnal chiliasm, and Dionysius' notice that some of his predecessors had rejected the book of Revelation as unintelligible and as authored by the heretic Cerinthus. Epiphanius may have lumped these all together to deduce the existence of a sect which rejected these Johannine books (if any source before him connected the two, we no longer have a record of it) and attributed them to Cerinthus; then he may have brought in certain objections which he knew had been raised (some even by Origen) against each of these Johannine books, giving his own defences of the truth, in some cases no doubt relying on previous exegetical tradition.

---

[62] Also 51. 30. 14 at the conclusion, 'the Gospels are in agreement, and no evangelist contradicts another'.

'Legitimate' Results

It is understandable that some may want to withhold full endorsement of Brent's position, pending further studies. But it should be clear in any case that we can no longer simply accept at face value the earlier reconstructions of the controversy based on the assumption of the authenticity of a lost work against Gaius by Hippolytus, known in common to Epiphanius and Dionysius bar Salibi. While holding Brent's conclusions somewhat lightly, what can we legitimately say about Gaius and the controversy over the Johannine literature which surfaced around the beginning of the third century?

IRENAEUS' JOHANNOPHOBES

First, under the newer or the older reading, the group mentioned by Irenaeus is a red herring in this debate. These people are indeed perhaps the first *bona-fide* Johannophobes known to us,[63] but Irenaeus considers them to be as much outsiders to the true faith as the Marcionites and the Valentinians. Very likely they are themselves adoptionists like Cerinthus, as well as being deniers of the Paraclete's work in the Church and, in Irenaeus' view, blasphemers against the Holy Spirit. To connect them with Gaius of Rome or with any opposition to the Johannine writings supposedly emanating from orthodox circles is simply unsupportable.

'GAIUS' AND THE 'GNOSTICISM' OF JOHN

Second, in all the back-and-forth about who said what about the Fourth Gospel and the Apocalypse, we cannot lose sight of the fact that no one in any corner of these debates, be it Irenaeus' Johannophobes, Gaius, or the Alogi, lays any charge of gnosticism or docetism against this Gospel. This absence of allegations of gnosticism has also been a constant feature of the evidence and does not rely upon acceptance of either Smith's or Brent's reconstructions. When Sanders said that the Alogi 'virtually admitted the correctness of Valentinian exegesis of the Gospel',[64] he was being carried along by a theory; he was not responding to the data surrounding the opposition to the Fourth Gospel in antiquity. In order to find a link between John and gnosticism connected with Gaius one must either speculate on the mental processes of those long dead,[65] or assert a dubiously close relation-

---

[63] It is entirely possible that they could be the only *bona-fide* Johannophobes to emerge from this whole debate. The two objections lodged by Epiphanius' Alogi against the Fourth Gospel, even if representing genuine objections, may have as their ultimate source either the pagan criticisms of critics like Celsus and Porphyry, or may be from the writing desks of Christian scholars like Origen interested in critical questions which were of little or no broader concern.

[64] J. N. Sanders, *The Fourth Gospel in the Early Church* (Cambridge, 1943), 66.

[65] W. Bauer, *Orthodoxy and Heresy in Earliest Christianity* (Philadelphia, 1971), 207–8, 'He reproaches it for its contradictions with the other gospels, plays Mark off against John (Epiphanius *Her.* 51. 6),

ship between gnosticism and Montanism,[66] or simply assume it from the mere attribution to Cerinthus. But as we have seen, the charge that Gaius actually made this attribution is almost certainly bogus. Whatever link was made between Cerinthus and the Johannine literature was made originally concerning the Apocalypse, not the Gospel, and had to do with the question of chiliasm. It could only have been applied to the Gospel on the supposition of a common authorship of the two works. But this is probably beside the point, for even Smith concludes that Gaius never did attribute any of the Johannine works to Cerinthus.[67] Smith thinks the false charge that he did so came from the excesses of Hippolytus' passionate attack on Gaius. Brent would credit the illusion to the historicizing efforts of Epiphanius (which is where I would tend to place it). It is not until Epiphanius that we hear of such a charge against the Fourth Gospel, and not until bar Salibi that it is attributed to Gaius.

Gaius and the Gospel according to John

Here I should also point out that the very notion that Gaius rejected or opposed the Fourth Gospel is by no means secure. The first explicit notice of it is from bar Salibi in the twelfth century, though he may be relying on older information, of the inherent trustworthiness of which we have already gained some idea. It is possible, though by no means certain, that Dionysius of Alexandria had read Gaius' *Dialogue with Proclus*. But the only writer in antiquity of whom we can be certain that he read Gaius' *Dialogue* and wrote about it, is Eusebius of Caesarea. It is easy to say that Eusebius wanted to conceal a respected, ecclesiastical author's opposition to the Fourth Gospel because of the embarrassment it would cause. And yet there are good reasons to think that, if Gaius had opposed this Gospel in his *Dialogue*, Eusebius would have reported it. Gaius, as Eusebius calls him an ἐκκλησιαστικὸς ἀνήρ (*HE* 2. 25. 6; cf. 6. 20. 1, 3), is just the sort of

---

and betrays in general an extraordinary sympathy for the earthly life of Jesus as presented by the synoptics. Of course, the reasons thus advanced are not the true cause for his rejection of John. Rather, he sensed in the gospel of John a spirit of heresy with which his Roman-ecclesiastical attitude could not be reconciled.'

[66] Haenchen, *John 1*, 23–4. Where do we find Haenchen's anti-gnostic churchman 'training his guns' on a gnostic Gospel (18)?

[67] I observe again that the criticisms themselves in Epiphanius and bar Salibi do not link the Gospel, or the Apocalypse, with Cerinthus, and that some of them seem to point in another direction. The fragment from bar Salibi's *Commentary on the Gospel of John* reads as follows: 'A certain heretic [Gaius] censured John because he did not agree with his companions when he says that after the baptism he went into Galilee and performed the miracle of the wine at Cana'. Here the critic speaks of 'John' and his 'companions', not of Cerinthus. Similarly in *Panar*. 51. 22. 1, 'Again, they also accuse the holy evangelist—or rather, they accuse the Gospel itself—because, they say, "John said that the Savior kept two Passovers over a two-year period, but the other evangelists describe one Passover."' Cerinthus is not mentioned, only John, as if he is author. Cf. 51. 32. 1 on Rev.

person in whose 'canon' of scripture Eusebius would have been interested. He announces already in 3. 3. 2 that, as his narrative proceeds, 'I will take pains to indicate successively which of the ἐκκλησιαστικῶν συγγραφέων in each period used any of the doubtful books, and what they said about the canonical and accepted scriptures (περὶ τῶν ἐνδιαθήκων καὶ ὁμολογουμένων γραφῶν) and what about those which are not such.' In this very section he makes a point about the book of Hebrews which appears to have to do directly with Gaius: 'And the fourteen letters of Paul are obvious and plain, yet it is not right to ignore that some dispute the Epistle to the Hebrews, saying that it was rejected (ἠθετήκασι) by the church at Rome as not being by Paul, and I will expound at the proper time what was said about it by our predecessors' (3. 3. 4–5). When Eusebius introduces Gaius in his own context (his previous citations from the *Dialogue* had been made to illustrate earlier persons referred to in the work), he begins by informing the reader, 'Now there flourished at that time many λόγιοι καὶ ἐκκλησιαστικοὶ ἄνδρες, and the letters which they penned to one another are still extant and easily accessible' (6. 20. 1), and Eusebius says these letters are preserved in the Jerusalem library equipped by Alexander. Of such men he mentions Berylus of Bostra and Hippolytus, 'who also presided over another church somewhere'. And then he informs us of Gaius,

And there has reached us also a Dialogue of Gaius, a very learned person (λογιωτάτου ἀνδρός) (which was set a-going at Rome in the time of Zephyrinus), with Proclus the champion of the heresy of the Phrygians. In which, when curbing the recklessness and audacity of his opponents in composing new Scriptures, he mentions only thirteen epistles of the holy Apostle, not numbering the Epistle to the Hebrews with the rest; seeing that even to this day among the Romans there are some who do not consider it to be the Apostle's. (3. 20. 3)

Thus we see that Eusebius did consider Gaius to be one of the 'ecclesiastical men' whose views on the NT books interested him, and his notice in 3. 3. 4–5 about some not accepting the Epistle to the Hebrews as Paul's due to a position held at Rome had to do with Gaius himself. In this light, Eusebius' 'silence' about any possible rejection of the Johannine literature, the Gospel in particular, would be genuinely puzzling. He was not averse to recording exceptional positions on New Testament books, and did in fact do so with regard to Gaius and his omission of Hebrews.

If Gaius ever lodged the sort of complaints about the Fourth Gospel's discrepancies with the Synoptics that appear in Epiphanius and bar Salibi, we may be virtually certain that it came in some book other than the *Dialogue with Proclus*. But that these objections may have come from disparate sources and not have been connected with Gaius at all is a position which, particularly since Brent's work, must be taken seriously. Then Gwynn's old observation about 'Hippolytus' referring to John 10: 11 and

12: 35–6 in the first of his replies to the objections of 'Gaius' to the Apocalypse, implying his 'opponent's' reception of John,[68] might just be an observation of one of the 'seams' still visible in the artificial assemblage.

If it was the threat of Montanism which drove Gaius to reject the Johannine books, as Smith thinks, then at the very least it is doubtful whether many of his contemporaries would have followed his course. The idea that the Gospel discrepancies in question could by themselves have stirred such passion as to force many Church members to abandon the Fourth Gospel, even if moved by the threat of Montanism, has inherent implausibilities. Three specific objections against John's contents survive which possibly arose from such a campaign, and two of these are aspects of the same objection. That Christian teachers before Gaius encountered difficulties like these in reconciling the Fourth Gospel to the Gospels of Matthew, Mark, and Luke in the second century is only natural, and it can be documented, so I shall later argue, from the time of Papias (*HE* 3. 24. 5–13; 3. 39. 15–16). This can also be plainly seen in writers such as Irenaeus, Clement of Alexandria, the *Muratorian Fragment*, and Origen. Such problems seem to have been exploited by pagan critics like Celsus. But, so far as we can tell from these other sources, the questions were not seen as posing a particular problem for John, as opposed to the other Gospels. It in fact appears that the advantage was at times held to rest if anywhere in John's favour, as it is Mark's 'order' which needs to be explained in the tradition cited by Papias in *HE* 3. 39. 15. Second, given even the wide usage of the Fourth Gospel observed so far, we shall have a hard time believing that these differences by themselves could have forced many within the Church to conclude along with 'the Alogi' that John is uncanonical (ἀδιάθετον) or unacceptable.[69] Finally, whether or not Gaius did turn against the Johannine Gospel and Apocalypse in his battle against the New Prophecy, it is a fact that other ecclesiastical antagonists made use of these Johannine books in battling the same foe (Epiphanius' anonymous source, *Panar.* 48. 10. 1–2; Apollonius of Ephesus, Eusebius *HE* 5. 18. 14).

GAIUS' ORTHODOXY AND ECCLESIASTICAL OFFICE

As to Gaius himself, if he ever did critique any portion of the Johannine literature on the basis of alleged contradictions with the rest of scripture (and this is very doubtful, at least as regards the Gospel), we may be sure he did not do so as a representative of the Roman hierarchy. As we know by now, the significance of Gaius for twentieth-century attempts at gauging the (non-)reception of the Fourth Gospel in Rome during the second century is

---

[68] Gwynn, 'Heads', 406, 408; also Brent, *Hippolytus*, 145.

[69] *Panar.* 51. 18. 6, 'But these people say that the Gospel according to John is non-canonical (ἀδιάθετον) because it did not mention these events—I mean the events of the forty-day temptation—and they do not see fit to accept it...'

hard to overstate. And this has had to do not only with a particular construal of what he taught, but also with his orthodoxy and his ecclesiastical
status as presbyter or even as bishop.[70] The inference is usually drawn that
the position of the Johannine Gospel in the orthodox churches, at least in
Rome, at the beginning of the third century must have been quite precarious if a presbyter, or bishop, in Rome could disparage and reject them
without fear of consequences.[71] But there are several aspects of both the
premises and the inference which call for some attention.

First, all we know about Gaius' orthodoxy is deduced solely from Eusebius[72] who calls him 'an ecclesiastical man' (ἐκκλησιαστικὸς ἀνήρ, *HE*
2. 25. 6) and obviously appreciates his learned disputation with Proclus the
Montanist. There is no question that from his *Dialogue* Eusebius judged
Gaius to be of sound ecclesiastical credentials. Gaius' omission of Hebrews
from his canon of New Testament scripture did not disqualify him, for this,
Eusebius thought, was characteristic of many in Rome, and Gaius at least
had an 'ecclesiastical' understanding of scripture as a closed corpus of authentic books,[73] not subject to addition through Montanist revelations (*HE*
6. 20. 3).

Second, what do we really know about Gaius and his ecclesiastical rank,
so much stressed by modern writers? Scholars should at least be aware that
bearing the title of presbyter at this time in Rome would not have guaranteed anyone's widespread reputation as a 'venerated ecclesiastical leader'
among the orthodox. For we know that many claimed the title who were at
variance in some way with the recognized episcopal authorities.[74] More

---

[70] Haenchen, *John 1*, 23–4.

[71] Bauer, *Orthodoxy and Heresy*, 207, 'It was thus permissible for a Roman Christian from these
circles, and an officeholder as well, to consider not only the Apocalypse but even the gospel of John
as a forgery of the gnostic Cerinthus'. Smith, 'Gaius', 427, regards it as 'one of the paramount
results' of his study to restore Gaius 'to his rightful status as an "*orthodox*" and venerated ecclesiastical leader of the church at Rome at the beginning of the third century A.D.' Culpepper, *John*,
121, insists that 'Gaius's standing as a leader of the church at Rome shows that the authority of
John and the apostolic authorship were not so firmly established (at least in Rome...) that it could
not be challenged by one of the scholars of the church'.

[72] The positive press Gaius received from later writers came from writers who knew nothing
more about him than what they read in Eusebius, who therefore report only on Gaius' anti-
Montanist work against Proclus and perhaps his enumeration of only thirteen epistles of Paul, and
are unaware of any controversy with Gaius about either the Apocalypse or the Gospel. These
include Jerome (*De vir. illustr.* 59; cf. Lightfoot, *AF* i/2. 378); Theodoret (*Haereticae Fabulae* 2. 3; 3.
3); and the report cited by Photius (*Bibliotheca* 48; see below).

[73] Cf. 3. 25. 6 where Eusebius speaks of writings which are true, genuine, and recognized,
κατὰ ἐκκλησιαστικὴν παρόδοσιν.

[74] We know of at least two Roman presbyters who, only a few years before Gaius, claimed this
title while 'trying to introduce innovations about the truth in their own way' (Eusebius, *HE* 5. 15.
1), namely Florinus and Blastus. Irenaeus addressed theological treatises (in the form of letters) to
each of these (*HE* 5. 20. 1); one, against Blastus, was entitled *On Schism*. In another letter he urged
Victor of Rome specifically to banish the books of Florinus and others, indicating that Florinus
'boasts himself as being one of your company', and as being a presbyter (a fragment of the Nitrian
Collection in the British Museum, *ANF* i. 576, Fr. LI; cf. W. W. Harvey, *Sancti Irenaei Episcopi
Lugdunensis Libros Quinque Adversus Haereses*, 2 vols. (Cambridge, 1862), ii, 457, no. xxviii). There was

importantly, just what rank did Gaius possess—presbyter, bishop, or both—
and how do we know that he possessed it?

Eusebius, who had read the *Dialogue with Proclus*, calls Gaius very learned
(λογιωτάτου, *HE* 6. 20. 3) and a man of the Church (ἐκκλησιαστικὸς
ἀνήρ, *HE* 2. 25. 6), but does not attribute to him an ecclesiastical office. Nor
did Jerome read into Eusebius' phrase ἐκκλησιαστικὸς ἀνήρ any kind of
official title (*De vir. illustr.* 59).[75] Epiphanius does not name any of his 'Alogi',
and the only title for him found in Dionysius bar Salibi is the title of heretic. If
bar Salibi is relying on an authentic Hippolytan source, then Hippolytus
called Gaius a heretic. As I pointed out earlier, the report that Gaius was a
presbyter, and that he had been ordained 'bishop of the nations' comes from a
single source, Photius of Constantinople, writing in about AD 850 (*Bibl.* 48).
And Photius got this information from a note written in the margins
(ἐν παραγραφαῖς)[76] of a book entitled *On the Essence of the Universe*
(Περὶ τῆς τοῦ παντὸς οὐσίας). The note ascribed *On the Essence of the Universe*, along with two other works known as *The Labyrinth*, and *Against the Heresy
of Artemon*, and finally a *Dialogue with Proclus* the Montanist, to Gaius, a certain
presbyter who lived in Rome. The author of the note observed that the work
On the Essence of the Universe, left anonymous, was in some manuscripts assigned
to Joseph(us?),[77] in others to Justin the martyr, in others to Irenaeus, just as
The Labyrinth was attributed in some manuscripts to Origen.[78] The note

another schism in Rome contemporary with Gaius, 'the heresy of Artemon', begun in the time of
Victor but flourishing for at least some decades and known for its corruption of the divine scriptures
and its denial of the deity of Christ (which is, by the way, nowhere in the scriptures more plainly set
forth than in the Fourth Gospel and the Apocalypse). This group too had its own presbyters and
bishops (Eusebius, *HE* 5. 28). We have already been forced to conclude that if Gaius was connected
with the group of Johannophobes mentioned by Irenaeus in 3. 11. 9 (and this is more than
doubtful), he was presbyter of a heretical group! Tertullian names the Monarchian Praxeas as a
presbyter (*Prax.* 1). Hippolytus, in *Ref.* 9, of course, charges the bishops Zephyrinus and Callistus
with false teaching and sordid lifestyles.

[75] Jerome has *Gaius sub Zephyrino, Romanae urbis episcopo*. The *NPNF* edn. mistranslates Jerome
here, ascribing the title of bishop to Gaius instead of to Zephyrinus.

[76] Text reprinted in Lightfoot, *AF* i/2. 347–8.

[77] Hence the source of Pierre Nautin's ascription of some of the works commonly ascribed to
Hippolytus to a man named Joseph (P. Nautin, *Hippolyte et Josipe* (Paris, 1947); see also his 'Hippolytus' in *EEChurch*, i. 383–5). A fragment of a treatise loosely fitting the description of this work
(preserved by John of Damascus in his *Sacra Parallela*) has sometimes been printed among the works
of Josephus the Jewish historian. The same work has been identified as the *On the Essence of
the Universe*, in which this marginal note appeared, and has been more commonly attributed
to Hippolytus. See C. E. Hill, 'Hades of Hippolytus or Tartarus of Tertullian: The Authorship of
the Fragment *De universo*', *VC* 43 (1989), 105–26.

[78] In the middle of the 5th cent., Theodoret (who elsewhere, *Haereticae Fabulae* 3. 3, assigns only
the *Dialogue with Proclus* to Gaius), speaks of a work called *The Little Labyrinth*, which he says some
wrongly attribute to Origen, and which he identifies as a work against the heresy of Artemon
(*Haereticae Fabulae* 2. 5). This agrees with Photius' marginaliast, who links a work *Against Artemon*
(commonly identified as the work cited by Eusebius in *HE* 5. 28) with *The Labyrinth*, which some
also had ascribed to Origen, as products of the same author. When the MS containing the work
entitled *Philosophumena*, otherwise known as the *Refutation of All Heresies* (attributed today to Hippolytus) was discovered in 1842, it bore the name of Origen.

informs us that, near the end of the book *The Labyrinth*, its author refers to another work of his, *On the Essence of the Universe*. This, by the way, is what identifies *The Labyrinth* as the *Refutation of All Heresies*, or at least the tenth book of that work, commonly ascribed now to Hippolytus of Rome, for just such a reference is contained near the end of its tenth book. But just where the name Gaius has entered the picture is not immediately clear. Lightfoot insightfully theorized that the works linked together in the marginal note reported by Photius might have been bound together at one time in the same volume, and that the *Dialogue with Proclus* contained the only clear indication of the name of its author.[79] Photius then tells us that the note went on to say 'that this Gaius was made presbyter of the church in the time of the highpriesthoods (ἀρχιερέων) of Victor and Zephyrinus, but was ordained also bishop of the nations (ἐθνῶν ἐπίσκοπον)'. The same marginal note, then, which for the first time gives Gaius an ecclesiastical title (two, it would seem, 'presbyter' and 'episcopos of the nations') also makes Gaius the author of these three other works,[80] at least two of which nineteenth- and twentieth-century scholarship has thought securely to have placed in the hands of Hippolytus.[81] Neither Photius nor the author of the marginal note gives us any reason to think either had read the *Dialogue with Proclus*, or Hippolytus' refutation of Gaius, or were aware of any controversy over the Johannine literature.

Now, it is certainly possible that the unknown author of the note, even if he was wrong in attributing these other works to Gaius, could have yet obtained from some source trustworthy information about Gaius' identity. It would seem that he had access to some source besides Eusebius, who attributes no ecclesiastical office to Gaius. We are in a position, I believe, to say what that source was. In the book known to Photius as *The Labyrinth*— what we now know as the tenth book of the *Refutation of All Heresies* ascribed to Hippolytus of Rome—we find the following self-attestation by the author:

Such is the true word concerning the Divinity, O Hellenic men and barbarians, Chaldeans and Assyrians, Egyptians and Libyans, Indians and Ethiopians, Celts and Latin generals, and all those dwelling in Europe, Asia, and Libya—to whom

---

[79] Lightfoot, *AF* i/2. 384. Lightfoot at this point was attempting to ascribe all of these works to Hippolytus and to suggest that Gaius and Hippolytus were one and the same. One might conjecture instead that Eusebius came across just such a codex in the library at Jerusalem, the one in which he found Gaius' *Dialogue*. If this work was bound with these other, anonymous, Roman works, Eusebius may have recognized at least one (the *Labyrinth*) as the *Against All Heresies* of a man he knew as Hippolytus (*HE* 6. 22. 1), and this recognition may well have been what prompted him to mention Hippolytus, as bishop of some city, just before mentioning Gaius in *HE* 6. 20. 2–3.

[80] Smith, 'Gaius', 16, admits that 'the evidence of Photius concerning the author of these writings is suspect, because there is reason to believe that these same works were actually written by Hippolytus', but on p. 14 he had accepted Photius' notice, from the same source, about Gaius being a presbyter and 'a bishop of the Gentiles'.

[81] Hence the source of Lightfoot's ultimately retracted theory that Gaius and Hippolytus were one and the same.

I myself become counselor (οἷς σύμβουλος ἐγὼ γίνομαι),[82] being a disciple of the philanthropic Word and *philanthropos* myself—in order that you may hasten and may be taught by us, who the real God is. (*Ref.* 10. 34. 1).

Thus the marginaliast's information about 'Gaius' being an 'overseer to the nations' was taken directly from *The Labyrinth*[83] (and possibly from the *Against Artemon*)[84] on the (mistaken) assumption that it was written by the same person, Gaius of Rome, who wrote the *Dialogue with Proclus*! The only way to maintain the attribution of office to Gaius is thus to identify him as the author of these other works (as the marginaliast has done), and if that is done, it would have to put to rest forever the idea that Gaius was an inveterate opponent of the Fourth Gospel, for that Gospel is used as an authority throughout the ten books of the *Refutation of All Heresies*. As to Victor and Zephyrinus, the author of the *Refutation* (*The Labyrinth*) calls Victor (189–99), 'the blessed Victor, who was at that time a bishop of the Church' (*Ref.* 9. 12. 10), but has a scathing report about Zephyrinus. Needless to say, if the marginaliast's information is discredited it leaves us with no attestation of an ecclesiastical office for Gaius.

For all we know, Gaius might have been a presbyter in one of the Christian communities in Rome; but there is simply no record of this. In the end it perhaps matters little whether Gaius held ecclesiastical office or not. But I have taken the time to examine the question because of the weight which has often been attached to Gaius' supposed office in the Church, either as qualifying him to represent the hierarchy of the Roman church in the matter of the status of the Johannine writings, or as showing how tenuous the authority of the Gospel of John must have been if a holder of high office could attack it with impunity. Whatever added weight Gaius' high office has been thought to imply, then, must be dropped.

THE SUCCESS OF 'GAIAN' JOHANNOPHOBIA

Fifth, if anyone in the Roman church mounted an offensive against the Johannine Gospel, their efforts were isolated and very ineffective in the ancient Church. Gaius' case is often cited to prove that it was within bounds for an orthodox writer to attribute the Fourth Gospel and the

---

[82] Cf. *Ref.* 9. 7. 2, where Callistus is called Zephyrinus' σύμβουλος τοῦ κακῶν.

[83] In the preface to the first book of the *Refutation*, the author claims to be among the successors of the apostles, 'obtaining the same grace, partaking in both the highpriesthood (ἀρχιερατείας) and the teaching, and being considered guardians of the Church', a comment which most interpreters have accepted as indicating an episcopal office for the author (he also evidently had the authority to excommunicate Church members, 9. 12. 21). It is probably from this very passage in the preface that the author of the marginalia took the word ἀρχιερατεία, which he uses for the offices of Victor and Zephyrinus. The author of the *Refutation* speaks of the times of these men, in relation to Callistus and himself, particularly in book 9. 11–13.

[84] The author of the *Against Artemon* also writes about the times of Victor and Zephyrinus in Rome. See Eusebius, *HE* 5. 28.

Revelation of John to a notorious heretic, and therefore that the status of these books must have been precarious up until that time. But of course we really do not know whether it was within bounds or not because we simply do not know what happened with Gaius after he (allegedly) put forth his disparaging views on the Fourth Gospel. On D. J. Smith's construal of the evidence, Gaius was soon condemned as a heretic by Hippolytus, the author of the *Heads against Gaius*.[85] For all we know, Gaius might have been disciplined, or might have retracted his views after being confronted (as Tertullian, *Prax.* 1, says Praxeas did, in writing). The point is that we have no church records from Rome which can tell us about Gaius; the best we can do is to ask how the views he is supposed to represent might have been received among his contemporaries and by immediately subsequent writers.

It is just possible that the criticism of Gaius was known already to the author of the *Muratorian Fragment*.[86]

And so, although different beginnings (*varia...principia*) might be taught in the separate books of the Gospels, nevertheless it makes no difference to the faith of believers, since all things in all [of them] are declared by the one sovereign Spirit—concerning his nativity, concerning [His] passion, concerning [His] resurrection, concerning [His] walk with His disciples, and concerning His double advent: the first in humility when He was despised, which has been; the second in royal power, glorious, which is to be. What marvel, then, if John so constantly brings forward particular [matters] also in his Epistles, saying of himself: 'What we have seen with our eyes and have heard with [our] ears and our hands have handled, these things we have written to you.' For thus he declares that he was not only an eyewitness and hearer, but also a writer of all the wonderful things of the Lord in order (*per ordinem*).

But the reference is too vague to support any specific correlation with any of the known points of criticism associated with Gaius, particularly the events following the baptism of Jesus by John. Its mention of John writing all the wonderful things of the Lord in order (*per ordinem*) also recalls the discussions we know were taking place as early as the sources used by Papias.[87] Likewise it is possible that the place of the Apocalypse at the end of the document indicates that questions had been raised, perhaps by Gaius. But this is doubtful, and the author's own esteem for the book is very much on the surface (see the discussion in Chapter 3). Authorship of the received writings was of obvious importance for the author of the *MF*, yet he makes no allusion to a question about authorship either of the Gospel or the Apocalypse. Thus the *MF* witnesses to the awareness of difficulties arising from the differences between the order and contents of the four Gospels, but we cannot be very confident that it knows any of the specific charges eventually associated with the name of Gaius.

[85] See Smith, 'Gaius', 361–4, who would date this work to AD 204–7.
[86] So Culpepper, *John*, 129, following D. J. Smith.
[87] Eusebius, *HE* 3. 39. 15–16; and 3. 24. 3–13, on which see the sections on Papias in Ch. 7.

In Chapter 3 a resemblance was noted between the *Muratorian Fragment* and a statement made by Tertullian in *Adversus Marcionem* 4. 2. 2 on the agreement of the Gospels in the essential matters, despite certain differences in order.[88] This, I suggested, may indicate Tertullian's knowledge of the *MF*, though it may or may not have to do with a criticism of John's Gospel which has come to be associated with Gaius. Here there is certainly no mention of Gaius' name, and the 'variations in the order of their narratives' noted by Tertullian do not single out John for scutiny but involve all four Gospels together, just as in the *MF*.

I have also already cited the words of Origen from his *Commentary on John*, in which he mentions a problem of Gospel disharmony which Epiphanius' Alogi bring up against John. It is possible that Origen is thus a witness to Gaius' earlier criticism. And yet it could be that it is Epiphanius who is only aware of the problem from reading Origen (whom he disliked). Origen does indicate that the difficulty of there being no place for the forty-day temptation in John's account is a potentially serious one for the student who cannot get beyond the material letter, and this could suggest that it was a difficulty which had forcefully been alleged by some critic. But not only does Origen not mention Gaius' name, or associate the problem with an attack on John or the Johannine literature, but, like the *MF* and Tertullian, he does not seem to see the problem as implicating John any more than the other Gospels.

I introduce now, however, another intriguing possibility which does in fact involve Gaius' name. There may be an unnoticed reference to Gaius in Tertullian's *De praescriptione haereticorum* 33. 10, written between 200 and 203,[89] very close to the time when Gaius published his *Dialogue*.[90] In a section in which he is pointing to examples of heresies encountered by the apostles, Tertullian says, 'John, however, in the Apocalypse is charged to chastise those "who eat things sacrificed to idols," and "who commit fornication." There are even now another sort of Nicolaitans. Theirs is called the Gaian heresy (*Gaiana haeresis dicitur*).'

There has been disagreement, however, over the original reading. All the extant manuscripts (A P X) read *Gaiana*, and this was the reading printed by Rhenanus in his *editio princeps* of Tertullian's works in 1521.[91] But in Rhenanus' third edition he printed *Cainana* (Cainites), which was then repeated in all the remaining sixteenth- and seventeenth-century editions of Tertullian's

---

[88] 'These all start with the same principles of the faith, so far as relates to the one only God the Creator and His Christ, how that He was born of the Virgin, and came to fulfil the law and the prophets. Never mind if there does occur some variation in the order of the narratives, provided that there be agreement in the essential matter of the faith, in which there is disagreement with Marcion.'

[89] Quasten, *Patrology*, ii. 272, AD 200; Barnes, *Tertullian*, 55, AD 203.

[90] Eusebius places the *Dialogue* in Rome at the time of Zephyrinus (199–217) (*HE* 2. 25. 7; 6. 20. 3). If this is so, then the debate may have taken place just after the new bishop was elected.

[91] B. Rhenanus, *Opera Q. S. Fl. Tertulliani* (Basle, 1521); 3rd edn. 1539.

works.[92] This seems to have been simply his conjecture,[93] based perhaps on an inability to identify a group of 'Gaians', and on the fact that Tertullian elsewhere reports that a female representative of the heresy of the Cainites, whom Tertullian calls a viper, had a few years earlier come to Carthage and had 'carried away a great number with her most venomous doctrine' (*De bapt.* 1. 2). But here there is a textual problem as well! Codex Trecensis 523 (12th cent.), the only manuscript of *De baptismo* now surviving, has *de canina haeresi vipera*, but the edition of Martin Mesnart from 1545, curiously, has *de Gaiana haeresi vipera*.[94] Quasten writes that the text of *De baptismo* in Mesnart's edition, taken from an unidentified and now lost manuscript, is inferior to that of Trecensis. Based on a passage from Jerome, where he speaks of *Caina haeresis* and calls it a viper, Harnack in 1914 proposed that the true reading in both *De praescriptione* and *De baptismo* must have been *Caina*.[95] This corresponds perfectly with the reference in *De baptismo* 1. 2 and is fairly taken as evidence that the text of Tertullian known to Jerome had *de Caina haeresi* there. What is more, the reference to vipers would be fitting in the case of a Cainite, as the Cainites are associated with the Ophites in Ps. Tertullian, *Against All Heresies* 2 (cf. Irenaeus, *AH* 1. 30, 31).[96] But does this decide the case as well for *De praescriptione* 33. 10, as assumed by Harnack and others?[97] The immoral practices of the Cainites, hinted at by Irenaeus (*AH* 1. 31. 2), might be seen as analogous to the practices of the Nicolaitans censured by John, to which Tertullian is comparing the heresy in question in *De praescriptione* 33. 10. On the other hand, in *De baptismo*, where Tertullian is faced with problems arising from the Cainites, he never refers to their morals (nor are bad morals mentioned in Ps. Tertullian). And the united reading of the three extant manuscripts of *De praescriptione*,[98] *Gaiana*, is a reading which, unlike *Cainana*, is unlikely to have arisen through a conscious scribal attempt to make sense of an otherwise inscrutable reference. In addition, there is the matter of the reading of the lost text of *De baptismo* 1. 2 used by Mesnart in 1545, which evidently read *de Gaiana haeresi vipera*. If we presume that the original of this text read *Caina*, we must

---

[92] Martin Mesnartius (Paris, 1545, considered a 4th edn. of Rhenanus); S. Gelenius (Basle, 1550, considered a 5th edn. of Rhenanus); J. Pamelius (Paris, 1583/Antwerp, 1584, considered a 6th edn. of Rhenanus); N. Rigaltius (Paris, 1634). (Note the helpful annotations on early edns. by Roger Pearse, 'Early Editions 1450–1859', at www.tertullian.org/editions/editions.htm.)

[93] It is possible that this was the reading of codex Gorziensis, which Rhenanus collated in the 3rd edn. but which is now lost. But the editor of the CCL edn. does not list it as a reading of Gorziensis as detectible from Rhenanus' 3rd edn.

[94] None of the MSS which contain *De Praescr.* has *De Bapt.*

[95] A. von Harnack, 'Tertullians Bibliothek christlicher Schriften', *Sitzungsberg. d. kön. Preuss. Akad. d. Wiss. zu Berlin* (1914), 303–34, at 323. Jerome's text reads, *et consurgit mihi Caina haeresis atque olim emortua vipera contritum caput levat* (*Epp.* 59. 1). See Barnes, *Tertullian*, 279.

[96] Barnes, *Tertullian*, 280.

[97] CCL 2. Barnes, *Tertullian*, 279, also assumes this reading

[98] Codex Parisinus Latinus 1622 (Agobardensis), 9th cent. (A); Codex Paterniacensis 439, 11th cent. (P); Codex Luxemburgensis 75, 15th cent. (X), though X is a descendant of P.

imagine that a Gaian heresy made more sense to some copyist than did a Cainite one. It is unlikely that Mesnart himself made this change, because in his edition of *De praescriptione* 33. 10, he had followed Rhenanius' third edition in reading *Cainana*, not *Gaiana* which the surviving texts have. Thus, to account for the possibility of an original *Gaiana* in *De praescriptione* 33. 10 and an early scribal change from *Caina* to *Gaiana* in *De baptismo* 1. 2, we may now say that we know of a Gaius who might have shown himself, in Tertullian's eyes, no less an enemy of the apostle John and his Revelation than the Nicolaitans were in John's own day. It is also potentially important that whatever Gaius might have said about the Apocalypse of John (note that the Gospel is not here implicated!) was said in a *Dialogue* with a man named Proclus, a Montanist teacher whom we know Tertullian later came to hold in very high esteem (*Val.* 5; *Scap.* 4. 5).[99]

If *Gaiana* is the original reading of *De praescriptione* 33. 10—and I must emphasize that this is not certain—we then surely have an extremely important, contemporary evaluation of the views (some views) of someone named Gaius.[100] It is interesting that Tertullian mentions 'the Gaian heresy' in a reference to the Apocalypse, not in a reference to the Gospel. The only fragment from Gaius' *Dialogue* we possess which possibly bears on the Johannine literature is his comment which seems to link the Johannine Apocalypse with the carnal millennialism of Cerinthus. If *Gaiana* is the correct reading, the importance of this short comment lies not only in confirming that Gaius said something about Revelation (as he likely did in the *Dialogue*) which was known by Tertullian in Carthage at least as early as 200–3, but in revealing Tertullian's dismissal of Gaius' position on the Apocalypse as a heresy, as a fitting successor to the disgusting practices of the Nicolaitans. Whether it was already known by the name 'the Gaian heresy' or whether this was Tertullian's own coinage we cannot of course tell. But this text would offer the earliest witness to Gaius' views on the Apocalypse from orthodox quarters, and that witness is unarguably negative.

There are critical questions surrounding both the alleged response by Hippolytus to Gaius and this possible reference to Gaius by Tertullian. But, such as they are, they are our only potentially contemporary responses[101]

---

[99] *Praescr.* was written before Tertullian's conversion to Montanism. But his later reverence towards Proclus could suggest a sympathy towards this man even from the time of his reading of Gaius' *Dialogue*. Perhaps it played a role in Tertullian's eventual adoption of the New Prophecy.

[100] There is, finally, one more possible reference to Gaius in the writings of Tertullian. In an ironical jab in *Val.* 32. 4 Tertullian mentions a 'Marcus or a Gaius' as ending up the brides and parents, by some angelic aeon, of aeonic offspring. But rather than being a reference to real people (Marcus the Valentinian and someone named Gaius) these appear to be names for common men (slaves, according to the note in the *ANF*).

[101] It is possible that Gaius' criticism was known already to the Ephesian Apollonius, who in his own refutation of Montanism in about AD 200 establishes the role of John in Asian Christianity. I have observed above that, unlike Gaius, Apollonius evidently used the Johannine Apocalypse positively against Montanism. If Apollonius wrote after Gaius and in knowledge of his work, he obvi-

and they unite in discouraging the idea that Gaius could have been representing a traditional position of the orthodox in Rome in charging that the Apocalypse of John taught the carnal chiliasm associated with Cerinthus, or in criticizing the contents of either Johannine work. On the contrary, they would be consistent with the results of the earlier portion of this study, which indicated that, based on the circumstantial evidence of various writers who had connections with Rome, both the Fourth Gospel and the Apocalypse must have been highly regarded by the major representatives of the Church there for quite some time prior to Gaius' *Dialogue*.

A later portion of this study will follow the fortunes of the Johannine literature through the fourth century or so. Here it may be said that, though Gaius may indeed stand at the beginning of a chain of events which would have negative consequences for the recognition of the Apocalypse of John in areas of the Christian Church, what is ironic, in the light of the OJP, is that he had no such effect on the continuing reception of the Gospel according to John. Outside of the 'Alogi' and Dionysius bar Salibi's 'Gaius', I do not know of a defender of the position attributed to these figures, inside or outside the Church. This could be one more indication that Gaius indeed did not criticize the Gospel and that the legacy which has grown up around him is unhistorical. But if he did reject the Fourth Gospel, either simply as being in conflict with the other three or also as being the product of the heretic Cerinthus, we shall have to agree with Hengel in pronouncing his enterprise of Gospel criticism a colossal failure in the ancient Church. Its path to success did not begin until AD 1888.

Summary and Conclusions

The findings of this study regarding the Fourth Gospel's place among Great Church writers in the period 170–200 have been summarized above. The main points may be restated briefly: the Fourth Gospel was widely used as an authoritative and scriptural source in this period, not only by Church leaders and authors but also among the non-literary laypeople. Most curious is the absence of any signs of struggle from an alleged takeover from the Gnostics. There are no defences of the Fourth Gospel from charges or suspicions of heresy; there are only battles over interpretation mainly on the part of Irenaeus and Clement of Alexandria. Of the 'many pre-Nicene critics' who are said to have opposed this Gospel I have found only the group mentioned by Irenaeus in *AH* 3. 11. 9; *Dem.* 99–100, and these can hardly be viewed as orthodox but show more resemblance to

---

ously did not agree with the Roman in his evaluation of the Apocalypse. If on the other hand Apollonius' treatise was written before Gaius' *Dialogue*, it will be seen as one more part of the consensus Gaius had to try to overthrow.

tendencies seen in the *Apocryphon of James*. One of the more enlightening results has concerned Rome, the supposed fortress of anti-Johannine suspicion and resentment. The evidence, on the other hand, though very limited, still presents only a positive reception of the Fourth Gospel in Hegesippus, the *Muratorian Fragment*, in catacomb art, and indirectly in the correspondence with official Rome on the part of the *Epistle of Vienne and Lyons*, Polycrates, and Irenaeus. The orthodox sources of the period not only use this book as scripture but they give us many clues about previous use both among gnostics and among their orthodox forebears. It has also become clear from these writers' use of at least the Gospel, the Apocalypse, and First Epistle of John, all used in a similar way and attributed to a single author, that it is fair to speak of an ecumenical recognition of a Johannine corpus in this period.

Is there anything in the complex universe of matters pertaining to Gaius of Rome which would disrupt these findings? In particular, does Gaius, and any opposition to the Fourth Gospel or to the Apocalypse in which he may have participated, give grounds for the claim that this Gospel had long been rejected or treated with mistrust in Rome? To both questions the answer is no. It is not impossible that Gaius found in the group of Johannophobes mentioned by Irenaeus a seed from which he might have developed his own formulations. But because of serious critical questions both about the strictness of Epiphanius of Salamis' historical interests in his chapter on the Alogi, and about the authenticity of the Hippolytan source cited and summarized by Dionysius bar Salibi in the twelfth century, it is not easy to be confident about what Gaius actually taught, particularly about the Johannine Gospel. We cannot be at all sure that Gaius ever rejected or opposed John's Gospel, and if he did there is very grave doubt about whether he ever attributed it to Cerinthus. Without doubt, however, we can say that neither Gaius nor anyone else remotely connected to his life and times seems ever to have charged John's Gospel with being gnostic, docetic, or with supporting such tendencies. And despite the authority commonly accorded to Gaius and his alleged rejection of John due to his position as presbyter, or bishop, in the church at Rome, the evidence for his Churchly office is based on a case of mistaken identity (as should have been realized long ago) and has to be discarded. The common portrayal of Gaius, as a conserver of orthodox sensibilities in orthodox Rome who wanted to enforce a long-held suspicion of the gnostically tainted Johannine Gospel, is a figment of the modern, critical imagination, attributable mainly to Walter Bauer. Whatever he taught about the Fourth Gospel, Gaius cannot be propped up as a representative of long-standing orthodox Roman antipathy towards that Gospel. Nor did such views—if any historical person ever held them—have any apparent success in winning adherents. The figure of 'Gaius the opponent of the Johannine literature' achieved his greatest following in the twentieth century.

5

John and 'the Gnostics'

As we have seen, for a long time the consensus of scholarship has held that gnostic and other heretical groups held a virtual monopoly on the Fourth Gospel throughout much of the second century. Here again are Melvyn Hillmer's conclusions reached in 1966,

At a time in history when the Apologists were using John very sparingly, with only incidental citations, these gnostic writers were writing commentaries on the text. This seems to be clear indication that John was first fully accepted and used as authoritative in gnostic circles; not until Irenaeus does it have the same kind of position in other than gnostic writers.[1]

The Commentaries of Ptolemaeus and Heracleon from the second generation of Valentinianism, give the earliest clear indication of the acceptance of the Gospel of John as canonical and worthy of verse by verse comment. The interpretation in these commentaries is in terms of Valentinian gnosticism but nevertheless demonstrates a final stage in the recognition of the gospel as a writing which has scriptural authority. It is significant that this position is first accorded to John in the work of Valentinian teachers, who were able with relative ease to interpret the Fourth Gospel in terms of their own theological system.[2]

The more recent formulation of J.-D. Kaestli states,

1) On one side, we have underscored the lack of clear attestation of a use of the fourth gospel in the texts and with the authors who have been considered afterwards as the representatives of 'orthodox' Christianity. One must await the last quarter of the second century, with Irenaeus and Theophilus of Antioch, to find the first sure witnesses attesting to the full acceptance of John in the 'canon' of the Great Church.
2) On the other side, contrasting with this absence of attestation, we have recovered the place of choice which the gospel of John held with the gnostics of the Valentinian school, with Heracleon in particular.[3]

In this section I shall not attempt to present an exhaustive, systematic examination of the borrowings from the Fourth Gospel in gnostic or gnostic-related literature from the second century. The task has to be more focused. First of all, just how much did the Valentinians and gnostics of the

---

[1] M. R. Hillmer, 'The Gospel of John in the Second Century' (Th. D. dissertation, Harvard Univ. Apr. 1966), 169.
[2] Ibid. 172.
[3] J.-D. Kaestli, 'Remarques sur le rapport du quatriéme évangile avec la gnose et sa réception au IIe siècle', in Kaestli et al. (eds.), La Communauté johannique et son histoire (Paris, 1990), 352–3.

period use the Fourth Gospel? Is their use of it seen 'on every side'? Also, how did the Valentinian and gnostic writers use the Johannine Gospel? For example, did they tend to use all of it or did they have favourite parts? Did they use it as scripture? What interested them about this Gospel? Why did they feel a 'peculiar kinship' with it? Was it John's soaring Christology, its pneumatology, or its general, 'proto-gnostic' ambience? But most of all I shall be interested here in the question of whether and to what extent gnostic use of the Fourth Gospel is likely to have contributed to a sense of Johannophobia, a reluctance to use John or an antipathy towards it, on the part of their ortho-dox contemporaries. This is at the heart of the paradigm that has dominated scholarship for decades, and an examination of the question has the potential of clearing up the mystery of why the gnostics (allegedly) favoured the Fourth Gospel, and why the orthodox (allegedly) did not.

Before the relevant evidence is examined, brief mention should be made of two tendencies often seen in the literature on this subject. First is the tendency to assume that the use of a book by Christian heretics necessarily must have advertised against that book in the eyes of the orthodox.[4] It is certainly possible that it did, but there might well be other possibilities. It is antecedently just as possible that sectarian use of a book should have very little effect upon the orthodox, for such use conceivably could reflect and depend upon an already high regard for the book within the orthodox mainstream. What the OJP has done is to set up the boundaries in such a way that few scholars entertain this possibility because it is considered an established fact that the orthodox were simply not using the Fourth Gospel at this time, or were using it 'tentatively', or furtively, as if using someone else's prized property. But, freed of preconceptions on this matter, one could envision a situation in which a book had to be used by proponents of a competing view if they wanted to make any headway in reaching or converting or even refuting people from the Great Church. These two may not be the only possibilities, and they may not be mutually exclusive, but we should at least be aware that the preferred explanation is often simply assumed without consideration of any alternative.

The other tendency worth mentioning here is the tendency to assume that any use of a book (at least, any gnostic use of the Fourth Gospel) always denotes an unqualified, positive evaluation and reception of that book. We shall come to see, I believe, that other possibilities exist in this case as well and cannot be ignored.

---

[4] To demonstrate the invalidity of the assumption one might ask whether the reverse was true as well. If heretical use of a book advertised against it for the orthodox, did heretical rejection of a book commend it? Did Marcion's positive rejection of the Johannine books (this is specifically attested by Tertullian, *Marc.* 4. 5) have the effect of commending these books to the orthodox? Which then should we presume was a more powerful force upon the minds of the orthodox, Valentinian acceptance or Marcionite rejection?

Second-Century 'Gnostic' Movements

INDIVIDUAL GNOSTIC TEACHERS

Heracleon

It is obvious from the many representations of the OJP cited at the beginning of this book that a major plank in the paradigm comes directly from the commentary on the Fourth Gospel by Heracleon the Valentinian. Other Valentinians and 'gnostics' certainly played their parts, but the one name most frequently associated with orthodox suspicion, avoidance, or rejection of John is that of Heracleon, who is supposed to have 'tainted' the work by his commentary on it.[5]

And yet, despite the prevalence of the assumption, there are immediate problems with asserting such an influence flowing from Heracleon's work. The first is that we cannot document anything of the sort. Irenaeus quite obviously did not experience any poisonous effects of Johannophobia from Heracleon's work. His reaction to the Valentinian use of John is one of indignation at their misusing a book which is part of the catholic scripture and which is illegitimately used to support Valentinianism:

> striving, as they do, to adapt the good words of revelation to their own wicked inventions. And it is not only from the writings of the evangelists and apostles that they endeavour to derive proofs for their opinions by means of perverse interpretations and deceitful expositions: they deal in the same way with the law and the prophets... and others of them, with great craftiness, adapted such parts of Scripture to their own figments, lead away captive from the truth those who do not retain a steadfast faith in one God, the Father Almighty, and in one Lord Jesus Christ, the Son of God. (*AH* 1. 4. 5)

The danger here mentioned by Irenaeus is not that theologians or Church leaders might come to question the authenticity of John, but that those with an unsteady faith in one God and one Lord might be led astray by the Valentinians' crafty adaptations of scriptures *already accepted* by the faithful. It might be objected, however, that Irenaeus may not have read the commentary of Heracleon on the Fourth Gospel. This in fact, I believe, was indeed the case. Irenaeus mentions Heracleon but once (*AH* 2. 4. 1), as a follower of Valentinus, but never alludes to any of his comments on John, while on the other hand he deals extensively with those of another Valentinian writer, identified in the Latin text as Ptolemy (1. 8. 5). If Heracleon's commentary on John was written in Rome or in Italy by this time,[6] it is unlikely that Irenaeus

---

[5] Hillmer, 'Second Century', 79–80; T. E. Pollard, *Johannine Christology and the Early Church* (Cambridge, 1970), 39; E. Haenchen, *John 1* (Philadelphia, 1984), 18–19; D. M. Smith, 'The Problem of John and the Synoptics', in A. Denaux (ed.), *John and the Synoptics* (Leuven, 1992), 157; J. H. Charlesworth, *The Beloved Disciple* (Valley Forge, Pa., 1995), 407.

[6] G. Salmon, 'Heracleon', *DCB*, ii. 897–901 at 900, thinks Heracleon, who Hippolytus says was a member of the Italian school of Valentinians, must have taught in south Italy, as he is not

would not have known it. That he did not know it would also seem to be supported by the fact that when Irenaeus mentions, in his famous remark, that the Valentinians used John because they found support in his Prologue for their syzygies (3. 11. 9), he thus mentions a factor that characterizes 'Ptolemy's' exegesis of John's Prologue but not Heracleon's.[7] Heracleon's work on John was evidently later than Ptolemy's, and probably was unknown to Irenaeus because it was not written till perhaps the late 170s, or the 180s, or even later.[8] Even Clement, writing in the 190s, who knows Heracleon as a Valentinian teacher, shows no signs of having read the now-famous commentary. But the OJP asks us to believe that many orthodox Christians had read or heard about Heracleon's commentary on the Gospel according to John, and that most of them as a result came to view that Gospel as not 'reliable and authentic',[9] if they did not already view it as such.

This brings us to a second problem, a basic and confounding flaw in this thesis that nevertheless routinely goes untreated. The invocation of Heracleon's commentary by proponents of the OJP ignores the fact that the time of the publication of Heracleon's commentary is the very time from which—even by their own admission—the Fourth Gospel is in the ascendancy among the orthodox. Without yet exploring the signs of earlier use in their works, we have already seen that from some time in the 170s until the end of the second century such representatives of the 'Great Church' as Theophilus in Antioch, Athenagoras in Athens, Hegesippus, probably the author of the *Muratorian Fragment*, and the officials in charge of the Christian cemeteries in Rome, the author of the *Epistle of Vienne and Lyons* and Irenaeus in Gaul, Melito in Sardis, Polycrates and Apollonius in Ephesus, Clement and the laity in Alexandria, and Tertullian and the martyrs in Carthage, were assuming essentially a scriptural status for the Fourth Gospel in the Church at large. By the end of the century, as even Haenchen and most others will say, the apostolic authority of this Gospel is generally acknowledged among the orthodox.[10] This brings up a related point. At least since Hillmer, scholars have cited the mere writing of a commentary on John by Heracleon as proof that Heracleon regarded John

mentioned by any Roman authority. C. Bammel, 'Herakleon', *Theologische Realenzyklopädie*, xv (Berlin, 1986), 54–7 at 54, says that any activity of Heracleon in Alexandria is doubtful.

[7] Salmon, 'Heracleon', 900; Elaine Pagels, *The Johannine Gospel in Gnostic Exegesis* (Nashville, Tenn., 1973), 46–7.

[8] Tertullian lists Heracleon after Ptolemy but before Secundus and Marcus (*Val.* 4); Ps. Tertullian, *Adv. omn. haer.* 4 lists Heracelon after Ptolemy and Secundus. R. A. Culpepper, *John, The Son of Zebedee* (Columbia, SC, 1994), 116, places Heracleon's commentary at *c.*170, but he assumes that it was known to Irenaeus. Heracleon was evidently not a personal disciple of Valentinus (Markschies, 'Valentinian Gnosticism', in J. D. Turner and A. McGuire, *The Nag Hammadi Library after Fifty Years* (Leiden, 1997), 430, 433–5, though Markschies too speculates, 430, that Heracleon's commentary on John was written 'perhaps around 170 CE').

[9] Charlesworth, *Beloved Disciple*, 407.

[10] Haenchen, *John 1*, 14; G. M. Hahneman, *The Muratorian Fragment and the Development of the Canon* (Oxford, 1992), 102.

as scriptural, in supposed contrast to the orthodox.[11] Certainly, Heracleon seems to have assumed that the very words of the Gospel are significant and even sacred. But the likely date for Heracleon's commentary is after Irenaeus' *Against Heresies*. Shall we argue that Heracleon had a greater respect for the scriptural character of John than did Irenaeus? It is, in my opinion, most probable that Heracleon's commentary was written partly in reaction to Irenaeus' refutation of 'Ptolemy'. But in any case the two writings must be closely contemporary. And even if Heracleon wrote closer to 170, it will make little difference. In 1880 Salmon, who believed the centre of Heracleon's activity should be fixed in the decade 170–80, wrote about its relevance for determining the relative status of the Gospel among the Valentinians and the orthodox,

Considerable interest attaches to the determination of the date of Heracleon on account of his use of St John's Gospel, which clearly had attained so high an authority when he wrote that it must then have been a work of considerable standing. It seems to us, however, that the mere fact that the book was held in equal honour by the Valentinians and the orthodox proves that it must have attained its position before the separation of the Valentinians from the church; and, therefore, that as far as the controversy concerning the fourth Gospel is concerned, it is of less importance to determine the exact date of Heacleon.[12]

The consensus view about Johannophobia then appears to be mistaken, at least as it regards the influence of Heracleon, and, really, any other gnostic teacher or school which flourished after about 170 or so. Heracleon's commentary may of course have been despised by the orthodox. It may have been scorned, feared, perhaps it was burnt (or cast into rubbish heaps). But we shall be hard pressed to show that it contributed to any significant Johannophobia among the orthodox in the first decades after it was published.

And what about thereafter? Surely one should see in Origen's somewhat copious use and refutation of Heracleon's commentary in the 230s an admission that it was regarded by the orthodox as a threat. It might be argued that the very fact that he and others mention Heracleon and contend against him presumes that some in the Great Church were being seduced by Heracleon, otherwise there would be no need to refute him.[13] This is certainly possible, but at least three observations should also be made.

First, it does not necessarily follow that whatever threat was posed by Heracleon's commentary was a particularly serious one.[14] Sometimes fairly

[11] Hillmer, 'Second Century', 169, who assumes that Heracleon wrote his commentary long before Irenaeus began to write; Culpepper, *John*, 118.
[12] Salmon, 'Heracleon', 900.
[13] J.-M. Poffet, 'Indices de réception de l'Évangile de Jean', in J.-D. Kaestli *et al.* (eds.), *La Communauté johannique et son histoire* (Paris, 1990), 316, indicates that Origen wrote 'précisément pour réfuter cette lecture jugée par lui ruineuse pour la foi chrétienne'.
[14] *Pace* Poffet, 'Indices', 316, who says that Origen's entire 32+ volume commentary on John was devoted to the refutation of Heracleon.

inconsequential people or heresies are refuted for the sake of completeness (as in Epiphanius, often), for the furnishing of historical backgrounds to present problems (as in Irenaeus on the Barbeloites), or to answer the criticism of pagan writers (as in Origen on the Ophites in answer to Celsus). Before Origen specifically cites passages from Heracleon's 'not very detailed'[15] commentary in the 230s, several authors, including Irenaeus, Clement, Tertullian, Hippolytus, and probably Ps. Tertullian, had mentioned Heracleon's teaching without ever mentioning or quoting from a work on John. Clement, in fact, only seems to know Heracleon's exegesis of passages in Luke (*Strom.* 4. 9. 73–5; *Ecl. Proph.* 25), which has caused some to think that Heracleon also wrote a commentary on Luke. If Origen had never written his own commentary on John, or if it had perished, we would not in fact know Heracleon had written one.[16] One of Origen's comments even makes it uncertain whether Origen himself was able to obtain a full copy of Heracleon's commentary,[17] which itself would call into question the accessibility of the work to great numbers of Christians. This nearly complete silence of orthodox authors about Heracleon's commentary at least shows us that wide estimates of its influence are highly conjectural, at best, and are flimsy support for the supposed phenomenon of orthodox Johannophobia in the second century.

Second, and more to the point for present purposes, it does not follow that Heracleon's 'threat', however serious it was, was a threat to orthodox use of John. In the case of Origen himself, presumably no one will claim that his exposure to Heracleon's commentary on John engendered in him any Johannophobic sentiments. And as I have already observed, by the time Heracleon published his commentary the place of the Fourth Gospel in the Great Church was quickly becoming or had already become immovable. And apart from the dubious case of Gaius of Rome there is no indication that this changed after AD 200. Whatever seductive power Heracleon's teaching might have exerted among members of these churches, its attractions would be more likely to have drawn one towards Heracleon's distinctive views, or to the Valentinian church (or school), rather than away from an appreciation of John's Gospel, which was by now prized by both friends and foes of Valentinianism.[18]

---

[15] C. Bammel, 'Herakleon', *Theologische Realenzyclopädie*, x (Berlin, 1986), 55. It is, as Bammel says (p. 54), not at all certain whether Heracleon commented on the whole of the Fourth Gospel. Origen's excerpts do not go beyond John 8.

[16] Photius cites a comment of Heracleon's on John 1: 17, but Salmon, 'Heracleon', 898, is probably correct that this was taken from one of the lost books of Origen's John commentary.

[17] ἐν οἷς καταλέλοιπεν ὑπομνήμασι. See Salmon, 'Heracleon', 898.

[18] Ibid. 899, 'Instances of this kind where the interpreter is forced to reject the most obvious meaning of the text are sufficiently numerous to shew that the gospel was not written in the interests of Valentinianism; but it is a book which Heracleon evidently recognized as of such authority that he must perforce have it on his side.'

Finally, another factor about Heracleon's commentary needs to be emphasized. Sweeping assertions about the dramatic effects of Heracleon's
comments on John usually bypass any discussion of the character of those
comments. It is known, however, that Heracleon's exegesis was much
'toned down', its strictly Valentinian and 'pleromatic' character to a great
extent obscured, at least as compared with Ptolemy's (or what has been
considered Ptolemy's).[19] His penchant for 'spiritual' exegesis is not so
much at odds with Origen's own,[20] and Origen even at times acknowledges
the worth of his adversary's comments. This makes it quite possible to
maintain that Heracleon had himself been influenced to a considerable
extent by orthodox writers such as Irenaeus to abandon the openly 'pleromic' exegesis advocated by his Valentinian predecessor cited by Irenaeus
in *AH* 1. 8. 5.[21] If so, this would only have been in order to make his
work more appealing to orthodoxy. This too works against any thesis
which would seek to credit Heracleon's commentary with a great
defection from the Fourth Gospel among the Great Church. Instead,
Salmon's conclusion that Heracleon saw in John's Gospel 'a book which
Heracleon evidently recognized as of such authority that he must perforce
have it on his side',[22] though hopelessly out-of-step with the prevailing
paradigm of today, still has to be regarded as eminently more agreeable
with the data.

Theodotus

It should be apparent that, if the notion of orthodox Johannophobia caused
by gnostic use of or association with John is to be saved at all, it will have to
be done by essentially restricting it to a time before the last thirty years or
so of the second century. This realization impinges as well upon the work of
another Valentinian teacher whom we have encountered already in a work
of Clement's, Theodotus, a representative of the so-called eastern school
of Valentinianism who evidently taught in Alexandria. He is not
mentioned by Irenaeus and, like Heracleon, probably wrote some years

[19] J.-D. Kaestli, 'L'Exégèse valentinienne', in Kaestli *et al.* (eds.), *La Communauté johannique*,
323–50.

[20] Salmon, 'Heracleon', 899, 'Heracleon's doctrine is not orthodox, but his principles of interpretation cannot be said to differ essentially from those of Origen himself. Many orthodox parallels,
for instance, could be adduced to Heracleon's exposition'; cf. Bammel, 'Herakleon', 55.

[21] Several have in fact maintained this, among them, E. De Faye, A. E. Brooke, and W. von
Loewenich, *Das Johannes-Verständnis*, according to Pagels, *Gnostic Exegesis*, 25 (see Pagels's own view
on p. 26). Similarly, Kaestli, 'L'Exégèse valentinienne', 350, has recently said that Heracleon did
not ignore or eliminate the myth of the aeons and Wisdom, 'mais qu'il l'a délibérément laissé de
côté parce que son commentaire s'adressait à un public pas encore initié à toutes les dimensions du
mythe'. Sanders, *Fourth Gospel*, 65, acknowledged the differences but preferred to say simply that
Heracleon's 'Valentinianism was profoundly modified by his understanding of the Fourth Gospel'.
Whatever the true cause, it remains apparent that the non-pleromic interpretations seem to be later
than the pleromic ones, and that, whether intentionally or not, they avoid the interpretations which
Irenaeus criticized in the 'commentary' usually attributed to Ptolemy in *AH* 1. 8. 5.

[22] Salmon, 'Heracleon', 899

after Ptolemy.[23] By the time he wrote, then, the Fourth Gospel was already well established in orthodox theology and piety. As evidence for a high Valentinian regard for the Fourth Gospel, Poffet points out that Theodotus cited from it *ad litteram*.[24] But the citations in *Theod.*[25] certainly show no higher regard for the Fourth Gospel than is exhibited by Clement, who also cited it *ad litteram* at times—not to admit, however, that literal citation necessarily denotes a higher regard than adapted citation or embedded allusion. And it is worth observing again that the combined labours of Theodotus, Heracleon, Ptolemy, and all other Valentinians known to Clement failed to poison his mind against the Fourth Gospel or to deter him from using it as an authoritative, scriptural book. To maintain that Theodotus' work did have such an effect on other orthodox scholars or on ordinary church members is speculation, and not particularly well-conceived speculation. I have noted above that Clement knew of orthodox church members, evidently in Alexandria, who, on the authority of Jesus' words in John 10, objected to the use of pagan philosophers—'thieves and robbers' who came only to kill and to destroy—in Christian theology. In fact, it appears that all the evidence of the period, both from Christian leaders and from the laity, is against such speculation.

Ptolemy

In the section on Irenaeus I dealt briefly with the exegesis of the Prologue of John's Gospel contained in a Valentinian work known to Irenaeus and traditionally assigned to Ptolemy the Valentinian. I mentioned in passing a controversy over whether this should rightfully be assigned to Ptolemy or not. There has long existed a question of how to relate this piece to the other work which has come down to us under Ptolemy's name, his *Letter to Flora*, which we have thanks to Epiphanius (*Panarion* 33. 3. 1–33. 7. 10). But now Christoph Markschies has argued that only the latter is genuinely Ptolemaean.[26] I shall return to this matter after a look at the *Letter* itself.

---

[23] F. Sagnard, *Clément d'Alexandrie, Extraits de Théodote: Texte grec, introduction, traduction et notes* SC (Paris, 1948), 7, suggests that he was contemporary with Ptolemy and taught between 160–70 (accepted by Culpepper, *John*, 117). This is hard to establish, however, as no one mentions him before Clement of Alexandria writing in the 190s or after the turn of the 3rd century. Even if Theodotus wrote as early as the 160s, however, it makes little difference. Negative effects on the use of John among the mainstream churches, if in fact there were any, could not have been great.

[24] Poffet, 'Indices', 315. The rest may have come from Ptolemy or some other Valentinian source or sources.

[25] Remember that, in the judgement of R. P. Casey, *The Excerpta ex Theodoto of Clement of Alexandria* (London, 1934), 5, as to Thedotus' use of the Fourth Gospel, only the references to the Paraclete in *Theod.* 23. 1–2 and to John 1: 9 in *Theod.* 41. 3 come from material which can be attributed to Theodotus himself. Material in *Theod.* 6–7 has probably come from Ptolemy (or the same source used by Irenaeus). The rest apparently comes either from this latter source or from some other product of the Ptolemaic school.

[26] '[T]he only reliable source for a reconstruction of the teachings of the Roman theologian Ptolemy is the Epistle to Flora. The system developed in Irenaeus' so-called "grand notice" cannot

The *Letter to Flora* is a letter-treatise[27] which sets out to develop an inter-pretative approach to the Law of Moses. This letter, like the Valentinian cited by Irenaeus in *AH* 1. 8. 5, also uses the Prologue to John's Gospel, though not in any programmatic way and without giving any openly plero-matic exegesis. His one clear allusion to it is as follows: 'And further, the apostle states that the craftsmanship of the world is his, and that "all things were made through him, and without him was not anything made" (Jn. 1. 3), thus anticipating these liars' flimsy wisdom' (*Panar.* 33. 3. 6).[28] Ptolemy's purpose in this citation is to confound those who would attribute the creation of the physical world and the giving of the law of Moses to 'the adversary, the pernicious devil' (probably a caricature of a Marcionite[29] or a 'gnostic' position). Ptolemy opposes just as sharply the view of those who attribute creation and the OT law to the highest Father. To him the Creator and Lawgiver, being an intermediate being (33. 7. 4), was just, but neither good nor evil (33. 7. 5). However one seeks to integrate Ptolemy's use of John 1:3 here with the more openly pleromatic exegesis of the Johannine Prologue in the treatise cited by Irenaeus, this certainly shows that he used at least parts of the Fourth Gospel as apostolic and as positive supports for his views. But just as certainly one cannot speak of any special reliance upon John, with regard to this letter. Ptolemy's lone citation of John, for example, is far outweighed by his ten citations of or allusions to Synoptic material, probably exclusively from Matthew.[30] He treats the words of Jesus recorded in Mat-thew's Gospel as authentic words of 'the Saviour' which he takes to support his position on the law. Moreover, he cites 'the apostle Paul',[31] by name, just as authoritatively (33. 5. 15; 33. 6. 6) for his own teaching (references to Rom., 1 Cor., and Eph.). As Markschies points out, Ptolemy's treatment 'takes it for granted that the readers of the Epistle knew the Bible and Jewish–Christian customs very well'.[32] Known to both Ptolemy and his readers in common is surely the Fourth Gospel, but also the First Gospel, the Letters of Paul, and no doubt more. This much, at least, conforms well to our observations about the Christian sources used in the work traditionally ascribed to Ptolemy in *Against Heresies* 1.8.

be called "Ptolemaeic" without further thought and, accordingly, the Epistle cannot be interpreted in the light of this system' (C. Markschies, 'New Research on Ptolemaeus Gnosticus', *ZAC* 4 (2000), 252).

[27] On its form and genre, see Winrich A. Löhr, 'Ptolemäus, *Gnostiker*', in *TRE* ii. 27 (Berlin, 1997), 699–702 at 699; Markschies, 'New Research', 228–33, who says it fits the description of a διαιρετικαὶ εἰσαγωγαί.

[28] B. Layton's translation in *The Gnostic Scriptures* (New York, 1987).

[29] So Löhr, 'Ptolemäus', 699; Markschies, 'New Research', 234, 237.

[30] Matt. 12: 25 in 33. 3. 5; Matt. 11: 27 in 33. 3. 7; Matt. 19: 8 and 19: 6 in 33. 4. 4; Matt. 19: 7 in 33. 4. 5; Matt. 15: 4 in 33. 4. 11 and again in 33. 5. 7; Matt. 15: 5 in 33. 4. 12; Matt. 15: 8 in 33. 4. 13; Matt. 5: 38 in 33. 5. 4.

[31] Layton, *The Gnostic Scriptures*, 313 n. g, says, 'Valentinians considered Paul to be the ultimate source of their esoteric tradition'.

[32] Markschies, 'New Research', at 238.

This brings us back to the question of authenticity. Any definitive determination about the authenticity of the work cited by Irenaeus is beyond the
scope of the present study. Before endorsing either position, the relevance of
each for this study may be explored briefly. Markschies writes that an
implication of his research is that the records at our disposal now

> allow the hypothesis that Ptolemy was closer to the consent of the theology of the
> city of Rome than his followers—similar to the namegiving Valentinus, who was
> closer to the consent of Alexandrine Theology than his followers. From this hypoth-
> esis two conclusions follow: first, Valentinus and Ptolemy are likely to be closer
> connected than I claimed in my book seven years ago. And second, the real origin-
> ators of the 'classical' Valentinian myth are neither Valentinus nor Ptolemy, but
> gifted and imaginative thinkers among their followers of whom we do not know the
> names.[33]

He writes further that the mentality of Ptolemy's Epistle is that of 'the
group of Christian theologians in the second century to which the Apologists and mainly Justin belonged. Ptolemy's insisting on the "teachings of
the saviour" and the "apostolic tradition"...(7, 9)—goes with this'.[34] Thus
the *Letter to Flora* and its 'less Valentinian' teaching would leave us with a
use of the Fourth Gospel that was, if Markschies is right, possibly non-
controversial among the orthodox in Rome. And it would mean that the
treatise known to Irenaeus, which explicitly links John 1: 1–18 to the names
and the generations of the pantheon of Valentinian aeons, is from a later
Valentinian who had developed the thought of Valentinus and Ptolemy
along lines not taken by them. This would most likely place the writing of
this unknown Valentinian even closer in time to Irenaeus himself than
previously thought. This in turn would provide even less room for Johannophobia to take hold in orthodox circles which responded negatively to the
development.

I have to admit to being somewhat sceptical about aspects of Markschies's
proposal. This goes for the assumption that the words *et Ptolomaeus quidem ita* in
the Latin version at the end of *AH* 1. 8. 5 are necessarily spurious[35] *and*

---

[33] Ibid. 252.

[34] Ibid. 253.

[35] Rousseau (SC 263, 218, n. 2) says Epiphanius probably omitted these words because he
placed this material in his section on Valentinus, not on Ptolemy. Markschies, 'New Research',
249–50, has contested this, arguing that Epiphanius did not have the words in his Greek
exemplar, for Epiphanius ends his citation of this section of Irenaeus with the words
πεπλήρωται τὰ Εἰρηναίου κατὰ τῶν Οὐαλεντίνων (GCS Epiphanius i. 435, 9 Holl) and in a
later section on Ptolemy (*Panarion* 33. 1. 2–2. 5) reproduces not *AH* 1. 8. 5 but 1. 12. 1, where
Irenaeus attributes the teaching to 'the followers of Ptolemy'. He proposes that the words are an
explanatory gloss supplied by the 4th-cent. Latin translator. But another explanation is possible. We
notice from Rousseau's SC edn. that at *Panar.* 33. 1, where Epiphanius purports to give teaching
from Ptolemy, his text differs from that of Hippolytus and the Latin version of Irenaeus 12. 1. The
text in Hippolytus, agreeing with the Latin, attributes the material only to 'the more experienced
followers of Ptolemy' (Οἱ δὲ περὶ τὸν Πτολεμαῖον ἐμπειρότεροι...λέγουσιν), while Epiphanius

mistaken.[36] One should also want to question the alleged compatibility between the thought of Ptolemy in the letter and that of Justin and his associates,[37] and the supposedly unproblematic nature of his use of John 1: 3 there. Can the theology of the letter be closer to Justin than to the Valentinian excerpts in *AH* 1. 8? I do not think so. But in any case, even if we should reject Markscheis's proposal, the import of the Ptolemaean heritage does not give more than a marginal foothold for the OJP. Ptolemy's use of John in the *Letter to Flora* would not have drawn as much attention as would his ten references to Matthew, and so it provides no incentive for a theory of orthodox Johannophobia which does not also advance a theory of orthodox Mattheophobia. And even if we were able to be confident about a date for one or both of these 'Ptolemaean' works as early as the early 160s,[38] we would still have to conclude that neither the *Letter to Flora* nor any other works he might have authored, including the exposition of the Johannine Prologue known to Irenaeus, can have had a great effect in orthodox circles—unless the effect was to stimulate Johannophilia instead of Johannophobia. For we are still very close to the time from which, by all accounts, and particularly as the demonstration above makes plain, orthodox use of this Gospel begins to show itself strong. After reviewing the evidence of Melito of Sardis, Claudius Appolinarius of Hierapolis, Tatian, and others, I shall be able to speak more definitely about the decade of the 160s itself. For now I only reiterate my former observation that the use of John's Prologue in the Valentinian work explicitly treated by Irenaeus had no deleterious effect on Irenaeus' appreciation for the Fourth Gospel. It appears that this 'Ptolemaean' exegesis was also known to Clement,

attributes it to Ptolemy and his followers (οὕτως τοίνυν ὁ Πτολεμαῖος καὶ οἱ σὺν αὐτῷ) and changes the plural verbs to singulars. That Hippolytus and the Latin are correct against Epiphanius is proved also by Tertullian, who in *Val.* 33, says, *hunc malui in locum distulisse aliter atque aliter commendata ab emendatioribus Ptolemaei. Exstiterunt enim de schola ipsius discipuli super magistrum....* Why then did Epiphanius change Irenaeus' report and attribute this material to Ptolemy himself? It may be that, having realized that he had already reproduced the Ptolemaean material from 1. 8 in a section on Valentinus (perhaps he only realized it when he got to the end of 1. 8. 5), Epiphanius presented the views Irenaeus attributed to followers of Ptolemy as those of Ptolemy himself.

[36] Markschies's view requires not only that the words are interpolated but that they are also incorrect. But it is worth stating that, even if the attribution to Ptolemy at the end of 1. 8. 5 is not original, this does not necessarily mean it was mistaken. It could be that the translator had located the true source of the citation and included it for the benefit of the reader.

[37] Although the defection of Justin's student Tatian to something resembling Valentinianism might form a bridge. Markschies, 'Valentinian Gnosticism', 425, 427; 'New Research', 244–9, takes seriously Harnack's contention that this Valentinian Ptolemy is the same man mentioned by Justin in *2Apol.* 2 as a teacher in Rome (recently revived by G. Lüdemann, 'Zur Geschichte', *ZNW* 70 (1979), 100–2), though he is, I believe, rightly sceptical. As he observes, 'Valentinian Gnosticism', 425 n. 100, 'it would be strange if Justin branded the "Valentinians" as heretics [in *Dial.* 35. 6]...and at the same time wrote, without any commentary, in support of the Valentinian Ptolemy'.

[38] Trying to date Ptolemy's works cannot produce exact results, but it must be remembered that 'Nowhere do we find the claim that Ptolemy was *personally* a disciple of Valentinus' (Markschies, 'Valentinian Gnosticism', 426). Markschies (ibid. 428), also observes that Irenaeus 'discusses, in sequence, Valentinus (11. 1), Secundus (11. 2), the other anonymous teacher (11. 3) and finally those of Ptolemy's school (12. 1)'. Ptolemy's *Letter to Flora* presupposes the existence of Marcionite teaching.

and it certainly had no such effect on him, nor upon Hippolytus, Tertullian, or Origen, the only fairly contemporary authors who we know may have had access to it.[39] If someone wants to insist, in spite of this, that it must have tended to turn many other Christians away from the Gospel according to John (and, if consistent, the Gospel according to Matthew), he or she should be obliged to produce evidence.

Valentinus

As for Valentinus himself, despite what one might expect, some experts have confessed that 'Whether Valentinus himself knew and used the gospel [of John] is uncertain'.[40] Of the handful of fragments of his work which have been preserved by others, some contact with John has been claimed with regard to two of them, but in each case the claim is dubious. Bentley Layton has suggested that John 6: 27 lies behind Valentinus' statements about Jesus' physical qualities in an excerpt from his *Epistle to Agathopoda* preserved by Clement of Alexandria (*Strom.* 3. 59. 3; Völker's fragment 3; Layton's fragment E).[41] Here, in Layton's translation, Valentinus says, 'He was continent, enduring all things. Jesus digested divinity (θεότητα 'Ιησοῦς εἰργάζετο): he ate and drank in a special way, without excreting his solids.'

Layton writes that Valentinus' 'exaggerated statement about Jesus' digestion may be based on a New Testament story of Jesus' command to the people of Tiberias in John 6: 27, playing upon the double meaning of the Greek verb 'to labor for,' which can also mean 'to digest': 'Jesus answered them ... "Do not *labor for* (or *digest*) the food which perishes, but for the food which endures to eternal life, which the son of man will give you"'.[42] This, however, seems fairly far-fetched. Besides the question of the proper way to translate Valentinus' εἰργάζετο,[43] the food Jesus speaks of in John 6: 27 is 'the bread of life' (6: 35), while Valentinus is obviously talking here about a special ability of the body of Jesus to process and retain real, physical victuals in a supernatural way.[44] Markschies rejects Layton's interpret-

---

[39] According to Mark T. Riley, 'Q. S. Fl. Tertulliani Adversus Valentinanos. Text, Translation, and Commentary' (Ph.D. dissertation, Stanford University, 1971), 16, 'There is no evidence that he [i.e. Tertullian] knew anything about the Valentinians apart from what Irenaeus says'. And Tertullian does not repeat the specific material on the Johannine Prologue from *AH* 1. 8. 5. While this may not bode well for Tertullian's reputation as a scrupulous researcher, nor does the fact that Tertullian did not have a Valentinian treatise in front of him encourage the idea that these treatises, including the exegesis of John 1: 1–18, were widely available.

[40] Pagels, *Gnostic Exegesis*, 24, who cites for this also von Loewenich, *Das Johannes-Verständnis*, 72–4, and Sanders, *Fourth Gospel*, 33–4. Von Loewenich, *Das Johannes-Verständnis*, 71 n. 1, says 'Es ist fraglich, ob schon die ältesten Valentinianer das Joh-Ev gekannt haben'.

[41] W. Völker, *Quellen zur Geschichte der christlichen Gnosis* (Tübingen, 1932), 60; Layton, *The Gnostic Scriptures*, 239.

[42] Layton, *The Gnostic Scriptures*, 238.

[43] See C. Markschies, *Valentinus Gnosticus? Untersuchungen zur valentinianischen Gnosis mit einem Kommentar zu den Fragmenten Valentins*, WUNT 65 (Tübingen, 1992), 91–8.

[44] E. Procter, *Christian Controversy in Alexandria* (New York, 1995), 69–70 observes that Clement, in *Strom.* 6. 71. 2–3, actually takes over basically the view of Valentinus as his own, after criticizing

ation,[45] preferring the translation, 'Jesus *verwirklichte* seine Gottheit', Jesus realized, actualized, practised, or exercised, his deity.[46] Yet, of this translation, he writes, 'ist zumindest nicht ausgeschlossen, daß dabei auch eine biblische Anspielung auf die johanneische Vorstellung vom *Werk des Vaters* vorliegt, das der Logos und Sohn tut: Jesus praktizierte, übt die Gottheit als Werk aus', referring to John 5: 20, 36; 7: 3, 21; 9: 3, 4; 10: 25, 32, 37, 38; 14: 10, 11; 15: 24.[47] While it is certainly possible that such a concept of Jesus 'practising' or 'exercising' his deity might reflect a knowledge of this Johannine theme, the connection is not overt or unambiguous.

Another possible Johannine allusion has been claimed from Völker's fragment 7 (Layton's A),[48] preserved by Hippolytus (*Ref.* 6. 42. 2): 'For Valentinus says he saw a newborn babe, and questioned it to find out who it was. And the babe answered him saying that it was the Word (λόγος). Thereupon, he adds to this a certain pompous tale, intending to derive from this his attempt at a sect.' Robert M. Grant suggested an allusion here to John 1: 1.[49] Markschies, on the other hand, points out that the extract is too brief for us to tell whether Valentinus, like Justin, had a 'Logos-Theologie' or, if he did, what role it might have played in his own theology.[50] But he suggests another link to John in the presumed answer of the infant, behind Hippolytus' report, which would have begun with ἐγὼ εἰμι.[51] The report is of a vision which, according to Hippolytus, Valentinus claims he had, which gives the appearance of documenting the origins of Valentinus' system as the result of a revelation. The Logos mentioned here seems to be a manifestation of the Logos of the pleroma. This would be confirmed by analogy with the vision which Marcus, 'imitating his teacher', also claimed to have, as Hippolytus reports in the same passage. 'Marcus, making a similar attempt...asserts that the Tetrad came to him in the form of a woman'.[52] This Tetrad then related a story about the genesis of the aeons, the first of which to be emitted from the mouth of the self-existent Father was the

Valentinus in 3. 59. 3. Clement did modify Valentinus' idea, however, by insisting that Jesus' body was flesh and not merely of psychic substance, holding, however, that the Saviour ate and drank merely 'to prevent his disciples from thinking that he did not have a real physical body' (70).

[45] Markschies, *Valentinus Gnosticus?* 92.
[46] R. M. Grant, *Gnosticism: An Anthology* (London, 1961), 144, translates, 'Jesus exercised his divine nature'.
[47] Markschies, *Valentinus Gnosticus?* 97.
[48] W. Völker, *Quellen zur Geschichte der Christlichen Gnosis* (Tübingen, 1932) 59; Layton, *The Gnostic Scriptures*, 231. The translation here is Layton's.
[49] Grant, *Gnosticism*, 141, 'it can be imagined that the Logos is the Logos of Jewish speculation and the Fourth Gospel'.
[50] Markschies, *Valentinus Gnosticus?* 212.
[51] Ibid. 213.
[52] Ibid. 205–7, following L. Abrahamowski, 'Ein gnostischer Logostheologe: Umfang und Redaktor des gnostischen Sonderguts in Hippolyts "Widerlegung aller Häresien"', in *Drei christologische Untersuchungen*, BZNW 45 (Berlin, 1981), 18–62, sees this analogy as raising doubts about the historicity of the report about Valentinus, as if it might have been made up for the purpose of forming an antecedent for Marcus. This seems rather too sceptical.

Logos. Here again it is a representative of the pleroma which came to the Valentinian adept in human form, and here again the Logos in question is the heavenly aeon. If so, though a knowledge of John 1 may be presupposed, as it seems to have been in the Valentinian version of the pleromatic myth (see below), any possible allusion to John 1: 1 would be quite indirect. Hippolytus gives no indication that he recognized it as an allusion to John 1: 1. But if it ever was recognized as such, one must then reckon with the way Valentinus has used this prime Christological text and its intended and likely effects on an orthodox reader. If an orthodox reader were to make a connection with John 1: 1 (the Word being with God and being God), and possibly to John 1: 14 (the Word becoming flesh), or to John 1: 18 (the Word revealing the Father), the effect on that reader would most likely not have been a sudden revelation that the Fourth Gospel taught Valentinianism, but rather shock and revulsion that Valentinus should present the Logos, who was in the beginning with God and was God, who became flesh and dwelt among his people, full of grace and truth, who is in fact none other than the person of Jesus Christ, in the form of an otherworldly, aeonic visitor to Valentinus, come in the form of an infant to reveal the mysteries of the Valentinian system. We may reasonably guess that it would have struck the average Christian in Rome much as Valentinian exegesis struck Irenaeus in Gaul. If this represents Valentinus' appropriation of the Fourth Gospel's doctrine of the Logos, we may hardly hesitate to see in it a contempt for, even a mockery of, that doctrine. Such a use, as we shall later see, would indeed have parallels with other writers and is by no means out of the question historically. In this case, then, Valentinus' use of the Fourth Gospel might be proved, but with no credible or likely supportive consequences for the OJP. Even so, we probably should be cautious about drawing inferences from this brief and almost contextless (and contested) excerpt in any direction.

If we were to limit our sources for understanding Valentinus and his teaching to the small fragments extracted from his works, we should have doubtful cause to affirm that Valentinus 'received' the Fourth Gospel at all,[53] and should have to say that, if he did, he seems to have used it in rather an 'unreceptive' way. Some have supposed that Valentinus was the author of the Nag Hammadi work, the *Gospel of Truth*. If true, this would enable us to affirm with certainty that he used the Fourth Gospel. But the attribution is quite doubtful, as the text itself is anonymous and as nobody, including Irenaeus, who seems to have known this work, attributes it to him. I shall thus reserve comment about the *Gospel of Truth* until a later point. But because his later followers certainly used the Fourth Gospel, because we have seen enough evidence already (without yet examining

---

[53] Hengel, *Question*, 146 n. 43; Culpepper, *John*, 115, 'The fragments of Valentinus's work contain no clear evidence that he used the Gospel of John'.

Justin's writings) to make it virtually certain that the Fourth Gospel was being used in Rome by the orthodox at about this time, because the general tendency of the Valentinians, according to Irenaeus and Tertullian, was to use all of the Church's scriptures (*Praescr.* 38), and because of the likely, though not conclusive, evidence from the fragments cited above, we may, I think, be reasonably sure that Valentinus did use it. For positive evidence of this, however, we are left with secondary summaries of his system, ostensibly dependent upon some written work which has not survived independently, and about which there is now controversy about their true attribution. In *AH* 1. 11. 1 Irenaeus ascribes a version of the gnostic myth to Valentinus himself, 'who adapted the principles of the heresy called "Gnostic" to the peculiar character of his own school' (he connects it at one point with the summary he had made in 1. 1). It definitely appears that the names bestowed on certain members of the pleroma in this work have been derived from John's Prologue. Five of the six members of the primary Ogdoad who are the progeny of the primary (non-Johannine) duo, Arrhetus and Sige, have names which occur in John 1: 1–18: Pater and Aletheia, Logos and Zoe, and Anthropos (though not his consort Ecclesia). Some of the names of the remaining twenty-two aeons mentioned in 1. 1. 1 (to which Irenaeus refers in 1. 11. 1) are also arguably inspired by the Fourth Gospel (particularly Paracletos, Pistis, Agape). And the brief exposition attributed by the Latin text to Ptolemy in 1. 8. 5, which relates the Ogdoad directly to John's Prologue, would bear this out. In the system of 1. 8. 5 certain name changes make the connection more explicit. The name of Pater is taken from the second masculine aeon and given to Arrhetus instead. It is replaced by Monogenes, another name from John 1.[54] The name of Sige is replaced with Charis, which also occurs in John 1. The name Ecclesia, which does not itself appear in the Prologue or anywhere else in John's Gospel, is also defended by this author (Ptolemy?) as being implied in John 1: 4, in its mention of Anthropos, the putative conjunctive partner of Ecclesia. Thus it would appear that the 'Ptolemaean' scheme of 1. 8. 5 has been able to work all of the elite eight into the Johannine Prologue.[55] From Irenaeus' presentations in 1. 8. 5 and 1. 11. 1 it would seem that Valentinus, in his makeover of 'gnostic' pleromatic mythology, adapted it to John's Prologue by taking names from the Prologue and giving them to members of the pleroma,[56] and that this process was perfected by his disciple 'Ptolemy'. It should be recalled that later, in 3. 11. 7, Irenaeus will say that the followers of Valentinus used John copiously to illustrate

---

[54] Tertullian points out in *Val.* 7 that the name Monogenes for this figure is improper because he was not the only offspring of his father. This seems to be another sign that the name was not original to the system but was taken from an alien source.

[55] Cf. Pagels, *Gnostic Exegesis*, 37.

[56] See my comments on the *Apocryphon of John* below.

their 'conjunctions'. This is just what is apparent from the accounts in *AH*
1. 1. 1; 1. 8. 5; 1. 11. 1.

It appears then that the author of the system summarized by Irenaeus in
AH 1. 11. 1, whether Valentinus himself or a later follower, did certainly
know and use the Fourth Gospel. As far as our evidence goes, this reliance
is attested mainly or only from John's Prologue. And it is virtually restricted
to the pleromatic aspect of the Valentinian myth. That is, as we have seen
above in the section on Irenaeus, there is not a preponderance of influence
from the Fourth Gospel in other areas of Valentinianism as reproduced by
Irenaeus. Now comes the delicate matter of trying to ascertain when this
'adaptation' of the gnostic myth with help from the Johannine Prologue was
made. Let us start with Valentinus himself. Irenaeus tells us that Valentinus
came to Rome in the time of Hyginus (136–40; *AH* 3. 4. 3), flourished
under Pius (140–54(5)), and remained until Anicetus (154(5)–66). Irenaeus
certainly had good contacts with Rome and was interested in the history of
the church there, and there is no reason to think that his basic timeline is
far askew.[57] Tertullian would later claim that Valentinus at one time
expected to be made bishop, and that when these expectations were dashed
he broke with the Church (*Val.* 4). If this is true the break probably came
shortly after 140, following the election of Pius. We certainly would be on
shaky ground to maintain that any radical departure from standard Christian theology such as is represented by Irenaeus' summary in *AH* 1. 11.
1 could have been publicly made before the early 140s, and it may well be
that the distinctive views which now characterize what is known as the
Valentinian system were not in place for some years after that. At this point
the researches of Christoph Markschies come back into play. Markschies
has argued that Valentinus himself never was very 'Valentinian'. Because of
certain questionable aspects of the secondary reports of his teaching by
Irenaeus and others, and because these reports do not match up exceptionally well with the fragments of Valentinus' own writings which have survived, Markschies argues that we may not rely upon the former for our
understanding of Valentinus but should regard them as reporting the views
of later followers.[58] If Markschies is correct, the 'gnostic myth' was never

---

[57] I am not sure of Markschies's reasons, 'Valentinian Gnosticism', 420, for saying that 'Valentinus left Rome perhaps already in 155, at the latest in 161' and for saying that Irenaeus' visit to
Rome in 177/8 was probably his first visit to the city. See my comments above on Irenaeus'
connections with Rome. It appears he was in Rome at the time of Polycarp's death and probably
also when Polycarp had visited Rome in 154/5. Thus Irenaeus would have been in Rome almost
certainly while Valentinus was still alive and probably in Rome.

[58] Markschies, *Valentinus Gnosticus?* Idem, 'Das Problem des historischen Valentin: Neue Forschungen zu Valentinus Gnosticus', in E. A. Livingstone (ed.), *Studia Patristica*, 24 (Leuven, 1993), 382–9.
In 'New Research', 225, he reports on his work, 'an utterly elementary rule of text-interpretation
was applied to the short passages which were mainly recorded by Clement of Alexandria and
Hippolytus'; 'A premise for this kind of interpretation however is that one does not ascribe anonymous treatises such as the so-called *Evangelium Veritatis* to Valentinus, and that one does not take
the statements of the later anti-heretic authors of the established church Irenaeus, Clement and

appropriated by Valentinus at all but only by later followers. This means that 'the main period of formation of what we call "Valentinian Gnosticism" must have been after the middle of the fifties of the first [*sic*, i.e. second!] century',[59] that is, some time after Valentinus' death, which Irenaeus placed under Anicetus, between 155 and 166. On this supposition, then, we have no reason to think Valentinus made any special use of the Fourth Gospel (unless it was a derisory one), and will have to say that the Valentinian practice of illustrating their conjunctions from the Fourth Gospel came some time later than 155 and perhaps not until after 166. Though we would still have no definitive date for the adoption of the full 'gnostic myth' of aeons by members of the Valentinian school, and the takeover of names from the Johannine Prologue for them, Markschies' conclusions would deliver an added blow to the theory that Valentinian use of John caused or increased orthodox Johannophobia. For these conclusions would tend to allow even less time between the adaptation of the Johannine Prologue by later Valentinians to illustrate their syzygies and the recognized widespread emergence of Johannine use on the part of the orthodox.

Certain doubts remain, it must be said, about Markschies's reconstruction of the history of Valentinianism. As we saw above, his understanding of Ptolemy relies on the phrase *et Ptolemaeus quidem ita* in the Latin of 1. 8. 5 being a much later and erroneous gloss. For Valentinus, it relies on Irenaeus being mistaken, or dissembling, in attributing the summary account of *AH* 1. 11. 1 to Valentinus. But Irenaeus distinguishes several varieties of Valentinian teaching, and had no need to make an uncertain attribution to Valentinus. The strength of Markschies's position, it seems to me, is that it takes seriously the differences between the extracts of Valentinus and Ptolemy's *Letter to Flora* on the one hand, and the reports of their systematic developments of the gnostic myth in Irenaeus and the heresiologists on the other, and it places before us the real possibility of evolution in Valentinus' own thought and in the early thought of his school. There may be other plausible ways to account for the difficulty. Irenaeus stresses the evasive and secretive habits of Valentinians in his day, confessing one thing in public but reserving a different meaning for the words (*AH* 1. 31. 4), which may have carried on the practices of their founder.[60] Alternatively, the evolution in Valentinus' own thought may indeed have been quite radical. Certainly by the time Justin published his *Dialogue with Trypho*, probably in *c.*155–60,

---

Hippolytus concerning Valentinus too seriously'. He states that 'In fact, Irenaeus hardly knew anything about Valentinus, and Clement and Hippolytus only knew fragments of texts from a later Valentinian commentary' (Ibid. 226).

[59] Markschies, 'New Research', at 226; for this statement he refers to *Valentinus Gnosticus?* 392–402.

[60] Procter, *Controversy*, 2–3, 'Apparently, Valentinus remained a member of the established Christian churches, reserving his radical interpretation of the scripture for selected disciples in a school setting outside the regular worship services'. Markschies, of course, rejects this approach to Valentinus.

when Valentinus was probably still alive or only recently deceased, there was an identifiable group called 'Valentinians' (οἱ Οὐαλεντινιανοί) because their doctrine originated with a man by that name (*Dial.* 35. 6).[61] Justin considers them false Christians and places them among others who 'blaspheme the Maker of all things, and Christ who was foretold by Him as coming ... with whom we have nothing in common, since we know them to be atheists, impious, unrighteous, and sinful, and confessors of Jesus in name only, instead of worshippers of Him'.

But even if we reject Markschies's reconstruction outright, there is perhaps nothing to connect Valentinus to the Fourth Gospel beyond an apparent borrowing of names from the Johannine Prologue, unless it is a disparaging replacement of the Prologue's Logos doctrine with another quite foreign one. It is still only with regard to Valentinus' pupils, Ptolemy (possibly), Theodotus, and Heracleon, writing probably in the 160s, 170s, and 180s, and possibly later, just about contemporaneously with Hegesippus, Theophilus, Irenaeus, and Clement, that we can say Valentinian use of John flourished in any sense. And by now the floodgates of the Great Church's use of John's Gospel are already opened. From the presentation above it is clear that from at least the 170s Valentinian use of this Gospel could not have produced much negative reaction against it among the orthodox. In due time we shall be able to speak more clearly about the 160s and earlier.

Tatian

Tatian's *Diatessaron* was a Gospel harmony based on the four Gospels of Matthew, Mark, Luke, and John. Yet I have noted that many scholars do not regard this as an indication of orthodox but of heterodox approval of the Fourth Gospel. Bauer wrote,

> To be sure, Justin's disciple Tatian placed the gospel of John on the same level as the synoptics, but he also broke with the church on account of profound differences in faith—poisoned, so Irenaeus thought, by the Valentinians and Marcion (AH 1. 28. 1 [= 1. 26. 1])—and he left the world capital to move once again toward the East. Thus Tatian cannot provide us with a satisfactory testimony concerning the moods and conditions within the 'church' at Rome ...[62]

Raymond Brown too, while acknowledging the status of the Fourth Gospel in the *Diatessaron*, objected that 'Tatian was an encratite who played down the value of the flesh, and so he should be reckoned on the heterodox side of the usage of John'.[63] Thus both these scholars, like others, regard Tatian's work as one more piece of evidence for the heterodox monopoly

---

[61] As Markschies, 'Valentinian Gnosticism', 414, points out, these people probably simply called themselves 'Christians' and were called Valentinians by others.

[62] Bauer, *Orthodoxy and Heresy*, 206–7.

[63] Brown, *Community*, 148. Also Barrett, *John* (1978), 125.

on John. The main problem, unacknowledged by these authors, however, is that their assessment requires a relatively late dating of the *Diatessaron*, after Tatian's adoption of encratism. This, as we shall see, is quite questionable. Many have concluded that Justin himself used a synthetic compilation of at least the three Synoptic Gospels, and the more complete work of Tatian may simply have been a continuation of this effort. The second problem is that, even if the *Diatessaron* is from his 'heretical' period, it does not necessarily follow that his inclusion of John was done from heretical motives. Did the encratites too claim John as their 'special Gospel'? This has not yet been alleged. Further, just as important as Tatian's *Diatessaron* is his treatise, *Oratio ad Graecos*, in which he clearly used the Fourth Gospel, particularly the Prologue, several times (chs. 4 (John 4: 24), 5 (John 1: 1), 13 (John 1: 4, 5), 19 (John 1: 3). For the positions of Bauer and Brown to hold, it must also be maintained that this work too comes from Tatian's later, heretical period. But this, as we shall see, is apparently impossible. I shall deal with the important questions of the dating and the orthodoxy of Tatian's works in more detail at a later point. I only observe now that Tatian's value in supporting the OJP relies upon the strength of the case for a late dating of both of these works, after Tatian's defection from the catholics.

And as to Tatian's potential for inciting any orthodox Johannophobia, we must also keep the following in mind: the earlier the dates of the *Diatessaron* and the *Oratio ad Graecos*, the more clearly they indicate orthodox reception of John, and the later the dates, the more likely they *may* indicate heterodox use, but the less likely they could have been a significant cause of Johannophobia among the orthodox. We may have to conclude that the use of John in the *Diatessaron* does not indicate a heretical predilection for it any more than the use of Matthew, Mark, and Luke in the same work indicates a predilection for them.

It appears that the consensus view about the extent of orthodox Johannophobia must undergo yet more drastic revisions, if it is to survive at all. It should be clear that it can no longer rest its fortunes on Heracleon's commentary, or upon Theodotus' excerpts, or even on Ptolemy's exegesis of the Prologue, and that only limited help, if indeed any, can be derived from Valentinus himself. Nor can Tatian the encratite be considered a reliable crutch. Yet it is also true that most scholars believe the connections between the Fourth Gospel and gnosticism go back to a much earlier time, and that Johannophobia's chilling effects were felt from the time of the Gospel's origin until these Valentinian and encratite teachers began writing. But if this is the case, it is still not unreasonable to ask for evidence.

If such evidence exists, it is likely to be found in gnostic sources which have some reasonable claim to predating 170, and for them to be considered as strong forces they should predate 170 by some distance. I shall begin, then, with the earliest known gnostic systems of the second century and work back up to Ptolemy and Irenaeus.

Basilides

From the scholars cited at the beginning of this study in support of the OJP there is no claim of a particular knowledge or use of the Fourth Gospel by the heresies of the Samaritans Simon and Menander, or by the Antiochene Saturninus. Certainly from the descriptions of their systems in Irenaeus and other early heresiologists we would have no reason to think that any of them valued or even knew the Fourth Gospel. Of known gnostics, the first to be named as being in any way partial to John is Basilides of Alexandria, who is mentioned by Sanders and Gamble, and probably alluded to by others.[64]

According to Eusebius, Basilides taught in Egypt in the reign of Hadrian (117–38); according to Clement (*Strom.* 3. 75. 13–16; 7. 106. 4), Basilides lived in the time of Antoninus Pius.[65] That Basilides at this early time and in Egypt may have known John's Gospel is not at all, in my opinion, unlikely. He is contemporary with Papias, who knew the Fourth Gospel and, as I have argued, attributed it to John the apostle.[66] The papyrus fragment of John $\mathfrak{P}^{52}$ may date from around this time, and was found in Egypt. We cannot be sure that it was copied in Egypt or when it arrived there, but most have seen it as evidence of the early inroads made by the Fourth Gospel among Christians in Egypt, and so it would offer some support for this possibility.

Basilides' use of John's Gospel, however, is known only from the account of his teaching given by Hippolytus of Rome in his *Refutation of All Heresies*, in the third or fourth decade of the third century. And there is a real problem here, because Hippolytus' account differs so markedly from those of Irenaeus and Clement of Alexandria (whose accounts contain no clear contacts with the Fourth Gospel) that most scholars now believe it reports the views not of Basilides himself but of some later followers (perhaps Isidore?).[67] It does not appear, then, that we can safely attribute the use of John's Gospel evident in Hippolytus' fragments to Basilides himself or to gnostic use in the reign of Hadrian. This aspect of the cases of Sanders, Gamble, and others for the OJP, then, does not appear solid. Still, if followers of Basilides later in the second century did use John, it may be instruct-

---

[64] Sanders, *Fourth Gospel*, 65. Gamble, *Canon*, 33.

[65] He may be, as Procter, *Controversy*, 1, says, 'the first Christian in Egypt about whom we have any certain knowledge'.

[66] C. E. Hill, 'What Papias Said about John', *JTS* ns 49 (1998), 582–629, and see below.

[67] Layton, *The Gnostic Scriptures*, 418–19 n. 2; G. Filoramo, *A History of Gnosticism*, tr. A. Alcock (ET: Oxford, 1990), 160–1; Procter, *Controversy*, 5 n. 4; W. A. Löhr, *Basilides unde seine Schule: Eine Studie zur Theologie- und Kirchengeschichte des Zweiten Jahrhunderts*, WUNT 83 (Tübingen, 1996), 284, 322–3, who cites also G. May, *Schöpfung aus dem Nichts: Die Entstehung der Lehre von der creatio ex nihilo*, Archiv für Kulturgeschichte, 48 (Berlin, 1978), 66–7. Löhr, *Basilides*, 304 n. 76, thinks the reference to John 1: 9 in *Ref.* 7. 22. 4 in particular is not from Basilides but from a redactor. In developing his theory Sanders, *Fourth Gospel*, 51–5, however, explicitly favoured Hippolytus' account over that of Irenaeus; Hillmer, 'Second Century', 132–5, was more doubtful, concluding that it was unlikely from the work of Basilides.

ive for us to examine the report of Hippolytus to see the scope of their usage.

The first of the two 'citations' found in Hippolytus' account is a bit clouded by the question of its correct punctuation: 'And this, he says, is that which has been stated in the Gospels: "He was the true light, which lighteth every man that cometh into the world"' (*Ref.* 7. 22. 4). On this punctuation, the reference to John 1: 9 would be from the follower of Basilides, but the reference to 'the Gospels' would be from Hippolytus. Or should the text be punctuated, '"And this", he says, "is that which has been stated in the Gospels: He was the true light, which lighteth every man that cometh into the world"'? In this case the reference to 'the Gospels' comes from the Basilidean. Hippolytus' normal practice of copying from his sources verbatim, as observed by Marcovich,[68] would suggest the latter alternative. The other apparent citation comes in *Refutation* 7. 27, 'And that each thing, says (Basilides), has its own particular times, the Saviour is a sufficient (witness) when He observes, "mine hour is not yet come" (Jn. 2. 4)'. This, combined with either reading of *Refutation* 7. 22. 4 allows us to conclude that this writer did know John's Gospel.[69] And if we assume the second punctuation of the earlier citation in 7. 22. 4, it will have to be admitted not only that he knew John's Gospel, but that he refers this Johannine material to what is stated 'in the Gospels', as if referring to some well-known collection, of which John is an acknowledged member.[70] These quotations then would need to be seen as reflecting a fairly definite conception of John as an authoritative source of information about Jesus, however interpreted.

Some Basilidean author, then, certainly knew and used the Gospel according to John, though his placement in the second century is vague. But if this author thought John was a 'gnostic' Gospel he must have thought two or three of the Synoptic Gospels were too, for according to Irenaeus, Basilides himself must have known the Synoptic account of Simon of Cyrene carrying the cross in the stead of Jesus (Irenaeus, *AH* 1. 24. 4).[71] And Clement of Alexandria actually says that the Basilideans 'boast of

---

[68] M. Marcovich (ed.), *Hippolytus. Refutatio Omnium Haeresium*, *PTS* 25 (Berlin, 1986), 33, 50, 'That simply means that *Hippolytus' passion for plagiarizing his sources is a blessing for us*, since we can be reasonably sure that he is, as a rule, faithfully copying his source'.

[69] Though taking the first reading of *Ref.* 7. 22. 4 one might approach the matter as Helmut Koester approaches the matter of the Johannine material contained in the writings of Justin Martyr, that is, by attributing the Johannine material instead to a floating tradition used by both the Basilideans and the author or redactor of the Fourth Gospel. One might deal similarly with the other apparent citation, in *Ref.* 7. 27. But the correspondence with the Gospel seems too close for such a theory to be convincing, particularly if the writing on which Hippolytus depends is from the latter half of the 2nd cent.

[70] This is why Hillmer, 'Second Century', 133, thought it unlikely that this is from Basilides himself but from some followers after the middle of the 2nd cent.

[71] His use is apparently from Mark rather than Matthew or Luke (B. A. Pearson, 'Pre-Valentinian Gnosticism in Alexandria', in B. A. Pearson (ed.), *The Future of Early Christianity: Essays in Honor of Helmut Koester* (Minneapolis, 1991), 455–66, at 462)

adducing the opinion of Matthew', not of John (*Strom.* 7. 17 ANF). And in the account given by Hippolytus there is a clear allusion to Matthew 2: 1–2 (Hippolytus, *Ref.* 7. 27. 5) and a citation of Luke 1: 35 (Hippolytus, *Ref.* 7. 26. 9). Along with a gnostic John, then, we must also be willing to speak of a gnostic Matthew and a gnostic Luke; also a gnostic Genesis (Hippolytus *Ref.* 7. 22. 3; 23. 1; Clement Al, *Strom.* 4. 165. 3); a gnostic Exodus (Hippolytus, *Ref.* 7. 25. 4); a gnostic Job (Clement Al., *Strom.* 4. 83. 1); a gnostic Psalms (Hippolytus, *Ref.* 7. 22. 3, 15; 26. 2, 4); a gnostic Isaiah (Hippolytus, *Ref.* 7. 25. 3; 27. 3); a gnostic Acts of the Apostles (Hippolytus *Ref.* 7. 20. 1);[72] a gnostic Romans (Hippolytus, *Ref.* 7. 25. 1, 2; Origen, *Comm. Rom.* 5. 1); a gnostic 1 Corinthians (Hippolytus, *Ref.* 7. 26. 3); a gnostic 2 Corinthians (Hippolytus, *Ref.* 7. 26. 7); a gnostic Ephesians (Hippolytus, *Ref.* 7. 20. 3; 25. 5; 26. 4, 7); a gnostic Colossians (Hippolytus, *Ref.* 7. 25. 3); and probably a gnostic 1 Peter (Clement Al., *Strom.* 4. 81. 2–83. 2),[73] for all of these books, and surely more,[74] were apparently used in second-century expressions of Basilidean teaching.[75]

And no matter when Hippolytus' Basilidean author wrote, we should have to conclude that on the most generous of allowances there is certainly no preponderance of Johannine influence in his system, nothing which could justify thinking that John was specially prized by the Basilideans or regarded as unusually conducive to their system of thought. The citations of Basilidean teaching, some from Basilides' son Isidore, given by Clement of Alexandria, contain several references to the OT, to Matthew, and to 1 Corinthians, but none to John.[76] The citations in Hippolytus' account might indicate a 'reception' of the Fourth Gospel, but they show no close affinity with its thought. And this indeed is what we might expect from their own claims of apostolic succession. The Basilideans, we are told by Clement and Hippolytus, claimed to be the direct heirs of secret apostolic tradition, but the apostles whom they claimed as their progenitors were Peter, whose interpreter was Glaucias, the instructor of Basilides, and the replacement apostle, Matthias (*Strom.* 7. 106. 4; 7. 108. 1; cf. 3. 26. 3; *Ref.* 7. 20. 1). Their list of apostolic predecessors evidently did not include John. We are thus left with precious little on which to construct a theory that Basilides or his followers frightened off other Christians from using John.

---

[72] Whence he must have learnt about the disciple Matthias.

[73] Cf. Layton, *The Gnostic Scriptures*, 440–1.

[74] Including a gnostic Homer, whose help is enlisted in Hippolytus, *Ref.* 7. 22. 8.

[75] The use of these NT works in Hippolytus' treatment is precisely one reason Löhr, *Basilides*, 313 gives for regarding Hippolytus' *Vorlage* as from a later representative writing after 150, and not from Basilides himself. Taking as his base instead only the eight extracts made from Basilides' work by Clement and Origen (and collected by Layton), Pearson, 'Pre-Valentinian Gnosticism in Alexandria', 462, writes, 'The fragments of Basilides ... show knowledge and use of the Pauline epistles (frg. F) and the Gospel of Matthew (frg. G)'. The last-named fragment, the most extensive one preserved, is from book 23 of Basilides' lost *Exegetica* and may constitute part of a commentary on 1 Peter 4.

[76] See Procter, *Controversy*, 7–9, 31–7, 65–6, 87–96, and notes.

It is more realistic to believe that the later Basilideans known to Hippolytus, like most of the second-century sects, besides using their own compositions, took over whatever parts of the more widely accepted Christian writings they believed could be used to advance their views or to add plausibility to their movement in the eyes of the general Christian population.

Carpocrates

About contemporary with Basilides and also hailing from Egypt is the teacher Carpocrates, whose followers included a certain Marcellina who came to Rome during the episcopate of Anicetus (155–66) (*AH* 1. 25. 6). Carpocrates is one of the few heretics whose followers 'style themselves Gnostics', according to Irenaeus. This is of especial interest because his system evidently did not utilize the so-called basic 'gnostic myth'.[77] Yet the Carpocratians did teach a sort of adoptionism, somewhat like that of Cerinthus, and could be regarded as forerunners of Valentinus on this point. On the matter of Carpocrates' written authorities Birger Pearson says,

What is of primary importance for the present discussion is the written sources used by Carpocrates, to the extent that we can ascertain them from the account presented by Irenaeus. These sources turn out to be, chiefly, New Testament books. The dominical saying about agreeing with one's adversary (Matt 5: 25–26; Luke 12: 58–59) is used to bolster the doctrine that all sins must be completed in this life in order to escape reincarnation (Adv. haer. 1. 25. 4). A saying in the Gospel of Mark (4: 10–11) is used to bolster the Carpocratian claim to be in possession of Jesus' esoteric teaching (Adv. haer. 1. 25. 5). And there is an allusion to the (deutero-) Pauline doctrine of salvation by faith (Eph 2: 8), cited as a basis for Carpocratian ethics (Adv. haer. 1. 25. 5).[78]

So far, there is no mention of Carpocrates' use of the Fourth Gospel. Pearson says, 'The Gospel of Matthew, at least, seems to have been used, as well as a version of the Gospel of Mark', and possibly, *The Secret Gospel of Mark*.[79] The last-mentioned work, has, of course, come up because of Morton Smith's discovery of a letter attributed to Clement of Alexandria in which Clement speaks of a *SGM* and gives two excerpts from it.[80] Both of these excerpts arguably contain material which is reminiscent of certain features of the Fourth Gospel, mainly its account of Jesus' raising of Lazarus. A cloud hangs over this whole problem, for many scholars dispute the authenticity of the Clementine letter. And if one accepts it, there are many questions about the apocryphal Gospel which have been variously

---

[77] Layton, *The Gnostic Scriptures*, 199.

[78] Pearson, 'Pre-Valentinian Gnosticism in Alexandria', 464.

[79] Ibid.

[80] M. Smith, *Clement of Alexandria and a Secret Gospel of Mark* (Cambridge, Mass., 1973); *The Secret Gospel: The Discovery and Interpretation of the Secret Gospel According to Mark* (New York, 1973); 'Clement of Alexandria and Secret Mark: The Score at the End of the First Decade', *HTR* 75 (1982), 449–61.

answered by scholars. In particular, though 'Clement' says the apocryphal Gospel was written by Mark himself, no scholar of whom I am aware accepts this at face value,[81] and the work may or may not have antedated Carpocrates. Smith himself argued that the author of the *SGM* did not know John's Gospel but that the two had a common source. Raymond Brown contested this, arguing persuasively that the author or compiler of *SGM*, whom Brown would place at around the middle of the second century, was familiar with the Fourth Gospel itself. He compares the method of the compiler with that of the author of the Egerton Gospel and Tatian's *Diatessaron*. '[I]t is closer in technique to Egerton which weaves together into a consecutive narrative sentences and phrases from the four Gospels and an agraphon'.[82] The parts which Brown thinks are borrowed from John are 'recast' in Markan style to conform to the rest of the work, so that they do not preserve the distinctive vocabulary of John nor, of course, their original setting in the Johannine narrative. Franz Neirynck, writing more recently, agrees, 'The complexity of Synoptic and Johannine reminiscences and the combination of the parallels do not allow for the reconstruction of a pre-Markan or a pre-Johannine source. The contacts with the Lazarus story are undeniable (Jn 12,1; 11,1 Bethany, 2 ἧς ὁ ἀδελφός, 32 fell at his feet, μου ἀπέθανεν ὁ ἀδελφός) but scarcely enough to form a coherent story.'[83]

If we accept the authenticity of the Clementine letter, it must also be remembered that Clement is writing to Theodotus about Carpocratian re-interpretation of the *SGM* and falsification through a number of additions; the *SGM* itself, a copy of which is accessible to Clement, is neither Carpocratian nor heretical. At the most, then, we have a report about (later) Carpocratians using an apparently orthodox work which used the Fourth Gospel. By the time Clement wrote (probably the mid-190s or later),[84] however, I must emphasize again, there was no longer any real danger (if there ever was) of the Fourth Gospel being shunned by the orthodox because of supposed gnostic affinities or connections. The adoption of Johannine material in the *SGM* then can add nothing to the previous conclusion about the Carpocratians derived from the extant information in Irenaeus and other heresiologists. The portions of the *SGM* which offended Clement and Theodore are, after all, Carpocratian additions to what was alleged to be a modified version of Mark. If they were to cast shadows upon the

---

[81] Smith, 'Score', 457, wrote in 1982 that 'Clement's attribution of the gospel to "Mark" is universally rejected".

[82] R. Brown, 'The Relation of "The Secret Gospel of Mark" to the Fourth Gospel', *CBQ* 36 (1974), 466–85 at 477.

[83] F. Neirynck, 'The Apocryphal Gospels and the Gospel of Mark', in J.-M. Sevrin (ed.), *The New Testament in Early Christianity: La Réception des écrits néotestamentaires dans le christianisme primitif*, BETL 86 (1989), 123–75, at 170.

[84] If Clement's letter is authentic, it is likely later than book 3 of the *Stromateis*, where Clement's treatment of the Carpocratians bears no signs of any knowledge of the apocryphal Mark issue.

orthodox use of any Christian Gospel, it would surely have been Mark, not John.

We appear to have in the Carpocratians, then, an early Egyptian gnostic group which has left scarcely a trace of any use of the Fourth Gospel at all. Were they too, like the orthodox, scared off by other gnostics from using John? Were they perhaps scared off by the orthodox? We cannot now know, but here is one gnostic group at least which apparently could not have contributed to the phenomenon of orthodox Johannophobia.

Cerinthus

Though the heretic Cerinthus, according to Irenaeus contemporary with the aged apostle John himself, has left no writings and cannot be cited as a direct example of the gnostic appropriation of John, his name surfaces at several points in the second and third centuries and some scholars have not hesitated to draw him into the history of the Johannine community.[85] 'Cerinthian thought', writes Raymond Brown, 'may represent a development of the interpretation of John advocated by the secessionists described in 1 John—a development as they moved down the path toward gnosticism'.[86] It is justifiable to think that there must have been some historical nexus between Cerinthus, at least the Cerinthian legacy, and the Johannine tradition.[87] This arises not only from the striking similarity between some of the aspects of Cerinthus' teaching as recorded by Irenaeus (*AH* 1. 26. 1) and the apparent views of the 'seceders' mentioned in 1 John.[88] Irenaeus reports the Polycarpan story of John and Cerinthus at the Ephesian baths (*AH* 3. 3. 4). He claims further that John wrote his Gospel and hints that he wrote his First Epistle to dispel Cerinthus' poison (*AH* 3. 11. 1; 16. 5).

In this context the *Epistula Apostolorum*, which sets itself explicitly against the teaching of Cerinthus and Simon, and which relies so heavily upon the Fourth Gospel, takes on a real significance. I have also suggested above that the Nag Hammadi document *Apocryphon of James*, with its notion of a cessation of prophecy which approximates that of the Johannophobes known to Irenaeus (*AH* 3. 11. 9), has ties with the Cerinthian heritage. This nexus so far observed is one of mutual antagonism between the Johannine and Cerinthus legacies. With Gaius, as we have seen, there is the somewhat ambiguous association of Cerinthus' chiliastic views with the Revelation of John, an association which at any rate is clearly seen in Dionysius' report of some who had charged that the heretic was the ghost author of Revelation. Growing out of the second-century context, even this bogus charge is based

---

[85] Brown, *Community*, 24, 149; *The Epistles of John*, 771.
[86] Brown, *The Epistles of John*, 771; cf. his *An Introduction to the New Testament* (New York, 1997), 391.
[87] This nexus, it is hoped, will be the subject of a future study.
[88] See Brown's list, *The Epistles of John*, 65, of modern scholars who connect the opponents in some way to Cerinthus.

on the supposition of an irreconcilable disparity between Cerinthus and John the Apostle, though it was made in an effort to discredit the Apocalypse and its supposed chiliasm as coming from John. Some scholars have posited on the other hand that it was Irenaeus, in an effort to claim the witness of the Fourth Gospel, who cunningly concocted the legend of the Ephesian bath-house and whose tendentious claim about John's motives in writing the Gospel masked the reality of an abiding, deep affinity between Cerinthian and Johannine thought.[89] The evidence of the *Ep. Apost.* and the *Ap. Jas..*, however, independently tends to support Irenaeus, as does the evidence of 1 John. We also are reminded that the Dionysian report associates only the Apocalypse, not the Gospel, with Cerinthus, and that it does so in terms of Cerinthus' chiliasm, not his docetism or gnosticism. It is only the later and somewhat dubious accounts of Epiphanius and Dionysius bar Salibi, which associate Cerinthus with the Gospel.

It is enough to point out here that the earliest evidence, from 1 John, *Ep. Apost.*, *ApocJas.*, and Irenaeus (Polycarp)[90] establishes a mutual antagonism between the Cerinthian and the Johannine traditions, and that the later evidence of Gaius, Dionysius of Alexandria, and even later writers, is consistent with this. I shall have some opportunity to touch upon this again when I consider the *Apocryphon of James* on its own. But the potential significance of such an antagonism, particularly if it can be seen as going back as far as the production of any of the Johannine writings, but even if it only pertains to the immediate Johannine and Cerinthian legacies, should be obvious. It constitutes a formulation derived from the sources themselves, a mapping-out of the theological terrain with regard to Johannism and gnosticism, which directly challenges the status quo of modern Johannine studies. The full import of its challenge, I think, has not yet been realized.

OTHER GNOSTIC GROUPS MENTIONED BY THE HERESIOLOGISTS: OPHITES, NAASSENES, PERETAE

Also roughly contemporary with Basilides and Carpocrates are various groups known to later writers by the names of Barbeloites, Ophites, Naassenes, Sethians, Cainites, and Peratae. Whether or not they were actually distinct groups, these all share an adherence to an early and originally pre-Valentinian form of the 'basic gnostic myth', and may be termed gnostics proper.[91] Irenaeus seems to describe three of these in successive chapters of

---

[89] e.g. Haenchen, *John 1*, 23–4. Even Brown's understanding of the seceders and their relation to Cerinthus requires that the early Cerinthians had a viable interpretation of the Johannine Gospel.

[90] C. E. Hill, 'Cerinthus, Gnostic or Chiliast?', *JECS* 8 (2000), 135–72, at 155–8.

[91] Layton, *The Gnostic Scriptures*, p. xv; M. J. Edwards, 'Gnostics and Valentinians in the Church Fathers', *JTS* ns 40 (1989), 26–47. Presumably these came into being in Egypt, but this is not certain. Jerome in 387 mentioned Ophites and Borborites in his day in the province of Galatia (Preface to book 2 of his commentary on Galatians).

AH: the Barbeloites (*AH* 1. 29), the Ophites (*AH* 1. 30) and the Cainites (*AH* 1. 31. 1–2).[92] In the system of the Cainites and the Barbelo-gnostics as described by Irenaeus there is nothing which is reminiscent of Johannine themes. But the source of Irenaeus' description of the Barbeloites has been found in (some version of) the Nag Hammadi text entitled *The Apocryphon of John*. As the title indicates, it is presented as a revelation made to John, and this John is the son of Zebedee (1. 5–8). Though this work seems to know the attribution of the Apocalypse to John the son of Zebedee (2. 16–17), it shows only debatable signs of influence from the Fourth Gospel but is a full and classic presentation of the gnostic myth (or a portion of it). This text will be examined below, but simply from the description given by Irenaeus, one would have trouble arguing that 'Barbeloite' gnostics would have been the cause of any Johannophobia among the orthodox.

From the reports of the heresiologists there is also nothing in Ophite teaching which savours of Johannine theology and no good reason to imagine that John was specially prized by them in any way. The first report that they knew the Fourth Gospel comes not until the middle of the third-century when Ps. Tertullian tells us that they found a justification for their adoration of the serpentine form from Jesus' own words in John 3: 14: 'Christ himself (they say further) in his gospel imitates Moses' serpent's sacred power, in saying: "And as Moses upreared the serpent in the desert, so it behoveth the Son of man to be upreared (Jn. 3. 14)"' (*Adv. omn. haer.* 2).[93] From Irenaeus' account, the earliest we still have,[94] we may be confident that the Ophites know the Gospel of Luke, for they know about 'the barren Elizabeth', mother of John the Baptist (*AH* 1. 30. 7). They also know Paul's first letter to the Corinthians (*AH* 1. 30. 13). But above all, it is clear from all accounts that the Ophites made very heavy use of the book of Genesis and of the whole Old Testament (*AH* 1. 30; *C. Cels.* 6. 31–2). Of course their reading of the OT was a reading 'against the grain', an inversion of its concepts of good and evil, of the divine and the demonic. But just as subversive was their reading of the NT. Whatever possible effect their teaching could have had on the use of John in the Church is at least as likely for Luke and Paul, and that likelihood would have to be multiplied many times with regard to the OT.

But Origen's report that the great majority of Christians 'neither are acquainted with, nor concern themselves about, such matters' as the arcane mysteries of Ophite teachings (*C. Cels.* 6. 31), cannot be swept aside.[95]

---

[92] See now A. H. B. Logan, *Gnostic Truth and Christian Heresy* (Edinburgh, 1996), 1–29.

[93] Though Hippolytus affirms the use of this text by the Peratae, see below.

[94] Irenaeus does not use the term 'Ophite', though it is used by Theodoret who has preserved Irenaeus' Greek account. It is also apparent from the remarks of Celsus that he had come across Ophite teaching.

[95] *C. Cels.* 6. 31. Origen affirms that the Ophites 'neither acknowledge Jesus as Saviour, nor God, nor Teacher, nor Son of God' (*C. Cels.* 6. 30). A. B. Scott, 'Churches or Books? Sethian Social Organization', *JECS* 3 (1995), 109–22, at 118, points out that 'So far as we can tell from Origen's

Though Origen, writing in the third century, may not be the final authority on Christian society in the middle or later part of the second century, it is unlikely that the Ophites ever played a very influential role in the beliefs and practices of very many Christians, about the Gospel of John or about anything else. It has even been questioned whether they can be viewed as socially organized 'groups' at all, or whether they were instead scattered individual authors writing without the benefit of any social, cultic movements.[96] The chief importance of these groups, or individuals, as far as understanding early Christianity is concerned, is no doubt that they served in some way as sources for the great gnostic–Christian synthesizers and popularizers, the Valentinians.[97] And again, any extrapolations based upon their use of John 3: 14 have to be tempered by the fact that they also used other biblical books in very similar ways to support their distinctive ideas.[98] Their use of John along with other biblical books such as Genesis, Matthew, Luke, and 1 Corinthians is in fact more consistent with the judgement that John must have held a position comparable to these other books among the churches which customarily used them, from which churches the Ophites got the idea for using these books.

Our only knowledge of the sect known as the Naassenes comes from Hippolytus of Rome in *Refutation* 5. 6. 3–11. 1; 10. 9. 1. The Naassene document he used is of uncertain date, but is probably contemporary with Irenaeus.[99] It is quite obvious that its author knew the Gospel of John, as he is recorded as referring to at least ten passages of that Gospel.[100] The Naassenes are thus often cited as evidence of the gnostic predilection for

corpus, many of the groups which have often been regarded as the source of gnosticism did not exist in significant numbers in the third century, and this conclusion is supported by reports from a later date by Epiphanius and Theodoret who also say that such groups as the Sethians, Simonians and Cainites in their day have few if any members. Though it is not impossible that they could have existed as cult movements which simply had died out, this is also what we would have expected if they had existed as what Stark and Bainbridge would call an audience cult, since in this case the sense of group commitment would never have been strong'.

[96] See Scott, 'Churches or Books?', 120, 'Rather than viewing Sethianism [i.e. pre-Valentinian gnosticism] as a group with a strong sense of its own boundaries, we conclude that its organizational structure may have been inherently weak'.

[97] Edwards, 'Gnostics and Valentinians', 46, observes that 'while Irenaeus could write of the Gnostics [i.e. Ophites and the like] as though the mere rehearsal of their opinion would render them odious, the Valentinian heresy, which because it was both more profound and more orthodox, was much the more alluring, could be refuted only by longer arguments and an exposure of its real or supposed antecedents.'

[98] Pagels, *Gnostic Exegesis*, 15, 'In Hippolytus' discussion of their exegesis, references to John and Matthew occur frequently; they also cite Luke, Mark, and the Pauline letters'.

[99] Hillmer, 'Second Century', 116 n. 33, cites A. D. Nock in *Journal of Hellenic Studies*, 49, 115, for establishing that it must be from the Hadrianic period or later, for it comments on the Hymn to Attis, which is dated to that period. G. Salmon, 'Ophites', in *DCB* iv. 86, believes, probably correctly, that the author of this tract was not one of the originators of his sect but a later follower. J. Frickel, *Hellenistische Erlösung in christlicher Deutung: Die gnostische Naassenerschrift. Quellenkritische Studien—Strukturanalyse—Schichtenscheidung—Rekonstruction der Anthropos-Lehrschrift*, Nag Hammadi Studies, 19 (Leiden, 1984), 160–71, places it between 150 and 190.

[100] For a detailed analysis of each, see Nagel, *Rezeption*, 299–315.

John. Just as we have seen with a number of other gnostics,[101] however, it is just as clear that this Naassene author knew the Gospel of Matthew, which is used even more copiously than John in this account,[102] Luke, Romans, 1 and 2 Corinthians, Galatians, Ephesians, and most of the Old Testament, not to mention a certain *Gospel of Thomas* and the *Gospel according to the Egyptians*, as well as Homer and other non-Christian writings. In fact, to gain an idea of the character of this document, the description given by C. H. Dodd is instructive.

> ...the Naassene document cited at considerable length by Hippolytus (*Refut.* V. 1–11) appears to be in substance a commentary upon a hymn to Attis, the text of which is quoted (v. 9). In this hymn Attis, in the syncretistic fashion of the times, is identified with other divine figures, such as Pan, Osiris and Adonis. The writer takes the various names and titles given to the god in the hymn, and illustrates them by reference to other mythologies. His examples range over a wide field. Among other religions, he is acquainted with Judaism and Christianity, and as he quotes Homer, Empedocles and Anacreon, so he quotes the Old Testament, the canonical gospels, and apparently the apocryphal Gospel of Thomas. The work is in no sense an interpretation of Christianity. In so far as it has any particular religious aim, it would seem to be to show that all religions are manifestations of the one esoteric truth.[103]

Once again we can observe a familiar pattern of gnostic groups taking over books used among the catholics, along with a varying assortment of other texts, bits and pieces of which could be used in support of their teachings.[104] This Naassene author's use of the Fourth Gospel, like his use of the Bible generally, is often connected with his flesh/spirit dualism.[105] Thus his citation of John 3: 6, 'That which is born of the flesh is flesh, and that which is born of the spirit is spirit' in *Ref.* 5. 7. 40. His freedom with texts is seen in his manipulation of John 5: 37 (if indeed it is an allusion to this

---

[101] The Naassenes, according to Hippolytus, *Ref.* 5. 6. 4, did use the term γνωστικοί for themselves.

[102] Salmon states, 'Ophites', 85, 'The writer...makes free use of the New Testament. He seems to have used all the four Gospels, but that of which he makes most use is St. John's'. By my own count, however, John is cited almost but not quite as frequently as Matthew (Hillmer, 'Second Century', 118, agrees). In any case Pagels, *Gnostic Exegesis*, 16, is quite mistaken when she writes that 'the Naassenes and Peratae referred to the fourth gospel to the virtual exclusion of the synoptics' (Ref 5–7), a statement echoed by Sloyan, 'Gnostic Adoption', 125.

[103] C. H. Dodd, *The Interpretation of the Fourth Gospel* (Cambridge, 1953), 98–9.

[104] Salmon, 'Ophites', 85, mentions the Naassene author's 'tyrannical method of Scripture exegesis by which he can prove any doctrine out of any text'. Speaking of Hippolytus' Naassenes and Peratae, Pagels, *Gnostic Exegesis*, 15, says, 'they approach both Jewish and Christian writings as they approach classical poetry—as a corpus of symbolically written sacred literature'. Maria Grazia Lancellotti, *The Naassenes: A Gnostic Identity Among Judaism, Christianity, Classical and Ancient Near Eastern Traditions*, Forschungen zur Anthropologie und Religionsgeschichte, 35 (Münster, 2000), 285, 'As is the case for "pagan" sources, the Scriptures are also used by the Naassenes as a field of research in which to look for those "seeds of truth" which only they are able to recognize.' See Lancellotti's list of scriptural passages used in the Naassene sermon (285–7).

[105] Nagel, *Rezeption*, 300–1, who cites Frickel, *Erlösung*, 173.

text) to make it serve the interests of his brand of docetism.[106] John 5: 37, where Jesus speaks of the Father, 'His voice you have never heard, his form you have never seen',[107] becomes a statement about the descending redeemer spoken on the part of believers,

This, says he, is what is spoken: "We have heard his voice, no doubt, but we have not seen his shape."[108] For the voice of him that is set apart and portrayed is heard; but (his) shape, which descends from above from the unportrayed one,—what sort it is, nobody knows. It resides, however, in an earthly mould, yet no one recognises it. (*Ref.* 5. 8. 14)[109]

That this author had access to a copy of John's Gospel, that he seems to have regarded it as in some sense a 'sacred' text, can hardly be denied. Even so, in the light of his prolific use of other scriptures we cannot say there is a special attachment to John in this work, certainly no more than to Matthew. It may be that John's own spirit/flesh dualism was found particularly congenial, though the dualism of the Naassene author is more metaphysical than ethical. But his acquisition of John and the other Christian writings may also simply reflect the greater accessibility of these particular writings in his locale in the second half of the second century. In any case, there is no reason to imagine that the Naassenes would have brought to the small numbers of Christians who might have paid attention to their writings more opprobrium onto John than onto Matthew or any of the other biblical books used by them.

The Peretae mentioned by Hippolytus and Clement are very probably not a group separate from the Naassenes (which in turn are probably not far removed from the Ophites described by Irenaeus), though their descriptions are based upon different exemplars.[110] Hippolytus twice informs his reader that prior to his exposure of it this heresy had gone unnoticed (5. 12. 1; 18. 1).[111] From the quotations of their treatises preserved by Hippolytus, their knowledge of at least Matthew, John, and Colossians, beyond the OT, is quite evident.[112] And they certainly must have known more biblical books, particularly if they are to be identified with the Naassenes. Whether they are to be considered separate from the Naassenes and Ophites or not,

---

[106] Hillmer, 'Second Century', 122.

[107] Ὄυτε φωνὴν αὐτοῦ πώποτε ἀκηκόατε οὔτε εἶδος αὐτοῦ ἑωράκατε.

[108] Φωνὴν μὲν αὐτοῦ ἠκούσαμεν, εἶδος δὲ αὐτοῦ οὐχ ἑωράκαμεν.

[109] *ANF* translation (5. 3).

[110] Origen, *C. Cels.* 6. 28, says that the Ophites were founded by one Euphrates. This is the name given by Hippolytus as the founder of the Peratae (*Ref.* 5. 13. 9). Salmon, 'Ophites', 84–7, has satisfactorily shown that the Peratae and the Naassenes mentioned by Hippolytus are one and the same group.

[111] Salmon, 'Ophites', 86, 'The works which Irenaeus refutes were in open circulation but in the time of Hippolytus the Gnostic sects were burrowing underground, and it is his pride to drag to light their secret documents, of which he was evidently an ardent collector'.

[112] Like the Ophites mentioned by Ps. Tertullian, *Adv. omn. haer.* 2, the Peratae according to Hippolytus cited John 3: 14 in support of the serpent (*Ref.* 5. 16. 11).

it is not likely that a group which Hippolytus had to introduce to his readers as his own discovery could be credited with dissuading numbers of Christians in the early second century from using the Gospel of John.

Irenaeus knew at least some writings of some of these groups, and it is only with regard to the Valentinians that he speaks of a 'copious use of that [Gospel] according to John, to illustrate their conjunctions' (*AH* 3. 11. 7). And this seems to have specific reference to the exegetical work of Ptolemy (or a later Valentinian) on John 1 which, as I have observed above, could, under the most favourable conditions, have produced but little orthodox Johannophobia, and most probably produced none. And so it is also with regard to non-Valentinian gnosticism, cited in patristic sources. These too have left us, so far, with a paralysing inability to affirm that the Fourth Gospel was 'especially favored in the second century by gnostic Christians',[113] that 'the gnostics adopted it as their special gospel,'[114] or that it was 'much the preserve of heretics'.[115] This translates to an inability to affirm the basis for a theory of widespread orthodox Johannophobia.

Surviving Gnostic Texts

Our knowledge of second- and third-century sects which are today commonly labelled gnostic is of course quite piecemeal. There must have been many writings, now lost to us, which would have improved our understanding of these sects significantly. While several gnostic or semi-gnostic texts were available at the time when J. N. Sanders wrote his book on the Fourth Gospel in the early Church, a new discovery was made shortly thereafter which promised to do just that. Indeed the Nag Hammadi finds were soon exploited by Hillmer, Barrett, Brown, and many others and have contributed inestimably to the current state of Johannine studies. Nor is it surprising that most experts initially concluded that these new finds supported the orthodox Johannophobia theory, for this theory has provided the working paradigm for the bulk of research. In support of the thesis 'that a wide acceptance of the Fourth Gospel came earlier among heterodox rater than among orthodox Christians', Raymond Brown pointed not only to Heracleon and Ptolemaeus, but to Nag Hammadi.

There is abundant evidence of familiarity with Johannine ideas in the recently published gnostic library from Nag Hammadi...For instance, there is a Word (*Logos*) christology in the *Tripartite Tractate*, and 'I AM' christology in the *Second Apocalypse of James*; also in *The Thunder, the Perfect Mind*, and in the *Trimorphic Protennoia* (where it is joined with a docetic account of the death of Jesus).[116]

---

[113] Gamble, 'Canonical Formulation of the New Testament', 185.

[114] Charlesworth, *Beloved Disciple*, 382.

[115] Trevett, *Ignatius of Antioch*, 197.

[116] R. E. Brown, *The Community of the Beloved Disciple* (New York, 1979), 147–8.

Koester notes also that 'Some of the earlier writings from Nag Hammadi also display usage of the Fourth Gospel, e.g., the *Gospel of Philip*...the *Testimony of Truth*.'[117] What James M. Robinson says about Ernst Haenchen, that he 'recognized in the Gnostic Gospels from Nag Hammadi the opportunity to trace the outcome of the Gnosticizing trajectory in which the Gospel of John is in some way involved, as a new way of casting light on John itself', would pertain also to many students of these texts.[118] The discovery and publication of the Nag Hammadi texts has presented an opportunity hitherto unknown for illuminating the relationship between John and various forms of gnostic thought. In this chapter I shall examine surviving 'gnostic' texts, most of which come from Nag Hammadi, to see what light they cast upon the subject.

TEXTS WHICH ARE TOO LATE

Navigating with the Nag Hammadi tractates, of course, poses several special problems. Chief among these is always that most of the texts are not easy to date or to locate within a socio-religious context. Only a portion have any serious claim to the second century, and, obviously, if the work in question is not from the second century it cannot have affected second-century orthodox use.[119] In fact, from all that we have seen above, we should have to stipulate that if a given Nag Hammadi or other gnostic text was not in fairly wide circulation from a time well before *c*.170–5, when scholars today acknowledge that the Church's use of the Fourth Gospel was burgeoning, it did not have much effect on orthodox use of John—unless its effect was to promote Johannophilia instead of Johannophobia.

This critical chronology has direct implications for the first document mentioned by Brown in the quotation above, the *Tripartite Tractate*. In their introduction to the work in the third edition of the *NHLE*, Attridge and Pagels state that, 'Since the doctrine of the text represents a revised form of Valentinian theology which may be a response to the criticism of orthodox theologians such as Irenaeus or Hippolytus, the work was probably written in the early to mid third century.'[120] If these Nag Hammadi scholars are correct, this work exampled by Brown fails the first test, the test of chronology. Orthodox Christians in *c*.170 or before have never seen it and cannot have been dissuaded from using the Fourth Gospel because of it.

---

[117] H. Koester, *Ancient Christian Gospels* (Philadelphia, 1990), 245–6, n. 6.

[118] J. M. Robinson, 'Foreword', in E. Haenchen, *John 1* (Philadelphia, 1984), p. xi.

[119] M. Hengel, *Die Johanneische Frage* (Tübingen, 1993), 45, thinks that the Nag Hammadi texts which use the Fourth Gospel, 'in großer Mehrzahl in die 1. Hälfte des 3. und die 2. Hälft des 2. Jahrhunderts gehören dürfen'.

[120] *NHLE*[3], 58. The same authors in *CGL* i. 178, say 'the first half of the third century A.D., although a date in the late third or early fourth century cannot be excluded'.

The same may probably be said about a work, the *Gospel of Philip*, which both Schnackenburg[121] and Koester cite as an early work which knows the Fourth Gospel. When Schnackenburg wrote, Robert McL. Wilson had recently dated it to the second half of the second century,[122] but as scholarship has progressed the tendency has been to view the work as coming from a generation or two later. J.-E. Mènarde placed it, 'tout au plus au IIIe siècle'.[123] W. W. Isenberg thinks it was originally written probably in Syria, 'perhaps as late as the second half of the third century C.E.'.[124] Schenke dates it a little earlier, somewhere around 200, or even in the late second century, but certainly removed some distance from the first generation of Valentinian teachers.[125] But in any case, Röhl argues that its use of material from the Fourth Gospel is rather incidental and unreflective of the actual content or setting of the Gospel,[126] and even if the work could be as early as, say, 160–70, we now know that it could not have had a profound negative influence on the use of John among the churches.

The Letter of Peter to Philip is a Valentinian work which has been said to contain a paraphrase of the Johannine Prologue.[127] The resemblances, however, seem quite general and thematic only. Röhl agrees, saying that the author's allusions to the Fourth Gospel are 'eher akzidentiell'.[128] This 'epistle' also knows at least Matthew, Luke, and Acts,[129] and it too is probably post-Irenaean[130] and so could not have engendered any significant Johannophobia among the orthodox.

Here then is a group of Nag Hammadi texts which we may eliminate from consideration as having spawned any measurable Johannophobia among the orthodox. One may always argue the hypothetical possibility that later gnostic texts like these may reflect a use of John that went back much further into the second century. It may be merely accidental that similar texts do not survive from an earlier period. But such an argument if applied to the ques-

---

[121] R. Schnackenburg, *The Gospel according to St John* (London, 1968), 148–9, 195.

[122] R. McL. Wilson, *The Gospel of Philip. Translated from the Coptic Text, with an Introduction and Commentary* (London, 1962).

[123] J.-E. Mènarde, *L'Évangile selon Philippe: Introduction, Texte-Traduction, Commentarie* (Paris, 1967), 35.

[124] W. W. Isenberg, 'The Gospel of Philip (II, *3*)', in *NHLE*³ 139–41 at 141.

[125] H.-M. Schenke, 'The Gospel of Philip', *NTA*² i. 179–87 at 182–3.

[126] G. Röhl, *Die Rezeption das Johannesevangeliums in christlich-gnostischen Schriften aus Nag Hammadi* (Frankfurt am Main, 1991), 162–3.

[127] K. Koschorke, 'Eine gnostische Paraphrase des johanneische Prologs', *VC* 33 (1979), 383–92.

[128] Röhl, *Rezeption*, 186. See here also his evaluation of Koschorke's claim.

[129] G. P. Luttikhuizen, 'The Letter of Peter to Philip and the New Testament', in R. McL. Wilson (ed.), *Nag Hammadi and Gnosis* (Leiden, 1978), 96–102, at 96, says that the author was 'thoroughly acquainted with' passages in Matthew, Luke, and Acts, 'and made free use of them; he does not quote literally'. See also M. Meyer, 'The Letter of Peter to Philip (VIII, *2*)', in *NHLE*³ 431–3 at 432, who thinks the reference to the 'four words' in 140, 25 is a reference to the four Gospels.

[130] Meyer, *NHLE*³ 433, 'On the basis of the parallels with *The Apocryphon of John* and Irenaeus, we suggest that *The Letter of Peter to Philip* was written around the end of the second century C.E. or into the third'. H.-G. Bethge, 'The Letter of Peter to Philip', *NTA*² i. 342–7 at 344 agrees.

tion of orthodox Johannophobia has to cut both ways. For one must then allow for the possibility (and this will be a much more likely possibility, as we shall see later) that later orthodox use, such as is found in Theophilus, Irenaeus, and Tertullian, also reflects a much earlier orthodox use.

Superficial, Incidental, or Questionable Use of the Fourth Gospel

The test of chronology will necessarily reduce the number of texts which might be legitimately used to claim an early, widespread use of the Fourth Gospel among heterodox groups, and a cause for orthodox Johannophobia. Most of the Nag Hammadi texts cannot be said with any confidence to pass this test. Even for those texts which may not be disqualified by a probable date after 170 or so, several problems remain. Some texts which are sometimes invoked, such as the *Gospel of Philip* mentioned above, display only a superficial or questionable acquaintance with the Fourth Gospel such that any 'adoption' of the Fourth Gospel would not necessarily have been easily perceived by the reader/hearer. Naturally, if the adoption of the Fourth Gospel was so subtle (or if the reader was not sufficiently familiar with the Fourth Gospel) that the reader did not recognize it, then the tractate could hardly have provoked any Johannophobia among the orthodox. In this category I may mention a few more texts.

The Thunder, the Perfect Mind

Brown cited this text as an example of gnostic use of the Fourth Gospel and thus as generally supporting the theory of orthodox Johannophobia. The indications of the date of *The Thunder, the Perfect Mind* are ambiguous enough to allow for the possibility that it could have been written prior to *c*.170. On the other hand, there is no record of any mention of this work in the second century, and no trace of its effects. But if we assume that it was written sometime prior to 170 and that it was read by orthodox Christians, we may, I suggest, be quite confident that the average orthodox reader would have missed the 'I AM' Christology which Brown found in this work. The 'I AM' form of speech is used, to be sure, but its use hardly adorns or designates a 'Christology'. The speaker, according to George MacRae, is 'a female figure who is, except possibly for the title, otherwise not specifically identified'.[131] Douglas Parrott says, 'In the tractate, Thunder is allegorized as Perfect Mind, meaning the extension of the divine into the world (1, 1–2). The understanding of Perfect Mind appears to owe much to the Stoic notion of cosmic Pneuma, the active, intelligent element in all things, made up of air and fire.'[132] MacRae says this work 'contains no distinctively

---

[131] G. W. MacRae, 'The Thunder: Perfect Mind (VI, 2)', *NHLE*[3], 295.

[132] *NHLE*[3], 296. Layton, *The Gnostic Scriptures*, 77, however, thinks she is 'afterthought—also known as "life" (Zoe), the female instructing principle, and the holy spirit'.

Christian, Jewish, or gnostic allusions and does not seem clearly to presuppose any particular gnostic myth'.[133] Parrott agrees that it is not really appropriate even to classify this work as 'gnostic'.[134] If it is unlikely that the author's intent was to wean anyone away from 'mainstream' Christianity to some form of gnosticism, it is doubly unlikely that any orthodox Christian readers it might have had in the second century would have associated its 'I am' statements with their allegedly gnostic parallels in the Fourth Gospel. Therefore, *The Thunder, the Perfect Mind* is no evidence for gnostic use of John and it is, to say the least, unlikely that this work would have been the cause for any Johannophobia.

Apocryphon of John

The next example has a somewhat better claim to knowledge of the Fourth Gospel. Even here, however, there is nothing resembling a 'citation' of the sort which advocates of the OJP typically want to require of orthodox writings. This is why Hillmer in fact denied that the parallels with John were 'clear and definite enough to allow a firm conclusion'.[135] He preferred to say that the two works were joined by a common tradition about a Revealer figure.[136]

It has long been apparent that Irenaeus in *Against Heresies* 1. 29 is familiar with a type of gnostic mythology which is closely related to the literary composition now known as the *Apocryphon of John*, known in three versions from Nag Hammadi and from the famous Berlin Codex (Papyrus Berolinensis no. 8502), discovered in 1896 though not published until 1955. All of these are in Coptic, though the original is thought to have been written in Greek. It is generally thought today that all four of our present texts of the *Apocryphon*[137] represent a somewhat later redaction than that which was known to Irenaeus around 180.[138] The *Apocryphon of John* contains 'one of the most classic narrations of the gnostic myth'.[139]

---

[133] *NHLE*[3] 296.

[134] Ibid.

[135] M. R. Hillmer, 'The Gospel of John in the Second Century' (Th.D. diss., Harvard University, Apr. 1966), 144. 'The dialogue section following the monologue in which John asks questions and Jesus replies, gives no indication of dependence on John or any close relationship with the gospel' (137); 'In the monologue [the part evidently known to Irenaeus] there are no explicit references to John and no clear quotations, but there are a number of important words which are also key terms in the Fourth Gospel' (137); on the 'frame' section, 'The similarities in all this material and the kind of situation in which they are presented are in no instance close enough to the Gospel of John to postulate direct dependence, and in addition have parallels in traditional gnostic materials' (143).

[136] Ibid. 144.

[137] Codex III, 1 and BG (Berolinensis 8502) are translated from a short Greek recension, Cod. II, 1 and IV, 1 are from a longer Greek recension.

[138] Michael Waldstein and Frederik Wisse, *The Apocryphon of John: Synopsis of Nag Hammadi Codices II, 1; II, 1 and IV, 1 with BG 8502, 2*, Nag Hammadi Studies, 33 (Leiden, 1995), 1, say, 'Irenaeus... did most likely not know AJ but rather a Gnostic document which was the apparent source of the first part of the main revelation discourse in the book. AJ was written in Greek probably during the early part of the Third Century.'

[139] Layton, *The Gnostic Scriptures*, 23.

A. H. B. Logan argues plausibly that both the *Apocryphon of John* and an apparently earlier myth quoted by Irenaeus in *AH* 1. 29 were influenced by John's Prologue. 'In its present form the *Apocryphon* is clearly dependent on the fourth Gospel and the concerns of the Johannine circle and its interpreters.'[140] While we may agree that the *Apocryphon* and its earlier form known to Irenaeus may be dependent in some way on the Fourth Gospel, it is extremely unclear in what sense we may speak of the *Apocryphon* representing the concerns of any 'Johannine circle'. In any case, in describing the development of the myth in the *Apocryphon of John*, Logan argues,

that it is the growing influence of the Fourth Gospel and its Prologue in particular which has messed up what was a clear and orderly myth of the Father, Mother and Son. That myth, I would argue, originally had no Ennoia, or Logos, or Autogenes, or Truth; it involved the Father, the Invisible Spirit, deciding to reveal himself to Barbelo, i.e. the heavenly Wisdom or Sophia of the Wisdom of Solomon, a virginal spirit acting alone... As a result, and here the fundamentally *Christian* character of the myth comes into view, she, Barbelo, the *Virgin* Spirit, in a typical Gnostic projection of historical earthly beings and events into the heavenly world, as the archetype of the obedient virgin Mary, delighted with the heavenly revelation and visitation, conceives purely spiritually the (*monogenes*) Son...

What I submit has happened is that under the influence of the Fourth Gospel and its distinctive themes, the Son, Christ, has been assimilated to the male paternal characteristic, Light (the Light, which is Christ), so that the latter and the following characteristic, Thelema, have been omitted in Irenaeus's account. At the same time Logos has been added on to the end, with an appropriate female counterpart, Ennoia, being inserted before Prognosis and united with Logos.[141]

Logan goes on to suggest that Autogenes, who is the emission of Ennoia and Logos, 'is best seen as the heavenly archetype of John the Baptist, later than the Logos and witnessing to the Great Light... The presence of Truth as his consort, obscured, as much else in the *Apocryphon*, by its later identification of Christ and Autogenes, is also due to Johannine influence.'[142] We may see that this parallels and confirms what we have seen above with respect to Ptolemy and Heracleon, namely, that the Johannine Prologue was mined by those in the 'gnostic'/Valentinian tradition for names to be secondarily applied to the various members of the pleroma. As Logan says, 'What is important is the attempt to demonstrate how the myth has developed and how Johannine influence is secondary.'[143] This is surely a

---

[140] A. H. B. Logan, 'John and the Gnostics', *JSNT* 43 (1991), 41–69, at 56. Logan himself argues that the myth in question has also been influenced at its formative stage by the birth narrative of Luke and perhaps by Hebrews 1–2 (54).

[141] Ibid. 52–3.

[142] Ibid. 53.

[143] Ibid. 54.

more realistic and less theory-driven analysis than has sometimes been given of the *Apocryphon of John* and other gnostic texts.[144]

In passing, it is hard to overestimate the importance of the fact that this secondary Johannine influence is not used for primarily Christological reasons, but for 'Christianizing' a pleromatic mythology. It too fits quite well under Irenaeus' description of Valentinian use of John, which he said was characterized by the attempt to illustrate their 'conjunctions' or syzygies, except that with the Ptolemaean exegesis there was at least an explicit attempt to relate the myth to the Johannine text as a literary text.

This means that orthodox readers who came into contact with either the *Apocryphon of John* or the earlier version known to Irenaeus may *possibly* have recognized certain words characteristic of the Prologue of the Fourth Gospel taken over for the pleromatic aeons, as they may have recognized them in Valentinian works. But if so, if they were familiar with both works, it is likely that they also noticed how the Johannine terminology had simply been lifted out to serve the alien mythology of the *Apocryphon*—and was treated with no greater kindness than was the Genesis terminology and the story of the early chapters of Genesis.[145] If Irenaeus recognized the Johannine terminology, he did not conclude that the apocryphon's author was in the same 'trajectory' with the Fourth Gospel, and it certainly produced no Johannophobia in him. It has yet to be proved that the probable reaction of the typical orthodox reader would have been radically different, resulting in a recoiling away from the Fourth Gospel, particularly in view of the relatively superficial awareness of the Fourth Gospel which this work evinces. It is more probable that any recognition of the vocabulary of the Prologue in this document or any of its proposed ancestors would have been accompanied by the recognition that that vocabulary had been put to very questionable use, and would have provoked a reaction similar to the reaction

---

[144] This brings me to an example of a 'gnostic–John' paradigm controlling research. As Logan, 'John and the Gnostics', 49–50, summarizes the work of M. Tardieu, *Ecrits gnostiques: Codex de Berlin, Sources gnostiques et manichéennes*, 1 (Paris, 1984) at 10, 33, 35–9, the latter thinks the *Ap. Jn.* 'is a *Christian* text composed of the same material as the Fourth Gospel... that it takes up a position at the heart of the Johannine school, and represents the manifesto of those who refused to compromise with Judaism... He would see the Pronoia hymn as going back to a dissident esoteric circle within the Johannine community, around the time of the final redaction of the Fourth Gospel (c. AD 120), and forming the basis of the threefold structure of our present *Apocryphon*'. But what cause is there to see the position of the *Apocryphon* as at the heart of the Johannine school, except the presupposition that it was so? The use of the Fourth Gospel in this apocryphon is practically confined to its use of the Prologue. And its use of the Prologue is essentially predatory, for the purpose of plastering over the pre-existing names of the pleromatic aeons with theological terms derived from a respected Christian source. This is just about the extent to which the *Ap. Jn.* is 'composed of the same material as the Fourth Gospel'.

[145] We have observed this phenomenon in relation to the Ophites above. Irenaeus' summary stops at the beginning of the section of the *Ap. Jn.* in which 'exposition' of the first chapters of Genesis begins. However, his summary betrays knowledge of at least some portion which explained the first verses of Gen. 1, as well as a portion (Cod. II, 11. 19–21; 13. 8–13; BG 44. 13–18) which contained the Isaianic prooftext (Isa. 45. 5) of the Creator's ignorant arrogance.

Irenaeus had to this work and to the work of the Ophites, of Ptolemy, and of others.

CRITICAL OR ADVERSARIAL USE OF THE FOURTH GOSPEL

Taking away such texts which could not have been written prior to *c.*170 or so and those which show only superficial or questionable use of the Fourth Gospel leaves us with relatively few texts. I shall examine in this section five texts for which a plausible case can be made for their existence and circulation prior to this time and which seem to show clear and credible signs of a knowledge of the Fourth Gospel. These are the *Trimorphic Protennoia*, the *Second Apocalypse of James*, the *Apocryphon of James*, the *Acts of John*, and the *Gospel of Thomas*. But that these texts therefore prove or illustrate (*a*) a heterodox affinity with and preference for John or (*b*) the probability that they or any other similar works engendered Johannophobia on the part of the orthodox, cannot be concluded. What is often overlooked is that several works which display an unmistakable knowledge of the Fourth Gospel show just as unmistakably a critical attitude towards it, or against some key aspect of it. Thus, despite the sweeping statements of some scholars, the use of the Fourth Gospel in a heterodox source does not necessarily denote a high admiration for that Gospel. It may indicate a 'reception' on the part of somebody, but not necessarily on the part of the authors of these works.

Trimorphic Protennoia

Brown also mentioned the *Trimorphic Protennoia* as a Nag Hammadi work which contains ' "a Word (*Logos*) christology" and an "I AM" christology, combined with a docetic account of Jesus' death'.[146] This is regarded by him as part of the evidence 'that a wide acceptance of the Fourth Gospel came earlier among heterodox rather than among orthodox Christians'.[147] The *Trimorphic Protennoia*, the first tractate in Codex XIII of the Nag Hammadi library, has in fact become for some the long-sought 'missing link'[148] which is thought to connect the Johannine Prologue to 'gnosticism'. According to George MacRae, 'The most clearly focused and concrete contribution to the discussion of a possible Gnostic background to the Fourth Gospel is the suggestion that the Johannine Prologue is related to

---

[146] Brown, *Community*, 147–8.

[147] Ibid. 147.

[148] The phrase was applied by Logan, 'John and the Gnostics', 46, who, however, does not agree with such an analysis. It was used by James M. Robinson in the discussion following his paper at the 1978 Yale conference on gnosticism in the following way, 'Perhaps the triad in the *Trimorphic Protennoia* provides the missing link in explaining the development from the female Sophia of the Jewish Wisdom literature to the male Logos of the Johannine prologue, as well as accounting for the prominence of the Logos in the prologue' (J. M. Robinson, 'Sethians and Johannine Thought: The *Trimorphic Protennoia* and the Prologue of the Gospel of John', in B. Layton (ed.), *The Rediscovery of Gnosticism*, ii (Leiden, 1981), 642–70, at 663).

the mythological scheme of the Nag Hammadi *Trimorphic Protennoia* NHC XIII,1.'[149]

But not all scholars agree on just how the two are related.[150] It is widely agreed that the *TP* as it now stands is from the middle or latter part of the second century, or somewhat later (many believe it is a product of a 'Sethian' or 'Barbeloite' school), and is dependent upon the Fourth Gospel. But many scholars regard the *TP* as a multi-stage composition. In its earliest stage of existence it is thought to have been a non-Christian, 'gnostic' document already related to the Johannine Prologue as twin products of 'gnosticizing' sapiential speculation.[151] Gesine (Schenke) Robinson believes that even in its first stage there were deep structural and verbal affinities with the Fourth Gospel which show both works shared an ultimate gnostic framework, and that the Johannine Prologue is a derivative adaptation of that gnostic outlook.[152] She sees minimal 'Christianization', in the final form, virtually limited to a few interpolations. But even if one supposes such an early and self-standing stage of composition, the resemblance to the Prologue of the Fourth Gospel at this stage may have been quite general.

[149] G. W. MacRae, 'Gnosticism and the Church of John's Gospel', in C. W. Hedrick and R. Hodgson, jun., (eds.), *Nag Hammadi, Gnosticism, and Early Christianity* (Peabody, Mass., 1986), 89–96, at 91. See also G. Robinson, 'The Trimorphic Protennoia and the Prologue of the Fourth Gospel', in J. E. Goehring (ed.), *Gnosticism and the Early Christian World: In Honor of James M. Robinson* (Sonoma, Calif., 1990), 37–49; E. Pagels has recently upheld this common 'religious milieu' in the appendix to her 'Exegesis of Genesis 1 in the Gospels of Thomas and John', *JBL* 118 (1999), 477–96, at 492–6.

[150] For a very helpful review of the history of scholarship on the relationship see now Nicola F. Denzey, 'Genesis Traditions in Conflict? The Use of Some Exegetical Traditions in the *Trimorphic Protennoia* and the Johannine Prologue', *VC* 55 (2001), 20–44.

[151] See Berliner Arbeitskreis für koptisch-gnostische Schriften, ' "Die dreigestaltige Protennoia": Eine gnostische Offenbarungsrede in koptischer Sprache aus dem Fund von Nag Hammadi', *TLZ* 99 (1974), 731–46, at 733–4 (written by G. Schenke). Since the publication of Michael Williams's book, *Rethinking 'Gnosticism': An Argument for Dismantling a Dubious Category* (Princeton, 1996), we are witnessing a greater circumspection among scholars about the use of the terms 'gnostic' and gnosticism' (e.g. Pagels, 'Exegesis of Genesis 1'; Denzey, 'Genesis Traditions').

[152] G. Robinson, 'Trimorphic Protennoia and the Prologue'. To enter into the details of this proposal here would take a great deal of space. Some of the debate is subjective and regards perceptions deriving from a precommitment to a Bultmannian paradigm about the influence of a pre-Christian gnosticism. Robinson's oft-quoted sentence, 'One has the impression that the relevant statements of Protennoia stand in their natural context, whereas their parallels in the Johannine Prologue, as we find it in the fourth gospel, seem to have been artificially made serviceable to a purpose really alien to them' ('Die dreigestaltige Protennoia', col. 733, cited in J. M. Robinson, 'Sethians and Johannine Thought', 651, and repeated by a number of authors), is a case in point. It is certain that not every 'one' has come away from a study of the two works with that same 'impression'. Part of the debate concerns 'hard data', such as the hard data which are still lacking to prove the existence, let alone the wide circulation, of a pre-Johannine, 'Sethian' gnosticism which could have been a common source for the *TP* and the Prologue of the Fourth Gospel. What does 'one' see in the remainder of the Fourth Gospel, or in the Johannine Epistles, or in Ignatius, or Polycarp, of the highly developed myth of aeons in the Godhead which we see in 'Sethianism'? There is a kind of docetism in the background of these documents, against which they react, and perhaps a variety of speculative exegeses of Genesis, etc., but not 'gnosticism' in the pleromatic sense. There is still a ponderous gap between various strands of Jewish 'wisdom speculation' which spoke of Wisdom's descent to the world and the 'Sethian' conception of a plurality of divine aeons.

John Turner believes a first stage of writing, which he would place in the late first century, would have shared 'the same pattern that underlies the Johannine Prologue, which...was likely also a product of a similar form of wisdom speculation'. That basic pattern has to do with the descent of a heavenly personification of divine wisdom into the lower world for the ultimate salvation of souls, and may bear no relationship to the Fourth Gospel beyond the basic similarity of the descent motif. Turner theorizes that the *TP* then underwent a Christianization, in which the Barbeloite editor drew upon material common to *The Apocryphon of John* and Irenaeus, *AH* 1. 29. Turner then suggests a further Christian supplementation in which the primary interaction with Johannine material comes. Thus, some who speak of multiple stages of production for the *Trimorphic Protennoia* recognize that it is precisely the later 'Christianized' stages, in which the work closely resembles the *Apocryphon of John* (probably known to Irenaeus in some form), which contain the most striking Johannine parallels.[153]

Still others, however, discount such compositional theories and regard the entire document as composed under Christian, and even Johannine, influence.[154] Logan, for instance, believes the work is post-Irenaean and a later elaboration of the *Apocryphon of John*.[155] He sees Johannine influence not only in allusions but in 'the underlying structure which the myth presupposed'; 'thus it is not simply a matter of direct literal influence from John's Gospel, but rather of that Gospel as a source among others, working at various levels, offering fresh perspectives in a continuing process of remythologization'.[156]

[153] Y. Janssens, 'The Trimorphic Protennoia and the Fourth Gospel', in A. H. B. Logan and A. J. Wedderburn (eds.), *The New Testament and Gnosis: Essays in Honor of Robert McL. Wilson* (Edinburgh, 1983), 229–43, at 242; E. Yamauchi, 'The Issue of Pre-Christian Gnosticism Reviewed in the light of the Nag Hammadi Texts', in J. D. Turner and A. McGuire (eds.), *The Nag Hammadi Library after Fifty Years* (Leiden, 1997), 85.
[154] A key study tending to show *TP*'s dependency upon John was done by J. Helderman, ' "In ihren Zelten..." Bemerkungen bei Codex XIII Nag Hammadi p. 47: 14–18, im Hinblick auf Joh i 14', in T. Baarda, A. F. J. Klijn, and W. C. van Unnik (eds.), *Miscellanea Neotestamentica* (Leiden, 1978), i. 181–211, esp. 208–11. See Y. Janssens, 'Le Codex XIII de Nag Hammadi', *Le Muséon*, 7 (1974), 341–413; idem, *La Protennoia Trimorphe (NH, XIII,1)*, BCNH 4 (Quebec, 1978), written without knowledge of the views of the Berlin Arbeitskreis, and idem, 'Une source gnostique du Prologue', in M. de Jonge (ed.), *L'Evangile de Jean: Sources, redaction, théologie*, BETL 44 (Gembloux, 1977), 355–8, where she still decides on Johannine use by the *TP*. Her conclusions on this, however, are more guarded in 'The Trimorphic Protennoia and the Fourth Gospel'. For a review up to 1981 and statement of the issues, see E. M. Yamauchi, 'Jewish Gnosticism? The Prologue of John, Mandaean Parallels and the Trimorphic Protennoia', in R. van den Broek and M. J. Vermaseren (eds.), *Studies in Gnosticism and Hellenistic Religions Presented to Gilles Quispel on the Occasion of his 65th Birthday* (Leiden, 1981), 467–97, at 480–4, and to 1991, see Logan, 'John and the Gnostics'.
[155] Logan, 'John and the Gnostics', 56–7, 'My simple point is this: the form of the myth presupposed by the *Protennoia*, particularly in the cosmogonic section of the first part...is a more developed version of that underlying the *Apocryphon*.' He points out that, in the *TP* 37. 3–20, 'Christ' is 'explicitly identified with the (Johannine) Word', and that Barbelo's titles from the *ApJ* are assimilated to the Word' (57). Both these works, he argues, 'represent secondary elaborations of the more primary form of the myth found in Irenaeus' (57)
[156] Logan, 'John and the Gnostics', 57.

At any rate, the final form of the *TP* does appear to interact with Johannine material.[157] Turner writes,

> In the third subtractate, traditional Christological titles such as Christ, Beloved, Son of God (i.e., 'Son of the Archigenetor') and Son of Man are polemically interpreted in a consciously docetic fashion so as to suggest that these titles were inappropriately applied to the human Jesus by the apostolic church. By implication, the apostolic Jesus is shown actually to be the Christ of the evil archons; the apostolic beloved is actually the Beloved of the archons; the apostolic Son of God is the Son of the ignorant world creator; and the apostolic Son of Man is only a human being among the sons of men.[158]

Turner then makes the critical observation, 'It is interesting that most of these reinterpretations of the Christology of the apostolic church in the *Trimorphic Protennoia* seem to depend on key passages from the Gospel of John to score their point in any acute fashion.'[159] Regardless of the accuracy of his theorized prehistory of the *TP*,[160] Turner is undoubtedly correct in that the final form, the form which definitely seems to know the Fourth Gospel, 'involved a deliberately polemical incorporation of Christian, specifically Johannine Christian, materials'.[161]

---

[157] Denzley, 'Genesis Traditions', has provided a valuable corrective to studies which have tended to consider the question of the relationship in too narrow terms. She has shown that much of the terminology, particularly the creation terminology, shared by the two texts is to be traced to their different ways of interpreting a common text, Genesis 1. This cannot account for all of the Johannine parallels, however, particularly the points at which the *TP* deals not simply with creation motifs, but also with soteriological 'incarnational motifs' (in the *TP*'s case, soteriological 'non-incarnational' motifs), some of which will be noted below. As is the case with J. D. Turner, 'Trimorphic Protennoia (XIII,*1*)' in *NHLE*[3] 511–13, Denzey's assumption (42) of some unspecified later, Christianizing redactions of the *TP* appears to leave room for actual literary dependence at the redactional level.

[158] Turner, *NHLE*[3] 512.

[159] Ibid. Other writers such as G. Robinson, MacRae, and C. A. Evans, 'On the Prologue of John and the *Trimorphic Protennoia*', *NTS* 27 (1981), 395–401, apparently assume that these elements belong to the earlier substratum and are independent of any knowledge of the Fourth Gospel. But even if many of the creation and revelation parallels cited by Evans, 'Prologue', 397, may be assigned to an independent exegetical approach to Gen. 1 (Denzey, 'Genesis Traditions'), certain structural similarities and particularly the Christological parallels (or 'anti-parallels' as the case may be) cannot be traced to Genesis and presuppose a Christian source or sources. Whether this belongs to the original writing or only to a later redaction is the question to be answered.

[160] While there may or may not have been a pre-existing, non-Christian descent motif, it is by no means necessary to assume that this was ever represented by a documentary stage of the *TP*. I am personally not convinced that the theory of literary stages is necessary, despite G. Robinson's attempts. See Logan, 'John and the Gnostics'; idem, *Gnostic Truth and Christian Heresy*, (Edinburgh, 1996), 30, who argues that the *TP* (presumably the entire *TP*) is post-Irenaean.

[161] Turner, *NHLE*[3] 512–13. G. Robinson, 'Trimorphic Protennoia', 43, on the other hand, thinks that the secondary Christianization 'took place in a rather superficial way'. But she still regards 49. 6–22 as part of the Christianization: 'The point being scored is that such titles as Christ, Beloved, Son of God, Angel, and Son of man do not really belong to Jesus. They are conferred upon Jesus only because of a failure to recognize the true Redeemer' (44). She thinks 'the orthodox concept of Jesus "sitting at the right hand of God" seems to have been corrected in terms of the Sethian view, namely: After the resurrection Jesus neither sits at the right hand of the biblical God, Yaldabaoth, nor at the right hand of the highest unknown God, but rather at the right hand of his own father Seth in his light Oroiael where he belongs!' (44).

Here is why Turner's observations with regard to the Fourth Gospel make sense, and why Janssens could say that 'while identical terms occur in *Trimorphic Protennoia* and the Fourth Gospel, they do not have the same meaning'.[162] Despite the many apparent allusions to Johannine themes,[163] despite the main figure of the *TP* using 'I am' statements,[164] and despite his/her testifying, in terms of John 1: 1, that he/she is 'the Word' (46. 5, 14; 47. 15), there is no corresponding declaration that this Word 'became flesh' (John 1: 14; cf. 1 John 4: 2; 2 John 7). In its place we read the following:

The third time I revealed myself to them [in] their tents as Word and I revealed myself in the likeness of their shape. And I wore everyone's garment and I hid myself within them, and [they] did not know the one who empowers me. (47. 13–19)

... in that place I clothed myself [as] the Son of the Archigenetor, and I was like him until the end of his decree ... (49. 12–14)

And among the Angels I revealed myself in their likeness, and among the Powers as if I were one of them, but among the Sons of Man as if I were a Son of Man, even though I am Father of everyone. (49. 15–20)

As for me, I put on Jesus. I bore him from the cursed wood, and established him in the dwelling places of his Father. And those who watch over their dwelling places did not recognize me. (50. 12–16).

Helderman appears to be correct that the use of the word 'tents' in 47. 15 cited above (where the Coptic translator simply transliterates instead of translating Greek σκηνή) reflects not only a use of John 1: 14 ('and the Word became flesh and ἐσκήνωσεν among us') but a deliberate, polemical transformation of the Johannine conception into a 'pure docetism'.[165] The

---

[162] Janssens, 'The Trimorphic Protennoia and the Fourth Gospel', 242. Cf. Denzey, 'Genesis Traditions', 42, 'Although similar in form and language, the *Trimorphic Protennoia*'s orientation differs radically from the Johannine Prologue'.

[163] See Y. Janssens, 'Une source gnostique du Prologue?' in M. de Jonge, *L'Évangile de Jean* (Gembloux, 1977), 355–8; Yamauchi, 'Jewish Gnosticism?', 482–3.

[164] Janssens, 'The Trimorphic Protennoia and the Fourth Gospel', 236, cites MacRae's ambiguous conclusions about the Johannine connections and says, 'I do not think that the use, although frequent, in both Trimorphic Protennoia and the Fourth Gospel, of the self-proclamation formula is sufficient proof of the influence of one of the two texts on the other.'

[165] 'Hierbei ist in *PT 47:14.15 die Pointe von Joh. i 14 absichtlich umgedeutet*', Helderman, 'In ihren Zelten...', 206–7; 'dafür ist die Umdeutung zu bewusst *polemisch* im Hinblich auf Joh. i 14!', 208; cf. also 189, 195–7. Cf. Yamauchi, 'Jewish Gnosticism?', 483; Janssens, 'The Trimorphic Protennoia and the Fourth Gospel', 240–1; Nagel, *Rezeption*, 455. On *TP* 47. 16–17 see Helderman, 'In ihren Zelten...', 201–5. G. Robinson, 'The Trimorphic Protennoia and the Prologue', 48, attempts to minimize the reversal, actually viewing the Johannine Prologue as 'summarizing' the last stage of Protennoia's revelation with the words 'the Logos became flesh', a summation which she alleges 'must have resulted of necessity' in 'a kind of docetism'. Denzey, 'Genesis Traditions', 40–1, is clear on the contrast between John 1: 14 and *TP* 45. 14–15, though she does not admit a literary relationship.

Logos did not tabernacle among them as flesh, but only revealed himself to them 'in their tents' and in 'the likeness of their shape'.

In addition, the *TP* espouses a notion of the Godhead and of creation quite different from that of the Prologue of the Fourth Gospel: 'And the great Demon [Yaltabaoth] began to produce aeons in the likeness of the real Aeons, except that he produced them out of his own power' (40. 4–7); 'And the Archigenetor of ignorance [Yaltabaoth] reigned over Chaos and the underworld and produced a man in my likeness' (40. 22–5). By contrast, the Prologue says of the Logos, 'All things were made through him, and apart from him nothing was made' (John 1: 3). If any reader was alert enough to catch the Johannine parallels, she[166] would surely know that what she was now reading undermined and sought to overthrow the teaching of the Johannine Prologue. That these points about creation would likely have been recognized in the second century is confirmed by Irenaeus, who used the Johannine Prologue to argue that John refutes the heretics on precisely these points in *AH* 3. 11. 1–3.[167]

What does all this mean for the question of the reception of the Fourth Gospel? With so many apparent borrowings from the Fourth Gospel, the docetic inversion of its incarnational Christology is all the more dramatic. Turner remarks that this final form of the *TP* should be assigned 'to the period of struggle over the interpretation of the Christology of the Fourth Gospel witnessed by the New Testament letters of John, perhaps the first quarter or half of the second century'.[168] This of course assumes that there was such a struggle. It would seem that the author of the *TP*, or its 'Christianizer', was at pains not merely to use but also to distance himself from the theology of the Fourth Gospel. In other words, he seems to be abandoning any struggle *for* the Fourth Gospel and its Christology (if there ever was one, which is more than doubtful), and instead trying to do it one better. In any case we have in the *TP* a work of which it can finally be said that it is a 'gnostic' production which knew and used the Fourth Gospel in a substantive way. And in it we see no simple claiming of that Gospel's authority, but a critical and antagonistic use of its expressions in the service of an opposing Christology!

This gnostic (Barbeloite or Sethian?) work then assumes a peculiar attitude towards the Fourth Gospel. It appropriates from John titles for Christ,

---

[166] It is perhaps fitting to use the example of a female reader, since some orthodox writers complained that certain gnostic teachers made female church members their special target (Irenaeus, *AH* 1. 13. 3).

[167] '"All things," he says, "were made by him;" therefore in "all things" this creation of ours is [included], for we cannot concede to these men that [the words] "all things" are spoken in reference to those within their Pleroma. For if their Pleroma do indeed contain these, this creation, as being such, is not outside, as I have demonstrated…but if they are outside the Pleroma, which indeed appeared impossible, it follows, in that case, that their Pleroma cannot be "all things:" therefore this vast creation is not outside [the Pleroma]' (*AH* 3. 11. 2).

[168] Turner, *NHLE*³ 513.

mainly but not exclusively from the Prologue, but applies them to the pleromatic aeon as well as to the descending Saviour who united himself temporarily with the human Jesus. Its employment of Johannine terms thus has affinities with that of the *Apocryphon of John* and the Valentinians. Central to its purpose in using this Gospel is the effort to 'supersede' it in a way which approaches the way the Ophites and others used the books of Genesis and Isaiah. It may not at this point be quite as negative, but it is certainly similarly predatory.

Not only, then, does the *Trimorphic Protennoia* with its 'deliberately polemical incorporation of Christian, specifically Johannine Christian, materials'[169] fail to provide a credible rationale for orthodox Johannophobia, it is much easier to regard it as tending to the opposite result. If our hypothetical orthodox reader is favourably impressed with this document, she is inclined to adopt its thoughts and attitudes, including its implied attitude towards the incarnational Christology of the Fourth Gospel. That Gospel could only be 'received' by this author and his sympathetic readers with a very large amount of 'correction', the kind which involved gnostic, supersessionary exegesis. Thus, if our reader is in danger of developing a case of Johannophobia, the virus only grips her as she retreats from orthodoxy and joins herself to the supposedly superior doctrines of the *Trimorphic Protennoia*. The net result would be a stronger identification of the Fourth Gospel and its incarnational Christology with the orthodox circles she is leaving behind. If on the other hand our reader finds herself disagreeable to the contents of this work, her tendency, like that of Irenaeus, will be to be more firmly established in her orthodoxy and to appreciate what the *TP* depreciates. In this case her esteem for John's Gospel can only grow. If there is any Johannophobia likely to be produced here, it is a heterodox, not an orthodox, strain.[170]

Second Apocalypse of James

About the date of another text mentioned by Brown, the *Second Apocalypse of James*, 'little can be said with certainty', according to Charles Hedrick.[171]

---

[169] Turner, *NHLE*[3], 512–13.

[170] I have found no good reason to follow the approach of the post-Bultmannian line of scholars, who try to place the Fourth Gospel and particularly its Prologue in the trajectory of a pre-Christian gnosis, now being adapted to Christianity. But it may not be unprofitable to consider where their analysis might lead us. If these scholars were correct, the Fourth Gospel's Prologue would be indebted to the same kind of gnosticism as we see in the earliest stage (whatever that was) of the *TP*. But if so, scholars like G. Robinson seem to neglect or downplay the important, demythologizing departures of the Prologue. The modifications made in the Prologue, chiefly in terms of its incarnational Christology but also in its monotheistic conception of God, its version of creation (all three of which, incidentally, Irenaeus points to as contradicting his heretical opponents, *AH* 3. 11. 1–3), and even in its view of John the Baptist, all clearly demonstrate the distance it would place between this 'gnostic' background at its own testimony. In other words, in this case it is the Fourth Gospel which is staking out a polemical stance over against the 'gnostic' tradition. Such an antagonistic stance is likely to have made it not less but more acceptable to orthodox audiences.

[171] *NHLE*[3] 269.

Hedrick writes that 'the absence of allusions to the later developed gnostic systems, and the almost total absence of allusions to the New Testament tradition suggest an early date for the origin of the tractate'.[172] But just how early this might be, we cannot tell.

Brown has pointed to its use of 'I AM christology' as an indication of its knowledge of John. The first-person 'I AM' style is, however, employed in the Nag Hammadi Library by speakers other than Jesus (in *The Thunder, the Perfect Mind* and *Trimorphic Protennoia*, as we have seen). Thus it is entirely possible that the average reader might not have made any connection to the Jesus of the Fourth Gospel. The author of *Sec. Apoc. Jas.* certainly employs this style: 'I am he who received revelation from the Pleroma [of] Imperishability' (46. 6–8); 'I am the [...] whom I knew' (47. 14–16); 'I am surely dying, but it is in life that I shall be found' (48. 8–9); 'I am the brother in secret, who prayed to the Father...' (48. 22–4). But so far there is nothing which would instinctively bring the Fourth Gospel to mind. Soon, however, we meet a string of 'I am's, 'I [am the] first [son] who was begotten... I am the beloved. I am the righteous one. I am the son of [the Father]' (49. 5–12); and then, 'I am the stranger, and they have no knowledge of me in [their] thoughts' (51. 7–9). Though there are no quotations here, it is possible that an alert reader might have been vaguely reminded of statements of Jesus in John's Gospel. Perhaps even more likely to send her mind in the direction of John 1. 4 is what she saw in *Sec. Apoc. Jas.* 58. 6–8, 'He was [this one who] is the life. He was the light.' But in this case our orthodox reader will also have read in the immediately preceding words, 'He was that one whom he who created the heaven and the earth, and dwelled in it, did not see' (58. 2–6), a typically disparaging comment about the Creator. And at this point, if indeed not before, if she was alert enough to pick up the *possible* allusions to the Fourth Gospel's Prologue, she would have realized that the author she was now reading was not advancing the Fourth Gospel's 'trajectory' but was in fact attacking its doctrine. For that Gospel has the Word, who later became flesh, as the one through whom 'all things were made' and without whom 'was not anything made' (John 1: 3). Indeed, the reader had read only a page earlier, in 56. 20–57. 1, the author's use of Isaiah 45. 5, that classic gnostic prooftext for the ignorance and hubris of the Creator (used also by the anti-Johannine *Trimorphic Protennoia* and by the *Apocryphon of John*): 'I am the LORD, and there is no other, besides me there is no God' (Isa. 45: 5, etc.).

The *Sec. Apoc. Jas.* leaves us just about where the *TP* left us, with an early gnostic work which seems to know and to have been influenced at some level by the Fourth Gospel but which shows an overall negative, antagonistic, or supersessionary, attitude towards that Gospel. It is not easy to see how we should regard this as a legitimate 'trajectory' of the Fourth Gospel.

---

[172] Ibid. 270.

And how does this play out for the question of orthodox Johannophobia? There are no known traces of the knowledge of the *Sec. Apoc. Jas.* in the second century, leaving us with no evidentiary basis upon which to judge the effects which the *Sec. Apoc. Jas.* might have had on second-century orthodox believers. But from the text itself one would have to observe that, as with the *TP*, the impression most likely given to the orthodox reader, if any was given at all on this matter, would be that *Sec. Apoc. Jas.* does not ally itself with the Fourth Gospel but opposes it. And again, as with the *TP*, this would likely only have made an avowed orthodox reader more indignant in her support of the Fourth Gospel. If, on the other hand, she found the views of the *Sec. Apoc. Jas.* attractive and eventually converted to its form of Christianity, she is likely to have adopted the text's superior attitude towards several aspects of her old orthodox faith, including its view of the Fourth Gospel. The net result in either case is that a close adherence to the authority of the Fourth Gospel comes to be associated more clearly with orthodoxy, not with gnosticism.

The *Second Apocalypse of James*, then, like (at least the final form of) the *Trimorphic Protennoia*, seems to assume the prior recognition of the Fourth Gospel in the Great Church and a fairly general knowledge of its contents. It is on the basis of this recognition that each develops its own more or less radical departures from the Fourth Gospel's theology.

Apocryphon of James

These observations about the *Trimorphic Protennoia* and the *Second Apocalypse of James* bring us to a Nag Hammadi text not mentioned by Brown, but mentioned by Hillmer and Culpepper,[173] whose knowledge of the Fourth Gospel and at least the First Epistle of John is very well attested. The *Apocryphon of James*, which I argued above may have connections with the group mentioned by Irenaeus in *AH* 3. 11. 9, purports to be a letter from James to a disciple, recording an encounter between Jesus and his twelve disciples 550 days after his resurrection.[174] In the story, James and Peter are selected by the Saviour to be 'filled' with the Holy Spirit and to receive new revelation consisting of parables, woes, and discourses, some of which have parallels with canonical Gospel materials. At the end of the revelatory section Jesus ascends to the Father and the two disciples follow him to the third heaven but are prevented from seeing the Majesty because the other disciples call them back. James and Peter relate part of their encounter to

---

[173] Hillmer, 'Second Century', 86–96; Culpepper, *John*, 118, who agrees with Cameron (see below) that 'the sayings of Jesus in this document may have been collected and composed prior to Irenaeus, during the first half of the second century'.

[174] Cf. the 445 days mentioned in *Ascension of Isaiah* 9. 16 and the eighteen months during which Irenaeus reports that the Valentinians said the Lord conversed with his disciples, according to Irenaeus, *AH* 1. 3.2; 30.14.

the other disciples, who are sent away by James, who then departs for Jerusalem.

The provenance of this work is under dispute, with dates ranging from the beginning of the second to the beginning of the third century, and Asia Minor, Syria, and Egypt all receiving some support as places of origin. Several scholars have noticed certain coincidences with the orthodox apocryphon *Epistula Apostolorum*, which they explain variously.

There has been a significant divide on the possible relationship between the *Ap. Jas.* and the canonical Gospels. Many, including Tuckett, Perkins, and Janssens, have regarded the similarities as a rather obvious indication that the *Ap. Jas.* knew these Gospels.[175] Others, such as Koester, Cameron, and Kirchner, argue on the basis of their form-critical methods that the *Ap. Jas.* delivers traditional sayings of Jesus independently of the four Gospels and usually in a more primitive form.[176] While both Tuckett and Perkins accept that the author may know independent tradition,[177] neither believes this can account for all the substantial parallels. I cannot here undertake a full review of the evidence, but shall instead point to a consideration which has been ignored by the proponents of an early, independent tradition in the *Ap. Jas.* and which seems to provide an essential part of the context for the question. That consideration is the open apologetic stance of the document, positioning itself against a perceived 'apostolic' or orthodox consensus, to the advantage of an allegedly superior point of view. In other words, it presupposes the existence of the majority Church and its ecclesiastical and 'canonical' paraphernalia, against which it is mounting its campaign for an alternative.

To illustrate this we need only look at the opening scene of the apocryphon, which relates an occasion 550 days after the resurrection, when the disciples were gathered and Jesus appeared to them: 'Now the twelve disciples [were] sitting all together at [the same time] and remembering what the Savior had said to each one of them, whether secretly or openly, they were setting it down in books. [And] I was writing what was in [my book][178] ...'

---

[175] C. M. Tuckett, *Nag Hammadi and the Gospel Tradition: Synoptic Tradition in the Nag Hammadi Library* (Edinburgh, 1986). Tuckett concludes that 'ApocJas seems to presuppose Matthew's finished gospel. Lukan material (e.g. Lk 15. 8–10) is also known and this is probably due to knowledge of Luke's gospel itself. There is no evidence to suggest that Mark's gospel was known, but equally nothing to suggest that it was unknown' (97); P. Perkins, 'Johannine Traditions in *Ap. Jas.* (NHC I, 2)', *JBL* 101 (1982), 403–14; idem, *Gnosticism and the New Testament* (Minneapolis, 1993); Y. Janssens, 'Traits de la Passion dans l'*Epistula Iacobi Apocrypha*', *Le Muséon*, 88 (1975), 97–101, which details a dependence upon Luke in one section of the work.

[176] H. Koester, *Introduction to the New Testament*, ii (Berlin, 1982), 225; R. Cameron, *Sayings Traditions in the* Apocryphon of James, HTS 34 (Philadelphia, 1984); D. Kirchner, 'Apocryphon of James', *NTA*² i. 285–91 at 287.

[177] C. M. Tuckett, *Nag Hammadi and the Gospel Tradition* (Edinburgh, 1986), 97.

[178] Assuming the correctness of this restoration of the text, this reference to another book by James perhaps is to be connected to his mention of another 'secret book' sent to the addressee 'ten months ago' in 1. 30. F. E. Williams, 'The Apocryphon of James: I, 2: 1.1–16.30' in H. W. Attridge

(2. 7–16).[179] Based on his lengthy examination of the practice of 'remembering' the words of Jesus in the early Church, Cameron believes this demonstrates that the *Ap. Jas.* was written at 'a time in which written texts with
"scriptural" authority were not yet normative',[180] when oral tradition could
be safely appealed to and relied upon to the exclusion of anything written.[181]
Koester says more specifically that ' "Remembering" what Jesus had said, is a
key term for the oral tradition'.[182] Cameron concludes,

> In this scene [2. 7–16], the technical term of 'remembering' is used in a program-
> matic way to introduce those sayings which compose the body of discourse and
> dialogue in the *Ap. Jas.* The hermeneutical moment of 'remembering' what the
> Savior had said is disclosed when the Savior appeared; the manifestation of
> the 'openness' of Jesus' teaching, therefore, is simultaneous with the 'appearing'
> of the risen Lord. Accordingly, the term 'remembering' is understood here as the
> introduction to a collection of 'secret sayings' of Jesus, and is used to refer to the
> composition of these sayings in 'secret books,' of which the *Ap. Jas.* is one.[183]

But this is clearly mistaken. The remembering activity in 2. 10 is coupled
with a scribal activity, and refers to books being written by the twelve *before*
the appearance of the Saviour on the 550th day.[184] The activity of the
twelve of recording in books what they are remembering cannot therefore
have to do with what is about to be 'revealed' to them by the Saviour, and
is not to be identified with any 'sayings traditions'[185] which might follow in
the *Ap. Jas.* This is supported by the fact that the parables Jesus tells them,

---

(ed.), *Nag Hammadi Codex I (The Jung Codex): Introductions, Texts, Translations, Indices*, Nag Hammadi
Studies, 22 (Leiden, 1985) (hereafter, Williams, NHS 22), 13–53, at 20, thinks the mention of a
previous book is a fictitious detail 'added for the sake of atmosphere'.

[179] Cameron's translation, *Sayings*, 91.

[180] Ibid. 92, where he is citing his own words from 'Apocryphon of James', 56.

[181] Also Kirchner, *NTA*[2] i. 287, 290; F. E. Williams, 'The Apocryphon of James (I, 2)', in
J. M. Robinson (gen. ed.), *The Nag Hammadi Library in English*, 3rd, completely revised edn. (San
Francisco, 1988), 29–30 at 30 (hereafter Williams, *NHLE*[3]). Kirchner calls the phrase, 'recall the
words of the Lord', a 'transmission formula'. It rather appears to have to do with a polemical
upstaging of the orthodox claim that their traditions, and particularly their Gospel writings, went
back to authentic apostolic reminiscences of the Lord's deeds and words. In the light of this, and
more especially in the light of Perkins's demonstration of a high saturation of Johannine allusions
('Johannine Traditions'), it is strange that Kirchner would also say that 'the treatment of the sayings
tradition in Ap. Jas. . . . does not yet reveal any dependence on canonised texts' (287).

[182] Koester, *ACG* 189.

[183] Cameron, *Sayings*, 129.

[184] Observed by Perkins, 'Johannine Traditions', 404, 'The opening scene suggests that they
wrote their accounts even before receiving gnosis from Peter and James'.

[185] Cameron, *Sayings*, 92, '*Ap. Jas.* 2. 7–16 intimates that it understood "remembering" as critical
production and reproduction. An examination of the use of this technical term in early Christian
literature will help clarify the ways in which sayings traditions that were available to the *Ap. Jas.*
were understood and utilized in the composition of this document'. But the reference to remembering in 2. 10 has nothing to do with the 'sayings' delivered later. How does *Ap. Jas* use 'remember'
elsewhere? In 3. 12–16 Jesus says, 'remember that you have seen the Son of Man, and spoken with
him in person, and listened to him in person'. This may have to do with sayings of Jesus, but
Kirchner points to an 'ironical' edge in this reminder. 'By taking, for instance, the formula as it
occurs on p. 3 in an ironical-paradoxical sense, it becomes possible to appreciate the following woe

of the date palm (7. 22–35), of the grain of wheat (8. 10–27), and the ear of grain (12. 22–7), are presented as new parables, not as mere interpretations of parables the disciples were 'remembering'. The author does not expound but merely refers by name to parables from the canonical Gospels,[186] parables obviously well known to the author and his readers: 'It was enough for some <to listen> to the teaching and understand "The Shepherds" and "The Seed" and "The Building" and "The Lamps of the Virgins" and "The Wage of the Workmen" and "The Didrachmae" and "The Woman"'.[187] 'It was enough for some', that is, for the common lot of Christians, but obviously not for James and Peter who are now the privileged recipients of extra revelation, which they could not have been 'remembering' at the opening of the scene.[188]

The connection in *Ap. Jas.* 2. 10's 'reminiscences' both with the apostles and with books cannot be ignored. Fifteen times Justin Martyr refers to the Church's Gospels as 'the memoirs of the apostles' or 'the memoirs which I say were drawn up by His apostles and those who followed them'.[189] In *Dial.* 106. 3 he refers to 'his memoirs', meaning Peter's, when citing information which is contained only in Mark. This of course relates to what Papias had said earlier about the nature of Mark's Gospel (*HE* 3. 39. 15). And it is not Papias' remembering of still unwritten sayings of Jesus that forms the parallel to the *Ap. Jas.*, but Mark's, or rather, Peter's

and benediction with their contrary import. The recollection formula is used in order to interpret sayings traditions through the form of revealed sayings. Sayings which according to Ap. Jas. derive from the earthly Jesus are rejected, since the Jesus of before Easter did not possess the character of revelation' (Kirchner, *NTA²*, 290). In 5. 33 Jesus says, 'Remember my cross and my death, and you will live!' This has no reference to sayings but to events, or narratives. In 10. 6 it is Jesus who has 'remembered' the disciples' tears and mourning and anguish. In 12. 35 Jesus urges the two disciples to 'remember me. And remember me because when I was with you, you did not know me'. This too has no direct reference to sayings.

[186] Even Koester, *ACG*, 197, agrees that this list refers to parables from the canonical Gospels. It is, he says, 'the only strong indication for a use of canonical gospels in this writing'. But, too predictably, he concludes that 'it is probably an interpolation'. On the contrary, the list of canonical parables is mentioned in order to give a rationale for the revelation of new ones. Koester supports his interpolation theory by observing Jesus' staying for 'eighteen days' with the disciples in 8. 3, just prior to the list. This is seen as a contradiction of the 550-day period after the resurrection, mentioned in 2. 19–21, and therefore is claimed as evidence of an interpolation. Kirchner's translation in *NTA²*, however, regards the word 'days' to be a slip and restores to 'eighteen months', which then corresponds well with the 550 days of ch. 2. D. Rouleau, *L'Épitre apocryphe de Jacques* (Quebec, 1987), 115, suggests that the original read 'eighteen months of days'. This would also make an exact parallel to the Valentinians cited by Irenaeus, *AH* 1. 3. 2; 30. 14.

[187] The canonical sources, according to Koester, *ACG*, 196–7: The Shepherds, Luke 16: 4–6; The Seed, Mark 4: 3–9 or 4: 26–9 or 4: 30–2 (=Q 13. 18–19); The Building, Matt. 7: 24–7; Luke 6: 47–9; The Lamps of the Virgins, Matt. 25: 1–12; The Wage of the Workmen, Matt. 20: 1–15; The Didrachmae, Luke 16: 8–9; The Woman, Luke 18: 2–8.

[188] Perkins, *GNT*, 72, '*Apocryphon of James* intends to invoke the authority of the canonical Gospels to bolster the esoteric, gnostic teaching presented in the treatise.'

[189] *1 Apol.* 66. 3; 67. 4; *Dial.* 100. 4; 101. 3; 102. 5; 103. 6, 8; 104. 1; 105. 1, 5, 6; 106. 1, 3, 4; 107. 1. In addition, Justin attaches to his conflation of Luke 1: 31–2; Matt. 1: 20–1 in *1 Apol.* 33. 5 the words, 'as they who have remembered all that concerns our Saviour Jesus Christ have taught (οἱ ἀπομνημονεύσαντες πάντα τὰ περὶ τοῦ σωτῆρος ἡμῶν Ἰησοῦ Χριστοῦ ἐδίδαξαν)'.

remembering. Though Papias does not say explicitly that the Gospel of Mark is Peter's memoirs, he says it is either Mark's 'remembrances' of what Peter taught or, more probably, Mark's record of what Peter remembered. And if Papias reports that Mark wrote down accurately what he remembered of Peter's teaching (*HE* 3. 39. 15), then the written document already in Papias' day, and already in the day of the Elder whom Papias is here quoting, is known by its character as a 'memoir' or book of reminiscences. In a story of Mark's origin which Eusebius attributes to Clement of Alexandria and Papias, it is said that Peter's hearers besought Mark, 'seeing that he was Peter's follower, to leave them with a ὑπόμνημα of the teaching given them verbally' (Eusebius, *HE* 2. 15. 1). Whether Clement has another source for this besides Papias or not, this tradition characterizes Mark's Gospel as a record of Peter's reminiscences.

Thus when *Ap. Jas.* begins with a scene in which the apostles are not only 'remembering' what the Lord had said to them but are putting into books what they remember, this appears to be a tacit acknowledgement of what we find among Church writers from the early part of the second century on, namely that the Church had in its possession books which were generally accepted as the memoirs of the apostles about the life and teaching of Jesus. The 'revelation' to James and Peter which follows in the *Ap. Jas.* of course comes with the intention of doing the catholics one better.[190] The familiarity of *Ap. Jas.*'s author with early Christian tradition about its received Gospels may well be signified again when he has James remark that he has written this tract 'in Hebrew characters' (1. 16). This has the appearance of being aimed at offsetting the claim recorded by Papias (evidently from the same Elder who spoke of the origins of Mark) that Matthew first wrote his Gospel in Hebrew (Papias, in Euseb., *HE* 3. 39. 16). Cameron recognizes that 'In both cases, this reference is meant to guarantee the authority and secure the reliability of their respective gospel texts.'[191] The author's familiarity with the traditions contained in Papias even justify the suspicion that he knew Papias' work, or at least the tradition on which it is based, which may have been fairly commonly known by the time he wrote.

The entire character of the work thus bears out what Perkins says about the author of the *Ap. Jas.*, that he appears 'to recognize that the Gospel canon and apostolic authority must be claimed for gnostic exegesis'.[192] 'Gnostic Christians might even accept a canon of four Gospels and Acts as public teaching. But that canon will not lead to knowledge of the Father

[190] Rouleau, *L'Épitre apocryphe de Jacques*, 99.
[191] Cameron, *Sayings*, 121–2: this claim 'is intended to locate this text in the earliest stages of the tradition. In this respect, the *Ap. Jas.* is to be compared with Papias's statement that the Gospel of Matthew was composed "in Hebrew."' But this raises the question of whether the author of the apocryphon (or the redactor of this final stage) does not then know the tradition given by Papias (which evidently is to be traced to his source, the Elder).
[192] Perkins, *GNT* 194.

unless the revelations of the heavenly Christ are used to interpret its content.'[193] Whether or not there was when the author wrote any access to 'free tradition' of any age, this apocryphon bears witness to the existence of written documents thought to have been authored by apostles and which were well-known and probably even considered by its opponents as having a scriptural authority. Thus the author's polemic can be seen more clearly as an attempt to utilize but transcend the authoritative texts of the Church at large.

Perkins then is surely correct that this work presupposes the four Gospels and that it knows the Fourth Gospel particularly well. She comments only on its positive use of Johannine material, even suggesting that the author's use of John and 1 John amounts to a self-legitimization.[194] This may be true to a degree, but it is even clearer that the author's use of Johannine texts is at times quite critical. Perkins reads *Ap. Jas.* 11. 12–13 as signifying that 'the gnostics also claim that they are the ones for whom the Paraclete of 1 John 2: 1–2 intercedes. "Those without a Paraclete" (11, 12–13) are condemned.'[195] But this seems to rest on a mistranslation. 'Woe to you who need an advocate! Woe to you, who stand in need of grace!' (*NTA*), is Kirchner's translation. 'Malheur à vous qui avez besoin d'un défenseur. Malheur à vous qui avez besoin de la grâce', is given by Rouleau.[196] Says Kirchner, '*Ap. Jas.* even pronounces a woe to those who think that they need an advocate, and extols those who earn grace through their own efforts'.[197] Such a judgement could hardly be more antagonistic towards the teaching of 1 John 1: 9; 2: 1–2.

This attitude towards Johannine teaching is not found only with regard to 1 John. In 2. 28–33 the Saviour says, 'Verily I say unto you, no one will ever enter the kingdom of heaven at my bidding, but (only) because you yourselves are full'. This should be compared to John 14: 6, 'Jesus said to him, "I am the way and the truth and the life; no one comes to the Father except through me"'. Against the testimony of Jesus in the Fourth Gospel, the author of *Ap. Jas.* does away with the need to come to the Father through Jesus. He who is 'full' can enter on his own. Jesus is a guide who has taught his disciples what to say to the archons on their way (8. 36). But he is not himself the way, the truth, and the life.[198] Though there is a

---

[193] Ibid.

[194] Perkins, 'Johannine Traditions', 413.

[195] Ibid. 411.

[196] Rouleau, *L'Épitre apocryphe de Jacques*, 124–5. Rouleau relates the Paraclete here to the Spirit promised in John 7: 39; 14: 16, 26; 16: 7–11. But this fails to observe that (*a*) a filling with the Spirit is definitely encouraged in 2. 35–3. 20, and (*b*) this malediction follows directly upon the disciples' satisfaction at the word that the Saviour would intercede for them.

[197] Kirchner, *NTA*[2] 290. Cf. Williams, NHS 22, 23, 'the emphasis on salvation by one's own effort is notable'.

[198] Koester, *ACG*, 191.

significant overlap with the Fourth Gospel in conceptions and terminology, there is a clear distancing represented here.

Even more striking is what we read in 3. 17–25, 'Woe to those who have seen the So[n of M]an! Blessed will they be who have not seen the man, who were not together with him, who did not speak with him, who did not listen to anything from him. Yours is life.' This is not a simple restating of the blessing of those who believe without having seen, as Jesus tells Thomas in John 20: 29,[199] and a legitimization of the author's group based on that Johannine passage, as Perkins suggests.[200] It is a woe pronounced upon the one who has seen, heard, conversed with the man Jesus, as if to say that such people have only known with their outward senses the earthly and not the heavenly being.[201] A comparison with the orthodox apocryphon *Ep. Apost.* 29 is instructive, 'And we said to him, "Blessed are we, for we see and hear you as you speak to us, and our eyes have seen such mighty deeds that you have done." And he answered and said to us, "But much more blessed will they be who do not see me and (yet) believe in me…"' (Eth.).[202] Here is a positive reflection on the same Gospel passage, John 20: 29, where both those who saw and heard Jesus and those who believe without sight are 'blessed', combined with a positive, probable appropriation of 1 John 1: 1–3. The difference between a blessing and a woe shows in the use of Johannine materials by the two authors a definite contrast in approach.

Perkins also saw in 3. 17–25 an allusion to 1 John 1: 1–3, 'That which was from the beginning, which we have heard, which we have seen with our eyes, which we have looked upon and touched with our hands, concerning the word of life…we proclaim also to you, so that you may have fellowship with us; and our fellowship is with the Father and with his Son Jesus Christ'. She does not observe, however, that *Ap. Jas.* 3. 17–25 seems the very inverse of that text!

---

[199] Koester, *ACG*, 192. F. E. Williams, 'NHC I, 2: The Apocryphon of James', in H. W. Attridge (ed.), *Nag Hammadi Codex I (The Jung Codex): Notes*, Nag Hammadi Studies, 23 (Leiden, 1985), 7–37 (hereafter, Williams, NHS 23), 31, says 'If correctly restored, this is the tractate's most direct quotation of a NT passage'.

[200] Perkins, 'Johannine Traditions', 411.

[201] Williams, NHS 23, 11, 'The woe is directed against orthodox Christians, whose religion is founded on the canonical Gospels'; 'though James and Peter have had this sort of experience of the Son of Man, their previously inadequate knowledge is now in process of enlargement'; J. van der Vliet, 'Spirit and Prophecy in the Epistula Iacobi Apocrypha (NHC I, 2)', *VC* 44 (1990), 30, 'Thus, in our passage "hearing" refers without a shade of doubt to the disciples' imperfect, external perception of Christ, which did not yet develop into belief and knowledge'.

[202] A similar view was known to Origen. He criticizes those who say that 'those are more blessed who have not seen and yet believe, than those who have seen and have believed, and for this they quote the saying to Thomas at the end of the Gospel of John, Blessed are they that have not seen and yet have believed. But it is not said here that those who have not seen and yet have believed are more blessed than those who have seen and believed. According to their view those after the Apostles are more blessed than the Apostles; than which nothing can be more foolish' (*C. John* 10. 27, *ANF*).

'Blessed are they who have not been ill and have known relief before falling ill; yours is the kingdom of God' (3. 30–4). Helderman notes that this involves the idea of salvation as healing.[203] Others need 'healing' from their miserable state, but those are blessed who never needed healing from illness, but have always known rest. Deprived of the metaphor, this could easily be read as a positive statement of the doctrine which is denounced in 1 John 1: 8–10: 'If we say we have no sin, we deceive ourselves, and the truth is not in us ... If we say we have not sinned, we make him a liar, and his word is not in us.' In this case the author of *Ap. Jas.* would not be denying that Jesus can give rest to those who have the illness, but he would be claiming that there are some who have not known the illness.

'Or do you perhaps think that the Father is a lover of mankind, or that he is won over by means of prayers, or that he bestows grace on someone because of another, or that he listens to someone who asks (something of him)?' (11. 29–34). The NHLE[3] translation is milder,[204] but still poses an antithesis with 1 John, which teaches that one may indeed be given grace 'because of another', whether that other is Jesus Christ who became a propitiation for the sins of others (1 John 2: 1–2), or whether it be another believer, who asks on behalf of the sinning brother and is granted life (1 John 5: 14, 16).

Finally, I make an observation about the pseudepigraphy. That the selection of only two disciples, James and Peter, is polemical is generally admitted.[205] The author 'insists that the Lord did not wish to make its contents known to "the twelve"'.[206] But why, if the author knows the Gospel and First Epistle of John so well, has he not included John among the disciples selected for a new, superior revelation? Whether the James in view is the Lord's brother, as most have assumed, or is the son of Zebedee,[207] the omission of John hardly seems innocent. In the canonical Gospels it is Peter with James and John the sons of Zebedee who constitute the inner circle of Jesus' disciples. In Acts and Galatians, it is Peter, with James of Jerusalem and John son of Zebedee who are the pillars of the Church.[208] In either

---

[203] J. Heldermann, 'Anapausis in the Epistula Jacobi Apocrypha', in R. McL. Wilson (ed.), *Nag Hammadi and Gnosis*, NHS 14 (Leiden, 1978), 36–7.

[204] *NHLE*[3] has 'without prayers' instead of 'by means of prayers'.

[205] Williams, NHS 22, 20–1, points to the author's elevation of James above Peter. 'One suspects that Peter, the typical representative of orthodox Christianity, has been introduced to lend authenticity to the variant tradition taught by our tractate. The observation that all twelve disciples "believed the revelation" (16. 2–5) may be there for the same purpose'. Cf. Rouleau, *L'Épitre apocryphe de Jacques*, 100.

[206] Perkins, *GNT* 182. Also, Williams, *NHLE*[3] 30, 'The reporting of a special postresurrection appearance of Jesus, and the appeal to James as a source of secret and superior tradition, are means Gnostics often used to legitimate their message.'

[207] W. C. van Unnik, 'The Origin of the Recently Discovered "Apocryphon Jacobi"', *VC* 10 (1956), 146–56, 154, says, 'it is equally possible that James, the son of Zebedee, was meant, he belonging with Peter and his brother to the inner circle of Jesus' Disciples' Also Koester, *ACG* 188.

[208] Clement of Alexandria, according to Eusebius (*HE* 2. 1), records in his *Hypotyposeis* the view that 'The Lord after the resurrection delivered the gnosis to James the Just and John and Peter.

association of Peter and one or the other James, John holds a firm place. In a text which knows so much Johannine tradition and, as we have seen, engages important parts of it in an adversarial way, we can hardly avoid reading such an omission as part of the stance of the author and his group, a stance which on the one hand shared general Johannine conceptions but which saw itself as at odds with its chief representatives. The author's use of so much Johannine material in an inverted or antithetical way would appear to be no less than a spurning of the apostle John. This forms a corollary to what I have already observed, that the *Ap. Jas.* had much in common with the group mentioned by Irenaeus in *AH* 3. 11. 9 which rejected the Fourth Gospel.

Far from being essentially a rival claimant of the mantle of Johannine Christianity, the *Apocryhon of James* instead manifests a settled and pronounced reaction against it. The apocryphon's repetition of certain Johannine concepts shows that these concepts were simply part of the playing field for anyone wanting to compete for adherents from among orthodox Church members. Certain things had to be taken for granted—at least ostensibly. It would not do, in these circles, to deny that certain men had heard Jesus, seen him, touched him, or that some of these men had handed down their records of Jesus' words and ministry to the Church. These things were apparently too well established and were not in dispute. The route taken by this author, and by Valentinian and other rivals generally, was to use but also supersede the apostolic testimony by one means or another, here, by selective, superior revelations.

The supersessionary attitude of this author towards the mainstream Church is in some ways clearer than is that of the *Second Apocalypse of James* or the *Trimorphic Protennoia.*[209] His predatory and polemical use of the Fourth Gospel and the First Epistle of John is even more pronounced. Thus, the reading of this work by our imaginary orthodox reader is even less likely to have provoked in her any Johannophobic sentiments, unless they are produced in her as a result of her acceptance of the author's 'advances' upon apostolic Christianity.

Acts of John

Another clear example of a 'gnostic' reaction to the Fourth Gospel is contained in a work not found at Nag Hammadi, the *Acts of John*, a lengthy, romantic, and at crucial points heterodox portrayal of the son of Zebedee's

These delivered it to the rest of the Apostles...' In this recounting of 'gnostic' tradition John is still in the favoured fraternity.

[209] Yet D. Rouleau, *L'Épitre apocryphe de Jacques*, 17, observes that the polemic of this work is milder than is contained in *The Second Treatise of the Great Seth* and *The Testimony of Truth*, 'mais elle n'en est pas moins réelle et efficace'. Rouleau reads the inclusion of Peter as a sign of deference to 'la Grande Église, l'Église de Pierre'. He thinks it is most critical not of the Great Church *per se*, but of its hierarchical structures and mechanisms of institutional mediation (18).

ministry in and around Ephesus. As with most other gnostic texts, it is not possible to be precise or certain about its origins. Most however regard it as a composite document. In a major, recent study, P. J. Lalleman, following the lead of E. Junod and J.-D. Kaestli, divides the text into three parts: section A, chs. 18–86, 106–8, 110–15; section B, 87–93, 103–5; and section C, 94–102 and 109,[210] with at least two authors, one responsible for A and B, one for C. All agree that at least section C should be characterized as 'gnostic'.[211] It appears that an existing, somewhat heterodox 'novel', or 'novelistic biography', was taken over and supplemented by a more blatantly 'gnostic' writer as a platform for his views. Many scholars would place the composite document in the late second century or later, but Lalleman has recently argued for 'a date in the second quarter of the second century for the redaction of the final text'.[212] Based on similarities with the *ApocJas.* and the *Ep. Apost.*, I think this proposal has merit, though I would place the work just before or after 150.[213]

Like the other texts considered in this section, the *AJ* without a doubt knows the Fourth Gospel;[214] it even assumes the attribution of that Gospel

[210] P. J. Lalleman, *The Acts of John* (Leuven, 1998), 25, etc.; Eric Junod and Jean-Daniel Kaestli, *L'Histoire des Actes apocryphes des apôtres du IIIe au IXe siècle: Le Cas des Actes de Jean*, Cahiers de la Revue de Théologie et de Philosophie, 7 (Geneva, 1982); idem (eds.), *Acta Iohannis*. Tomus 1: *Praefatio—Textus*; Tomus 2: *Textus alli—Commentarius, Indices*, Corpus Christianorum Series Apocryphorum 1, 2 (Turnhout, 1983). The original beginning is lost; the present chs. 1–17 are considered to be later, 4th or 5th cent., Lalleman, *Acts of John*, 12–13. Lalleman characterizes sections B and C together as a 'gospel' (45).
[211] Lalleman, *Acts of John*, does not think sections A and B are gnostic, agreeing with Junod and Kaestli. He points out that Zahn, 'Die Wanderungen des Apostels Johannes', *Neue Kirchliche Zeitschrift* 10 (1899), 191–218 at 215, thought the author concealed his gnostic views in the first parts and revealed them at the end.
[212] Lalleman, *Acts of John*, 270, 272. He believes it must be older than and used by the *ApocJn.* and probably the *Acts of Paul, Acts of Peter*, and *ApocPet.* (137, 151). The Johannine parallels make Lalleman think the work came from Asia Minor. Most others have favoured either Egypt or Sryia. See K. Schäferdiek, 'The Acts of John', in *NTA*² ii. 152–71, at 166–7.
[213] See C. E. Hill, 'The *Epistula Apostolorum*: An Asian Tract from the Time of Polycarp', *JECS* 7 (1999), 1–53. For this date for the *Acts* see also Braun, *Jean le Théologien*, 200–4.
[214] Schäferdiek, *NTA*² ii. 164, observes that the itinerary of John's travels in chs. 55–9 begins from Ephesus and proceeds to Smyrna, then to various unnamed towns and finally to Laodicea, thus mirroring the order of the seven churches given in Rev. 2–3. This was also held by T. Zahn, C. Schmidt, M. Blumenthal, and Hengel, *Frage*, 53. If correct, this also amounts to a recognition of the tradition which identified the author of the Fourth Gospel and the Apocalypse as the same John the apostle. But Lalleman, *Acts of John*, 18–19, rejects the idea that the mention of John's travels to Ephesus, Smyrna, and Laodicea, where material is missing between his time in Smryna and in Laodicea, indicates a knowledge of Revelation. He says that 'the present research has not rendered a single indication that the author of the AJ knew Rev', and proposes an alternative model for John's route in the annual assize tour of the Roman governor of Asia, in which the governor administered justice. Yet, in citing for this idea E. Plümmacher, 'Apostolische Missionsreise und statthalterliche Assisetour', *ZNW* 85 (1994) 259–78, he says that Plümmacher's thesis 'implies that the route of John's Asiatic tour spanned the same cities as the governor's, which probably covered 13 or 14 cities, among which Miletus, Pergamon, Apameia, Laodicea, Smyrna and Ephesos, in a random order. Among these cities, Ephesos and Smyrna were most important for our author' (19 n. 75). Yet it remains that the *AJ* does not mention any of the other cities, only ones mentioned by Revelation.

to John the son of Zebedee.[215] This has been demonstrated many times and need not be reiterated here. But this is not evidence of gnostic love for this Gospel and, despite its common citation by supporters of the OJP, it can only give them cold comfort. The attitude of this author towards the Fourth Gospel has been observed by other scholars, and it is quite comparable to the attitude of other gnostic authors canvassed in this section. Luttikhuizen writes that in *AJ* 97–102, 'the relation to the Gospel accounts, especially the Fourth Gospel, is oppositional: in clear contrast to the Gospel, Christ (the descended saviour) reveals to John, who had fled from the crucifixion scene unto the Mount of Olives, that he, Christ, is not the one who is crucified on the wooden cross in Jerusalem... the story concludes with the report that John laughs at the people around the cross in Jerusalem'.[216] Similarly, Lalleman concludes, 'From the viewpoint of the later canon and of Orthodoxy, the type of intertextual relationship between John's Gospel and the AJ is that of distortion. Our author's specific outlook opposes "orthodox" readings of the Gospel.'[217]

One of the most telling examples of this author's use of John is in 101. 8–9, where he denies that blood flowed from Jesus on the cross, in contradiction of John 19: 34: 'You hear that I suffered, yet I suffered not; and that I suffered not, yet I did suffer; and that I was pierced, yet I was not lashed; that I was hanged, yet I was not hanged; that blood flowed from me, yet it did not flow...' Lalleman observes, 'This is unmistakably a form of substitution which implies a direct refutation of the verse from John...[218] The pattern of the literary relationship is clearly polemical.'[219]

---

[215] Note 89. 11, 'when I reclined at table he would take me to his breast' (ἀνακείμενον ἐμὲ ἐπὶ τὰ ἴδια στήθη ἐδέχεται); and 90. 4, 'Then I, since he loved me (ἐγὼ δὲ οὖν, ἐπειδὴ ἐφίλει με), went quietly up to him'. Lalleman has even pointed to a portion of the *Acts* which probably alludes to John's writing of the Gospel. In 88. 3–5 we read, Ἐγὼ μὲν ὑμῖν οὔτε προσομιλεῖν οὔτε γράψαι χωρῶ ἅ τε εἶδον ἅ τε ἤκουσα (cf. 88. 6). Note the use of the word χωρεῖν, which is an apparent reflection on Jn. 21. 25.

[216] G. P. Luttikhuizen, 'The Thought Pattern of Gnostic Mythologizers and their Use of Biblical Traditions', in J. D. Turner and A. McGuire (eds.), *The Nag Hammadi Library after Fifty Years: Proceedings of the 1995 Society of Biblical Literature Commemoration*, Nag Hammadi and Manichaean Studies, 44 (Leiden, 1997), 89–101 at 92–3. Luttikhuizen writes of three gnostic texts in which the NT accounts of Jesus' suffering on the cross are overturned, the *Letter of Peter to Philip*, the *Apocalypse of Peter* from Nag Hammadi Codex VII, and the *Acts of John*.

[217] Lalleman, *Acts of John*, 122. R. Pervo, 'Johannine Trajectories in the Acts of John', *Apocrypha*, 3 (1992), 47–68, sought to show that the *AJ* as a whole was a parodying commentary on the Fourth Gospel.

[218] Cf. the statement preserved in *Theod.* 62. 2 which, in reference to John 19: 37, says 'but they pierced the appearance'.

[219] Lalleman, *Acts of John*, 116. Writing later of *AJ* 101, he says the words 'blood flowed from me, yet it did not flow' demonstrate that the author 'knew or supposed that the flowing of the blood and the water in the Gospel of John were literally meant. The AJ deletes the element blood from the pair water and blood found in the Gospel, thus suggesting that "Christ came in water only". This is exactly the otherwise unattested thought of the Johannine adversaries! These adversaries, whose beliefs are expressed in the AJ, held that Christ had only apparently or not at all been human' (250). I think, however, that the point is not that 'water' flowed instead of blood, but simply that blood did not flow from the 'true' Lord, the one that speaks to the 'Lord' in ch. 92.

Both the gnostic and the anti-Johannine tendencies are, as all agree, most prominent in what Lalleman calls section C. He continues, 'On the whole, section C of the AJ is both familiar with the Gospel of John and opposed to it. It is a critical revision of the gospel.'[220] Lalleman believes that

Section B as a whole is an effort to replace other gospels, an act that has authority because it is allegedly carried out by one of the previous evangelists, John. Instead of a straightforward contradiction of these gospels, the author opts to reveal new knowledge that had not yet been expressed in writing before. But again we encounter a characteristic of the chapter's intertextual references: readers who do not know any other gospel will hardly notice the polemical attitude towards the Fourth Gospel; for them the AJ can well serve as *the* gospel.[221]

That it was intended to serve as 'a gospel' in the same sense in which the four Gospels were serving in the orthodox churches at this time is, however, highly questionable. It is not likely that the same attitude was required by the author of his readers towards any text, including his own. But Lalleman does appear to be correct in saying that even section B but especially section C adopt a polemical and supersessionary stance over and against the Fourth Gospel (while in no way denying its attribution to the apostle John). This is in fact quite similar to the *Apocryphon of James*, which, as we have seen, presupposes the existence and use in the Church of apostolic recollections of Jesus' words and ministry.

Lalleman's recent analysis is important for its bringing to light the antagonistic elements in the *AJ* with respect to the Fourth Gospel. To this extent he certifies for the *AJ* the tendencies which have been noted above with regard to other heterodox documents. Unfortunately, he follows a reconstruction of the literary and community history of the work which has little empirical basis. Following in the train of Koester, Kaestli, Pervo, and others, he argues that the *AJ* is part of a Johannine 'trajectory', where the word trajectory 'is used for a theological tradition which has socio-historical as well as literary features'.[222] Lalleman concludes that the differences between the Fourth Gospel and the *AJ* 'point to the existence of great theological differences among members of one "family", i.e. among recipients of the Fourth Gospel. Section C is a critical revision of that Gospel.'[223] If this

---

[220] Lalleman, *Acts of John*, 116.

[221] Ibid. 115.

[222] Ibid. 111, which see for bibliography. His assumptions are based to a degree on his view that the *AJ* reflects almost exactly the views of the opponents mentioned in the Johannine Epistles. See his arguments on pp. 246–52 which I shall consider elsewhere.

[223] Lalleman, *Acts of John*, 111. Cf. Pervo, 'Johannine Trajectories', who speaks of the authors of the *AJ* as members of 'johannine "schools" or circles' (58; 68); as representing 'one wing of the johannine tradition (61). He regards the material in chs. 87–105 as 'intra-johannine development, as the result of fresh interpretation of and meditation upon the message contained in the Gospel. All of its tendencies have their roots within the multi-faceted aspects of johannine thought' (67). Nevertheless, Pervo everywhere observes the sometimes radical nature of this 'intra-johannine development'. He speaks of the author of chs. 94–102, the most 'gnostic' section, as an 'Anti-Ecclesiastical Redactor' (63). But why then is he not also an 'Anti-Johannine Redactor'?

'family' could be defined as loosely as 'readers of the Fourth Gospel', this may be true. But the assumption that the *AJ*'s author and his community were somehow in a direct 'socio-historical' line descending from the author and original recipients of the Fourth Gospel is a serious begging of the question.[224] Lalleman rightly rejects the speculative conclusion of Kaestli that section C of the *AJ* goes back to a time before the Fourth Gospel had been made 'orthodox'.[225] He rather prefers to think of the *AJ* as developing in a community which has grown a bit apart from its original Johannine context.

The AJ can be situated on the road from the Fourth Gospel to a form of Gnosticism, as it gives voice to groups such as those combated in the Johannine Epistles and by Ignatius in his Letters to the Smyrnaeans and the Trallians. The second, Gnostic part of the AJ gives us a view of the fate of this ultra-Johannine group at a later moment in its history: it has become so radical that it contradicts the very contents of the Gospel which had been at the root of its existence. The AJ may have originated at the same time as the Johannine and Ignatian Epistles, or later, in case the AJ's spiritualising type of Christology survived.[226]

But who is to say that this road started from the Fourth Gospel, or at what point it passed through the Fourth Gospel? The Fourth Gospel could have been a relatively late stop.[227] One can certainly count up points of commonality between the two documents, such as the lack of overt concern for Church order; a soft-pedalling of sacramental theology, a view of the miracles of Jesus as 'signs' pointing beyond themselves, the use of contrasting pairs. In this, and perhaps more, the *AJ* may indeed have been influenced by John.[228] But this is little more than would be expected in a situation in which the Fourth Gospel is already a familiar part of the ecclesiastical situation, and a necessary read for any who would compete with the orthodox interpretation of Christianity. If it points to anyone's prior claim on the Fourth Gospel that group would be the one opposed by the *AJ*. As Lalleman rightly observes, 'The polemics imply that the AJ also

[224] See also J. D. Kaestli, 'Remarques sur le rapport du quatriéme evangile avec la gnose', in Kaestli *et al.* (eds.), *La Communanté johannique et son histoire* (Paris, 1990), 355, who says that group that produced the *AJ* '*fait partie de la postérité directe du mouvement johannique*' (emphasis his).

[225] Lalleman, *Acts of John*, 118.

[226] Ibid. 255.

[227] 'The ultra-Johannine group which presents itself in section C is forced to combat the very Gospel that was formative of their thought' (122). But in what sense was it ever formative for their thought? 'As members of a Johannine community, acquainted with the Fourth Gospel, the adversaries laid extreme stress on its high Christology' (251). But, does it lay stress on the Fourth Gospel's high Christology, or on its own?

[228] Apart from the author's chosen subject matter (probably simply taken over by B and C from A), is his attachment to the Fourth Gospel really that much greater than his attachment to the Synoptics? Lalleman, *Acts of John*, 45, produces a chart which counts 27 references to John in section C, but also counts 14 references to Matthew, 10 to Mark, and 11 to Luke. He says, 'its familiarity with the Fourth Gospel does not hamper its knowledge of other Gospels' (246).

testifies to the fact that the Fourth Gospel was accepted and used in the non-Gnostic part of the church.'[229]

This fact further calls into question the argument that the *AJ* is part of an authentic 'Johannine trajectory', particularly if one is assuming a socio-historical dimension. Lalleman concludes, 'From the viewpoint of the later canon and of Orthodoxy, the type of intertextual relationship between John's Gospel and the AJ is that of distortion. Our author's specific outlook opposes "orthodox" readings of the Gospel and has rightly been called ultra-Johannine.[230] Conversely, the author of the AJ would probably argue that his spiritualisation is the legitimate continuation of the trajectory.'[231] The obvious question here is, in what sense can something that admittedly distorts and opposes John be called ultra-Johannine?[232] The author's method goes beyond, let us say, taking one Johannine theme to an extreme, to the neglect of another. He actually takes up certain teachings of the Johannine Gospel, such as the piercing of Jesus and his bleeding on the cross, and openly contests them. It is thus far from clear that the author, given his polemical and supersessionist attitude towards the Fourth Gospel, thinks his 'spiritualization' is the legitimate 'continuation' of the Johannine trajectory. More likely he thinks it is the legitimate *alternative* to the Johannine trajectory. After all, he is not simply contesting, for instance, 1 John or Irenaeus about the interpretation of the Fourth Gospel; he is contesting the Fourth Gospel. Instead of speaking of the *Acts of John* (particularly chs. 94–102; 109) as an initiation into Johannine gnosticism, it would be more accurate to call it an initiation into *anti-Johannine* gnosticism.

The date of the *AJ* is still uncertain. But as it stands it belongs a group of 'gnostic' or 'gnosticizing' texts which may be as early as the second century, perhaps as early as the first half of the second century, which have at least this much in common, that they display an essentially antagonistic attitude towards the Fourth Gospel.

---

[229] Ibid. 122. This is probably seen as well in the author's acceptance of the tradition that the Fourth Gospel was written by John the apostle, who resided in Ephesus. Both of these elements of the tradition are dismissed as legendary by the majority of scholars today. If the community behind the *AJ* had real socio-historical links to the original 'Johannine community', which was not led by John and was not situated in Ephesus, why did they accept, or perhaps invent, this tradition? They might conceivably invent such a tradition if they wanted to legitimate themselves through this Gospel. But such a motivation is called into question by the fact that they had to take such deep exceptions to this 'legitimating device'. This suggests that these elements of the tradition were already in place when this author took them over.

[230] By P. Vielhauer, *Geschichte der urchristlichen Literatur* (Berlin, 1975), 472.

[231] Lalleman, *Acts of John*, 122. Again, 'This author even has to contradict the text of the Gospel in order to convey his spiritualising interpretation of it' (255).

[232] Pervo, 'Johannine Trajectories', 65, suggests 'This theologian has done to *John* something similar to what Marcion did to Paul, and, as in the case of Marcion, complaints about tampering with the johannine tradition ought not overlook similar tampering from another viewpoint. The author could quite probably claim that the object was to save the particularity of the johannine witness.' If so, while Marcion 'saved Paul' by means of 'editing', this author practised salvation by parody and contradiction. It still appears that supersession is the better model.

Gospel of Truth

Another Nag Hammadi tractate which was surely influenced by the Fourth Gospel is the *Gospel of Truth*, a work which Bentley Layton calls 'One of the most brilliantly crafted works of ancient Christian literature'.[233] The tractate has no title in Codices I or XII of the Nag Hammadi texts where it occurs. Its first line, 'The gospel of truth is joy', however, makes it at least likely that it went by the title *Gospel of Truth*, and this happens to be the title of a Valentinian book mentioned by Irenaeus in *AH* 3. 11. 9. Thus it may be from as early as the mid-140s, or as late as about 180.

There seems to be now no consensus on how this Nag Hammadi work is related to Valentinianism. Many modern scholars have indeed concluded, based in part on parallels with fragments of Valentinus' works conserved in other places, that the *GTr.* bears the fingerprints of the founder of that movement himself. But it must be admitted that neither the text itself nor the words of Irenaeus give any indication of this. Others have commented on the *GTr*'s failure to record the Valentinian pleromatic myth, or clearly to articulate Valentinian principles. Does it then reflect an early, underdeveloped form of Valentinianism? Or is it instead a later form which has toned down its overtly Valentinian features in response to orthodox criticism? Is it in fact Valentinian in any sense? Each position has had defenders. Harold Attridge has offered what appears to me to be a very plausible explanation of the character of the *GTr.* in the light of these factors. He believes it is a text which 'deliberately conceals whatever might be the particular theology of its author, although there are abundant hints that this theology is a developed form of Valentinian speculation'.[234] And why the concealment? 'The presupposed theology is concealed so that the author may make an appeal to ordinary Christians, inviting them to share the basic insights of Valentinianism. Thus the text should be considered more exoteric than esoteric.'[235] As such, he argues, it was 'a text designed to be read and understood by people who do *not* share the fundamental theological presuppositions of its author'.[236] It undertakes its task, Attridge maintains, by taking aspects of the faith familiar to the ordinary Christian reader and reinterpreting them 'with unfamiliar metaphors'[237] which present an attractive face for Valentinianism. In this the *GTr.* is not very different from the other works considered in this section, though it may approach its task a bit more self-consciously and perhaps executes it a bit more skilfully.

---

[233] Layton, *The Gnostic Scriptures*, 250.

[234] H. W. Attridge, 'The Gospel of Truth as an Exoteric Text', in C. W. Hedrick and R. Hodgson, jun., *Nag Hammadi, Gnosticism, and Early Christianity* (Peabody, Mass., 1986), 239–55, at 239–40.

[235] Ibid. 239–40.   [236] Ibid. 242.   [237] Ibid. 245.

What may we now say about the *GTr.*'s use of the Fourth Gospel and the rest of the Johannine literature? Koester is certainly in a small minority when he concludes that 'dependence upon the Gospel of John is not clear'.[238] His judgement is due not to any inability to find parallels with Johannine materials, however, but to his theory of the development of the Johannine tradition, according to which the Gospel of John is perceived as a very late production which relied on oral and written traditions which happen to show up independently in a fairly surprising variety of places (as we have already seen and will continue to see), the *GTr.* being but one. In a very helpful study of the author's use of biblical texts, on the other hand, Jacqueline Williams finds frequent references to the Gospel of John in this work, eleven of which she lists as probable, five as possible (one dubious).[239] The portions of the Fourth Gospel used range from the first to the twentieth chapters, though she emphasizes that 'it is sometimes difficult to be certain which texts are used', for some motifs occur several times in John.[240] This author knew not only the Fourth Gospel but also 1 John and the Revelation of John.[241] Williams's study seems to show that the entire Johannine corpus was important in the setting in which this author wrote, as was the Pauline, as was the Gospel according to Matthew, and the epistle to the Hebrews.[242] This apparently wide familiarity with what we now call New Testament texts[243] is an important aspect of the document. That the author could use Matthew and the book of Revelation at least seems to undermine the idea that whatever it cites or alludes to should be presumed to have gnostic affinities.

One might agree with Maurice Wiles that some aspects of the interpretation of John evident in the *GTr.* 'incorporate amongst other features a real grasp of some of the central themes of the Gospel'.[244] Perhaps one of these

[238] Koester, *ACG*, 245–6 n. 6.

[239] Jacquelin A. Williams, *Biblical Interpretation in the Gnostic Gospel of Truth from Nag Hammadi*, SBL Dissertation Series, 79 (Atlanta, Ga., 1988). Probable: *GTr.* 18. 18–21/John 14: 6; 21. 10–14, 20–23/John 12: 32; *GTr.* 22. 13–15/John 3: 8. Possible: *GTr.* 21. 32–4/John 10: 3 (64–6). Possible: *GTr.* 22. 2–4/John 3: 31 (67–9). See further C. K. Barrett, 'The Theological Vocabulary of the Fourth Gospel and the Gospel of Truth', in *Essays in John* (London, 1982), 50–64.

[240] Williams, *Biblical Interpretation*, 185.

[241] See Williams's caveats, *Biblical Interpretation*, 185–6.

[242] She finds only two dubious references for Luke and none for Mark. Others, such as Attridge, 'Exoteric', 242 n. 16, do see allusions to Mark and Luke.

[243] See the early and seminal study of W. C. van Unnik, 'The "Gospel of Truth" and the New Testament', in F. L. Cross (ed.), *The Jung Codex* (London, 1955), 79–129. Layton, *The Gnostic Scriptures*, 251, says 'It has been demonstrated that in GTr Valentinus [*sic*] paraphrases, and so interprets, some thirty to sixty scriptural passages, almost all from New Testament books (Gn, Jn, 1 Jn, Rv, Mt, Rm, 1 Co, 2 Co, Ep, Col, and Heb)'. Layton thinks that 'Of these, it has been shown that the Johannine literature (including Rv) has had the most profound theological influence upon Valentinus's thought; the Pauline literature, less so; and Mt hardly at all. To a large degree the paraphrased passages have been verbally reshaped by abridgement or substitution, to make them agree with Valentinus's own theological perspective'.

[244] M. F. Wiles, *The Spiritual Gospel: The Interpretation of the Fourth Gospel in the Early Church* (Cambridge, 1960), 97, which see for some examples.

might be the important theological affirmation of the unity of the Father and the Son (John 10: 30, etc.). But as Williams reports, the *GTr.* also tends to blur the distinction between the Son and the Father. And this tendency is seen in his interpretative use of verses from Matthew, Philippians, Hebrews and Revelation, as well as from John.[245] Whether or not the Fourth Gospel, compared to other NT works, had a more or a less profound effect on him, the way this author uses John is not appreciably different from the way he uses other early Christian texts. Williams says that the interpretation reflected in his biblical allusions 'is not based on the original context',[246] but that he regularly employs various but intelligible methods to revise those original contexts in accord with pre-existing ideals.[247]

A few specific Johannine allusions call for attention. 'When the Word appeared, the one that is within the heart of those who utter it—it is not a sound alone but it became a body—a great disturbance took place' (*GTr.* 26. 4–9). Williams thinks the verse to which this text alludes, John 1: 14, 'And the Word become flesh and dwelt among us', was 'shocking' to our author, who intentionally substituted the word 'body' for 'flesh'.[248] This interpretative substitute may not at first sight seem to carry a greatly different meaning. It does not appear to be as drastic a change as we have seen in *TP* 47. 13–19, 'The third time I revealed myself to them [in] their tents as Word and I revealed myself in the likeness of their shape. And I wore everyone's garment and I hid myself within them, and [they] did not know the one who empowers me.' But it would accord well with Attridge's analysis of the aims of the author to present a more appealing side to the orthodox reader, presenting subtle shifts of meaning on the surface which may conceal greater ones beneath. What may lie beneath is what Irenaeus reports in *AH*. 1. 9. 3,

For, according to them, the Word did not originally become flesh. For they maintain that the Saviour assumed an animal body (ἐνδύσασθαι σῶμα ψυχικόν), formed in accordance with a special dispensation by an unspeakable providence, so

---

[245] Williams, *Biblical Interpretation*, 194.
[246] Ibid. 189.
[247] Ibid. 190–9. William Nelson, 'The Interpretation of the Gospel of John in the Gnostic "Gospel of Truth": A Study in the Development of Early Christian Theology' (diss. Princeton University, 1963), 130–1 (cited from Röhl, *Rezeption*, 104–5) describes the author's heavy use of Johannine terminology while showing a 'drastic departure from the thought of the Gospel'. Nelson goes on to demonstrate the contrasting views of (*a*) man before God, (*b*) the redemptive work of Christ, (*c*) the appropriation of eternal life, in the Fourth Gospel and the *GTr*. Nelson writes, 'Thus, it is quite clear that the author of the Gnostic treatise is using the *terminology* of the Fourth Gospel to suit his own particular theological purpose. For this reason he consciously emphasizes only those aspects of the Johannine teaching which can be made to fit into his own Gnostic system' (130–1). While Röhl does not disagree with this overall assessment, he criticizes Nelson for a one-sided commitment to the Fourth Gospel as the postulated conceptual background for the relevant portions of the *GTr*. In the end, Röhl himself finds much less influence from the Fourth Gospel and he strongly contests the notion that the *GTr.* is some kind of natural development of the Fourth Gospel (108–30).
[248] Williams, *Biblical Interpretation*, 203.

as to become visible and palpable. But flesh is that which was of old formed for Adam by God out of the dust, and it is this that John has declared the Word of God became.

That is, the seemingly subtle shift from 'flesh' to 'body' may indeed mask a great deal of Valentinian theology—perhaps an example of how, to Irenaeus' mind, 'their language resembles ours, while their sentiments are very different' (Irenaeus, *AH* 1, *praef.* 2). At a later point the author reproaches the 'material' or 'hylic' ones for not recognizing the Son's true likeness: 'For the material ones were strangers and did not see his likeness and had not known him. For he came by means of fleshly form, while nothing blocked his course because incorruptibility is irresistible' (31. 1–8). His 'fleshly form' is what was seen by the hylics, who did not recognize him. This seems to confirm the author's docetism[249] and that there is a substantial difference intended in the change from 'flesh' to 'body' in *GTr.* 26. 4–9.

Another interesting example of the author's use of Johannine material is found in *GTr.* 21. 14, 20–3, 'all must go to him (the Father). Then, as <each> person gains knowledge, he receives his own, and he draws them to himself.... and all must go to him and each person receive his own',[250] cf. John 12: 32, 'and I, when I am lifted up from the earth, will draw all men to myself'. Williams writes,

Because the context of GTr does not refer to the death of Jesus as did John, the emphasis of the passage has been changed considerably. This is also true because the passage refers to the Father rather than to Jesus...Moreover, no resolution is offered of the ambiguous word 'all,' but the meaning is apparently that all who have knowledge (which comes from Jesus, 20: 34–21: 8) return to their origin within the Father.[251]

This removes the cross as the setting for Jesus' drawing of all men to himself and in fact removes Jesus from any instrumentality in this act, placing it in the hands of the individual and in the individual's acquisition of knowledge, even implying 'that this drawing is not dependent upon the Father's initiative'.[252] The distortion of John's doctrine here is a bit more pronounced than what is usual in *GTr.* In its tendency towards auto-soterism, denying the necessity of the redeeming work of Jesus, and doing so through interpretative distortion of Johannine texts, it is much like

[249] Braun, *Jean le théologien*, 119; Raymond Kuntzmann and Michèle Morgen, 'Un exemple de réception de la tradition johannique: 1 Jn 1, 1–5 et Évangile de Vérité NHI, p. 30, 16–31, 35', in A. Marchadour (ed.), *Origine et Postérité de l'Évangile de Jean: XIIIe Congrès de l'ACFEB Toulouse (1989)* (Paris, 1990), 265–76. The notes in *Nag Hammadi Codex I (The Jung Codex): Notes*, Nag Hammadi Studies, 23 (Leiden, 1985), 'NHC I,3: The Gospel of Truth', 39–135, at 88–9, by H. W. Attridge and G. W. MacRae, downplay this interpretation, but it would fit Attridge's overall explanation of the *GTr.* as an exoteric Valentinian text to a tee.
[250] Williams's translation.   [251] Williams, *Biblical Interpretation*, 61–2.   [252] Ibid. 193.

the *Apocryphon of James* 2. 28–33; 3. 30–4; 11. 12–13, 29–34, as observed above.

GTr. 18. 18–21 says '…Jesus, the Christ, enlightened those who were in darkness through oblivion. He enlightened them; he showed (them) a way; and the way is the truth which he taught them.' This seems to rely on John 14: 6, 'And Jesus said to him, "I am the way, and the truth, and the life; no one comes to the Father, but by me"'. Here the alterations again seem minor on the surface: it is after all still Jesus the Christ who enlightens and shows the way, that is, the truth which he taught them. Yet in John it is Jesus himself who is the way, the truth, and the life. He is the only way to the Father. Here again the *GTr.* is reminiscent of *ApocJas.* 11. 12–13 (see above). This is one of several Johannine allusions in *GTr.* which actually have the effect of diminishing John's emphasis on Jesus in one way or another, sometimes by transferring attention to the Father (*GTr.* 24. 9–14,[253] cf. John 1: 18; *GTr.* 27. 8–9, cf. John 1: 18), sometimes to the believer (*GTr.* 21. 14, 20–3, cf. John 12: 31; *GTr.* 22. 2–4, cf. John 3: 31). In this sense, at least, one may say that the *GTr.*'s Christology is 'lower' than that of the Fourth Gospel, and lower than that of Irenaeus.

That this author knows John's Gospel, then, is certain; this Gospel is apparently well known in his context and familiar to many of his intended readers. But we have seen enough to show us that this author's use of the Fourth Gospel is anything but uniformly positive. We recognize elements of the critical appropriation of John which have been observed in *Trimorphic Protennoia, Second Apocalypse of James, Apocryphon of James*, and *Acts of John*. The opposition may be somewhat less direct in *GTr.*, the changes more subtle, but the ultimate aim does not seem to be very much different. This is directly contrary to the conventional wisdom about the *GTr.* and gnosticism in general and its relationship to the Fourth Gospel. That conventional wisdom also often lays down that that relationship was different as regards 1 John, which is presumed to have been less inviting to gnostic groups because, unlike the Fourth Gospel, it was written to combat incipient gnostic tendencies.[254] This also is not supported by *GTr.*, as we now shall observe.

GTr. 30. 26–32, 'For, when they had seen him and had heard him, he granted them to taste him and to smell him and to touch the beloved Son', seems to play on the words of 1 John 1: 1–2, 'That which was from the beginning, which we have heard, which we have seen with our eyes, which we have looked upon and touched with our hands, concerning the word of life—the life was manifest, and we saw it, and testify to it, and proclaim to you the eternal life which was with the Father and was made manifest to

[253] With regard to this, Williams, *Biblical Interpretation*, 76, says, 'The import of the two passages is quite different. GTr does not state that the Son makes the Father (or God) known, as John does, but that the Father manifests the Son'.

[254] e.g. Kuntzmann and Morgen, 'Un exemple de réception', 267.

us...'. At first glance, *GTr.* here does not so much contradict 1 John as transcend it regarding the supposed level of intimacy between the spiritual believer and the Son.[255] But Williams thinks that 'if Valentinus has used this passage, he has separated seeing and hearing the beloved Son from tasting, smelling, and touching him. He may wish to separate Jesus' earthly life from his resurrected life... In this case, sight and hearing would refer to Jesus' earthly life and taste, smell, and touch would refer to Jesus' post-resurrection state.'[256] These experiences would refer to the post-resurrection state and would be figurative expressions. That is, the 'touching' of the Saviour would thus be transferred from the pre-resurrected state of Jesus' incarnation in 1 John to a spiritual touching, tasting, and smelling of Jesus after his resurrection. Later in the same context the author refers to the 'fleshly form' of the Son, which, as Kuntzmann and Morgen point out, also contrasts with the emphasis in 1 John 1: 1–5 on the reality of the incarnation.[257]

Williams sees a probable allusion to 1 John 1: 5 in *GTr.* 35. 5–6, 'While their hope, for which they are waiting, is in waiting—they whose image is light with no shadow in it—then, at that time, the pleroma is proceeding to come'. Here, as in 1 John 1: 5, light is connected to divinity, though in *GTr.*, it is the divinity of the believer. Williams observes that here, ' "Light," however, is no longer an ethical image [as in 1 John]... which is contrasted with darkness. Rather, it is a metaphysical image which is contrasted, not with its logical or diametrical opposite ("darkness") but with "shadow," imagery which suggests a deficiency of (or in) light'.[258] Thus the author does not hesitate to invoke language which was probably familiar from 1 John, while applying it to a system of thought quite alien to that of 1 John.

In each allusion something is changed from the Johannine context, following the normal tendency of this author, producing a reorientation sometimes more, sometimes less extreme. What does stand out is that the author's treatment of the Fourth Gospel is essentially no different from his treatment of 1 John, and indeed, hardly different from his treatment of other texts which now make up the New Testament. There is certainly some kind of 'authority' invoked in each allusion, some form of legitimization is implicitly being sought. But the author's treatment increases the overall impression that he regards these existing 'authoritative' texts as quite pliable and, most importantly, subordinate to his own interests and agenda. This suggests (as indeed Attridge acknowledges) that the authority

[255] 'Le vocabulaire kérugmatique de 1 Jn 1, 1–5 entre ainsi au service de la mystique gnostique d'identification avec le Sauveur', ibid. 274. Kuntzmann and Morgen prefer to think of *GTr.* as using Johannine elements without knowledge of 1 John.
[256] Williams, *Biblical Interpretation*, 109.
[257] Kuntzmann and Morgen, 'Un exemple de réception', 275.
[258] Williams, *Biblical Interpretation*, 146.

invoked when alluding to these texts is one which was recognized by others and may not have pertained in the same way to the author himself.

From this survey of its use of the Johannine material, it is also evident that *GTr.* is unlikely to have engendered any orthodox Johannophobia. If the *GTr.* was, as Attridge thinks, 'a text designed to be read and understood by people who do *not* share the fundamental theological presuppositions of its author',[259] it certainly found such a reader in Irenaeus of Lyons. But Irenaeus, of course, was swayed by his reading of *GTr.* towards a negative view not of the Fourth Gospel, but of the *GTr.* One might suppose that Irenaeus was not representative of the likely orthodox readership in his day, being better trained to spot heresy in *GTr.*'s subtleties and perhaps more inclined to condemn it out of hand. But, as with other texts in this section, it appears that the only way an orthodox reader might slide into a negative attitude towards the Fourth Gospel is as she begins to adopt the views of the author of the *GTr.* If this was her reaction, she is just as likely to have taken up the same attitude towards Matthew, the Pauline Corpus, 1 John, and Revelation, for all of these are used by the *GTr.*, and in much the same way.

Layton writes, '*The Gospel of Truth* . . . is . . . one of the earliest witnesses to the contents of the proto-orthodox canon—in it Valentinus takes pains to express himself by paraphrasing and alluding to the New Testament passages, sometimes almost gratuitously'.[260] Layton also concludes that 'Valentinian canonical scripture in the proper sense was simply the proto-orthodox canon'.[261] It may be a misnomer to call anything 'Valentinian canonical scripture', but Layton's main point is no doubt correct: Valentinian use of written religious authorities, at least as instanced in the *GTr.*, witnesses to the prior existence of a body of new and authoritative Christian literature which was functioning as scripture in the churches from which Valentinians sought converts. The use of the Fourth Gospel in the *GTr.*, and perhaps in Valentinian exegesis in general, then, seems to say much more about the place it already held in the non-Valentinian churches than about any natural congruency between it and the Valentinian system.[262]

Gospel of Thomas

There is probably no better known or discussed Nag Hammadi work than that which is known as the *Gospel of Thomas*. Occasionally this pseudepigraphon and its (alleged) knowledge of the Fourth Gospel are mentioned

---

[259] Attridge, 'Exoteric', 242.

[260] Layton, *The Gnostic Scriptures*, p. xxii.

[261] Ibid., p. xxiii; cf. W. van Unnik, 'Gospel of Truth', 124.

[262] This in fact closely resembles the conclusion of F.-M. Braun over five decades ago. Braun, *Jean le théologien*, 130, 'Quoi qu'il en soit, si, comme son affectation d'orthodoxie le montre, l'auteur de l'*Évangile de Vérité* s'adressait aux fidèles, la conclusion qui'il me paraît impossible d'élude est que, en faisant implicitement appel au quatrième Évangile, il le tenait pour un des écrits les plus chers au coeur de chrétiens.'

as evidence for the gnostic preference for that Gospel.[263] Conceivably, then, the *Gospel of Thomas* could have contributed to an orthodox avoidance of John.

The conclusion of an early study by Raymond Brown was that the *Gospel of Thomas* had indeed been influenced by John.[264] But today, over fifty years after the discovery of its full text and after countless studies, the origin of the *GT*, its date, character, and relation not only to John but to each of the canonical Gospels (and their alleged sources), are matters still warmly disputed by scholars. There is widespread agreement that the *GT* originated in Syria; the use of the name 'Judas Thomas', the special name for the apostle in that region, alone points to this conclusion. But Helmut Koester, following Giles Quispel, thinks 'the tradition of sayings of Jesus preserved in the *Gospel of Thomas* pre-dates the canonical Gospels and rules out the possibility of a dependence upon any of these Gospels'.[265] Koester is joined by a number of scholars in this view. Ismo Dunderberg would place both *Thomas* and John later than the Synoptics and nearly contemporaneous with each other, based on the way they use 'authenticating figures such as the Beloved Disciple in the Gospel of John and Thomas in the *Gospel of Thomas*'.[266] But Dunderberg also allows for the possibility that 'Although the form of this gospel may be more archaic than that of the Johannine discourses, it does not necessarily follow that all the materials included in the extant *Gospel of Thomas* are archaic'.[267] That is, some of the Johannine parallels might belong to a secondary development in *Thomas*'s literary history. Stevan Davies has argued that *Thomas* comes from the Johannine community itself, at a stage earlier than the Fourth Gospel.[268] Many other scholars, on the other hand, have held that *Thomas*, as a literary work, is entirely a 'secondary' Gospel which used all four canonical Gospels, including John.[269]

---

[263] Barrett, *John* (1978), 66.

[264] Though the influence, Brown thought, was through an intermediary source. See R. E. Brown, 'The Gospel of Thomas and St John's Gospel', *NTS* 9 (1962–3), 155–77. J. Sell, 'Johannine Traditions in Logion 61 of the Gospel of Thomas', *Perspectives in Religious Studies*, 7 (1980), 23–37, argues that there was no intermediary source and that the dependence was on the finished form of John. Both these authors are criticized by I. Dunderberg, '*Thomas*' I-sayings and the Gospel of John', in Risto Uro (ed.), Thomas *at the Crossroads: Essays on the* Gospel of Thomas (Edinburgh, 1998), 33–64, at 35–7.

[265] Koester, *ACG* 85–6. Beginning with his 'The Gospel of Thomas and the New Testament', *VC* 11 (1957), 189–207, the list of Quispel's works on *Thomas* would take up a great deal of space (J. K. Elliott, *The Apocryphal New Testament: A Collection of Apocryphal Christian Literature in an English Translation* (Oxford, 1993), 124, says there are at least thirty-five).

[266] I. Dunderberg, '*Thomas* and the Beloved Disciple', in Risto Uro (ed.), Thomas *at the Crossroads: Essays on the* Gospel of Thomas (Edinburgh, 1998), 65–88, at 88.

[267] Dunderberg, 'I-sayings', 38–9.

[268] Stevan L. Davies, *The Gospel of Thomas and Christian Wisdom* (New York, 1983); idem, 'The Christology and Protology of the Gospel of Thomas', *JBL* 111 (1992), 663–82. Dunderberg, 'I-sayings', 39–40, criticizes Davies's theory as resting 'on a plethora of conjectures'.

[269] Koester, *ACG* 85, lists many, including the following. R. M. Grant, 'Notes on the Gospel of Thomas', *VC* 13 (1959), 170–80; E. Haenchen, *Die Botschaft des Thomas-Evangeliums* (Berlin, 1961);

H. J. W. Drijvers, writing about the well-known common variants found in *Thomas* and the *Diatessaron*, notes that

Instead of assuming an independent Jewish–Christian gospel that was used as well by the author of the *Gospel of Thomas* as by Tatian, it seems a much simpler and more satisfying explanation to assume that the author of the *Gospel of Thomas* used Tatian's *Diatessaron*; at least this would apply to the author of an original Syriac version that might have been different from the preserved Coptic version. It is of course quite possible that Tatian and, consequently, the author of the *Gospel of Thomas* knew and made use of extracanonical traditions that can be old and authentic, but that does not mean that the *Gospel of Thomas* as such is a representative of an independent gospel tradition.[270]

Drijvers thus favours a date of *c*.200 for the *GT*. An important, recent monograph by Nicholas Perrin makes an extremely strong case that the original Syriac *Thomas* is dependent on the Syriac *Diatessaron* and can be dated no earlier than the late second century.[271] If the author of *Thomas* used the *Diatessaron*, even if he did so some years before 200, it is plain that he could not have had much of a deleterious effect on the orthodox use of John. The same goes, needless to say, if Wolfgang Schrage's much criticized theory is correct that *Thomas*'s Synoptic parallels are based on the Coptic translation of these Gospels.[272]

The conclusions of scholars about this work, its community, date, composition, character, and relation to the Fourth Gospel or the Johannine community are indeed baffling in their diversity. Dunderberg has helpfully clarified some of the conflicting methods of scholars in this area[273] and

---

J. E. Ménard, *L'Évangile selon Thomas*, NHS 5 (Leiden, 1975); idem, 'La Tradition synoptique et l'Évangile selon Thomas', in F. Paschke (ed.), *Überlieferungsgeschichtliche Untersuchungen*, TU 125 (Berlin, 1981), 411–26; B. Dehandschutter, 'L'Évangile selon Thomas: Témoin d'une tradition prélucanienne?', in F. Neirynck (ed.), *L'Évangile de Luc*, BETL 32 (Gembloux, 1973), 287–97; idem, 'L'Évangile de Thomas comme collection des paroles de Jésus', in J. Delobel (ed.), *LOGIA: Les paroles de Jésus—The Sayings of Jesus: Memorial Joseph Coppens*, BETL 59 (Leuven, 1982), 507–15; J.-M. Sevrin, 'L'Évangile selon Thomas: Paroles de Jésus et révélation gnostique', *RTL* 8 (1977), 265–92; K. R. Snodgrass, 'The Gospel of Thomas: A Secondary Gospel', *The Second Century*, 7 (1989–90), 19–38.

[270] H. J. W. Drijvers, 'Facts and Problems in Early Syriac-Speaking Christianity', *The Second Century*, 2 (1982), 157–75, at 173.

[271] Nicholas Perrin, *Thomas and Tatian: The Relationship between the* Gospel of Thomas *and the* Diatessaron (Atlanta, Ga., 2002). He examines the text of *Thomas* in terms of 'catchwords' which would have occurred in a Syriac original. This also results in a convenient explanation for the arrangement of the sayings (i.e. that it was influenced by catchwords or puns) (ibid. 169, 171–72). He finds also that the supposition of a Syriac (even as opposed to a western Aramaic) text often explains the origin of an odd Coptic word or phrase in the present Coptic text. Perrin finds evidence of a relation between *Thomas* and Tatian in the affinities between their encratistic tendencies, in their shared textual peculiarities (noted by many authors, such as Quispel and Drijvers), and in their shared sequences of sayings (ibid. 188–9).

[272] W. Schrage, *Das Verhältnis des Thomas-Evangeliums zur synoptischen Tradition und zu den koptischen Evangelienübersetzungen*, BZNW 29 (Berlin, 1964). Later scholars have accounted for the similarities by attributing them to Coptic redaction and emphasizing the possibility that certain sayings in *Thomas* were added later, while pointing to the Greek fragments from Oxyrhynchus as proof of an earlier, Greek, recension. See the bibliography in Koester, *ACG* 85–6.

[273] Dunderberg, 'I-sayings', 41–3.

cautions against generalizing with regard to this document. 'Since it is possible that each saying of the *Gospel of Thomas* has a tradition history of its own, the extant *Gospel of Thomas* might show variation in its relationship to the canonical gospels'.[274] With this understood, there is no objection to the possibility of *GT* containing material which predates the Fourth Gospel. On the other hand, both the Diatessaronic agreements and the choice of Judas Thomas as the authenticating figure[275] seem to point to a late second-century Syrian environment. Perrin's recent work on *Thomas* and the *Diatessaron* substantiates this theory very significantly. And despite Koester's astounding assertion that the attestation for *Thomas* is 'just as strong as that for the canonical Gospels',[276] it does not appear that the existence of *Thomas* before *c*.200 can be proved from the evidence.[277] Thus, while the *GT* may contain some traditional sayings which had been ascribed to Jesus

[274] Ibid. 42–3.

[275] A. De Conick, '"Blessed are those Who Have Not Seen" (John 20: 29): Johannine Dramatization of an Early Christian Discourse', in John D. Turner and Anne McGuire (eds.), *The Nag Hammadi Library after Fifty Years: Proceedings of the 1995 Society of Biblical Literature Commemoration*, Nag Hammadi and Manichaean Studies, 44 (Leiden, 1997), 381–98, at 397, writes 'The assumption of this methodology is that the Johannine author is not painting an arbitrary picture of the apostle Thomas, the hero of Syrian Christianity, when he portrays him as a false hero whose mystical soteriology is corrected by Jesus'. But when exactly did Thomas become the hero of Syrian Christianity? Was it before the Fourth Gospel was written? And the name 'Didymos Judas Thomas' preserved in *GT*, as Drijvers points out, is a combination of the Lord's brother Judas with the apostle Thomas, whose name, as marked by the additional name Didymos, means twin. This extension of the name is a secondary development and seems to coincide with the kind of theology present in the *GT*, the *Acts of Thomas*, and in Tatian, whereby the believer becomes identified, as Thomas the twin was, with Jesus (Drijvers, 'Early Syriac-Speaking Christianity', 171–2; idem, 'East of Antioch. Forces and Structures in the Development of Early Syriac Theology', in Hans J. W. Drijvers, *East of Antioch. Studies in Early Syriac Christianity* (London, 1984), 1–27 at 15–16; idem, 'The Acts of Thomas', *NTA*², 324–5.

[276] Koester, *ACG*. 77, referring to his article, 'Apocryphal and Canonical Gospels', *HTR* 73 (1980), 107–12. In the latter article, which gives Koester's view of the attestations of early Christian Gospel or Gospel-like materials in literary and documentary sources, one can find only four mentions of the *GT*: POxy. 1, dated 'End of 2c century and beginning of 3d century A.D'; POxy 654 and 655, both dated 'Third century'; and Tatian, whose use of *GT* in his *Diatess.*, Koester admits, is 'possible but not certain' (110 n. 18). From the same period Koester lists for John 𝔓⁵², dated 'First half of the 2d century A.D'; 𝔓⁶⁶, dated 'End of 2d century and beginning of 3d century A.D.'; 𝔓⁵, ⁹, ²², ²⁸, ³⁹, ⁴⁵, ⁷⁵, ⁸⁰, dated 'Third century'; and then 'Valentinians', Clement of Alexandria, Tatian, and Irenaeus. Even from his own quite defective and tendentious list Koester's assertion cannot be supported. Nor does Koester mention here that the first 'attestations' to a 'Gospel according to Thomas' by name, by Hippolytus, Origen, and Eusebius, are all negative. It must be said, finally, that there exists a variant tradition under the name of Koester, 'Introduction', to 'Tractate 2. The Gospel according to Thomas', in B. Layton (ed.), *Nag Hammadi Codex II, 2–7 together with XIII, 2*, Brit. Lib. Or.4926(1), and P. Oxy. 1, 645, 655*, Nag Hammadi Studies, 20 (Leiden, 1989), 38–49, concerning the *GT* which reads, 'All attestations before the third century are uncertain'.

[277] This was the conclusion of Tjitze Baarda in a paper read at the 1997 Society of Biblical Literature Meeting. Baarda specifically took Koester, Crossan, and others to task for their 'preconceived' notion of *Thomas*' independence of the canonical Gospels. The earliest firm attestation is P. Oxy. 1, dated by Grenfell and Hunt to *c*.200, the other two Oxyrhynchus fragments coming from around the middle of the 3rd cent. Baarda pointed out that Hippolytus' quotation (*Ref.* 5. 7. 20–22a) from a εὐαγγελίον κατὰ Θωμᾶν as used by the Naassenes does not really correspond to anything in the present text of our *GT*, even to saying 4, to which it is customarily compared. Both these speak of 'a child of seven', but Hippolytus has 'seven years', while *GT* has 'seven days', and

from a much earlier time, even possibly from before the publication of the
Fourth Gospel, and while some of the theological tendencies of the *GT* may
be as early as or earlier than this time, the literary work identifiable as the
Gospel of Thomas is not likely to have been compiled and published until after
the middle of the second century, very probably after the *Diatessaron*. It thus
seems to me that the parallels often cited which do demonstrate that the
author knew the Fourth Gospel, at least at a secondary level, come, as likely
as not, only from the *Diatessaron*.

But what if one should want to credit a theory of pre-canonical, Jesus-
tradition history like Koester's,[278] and regard the bulk of *Thomas* as containing Jesus material which is at least as early as and independent of the
canonical Gospels? If it also existed as a literary document before John one
will have to concede that its earliest readers, at least, could not have
thought it reflected unfavourably on John, for the latter would not yet have
been in existence. And what about readers in the second century? Regardless of which Gospel was written first, and even without coming to any firm
conclusion with regard to literary dependence, or even about the common
use of unwritten tradition, would a second-century member of the mainstream Christian Church who knew both Gospels have recognized in
John a dangerous kindred spirit with *GT*? This would in any case be
extremely doubtful. First of all, Koester identifies only six or eight out of
114 sayings in *GT* which are specially close to John.[279] This compares with
'seventy nine units in the *Gospel of Thomas* which have parallels in the Synoptic Gospels', forty-six of which are parallels with 'Q' and twenty-seven
with Mark.[280] This general picture is confirmed by J. K. Elliott[281] and

the contexts are quite different, though it is possible that the text was manipulated by the Naassenes, by Hippolytus, or by both. There is also no way to tell if τὸ κατὰ Θωμᾶν Εὐαγγέλιον
mentioned by Origen in *HomLuc.* 1. 5. 13 is a reference to our *GT*, particularly in the light of the
Hippolytan reference.

[278] One should better speak of numerous particular theories regarding the original settings and
forms of numerous individual sayings of Jesus, coupled with a complex theory of the Gospel
according to John as 'the end product of a long development of the tradition about Jesus in the
Johannine church' (*ACG* 123). Dunderberg observes that Koester's overall view of the development
of sayings traditions 'seems to determine Koester's method and results as well…Scholars who
presuppose a different view have been led to opposite conclusions by using the same method' ('I-
sayings', 38, citing as an example J. H. Charlesworth and C. E. Evans, 'Jesus in the Agrapha and
Apocryphal Gospels', in B. Chilton and C. E. Evans (eds.), *Studying the Historical Jesus: Evaluations of
the State of Current Research*, NTTS 19 (Leiden, 1994), 479–533).

[279] H. Koester, 'The Gospel of Thomas (II, *2*)' in *NHLE*³, 124–6 at 124–5, sayings 13, 19, 24,
38, 49, 92. From *ACG* one could add also sayings 1 and 108 (sayings 18b, 19c, and 111 concur only
in the use of the metaphor of 'seeing' or 'tasting' death; sayings 24b, 50a, and 77a, along with John
11: 9–10; 12: 35–6; 8: 12, are said to be independent developments of 'the synoptic sayings about
the light' (117)) (for another interpretation of the light imagery in logion 77 and elsewhere, see
Pagels, 'Exegesis of Genesis 1', 483–8). Other parallels are more questionable.

[280] Koester, *ACG*. 87, 109; see his treatment, ibid. 86–113.

[281] Elliott, *ANT*, 133–34, identifies six parallels with John, though his lists differs somewhat: 1,
31, 38, 59, 71, 108. Of these, only 1 ('And he said, "He who finds the interpretation of these
sayings will not taste death"'; cf. John 7: 37), 59 ('Jesus said, "Look upon the Living One as long as

others.[282] Whatever in *Thomas* might have reminded the orthodox reader of John, or whatever in John might have reminded her of *Thomas*, must have paled in importance compared to the questions which would have arisen from the use made by *Thomas* of materials she knew from the Synoptic Gospels.

And if somehow these questions blew past our reader and her attention was somehow stuck instead on the much fewer Johannine parallels, what is her reaction likely to have been? She no doubt would have perceived that the two authors were interpreting the sayings of Jesus in radically different ways, and that John's way was more clearly in line with the 'orthodoxy' she knew, while *Thomas*'s was heading in another direction.[283] For as Koester says, 'If Thomas is dependent upon John, one must conclude that he deliberately generalized John's statements about the heavenly origin of Jesus and transformed them into the announcement that everyone who gains true knowledge can claim divine origin and return to it.'[284] And if on the other hand John is reacting to tradition independently developed by *Thomas*, then 'John already presupposed this generalized belief and rejected it deliberately. The believers do not arrive at salvation through knowledge about themselves, but through knowledge of Jesus.'[285] We may see some of the important divergences between John and *Thomas* in the following places.

---

you live, lest you die and seek to see him and you cannot see" '; cf. John 7: 34; 8: 21; 13: 33), and 108 ('Jesus said, "He who drinks from my mouth will be as I am, and I shall be that person, and the hidden things will be revealed to him" '; cf. John 7: 37), do not also have Synoptic parallels.

[282] B. Blatz, 'The Coptic Gospel of Thomas', *NTA*[2], 110–16, at 113, 'Roughly half of the sayings have parallels in the Synoptic Gospels'. Until recently, the literature on *Thomas* reflected this imbalance. Charlesworth, *Beloved Disciple*, 371, only a few years ago was able to lament that 'Not one monograph . . . is devoted to a study of the GosJn and this apocryphal gospel'. He observes that 'The most striking literary parallels are with Mt, then Lk, less with Mark, and very few with the GosJn. The links with the GosJn are more in terms of the proto-gnostic social environment and are ideological' (371 n. 61).

[283] And this is indeed consistent with what evidence we have for the early knowledge of the *GT*. We have no evidence of its existence from the 2nd cent., but some document, or documents, known as 'Gospel according to Thomas' begins to be noticed in the 3rd cent. If it is the book mentioned by Hippolytus (and as we have seen, this is doubtful) writing in Rome some time between 222 and 235, it is associated with the Naassenes (*Ref.* 5. 7. 20). Origen in Alexandria, only slightly later, would list the Thomasine Gospel as spurious (*Hom. Luc.* 1. 5. 13); Eusebius not only as spurious, but to be 'shunned as altogether wicked and impious' (*HE* 3. 25. 6). These writers do not link it in any way with John and certainly show no signs of suffering from Johannophobia themselves. Their negative judgements of the *GT* and positive appreciations of the Fourth Gospel are our only empirical evidence of the possible effects of *GT* on orthodox regard for John.

[284] Koester, *ACG*, 119.

[285] Ibid. 'The saying about "seeking me and not finding me" (John 13: 3) is then used to reject both the notion of Jesus as the paradigm for the Gnostic believer and the concept of the discovery of one's own divine origin' (ibid. 120). The reason for the concentration of parallels in the farewell discourses and in John 7: 38–8: 56 is that 'John is here discussing a tradition of sayings which proclaim a salvation that is based upon the knowledge of one's origin', sayings which he then altered.

GOSPEL ACCORDING TO THOMAS	GOSPEL ACCORDING TO JOHN
#49 Blessed are the solitary and elect, for you will find the kingdom. For you are from it and to it you will return.	16.28 I came from the Father and have come into the world; again, I am leaving the world and going to the Father.
#50a If they say to you, 'Where did you come from?', say to them, 'We came from the light, the place where the light came into being on its own accord...'	19.8 When Pilate heard these words, he was the more afraid; 9 he entered the praetorium again and said to Jesus, 'Where are you from?'
	1.9 The true light that enlightens every man was coming into the world.
	8.12 Again Jesus spoke to them, saying, 'I am the light of the world...'
#19a Blessed is he who came into being before he came into being.	8.58 Jesus said to them, 'Truly, truly, I say to you, Before Abraham was, I am'.

Other important ways in which John and *Thomas* part company have been noted by several recent scholars.[286] 'Davies focuses primarily on similarities between Thomas and John', writes Elaine Pagels in a recent article, 'but what I find even more striking are the differences'.[287] I would agree. Indeed, could we perhaps be witnessing a certain maturing in Thomasine studies, even in Nag Hammadi studies in general, which is getting over the initial excitement created by the discovery of Johannine parallels and is settling in on asking how *Thomas* compares with John in the *use* of common traditions of various kinds, regardless of the legitimate but still unresolved matter of direct or indirect literary dependence? It seems to me, too, that when it is asked how John and *Thomas* use their common material, it is the distance between them which stands out most markedly. If indeed *Thomas* used John—and this holds to some extent even if it knew John only secondarily through the *Diatessaron*—it did so in a critical and adversarial way, transforming what John said about Jesus and generalizing it to the 'Thomasine' Christian, and shifting the focus from belief in Jesus to knowledge of

[286] See G. J. Riley, *Resurrection Reconsidered: Thomas and John in Controversy* (Minneapolis, 1995); idem, 'The Gospel of Thomas in Recent Scholarship', *Currents in Research*, 2 (1994), 227–52, at 240; A. D. De Conick, *Seek to See Him: Ascent and Vision Mysticism in the Gospel of Thomas*, VCSuppl. 33 (Leiden, 1996); eadem, 'Blessed are those who have not seen', 381–98; Pagels, 'Exegesis of Genesis 1', 477–96. Pagels sees John as 'actively engaged in polemic against specific patterns of Genesis exegesis he intended his prologue to refute' (479), patterns of exegesis which are present in *Thomas* (though, Pagels shows, not only in *Thomas*).
[287] Pagels, 'Exegesis of Genesis 1', 479. 'According to log. 24, Jesus himself rebukes those who seek access to God elsewhere, even—or perhaps especially—those who seek it by trying to follow Jesus himself. The disciples who ask Jesus to "show us the place where you are, since it is necessary for us to seek it" (log. 24), do not even merit a direct reply for so misguided a request... He directs the disciple not toward himself (as does the Jesus of John 14: 6) but toward the light hidden within' (487).

one's heavenly origin as the vehicle of salvation. If on the other hand John used *Thomas*, or if it simply interacted with traditions and ideas which eventually found expression in *Thomas*, then its interaction is predominantly critical.

The *Gospel of Thomas*, then, can hardly be regarded as evidence of a popularity of John's Gospel among 'gnostic' or heterodox Christians. If indeed it interacted with John, it stands alongside *Trimorphic Protennoia*, the *Second Apocalypse of James*, the Apocryphon *of James*, the *Acts of John*, and the *Gospel of Truth*, as examples of heterodox works which show a predominantly antagonistic—a Johannophobic—rather than congenial 'reception'.

This investigation obliges me to agree with some recent studies which have tended to lower the estimation of the number of second-century, gnostic-related figures or texts which used the Fourth Gospel. The information about Basilides fails to establish use of it on his part, though Basilideans later used it, along with many other scriptural texts. The Carpocratians do not appear to have used it. The *Apocryphon of John* may have got some names for its syzygies from the Prologue of John, a practice later perfected by the Valentinians, but apart from this it shows no interest in the Gospel. At the beginning of this chapter I noted two widespread assumptions in the literature: that gnostic use of the Fourth Gospel must have discouraged orthodox use, and that any gnostic use of the Fourth Gospel was evidence of a gnostic reception of and affinity with this Gospel. We can now see how misleading these assumptions can be and what bedevilment they have actually caused. First of all, many of the authors and texts often cited as instancing the gnostic monopoly on John come from a time after the orthodox reception of John is plainly visible. This goes most especially for the celebrated commentary of Heracleon, which is probably not from before about 180 (more likely a decade or more later) and seems to represent a Valentinian approach which has modified its exegesis based upon criticism of people such as Irenaeus. Some also of the Nag Hammadi texts often called upon are too late to have inhibited orthodox appreciation of John, and it is unlikely that they would have done so in any case. Others show only a superficial or questionable use of John. It is a characteristic of nearly all the texts examined, that they use the other canonical Gospels, Paul, and various portions of the Old and New Testaments in much the same way. Far from revealing an orthodox fear of the Fourth Gospel, these works instead seem to require that this Gospel was already being used and accorded a high status in the Great Church; that it simply formed part of the backdrop in the ecclesiastical settings in which these works were composed. This is particularly the case with those works just discussed, which exhibit a critical or adversarial approach to the Fourth Gospel, indicating that it must have been used and highly valued in the Great Church, with whom these authors were engaging in competition for adherents.

Thus the second assumption, that all gnostic use of John signifies gnostic affinity, or participation in a gnostic-Johannine trajectory, is shown to be equally false. The six works canvassed above demonstrate the surprising tendency of the earliest gnostic sources to use the Fourth Gospel in essentially an antagonistic or critical way. This seems in fact to be the case with every document I have found which plausibly predates *c.*170 and is not directly connected with Valentinian exegetical treatises[288] (it even may pertain to some of Valentinus' own work). This predominantly polemical use of the Fourth Gospel (and 1 John) which has now been documented in at least the *Trimorphic Protennoia*, the *Second Apocalypse of James*, the *Apocryphon of James*, the *Acts of John*, the *Gospel of Truth*, and probably in *Gospel of Thomas* has been observed by several individual scholars, but its import has not been realized for the matter of the reception of the Johannine Gospel in the second century. In fact the paradigm has exercised so strong an influence that even when the adversarial appropriation of John has been clearly recognized, some interpreters have sought to submerge the conflict and transpose it into an inter-Johannine, family squabble over the interpretation of the Fourth Gospel. But these works do not merely discredit the interpretations of John contained in 1 John or Irenaeus, they take issue with the teaching of John itself. And nowhere is this more pronounced than in the area of John's Christology. Thus the 'affinity' between these gnostic authors and John often appears quite affected, largely for the sake of making inroads among opponents, and sometimes in the bald attempt to supersede the authority of writings acknowledged to be apostolic.

The window on the orthodox provided by these works also has another consequence with which we shall have to reckon, namely, that the earlier these particular gnostic works are dated, the earlier we must recognize a fairly firmly established usage of John's Gospel in the Church at large.

Further, in works such as *Apocalypse of James* and the *Gospel of Truth* where there is an apparent knowledge of 1 John, we find no noticeable difference in the attitude displayed towards the Fourth Gospel and towards 1 John, as the currently predominant model would seem to require. These authors are no more accepting of the theological affirmations of the Fourth Gospel than of those of 1 John, which, among other things, privileges the witness of those who saw, heard, and touched the Word of Life (1 John 1: 1–4).

This evidence thus demonstrates that the assumption of a deep affinity for the Fourth Gospel among such individuals and groups as are represented by these texts has been by and large grossly mistaken. The strategies employed by these several authors are much more in line with the heterodox strategies which Irenaeus mentions at the beginning of *AH* 3, strategies

---

[288] Namely, the Ptolemaian work cited in *AH* 1. 8. 5 which interpreted the Johannine Prologue in terms of the Valentinian pleroma; the work of Theodotus (along with probably the source used by Irenaeus) cited by Clement; and Heracleon's commentary.

to supersede or 'improve upon' the apostles, interpreting apostolic scriptures with reference to secret 'tradition' passed down orally.

For it is unlawful to assert that they preached before they possessed 'perfect knowledge,' as some do even venture to say, boasting themselves as improvers of the apostles. (3. 1. 1)

When, however, they are confuted from the Scriptures, they turn round and accuse these same Scriptures, as if they were not correct, nor of authority, and [assert] that they are ambiguous, and that the truth cannot be extracted from them by those who are ignorant of tradition. For [they allege] that the truth was not delivered by means of written documents, but *vivâ voce* ... (3. 2. 1)

For [they maintain] that the apostles intermingled the things of the law with the words of the Saviour; and that not the apostles alone, but even the Lord Himself, spoke as at one time from the Demiurge, at another from the intermediate place, and yet again from the Pleroma, but that they themselves, indubitably, unsulliedly, and purely, have knowledge of the hidden mystery ... It comes to this, therefore, that these men do now consent neither to Scripture nor to tradition. (3. 2. 2)

With attitudes and approaches such as these in play, one did not have to follow Marcion in rejecting any of the Church's literature, but could by all means 'receive' each and every writing, if armed with a code for interpreting it and, as the ace up one's sleeve, with the notion that the apostolic writings themselves by no means held the last word.

   This phenomenon of an alleged supersession of the apostolic scriptures and traditions provides a better context also for viewing the group that Irenaeus mentioned in *AH* 3. 11. 9 which is said to have rejected John's Gospel. The ostensible reason Irenaeus gives in his brief account has to do with this group's aversion to the Johannine doctrine of the Paraclete Spirit. But in the literature reviewed here this makes sense as part of a polemic against 'official' or apostolic Christianity, which put great stock in the writings claimed to have been handed down by the apostles and their disciples. For the Paraclete in John's Gospel serves to authenticate the witness of the original disciples of Jesus by leading them in all the truth, declaring to them the things that are to come and the things that belong to Jesus, and giving them remembrance of all that Jesus said to them (John 14: 26; 16: 12–14). The earlier linking of the *Apocryphon of James* with the group mentioned by Irenaeus may now be affirmed, not in the sense of an absolute identification, but by way of acknowledging the close alignment of certain basic principles which belong to the setting of the heterodox–orthodox struggle in the second century leading up to Irenaeus.

   The only Johannophobia we have been able to document, then, is found not among orthodox writers, probably not even with Gaius, but in the anonymous group mentioned by Irenaeus and in the authors of the *Trimorphic Protennoia*, the *Second Apocalypose of James*, the *Apocryphon of James*, the *Acts of John* 94–102, 109, the *Gospel of Truth*, and the *Gospel of Thomas*. And contrary to the prevailing hypothesis, there is, as Hengel has already observed, no reason to think that gnostic use of John's Gospel (outside Valentinian circles) was ever widespread at all.[289] Even the Valentinians, while Irenaeus attests that they 'make copious use of that according to John, to illustrate their conjunctions' (*AH* 3. 11. 7), apart from their use of the Prologue, where they believed their 'conjunctions' were illustrated, show no more attachment to John than they do for Matthew or Paul (it is to be recalled that Heracleon also wrote exegetical comments, perhaps a commentary, on Luke). Indeed the Valentinians and works like the *Gospel of Truth* tended to use all the Church's Gospels and apparently whatever else might have constituted the Church's 'canon' at that time (much as Tertullian has reported).

John, the Gnostics' Gospel?

This, again, does not line up well with the nearly universal conviction that John was the 'special Gospel' of gnostics and heretics precisely because it was eminently conducive to their systems of thought, or because it shared with them some of their deepest religious commitments.[290] What are the gnostics supposed to have liked about John, or what constituted the ground of the unity which John is supposed to have shared with them? A judicious attempt at answering this question was made years ago by Maurice Wiles. We can still use his work as the basis for a fruitful discussion. Wiles summarized 'four important respects in which the Gnostic could find grounds within the Gospel itself appearing to support an interpretation along lines characteristic of his own peculiar way of thought'.[291] These are, (*a*) the philosophical character of the Prologue, (*b*) dualism, (*c*) docetism, and (*d*) determinism. Each of these aspects of John's Gospel, Wiles believes, provided some basis for Valentinian use, though in each case he concedes that their exegesis falls far short of discovering John's own views in these areas.

JOHN'S DETERMINISM

Of the four aspects named, it is probably John's 'determinism' which might most easily be seen as favouring the gnostics over the orthodox. At any rate, John's determinism presented certain problems for later orthodox theologians who developed the doctrine of free will in the face of Valentinian and then Manichaean determinism.[292] And yet, several factors prevent us from

---

[289] Certainly there is no reason to think it was 'the great battle-ground...between Gnosticism and Catholicism', Sanders, *Fourth Gospel*, 66.

[290] Against this see now J.-M. Sevrin, 'Le Quatrième Évangile et le gnosticisme: Questions de méthode', in J.-D. Kaestli *et al.* (eds.), *La Communauté johannique et son Histoire* (Paris, 1990), 251–68.

[291] Wiles, *Spiritual Gospel*, 98.

[292] Ibid. 107–11; note particularly Origen, *Comm. John* 20. 24, 28, 29, 33.

saying that gnosticism was some kind of natural outgrowth of 'Johannine determinism' or that that they necessarily came from a common stock.

First, if the Johannine tradition has a vital notion of predestination, so does the Pauline (Rom. 9: 6–29; Eph. 1: 3–6; 2: 10; 1 Thess. 1: 4; 2 Thess. 2: 13–14; Tit. 1: 1). In fact, any problems faced by later orthodox defenders of free will were problems handed to them not only by John and Paul but by other parts of the NT and orthodox tradition (Acts 2: 23; 4: 27–8; 13: 48; 1 Pet. 1: 2; 2 Pet. 1: 10).[293] The *Gospel of Truth* made use of the Johannine Apocalypse's image of the book of life to support its notion of predestination (19. 34–21. 3).

Nor do we even need to look outside first-century Palestinian Judaism for anticipations of John's understanding of predestination. Determinism among the Essenes and at Qumran is well documented. In fact, one proponent of the OJP is on record saying that he believes that the Jewish sect of the Essenes 'bequeathed to western civilization the concept of predestination', and that John was influenced by Qumran in this area.[294]

Secondly, a predestinarian outlook is not absent from the Christian antidocetic or anti-gnostic writers themselves. We see for instance that a very early anti-docetist, Polycarp, speaks of 'those who have been truly chosen (ἀληθῶς ... ἐκλελεγμένων) by God and our Lord' (*Ad Phil.* 1. 1), and, in very Johannine terms, of others who are 'of the devil' (*Ad Phil.* 7. 1; cf. John 8: 44). Polycarp reiterates the divine monergism of Ephesians 2: 5, 8, 9, 'by grace ye are saved, not by works but by the will of God through Jesus Christ' (*Ad Phil.* 1. 3), and clearly teaches that faith itself is a gift of God (3. 2; 4. 2). Another early anti-docetist, Ignatius of Antioch, addresses the church at Ephesus as 'predestined from eternity for abiding and unchangeable glory, united and chosen through true suffering by the will of the Father and Jesus Christ our God' (*Eph.*, praescr.).[295] Irenaeus too, though he may also write in ways which seem to contradict it, confesses that 'when the number is completed, which He had predetermined in His own counsel,

---

[293] Wiles, *Spiritual Gospel*, 107, points to the Basilideans' use of John 2: 4 ('My hour is not yet come'): 'Basilides therefore claims that Jesus himself is witness to the truth of the conception of fixed times for particular events' (Hippolytus, *Ref.* 7. 27. 5, see my treatment above). But in the context we find that the Basilideans (not Basilides himself) also claimed Rom. 8: 19–21 and Matt. 2: 1–2 as support for this conception. Nor is it clear that Hippolytus disagrees with the bare notion of 'fixed times for particular events' or with the NT verses used to support this it. He only objects to the Basilidean understanding of the 'times and events'.

[294] J. H. Charlesworth, 'The Dead Sea Scrolls and the Gospel according to John', in R. A. Culpepper and C. C. Black (eds.), *Exploring the Gospel of John* (Louisville, Ky., 1996), 65–97, at 83–4. Charlesworth says that he, M. Broshi (*The Dead Sea Scrolls* (Tokyo, 1979), 12–20), and Flusser (*The Spiritual History of the Dead Sea Sect* (Tel Aviv, 1989), 46) 'independently came to the startling conclusion that the Essenes bequeathed to western civilization the concept of predestination' (96 n. 78). See also, among others, J. C. VanderKam, *The Dead Sea Scrolls Today* (Grand Rapids, Mich., 1994), 109.

[295] ... τῇ προωρισμένῃ πρὸ αἰώνων εἶναι διὰ παντὸς εἰς δόξαν παράμονον ἄρεπτον, ἡνωμένῃ καὶ ἐκλελεγμένῃ ἐν πάθει ἀληθινῷ ἐν θελήματι τοῦ πατρὸς καὶ Ἰησοῦ Χριστοῦ τοῦ θεοῦ ἡμῶν ... cf. Eph. 1: 3–14.

all those who have been enrolled for life shall rise again' (*AH* 2. 33. 5). It is not as if a notion of divine election and predestination was the peculiar possession of gnostics and Valentinians. One has to inquire into the types of determinism which were being advocated.

This brings us to a third point. It will have to be admitted that differences between Johannine predestinarianism and Valentinian, in particular, are more than trifling. To be specific, John provides no support (apart from one's pre-acceptance of the Valentinian system and assuming John teaches it allegorically) for the distinctively Valentinian idea of what has been called 'substantive determinism', the gnostic threefold division of humanity into hylic, psychic, and spiritual natures, on the basis of which each will attain to a predetermined end.[296] Irenaeus charges that this sort of 'similar to similar' determinism, which places even God under its necessity,[297] agrees with the Stoics and others who are ignorant of God (*AH* 2. 14. 4). Not only does Irenaeus fail to see any link at all with John, he sees testimony to the volitional aspects of faith precisely in John 3: 16, among other places (*AH* 4. 37. 5). The orthodox were at least on firm ground when insisting that the Fourth Gospel teaches the necessity of a transition for the elect, who must be 'drawn' to the Son by the Father and must 'become' children of God by a new birth and by faith, not by a simple revelation of their essentially divine natures.[298]

Finally, it has yet to be shown that the Fourth Gospel was ever invoked by the gnostics to support their brand of 'determinism' in a particular or customary way, any more than were several other NT writings. The *Gospel of Truth* in fact finds support for its determinism not in the Fourth Gospel but in the book of life motif from the book of Revelation.

JOHN'S PHILOSOPHICAL PROLOGUE

With regard to John's Prologue, we may affirm without reservation a historically verifiable attraction to proponents of the 'basic gnostic myth'. But this appears to have begun as quite superficial, and to have remained so even with the Valentinians, who, however, at least gave attention to the text as a literary entity. And we have already seen how the persuasive power of pleromatic exegesis of John 1 appears dependent upon a prior acceptance

---

[296] See Pagels, *Gnostic Exegesis*, 48–9, 83–113; Sevrin, 'Le Quatrième Évangile et le gnosticisme', 265; W. A. Löhr, 'Gnostic Determinism Reconsidered', *VC* 46 (1992), 381–90.

[297] 'Then again, as to the opinion that everything of necessity passes away to those things out of which they maintain it was also formed, and that God is the slave of this necessity, so that He cannot impart immortality to what is mortal, or bestow incorruption on what is corruptible, but every one passes into a substance similar in nature to itself, both those who are named Stoics from the portico, and indeed all that are ignorant of God, poets and historians alike, make the same affirmation' (*AH* 2. 14. 4).

[298] Origen, *Comm. John* 19. 20 (John. 15: 19); 28. 21 (John 11: 51); 20. 33 (John 1: 12); see Wiles, *Spiritual Gospel*, 108–9.

of the gnostic myth and the distinctively Valentinian hermeneutic. According to the judgement of a wide variety of scholars, the great bulk of gnostic use of John was characterized by what would today generally be called an excessively 'eisegetical' approach.

Wiles himself observed that 'the difference between Irenaeus and the Gnostics...is between an approach which is under the strict control of historical fact and one which allows free rein to the speculative imagination'.[299] Pagels, who has made an admirable effort to enter sympathetically into the Valentinian frame of mind, emphasizes that Valentinian exegesis of John assumes a prior acceptance of Valentinian principles. As she says, 'The characteristically Valentinian exegetical practices, such as their selective use of passages to fit into the framework of the exegesis, the hypostatization of nouns, and their interpretation of events as symbols of spiritual processes can be shown, likewise, to derive from their theological outlook'.[300] The gnostic theologians 'recognized that to explicate the symbolic truths hidden in scripture would require nothing less than to develop a new hermeneutical method—and this is precisely what they have done'.[301] 'Knowledge of the myth and its theological basis forms the essential prerequisite' not only for understanding Valentinian theology, but 'for understanding Valentinian exegesis'.[302] In order to see how this worked, I cite Pagels at length.

We have already seen how Ptolemy interprets Jn 1 1–4, and how he (having decided on the pleromic framework for his exegesis) has selected for comment only those passages which he considers refer to the pleroma. His theological instruction into the 'mystery' of the tetrads enables Ptolemy to recognize that Jn 1. 4 signifies the second tetrad. It indicates, he explains, the emergence of Zoe in her syzygos Anthropos (AH 1. 8. 5). This indicates in pleromic terms how the elect emerge in the unfolding of the divine life. Another such passage that bears reference to the pleroma is Jn 1. 14. In this passage...Ptolemy finds hidden reference to the primary pleromic tetrad, consisting of the Father, Charis, Monogenes, and Aletheia. He perceives (according to his initiation into Valentinian theology) that in Jn 1. 14 John 'clearly sets forth the first tetrad, when he speaks of the Father and Charis, and Monogenes and Aletheia.' Secondly, Ptolemy notes that the verse may also refer to the savior as he appears in the kenoma, as 'fruit of the pleroma,' bearing within himself the powers of all the aions, so that he 'can be called by the names of all of them' (including Monogenes, Aletheia, and Charis). Thirdly, the verse may be taken to refer to the 'logos made flesh, whose glory we beheld,' that is, to the savior manifested in material form in the cosmos. As no corporeality exists either in the

---

[299] Wiles, *Spiritual Gospel*, 99. Cf. G. Salmon, 'Heracleon', *DCB* iv. 899, 'Instances of this kind [i.e. Heracleon's restriction of the word cosmos in John 1: 3 to the visible creation] where the interpreter is forced to reject the most obvious meaning of the text are sufficiently numerous to shew that the gospel was not written in the interests of Valentinianism'.

[300] Pagels, *Gnostic Exegesis*, 46.

[301] Ibid. 14.

[302] Ibid. 34.

pleroma or in the kenoma, the savior comes into visible form only as he enters into the cosmos and assumes the existence of the psychic Christ and the body of Jesus ... Not only is the visible logos himself not the Monogenes, but he is separated from him by whole realms of being.[303]

Without first adopting the pleromic myth and the 'new hermeneutical method' it enables, it is, to say the least, extremely doubtful that non-Valentinian Christians would ever have recognized the myth in the Fourth Gospel's Prologue,[304] let alone in its subsequent portrayal of Jesus' life and ministry.

Even Sanders conceded that 'the forced character' of Theodotus' comments on John's Prologue, 'ingenious though they are, makes it obvious that the main lines of the Valentinian system represent something independent of the Fourth Gospel'.[305] And yet Sanders still argued, in words that seem to have influenced many other scholars, that John and the gnostics 'employ the same religious and philosophical or theosophical terminology'.[306] This is already problematic, if we are to suppose that John meant by the concepts of Logos, Monogenes, Charis, etc., just what the Valentinians meant by them. But Sanders also went beyond this to suggest that the similar terminology 'may conceal a larger identity of ideology than one is inclined to admit'.[307] But the argument from terminology to ideology is neither straightforward nor safe, for at least three reasons. First, it is instructive to note that Valentinian pleromatic exegesis of the first chapter of John bears an uncanny resemblance to Ophite exegesis of the first chapters of Genesis (see Irenaeus, *AH* 1. 30). Apart from the greater chronological distance

---

[303] Pagels, *Gnostic Exegesis*, 37.

[304] M. Donovan, *One Right Reading?* (Collegeville, Minn., 1997), 36, observes about the Valentinian exegesis recorded by Irenaeus that it 'relates passages joined only by common words or allusions and does not hesitate to interpret texts apart from their obvious meaning in their context. This methodology has much in common with the approach Irenaeus himself uses. It is in the area of theological presuppositions that he and they part company.' But Donovan is being overly generous at this point, vastly overstating the similarities and minimizing the differences in the methods of Irenaeus and the Valentinians noted by other scholars. That Irenaeus too at times interprets more in accordance with theological preconception than in accordance with consistently applied 'natural' methods, still does not (*pace* Donovan) place his exegesis on quite the same level as that of the Valentinian interpreters he criticizes. The 'theological presuppositions' themselves, in this case, have a reciprocal relationship with a set of textual authorities, which results in the conclusion that some presuppositions are more textually legitimate than others.

[305] Sanders, *Fourth Gospel*, 65.

[306] Ibid.

[307] Ibid. See further, ibid. 56–7, 'But even if they are fully hyptostatised entities, it must be remembered that this is only carrying out to an extent unwarranted by any specifically *religious* need or experience the process begun in principle by the author of the Fourth Gospel when he wrote "In the beginning was the Word ... and the word became flesh". One must remember that the Christian origin of Valentinus and even his orthodoxy (in Alexandria) are unquestionable. It was only in Rome that his orthodoxy was challenged.' Sanders appears to be dependent here upon Tertullian's narrative of Valentinus' history. But as Tertullian tells it, it was not that Valentinus was always a Valentinian and it only happened to be noticed and challenged after he had spent several years in Rome. It was that he had remained orthodox and had not published any of his distinctive teachings until that time.

which separated them from the text involved, one could just as easily say that the Ophites shared with the author of Genesis the 'religious and philosophical or theosophical terminology' of Bythus, Light, Spirit, First Man, Eve, The Mother of the Living, Serpent, Iao, Sabaoth, Adoneus, Eloeus, etc. (all terms shared by the Ophites in Irenaeus, *AH* 1. 30. 1, 11, and the Genesis author or editor). Then one could note the remarkable similarity between Ophite terminology and that of Genesis, and just as easily propose that these conceal a larger identity of ideology than one is inclined to admit. These cases of gnostic exegetical exploitation are really quite similar and should be studied before assertions are made about John's affinity with Valentinians and Sethites on the basis of religious terms common to both of them.

Second, the terminological argument also cuts in another direction. If we are going to put stock in terminology, it should not be forgotten that the Fourth Gospel shares even more of its lexicon with 1 John, and probably no one has ever accused the author of that letter of being a gnostic.[308] For the author of 1 John, the words Arche, Logos, Zoe, Aion, Pater, Huios, Iesus, Christos (all contained in the first four verses of 1 John) bear no resemblance to Valentinian aeons—and by all appearances, the author of 1 John stands in a much closer relationship, both chronologically and theologically, to the author of the Fourth Gospel than does any of the trio, Ptolemy, Theodotus, or Heracleon.

Third, we have already seen that there is every reason to believe that the earliest forms of the gnostic myth themselves shared very little if any common terminology with the Prologue. Aeons which originally bore other names were given Johannine names in the Valentinian system, and this conformity increased from the system attributed to Valentinus in *AH* 1. 11 to that attributed to Ptolemy or one of his followers in 1. 8. 5.

---

[308] In Johannine studies one has to be careful before saying without qualification that any particular hypothesis has never been tried. Something approaching a 'gnostic' reading of 1 John has actually been given by Francois Vouga, who wants to argue that 'the Johannine Epistles with their particular polemical traits, could very well be understood as the precursors of the Gnostic polemic against the proto-Catholic church, such as we can observe so remarkably in the Apocalypse of Peter or in the Testimony of Truth' ('The Johannine School: A Gnostic Tradition in Primitive Christianity?', *Biblica*, 69 (1988), 371–85, at 380). Vouga elsewhere, relying on the fact that the early orthodox allusions to 1 John 4: 2–3 are not literal citations, and supposing that 1 John 5: 5–6 refers disparagingly not to a docetic heresy but to a eucharistic one, argues that both the Gospel and the Letters of John were the legitimate inheritance of the gnostics and were reclaimed by the orthodox only through some questionable interventions (F. Vouga, 'Jean et la gnose', in A. Marchadour (ed.), *Origine et postérité de l'évangile de Jean: XIIIe congrès de l'ACFEB Toulouse (1989)* (Paris, 1990), 107–25, at 119). Vouga is at least correct, against most, that the heterodox of the 2nd cent. show about the same attitude towards the First Letter as they do towards the Gospel. But he makes far too much of the paraphrastic reference to 1 John 4: 2–3; 2 John 7 in Polycarp and the textual variation of 1 John 4: 2 found in Irenaeus and Tertullian, and on the other hand takes no account of the antagonistic use of the Johannine books by several heterodox sources. Vouga also couches his exegesis of Johannine texts in terms, such as 'Révélateur', and concepts which are prejudicial towards the fashioning of lines of connection with later gnostic works.

Thus J. N. Sanders's idea that John was 'spoiling the Egyptians' by taking their gnostic terminology and clothing the original *kerygma* with it[309] appears to be just the opposite of what the sources reveal. We know that the Valentinians, and perhaps some of the 'gnostics' before them, 'spoiled' John's Prologue. Did John himself spoil some even earlier gnostic source, scramble their pleromatic syzygies, demythologize their gnostic content, and overlay them onto a basically historical and Jewish framework? Despite decades of scholarly energy spent on the question, we are still far from being able to affirm that anything like such a gnostic myth existed when the Prologue to the Fourth Gospel was written,[310] let alone that the author knew it, and let alone that he thought it important enough to require him to adapt it so rigorously and so artificially in his Prologue. Sanders's statement about spoiling the Egyptians was made before the discovery of the Qumran documents. And these latter show at least that a penchant for abstract nouns, the use of dualizing expressions of opposites such as darkness and light, truth and falsehood, and a robust notion of predestination cannot be seen as reliable indicators of a 'gnostic' intellectual milieu.

JOHN'S DUALISM

As to dualism as well, a general affirmation can certainly be made: both John on the one hand and the gnostics and Valentinians on the other held to some form of dualism. We have seen that the author of the Naassene document discovered by Hippolytus did call upon John 3: 14 in support of his flesh/spirit dualism. But as we have observed, the Jewish sectarians at Qumran also had an unmistakably 'dualistic' outlook,[311] and, more importantly, so did Paul and, more importantly still, so did the author of 1–3 John. Revelation too presents what is often called a 'stark dualism' in apocalyptic form.[312] The dualism of the Johannine Apocalypse has even been related to that of the Fourth Gospel by students of apocalyptic.[313] In

---

[309] Sanders, *Fourth Gospel*, 65.

[310] Sevrin, 'Le Quatrième Évangile et le gnosticisme', 262, 'One may doubtless speak of a pre-Christian gnosticism in the logical sense of the term, that is to say, a gnosticism Christianized secondarily and on the surface, but in the chronological sense, such a gnosticism remains to be discovered'. In the 1st cent. Sevrin thinks, one can only speak of isolated gnostic motifs.

[311] Charlesworth, 'Dead Sea Scrolls', 68–75, 81–3, who, again, argues for dependence of John on Qumran.

[312] Much of what Lattke, 'Gnostic Jesus', 151, says about the dualism of the Fourth Gospel could be said equally of the Revelation.

[313] C. Rowland, 'The Parting of the Ways: The Evidence of Jewish and Christian Apocalyptic and Mystical Material', in J. D. G. Dunn (ed.), *Jews and Christians: The Parting of the Ways A.D. 70 to 135* (Grand Rapids/Mich., 1999 repr. of 1992 orig.), 2213–38, at 228, 'The contrast between appearance and reality with the latter laid bare by the revelation, the drawing back of the veil which hides God's mysteries, is one of the fundamental aspects of apocalyptic. That epistemology is fundamental to the Fourth Gospel also. Since the discovery of the Dead Sea Scrolls we have becomes [*sic*] used to finding the background to these ideas in such sectarian sources. The Apocalypse's concern to offer the truth of the situation, whether it be the spiritual condition of the

fact, 'dualism' may be viewed so broadly as to encompass a great many expressions of both Christianity and Judaism in this period. The question is always about the kind of dualism which is signified. The 'historical dualism in which the Old Testament was associated entirely with the demiurge and the New was regarded as in radical opposition to it' is, as Wiles says, 'a less plausible interpretation of the Gospel than the cosmological one'.[314] As Wiles also says, the principal means used by the orthodox for meeting such a dualist interpretation was 'the demonstration of positive teaching in the Gospel, which showed Jesus to be utterly at one both with the God of creation and with the God of the Old Testament. In this task it was the Prologue which provided the most important evidence.'[315] This last sentence is as profound as it is shocking. The point to be observed here is that Valentinian and gnostic dualistic exegesis of John was still controlled by their underlying presupposition of what Wiles call a 'historical' dualism between the God of creation (and OT) and the highest God of the pleroma, and by their method of selective and allegorical exegesis. From this approach neither the Gospel of John, nor those of Matthew, Mark, or Luke, nor the writings of Paul, nor just about any other piece of literature the Valentinians set their eyes upon, could be entirely protected.

JOHN'S 'DOCETISM'

Of great importance for our study is the Valentinian case for docetism from John's Gospel. Where did the Gnostics find support for their docetism in John? The answer we should expect from reading much of twentieth-century scholarship would have to be quite simple: 'on every page'. After all, some have said that John's Christology itself clothes itself 'in the form of a naive docetism',[316] presenting 'God going about on the earth';[317] others, with more restraint, simply that 'the Gospel was readily susceptible of a docetic reading';[318] and others that 'John must be seen as one stage in the

churches or the reality of the unfolding of the divine purposes, is matched by the Fourth Gospel's dualistic contrasts which serve to thrown into the sharpest possible relief the impoverished character of the world and the blindness of its inhabitants. Here as elsewhere both Revelation and the Fourth Gospel are indebted to the apocalyptic tradition'.

[314] Wiles, *Spiritual Gospel*, 101. Even MacRae, 'Gnosticism and the Church', 94–5, concedes, 'Though I think it probable that the dualistic pattern of Johannine thought is indebted to contemporary Gnostic ideas, it is clear that the Fourth Gospel has adapted a cosmic dualism to its own purposes, which are not ultimately Gnostic'; 'the dualism of John by itself is not clear evidence of Gnostic influence'.

[315] Wiles, Spiritual Gospel, 102.

[316] E. Käsemann, *The Testament of Jesus: A Study of the Gospel of John in the Light of Chapter 17* (ET: Philadelphia, 1968), 26.

[317] Ibid. 9, citing the earlier work of F. C. Bauer, *Kritische Untersuchungen Über die kanonischen Evangelien* (1847), 87, 313; G. P. Wetter, *Der Sohn Gottes* (1916), 149; E. Hirsch, *Das vierte Evangelium* (1936), 138.

[318] J. Ashton, *Understanding the Fourth Gospel* (Oxford, 1990), 194.

development of full-blown gnosticism'.[319] These evaluations do nothing,
then, to prepare us for Wiles's unexpected confession that 'the Gnostics did
not always find it easy to derive their docetism from the text of the
Gospel'![320] In fact, Wiles has to go all the way to a fourth-century, Syrian,
fictional debate between an orthodox and a Manichaean to find a 'gnostic',
exegetical claim for a docetic Christology from John's Gospel.[321]

The surprising reality is that the very aspects of the Fourth Gospel usually held up by modern scholars as approaching (or in the case of Käsemann and others, as representing) a docetic Christology do not appear to
have been seen that way by the gnostics who allegedly found John so
conducive to their system of thought. A great part of Valentinian Johannine
exegesis was centred on the Prologue, where John's abstract theological
terms were metamorphosed into names for the Valentinian syzygies. It is
apparent that Valentinians must have read the rest of the Gospel, just as
they read the rest of the Church's Bible, assuming their Valentinian Christology, but it is not easy to see where they would have found passages which
offered promise for Valentinian Christological exegesis, particularly as support for their distinctive quadripartite Christology.[322]

While the authors of the *Gospel of Truth* and the *Gospel of Thomas* may have
been attracted to the Fourth Gospel's teaching on the unity of the Son with
the Father, it is also plain that they had to distort it in the direction of
blurring the distinction between Jesus and the Father, and by portraying
not only Jesus' heavenly origin and unity with the Father, but also the
believer's. We have observed that texts such as these certainly display a
'lower' Christology than that of the Fourth Gospel in that they deprive
Jesus of his uniqueness, both as divine and as redeemer, by opening these
categories to every enlightened believer. It is also apparent that several
authors in using the Fourth Gospel had to alter or attack its teachings

---

[319] Barrett, *John* (1955), 66. And yet, on the same page he wrote, 'it remains substantially true
that the gnostics used John because out of it, by exegesis sound or unsound, they were able to win
support and enrichment for preconceived theories and mythologies'. But if it was their 'preconceived theories and mythologies' that they were supporting, this does not excite confidence that
gnostic attraction to John was due to a strong common bond in religious experience and conceptions. It sounds more like they might have used John, as they used many other previously existing
Christian texts, adventitiously, exploiting it for their own purposes without a deep appreciation for
the author's original thought. So, if 'we should not be justified in speaking of second-century
gnosticism as in any sense a creation of John', in what sense can it then be maintained that 'John
must be seen as one stage in the development of full-blown gnosticism'?

[320] Wiles, *Spiritual Gospel*, 107.

[321] Ibid. 106, namely, Hegemonius, *Acta Archelaii*, 54. And this, as it turns out, is based as much
on what John does not say as upon what he does say. That is, John does not clearly refer to the
birth of Jesus, and refers to him as being 'sent' from heaven. One could imagine docetists hoping
for a clearer Johannine exegetical basis for their docetism.

[322] It has of course been maintained by others that John is in reality quite visibly anti-docetic.
See Sevrin, 'Le Quatrième Évangile et le gnosticisme', 265; U. Schnelle, *Antidocetic Christology in the
Gospel of John: An Investigation of the Place of the Fourth Gospel in the Johannine School*, tr. L. M. Maloney
(ET: Minneapolis, 1992).

about the incarnation and the real, bodily death of Jesus. In the apparently Ptolemaean exegesis preserved in the *Excerpta ex Theodoto* we find an obvious attempt at counter-interpretation of John 19: 34–7 (*Theod.* 61, 62),[323] denying that the body of Jesus which was pierced was real: 'but they pierced the appearance' (ἐξεκέντησαν δὲ τὸ φαινόμενον).[324] We have witnessed similar evasions of the teaching of John 19: 34–7 from the author of the *Acts of John* 101. 8–9, even implying 'a direct refutation of the verse from John'.[325] From these we would certainly get the impression that John was not an ally but a formidably enemy to these writers in these important matters of Christology.

EXPECTATION AND REALITY

This brings us to a very important realization which has, I think, rather profound implications. And that is the realization of a great gulf which exists between the expectation of gnostic use of the Fourth Gospel and the reality. In the face of the bulk of twentieth-century scholarship, why is the evidence for a docetic exegesis of John so miserably slim? Why does empirical reality not come anywhere close to meeting expectation? Two major, interrelated reasons can be identified. The first is that much of modern scholarship has approached the sources with an overly simplistic notion of Christological development in the Christian Church. That notion is essentially an evolutionary[326] one which moves on a more or less straight historical line from the conception of a purely human prophet/teacher/sage/revolutionary, etc., to the conception of a purely divine being, a heavenly revealer who came to earth to announce salvation of the heavenly elect. Generally speaking, the closer to the first end of that spectrum, the more primitive, Jewish, and original the Christology. The closer to the latter end, the more Hellenized and gnosticized the Christology. John's Gospel presents a Jesus who is much further along on the spectrum than do the Synoptics; hence, it is further along the line towards full-blown gnosticism. MacRae says that the Fourth Gospel

portrays Christ as a pre-existent, in some sense divine, figure who descends from the world of the Father into the created world for the purpose of offering salvation

---

[323] Cf. Kaestli, 'L'Exégèse valentinienne', 341.

[324] The opposition is noted by Hillmer, 'Second Century', 114, who says the author of this statement wrote 'in precise opposition to the meaning as represented in the gospel'.

[325] Lalleman, *Acts of John*, 116, who also concludes that the words 'blood flowed from me, yet it did not flow' demonstrate that the author 'knew or supposed that the flowing of the blood and the water in the Gospel of John were literally meant.

[326] Jack T. Sanders, 'Nag Hammadi, *Odes of Solomon* and NT Christological Hymns', in James E. Goehring (ed.), *Gnosticism and the Early Christian World* (Sonoma, Calif., 1990), 51–66, at 64–6, has some promising reflections on alternative evolutionary models which he applies to aspects of the question of the development of gnosticism *vis à vis* Christianity. The notion of direct trajectory here too comes out as decidedly inferior.

to humanity by revealing the Father. Apart from the question of the origin of this type of thought, one must recognize the fact that it resembles nothing in the ancient world so much as the Gnostic revealer myth.[327]

Nothing indeed, that is, except the '*orthodox* revealer myth'! MacRae has omitted to mention that the Fourth Gospel's soteriology is not purely revelational, but demands faith in Jesus, and pointedly includes his 'taking away the sin of the world' (1: 29), his death 'for the people' (11: 50), and the shedding of his blood (6: 54–6; 19: 34). To dismiss these elements as secondary or redactional begs the question. The fact is that Christ's divine and heavenly pre-existence, temporary earthly sojourn, and subsequent heavenly enthronement, were part of the common Christology well before John wrote, well before the rise of any of the identifiably 'gnostic' systems, and remained so throughout the whole of the second century and ever since.[328] If John's presentation exceeds the Synoptic Gospels on this score, it does not very far exceed other NT expressions which had led up to the situation for Christians in Asia Minor at the end of the first century.

Beginning even in the first verse of what is probably his first letter, Galatians 1: 1, Paul explicitly places Jesus Christ with God the Father as representative of divine agency, to be contrasted with human agency.[329] (If 1 Thessalonians is his first letter, we have there Paul's association of Jesus with God the Father in the conferring of blessing (1: 1) and in the supernatural ability to direct Paul's way to his readers (3: 11).) That the divine and pre-existent Lord Jesus Christ was God's agent in creation is stated in terms which sound uncannily Johannine in 1 Corinthians 8. 6, 'and one Lord, Jesus Christ, through whom are all things and through whom we exist' (cf. δι'οὗ τὰ πάντα here with John 1: 3, πάντα δι᾽ αὐτοῦ ἐγένετο). The pre-existence of Christ is assumed by Paul again in 1 Corinthians 10: 4, where he refers to Christ as the Rock which followed the Israelites in the wilderness. A full descent/ascent motif is plainly and uncontroversially assumed in Philippians 2: 5–11, which most scholars believe reflects an earlier hymnic or confessional expression. Whether the 'high Christology' of Colossians 1 is judged to be from Paul himself or not, it always belonged to the corpus of his writings and was in any case written before any of the second-century heterodox writers. Here the Son's pre-existence and role in creation (1: 16) is seamlessly connected to his incarnation and suffering (1: 20). Whether or not one wants to argue for some version of a pre-Pauline gnosticism, it will

---

[327] MacRae, 'Gnosticism and the Church', 93.

[328] Rom. 9: 5; 10: 9, 13; 1 Cor. 8: 6; Gal. 1: 1; Phil. 2: 4–11; Col. 1: 15–20; Heb. 1: 1–3. See N. T. Wright, *What St Paul Really Said: Was Paul of Tarsus the Real Founder of Christianity?* (Grand Rapids, Mich., 1997), 71, 'Paul, in short, seems to have held what generations of exegetes have imagined to be an impossibility; a thoroughly incarnational theology, grounded in a thoroughly Jewish worldview'.

[329] For Paul, see now R. Bauckham, *God Crucified: Monotheism and Christology in the New Testament* (Grand Rapids, Mich., 1998).

have to be recognized that a 'developed', divine Christology, including the idea of a coming of a heavenly redeemer and his return to heaven, is assumed by Paul himself and by itself could not have been considered 'gnostic' or 'heterodox' in the first century. The Epistle to the Hebrews, heavily used by Clement of Rome, also testifies to the acceptance of a divine–human Christology among first-century, mainstream Christian congregations (1: 1–14; 3: 5–6, etc.)—and this in a letter written to a church greatly influenced by the OT and by current Jewish norms of faith and cultus. The deity of Jesus Christ is assumed in the Johannine Apocalypse (*passim*) and a descent/ascent scheme (arguably combined with the idea of a virgin birth) is presupposed in the vision of 12: 1–6. A divine–human Christology is undebatably present in Ignatius, Polycarp, Aristides, and Hermas from the early years of the second century.[330] And so this prominent teaching in John's Gospel could hardly have stood before even its very first readers as a clear sign of some early form of docetism, particularly with its pointed indications of Jesus' humanity. Did the Valentinians welcome John's Jesus, who had descended straight from the Father to offer salvation by revealing the Father? Perhaps, though they had to deal with other impediments in John's account of the interval between Jesus' descent and his later ascent. But the welcome certainly could have been no less enthusiastic among the orthodox, who were eager to point out that the Fourth Gospel spoke not simply of some heavenly aeon who descended, but of 'Jesus Christ', who 'became flesh' (John 1: 14; Irenaeus, *AH* 3. 11. 2), who was crucified and bled and died, who also rose from the dead.[331]

A second reason for the disparity between expectation and reality in gnostic use of the Fourth Gospel, particularly with respect to any attempt to support docetism, is that there has been much confusion about the character of the docetism which might have played a role in the origins of some of the Johannine writings. The full evidence for this will have to be presented in another place, but here I can simply state that what many have regarded as the most docetic aspects of the Fourth Gospel—its striking representations of Jesus' heavenly origin and divine life on earth, which for some, places a true incarnation in question[332]—actually constituted for the author his strongest salvo against docetism. For the best conclusion we can draw

---

[330] Ignatius, *IEph.* praescr.; 7.2, etc.; Polycarp, *Ad Phil.* 12. 2; Aristides, *Apol.* 1; Hermas, *Shep.* Sim. 12; etc.

[331] It has been well said by J. D. G. Dunn, 'John and the Synoptics as a Theological Question', 306, 'For all the weight that John puts upon Jesus as revealer and as teaching by dialogue, these aspects can never be separated in John from the central fact that Jesus fulfilled his heavenly mission by dying and rising again. This motif is so persistent and so pervasive that it dominates the whole: for example, the persistent drumbeat references to the hour of his approaching death; the repeated motifs of his glorification, ascension, and uplifting on the cross; the Lamb that takes away the sin of the world; the flesh, given for the life of the world, which must be eaten and the blood, drunk; and so forth.'

[332] Käsemann, *Testament*, 9.

from the Johannine Gospel and Letters about its Christological opponents is that they held a kind of Cerinthian, adoptionist distinction between an earthly Jesus and a heavenly Christ. But John allows no such dichotomy, and presents on the one hand the divine Logos who 'became flesh', and on the other the human Jesus who was also divine; that he who suffered is he who arose and was glorified by his Father. Thus the assertions of Jesus' divinity and the depictions of his divine self-consciousness throughout the Gospel point out that the one who 'descended from heaven, the Son of man' (3: 13), who 'comes from above' and is above all (3: 31), is identical with Jesus the man and is not some separable, heavenly being. Not only is the 'Christ' human, but the man Jesus is divine. The significance of John's climactic purpose statement, 'but these are written that you may believe that Jesus is the Christ, the Son of God, and that believing you may have life in his name' (20: 31) may be that its identification of Jesus as the Christ and Son of God encompasses both the original sense of Christ as the Jewish Messiah, and also the later sense of pre-existent heavenly being, which the opponents in 1 John would not concede to the man, Jesus. To put it simply, Jesus is the Christ; he is not merely the Christ-bearer.

Ironically, then, this means that expressions of Jesus' deity in the Fourth Gospel are in fact, *contra* Käsemann, the strongest indicators of a non-docetic Christology. For the Cerinthians, Jesus was a man pure and simple, visited by a divine spirit. John's magnification of Jesus' divinity is not a movement in the direction of docetism but a movement directly against it. If the author of the Fourth Gospel wrote with a conscious awareness of the early stages of the Christological problem that is evident in 1 and 2 John, then it may be seen that his high Christology is not advancing a naive docetism but instead is denying probably the only form of docetism he knew. This in fact helps explain the way John's Gospel was used as a barrier against 'gnosticism', at least against Cerinthianism and Valentinianism, two forms of the adoptionist docetic Christology, throughout the second century. The language and theological themes of this Gospel are largely perpetuated by 1 and 2 John, whose docetic opponents bear a strong resemblance to later descriptions of Cerinthus' teaching (Irenaeus, *AH* 1. 26). The *Epistula Apostolorum* attacks a Cerinthian type of heterodoxy and uses the Johannine literature rather profusely. The *Apocryphon of James* and the gnostic parts of the *Acts of John* promote a religion which has many affinities to Cerinthian thought, and each uses the Fourth Gospel and First Epistle of John in a predatory, supersessionary, and sometimes hostile way. Irenaeus preserves the tradition, almost certainly passed down through Polycarp, that John wrote his Gospel (and by implication his First Epistle) against Cerinthus (*AH* 3. 3. 1). He relates Polycarp's story of a personal antagonism between John and Cerinthus (*AH* 3. 3. 4), and notes that a Cerinthian type of group (with resemblances to the *Apoc Jas.*) rejected John's Gospel and utilized Mark's to support their docetism (*AH* 3. 11. 9).

All this means that, rather than Irenaeus being the great innovator, as many have thought, pioneering an orthodox interpretation of the gnostic Gospel of John,[333] it appears that Valentinus, or more probably Ptolemy, was the creative genius who engineered a reinterpretation of the abstract nouns of the Johannine Prologue to adapt to a theory of pleromatic aeons and syzygies which had been borrowed from 'the gnostics'. Predominantly, the earliest appropriation of John on the part of gnostic writers was adversarial or supersessionary. In this sense it is they who appear to be the first Johannophobes. It was the Valentinians who found a new way of 'receiving' this Gospel, used by the mainstream Church, by finding names for its pleromatic aeons in John's 'philosophical Prologue'.

[333] Sanders, *Fourth Gospel*, 66.

6

John among the Orthodox, 150–*c*.170

In chapters 3–5 above we have encountered many signs which seem to demand that a recognition and reception of the Fourth Gospel, and indeed the Johannine Revelation and at least the First Epistle, must have taken place in orthodox churches much earlier than the 170s, perhaps far back in the second century. Both the orthodox and the heterodox sources seem to demand this. This is quite surprising in the light of the common explanation of the second century which states that very little orthodox use is to be found prior to about 170–80, and that what can be found is tentative or self-conscious. It is now time to examine the earlier portions of the second century.

From here I shall work backwards chronologically from just before the orthodox writers examined in Chapter 3 to see whether there are precedents for their use of the Fourth Gospel, and the rest of the Johannine corpus, and what the nature of these precedents might be.

Melito of Sardis

Melito was listed by Polycrates as one of the luminaries of the quartodeciman faith who slept in Asia (Eusebius, *HE* 5. 24. 2–6). His fame as an orator and a writer spread beyond his native Asia Minor, at least to Alexandria (Clement and Origen) and North Africa (Tertullian). Of his numerous writings we have only one in complete form and mere fragments of the others. His witness to the Fourth Gospel is related temporally to that of his contemporary, Apollinarius of Hierapolis, who, like Melito, also wrote a treatise with the title *Concerning the Passover*. Treating the date of the one will impinge upon the dating of the other.

At the top of Eusebius' list of the works of Melito known to him are 'two books *On the Passover*' (*HE* 4. 26. 2). He cites a passage from the beginning of this work to show when it was written (4. 26. 3). Scholars are not agreed as to just how this notice relates to the work *Peri Pascha* which was rediscovered in the twentieth century and is now securely attributed to Melito.[1] The latter appears to be only a single, self-standing book, not two books as Eusebius says, and it nowhere contains the fragment quoted by Eusebius as the beginning of the work. Still, there are various ways the discrepancies could be resolved. In the Eusebian fragment Melito cites the rise of a great dispute or

---

[1] For discussion, see S. G. Hall, *Melito of Sardis* (Oxford, 1979), pp. xix–xxii.

inquiry at Laodicea as the occasion for his work, 'In the time of Servillius Paulus, proconsul of Asia, at the time when Sagaris was martyred, there was a great discussion in Laodicea[2] about the Passover, which fell according to the season in those days, and this was written'. It could well be that the *Peri Pascha*, which shows no signs of such a controversy, is a homily on the subject which was perhaps published with a second volume appended in the wake of the said controversy. Eusebius' fragment places the work in the proconsulship of one 'Servillius Paulus'. This must be a copyist's mistake, however, since no such proconsul is known. If the man referred to is L. Sergius Paulus, as Rufinus thought, he 'could have been proconsul in Asia in 166–7 (May–May) or before 162'.[3] If on the other hand he is, as Perler suggested, Q. Servilius Pudens, who was consul in 166, 'he might have served in Asia after that year'.[4] In either case, we may conclude that the controversy referred to by Melito took place some time between 160 and 170. Lawlor and Oulton have reconstructed a plausible chronology, based not only on this but on several passages in Eusebius, and have concluded that the most probable date for the death of Sagaris, and therefore for the relative date of the *Peri Pascha* of Melito, at least the part devoted to the controversy, is around 164.[5] Because the homily we have shows no signs of this controversy, it is likely to have been written some time before this.

At any rate, the homily *Peri Pascha*, though it does not cite any New Testament books formally,[6] shows that Melito uses John's Gospel for his knowledge of the life and sufferings of Jesus as he does Matthew's. Melito alludes to the distinctive Johannine stories of the healing of the man born blind (John 9: 1–7; *P. Pasch.* 653–4), and of the raising of Lazarus, who was in the tomb four days (John 11: 17–44; *P. Pasch.* 552, 656), both as if well known to his hearers in Sardis. He clearly knows John's presentation of the passion of Jesus, alluding twice to John's account of Jesus' bones not being broken (John 19: 36; *P. Pasch.* 25; 501), placing the crucifixion after 'the sixth hour' (*P. Pasch.* 499), as does John 19: 14, and describing the inscription above the cross as a τίτλος (*P. Pasch.* 708) as does John 19: 19. His use of Johannine material is subtle and unaffected. It is significant that this specimen of Melito's work is not an apologetic or anti-heretical tract, but a homily delivered in the context of the community's worship.[7] For he is comfortable in using material from the Fourth Gospel, along with the

---

[2] The words 'in Laodicea' are in the text but absent from Lake's translation in the LCL edn.

[3] Hall, *Melito*, p. xxi.

[4] Ibid. In a later article, 'The Origins of Easter', *Studia Patristica*, 15/1 (1984), 554–67, at 560, Hall thus writes that '166–7 is the most likely date for the dispute, though a date before 162 is possible, and slight emendations make a later date likely'.

[5] Lawlor and Oulton, *Eusebius* (London, 1954), 186, with cross-references.

[6] Henry M. Knapp, 'Melito's Use of Scripture in *Peri Pascha*: Second-Century Typology', *VC* 54 (2000), 343–74, at 353.

[7] We may surmise that his book, *On the Incarnation of God* (Περὶ ἐνσωμάτου Θεοῦ, Eusebius, *HE* 4. 26. 2) also must have made good use of the Fourth Gospel.

Synoptic Gospels, seemingly oblivious to any inflammatory import of this textual selection. Was his congregation in Sardis accustomed to hearing appeals to gnostic literature? It seems that they and their pastor were as much at home in the Johannine Gospel as they were in the other three.

The *Peri Pascha* also seems to know the book of Revelation. In lines 792–3 Jesus is called 'the Alpha and the Omega . . . the beginning and the end', in the words of Revelation 21: 6 (cf. 1: 8). We know from Eusebius and Jerome (Eusebius, *HE* 4. 26. 2; Jerome, *De vir. illust.* 24) that Melito also wrote a work entitled *On the Devil and the Apocalypse of John*.[8] We do not know what this book contained, though it is likely it had to do with the powers of Satan in relation to his binding mentioned in Revelation 20: 1–3.[9] As the subject of one of his books, the Apocalypse of John must have been regarded very highly by Melito.

We know from another fragment preserved by Eusebius that Melito produced six books of extracts from the 'the books of the Old Testament' and that he travelled to Palestine once to ascertain the exact number and identity of the books in the Old Testament (*HE* 4. 26. 13–14). This is apparently the first surviving use of the term Old Testament in a literary sense of a finite collection of scriptural books. And this name, as many have observed, implies the existence of a parallel collection known as the New Testament. Given Melito's use of the Gospel according to John and the Revelation of John, it is likely that these books would have been included in Melito's category of 'New Testament' books.

Claudius Apollinarius of Hierapolis

Claudius Apollinarius, an early bishop of Hierapolis, according to Serapion, wrote during the reign of Marcus Aurelius (Eusebius, *HE* 4. 27; 5. 5. 4; 5. 16. 1; 5. 19. 1, 2). One of his treatises, an apology addressed to the emperor, must have been written between 171 and 177.[10] By the time Serapion of Antioch mentions him in *c*.190, he is deceased (*HE* 5. 19. 2). According to Eusebius, Apollinarius wrote several other works for which Eusebius says he was justly famous.[11] Unfortunately, all these are lost, save for a fragment preserved in the *Chronicon Paschale*.

In a treatise on the Passover written evidently several years earlier (see below) he wrote about Jesus being 'pierced in his holy side, who poured

---

[8] Though it is possible that τῆς Ἀποκαλύψεως is the title of a separate work, judging from the titles in Eusebius' list, if it were a separate work it would have been entitled Περὶ τῆς Ἀποκαλύψεως. Instead, the entire title seems to have been Περὶ τοῦ διαβόλου καὶ τῆς Ἀποκαλύψεως.

[9] C. E. Hill, *Regnum Caelorum*[2] (Grand Rapids, Mich., 2001), 104 n. 7.

[10] Lawlor and Oulton, *Eusebius*, 150, 162.

[11] Five books *Against the Greeks*, two books *On the Truth*, two books, *Against the Jews*, and treatises against Montanism (*HE* 4. 28).

forth from his side the two purifying elements, water and blood, word and spirit,[12] and who was buried on the day of the Passover, the stone being placed upon the tomb'. His reference to the water and blood pouring out from Jesus' side signifies his knowledge of the highly personalized account of the author of the Fourth Gospel, who alone mentions it and specially attests to seeing it firsthand (John 19: 34–5; cf. Irenaeus, *AH* 3. 22. 2; 4. 33. 2; 4. 35. 3). Apollinarius also interprets the significance of the blood and water.[13] He mentions in the same treatise the Gospel according to Matthew and 'the Gospels' as common authorities ('they quote Matthew as speaking in accordance with their view. Wherefore their opinion is contrary to the law, and the Gospels seem to be at variance with them').[14] We know then that Apollinarius in Hierapolis, a successor of Papias, used a collection of Gospels, including Matthew and John, as authorities. We now need to see how precise we can be about the date of his reference to John.

The date determined above for the *Peri Pascha* of Melito, around 164 or so, has a reflexive effect on that of the treatise of Apollinarius. The evidence for this begins with Eusebius, who mentions the two men together in *HE* 4. 26. 1, 'In their time, too, Melito, bishop of the diocese of Sardis, and Apollinarius, bishop of Hierapolis, were at the height of their fame'. When in the introduction to his work on the subject Melito mentions a 'great controversy' at Laodicea at about the time of (or perhaps, as Lawlor and Oulton suggest, the time of the anniversary of)[15] the martyrdom of Sagaris, this causes us to wonder whether Apollinarius, whose Hierapolis is only a few miles from Laodicea, might have been involved in the controversy–and on the side opposite Melito. We know that Melito and Sagaris held to the quartodeciman position, as Polycrates mentions them both as his predecessors (*HE* 5. 24. 5, 'And why should I speak of Sagaris, bishop and martyr, who sleeps at Laodicaea…and Melito the eunuch…?'). But apparently Apollinarius, who is not mentioned in Polycrates' list of quartodeciman predecessors, even though Philip and his two daughters who lie buried in Hierapolis are, did not.[16] It appears therefore that Apollinarius must have been involved in the 'great discussion' about the Passover which took place in Laodicea, to which Melito refers in the Eusebian fragment. If so, this means that Apollinarius' treatise on the Passover, which evidently taught or presupposed an Easter observance somehow at odds with many of his

---

[12] ὁ τὴν ἁγίαν πλευρὰν ἐκκεντηθείς, ὁ ἐκχέας ἐκ τῆς πλευρᾶς αὐτοῦ τὰ δύο πάλιν καθά ρσια, ὕδωρ καὶ αἷμα. Greek from *Chronicon Paschale*, ed. B. G. Niebuhr, vol. i, Corpus Scriptorum Historiae Byzantinae (Bonn, 1832), 14.

[13] Melito, his contemporary, twice alludes to John's account of Jesus' bones not being broken, in the same passage (John 19: 36; *P Pasch.* 25, 501).

[14] From the *Chronicon Paschale*, praef., translation from *ANF* viii. 772–3. The author of the *Chronicon Paschale* wrote in the 6th cent.

[15] Lawlor and Oulton, *Eusebius*, 148.

[16] J. Quasten, *Patrology* (Westminster, Md., 1984), i, 229.

brethren in Asia Minor, was probably written at about this time as well, in the mid-160s around the time of Sagaris' martyrdom.

We may conclude then from Melito and from the tiny fragment of a single work by Apollinarius of Hierapolis that the Fourth Gospel, in a collection of Gospels which also included Matthew, was used by Church leaders on both sides in the quartodeciman controversy in Asia Minor in the 160s well before this controversy spread through the entire Church in the 190s, and probably some fifteen or twenty years before *Against Heresies* was begun.[17] This adds one more layer to the growing evidence which shows that Irenaeus' practice of using the Fourth Gospel as an orthodox authority, even as scripture, was no departure from Asian norms, that he was not 'introducing' a foreign Gospel, and that he had no need to 'argue' for its use in orthodox circles. It confirms that when the Asian and Phrygian Christian émigrés left their homes and moved to the cities of Vienne and Lyons in Gaul, a conviction of the power and usefulness of the Gospel according to John was something they took with them.

Tatian

Both in his *Diatessaron* and in his *Oratio ad Graecos* 13. 1 (also probably chapters 4 and 5) Tatian shows that he acknowledges John's Gospel as scripture and as a partner with the three other ecclesiastical Gospels. But the witness of Tatian to the Fourth Gospel is often very carelessly handled and misjudged, due to his eventual advocacy of a heretical form of encratism.[18] The *Oratio* at least, if not also the *Diatessaron*, must be attributed to his 'orthodox' years, before he abandoned the views of his teacher Justin.[19] It is

[17] M. Hengel, *Die johanneische Frage* (Tübingen, 1993), 23 n. 28, 'The fragments show how very much Apollinaris esteemed the Fourth Gospel. For some time prior to the writing of his treatise on the passover it must have already been generally known in the Church, otherwise he could not have referred to it so decisively.'

[18] J. Bauer, *Orthodoxy and Heresy in Earliest Christianity* (Philadelphia, 1971), 206–7, 'To be sure, Justin's disciple Tatian placed the gospel of John on the same level as the synoptics, but he also broke with the church on account of profound differences in faith—poisoned, so Irenaeus thought, by the Valentinians and Marcion (AH 1. 28. 1 [= 1. 26. 1])—and he left the world capital to move once again toward the East. Thus Tatian cannot provide us with a satisfactory testimony concerning the moods and conditions within the "church" at Rome...'; R. E. Brown, *The Community of the Beloved Disciple* (New York, 1979), 148, 'Often it is noted that Tatian (*ca.* A.D. 170), a pupil of Justin, used the Fourth Gospel in his harmony of the Gospels, the *Diatessaron*; but Tatian was an encratite who played down the value of the flesh, and so he should be reckoned on the heterodox side of the usage of John.'

[19] The first record of his apostasy is that of Irenaeus, *AH* 1. 28. 1: 'A certain man named Tatian first introduced the blasphemy [i.e. that Adam, God's first-created, was not saved]. He was a hearer of Justin's, and as long as he continued with him he expressed no such views; but after his martyrdom he separated from the Church, and, excited and puffed up by the thought of being a teacher, as if he were superior to others, he composed his own peculiar type of doctrine. He invented a system of certain invisible Aeons, like the followers of Valentinus; while, like Marcion and Saturninus, he declared that marriage was nothing else than corruption and fornication. But his denial of Adam's salvation was an opinion due entirely to himself.'

true that the *Oratio* has been placed by Robert Grant in about 177–8,[20] but this is certainly too late. Already by the time Irenaeus writes book 1 of *Against Heresies* (*AH* 1. 28; cf. 3. 37), probably in *c*.180, he knows some of Tatian's later writings which give expression to his heterodoxy. This suggests that these writings must have been available for some time. Eusebius' *Chronicon* puts the founding of Tatian's heretical school in the twelfth year of Marcus Aurelius (172), which at least forms a good fit with Irenaeus' words.[21] But there is nothing in the *Oratio* which could have incurred Irenaeus' judgement, and that it comes from before Tatian's heretical period is shown by its defence of the bodily resurrection,[22] its attribution of creation (even calling it the δημιουργίαν) to the highest God,[23] and by its admiration for Justin (ch. 19). It is, moreover, referred to favourably by Clement, in *Stromata* 1. 101. 2, and when the orthodox author of a work against Artemon (*The Little Labyrinth?*) lists Tatian among those who wrote about Christ as divine (Eusebius, *HE* 5. 28. 4), he is no doubt referring to the *Oratio*. Finally, Peterson has called attention to 'the apparently recent date of Tatian's conversion (cp. *Or.* 35. 2)' at the time he wrote the *Oratio*.[24] Much more accurately, then, Bolgiani places the *Oratio* between 155 and 170;[25] Marcovich between 165 and 172.[26] In fact, the language of chapter 19 seems to imply that Justin is still alive and that Crescens's murderous designs on Justin had so far not met with success.[27] If this is so, a date just before the middle 160s would appear the most probable.

The use of the Fourth Gospel in chapters 4, 5, 13, 19 of the *Oratio* is certain. Grant summarizes:

At the beginning of chapter 4 he says that 'God is Spirit' (John 4: 24) and adds that 'God is the beginning of all.' In chapter 5 he returns to the opening verse, citing it as 'God was in the beginning.' John 1: 1 says that the Logos was in the beginning but immediately adds that the Logos was God. In chapter 19 he cites verse 3 as

---

[20] R. M. Grant, *Greek Apologists of the Second Century* (Philadelphia, 1988), 112–15. *Pace* William L. Peterson, *Tatian's Diatessaron: Its Creation, Dissemination, Significance, and History in Scholarship*, Supplements to Vigiliae Christianae, 25 (Leiden, 1994), 77.

[21] Epiphanius, *Panar.* 46. 1. 6, places this at around the twelfth year of Antoninus Pius (138–61). But Peterson, *Tatian's Diatessaron*, 71, points out that 'If...one substitutes the name of Marcus Aurelius Antoninus (reigned 161–180) for Antoninus Pius, then one arrives at a date of 172/3—virtually identical with the date given by Eusebius: 172'.

[22] Contrast with Fragment 2, *ANF* ii. 82, from Clement Al., *Strom.* 3. 12. 86.

[23] 4. 2, contrast fragment 7, *ANF* ii. 82, from Origen, *De orat.*; cf. Grant, *Greek Apologists*, 129.

[24] Peterson, *Tatian's Diatessaron*, 73, n. 120. Here Tatian gives a comment which might be made by pagan acquaintances, 'Do not get impatient with our culture and involve yourselves in fatuous and scurrilous controversy against us, saying: "Tatian is going one better than the Greeks and the countless hordes of philosophers with his newfangled barbarian doctrines!"' (Wittaker's translation). Peterson also gives evidence for the *Oratio* being written in response to laws which discriminated against Christians.

[25] F. Bolgiani, 'Tatian', in *EEChurch*, ii. 815.

[26] M. Marcovich, *Tatiani: Oratio ad Graecos* (Berlin, 1995), 3, 'Now, since Tatian's *Oratio* reports both the presence of Justin's teachings and the environment of Rome, I think it is highly likely that it was written in Rome between ca. A.D. 165 and 172'.

[27] Though Marcovich, *Tatiani*, 2, thinks otherwise.

'everything was made *by* him,' not 'through him,' since he is emphasizing the deity of the Logos. In chapter 13 he refers to 'what was said,' i.e., in scripture: 'The darkness does not overcome the light.' He uses the present tense in John 1: 5 because he takes the verse in a timeless sense as referring to the Logos (the light) and the human soul (the darkness).[28]

I only wish to expand here a bit on Tatian's treatment in *Oratio* 5.

5. 1   God 'was in the beginning' and we have received the tradition (παρειλή-φαμεν) that the beginning was the power of the Word. The Lord of all things who was himself the foundation of the whole was alone in relation to the creation which had not yet come into being. In so far as all power over things visible and invisible was with him, he with himself and the Word which was in him established all things through the power of the Word. By his mere will (θελήματι) the Word sprang forth and did not come in vain, but became the 'firstborn' work of the Father. Him we know as the beginning of the universe. 2. He came into being by partition (κατὰ μερισμόν), not by section (κατὰ ἀποκοπήν), for what is severed is separated from its origin, but what has been partitioned takes on a distinctive function and does not diminish the source from which it has been taken... 3. Just as the Word begotten in the beginning in turn begot our creation by fabricating matter for himself, so I too, in imitation of the Word, having been begotten again (ἀναγεννηθείς) and obtained understanding of the truth am bringing to order the confusion in kindred matter.[29]

I cite this reflection on John 1: 1–3 primarily to show two aspects which will become relevant when we examine Justin below. First, the aptness of Colossians 1: 15, where Paul applies to Christ the term πρωτότοκος, to Christian expositions of the Johannine Prologue, or the Christology therein, is seen here in Tatian as it was already in Athenagoras, *Plea* 10. 3. Second, there is another allusion to the Fourth Gospel in 5. 3, where Tatian testifies that he has been begotten again. Though the text of John 3: 3, 7, which uses the uncompounded verb γεννάω (in the passive) with the adverb ἄνωθεν, is utterly stable, there can be no doubt that Tatian's ἀναγεννηθείς is an allusion to these sayings of Jesus, given the context.

---

[28] See also M. McGehee, 'Why Tatian Never "Apologized" to the Greeks', *JECS* 1 (1993), 143–58. He emphasizes (ibid. 148) that the *Oratio* was not intended to be a complete theological exposition, but argues that its should be regarded as a *protrepticus*. '[W]e should not assume that what Tatian presents here was ever meant to be a systematic presentation of his thought on the Being of God, the nature of Christ, the internal dynamics of the Trinity, and so on. In fact, additional evidence such as Origen's *Against Celsus* 3. 50–53, suggests that theological education occurred in private and implies that protreptic discourses would not become too specific about the finer points of Christian thought'. Such finer points would certainly include discussions of the authoritative sources for Christian doctrine. McGehee later states (156), 'He quotes from or alludes to the Scriptures but seems to make little of their authority. Yet certainly they did matter to him. Tatian, after all, compiled the Diatessaron. Perhaps he did not believe that they would help in his persuasion. Since a pagan audience would have been unfamiliar (and probably unimpressed) with Christian texts, he might have considered that there was no advantage in quoting from them.' This is no doubt correct, as we have seen from the words and example of Tertullian above.

[29] The translation is that of Molly Whittaker, *Tatian, Oratio ad Graecos and Fragments* (Oxford, 1982).

The modification is probably simply for clarity to an audience uninitiated into Christian teaching, and gives no indication of being derived from a separate and unrelated baptismal liturgy. That Tatian never mentions the name of the author of this Gospel is irrelevant, for 'His New Testament quotations and allusions in the *Oratio* are all made without attribution to their authors'.[30]

We still do not know when Tatian published his *Diatessaron*, though it is often placed in or after the year 172, when, according to Eusebius, Tatian was expelled from the Roman church.[31] But given the fact that Justin appears to have made use of materials from the Gospels which had already been excerpted and harmonized, we are not obliged to think that it was late in Tatian's career. We know that it was composed from the four canonical Gospels, including John's.[32] It appears in fact that the work began with John 1: 1 and ended with John 21: 19–23 and Luke 24: 49. This causes Leloir to remark, 'Diverse indications, and notably the choice of the Evangelist John to commence and terminate the *Diatessaron*, permit moreover the conclusion that Tatian conceived of the Fourth Gospel as the key to the Synoptics'.[33] This also attests to the perceived authority of the Fourth Gospel. Nor can it be claimed that the inclusion was revolutionary, or innovative, based on what we have seen so far. Victor of Capua, writing a preface to the Codex Fuldensis (a Latin harmony of the life of Christ) in 546, says that Tatian gave the name of *Diapente* to his work. This has led to much speculation about a fifth source.[34] While we cannot rule this out, such borrowing, if it occurred, must have been on a small scale. Drijvers says, 'It seems to me extremely unlikely that Tatian made use of extracanonical material or even of an apocryphal gospel in composing his Diatessaron'.[35] Variations of the Gospel texts found in common between the *Diatessaron* and the *Gospel according to Thomas* or between the *Diatessaron*, and the *Odes of Solomon* (both with links to Syria), are

---

[30] Ibid., p. xviii.

[31] See W. L. Peterson, 'Tatian's Diatessaron', in Koester, *ACG* 403–30, at 429, who says that any time after Justin's death in *c.*163 and Tatian's in *c.*185 is possible, though most surmise that it was composed after his expulsion from the Roman church in 172 (assuming Eusebius is correct). Peterson believes Tatian composed it in Syriac, though this may have been done while still in Rome, and does not discount the possibility of two *Diatessarons*, a Roman and a Syrian.

[32] B. M. Metzger, *The Canon of the New Testament: Its Origin, Development, and Significance* (Oxford, 1987), 115, 'At a time when many gospels were competing for attention, it is certainly significant that Tatian selected just these four'.

[33] L. Leloir (ed.), *Ephraem, Commentaire de l'évangile concordant ou Diatessaron*, SC 121 (Paris, 1966), 16, cited from M. Hengel, *The Johannine Question* (London, 1989), 140–1 n. 14.

[34] See G. M. Hahneman, *The Muratorian Fragment* (Oxford, 1992), 98–9; J. Charlesworth, 'Tatian's Dependence upon Apocryphal Traditions', *HeyJ* 15 (1974), 5–17.

[35] H. J. W. Drijvers, 'Facts and Problems in Early Syriac-Speaking Christianity', *The Second Century*, 2 (1982), 173 n. 64. B. M. Metzger, *The Canon of the New Testament* (Oxford, 1987), 116 n. 5, says that several of these come from either the *Gospel according to the Hebrews* or from the *Protevangelium of James*. He points out that 'It is not known whether they were present in the *Diatessaron* from the beginning, or whether some were incorporated after Tatian had published his harmony of the four Gospels'.

plausibly explained by Drijvers by the theory that both these texts were dependent upon the *Diatessaron*.[36]

Most importantly, whatever purpose Tatian had in producing the *Diatessaron*, and whatever theological tendencies it may have exhibited, its acceptance and inclusion of John was not, as Bauer and Brown allege, a result of his turn towards heterodoxy. It was simply the continuation of his practice already signified in his orthodox works (and also known before him, as we shall see, in his predecessor Justin).

In Tatian's orthodox work dating from *c.*162–70 we have a clear attestation of the use of the Fourth Gospel as authoritative and as scripture. This happened outside Asia Minor, and well before Irenaeus wrote. The *Oratio*, at least, must be placed in Rome, and possibly so should the *Diatessaron*. This conclusion must stir up curiosity about the situation of the Fourth Gospel in the writings of Justin, Tatian's teacher, who is said to have made very little or no use of this Gospel. We shall come to Justin's witness before long.

The Egerton Gospel

The Egyptian papyrus containing what is known as the Egerton Gospel (Papyrus Egerton 2) was originally dated by Bell and Skeat at about the middle of the second century.[37] But the later discovery of another fragment of the text (Papyrus Köln 255)[38] has necessitated a redating of the text to about 200, a redating which has been accepted by Skeat himself.[39] A later dating of the papyrus does not necessarily require a later dating of the 'Gospel' represented by these papyrus fragments.

Helmut Koester, following the approach of Goro Mayeda,[40] has argued that the Egerton Gospel is not only earlier than the Fourth Gospel, but a direct source for it. He believes it reflects a stage of tradition which is earlier than the Synoptic Gospels as well.[41] It would seem, however, that Neirynck

---

[36] Drijvers, 'Facts and Problems', 173.

[37] H. I. Bell and T. C. Skeat, *Fragments of an Unknown Gospel and Other Early Christian Papyri* (London, 1935); idem, *The New Gospel Fragments* (London, 1935).

[38] M. Gronewald in *Kölner Papyri (PKöln)* vol. vi = Abh. RWA, Sonderreihe Papyrologica Coloniensia, 7 (Cologne, 1987). See also D. Lührmann, 'Das neue Fragment de PEgerton 2 (PKöln 255)', in F. Van Segbroek (ed.), *The Four Gospels 1992: Festschrift Frans Neirynck*, BETL 100 (Leuven, 1992), 2239–55.

[39] L. Hurtado, 'The Origin of the *Nomina Sacra*: A Proposal,' *JBL* 117 (1998), 655–73, at 657 n. 7, cites a personal letter from T. C. Skeat (21 June 1997).

[40] Goro Mayeda, *Das Leben-Jesu-Fragment Papyrus Egerton 2 und seine Stellung in der urchristlichen Literaturgeschichte* (Berne, 1946).

[41] H. Koester, *Introduction to the New Testament* (Berlin, 1982), 181–3; 'Apocryphal and Canonical Gospels', *HTR* 73 (1980), 105–30; *ACG* 205–16. Similar theories had circulated quite early after the first publication of the fragments. In their *editio princeps*, Bell and Skeat in 1935 had already rejected the idea that John had borrowed from Egerton (*Fragments of an Unknown Gospel*, 21). They had, however, suggested two possibilities, 'either that John and the new Gospel were alike drawing on some earlier source or that the latter was using a form of John earlier than that which we know and

has established that a major section of the fragment must be post-Synoptic.[42] Probably the majority of scholars, in fact, have concluded that Egerton is later than and dependent in some way upon the four Gospels.[43] Raymond Brown concluded that Egerton 'weaves together into a consecutive narrative sentences and phrases from the four Gospels and an agraphon'.[44] Hengel says Egerton 'represents a free cento of Johannine and synoptic texts'.[45] Jeremias thought that

the juxtaposition of Johannine (I) and Synoptic material (II and III) and the fact that the Johannine material is shot through with Synoptic phrases and the Synoptic with Johannine usage, permits the conjecture that the author knew all and every one of the canonical Gospels. Only he had no one of them before him as a written text.[46]

widely differing from it' (28). One of their main reasons for not preferring the simpler idea that Egerton was simply based upon John, however, was the reigning theory that the Fourth Gospel was perhaps as late as 120–30, giving scarcely enough time for the writer of Egerton, who, if he was reliant upon John, knew it quite well, to have come to know it and for it to have 'acquired a recognized position in the Church' (28). But as Bell and Skeat wrote, things were about to change. Bell would write in the very next year, 'scarcely had the new Gospel appeared when Mr. C. H. Roberts discovered in the Rylands collection a portion of a single leaf from a codex of St. John which must be at least as early as the British Museum papyrus [i.e. Egerton] and may be even older', and this fragment, now known as $\mathfrak{P}^{52}$, 'is valuable evidence of the existence and wide circulation of St. John's Gospel in the first half of the second century' (H. I. Bell, *Recent Discoveries of Biblical Papyri: An Inaugural Lecture Delivered before the University of Oxford on 18 November 1936* (Oxford, 1937), 20–1). In this publication Bell was able to say, 'It was suggested in the *editio princeps* that it might be, or might be derived from, one of the sources used by the author of the fourth Gospel. This idea has been rejected by almost all who have produced a detailed criticism of the edition, and their arguments have convinced me that it is untenable. We may, I think, accept it as established that the New Gospel is in part based upon St. John's Gospel, whether in its present or in some earlier form' (17). Bell's tentative conclusion was 'that the new text was written before the end of the first quarter of the second century; that the author knew St. John's Gospel and possibly, but if so less intimately, St. Luke's or some other Synoptic Gospel; that he had, however, access to other sources which have not survived elsewhere; and that, though he probably handled his material quite freely, he wrote in good faith, with no heretical axe to grind' (20).

[42] See F. Neirynck, 'Papyrus Egerton 2 and the Healing of the Leper', *ETL* 61 (1985), 153–60, though this did not gain Koester's assent, *ACG* 213 n. 1; also Neirynck's 'The Apocryphal Gospels and the Gospel of Mark', in J.-M. Severin (ed.), *The New Testament in Early Christianity*, BETL 86 (1989), 123–75, at 161–7.

[43] In Jan. 1936 C. H. Dodd published a study of the Egerton fragments in which he concluded that its author had used the Fourth Gospel ('A New Gospel', *BJRL* 20 (1936), reprinted separately by Manchester University Press, 1936). He could find no definitive signs that the author had used any of the Synoptic Gospels, however, and concluded, based on the finding of $\mathfrak{P}^{52}$ and Egerton in Egypt, and the supposed use of John by Basilides, Valentinus, Theodotus, that 'There was evidently in that Gospel [i.e. John] something that specially appealed to the Egyptian mind' (39). See also E.-M. Braun, *Jean le Théologien* (Paris, 1959), 87–94.

[44] Raymond Brown, 'The Relation of "The Secret Gospel of Mark" to the Fourth Gospel', *CBQ* 36 (1974), 477.

[45] Hengel, *Question*, 1.

[46] In J. Jeremias and W. Schneemelcher, 'Papyrus Egerton 2', in *NTA*² i. 96–9, at 97. Koester, *ACG* 213, seems to think that quotation 'from memory' is unlikely—not only here but in any 2nd-cent. author—and objects that if we allow for this possibility we must also allow that he is quoting oral, not written, tradition. Braun, *Jean le Théologien*, 92–3, on the other hand, thinks this is precisely the type of word connection which comes from memory, and points to 'l'attitude très libre que les anciens prenaient à l'égard des textes' (93).

304   *Johannine Writings in the Second Century*

In our relatively brief fragments we can see that there is 'Johannine' material from at least chapters 3, 5, 7, 9, and 10 of that Gospel. In Egerton 2 recto 43–59 the author seems to have adapted from John 3: 2 the phrase, 'Teacher Jesus, we know that thou art come <from God>', though it is placed in an entirely different context, as an introduction to the question about paying taxes to Caesar which occurs in Matthew 22: 15–22; Mark 12: 13–17; Luke 20: 20–6. Egerton 1 verso 7–20 (adding P. Köln 255) seems to be taken almost completely from John 39–40, 45; 9: 28–9; 5: 46. Egerton 1 recto 22–31 seems to conflate John 7: 30 and 10: 31, 39. Koester believes all these parallels show that Egerton is the more original, pre-Johannine version, which in some form was known to the Johannine author and expanded by him: 'What appears here is a language that is pre-johan-nine and pre-synoptic at the same time'.[47] It is more accurate to say that by themselves it is often almost impossible to say whether one author was expanding or the other was contracting. More determinative is surely the fact that we can note the presence in the Egerton fragments of two distinct-ive Johannine 'redactional' themes, the question 'whence Jesus is' (1 verso 20; see John 7: 27–8, 41–3, 52; 8: 14, 23, 42; 9: 29–30; 13: 3; 19: 9; cf. 2: 9; 3: 8), and reference to 'Jesus' hour' (1 recto 22–31; see John 7: 30; cf. 2: 4; 7: 5, 44; 8: 20; 12: 23; 13: 1).[48] These are no mere redactional elements[49] but *bona-fide* Johannine themes.

Have we discovered then in the Egerton Gospel the lost source for two of the seemingly unique traits of the Johannine author's account of the life of Jesus? Even more poignantly, are we to believe that the author (redactor) of the Fourth Gospel took from the Egerton Gospel, or from their common

[47] Koester, *ACG* 215.

[48] Koester, *ACG* 211, notices this one. He says 'The phrase "his hour had not yet come" might be considered to have been created by the author of the Gospel of John. In that case arguments for a dependence of *Papyrus Egerton 2* upon the Fourth Gospel would be persuasive. However... the use of the term "hour" in reference to the suffering and death of Jesus also appears in the Gethsemane pericope of Mark 14: 35... Thus it would seem quite possible that the reference to the "hour" of Jesus' betrayal appeared in a source of the Fourth Gospel. It is, then, preferable to explain John's multiple reference to failed attempts to arrest Jesus as reflections and usages of only one traditional report, such as the one which is preserved by *Papyrus Egerton 2*.' This is very unconvincing. First, the mention of 'the hour' in Mark 14: 35 is a simple metaphrasis for 'the time'. Mark does not have the distinctive dramatic element of 'the time' being 'not yet' and then climactically arriving, as we have in John. Egerton's statement that the hour of Jesus' arrest 'had not yet come' is characteristically Johannine. Second, it is hardly legitimate to restrict John's development of this theme to his 'multiple reference to failed attempts to arrest Jesus'. The theme of 'Jesus' hour' as 'not yet come' is found in Jesus' words to his mother at the wedding at Cana (2: 4) before it is related to the abortive attempts to arrest him by the Jewish authorities in chs. 7–8. The arrival of 'Jesus' hour' is the dramatic turning point in the Johannine narrative: 'And Jesus answered them, "The hour has come for the Son of man to be glorified ... And what shall I say? 'Father, save me from this hour'? Nor, for this purpose I have come to this hour. Father, glorify thy name"' (John 12: 23–8). It rather appears that Egerton's author has simply incorporated this distinctive Johannine idea, probably based specifically on its occurrence in John 7: 30, along with John's account of the attempt to stone Jesus in John 10: 31–9, into his narrative.

[49] Koester, *ACG* 212, 215, denies that Egerton contains any real redactional elements from any of the four Gospels.

source, only its 'Johannine' elements and scrupulously avoided any of its Synoptic elements?[50] Likewise, are we to believe that the authors of Mark and 'Q'[51] each presciently selected only those parts of the Egerton tradition which were somehow destined not to make it into the Johannine? It is no easier to imagine that Egerton's Synoptic and Johannine blend somehow got separated into two (or three, counting 'Q') hermetically sealed packages prior to the work of the other Evangelists and that only one package was known to each. Because of the seemingly casual appearance of two distinctive Johannine themes, and because of the extreme difficulty of conceiving of the clinical separation and preservation of Egerton's Synoptic and Johannine material into two or three streams, it is incomparably easier to agree with those scholars who recognize that the common material is borrowed by Egerton's author, directly or indirectly, from memory or by conscious adaptation, or both, from the four Gospels.

As to the nature of this Gospel, its fragmentary state makes any analysis tentative at best. Comparing it with the Secret Gospel of Mark, Raymond Brown wondered, 'if both may not reflect the clime of mid-2d-century Egypt when canonical material was being adapted to serve the interests of special groups'.[52] This may be, but it is no longer possible to determine what the interests of this special group were. Brown observes that Egerton 'does not share the secret initiatory purpose of the SGM passage'. But even this is difficult to say, given the small amount of text left. We cannot easily find any heterodox purpose in what is left, and this means we might be justified in treating it as a production of popular orthodox piety,[53] though we must always remain cautious about any judgement. What we can say is that the sort of amalgamating and reworking of material from the four Gospels is reminiscent of the kind of thing we see in different forms in the *Gospel of Peter*, and the *Epistula Apostolorum*, where it also is mixed in with other material, and is not altogether unrelated to the attempt in Tatian's *Diatessaron* to form an amalgamated and harmonized Gospel text. Placing this 'Gospel' in such a context makes its use of the four Gospels a bit more understandable. The Egerton Gospel, then, is one more second-century witness to the acceptability of the Fourth Gospel and of its natural place alongside the Synoptics as in some sense authoritative sources for the life of Jesus. Koester says that if this Gospel is from the early decades of the second century or even from *c*.200 (instead of, in his view, being much

---

[50] This mystery was already noted by Bell and Skeat in 1935, *Fragments of an Unknown Gospel*, 28, 'Above all, how came he to select from this Gospel only the non-Synoptic material which it contained?'.

[51] Neirynck, 'Apocryphal Gospels', 166, observes that Jesus' question in Egerton 2 recto, 'Why do you call me teacher with your mouth and do not do what I say', is a 'Q' saying (cf. Luke 6: 46; Matt, 7: 21).

[52] Brown, 'Relation of "Secret Gospel of Mark"', 477.

[53] Braun, *Jean le Théologien*, 94, thinks it is 'a product of ordinary Christianity. It witnesses to the seduction which the legendary tracts and thaumaturgical accounts exercised on the popular spirit'.

earlier), it 'would appear to be . . . a spectacularly early piece of evidence for the establishment of the four-gospel canon of the New Testament'.[54] Spectacular or not, I believe we shall see that it is not unique and probably not so unusual.

Gospel of Peter

The *Gospel of Peter* may have originated in Syria, or in Asia Minor; at any rate we know a work by this title was being read by believers in Rhossos in Cilicia, some 30 miles north-west of Antioch, by *c.*190 (Eusebius, *HE* 6. 12. 2–6). Two small fragments of what is evidently this work found at Oxyrhynchus (P. Oxy. 2949) date from *c.*200.[55] But our major representation of the *Gospel of Peter* derives from the so-called Akhmim Fragment, preserved in an amulet of the eighth or ninth century. Like the Egerton Gospel, this Gospel is difficult to date.[56] Hengel, following Mara, would place it in the first half of the second century.[57] Certain correspondences with Justin allow a general approximation of date but nothing more.

The influence of special material from the Fourth Gospel is apparent at several points in the portion of the work which has survived: Jesus' appearance at the tribunal (*GP* 3. 7; John 19: 13); the striking (ἐράπισαν) of Jesus (*GP* 3. 9; John 18: 22; 19: 3); the scourging (ἐμάστιζον) of Jesus (*GP* 3. 9; John 19: 1)—in both of these last two instances preserving vocabulary distinct to John as opposed to the Synoptics; the non-breaking of Jesus' bones (*GP* 4. 14; John 19: 32–3); the nails in Jesus' hands (*GP* 6. 21; John 20: 25); references to the 'fear' of the Jews (*GP* 12. 50, 52; John 19: 38; 20: 19); and the fishing expedition of the disciples after the resurrection (*GP* 14. 60; John 21: 1–3).[58] There are other possible parallels which may have come either from John or from the Synoptic Gospels (less likely, from oral tradition).

Despite what appear to be obvious indications of dependence upon John and the Synoptics, extensive efforts have been made in recent decades to claim that the *GP* represents an early source which was independent of the

[54] Koester, *ACG* 207. Koester had originally made this observation ('Apocryphal and Canonical Gospels', 120) with respect to J. Jeremias's position that Egerton was from the early decades of the 2nd cent. and 'knew all and every one of the canonical gospels' (from *NTA*[1] i. 95). He repeated it (*ACG* 207) after the discovery of Papyrus Köln 255.

[55] The identification was made by Dieter Lührmann, 'POx 2949: EvPt 3–5 in einer Handschrift des 2/3. Jahrhunderts', *ZNW* 72 (1981), 216–26.

[56] For the possibility that the Egerton Gospel is actually part of the *Gospel of Peter* see D. F. Wright, 'Papyrus Egerton 2 (The Unknown Gospel): Part of the Gospel of Peter?', *The Second Century*, 5 (1985–6), 129–50.

[57] Hengel, *Question*, 11, 148 n. 56; M. G. Mara, *Évangile de Pierre*, SC 201 (Paris, 1973), 217–18.

[58] See also R. E. Brown, 'The Gospel of Peter and Canonical Gospel Priority', *NTS* 33 (1987), 321–43; Peter M. Head, 'On the Christology of the Gospel of Peter', *VC* 46 (1992), 209–24. Koester, *ACG* 218, admits that 'Parallels with the passion and resurrection accounts of all four canonical gospels are numerous'.

four canonical Gospels,[59] that this source was used by all four canonical Gospels and was best preserved by the *GP*,[60] or that *GP* and the four Gospels are each independent developments (the *GP*, again, being the earliest) of an early but ambiguous 'exegetical tradition'.[61] But other scholars have been less impressed with theory-laden reconstructions, which often involve the 'backdoor' provision that unmistakable verbal correspondences with the canonical texts in proposed 'earlier' texts could be due to later copyists who 'could have been influenced by the texts of the canonical gospels'.[62] I would have to agree with Braun, Schneemelcher, and Hengel that these coincidences, some of them quite minute, make it much easier to believe that the *Gospel of Peter* knew John's account rather than vice versa, or rather than the hypothesis that each is reliant upon a common source or tradition.[63]

Although implicated as tainted by docetism in a controversy involving Serapion of Antioch, it may be that this apocryphon's support for docetism was unintentional; it certainly shows no signs of being a Valentinian or Marcionite production, and we can see no apparent signs of adherence to a pleromatic myth. Serapion said he had discovered 'that the most part of it

[59] J. Denker, *Die theologiegeschichtliche Stellung des Petrusevangeliums: Ein Beitrag zur Frühgeschichte des Doketismus*, Europäische Hochschulschriften, 23, Theology, 36 (Berne, 1975). Koester, *ACG* 218, summarizes Denker's thesis: 'the *Gospel of Peter* is dependent upon the traditions of interpreting Old Testament materials for the description of Jesus' suffering and death; it shares such traditions with the canonical gospels, but is not dependent upon the canonical gospels'.

[60] J. D. Crossan, *The Cross that Spoke: The Origins of the Passion Narrative* (San Francisco, 1988). Crossan asserts that the *GP* is actually a prime witness to a 1st-cent., independent, 'Cross Gospel', from which all four canonical Gospels drew.

[61] Koester, *ACG* 216–40.

[62] Ibid. 219. Crossan too allows that our present text includes elements (2. 3–5; 6. 23–4; 12. 50–13. 57; 14. 60) drawn from the canonical Gospels by a later redactor.

[63] See also Braun, *Jean le Théologien*, 140, 204–9, 221–3; J. K. Elliott, *ANT* 151; R. Kieffer, 'Les Premiers indices d'une réception de l'évangile de saint Jean', in F. Van Segbroeck et al. (eds.), *The Four Gospels* (Leuven, 1992), 2229. W. Schneemelcher, 'The Gospel of Peter: Introduction', in *NTA*² i. 216–22, at 219, thinks 'the verbal agreements between the Gos.Pet. and the canonical Gospels are too numerous to allow us to uphold so sharp a rejection of their knowledge and use' (as is proposed by Denker); Schneemelcher says that Koester's view 'seems to be contradicted by the fact that the author betrays no knowledge of the situation in Palestine in the time of Jesus, which one would expect to find at least in some way in an old tradition. In particular the Jewish institutions are evidently unknown to him (Mara has laid special stress on this)'; Hengel, *Question*, 148–9. n. 56, refers to Mara's collection of parallels with John (*Évangile de Pierre*, (Paris, 1973), 233–5): 'They are so numerous and so far-reaching that it is impossible for them all to be derived from a common source (which is completely hypothetical). In many respects the author follows the Fourth Gospel and the Apocalypse in his theology... In reality the author makes free use of all four Gospels and adorns them with legendary additions.' In *Frage*, 56 n. 159, Hengel goes on to criticize Crossan's 'phantastische Konstruktion einer Sündenbock-Tradition' and is astounded that Koester, *ACG* 220, follows it uncritically. Koester does criticize other aspects of Crossan's work (*ACG* 219–20); he is adamant that there is no single source upon which all four Gospels are dependent, particularly as to the resurrection and appearance narratives. Particularly interesting is that Koester calls a major aspect of Crossan's theory a 'fiction' (*ACG* 220)! Hengel sees the fully secondary character of the *GP* in the claim of authorship by Peter, who speaks in the first person, and in the fact that Jesus is crucified by the Jews at the command of Herod and not by the Roman soldiers at the command of Pilate (*Frage*, 56 n. 159).

(τὰ ... πλείονα) indeed was in accordance with the true teaching of the
Saviour, but that some things were added (προσδιεσταλμένα)' (*HE* 6. 12.
6). If he is correct, the docetic material had been added by docetists later.
Alternatively, the offending portions were original but were relatively innocent and only seized on later by the docetists in Rhossus. In any case its use
by docetists to make their case must have centred on only a few portions of
the work. In 4. 10, when Jesus is crucified it is said that he 'held his peace,
as if he felt no pain' (αὐτος δὲ ἐσιώπα ὡς μηδένα πόνον ἔχων). This
could be taken as a denial of his full humanity, though the 'as if' seems to
go the opposite way of conventional docetism.[64] And, as Peter M. Head
points out, it seems to conform to a heroic notion of endurance which had
parallels in second-century martyr accounts.[65] The Lord's cry from the
cross, 'My power, O power, thou hast forsaken me!' (5. 19) could easily
have been read by adoptionistic docetists as signifying that his spirit had
already departed, leaving the earthly Jesus on the cross. But this is not
obviously the meaning of the author and, strictly speaking, would break the
norm of such docetic presentations, which typically use the term 'Power' for
the supreme God, not for the heavenly being which temporarily adopted
the earthly Jesus. Besides, these words are placed in the mouth, not of an
abandoned vessel, but of 'the Lord', presumably the same Lord who is
spoken of both before and after the crucifixion.[66] And, arguing against an
original docetic intent of the author, the Lord's body (6. 21, 23, 24) and his
death (8. 28) are spoken of throughout the work in straightforward terms,
with no obvious, docetic double entendre. The question of the heavenly
voice, 'Hast thou preached to them that sleep?' (10. 41), though 'apocryphal', reflects a concern for the OT righteous, which is not a stock concern of docetist writers. Finally, the entire emphasis on the resurrection of
'the Lord' in this document is a major stumbling block to a patently docetic
motive. The 'docetic-sounding' elements, then, are better seen as 'indicative
of the popular nature of the document'.[67]

    The *Gospel of Peter* seems to retell the gospel story based upon the four
Gospels, perhaps with some apologetic import, perhaps with some harmonizing intent, perhaps with the intent to embellish and, one assumes, to edify.
If, as is doubtful, it was written as propaganda for a docetic Christology, its
use of the other canonical Gospels[68] and not merely or not distinctively
John means it is not likely to have engendered any Johannophobia on the
part of its orthodox critics. But the fragments which are left to us seem on

---

[64] Head, 'Christology', 212. At 221 n. 20, Head mentions similar statements by Origen, *C. Matt.*
125 and by Dionysius of Alexandria, *Comm. Luke* 22. 42–4 (Feltoe, 239), the latter, speaking of Jesus'
silent endurance ὥσπερ οὐδὲν πάσχων.
[65] Head, 'Christology', 213.
[66] Also noted ibid. 216.
[67] Ibid. 218.
[68] See F. Neirynck, 'Apocryphal Gospels', 140–52 and the literature cited there.

the other hand to reveal a Gospel which is, apart from a tendency to enhance the miraculous, a relatively unadorned retelling of the crucifixion and resurrection stories in an amalgamation of the four Gospels, and some other sources (including OT sources). It thus is at home among other attempts we know were being made at around or just after the middle of the second century to amalgamate or harmonize the Gospel accounts,[69] such as we see in different ways in the Egerton Gospel, in Justin, and most extensively and successfully, in Tatian's *Diatessaron*, and a bit earlier in the longer ending to Mark. Together with them it also attests to the special place of the Fourth Gospel among the Synoptics in the Christian communities of their authors.

Celsus and his Sources

In his later years, between 244 and 249 (Eusebius, *HE* 6. 36. 2) Origen wrote an eight-volume work against the philosopher Celsus, who in the 160s or 170s had written a powerful critique of Christianity. From the quotations from Celsus' *True Word* preserved in Origen's refutation much can be learnt about Celsus' knowledge of Christianity, or about what he thought he knew about it. One thing we learn is that Celsus the critic of Christianity knew that the Gospel according to John was one of the prime Christian Gospels. Several times he polemicized against something taught only in the Fourth Gospel, sometimes apparently even quoting it.[70] Celsus objected to the Christian idea that Jesus was divine by saying that 'the body of a god is not nourished with such food' (*C. Cels.* 1. 70), for Celsus was claiming to be able 'to prove from the Gospel narratives both that He partook of food, and food of a particular kind'. Such food included the Passover meal and, apparently, the piece of fish which Jesus ate, according to John 21: 13, after his resurrection. Celsus also mentioned the thirst that Jesus suffered by the well of Jacob (παρὰ τῇ πηγῇ 'Ιακώβ), obviously based upon knowledge of John's account of Jesus at the well in John 4: 4–42. Origen's words confirm that Celsus knew these Gospels as Gospels,[71] and that the material in question came ultimately from them (whether modified or misused by Celsus or not) and not from Christian oral tradition or from liturgical or catechetical sources. They also set the material in this section off from material Origen elsewhere says Celsus must have got from questionable sources and which was not

---

[69] Head, 'Christology', 218, 'The cumulative evidence for a second century date is strong and adds to the impression that GP is a redaction of the canonical material (perhaps also influenced by oral traditions)'.

[70] See Hengel, *Question*, 6, 142 n. 23.

[71] Also at one point (2. 74) Celsus' fictional Jew, arguing against the Christians, claims to have taken his information about Christianity 'from your own books, in addition to which we need no other witness; for ye fall upon your own swords'. It is evident that Celsus had ready access to what he considered were the treasured and self-authenticating books of the Christians.

representative of the catholic faith. Celsus knows and disdains the Christian teaching that Jesus is God (2. 30) and the Logos (2. 31), as contained in John 1: 1, 14. His ridicule of Jesus as having a body through which watery ichor flowed, in imitation of the gods, must depend upon a reading of John 19: 34–5, which Origen quotes in full to correct him (*C. Cels.* 2. 36; cf. 1. 66). His mention of Jesus' thirst on the cross seems to betray a knowledge of John 19: 28 (*C. Cels.* 2. 37). From the reply which he puts in the mouth of a Christian, to the effect that Jesus underwent death 'to bring about the destruction of the father of evil' it is reasonable to suppose that Celsus was familiar with one or more statements in the Fourth Gospel or 1 John (John 8: 44, 45, the devil as father; 16: 11, Jesus' victory over the devil) and perhaps with 1 John 3: 8, which says that Jesus' purpose in coming was to destroy the works of the devil. In a sarcastic account of the resurrection Celsus alludes to the episode with Thomas and the disciples, in which Jesus showed his disciples the nail prints in his hands[72] (John 20: 20, 25–7; *C. Cels.* 2. 55; see further 2. 61). He had some uncomplimentary words about a female witness to the resurrection, which must indicate a knowledge of John's story of Mary at the tomb of Jesus, also from John 20 (*C. Cels.* 2. 55). Celsus' familiarity with the Fourth Gospel then runs throughout the text, though his objections centre on the first and last parts of the Gospel. He also knew at least Matthew and Luke. Moreover, there is one fragment from Celsus' work which may indicate his awareness of a fourfold Gospel. At one point he is recorded as complaining about the 'threefold, and fourfold, and many-fold' form of the Gospel (μεταχαράττειν ἐκ τῆς πρώτης γραφῆς τὸ εὐαγγέλιον τριχῆ καὶ τετραχῆ καὶ πολλαχῆ καὶ μεταπλάττειν; *C. Cels.* 2. 27).[73] Chadwick offered another translation, 'some believers... alter the original text of the gospel three or four or several times over, and they change its character to enable them to deny difficulties in face of criticism', but his note acknowledged that 'He may mean the different gospel, *three or four* being a reference to the canonical four'.[74] Hengel remarks from this that Celsus thus becomes, next to Tatian and Irenaeus, an early witness for a four Gospel canon.[75] That a critic like Celsus was able to gather information from so many sources in John and in the Synoptics testifies to the circulation and to the authority of these Gospels among Christians in his locality at the time, and to their general availability even to unbelievers.

We cannot, however, pinpoint that locality and time with much assurance. Many place Celsus' *True Word* in the middle or late 170s[76] but others

---

[72] ...τὰ σημεῖα τῆς κολάσεως ἔδειξε καὶ τὰς χεῖρας ὡς ἦσαν πεπερονημέναι.

[73] Greek from M. Borret, *Origène* Contra Celse, 5 vols, *Introduction, texte critique, traduction et notes*, SC 132, 136, 147, 150, 227 (Paris, 1967–76).

[74] H. Chadwick, *Origen: Contra Celsum* (Cambridge, 1965).

[75] Hengel, *Frage*, 28 n. 48.

[76] Chadwick decides on 177–80; R. J. Hoffmann, *Celsus. On the True Doctrine. A Discourse Against the Christians* (Oxford, 1987), 30–3, following Keim, favours 177.

as early as 160, a date which seems to be favoured by Hengel.[77] It is usually assumed that Celsus lived and wrote in Rome, though Henry Chadwick has shown that a case can be made for Alexandria.[78] If Celsus wrote in Rome, his testimony takes on increased importance, given our general lack of witnesses from Rome in this period. Celsus' knowledge of John's story of Jesus and the Samaritan woman is also important in another respect. I have noted above that depictions of this scene are found on the walls of the oldest portions of the catacombs of Callistus and Praetextatus, which in all likelihood date to the first decades of the third century. Celsus would thus seem to confirm the knowledge of John 4 among the orthodox in Rome at least three or more decades earlier. In any case the seldom-cited witness of the critic Celsus points to the common acceptance among Christians in the third quarter of the second century, and almost certainly within the lifetime of Justin, of a fourfold Gospel canon, including the Fourth Gospel.

The Martyrdom of Sts Carpus, Papylus, and Agathonice

There has been some disagreement about the date of the martyrdom of these Christians, or at least about the date of the work which describes it. Eusebius (*HE* 4. 15. 48), writing of the time of the joint emperors, Marcus Aurelius and Lucius Verus (AD 161–9), says 'there are also memoirs (ὑπομνήματα) extant of others who were martyred in the city of Pergamon in Asia, Carpus and Papylus, and a woman, Agathonice, who died after many glorious confessions'. The Greek text does not date the martyrdoms but the Latin recension places them under Decius (250).[79] It is not easy to account for the Latin dating if it is not correct, but on the other hand it is unlikely that Eusebius would have been so mistaken about a martyrdom which, in this case, occurred almost in his own lifetime. Jan den Boeft and Jan Bremmer have apparently shown that the martyrdom must have taken place before 215, for Papylus, who according to the Greek version, came from Thyatira, was brought to Pergamum, which until that year had jurisdiction over Thyatira, for trial, but 'the emperor Caracalla granted to Thyatira the right to hold assizes after he had stayed there in 215. So after 215 an inhabitant of Thyatira, and certainly a proper citizen as Papylus was (Greek version par. 24), would have been tried in the city itself and no longer at

---

[77] Hengel cites H. U. Rosenbaum, 'Zur Datierung von Celsus' ΑΛΗΘΗΣ ΛΟΓΟΣ', *VC* 26 (1972), 102–11, and J. Schwartz, 'Du Testament de Lévi au Discours véritable de Celse', *RHPR* 40 (1960), 126–45 at 137. Lightfoot too provisionally assigned the writing to the time of Antoninus Pius (*AF* ii 1. 530–1).

[78] Chadwick, *Contra Celsum*, pp. xxviii–xxix.

[79] This date is accepted by V. Saxer, 'Martyr. III. Acts, Passions, Legends', in *EEChurch*, i. 533–4 at 533. Frend, *Martyrdom*, 296 n. 32, uses it as genuine but with the following reservation, 'It may be, as Delehaye has suggested (*Les Passions*, 137–41), that the *Acta* though based on the genuine ὑπομνήματα recorded by Eusebius have been re-edited much later'.

Pergamum.'[80] Lawlor and Oulton, Quasten, Frend, and Musurillo accepted Eusebius' date, as has more recently Bisbee.[81] If it is rightly dated by Eusebius it is thus roughly contemporary with the martyrdom of Justin and his companions in Rome.

In his statement, Carpus[82] makes a clear allusion to the words of Jesus reported in John 4: 23, 'The true worshippers, according to the Lord's divine instruction, those who worship God in spirit and in truth, take on the image of God's glory and become immortal with him, sharing in eternal life through the Word' (1. 7). The reference to John 4: 23 (in the passage about the Samaritan woman at the well) is unmistakable, and it is related to 'the Lord's divine instruction'. The Word as the agent of eternal life in all probability goes back ultimately to John 1: 1, 14. The teaching that believers may 'take on the image of God's glory...sharing in eternal life through the Word' harks back to John 17, particularly verses 1–3, 22, 24. The Fourth Gospel's unique presentation of the character of true worship, its Christological title, 'the Word', and its emphasis on glory and eternal life, are all referenced in this brief but remarkable confession.

The setting in Asia Minor is significant. Along with Melito of Sardis and Claudius Apollinarius of Hierapolis, Carpus the martyr gives us one more indication of the popularity of the Fourth Gospel throughout Asia Minor in the time before Irenaeus wrote.

Justin Martyr[83]

Justin Martyr was clearly a figure of some prominence among Christians in Rome around the middle of the second century. Trained as a philosopher, this Christian apologist attracted public notoriety in Rome, gaining detractors as well as admirers. He was not a bishop and probably not a presbyter, and thus does not necessarily represent the official hierarchy at Rome at the time. But he certainly was one of the most recognized orthodox and anti-

---

[80] J. den Boeft and J. Bremmer, 'Notiunculae Martyrologicae II', *VC* 36 (1982), 383–402, at 384–5. These authors also suggest that the martyrdom took place after the turn of the 3rd cent. based upon the proconsul's use, in Latin, of the term *principalis*, which is unknown as a legal category until Callistratus, who lived under Septimus Severus and Caracalla. But this depends on the judgement that that Latin text is the original.

[81] Lawlor and Oulton, *Eusebius*, ii. 137; Quasten, *Patrology*, i, 183, calls it a 'genuine, eye-witness account'; see Musurillo's introduction to the work; G. A. Bisbee, *Pre-Decian Acts of Martyrs and Commentarii*, Harvard Dissertations in Religion, 22 (Philadelphia, 1988), 82, 89, 107, too accepts it as a genuine second-century act.

[82] According to the Latin Recension, Carpus was bishop of Gordos, probably Gordos Iulia in Lydia. See H. Musurillo, *The Acts of the Christian Martyrs: Introductions, Texts, and Translations* (Oxford, 1972), 29 n. 10. Musurillo notes that the title of bishop is not in the Greek and may have been an augmentation by the Latin translator.

[83] Greek texts for the *Apologies* are taken from A. Wartelle, *Saint Justin. Apologies. Introduction, texte critique, traduction, commentarie et index*, Études Augustiniennes (Paris, 1987); for the *Dialogue* from M. Marcovich, *Iustini Martyris. Dialogue cum Tryphone*, PTS 47 (Berlin, 1997).

heretical teachers of his day in Rome or elsewhere and thus it should not be assumed that he was very far afield from whatever 'official' expressions were then current in Rome. His first *Apology* was written probably shortly after 150, and his second (if indeed it was a separate writing) at about the same time or not long thereafter.[84] As to the *Dialogue*, it is clear that in its present form it was not published until after the first *Apology* (to which he refers in 120. 6), that is, perhaps 154–60. But it purports to record a debate which probably took place some years earlier when Justin was in Ephesus, and parts of it may have been set down in writing long before the completed work was published. One portion in particular (chs. 98–107) has been thought by some to have been incorporated by Justin from an earlier work of his on the exegesis of Psalm 22.

Justin's status as a well-known Christian scholar and teacher then lends importance to his witness about the use of Christian written authorities. The question of his use of the Fourth Gospel, however, has not been satisfactorily solved, at least not in such a way as has drawn agreement among modern scholars. The evidence has drawn a wide range of judgements: Koester denies that Justin had 'any knowledge of the Fourth Gospel',[85] insisting that the parallels with that Gospel 'derive from an older tradition related to John, not from the gospel itself'.[86] Haenchen also held that 'it cannot be proved that Justin made use of the Gospel of John'.[87] Von Campenhausen did not rule out Justin's knowledge of the Fourth Gospel, but concluded that it was 'ignored' by him.[88] Henry Chadwick holds that Justin's knowledge of the Fourth Gospel is 'less than certain but still the most probable and simple hypothesis',[89] while Robert M. Grant says that it is 'virtually certain'.[90] John Prior thinks Justin knew John's Gospel but did not include it among the 'memoirs of the apostles', and did not regard it as canonical or as the work of an apostle.[91] This was also the view of J. N. Sanders,[92] and is approximately that of L. W. Barnard, who, however, concludes that 'Justin is tentatively feeling his way towards a recognition of the Fourth Gospel'.[93]

---

[84] Koester, *Introduction*, 342. Grant, *Greek Apologists*, 52–3, argues for *c.*156 as the date of composition.

[85] Koester, *ACG* 246.

[86] Koester, *Introduction*, 9.

[87] Haenchen, *John 1*, 13.

[88] Campenhousen, *Formation*, 172.

[89] H. Chadwick, *Early Christian Thought and the Classical Tradition: Studies in Justin, Clement, and Origen* (Oxford, 1966), 124–5.

[90] Grant, *Greek Apologists*, 58–9. Justin's knowledge of the Fourth Gospel is also affirmed by von Loewenich, *Das Johannes-Verständnis*, 45, who finds the similarities in 'Logologie' to reflect a natural development; Metzger, *Canon*, 146–7; Stanton, 'Fourfold Gospel', 330–1; Hengel, *Question*, 12–14.

[91] J. Pryor, 'Justin Martyr and the Fourth Gospel', *The Second Century*, 9 (1992), 153–69, at 157, 166, 169.

[92] Sanders, *Fourth Gospel*, 31, 'Justin's writings illustrate the first tentative use which was made of the Fourth Gospel by an orthodox writer, and this tentativeness makes it difficult to believe that Justin regarded the Fourth Gospel as Scripture or as the work of an apostle.'

[93] L. W. Barnard, *Justin Martyr* (Cambridge, 1967), 63.

Many would bring the gnostic factor into the equation. Koester suggests, 'It is not impossible that Justin rejected that gospel because it was particularly popular among his gnostic opponents'.[94] Culpepper allows that Justin seems to have known the Fourth Gospel but says he 'made only tentative use of it because its origin was suspect or because it had not gained widespread recognition as an apostolic writing',[95] concluding finally that 'it is reasonable to assume that his reticence about using the Gospel was influenced by its popularity among the Gnostics'.[96] Without mentioning Justin by name, many other scholars probably have him in view when they speak of the general Johannophobia which seized the orthodox in the second century.

Moreover, Justin's silence, or near silence, with regard to the Fourth Gospel has been seen as definitive not only for himself as a private Christian teacher and scholar, but for the church at Rome in the middle of the second century. Because, then, the witness of Justin is not only important in its own right, but also has been taken to be representative of the church in Rome in his day, as an instance of orthodox Johannophobia, it will be considered here at some length. It cannot be denied that Justin never mentions any John as the author of a Gospel, even though he explicitly attributes John's Apocalypse to Jesus' apostle John. On the other hand, it is not to be denied that Justin's naming of the author of the Apocalypse is unusual for him, and that his writings contain a not insignificant number of striking parallels with the Fourth Gospel. I remarked earlier that it seems one must either affirm that he indeed knew, and sometimes used, the Fourth Gospel, or agree with Koester, who posits that the Johannine parallels in Justin's writings 'derive from an older tradition related to John, not from the gospel itself'.[97] Now it is time to see which of these options does better justice to the evidence.

Though our cache of Roman Christian writing between Clement of Rome and the end of the second century is not at all plentiful, mere chronology casts this latter option into grave doubt. As we have just seen, Justin's one-time disciple, Tatian, was in no way reluctant to use the Fourth Gospel and treated it as scripture probably while Justin was still alive, and later incorporated it with the three Synoptic Gospels into his *Diatessaron*. Perhaps as early as the 160s Celsus, probably in Rome, can assume a fourfold Gospel in use by Christians. The contemporary *Gospel of Truth*, probably written in Rome before Justin died, also knows the Fourth Gospel, as it knows most of the present New Testament corpus. Hegesippus arrived in Rome from the East in *c.*155–60, at the time Justin was at the height of his publishing activity. We have observed Lawlor's persuasive argument that Hegesippus' *Memoirs*, published fifteen years or so later in Rome, identifies John the author of the Apocalypse as 'the Evangelist.'

---

[94] Koester, *Introduction*, 9.   [95] Culpepper, *John*, 112.   [96] Ibid. 119.
[97] Koester, *Introduction*, 9.

JUSTIN'S APOLOGETIC ENTERPRISE

But why does Justin not cite explicitly from John or mention him by name? This question, if it is seen as implying a negative judgement on the question of Justin's knowledge of John, does not take seriously the apologetic nature of Justin's surviving works.[98] That these works, ostensibly addressed to outsiders, were also intended to instruct Christians in exegesis and apologetic procedure is patent, but their character as addressed to unbelievers has to be recognized in order to put Justin's scriptural knowledge into perspective. This used to be commonly recognized as a complicating factor in the search for Justin's 'canon',[99] but has been quite ignored in some recent writers.[100] Justin's general approach is to accommodate himself as much as possible to the admitted authorities of his opponent, to stay as far as possible within the bounds imposed by them. This can be seen in his comments to Trypho about those OT texts which he charges were excised from the Hebrew Bibles: 'I have not attempted to establish proof about Christ from the passages of Scripture which are not confessed (μὴ ὁμολογουμένων) by you, which I quoted from the words of Jeremiah the prophet, and Esdras, and David; but from those which are even now confessed by you' (*Dial.* 120. 5, cf. chs. 68, 71–3). This is a principle that is, with certain exceptions, generally adhered to by all the early Christian apologists, and is reflected in the apologetic principles of Irenaeus.[101] Thus when Justin first refers to the

---

[98] For what follows, see also C. E. Hill, 'Justin and the New Testament Writings', in E. A. Livingstone (ed.), *Studia Patristica*, 30 (Leuven, 1997), 42–8.

[99] J. B. Lightfoot, *Essays on the Work Entitled* Supernatural Religion *Reprinted from* The Contemporary Review, 2nd edn. (London, 1893), 33, observed over a hundred years ago that, 'In works like these, addressed to Heathens and Jews, who attributed no authority to the writings of Apostles and Evangelists, and for whom the names of the writers would have no meaning, we are not surprised that he refers to those writings for the most part anonymously and with reserve'. Cf. A. H. Charteris, *Canonicity: A Collection of Early Testimonies to the Canonical Books of the New Testament* (Edinburgh, 1880), p. lv. See also Barnard, *Justin Martyr*, 63, 'This, no doubt, is to be explained by his apologetic purpose which prevented his appealing to purely *Christian* teachers and writings as authorities'. Compare Westcott's comment, 'if Justin differs in any way from other similar writers as to the mode in which he introduces his Evangelic quotations, it is because he has described with unusual care the sources from which he drew them. He is not less but more explicit than later Apologists as to the writings from which he derives his accounts of the Lord's life and teaching' (Westcott, *Canon of the New Testament*, 120). See the example of Cyprian (*Demetr.*), who is criticized by Lactantius (*D. Inst.* 5. 4) for citing the Gospels of Matthew and John (though without naming them) in a debate with an unbeliever who regarded such writings as 'vain, fictitious, and false'.

[100] C. H. Cosgrove, 'Justin Martyr and the Emerging Christian Canon: Observations on the Purpose and Destination of the Dialogue with Trypho', *VC* 36 (1982), 209–32, admits this with regard to Justin's *Apologies*, but thinks the *Dialogue* was written with no intention of it being read by outsiders. For a real apologetic motive, however, see *Dial.* 39. 2; 55. 3; 64. 2–3; 92. 6, 142. 2. And for comparison note Celsus' familiarity with another apologetic dialogue between a Jew and a Christian, the *Disputation of Papiscus and Jason* by Aristo of Pella written not long before Justin's Dialogue (Origen, *C. Cels.* 4.52). Further, Eusebius at least regarded Justin's *Dialogue* as 'a dialogue against (πρός) the Jews' (*HE* 4. 18. 6). Finally, even if it were intended only for Christian use, it was intended to instruct them in how to conduct a 'dialogue' with a Jew, and is hence still apologetic literature.

[101] See e.g. *AH* 1. 27. 4, when speaking of Marcion, 'I purpose specially to refute him, convicting him out of his own writings; and, with the help of God, I shall overthrow him out of those

teachings of Jesus in his debate with Trypho (*Dial.* 18. 1), he feels obligated to offer some special 'apology' for doing so. He excuses his practice to Trypho by alluding to the latter's previous admission that he had already carefully read the 'so-called Gospel' (10. 1). 'For since you have read, O Trypho, as you yourself admitted, the doctrines taught (τὰ ... διδαχθέντα) by our Saviour, I do not think that I have done foolishly in adding some short utterances of His to the prophetic statements.' When he later explicitly cites testimonies from 'the Gospel', he does not argue from them as inspired, religious texts (as he might well have held them to be), but seeks primarily to use them as historical accounts which can confirm the fulfilment of prophecy,[102] referring to them as 'memoirs' (ἀπομνημονεύματα, perhaps 'recountings') of the apostles of Jesus (twelve times in *Dial.* 98–107), such as might still be admissible under the constraints of his apologetic method. He never appeals to the apostle Paul, but in a debate with a Jew who surely would have regarded Paul as an apostate, this is not utterly surprising. Likewise, in his *Apologies* addressed to the emperor and the Senate he cites several instances of the teachings of Jesus in an effort to demonstrate that the ethical practices of the Christians are not reprehensible but pure and lofty, and in accord with the truth.

JUSTIN AND THE FOURTH GOSPEL

The Word made flesh

The evidence that Justin knew the Fourth Gospel and that it was important for his Christology in particular is, in my opinion, quite convincing, regardless of the fact that he does not quote the Gospel explicitly or as such, and regardless of the dismal evaluations of many scholars. I begin with observations on several texts which manifest his Logos Christology, none of which, by the way, is reviewed by Koester. Much has been written on Justin's Logos doctrine, which it is not necessary to assess here. It is only necessary to show that, while it is certainly true that the Fourth Gospel and Revelation cannot support every aspect of Justin's doctrine, there are undeniable indications that this Gospel did play a formative role in, perhaps was the impetus for, Justin's developments. This is because the points of contact with John's Logos doctrine are not confined to the term Logos used for

discourses of the Lord and the apostles which are of authority with him, and of which he makes use'. Also note his defence against the heretics in *AH* 3. 11. 7, where he says that the Ebionites can be refuted out of the very Gospel which they use, Marcion can be proved a blasphemer from the passages of Luke which he still retains, those who prefer Mark can be rectified by a true reading of that book, and the Valentinians 'shall be proved to be totally in error by means of this very Gospel' (John), of which they make special use. Since his opponents actually use some at least of the Church's writings as their own authorities, Irenaeus considers that when he refutes them from these writings, 'our proof derived from them is firm and true' (*AH* 3. 11. 7).

[102] For Justin's use of them as history, see Koester, *ACG* 38–42. Koester denies that these written texts could have been regarded as scripture by Justin.

Christ (which happens in the NT only in John's Prologue and in Revelation), but extend to expressions in the same contexts which recall the presentation of John's Prologue.

Justin uses the word Logos a few times early in his apology in the sense of 'reason'. He introduces another meaning, as a title for Jesus Christ as a divine being, in *1Apol.* 5. 'For not only among the Greeks did reason (ὑπὸ λόγου) prevail to condemn these things through Socrates, but also among the Barbarians were they condemned by Reason Himself (ὑπ'αὐτοῦ τοῦ Λόγου), who took shape, and became man (μορφωθέντος καὶ ἀνθρώπου γενομένου), and was called Jesus Christ' (*1Apol.* 5. 4). The pre-existent Logos himself became man, and was called Jesus Christ. This certainly recalls the Prologue of the Fourth Gospel, where, as far as we know, for the first time in literature (unless it be Revelation 19: 13) Jesus Christ is called ὁ λόγος, and specifically it recalls John 1: 14 (καὶ ὁ λόγος σὰρξ ἐγένετο), the first time the title is used in connection with the incarnation.[103] And as to Justin's notion that the Logos has played a guiding role in the reasonable doings of mankind (more explicit in *1Apol.* 46. 2), though it may not have been exactly the thought of the author of the Johannine Prologue, it is not hard to recognize it as an application of John 1: 9 (τὸ φῶς τὸ ἀληθινόν, ὃ φωτίζει πάντα ἄνθρωπον) to a Stoicizing philosophical anthropology. Would this have come simply from general Christian tradition, or Christian philosophical tradition (as a philosophical theme it is not found in Aristides or any Christian predecessor), apart from the impetus of the Fourth Gospel? Justin refers to this Word as divine: 'For the restraint which human laws could not effect, the Word, inasmuch as He is divine (ὁ Λόγος θεῖος ὤν), would have effected' (*1Apol.* 10. 6); ... who also, being the first-begotten Word of God, is even God (ὃς λόγος καὶ πρωτότοκος ὢν τοῦ θεοῦ καὶ θεὸς ὑπάρχει)' (*1Apol.* 63. 15).

The word θεῖος used in *1Apol.* 10. 6 to describe ὁ λογος and the statement that he exists as θεὸς (63. 15) are both reminiscent of John 1: 1, ἐν ἀρχῇ ἦν ὁ λόγος ... καὶ θεὸς ἦν ὁ λόγος, and again imply some kind of relationship with another point in the Johannine Prologue: 'For he gives the second place to the Logos which is with God (τῷ παρὰ θεοῦ Λόγῳ), who he said was placed crosswise in the universe' (*1Apol.* 60. 7). Here Justin is trying to make the case that Plato had read Moses. The subject of the sentence is Plato, but the language of the first clause does not come from Plato, in his *Timaeus* or anywhere else, but from the Fourth Gospel. Justin describes the Logos as τῷ παρὰ θεοῦ Λόγῳ, the Fourth Gospel says ὁ λόγος ἦν πρὸς τὸν θεόν (1: 1); ὡς μονογενοῦς παρὰ πατρός (1: 14); ὁ ὢν παρὰ τοῦ θεοῦ (6: 46). In the second apology he speaks similarly, and refers to the creation of the world through the Son. 'And his Son, who alone is properly called Son, the Word, who also was with Him and was

---

[103] A. Wartelle, *Saint Justin. Apologies* (Paris, 1987), 244.

begotten before the works, when at first He created and arranged all things by him, is called Christ, in reference to his being anointed and God's ordering all things through him' (*2Apol.* 6. 3, 4–5).[104]

Justin knows the Logos as God's only proper or rightful Son (ὁ μόνος λεγόμενος κυρίως υἱός, cf. John 1: 18, δόξαν ὡς μονογενοῦς πατρός), who was with him (συνών, cf. John 1: 1, 2, ἦν πρὸς τὸν θεόν)[105] at the beginning (τὴν ἀρχήν, cf. John 1: 1, 2, ἐν ἀρχῇ), through whom God created all things (δι' αὐτοῦ πάντα ἔκτισε, cf. John 1: 3, πάντα δι' αὐτῷ ἐγένετο). John is not quoted, but Justin's words are but a paraphrase of the Fourth Gospel's teaching about the Logos from its Prologue. Several times Justin speaks of the Word's becoming man or flesh in such a way as to confirm further Justin's knowledge of this passage. Three of these come in chapters 21–3 of the first apology.

…the Word, who is the first-birth (πρῶτον γέννημα) of God, was produced without sexual union (ἄνευ ἐπιμιξίας … γεγεννῆσθαι). (*1Apol.* 21. 1)

And if we assert that the Word of God was begotten of God in a peculiar manner (ἰδίως … γεγεννῆσθαι αὐτὸν ἐκ θεοῦ λέγομεν), different from ordinary generation, let this … be no extraordinary thing to you, who say that Mercury is the angelic word of God.[106] (*1Apol.* 22. 2)

…that Jesus Christ is God's only Son, begotten in a peculiar manner (μόνος ἰδίως Υἱὸς τῷ θεῷ γεγέννηται), being His Word and first-begotten (πρωτότοκος), and power; and, becoming man according to His will (καὶ τῇ βουλῇ αὐτοῦ γενόμενος ἄνθρωπος)[107] (*1Apol.* 23. 2)

The first matter which calls for attention is the way Justin describes Christ as 'Word' of God, as the 'first begotten' (πρῶτον γέννημα) of God, 'begotten of God in a peculiar manner', and 'God's only Son, begotten in a peculiar manner' (μόνος ἰδίως Υἱὸς τῷ θεῷ γεγέννηται). Along with probable influence from Colossians 1: 15 'firstborn of all creation' (πρωτότοκος πάσης κτίσεως),[108] these are quite explicable as permutations of John 1: 1, 14, where the author uses the distinctive title μονογενὴς παρὰ πατρός for the Logos, and possibly John 1: 18, where texts of the so-called Western tradition and citations in the Latin translation of Irenaeus read ὁ μονογενὴς υἱός.[109] Justin's notion of Christ as 'God's only Son, begotten in a peculiar manner' (cf. also *Dial.* 61. 1, 3; 76. 2) is more or less simply a repackaging of John's notion of the pre-existent, divine Word, the monogenes of the Father.

---

[104] Ὁ δὲ υἱὸς ἐκείνου, ὁ μόνος λεγόμενος κυρίως υἱός, ὁ λόγος πρὸ τῶν ποιημάτων καὶ συνὼν καὶ γεννώμενος, ὅτε τὴν ἀρχὴν δι' αὐτοῦ πάντα ἔκτισε καὶ ἐκόσμησε.

[105] Cf. also *Dial.* 62. 4, συνῆν τῷ πατρί.

[106] My translation.

[107] My translation; 'the only proper Son who has been begotten by God', *ANF.*

[108] Cf. the examples of Athenagoras, *Plea* 10. 3 and Tatian in *Oratio* 5. 1, as noted above.

[109] See NA[27]. The word υἱός could also reflect John 3: 16; 1 John 4: 9.

This language is not used by Justin to speak of the incarnation but of Christ's pre-cosmic generation from the Father. The incarnation comes into view in the next phrases, 'produced without sexual union' (*1Apol.* 21. 1), and 'becoming man according to His will' (*1Apol.* 23. 2), to which I now turn as further examples of Johannine influence. Justin's reference in *1Apol.* 21. 1 to Jesus being born 'without sexual union', that is, literally, 'without mixing' (ἄνευ ἐπιμιξίας), is strikingly reminiscent of the early 'Western' textual variation in John 1: 13, which takes it as a Christological statement, substituting ὅς . . . ἐγεννήθη for οἱ ἐγεννήθησαν: 'who was born, not of blood nor of the will of the flesh nor of the will of man, but of God'.[110] This is not to say that Justin had a text with this reading. In fact, his failure to cite the text verbatim may be due in part to his awareness that his Christological application was a 'reading between the lines' of the text. In any case, whether or not the Christological reading actually occurred in a manuscript he used,[111] it is this Johannine text which lies behind this and other passages in Justin's work. Justin's phrase 'without mixing' (ἄνευ ἐπιμιξίας), apparently goes back to the portion of John 1: 13 which speaks of a birth οὐκ ἐξ αἱμάτων, that is, not of the mixing of the blood(s) of a human male and female. This is confirmed later in the *Apology* when Justin speaks of Christ as having 'blood, though not of the seed of man, but of the power of God' (32. 9) as well as by other references in the *Dialogue* to Christ's 'blood not springing from the seed of man' (*Dial.* 54. 2; 63. 2). Likewise, the emphasis on the incarnation taking place through the will of God in *1Apol.* 23. 2 (καὶ τῇ βουλῇ αὐτοῦ γενόμενος ἄνθρωπος), or in *Dial.* 63. 2, where the Johannine language is even more striking, 'since His blood did not spring from the seed of man, but from the will of God' (ὡς τοῦ αἵματος αὐτοῦ οὐκ ἐξ ἀνθρωπείου σπέρματος γεγεννημένου, ἀλλ' ἐκ θελήματος θεοῦ),[112] can only indicate a reliance on the same Johannine source: 'who were born, not of blood or of the will of the flesh or of the will of man, but of God' (οὐδὲ ἐκ θελήματος ἀνδρὸς ἀλλ' ἐκ θεου ἐγεννήθησαν). Notwithstanding that Justin has a penchant for slightly varying his expression in almost every instance, the underlying foundation is unmistakably Johannine.

[110] Such a reading is presupposed in the Latin MS b, is apparently cited thus by Irenaeus and Tertullian, and known later to Ambrose and Augustine (B. H. Streeter, *The Four Gospels* (London, 1926), 70). In recent decades several scholars have argued for the singular reading as original. See the review and arguments for the originality of the plural in J. Pryor, 'Of the Virgin Birth or the Birth of Christians? The Text of John 1:13 Once More', *Nov. T.* 27 (1985), 296–318.

[111] Streeter, *Four Gospels*, 70, long ago proposed that this reading was known to Justin. The discussion in G. R. Beasley-Murray, *John*, WBC 36 (Milton Keynes, 1987), 2, note c, of the relation of the Christological reading to the matter of the virgin birth could be illuminated by Justin's words. The expression οὐκ ἐξ αἱμάτων would not rule out a participation in the blood of Mary. In Justin's interpretation, the plural, ἐξ αἱμάτων, refers to the mixing of the 'bloods' of the male and the female; it would thus not rule out the true participation of the 'begotten' in the human nature of a human parent.

[112] See also *1Apol.* 76. 1; *2Apol.* 6. 4–5;

That Justin's understanding of the incarnation is dependent upon John 1: 13 is further demonstrated by a work written some years earlier and known to rely heavily on the Fourth Gospel, the *Epistula Apostolorum*. In *Ep. Apost.* 3. 2 this author declares that, 'the Word which became flesh through the holy virgin Mary... was born not by the lust of the flesh but by the will of God'. It cannot be supposed that Justin in *Dial.* 63. 2, cited above, is dependent on the *Epistula* without knowledge of its source, John 1: 13, for a part of the verse included by the *Epistula* ('the will of the flesh') is never mentioned by Justin and two parts included by Justin ('the will of man'; born 'of God') are omitted by the *Epistula*. Nor is it credible to posit reliance upon a common source apart from the Fourth Gospel, for the *Epistula*'s thorough dependence upon that Gospel is patent throughout the entire work. Rather, Justin and the author of the *Epistula*, though they may or may not have had a text of John with this variant reading already in it, give unmistakable evidence that the verse and its Christological application were known to each of them (and indicate the motive which must have generated the variant).[113]

One more text from the first *Apology* shows a similar reliance upon the wording of John's description of the incarnation. 'And the first power after God the Father and Lord of all is the Word, who is also the Son; and of Him we will, in what follows, relate how He took flesh and became man (σαρκοποιηθεὶς ἄνθρωπος γέγονεν)' (*1Apol.* 32.10). Of this passage Wartelle says, 'This text seems certainly to be written with precisely the prologue of the Gospel of John in mind'.[114] Wartelle is apparently referring to the mention, again, of 'the Word, who is also the Son', and in particular the use of the word σαρκοποιηθείς, which irresistibly recalls John's unique and striking phrase, καὶ ὁ λόγος σὰρξ ἐγένετο (John 1: 14, cf. also 66. 2; *Dial.* 84. 2; 87. 2; 100. 2).

I take these passages from the first *Apology* to be conclusive already of the fact that Justin knew the Fourth Gospel, at least its Prologue. This passage seems to have played a formative role in his understanding of the pre-existent Christ as the Word of God, his only-begotten Son, begotten after a peculiar manner, and in his notion of the incarnation. Very similar language occurs in several places in the *Dialogue*, some of which will be examined below. At this point it must be mentioned that there is one place in the *Dialogue* where Justin's reference to the Word becoming flesh *seems* to give his source for the teaching: 'For I have proved that he was monogenes to the Father of all things, begotten of him in a peculiar manner as Word and Power, and later having become man through the virgin, as we have learned from the memoirs'.[115] (*Dial.* 105. 1, cf. 100. 2, 4). This comes near the end of a long exposition of Psalm 22, which, Justin seeks to show, refers at length to Jesus Christ. The occasion for the appearance of the word only-

---

[113] See also Irenaeus, *AH* 3. 19. 2, cited below.   [114] Wartelle, *Justin*, 271.
[115] My translation.

begotten (μονογενής) here in fact comes from the Greek translation of Psalm 22: 20, which Justin had cited in 98. 5. Yet the fact that Justin automatically understands this as a Christological title[116] (one which is approximated but not repeated verbatim, as we have seen above, in *1Apol.* 23. 2) seems to demand a cause such as is provided by John 1: 14, 18, 3: 16, 18 (cf. 1 John 4: 9). This is because in its context in the Psalm, the word monogenes is not a name for God's 'only-begotten', but the sufferer's! That Justin is being provoked by one or more of these Johannine sources is further supported by the following reference to the Word, and his becoming man, concepts which, as we have seen above, must be based in some way on the Prologue of the Fourth Gospel.

But the important new contribution of this text is that here Justin seems to inform us of his source for what he asserts about the Word: 'as we have learned from the memoirs'. Grant says, 'It is hard to restrict what the apostles taught to the virgin birth'.[117] That is, it seems, at least on the surface, that it should include also his being the Word, the 'only-begotten', and becoming man. On the other hand, Pryor has argued that what Justin attributes to the memoirs should indeed be restricted to the virgin birth. In opposition to D. M. Davey,[118] he writes,

Grammatically, the sentence can be so translated that 'as we have learned from the memoirs' is a reference not just to the virginal birth but also to the demonstration of Christ's status with the Father...I believe, however, that one test can be conducted to find Justin's meaning. He says that he has already demonstrated (προεδήλωσα) his case. It should be possible from a study of Justin's method of argument and demonstration to resolve our problem. If Davey is correct, we could find evidence of *direct* dependence on John 1 in the argument of the earlier chapters.[119]

Pryor does not find any direct quotations from the Fourth Gospel in Justin's preceding argument for the virgin birth, though he acknowledges allusions, while he does on the other hand find a narration taken 'from the Matthean and Lukan accounts' of the virginal conception and birth of Jesus in *Dial.* 78 (though even here these sources are not named, and there is no introductory formula).[120] Thus, he concludes that Justin meant to assert only that he had already proved from the memoirs that Jesus was born of a virgin, and that the memoirs included Matthew and Luke, but not John. And yet the matter cannot be so neatly resolved. Justin makes two assertions in this sentence: that he has proved something (that Jesus is God's mono-genes), and that he has found something in the memoirs (at least that Jesus became man through the virgin, and possibly also that he was God's mono-

---

[116] ...τὴν μονογενῆ μου, in parallelism with τὴν ψυχήν μου.
[117] Grant, *Greek Apologists*, 58.
[118] D. M. Davey, 'Justin Martyr and the Fourth Gospel', *Scripture*, 17 (1965), 117–22.
[119] Pryor, 'Justin Martyr', 156–7.
[120] Ibid. 157.

genes, divinely begotten in a peculiar manner).[121] Justin does not say that
he has 'proved' either of these assertions 'from the memoirs', only that he
has learnt something from the memoirs.[122] The plural, 'as we have learned
from the memoirs', evidently refers not to Justin and Trypho but to Justin
and other Christians.[123] Later in the same chapter he makes a similar
claim: 'For when Christ was giving up his spirit on the cross, he said,
"Father, into thy hands I commend my spirit," as I have learned also from
the memoirs' (105. 5). This, as the singular shows even more clearly here,
signifies something Justin has learnt, not what he can assume that Trypho
and his friends have learnt up to this point. In fact, in chapter 87 Trypho had
been careful to attribute these very beliefs mentioned in 105. 1 to Justin
alone and not to himself, 'and you maintain him to be pre-existent God,
and having become incarnate by God's will, to be born man by the virgin'.
Thus, what Justin speaks of in 105. 1 as something he has learnt from the
memoirs is not necessarily something he has demonstrated in the debate by
formal citation of the memoirs. As was mentioned, this might include 'that
he was monogenes to the Father of all things, begotten of him in a peculiar
manner as Word and Power', but it at least includes his 'later having
become man through the virgin'. If what he refers to the memoirs includes
the former, the unique relationship to the Father, then the memoirs must
surely include the Fourth Gospel, for such teachings—and most distinctively, Jesus as God's monogenes—appear clearly only there and in no other
source which could possibly be considered to be among 'the memoirs'. But
even if it should include only the latter, the virgin birth of God's monogenes, it unlikely that Luke 1: 35 (which he quoted in 100. 5) is the only
source in mind. This is because for Justin the birth of the Christ from a
virgin is only, so to speak, the middle act of a very long story. It does not

---

[121] The predicate of the sentence, that which Justin says he has already proved, is that 'he was
the only-begotten of the Father of all things'. Two participial clauses then follow, further describing
this monogenes of the Father as (a) generated from the Father after a peculiar manner as Word and
Power, and (b) having become man through the virgin. It is at least the incarnation, and possibly
the eternal divinity and generation of the monogenes, which is credited to the memoirs of the
apostles.

[122] Pryor is correct that ch. 78 contains a summary of the events surrounding the birth of Jesus
taken from Matthew and Luke. But even here, Justin does not name his Christian sources. Trypho
may well know that Justin is now relying on 'the so-called Gospel' to which he had referred in ch.
10, but neither 'the Gospel' nor 'the memoirs' are mentioned. He returns to the incarnation,
however, in ch. 100. The 'Gospel' and the 'memoirs of his apostles' are mentioned in this chapter,
but only Luke 1: 35 is cited explicitly for attestation of the incarnation. In this section, however, we
also seem to have Johannine allusions. In 100. 2 it is stated that Christians know Christ to be 'the
firstborn of God and to be before all creatures; likewise to be the son of the patriarchs, since he was
made flesh (σαρκοποιηθείς) by the virgin of their family, and submitted to become a man' (my
translation). As we have seen before in our consideration of *1Apol.* 32. 10; 66. 2 (in the *Dialogue* he
uses the word in 84. 2; 87. 2), this is based on John 1: 14 and belongs to a whole vocabulary of
ontological and incarnational terms which are indebted to John's Prologue.

[123] ἐμάθομεν in 105. 1; συνήκαμεν in 81. 3 and νενοήκαμεν in 75. 1; 100. 1, all refer to
something Justin and other Christians have learnt, understood, or perceived from the scriptures, but
which cannot be attributed to Trypho and his friends.

represent the beginning of the Christ's existence, but is the momentous transition to human flesh of the one who was pre-existent God, the Father's monogenes, begotten in a peculiar manner as Word and Power, who was made flesh not as a man of men, not by the mixing of human blood lines, but through the will of God.

That is to say, (a) Justin's understanding of the virgin birth is itself inseparable from his conception of the pre-existent, divine Word, a conception which is greatly indebted to the Prologue of John's Gospel, and (b) even Justin's understanding of the virgin birth itself has been profoundly influenced and, one must say, to a large degree formed, by the Prologue of the Fourth Gospel. We have seen this, I believe, from the *First Apology*, and it is the case in the *Dialogue* as well. I have already noted a tendency in Christian theology to amalgamate John's description of the incarnation from his Prologue with Luke's account of the annunciation to Mary observable in *Epistle of the Apostles* and in the Christian portions of the *Sibylline Oracles* 1 and 8. Justin's practice is of a piece with this.

The roots of this statement in *Dial.* 105. 1 go back at least to 54. 2 (there are two passing references to the virgin birth in 23. 3; 43. 1). It is here that Justin introduces his exposition of Jacob's blessing of Judah in Genesis 49: 11, 'he shall wash his garments with wine, and his vesture with the blood of the grape'. According to Justin's typological exegesis, this 'signified that he would wash those that believe in him with his own blood'. He continues,

That the Scripture mentions the blood of the grape has been evidently designed, because Christ derives blood not from the seed of man, but from the power of God. For as God, and not man, has produced the blood of the vine, so also [the Scripture] has predicted that the blood of Christ would be not of the seed of man, but of the power of God. But this prophecy, sirs, which I repeated, proves that Christ is not man of men, begotten in the ordinary course of humanity.

This exegesis of the blood of the grape, consistent with what we have seen above, depends on the text of John 1: 13 taken Christologically.[124] Then in *Dial.* 63. 2, when asked by Trypho to prove 'that he submitted to become man by the virgin, according to the will of his Father', Justin replies,

This, too, has been already demonstrated by me in the previously quoted words of the prophecies, my friends ... The passage, then, which Isaiah records, 'Who shall declare his generation? for his life is taken away from the earth' [Isa. 53: 8],—does it not appear to you to refer to one who, not having descent (τὸ γένος) from men, was said to be delivered over to death by God for the transgressions of the people?—of whose blood, Moses (as I mentioned before), when speaking in parable, said, that he would wash his garments in the blood of the grape; since his blood did not spring from the seed of man, but from the will of God.

---

[124] It is perhaps because he knows the Gospel text refers to the corporate body of those who believe in him, not directly to the Logos himself, that he does not quote this verse explicitly.

That the last part of this is indeed based on the Christological reading of John 1: 13 is shown more clearly by Irenaeus in *AH* 3. 19. 2, in a passage where he is refuting Jews, Ebionites, and Cerinthians who insist that Jesus was 'simply a mere man, begotten by Joseph' (3. 19. 1), where Irenaeus borrows the exegesis of both Isaiah 53: 8 and John 1: 13 from Justin:

> For this reason [it is said], 'Who shall declare his generation?' [Isa. 53: 8] since 'He is a man, and who shall recognise him?' [Jer. 17: 9] But he to whom the Father which is in heaven has revealed him, knows him,[125] so that he understands that he who 'was not born either by the will of the flesh, or by the will of man,' [John 1: 13] is the Son of man, this is Christ, the Son of the living God.

In other words, the text of John 1: 1–18 is eminent both in Justin's conception of Jesus as the monogenes of the Father, divinely begotten after a peculiar manner, through whom God created all things and endowed mankind with reason, and in Justin's conception of Jesus as humanly born, not as man of men (*Dial.* 54. 2), begotten not from the seed of man (*Dial.* 54. 2; 63. 2) but by an act of the Father's will (*Dial.* 61. 1; 63. 2). It thus will have to appear the most reasonable conclusion that when Justin says in passing that he, and other Christians, have learnt from the memoirs that Jesus is the Father's monogenes, who later became man through the virgin, he indeed has the Fourth Gospel in mind. This is particularly significant because of Justin's use of the plural, implying that this portion of the 'memoirs' was also known among his Christian companions for teaching these things.[126]

At any rate John's Prologue is a primary source for Justin's Christology, both in terms of ontology and incarnation.[127] Though Justin's general vocabulary is not replete with Johannine associations, we must none the less say that in these aspects of his Christology, and in the related development of his Logos doctrine, the Johannine Prologue has played a formative role. Probable allusions to John 1: 1, 2, 3, 9, 13, 14, and possibly 18, have been recognized in this role. If this is so, despite the lack of formal citation, one cannot regard the Fourth Gospel as a work of marginal importance to Justin.[128] It indeed appears from the passages considered above that John's

---

[125] An allusion to Matt. 11: 27/Lk. 10: 22; cf. Justin, *Dial.* 100. 1.

[126] Here he could not be referring to Valentinian Christians. If indeed the Valentinian attempt to use the Prologue to John's Gospel to illustrate their conjunctions had been made by this time (and this is at least doubtful), this approach did not glean from the Prologue a reference to Jesus as God's monogenes or his becoming man through a virgin.

[127] Pryor, 'Justin Martyr', 162–3, 'I believe it is right to conclude that Justin does know John's Logos doctrine, and indeed that the Johannine Logos is the starting point for his (and that of other second century apologists') developed Christology...There simply is no evidence that the apologists derived their initial impetus for developing a Logos Christology from any source except Johannine Christianity'. Cf. Hengel, *Question*, 13, who states that Justin's Logos Christology 'is inconceivable without the prologue of John'.

[128] Pryor, 'Justin Martyr', 162, concludes, 'In none of his writings could it have served his interests to quote from the 4G as an authority. Neither Trypho nor any pagan audience for the Apologies would have been impressed by the authority of that Gospel. But failure to cite it as an authority and failure to make extensive use of it are not the same thing.'

Gospel belonged to the group Justin called the 'memoirs of the apostles'. I shall return to this topic below.

Born again *(1Apol. 61. 4)*

In one section of his first apology Justin seeks to inform the rulers about 'the manner in which we dedicated ourselves to God when we had been made new through Christ' (*1Apol.* 61. 1). He proceeds to speak of the Christian baptismal practice as he knows it in Rome.

Then they are brought by us where there is water, and are regenerated in the same manner in which we were ourselves regenerated. For, in the name of God, the Father and Lord of the universe, and of our Saviour Jesus Christ, and of the Holy Spirit, they then receive the washing with water. For Christ also said, 'Except ye be born again, ye shall not enter into the kingdom of heaven' (Ἂν μὴ ἀναγεννηθῆτε, οὐ μὴ εἰσέλθητε εἰς τὴν βασιλείαν τῶν οὐρανῶν).

The resemblance to John 3: 3, 5 is undeniably close, but not verbally exact. Koester thus believes the words attributed to Christ by Justin are not beholden to the Fourth Gospel at all, but are derived instead 'from the free tradition' through a current baptismal liturgy.[129] In this he is agreeing with Bellinzoni and Hillmer.[130] But apart from the fact that the correspondence with neither of Jesus' two sayings in John 3: 3 and 5 is verbally exact,[131] something which is hardly out of keeping either with Justin's usual 'citation' habits,[132] or with the custom of the times,[133] there is no reason to suppress one's immediate impression that Justin is indeed referring to Jesus' words in this passage.[134] That Justin has 'born again' (ἀναγεννάω) instead of John's 'born from above' (γεννάω ἄνωθεν) may be due, as some have suggested, to confusion with some other source (1 Pet. 1: 3), or to a faulty memory of John 3: 3. And yet, in his study of quotations in philosophical works, Whittaker notes

---

[129] Koester, *ACG* 361. Koester cites Justin's use of the word ἀναγεννηθῆτε as evidence that his version of the saying is independent of and more original than John's (258, 362). Koester also alleges that the Johannine 'you cannot see' of John 3: 3, instead of 'you cannot enter' in Justin, is more evidence of a discrepancy (258), forgetting for the moment that John 3: 5 also has 'you cannot enter'.

[130] A. J. Bellinzoni, *The Sayings of Jesus in the Writings of Justin Martyr*, Suppl. Nov. T. 17 (Leiden, 1967), 136–7, 'Justin has independently preserved a liturgical baptismal text in a form older than that found in John and that John's text is probably based on the same or on a similar tradition'; Hillmer, 'Second Century', 54–8.

[131] John 3: 3, ἐὰν μή τις γεννηθῇ ἄνωθεν, οὐ δύναται ἰδεῖν τὴν βασιλείαν τοῦ θεοῦ; 3: 5, ἐὰν μή τις γεννηθῇ ἐξ ὕδατος καὶ πνεύματος, οὐ δύναται εἰσελθεῖν εἰς τὴν βασιλείαν τοῦ θεοῦ.

[132] Wartelle, *Justin*, 290. Pryor, 'Justin Martyr', 164, 'verbal variation of Justin from John 3 proves nothing'. Much of the disagreement about whether Justin here or elsewhere is dependent upon John goes to the criterion of exact reproduction, which is heavily relied upon by those who deny literary dependence. See the final section of Ch. 2 above.

[133] Whittaker, 'Indirect Tradition'.

[134] Wartelle, *Justin*, 290, who says this is 'an incontestable borrowing from the Fourth Gospel'.

the category of substitutions, in particular the substitution of cognate terms and synonyms. These constitute, in my experience, the commonest form of variation in the indirect tradition of philosophical texts.... excessively common are the substitution of compound verbs for simple verbs or *vice versa*, or the substitution of different compounds, variations in the degrees of comparison of adjectives and adverbs, the substitution of singular forms for plural or *vice versa*, or, more drastically, the substitution of cognate nouns or participles in place of verbs, or *vice versa*.[135]

It is likely that Justin simply felt the substitute word ἀναγεννάω would be less perplexing to a pagan audience than the expression 'born from above'.[136] At any rate he had already adopted ἀναγεννάω as his customary term for regeneration through baptism, having already used it three times in the first part of the paragraph,[137] and this modification in the text of John 3: 3, 5 is in keeping with this chosen theological vocabulary. As we have seen above, Tatian would soon use the same lexical modification of John 3: 3 or 5 in a context in which there are other explicit references to the Fourth Gospel (*Or.* 5. 3). Justin's substitution of οὐ μὴ εἰσέλθητε εἰς τὴν βασιλείαν τῶν οὐρανῶν for John's οὐ δύναται εἰσελθεῖν εἰς τὴν βασιλείαν τοῦ θεοῦ (John 3: 5) is probably due, as some have suggested, to a conflation, either conscious[138] or unconscious, with Matthew 18: 3 (οὐ μὴ εἰσέλθητε εἰς τὴν βασιλείαν τῶν οὐρανῶν).[139] It is a natural enough slip for those well acquainted with the similar saying in Matthew. Even the original scribe of codex ℵ wrote βασιλείαν τῶν οὐρανῶν as he was copying John 3: 5 from his archetype.[140] According to Romanides,[141] all citations of John 3: 3–5 before Origen, have 'kingdom of heaven' instead of 'kingdom of God'.

It is also important to notice that Justin does not cite these words of Christ as coming from the liturgy or as part of the liturgy; he cites them as words of Christ which justify and explain the practice of the Christians. Nor do any of the authors cited by Bellinzoni (Hippolytus, *Ref.* 8. 10; *Apost. Const.* 6. 15; Pseudoclementine, *Hom.* 11. 26, Pseudoclementine, *Recogn.* 6. 9)[142] as

---

[135] Whittaker, 'Indirect Tradition', 83, 84.

[136] Pryor, 'Justin Martyr', 165.

[137] 61. 3, 4. He also uses the noun ἀναγέννησις in 61. 3; 66. 1 and in *Dial.* 138. 2. Cf. τὸ μυστήριον τῆς πάλιν γενέσεως ἡμῶν in *Dial.* 85. 7. Ἀναγεννάω may have been, as J. S. Romanides thinks, 'Justin Martyr and the Fourth Gospel', *The Greek Orthodox Theological Review*, 4 (1958–9), 115–34, at 127, a technical term for the baptismal rite in Justin's day. At least it was the term Justin had adopted.

[138] Whittaker, 'Indirect Tradition', 89, speaks of a practice among philosophical writers of 'conflation into one reminiscence of disparate texts drawn from one or more authors'.

[139] Romanides, 'Justin Martyr and the Fourth Gospel', 131–2; Pryor, 'Justin Martyr', 165, 'surely by the second century, texts such as Matthew 18: 3 and John 3: 3, 5 would have been understood baptismally with a resulting fusing of texts!'

[140] See R. Swanson (ed.), *New Testament Greek Manuscripts: Variant Readings Arranged in Horizontal Lines Against Codex Vaticanus. John* (Sheffield, 1995), 28.

[141] Romanides, 'Justin Martyr and the Fourth Gospel', 130–1.

[142] Hippolytus, *Ref.* 8. 10. 8 ἐὰν μή τις γεννηθῇ ἐξ ὕδατος καὶ πνεύματος, οὐκ εἰσελεύσεται εἰς τὴν βασιλείαν τῶν οὐρανῶν; *Apost. Const.* 6. 15 ἐὰν μή τις βαπτισθῇ ἐξ ὕδατος καὶ

attesting to a common, 'traditional baptismal saying' allegedly known to them and to Justin, give the saying of Jesus as part of a baptismal liturgy, but rather as part of an explanation of baptism. All seem to conflate, in various ways, the two forms of Jesus' saying in John 3: 3 and 5, despite all having 'kingdom of heaven' instead of 'kingdom of God'. The discrepancies which exist between them would seem to make the search for single, common wording, if it is not John 3: 3, 5, rather hopeless.[143] This is not to mention the fact that early liturgical sources which do give instruction for baptismal practice, like *Didache* 7, the *Apostolic Tradition* 20–1 of Hippolytus, the latter pertaining to Rome, contain nothing which corresponds to this. And, in any case, why we should regard a hypothetical baptismal tract (Bellinzoni speaks in terms of written, not simply oral, tradition), which we do not know that anyone ever possessed, as a more probable source for these words than the Fourth Gospel, which we have good reason to believe that each of these authors possessed, is not easy to comprehend.

There is another crucial factor in this debate which is surprisingly ignored by Koester, Hillmer, and Bellinzoni (and consequently by scholars who rely on them). None of these scholars takes into account, or even reports, the words which follow immediately this saying of Jesus in the text of Justin's *Apology* (61. 5),[144] 'Now, that it is impossible for those who have once been born to enter into their mothers' wombs, is manifest to all', words which echo the dumbfounded reply of Nicodemus in John 3: 4[145] and which tend to show again that Justin is adapting his source, not directly quoting it.[146] Did the alleged baptismal tract contain these words as well? Certainly no correspondences can be found in the four parallel texts cited by Bellinzoni. Or shall we believe that Justin and the Johannine author

---

πνεύματος, οὐ μὴ εἰσέλθη εἰς τὴν βασιλείαν τῶν οὐρανῶν; *Clem. Hom.* 11. 26 ἀμὴν ὑμῖν λέγω, ἐὰν μὴ ἀναγεννηθῆτε ὕδατι ζῶντι, εἰς ὄνομα πατρὸς, υἱοῦ, ἁγίου πνεύματος, οὐ μὴ εἰσέλθητε εἰς τὴν βασιλείαν τῶν οὐρανῶν; *Clem. Rec.* 6. 9 *Amen dico vobis, nisi quis denuo renatus fuerit ex aqua viva, non introibit in regna coelorum.* The Clementine examples show that they are primarily based on Matt. 18: 3 even in the first part of the 'saying' (ἀμὴν ὑμῖν λέγω). Hippolytus and the *Apost. Const.* preserve John's ἐὰν μή τις γεννηθῆ [*Apost Const.* βαπτισθῆ] ἐξ ὕδατος καὶ πνεύματος. Justin is based on John here too, though he drops the indefinite singular pronoun to make the address to a second-person-plural audience.

[143] See also Nagel, *Rezeption*, 97–9.

[144] Bellinzoni (1962) and Hillmer (1966) did their dissertations at Harvard. Koester taught at Harvard for many years. This argues for the existence of a unique 'Harvard-text' of Justin Martyr which lacks *1Apol.* 61. 5. (An earlier form of this text may have been known as well to Sanders, *Fourth Gospel*, 27–8.)

[145] ὅτι δὲ καὶ ἀδύνατον εἰς τὰς μήτρας τῶν τεκουσῶν τοὺς ἅπαξ γεννωμένους ἐμβῆναι, φανερὸν πᾶσιν ἐστι (*1Apol.* 61. 5); πῶς δύναται ἄνθρωπος γεννηθῆναι γέρων ὤν; μὴ δύναται εἰς τὴν κοιλίαν τῆς μητρὸς αὐτοῦ δεύτερον εἰσελθεῖν καὶ γεννηθῆναι (John 3: 4).

[146] Hillmer, 'Second Century', 57, claims the supposed absence of characteristic Johannine features in Justin as 'a strong indication that Justin has received the saying independently of John'. But the reference to being born again (Ibid. 55–6), and the comment about the impossibility of entering one's mother's womb again, are characteristic Johannine features taken over by Justin.

came up with them independently?[147] That Justin writes these words immediately after repeating what is to all appearances a close paraphrase of
Jesus' words in John 3: 3, 5 shows instead that he is, as Grant so sensibly
says, simply 'following the line of argument in John 3: 3–4'.[148]

Justin's use of John 3: 3–5 in his explanation of Christian baptism in
1Apol. 61. 4–5 indicates that he considered John's narrative of Nicodemus'
encounter with Jesus to be the record of a historical event, and the words
there attributed to Jesus to be authentic—though he did not care to be
verbally exact in his reproduction of it. This Johannine passage was one of
several which informed Justin's theology of baptism, and it joins the Johannine Prologue in a group of Johannine texts which played key roles in both
his theology and his understanding of the sacrament.

Jesus' baptism

There is another apparent link to the Fourth Gospel in *Dial.* 88. 7.[149] To
catch the significance of this connection it is necessary to back up to the
previous chapter. Trypho is puzzled over Justin's assertion that Christ is 'pre-
existent God', in the light of the prophecy of Isaiah 11. 1–2, which predicts
that the Messiah would be 'filled with the powers of the Holy Ghost, which
the Scripture by Isaiah enumerates, as if He were in lack of them' (87. 2).
Justin's reply is that 'these enumerated powers of the Spirit have come on
Him, not because He stood in need of them, but because they would rest
in Him, i.e., would find their accomplishment in Him' (88. 3). At length
Justin comes to that event in Jesus' life wherein this was realized, his baptism
in the Jordan by John the Baptist. The amazing outward events which took
place at that time were necessary, he says, so that people could know who
indeed was the Christ. For some had supposed that John was the Christ,
'but he cried to them, "I am not the Christ, but the voice of one crying; for
he that is stronger than I shall come, whose shoes I am not worthy to bear"'.
Koester correctly points out, 'The answer "I am not the Christ" has a parallel only in the Gospel of John; the continuation of the Baptist's answer in
Justin ("but the voice of a crier") also recalls the text of the Fourth Gospel'.[150]
John, indeed, records not one but two instances of the Baptist's denial that he
is the Christ (1: 20; 3: 28), and the author himself writes in his Prologue that
'he was not the light, but came to bear witness to the light' (1: 8). Koester,
however, is unwilling to say that this signifies Justin's knowledge of the Fourth
Gospel,[151] suggesting instead that Justin might have put this together from

---

[147] As Culpepper, *John*, 113, does, 'The protest that one cannot literally be born again can be
made any time such metaphorical language is used. Here too, Justin need not be citing John 3: 3–5'.
[148] Grant, *Greek Apologists*, 59; cf. Wartelle, *Justin*, 290; L. W. Barnard, *St. Justin Martyr: The First
and Second Apologies*, ACW 56 (New York., 1997), 173. n. 370.
[149] Hillmer, 'Second Century', 59–62; Koester, *ACG* 391; Nagel, *Rezeption*, 100–2.
[150] Koester, *ACG* 391.
[151] Ibid., 'That Justin knew the Gospel of John, or the tradition about John the Baptist that was
used in this Gospel, cannot be categorically excluded. But this singular similarity with John's text is

the text of Isaiah 40: 3 (the voice of the crier) and Luke 3: 15 (who alone of the other three Evangelists says anything about John being considered the Christ). But by now it is becoming increasingly hard to believe that Justin could have obtained from so many disparate sources so many details found explicitly only in the Fourth Gospel—or that his mind could have taken independently the same courses already charted by the Fourth Gospel's author—and yet not have known this Gospel.

Nor should it be missed that these are not the only Johannine allusions in this passage. The notion of the Spirit of the Lord 'resting' (Isa. 11: 2) on Jesus, which was the subject of Trypho's original question, also seems to go to John's account of Jesus' baptism. According to Justin, that the Spirit of the Lord would rest upon the Messiah signifies not that he stood in need of the powers of the Spirit, but that 'they would rest in him, i.e., would find their accomplishment in him' (*Dial.* 88. 3). This was signified when at his baptism the Holy Spirit lighted on Jesus like a dove, and remained on him. Only the Fourth Gospel records the 'remaining' of the Spirit on Jesus, and it is a peculiar emphasis of the Baptist in this Gospel: 'And John bore witness, "I saw the Spirit descend as a dove from heaven, and it remained on him. I myself did not know him; but he who sent me to baptize with water said to me, 'He on whom you see the Spirit descend and remain, this is he who baptizes with the Holy Spirit'"' (John 1: 32–3). Again we find Justin emphasizing a point in the gospel history emphasized only by the author of the Fourth Gospel.

And here is another interesting point. Earlier in the chapter, when Justin referred to the Holy Spirit lighting on Jesus like a dove, he attested that this fact is something 'the apostles of this very Christ of ours wrote (ἔγραψεν)' (*Dial.* 88. 3). The account of the Spirit's descent at Jesus' baptism is recorded in all four canonical Gospels, but only Matthew and John are Gospels which, according to early Christian tradition, were actually written by apostles, Mark and Luke being written by followers of apostles. As we shall see later, Justin himself apparently knows this tradition. It is significant that Justin does not refer here to 'the memoirs' or to 'the memoirs of the apostles', names for the Gospels which would include apostolic reports written by a follower. He refers instead to things which Jesus' apostles themselves 'wrote'. Thus when Justin says he has gained information about the lighting of the Spirit on Christ at his baptism from accounts not merely 'handed down' by Christ's apostles but 'written' by them, it is likely that he is not simply speaking loosely. If he had vociferously derided the Fourth Gospel as the product of heresy (like one of Charlesworth's 'many pre-Nicene critics'), or perhaps even if there were no trace of influence from the Fourth Gospel in Justin's writings,

too weak to be a basis for the argument of Justin's acquaintance with the Fourth Gospel. It is possible that Justin developed the answer of the Baptist on the basis of Luke's text and the Isaiah prophecy.' But this 'similarity with John's text' is far from singular and is not the only basis for the argument. Koester does not begin to reckon with the extent of the evidence.

we might have grounds for doubting that Justin held to the common second-century tradition about the origin of the Fourth Gospel. But since we have seen, on the contrary, that this Gospel evidently was a key influence on Justin's sacramental and Christological thought, and particularly because the text of John's account of Jesus' baptism is in use *in this very context*, there is no reason to deny and every reason to affirm that Justin does have John's Gospel in mind at this point. This would certainly suggest that he considers this source to have been 'written' by an apostle of Jesus.

Jesus' crucifixion, and 'the acts'

In *1Apol.* 35 Justin mentions for the emperor several OT prophecies which were fulfilled in the events surrounding Jesus' crucifixion. There are three points he mentions here which parallel the Fourth Gospel specifically. The first comes in his interpretation of Isaiah 58: 2, 'They now ask of me judgment, and dare to draw near to God' (*1Apol.* 35. 4). In it there are parallels with John and with the *Gospel of Peter* which require some sort of relationship. Justin says, 'as the prophet spoke, they tormented him, and set him on the judgment-seat (αὐτὸν ἐκάθισαν ἐπὶ βήματος), and said, "Judge us"'. This seems to derive from a reading of John 19: 13, the only Gospel to speak of a βῆμα at Jesus' trial: 'When Pilate heard these words, he brought Jesus out and ἐκάθισεν on the judgment seat (ἐπὶ βήματος) at a place called The Pavement, and in Hebrew, Gabbatha' (John 19: 13). But instead of Pilate sitting on the βῆμα, Justin has read ἐκάθισεν as referring to Jesus.[152] This is in fact what allows Isaiah 58: 2 to be related to the events of the passion of Jesus. The same exegetical tradition, related again to the ἐκάθισεν of John 19: 13, apparently lies behind the *Gospel of Peter*, which says, 'And they put upon him a purple robe and set him on the judgment seat (ἐκάθισεν αὐτὸν ἐπὶ καθέδραν κρίσεως) and said, "Judge righteously, O king of Israel"' (3. 7). For convenience, the three accounts are laid out here.

1 APOL. 35. 6	GOSP. OF PET. 3. 6–7	JOHN 19: 13
καὶ γάρ, ὡς εἶπεν ὁ προφήτης, διασύροντες αὐτὸν ἐκάθισαν ἐπὶ βήματος καὶ εἶπον· Κρῖνον ἡμῖν.	καὶ ἔλεγον· σύρωμεν τὸν υἱὸν τοῦ θεοῦ ἐξουσίαν αὐτοῦ ἐσχηκότες· καὶ πορφύραν αὐτὸν περιέβαλον καὶ ἐκάθισαν αὐτὸν ἐπὶ καθέδραν κρίσεως λέγοντες· Δικαίως κρῖνε, βασιλεῦ τοῦ Ἰσραήλ.	ὁ οὖν Πιλᾶτος ἀκούσας τῶν τούτων λόγων ἤγαγεν ἔξω τὸν Ἰησοῦν καὶ ἐκάθισεν ἐπὶ βήματος εἰς τόπον λεγόμενον Λιθόστρωτον, Ἑβραιστὶ δὲ Γαββαθά.

---

[152] For modern commentators who have accepted a transitive meaning for ἐκάθισεν, see the commentaries of Barrett and Brown.

Koester believes Justin, the *GP*, and the Fourth Gospel must be based on a common written source.[153] But no such source is known, and it is much simpler to suppose that the common source for Justin and the *GP* is the Fourth Gospel, combined with an exegesis of Isaiah 58: 2. As Koester himself says, 'the *Gospel of Peter* cannot have been Justin's source, because he uses the word βῆμα for "judgment seat," like John 19: 13'.[154] But Justin could have been the *Gospel of Peter*'s source,[155] or they could simply represent two instances of an exegetical tradition based on John 19: 13[156] read in the light of Isaiah 58: 2.[157] We have already seen decisive evidence above for the *Gospel of Peter*'s dependence upon John.[158]

Justin then cites the words of Psalm 22: 16, 'They pierced my hands and my feet', and says this expression 'was used in reference to the nails (ἥλοι) of the cross which were fixed in his hands and feet' (35. 7). Psalm 22, of course, does not refer to any nails.[159] The nails are another detail mentioned in the *Gospel of Peter*, in its account of the descent from the cross, where the Jews are said to have drawn them out of Jesus' hands (6. 21).[160] That Jesus was held to the cross by nails (as opposed to rope, etc.), is mentioned by none of the Synoptic Gospels, but only in the Fourth Gospel's story of the encounter of Thomas with the risen Christ (20: 25, 27).[161]

Justin goes on to mention the dividing of Jesus' garments and the casting of lots, according to Psalm 22: 18, something all four of the canonical Gospels record. Though all of these Gospels clearly allude to this Psalm text in their description of the events, John's is the only one to cite it formally, as does Justin. In one of his references to the casting of lots for Jesus' garments (*Dial.* 97. 3) Justin substitutes the word λαχμός for the word κλῆρος, used in the LXX and in all four of the Gospels. The author of the *GP* does the same (4. 12). It may be significant then that of the four canonical Gospels John's is the only one to use a form of this word, when, before citing Psalm 22: 18, the author quotes the soldiers conversing about

[153] Koester, *ACG* 397.
[154] Ibid.
[155] The *GP*'s σύρωμεν, related to Justin's διασύροντες, would suggest this.
[156] On the tendency of particular 'misquotations' to show up throughout a commentary or expositional tradition, see Whittaker, 'Indirect Tradition'.
[157] The Δικαίως κρῖνε of the *GP* probably goes back directly to κρίσιν δικαίαν of the LXX.
[158] The purple robe mentioned in the *GP* also comes ultimately either from either Mark 15: 17 or John 19: 2.
[159] The word ὤρυξαν does not necessarily mean 'they pierced', but more precisely, 'they dug'.
[160] *Ps. Barn.* 5. 14 cites a condensation of Ps. 119: 120, 'nail my flesh' (καθήλωσόν μου τὰς σάρκας) in reference to the crucifixion; Ignatius, *ISmyrn.* 1. 1–2 also refers to Christ being nailed (καθηλωμένος) for us, and our being established in faith 'as if nailed to the cross of the Lord Jesus Christ'. See Koester, *ACG* 397.
[161] That John mentions them not in his account of the crucifixion but in the story of Thomas after the resurrection is hardly evidence, as Koester, *ACG* 397 n. 2, seems to think, against John being the source for Justin and the *GP*. Justin refers to the nails in the context of the crucifixion, but the *GP* in the descent from the cross. We have seen above that Celsus (Origen, *C. Cels.* 2. 55), perhaps in Rome, only a few years later knows John's account of Thomas and Jesus' nailprints.

Jesus' seamless tunic, 'Let us not tear it, but cast lots (λάχωμεν) for it to see whose it shall be' (19: 24). Another interesting detail should be mentioned here. In his first *Apology* when Justin cites the fulfilment of Psalm 22: 18, he cites only the second half of the verse, which refers to the singular ἱματισμόν in *1Apol.* 35. 5, 8; 38. 4.[162] This is in contradistinction to each of the Synoptic accounts, which cite only Psalm 22: 18a and the plural ἱμάτια (the *GP* 4. 12 too refers only to plural garments, but uses another word, τὰ ἐνδύματα). It is John's crucifixion account alone which has the story of the soldiers casting lots for Jesus' tunic. By recording this incident John shows that the second half of Psalm 22: 18 was fulfilled, which mentions casting of lots for a singular garment (ἱματισμόν). Thus, though Justin does not draw attention to the tunic itself, his citation of only Psalm 22: 18b and the singular 'garment' in the first *Apology*, combined with his use of the word λαχμός, seem to demonstrate his awareness of John's unique account.

Of these three points of contact with the Fourth Gospel from Justin's reflections on the prophetic background for the crucifixion, only the second might have been taken from general Christian tradition. But Justin's mention of the nails in this context, surrounded by other apparent Johannine allusions, suggests that it too comes ultimately from the same source from which he knows about Jesus 'sitting on the judgment seat' and the soldiers casting lots for Jesus' garment.

This brings up another interesting matter, of great importance for ascertaining Justin's sources and the place of John's Gospel among them. Justin solemnly attests at the end of *1Apol.* 35 (35. 9, and later in 48. 3) that the events he listed in this chapter as fulfilment of the prophetic oracles did happen, and that the emperor could learn of them from 'the acts which took place under Pontius Pilate' (ἐκ τῶν ἐπὶ Ποντίου Πιλάτου γενομένων ἄκτων). This reference must be to some written account. The identity of these 'acts' is not explicitly stated, and Justin's ambiguity has led to various theories. The attempt to relate them to later apocryphal 'Pilate literature', such as the *Acts of Pilate* which are now contained in the *Gospel of Nicodemus*, has proved unsuccessful.[163] Justin in fact does not speak of 'acts of Pontius Pilate' (despite the *ANF* rendering) but 'acts which occurred under Pontius Pilate'. The expression makes it possible that he is referring to official documents from the procuratorship of Pilate.[164] His word 'acts' (ἄκτων), a Latin loanword, seems to lend to this source an official character. And in the previous chapter he had referred the emperor to an official source, 'the

---

[162] He does cite the entire verse in his exegesis of the Psalm in *Dial.* 97, 104. His elaboration on the fulfilment in 97. 3 is not inconsistent with John's account, *pace* Pryor. Moreover, Justin's mention of the nails and the λαχμός in this very section would point to a knowledge of John's crucifixion narrative.

[163] See Koester, *ACG* 42; Wartelle, *Justin*, 273, on 35. 9.

[164] So Barnard, *Apologies*, 151, n. 242.

registers of the taxing made under Cyrenius, your first procurator in Judea'. But if this is the case, he could only mean that the events which he mentions as fulfilments of prophecy in this chapter were attested in these 'acts' in the most general way, and in fact, even this is stretching the language. For these events include Jesus' birth and growth to manhood, the gainsaying, denial and torture of him by his persecutors, their setting him on a judgment seat, his crucifixion, the soldiers' using nails to affix his hands and feet to the cross, and their casting of lots for his vesture. And his later reference to the 'acts' alleges that they contain documentation of Jesus healing diseases and raising the dead (*1Apol.* 48. 3). What Justin attributes to these 'acts', then, makes it impossible to conceive of them as any official Roman document chronicling the events of the procuratorship of Pilate.

Koester therefore appears to be correct in holding that these 'acts', which must have contained a great deal of specific material about the life of Jesus, were in fact 'gospel materials'.[165] By this Koester seems to mean materials which were part of the prehistory of, and which may have been used in the composition of, the canonical and other Gospels, but which cannot be identified as any one of these Gospels. Yet this solution too is quite problematic. Besides the noteworthy fact that no materials which fit this description have ever been found, that Justin refers to the record of these 'acts' as something not only current in his day but publicly available, and to which the emperor could easily have access,[166] makes it hardly credible that he is referring to such obscure, non-literary, and, to the present day, unidentifiable sources. If they are 'gospel materials' they are certainly the Gospels according to Matthew, Mark, Luke, or John, or a collection of one or more of these, which would have been publicly available in Rome in the middle of the second century. And as we have seen, several of the points mentioned by Justin in *1Apol.* 35 or in parallel accounts have close associations with John's unique material on the crucifixion and its aftermath and are apparently dependent upon them.

Thus it appears that Justin is referring not to official Roman records of Pilate's procuratorship but to the Church's Gospels as the written sources for 'acts', which *Jesus* accomplished and which 'took place' under Pontius Pilate. The Latin loanword (*acta*) in Greek characters could stand for one of the Greek words πραγμάτα, πρᾶξεις, πραχθέντα. It must be observed here that before the word Gospel became the universal standard and almost

---

[165] Koester, *ACG* 41–2.
[166] This assumed accessibility ties in with an interesting comment made recently by J. Eldon Epp, 'Issues in the Interrelation of New Testament Textual Criticism and Canon', in L. M. McDonald and J. A. Sanders (eds.), *The Canon Debate* (Peabody, Mass., 2002), 485–515 at 512. Commenting on the modest page sizes of the earliest NT papyri, Epp writes, 'This suggests that the media commonly used by and most appealing to early Christians were codices in the earliest attested form and sizes, which, in turn, rated high in portability, a feature not only valuable to early Christian travelers in their mission, but also convenient and practical in the dissemination of the writings they carried and used.'

exclusive form of reference to these books, other descriptive ways of referring to them or to their contents were evidently in use among Christians.
Justin gives us one, which we shall examine below, 'the ἀπομνημονεύματα of Jesus' apostles'. But there is good evidence that another way to
speak of them was as the records of the 'acts' of Jesus, or of 'things done' by
Jesus. In language which portends Justin's own, Ignatius, in fact, already
had spoken of the key events of Jesus' life as deeds done by Jesus which
took place under Pontius Pilate: 'be convinced of the birth and passion and
resurrection which took place (γενομένη) at the time of the procuratorship
of Pontius Pilate; for these things were truly and certainly done
(πραχθέντα) by Jesus Christ' (*IMagn.* 11. 1, cf. *ITrall.* 9. 1; *ISmyrn.* 1. 1).
Justin only makes clear that these things are recorded in written sources. At
roughly the same time as Ignatius, the elder known to Papias in Eusebius,
HE 3. 39. 15, used to speak of the Evangelist Mark writing down accurately
'the things either said or done (τὰ ... ἢ λεχθέντα ἢ πραχθέντα) by the
Lord'. In what I believe has been shown to be another portion of this
elder's recorded tradition, summarized and paraphrased by Eusebius in *HE*
3. 24,[167] Eusebius uses likewise the passive participle, aorist or perfect, of
πράσσω four times and the noun πρᾶξις three times to refer to the deeds
of Jesus as the definitive elements of the Gospels. According to this early
second-century tradition, the apostle John had observed that the first three
Gospels lacked only the account of 'what was done by Christ (τῶν
...ὑπὸ τοῦ Χριστοῦ πεπραγμένων) at first, at the beginning of the
preaching' (3. 24. 7); 'the three evangelists related only things done by the
Saviour (πεπραγμένα τῷ σωτῆρι) one year after John the Baptist had
been put in prison' (3. 24. 8); 'Luke, too, makes a similar observation before
beginning the acts of Jesus (τῶν τοῦ Ἰησοῦ πράξεων)' (3. 24. 10); 'They
say accordingly that for this reason the apostle John was asked to hand
down in the Gospel according to him the period passed over in silence by
the former evangelists and the things done by the Savior (τὰ ... πεπραγμένα τῷ σωτῆρι) during it' (3. 24. 11); (John) 'by mentioning the Baptist in the midst of the acts of Jesus (τῶν Ἰησοῦ πράξεων)' (3. 24. 11); 'thus
John in the Scripture of the Gospel according to him hands down the
things done by Christ (τὰ ... πρὸς τοῦ Χριστοῦ πραχθέντα) before the
Baptist had been thrown into prison' (3. 24. 12); 'that according to John
contains the first of the acts of Christ (τὰ πρῶτρα τῶν τοῦ Χριστοῦ
πράξεων)' (3. 24. 13). This very distinctive language (which may be indebted to Luke 1: 1–2; Acts 1: 1–2, and related to the title which came to
be used for Luke's second volume) shows that in the days of Papias and his
elder the four Gospels were referred to in terms of their being the records
of the acts of Jesus. It shows that what Justin must have meant by 'the acts
(of Jesus) which occurred under Pontius Pilate' is the record of the acts of

---

[167] Hill, 'What Papias Said about John', esp. 595–6, and see below.

Jesus contained in the memoirs of his apostles, the Gospels, from which the emperor, if he wished, could learn about the events in question. When we remember that these events include his birth and growth to manhood, the gainsaying, denial and torture of him by his foes, their setting him on a judgment seat, the soldiers' using nails to affix his hands and feet to the cross, their casting of lots for his vesture, Jesus' healing of diseases and raising the dead, this will have to appear by far the most consistent and reasonable way to understand his words. And it is substantiated by two other factors. First, besides the reference to official census registers in *1Apol.* 34, all other cases where Justin refers the emperor to written documents, the references are to Christian religious authorities ('our writings' in 28. 1; Moses' writings in 62. 4 and 63. 6).

Second, there is an instructive parallel for Justin's citation of Psalm 22: 18 in *Dial.* 104, a verse which, as we have seen, is prominent in *1Apol.* 35 and 38. In the latter Justin says that their fulfilment could be read out of the 'acts which took place under Pontius Pilate'. But in *Dial.* 104 he attests to Trypho that the fulfilment of Psalm 22: 15c–18 'is written to have taken place in the memoirs of his apostles' (ἐν τοῖς Ἀπομνημονεύμασι τῶν ἀποστόλων αὐτοῦ γέγραπται γενόμενον). This, I believe, seals the fact that what Justin refers to as 'the acts which took place under Pontius Pilate' are the acts of Jesus recorded in the Gospels, the 'memoirs' of the apostles.

This in turn confirms that it is these well-known, publicly available works, and not obscure and otherwise unknown 'gospel materials' which are Justin's named sources, the sources he commends to the emperor, for recording the fulfilment of prophecies about Jesus' 'acts'. And this make it morally certain that the several details in this section which correspond only to the Fourth Gospel and not to the Synoptics are indeed telltale signs of Justin's knowledge of and dependence upon that Gospel. Thus the Fourth Gospel is recognized as an important authority for Justin's views of Jesus' deity and incarnation and baptism, for his understanding of the meaning of Christian baptism, and for his understanding of the sufferings of Jesus in fulfilment of OT prophecy. It also confirms the conclusion drawn above from *Dial.* 105.1 that the Fourth Gospel was indeed among his collection of the 'memoirs of the apostles'.

Miscellanea

There are a number of other details in Justin's writings which appear to be signs of his knowledge of the Fourth Gospel. In *Dialogue* 69 Justin cites Isaiah 35: 1–7, a text which tells that when God comes to save his people, 'then the eyes of the blind shall be opened, and the ears of the deaf shall hear. Then the lame shall leap as an hart, and the tongue of the stammerers shall be distinct'. Justin attests that this is speaking of Christ, 'who also appeared in your nation, and healed those who were maimed and deaf, and lame in body from their birth, causing them to leap, to hear, and to

see, by his word' (69. 6). The detail added almost casually, that Jesus healed
those who had been thus afflicted 'from their birth' (ἐκ γενετῆς), has its only
apparent source in John 9: 1, 19, 20, 32, which magnify the fact that Jesus
healed a man blind 'from his birth' (ἐκ γενετῆς).[168] This is the only occurrence of the expression ἐκ γενετῆς in the NT. Again Justin preserves language from the Fourth Gospel which relates to Jesus' life and work.

Some have observed that while Justin's writings are cautious in citing
Christian authorities, his use of them is sometimes evident in his choice and
exposition of OT texts which match those of NT writings. This is usually said
in reference to his use of Paul and Pauline exegesis, but it pertains to John as
well. We have seen this with regard to Psalm 22: 18 above, which John alone
among NT writers cites. Mention should be made of Justin's references to the
prophecy of Zechariah 12: 10–14 in *Dial.* 14. 8; 32. 2; *1Apol.* 52. 12, which
is cited only by John 19: 37 and Revelation 1: 7 in the New Testament.
His form of reference also agrees with these Johannine texts where it disagrees
with the LXX text, as we now have it.[169] A similar case is found in Justin's
citation of Isaiah 6: 10 in *Dial.* 33. 1, which corresponds to the wording of
John 12: 40 (πωροῦν) instead of the LXX (παχύνειν).[170] Justin also cites
Moses' lifting up of the serpent from Numbers 21: 8–9 and the salvation it
foreshadowed, as does John (3: 14), alone among the Gospels (cf. *Ps. Barn.* 12.
5–7). By themselves these coincidences could not count for much, but in the
light of Justin's many traces of Johannine material they fill out an ever-clearer
picture of his knowledge of that Gospel.

The extent of Justin's debt to the Fourth Gospel is impressive. The connections with the Prologue of John's Gospel are too clear to leave any real
doubt that Justin knew that Prologue and used it as a key source for his
understanding of Jesus' eternal deity and incarnation. He knows Jesus'
saying about the new birth from John 3: 5, 7 and it informs his understanding of the meaning of Christian baptism. Justin knows details contained
only in John's account of Jesus' baptism and in his account of Jesus' crucifixion. He knows other scattered details recorded by the author of the
Fourth Gospel and cites several OT texts which are cited either uniquely
by John or in a unique way by John among the Gospels. To suppose then
that in about the years 150–5 Justin in Rome knew some pre-Johannine
source for John's Prologue without knowing the Prologue itself, to suppose
that he knew a baptismal liturgy used by the Fourth Gospel without knowing the Fourth Gospel itself, to suppose that he knew a pre-Johannine

---

[168] So also Pryor, 'Justin Martyr', 158. On 159 Pryor writes of *Dial.* 69 that, although some
material may have been shared by John and certain Jewish sources, 'when it is recognized that
within the space of a dozen lines of text there are possible allusions to as many as four or five
passages in John, one begins to suspect that perhaps the literary link can be more confidently
asserted'.

[169] See Nagel, *Rezeption*, 109–10 for a close comparison, with the alternatives.

[170] Ibid. 110–11.

source for the Johannine crucifixion account without knowing the Johannine crucifixion account itself, and to suppose that he put the same words into the mouth of John the Baptist as does the Fourth Gospel without knowing that Gospel, is to prefer supposition to reality.

Despite his lack of formal citation, despite his tendency to paraphrase or summarize, and despite his habit of conflating texts, Justin's knowledge of the Fourth Gospel has to be considered quite secure and really quite comprehensive. It remains true, of course, that Synoptic or Synoptic-like material appears in greater abundance in Justin's writing. But the subject matter of his surviving treatises certainly plays a role here, as Stanton has recently observed.[171] In a long section of the first *Apology* Justin cites many instances of Jesus' ethical teaching in order to show the pious, peaceable, and chaste precepts by which the Christians live. For this purpose the Synoptics provide much more material than does the Fourth Gospel. A major subject of debate between Justin and Trypho concerns Jesus' birth from a virgin in fulfilment of Isaiah 7: 14. And while we have seen that Justin's conception even of the virgin birth is anchored in John's Prologue, when searching for historical accounts of the birth itself and the events which surround it (the census, the Magi, Herod's tirade, the flight to Egypt, etc.), the Fourth Gospel (like the Second Gospel) can, of course, be of no service to him and he must rely upon Matthew and Luke.

John and the Apostolic Memoirs

I turn now to consider more closely the identity of the 'apostolic memoirs', the name given by Justin to what he says were commonly called the Gospels, 'For the apostles, in the memoirs composed by them, which are called Gospels, have thus delivered unto us ...' (*1Apol.* 66. 3).[172] These 'memoirs' (if that is a good translation of the term), Justin tells us, were publicly read and commented on by preachers in Christian services of worship on the day called Sunday (*1Apol.* 67. 3). Their importance in Rome at mid-century, not only with Justin himself but with some worshipping community to which he belonged, is therefore hard to gainsay. It is virtually agreed that as Justin uses the term memoirs it encompasses at least the Gospels of Matthew, Mark, and Luke[173] (though some would hold that Justin had these only in a

---

[171] Stanton, 'Fourfold Gospel', 330–1, 'Justin's failure to refer to John's Gospel more frequently is puzzling, but it may be related to his strong interest in infancy narratives, and in ethical teaching and futurist eschatological sayings—all in somewhat short supply in this Gospel' (330). On Justin's 'preference' for the Synoptics, see Hengel, *Frage*, 64–5, where he cites Chadwick *Early Christian Thought*, 124–5, who suggests that if Justin did use a Synoptic Gospel-harmony, John may not have been added to this as of yet.

[172] The term memoirs, as some have pointed out, is not a title in the same way as the term 'Gospel' is. See Barnard, *Justin*, 56.

[173] Koester, *ACG* 38, 'In each instance the materials quoted derive from written gospels, usually from Matthew and Luke, in one instance from Mark'.

harmony). But it is very often denied that it could also have included John. On the other hand, I have already concluded from the evidence above that Justin considered the Fourth Gospel to be among the 'apostolic memoirs'. It is now time to attempt to conduct a more complete investigation.

Justin once states that the memoirs were composed by 'Jesus' apostles and their followers' (*Dial.* 103. 8). This simple attribution prompted Hugh Lawlor to write long ago that it 'implies that at least two of the evangelists were apostles, and at least two were companions of apostles. He may be assumed to refer, on the one hand to Matthew and John, and on the other to Mark and Luke.'[174] To several scholars, at least, including Goodspeed, Grant, Davey, and Stanton,[175] this has appeared quite reasonable, and consistent with Justin's use of the term and his use of Gospel material. But others have rendered a negative judgement on the question of John's inclusion and John Pryor has advanced another interpretation of Justin's comment. His argument is based on *Dial.* 106. 3, where Justin refers to Jesus' changing of Simon's name to Peter and Jesus' changing of the names of the sons of Zebedee to Boanerges. The latter, he says, is written in 'his', that is, Peter's, memoirs. This incident, as it turns out, is recorded only by Mark (Mark 3: 17). Thus without mentioning the name or title of Mark, Justin identifies Mark's Gospel as in a real way the memoirs of Peter, in agreement with Papias (Eusebius, *HE* 3. 39). Pryor would read this, however, as a claim of joint authorship by an apostle and a follower (Peter and Mark). Thus the attribution of the memoirs to 'Jesus' apostles and their followers' in *Dial.* 103. 8 could be taken to mean that 'he is not consciously dividing the gospels into two groupings, but is, rather, being more precise in his description of a work like Mark's Gospel'.[176] Presumably, then, this could apply to other Gospels as well. Thus all that Justin would mean to affirm in *Dial.* 103. 8 is his belief that apostles and their followers co-laboured in the production of these writings; it would not give sole authorial responsibility for one or more Gospels to any apostle.

It should be observed first of all that even Pryor's interpretation cannot rule out the probability that Justin included John's Gospel in the memoirs. It would only mean that Justin cannot be read as attesting to (at least) two Gospels written by apostles and (at least) two by apostolic disciples. But this interpretation does not seem to take seriously the care with which Justin speaks of the origins of these memoirs elsewhere, nor does it regard the

---

[174] Lawlor, 'Eusebius on Papias', 202 n. 1.

[175] Grant, *Greek Apologists*, 59, 'I prefer to agree with E. J. Goodspeed that when Justin refers to Gospels composed by Jesus' apostles and by their followers, he has two of each class in mind'. Davey, 'Justin Martyr and the Fourth Gospel', 119. Stanton, 'Fourfold Gospel', 330–1, 'Since there is no clear evidence for Justin's knowledge of any gospels other than the canonical four, we can be all but certain that he had in mind Matthew, Mark, Luke, and John, no more, no less'. Most scholars who deny Justin's knowledge of the Fourth Gospel, including Haenchen, Koester, and Bellinzoni, do not deal with this text.

[176] Pryor, 'Justin Martyr', 155.

extent of his agreement with what Papias had already written on this subject. Both of these factors favour the interpretation of Lawlor (and others)
over that of Pryor.

Justin's acquaintance with what Papias had written on the origins of the
Gospels (or with the tradition that lay beneath it) is widely acknowledged.[177] Many believe that his choice of the word ἀπομνημονεύματα
for the Gospels is based on Papias.[178] And this connection works towards
the rejection of Pryor's thesis. For Papias does not speak of a joint authorship of Mark's Gospel, but of Mark, the follower, faithfully writing down
what his master Peter remembered and preached (Eusebius, *HE* 39. 15).
And in distinction to this, he speaks of Matthew's Gospel as being his own
writing, not a joint production in any way (there might be room for a
disciple to have translated Matthew from Aramaic to Greek, but Papias
does not assign this task to any one person). Justin's language is in fact a
fine summary of what Papias says, in terms of assigning one Gospel to an
apostle alone, and another to an apostle's follower. I have shown elsewhere
that Papias also wrote of John's and Luke's Gospels, and that Eusebius has
preserved this information, though not under Papias' name. These likewise
show that Papias attributed John to the apostle himself, and Luke to the
follower of an apostle.

And Justin's agreement with Papias goes beyond merely connecting the
Gospel of Mark with the apostle Peter, but extends even to much of the
same, distinctive vocabulary. Justin says in *Dial.* 103. 8 that the memoirs
were 'composed' or 'arranged' (συντετάχθαι) by the apostles of Jesus and
by those who followed them. Papias says that Peter did not make a
σύνταξις of the Lord's words but implies that Mark made one from Peter's
teaching (though not setting things 'in order' (τάξει), 3. 39. 15). He also
says that Matthew made an arrangement of (συνετάξατο) the Lord's
oracles in the Hebrew language (3. 39. 16). Justin refers to 'the apostles and
those who followed them' (τῶν ἐκείνοις παρακολουθησάντων) as being
responsible for the memoirs; Papias uses the same word for Mark, who
'followed' Peter (παρηκολούθησεν . . . Πέτρῳ). Justin calls these writings
ἀπομνημονεύματα; Papias refers to Peter 'recounting' (ἀπεμνημόνευσεν), and Mark writing (γράψας). The extent of this correspondence
alone means we should have to assume that Justin knew Papias' writing and
that he, like Papias, knew two Gospels written by apostles themselves, and
two written by disciples of apostles from apostolic preaching or testimony.

---

[177] See e.g. Koester, *ACG* 40; Metzger, *Canon*, 145.
[178] e.g. B. W. Bacon, 'Marcion, Papias, and "the Elders"', *JTS* NS 23 (1922), 134–60, at 154;
R. G. Heard, 'The Ἀπομνημονεύματα in Papias, Justin and Irenaeus', *NTS* 1 (1954–5), 122–9;
E. F. Osborn, *Justin Martyr*, BHTh. 47 (Tübingen, 1973); L. Abramowski, 'Die "Erinnerungen der
Apostel" bei Justin', in P. Stuhlmacher (ed.), *Das Evangelium und die Evangelien*, WUNT 28
(Tübingen, 1983), 341–53; cf. Koester, *ACG* 39–40.

This is also confirmed by Justin's almost uncanny scrupulosity when he alludes to the authorship and composition of the Gospels. The memoirs are said to have been 'composed' or arranged (συντετάχθαι) by the apostles and those who followed them (*Dial.* 103. 8). Here συντάσσω surely refers to actual authorship,[179] as is evident from his use of the term elsewhere[180] (and cf. Papias, as cited above). This notice of the activity of the followers of the apostles is the only one of its kind in Justin's writings, and the fact that he proceeds immediately to cite an incident recorded only in Luke's Gospel (Jesus' sweating like blood from Luke 22: 44), makes it appear that his notice pertains to this piece of information, which was recorded only by a follower of apostles. Likewise, as we have already observed, when he cites a detail contained only in Mark's Gospel, he assigns this to Peter's memoirs but does not name Peter as writer or composer (*Dial.* 106. 3). This verbal care is further maintained by an instance in which the authors of two of the Gospel accounts are mentioned, though in a distinctive way, 'as they who have recounted (οἱ ἀπομνημονεύσσντες) all that concerns our Saviour Jesus Christ have taught, whom we have believed' (*1Apol.* 33. 5). The plural here seems to indicate that he is aware that the information is found in (at least) two authoritative sources. It turns out that these are Matthew 1: 21 and Luke 1: 31–2. His introduction of the authors not as apostles, but as 'they who have recounted all that concerns our Saviour Jesus Christ', seems to indicate his awareness, again, that at least one of them was not an apostle.

Yet another example occurs in *1Apol.* 66. 3, 'For the apostles, in the memoirs which have come into being by their agency (ἐν τοῖς γενομένοις ὑπ' αὐτῶν ἀπομνημονεύμασιν), which are called Gospels, have thus delivered unto us what was enjoined on them (παρέδωκαν ἐντετάλθαι αὐτοις)'. The wording here too is peculiar and careful. His use of the passive γενομένοις with ὑπο, denoting ultimate agency, attributes the existence of the memoirs/Gospels to the apostles as ultimate authorities, and depicts them as handing down the contents of these works, without using a word like γράφω, συνγράφω, or συντάσσω which would specify that they actually 'wrote' each of the Gospels. What he goes on to say was so delivered is, 'that Jesus took bread and when he had given thanks, said, "This do ye in remembrance of me, this is my body;" and that, after the

---

[179] LSJ, σύντασσω, ii 3, p. 1725.

[180] The prophecies of the prophets were 'composed' or arranged (συντεταγμένας) into books 'by the prophets themselves' (*1Apol.* 31. 1). Justin uses the word as well for his own activity of composing a work against heresies (*1Apol.* 26. 8), and for his second apology (*2Apol.* 15. 2). He calls his *Dialogue* a σύνταξις (*Dial.* 80. 3) and his second apology 'this arrangement of words' (τήν τῶνδε τῶν λόγων συντάξιν, *2Apol.* 1. 1). Similarly he uses another nominal form of the same word, σύνταγμα, for Moses' writings in *1Apol.* 63. 11. He uses the word σύγγραμμα in a similar way, 'you may learn accurately from his writings (συγγραμμάτων) [Moses]', *1Apol.* 31. 3; 62. 4; 63. 6; 67. 3, for the writings of the prophets which are read in Christian gatherings, and in 28. 1 for 'our writings'.

same manner, having taken the cup and given thanks, he said, "This is my blood;" and gave it to them alone'. This is based on Luke's account (22: 19–20), though much of it is of course paralleled in Matthew and Mark.[181]

It is with this evident scrupulosity about the memoirs in mind then that we come back to a text already mentioned above, *Dial.* 88. 3. This is where Justin, after referring to the Holy Spirit lighting on Jesus like a dove at his baptism, claimed that this is something 'the apostles of this very Christ of ours wrote ἔγραψεν' (*Dial.* 88. 3). Justin seems to want to claim for the attestation of this event, as it was the fulfilment of Isaiah's prophecy, the authority of Jesus' apostles themselves, possibly as presumed eyewitnesses. And rather than saying simply that this was recorded in their memoirs, which might have covered the accounts written by Mark or Luke as well, Justin is careful to say that the apostles of this very Christ of ours 'wrote' this. The plural also seems to demand at least two apostolic writings. Moreover, we saw above that the context of *Dial.* 87–8 contains probably three allusions to specifically Johannine material. There is thus no reason to deny that Justin has in mind both Matthew and John as apostles who wrote accounts which described or mentioned the descent of the Spirit as a dove onto Jesus at his baptism. This is how, without actually mentioning any of the apostles' names, Justin sometimes indicates to the knowing Christian reader which Gospel or Gospels he has in mind. And the coherence with the tradition passed on by Papias and second-century tradition generally allows us today to make out with some certainty his use of Matthew, Mark, Luke, and John.

All of this works to confirm the reading of *Dial.* 103. 8 which Lawlor and others have accepted. That is, when Justin says the memoirs were composed by Jesus' apostles and their followers, Justin denotes (at least) two apostles, Matthew and John, and two followers, Mark and Luke, as 'writers' or 'composers' of the Gospels. The term 'apostolic memoirs' is useful for it allows Justin to claim full apostolic authority for these Gospels without having to claim that each particular Gospel was written by an apostle; each has one or more apostles as ultimate source, but may have been written by a follower of the apostles.

Finally, this conclusion also supports my examination above of two passages where John's inclusion in the memoirs seems certain. These are:

---

[181] Bellinzoni's study does not take up this issue in detail, but he renders his opinion that 'the words of institution recorded by Justin in *Apol.* 66: 3 are also from traditional liturgical forms older than the versions found in our synoptic gospels'. This is highly doubtful. It appears from his introductory statement ('delivered... enjoined') that Justin is also borrowing words from Paul in 1 Cor. 11: 23–6 ('delivered... received'). It would thus seem that Justin regards Paul as the apostle (or at least one of the apostles) from whom Luke received his account of the life of the Lord. Even though Paul was not with the historical Jesus, his words in 1 Cor. 11: 23, 'For I received from the Lord what I also delivered to you' were seen as indicating his direct reception of revelation from the Lord, revelation which he then delivered to his followers, including Luke, who wrote a Gospel. This is in full accord with what we have identified as Papias' tradition concerning Luke's Gospel (Hill, 'What Papias Said about John', appendix).

1Apol. 35, where Justin refers to 'the acts which took place under Pontius
Pilate' for information which he elsewhere says is contained in 'the
memoirs', and which includes several Johannine allusions; and *Dial.* 105. 1,
where Justin seems to attribute some of his Johannine conceptions to the
memoirs, 'For I have proved that he was monogenes to the Father of all
things, begotten of him in a peculiar manner as Word and Power, and later
having become man through the virgin, as we have learned from the
memoirs.'[182]

It is therefore safe to conclude that not only did Justin know the Fourth
Gospel, but he considered it to have been written by an apostle, and, along
with the Gospels of Matthew, Mark, and Luke, to be part of the Church's
collection of apostolic memoirs fit for homiletical exposition on the Lord's
day.

JUSTIN AND THE JOHANNINE APOCALYPSE AND LETTERS

We are in a fortunate position when we come to ask of Justin's knowledge
of the Johannine Apocalypse. This is because we have one rare, explicit
mention of this book and its author in *Dial.* 81. 4. If we did not have this
statement, the situation would be much like that which pertains to his use of
most other NT sources, where we must rely not on explicit or precise
quotations, with attribution and citation formulas, but on patches of partial,
often conflated or 'interpreted' citations or allusions, and inferences drawn
from Justin's redolent but sometimes annoyingly ambiguous style. And yet,
even apart from this one, explicit statement, his knowledge of the Apocalypse might still be surmised from a few passages, such as *Dial.* 39. 6 (cf.
also 70. 5; 103. 5) where his reference to the Serpent 'deceiving' and 'perse-
cuting' Christians has strong lexical connections to Revelation 12: 9, 13.
Building upon this is *1Apol.* 28. 1, where similar information about the devil
is given this time to a pagan audience, with a documentary notice: 'For
among us the prince of the wicked spirits is called the serpent, and Satan,
and the devil, as you can learn by looking into our writings'. While it is
certainly a natural inference, the actual identification of the chief wicked
spirit as the Serpent is not made in the OT but only in the New. And this is
done not even in the Gospels, where this spirit is never called 'serpent'. He
is referred to thus only by Paul in 1 Corinthians 10: 9; 2 Corinthians 11: 3
and by John in Revelation 12: 9, 14, 15; 20: 2. And it is this last text which
has almost an exact correspondence to Justin's words (ὁ ὄφις ὁ ἀρχαῖος, ὅς
ἐστιν διάβολος καὶ ὁ Σατανᾶς, Rev. 20: 2; ὄφις καλεῖται καὶ σατανᾶς
καὶ διάβολος Dial. 28. 1).[183] The significance of this passage enlarges

---

[182] My translation.
[183] That he is indeed referring to Revelation here is recognized by L. M. McDonald, *The
Formation of the Christian Biblical Canon* (Peabody, Mass., 1995), 151.

when it is realized that Justin's one explicit reference to the book of Revelation is to the very chapter, 20, in which this description of the devil is found (*Dial.* 81). I refer again to the citations of Zechariah 12: 10, 12 in *1Apol.* 52; *Dial.* 14; 32; 64; 118, which may well depend upon both John 19: 37 and Revelation 1: 7. Thus, without *Dial.* 81 a tolerably good circumstantial case could be made for his knowledge of Revelation, from the bulk of Justin's writings. But because for some reason Justin was goaded away from his usual tight-lipped style in *Dial.* 81. 4, we now can place these allusions in their proper perspective.

When Trypho questions Justin's belief in a future life in a rebuilt Jerusalem, where Christians will rejoice with the patriarchs and prophets, righteous Jews and proselytes, Justin has to assure him that he and other right-minded Christians believe there will be 'a resurrection of the dead, and a thousand years in Jerusalem, which will then be built, adorned, and enlarged, [as] the prophets Ezekiel and Isaiah and others declare' (80. 5) The thousand years come ostensibly from the 'obscure' prediction of Isaiah 65: 22 which says that 'according to the days of the tree of life (LXX; MT, a tree) shall be the days of my people'. Justin takes this to refer to the tree of life in the garden. And through a misidentification of this tree with the tree of the knowledge of good and evil, combined with a typological exegesis of Genesis 2: 17 ('for in the day that you eat of it you shall die'), exegeted in the light of Psalm 90: 4 (as Justin renders it, 'The day of the Lord is as a thousand years'),[184] Justin arrives at a promise of a thousand-year reign! This is probably a traditional association of texts, which originated in Jewish circles. Irenaeus certainly knows it from Justin and possibly from Papias. Then, in 81. 4, Justin adds an attestation for this conception from a Christian source,

further, there was a certain man among us (παρ ἡμῖν), whose name was John, one of the apostles of Christ, who prophesied, by a revelation that was made to him, that those who believed in our Christ would dwell a thousand years in Jerusalem; and that thereafter the general, and, in short, the eternal resurrection and judgment of all men would likewise take place.

There is no good reason to question Eusebius' statement that Justin's dialogue with Trypho took place at Ephesus (*HE* 4. 18. 6). Justin's words, 'a man among us', then, evidently refers to the apostle John's former residence in Ephesus. That the author of Revelation lived in Ephesus, of all the cities mentioned in Revelation, before or after his exile to Patmos, is something which is by no means stated in the text of that book. Likewise, though the author of Revelation gives his name as John, he does not, as many a modern commentator will remind us, identify himself as an apostle. How

---

[184] LXX has 'For a thousand years in thine eyes are as yesterday which has passed, and a watch in the night'.

then does Justin know that this John had been 'one of the apostles of Christ' and that he lived in Ephesus? We know that early Christian tradition identified John the author of Revelation with the author of the Fourth Gospel. We know that from at least Hegesippus, who arrived in Rome probably while Justin was still alive, Irenaeus, and Polycrates, this apostle John is thought to have made his home in Ephesus. Is this the view that Justin too presupposes?

It has already been established that Justin must have regarded the Fourth Gospel as written by an apostle. Though he does not come close to naming this man, there is only one Gospel which went by the name of an apostle of Jesus and which contained the 'Johannine' material that Justin's allusions contain, and that, obviously, is the Gospel of John. Moreover, if Justin is in line with Papias, whose writing he evidently knew, he will have identified this 'Johannine' Gospel as that of John the apostle. Thus we have every reason to believe that Justin too held to this tradition of the apostle John's residency in Ephesus, and his authorship of both the Fourth Gospel and the Revelation. And this pushes this unified tradition at least to the early 150s, and probably earlier, to the time when Justin and Trypho met some years prior.

As to the Johannine Epistles, though we have no formal citations and the allusions are few, they are reasonably clear. In *Dial.* 45. 4 Justin refers to Christ coming to earth so that 'serpent that sinned (ὁ πονηρευσάμενος) from the beginning, and the angels like him may be destroyed'. The resemblance to 1 John 3: 8, 'for the devil has sinned from the beginning. The reason the Son of God appeared was to destroy the works of the devil' (cf. also John 8: 44) certainly gives the impression that Justin knows this passage. His words in *Dial.* 123. 9 'so we from Christ, who begat us unto God . . . are called and are the true sons of God (θεοῦ τέκνα ἀληθινὰ καλούμεθα καὶ ἐσμέν), and keep the commandments of Christ' reproduce almost exactly the peculiar phrasing of 1 John 3: 1, 'See what love the Father has given us, that we should be called children of God; and so we are' (τέκνα θεοῦ κληθῶμεν, καὶ ἐσμέν). The idea that Christ begat us unto God is probably related to a passage like 1 John 2: 29, 'If you know that he is righteous, you may be sure that every one who does right is born of him', where 'him' is understood as Jesus. 'Keeping the commandments of Christ' also echoes John 14: 15, 23; 15: 10; 1 John 2: 3. Justin gives no indication in either of these instances that he is alluding to a source, but as with his Pauline allusions, he has worked the words and thoughts of these Christian sources into his own.

To summarize, we may regard it as certain that Justin knew not only the Johannine Apocalypse, but also the Johannine Gospel and at least the first Johannine Epistle. With hardly any less confidence we can be assured that the first two of these, at least, he attributed to the same man, the apostle of Christ named John.

JUSTIN'S ESTIMATE OF THE APOSTOLIC WRITINGS

I believe it has been established that the Fourth Gospel was known to Justin, and that while it was not often quoted by him in his extant writings, it did play a very important role in forming his Christology, his understanding of the sacrament of baptism, and his knowledge of the life and sufferings of Jesus; that it also was known as a 'Gospel', and that it belonged to what Justin calls the 'memoirs of the apostles'. We can surmise even that he thought it was written by an apostle. If this is true, it already challenges the widespread notion that no early Christian writing, whether the Fourth Gospel, the Apocalypse, the letters of John, or indeed any New Testament writing, was highly valued by Justin and his church.

It is commonly held that in Rome of Justin's day even the memoirs themselves possessed only a quite limited authority.[185] Koester insists that the memoirs of the apostles functioned as nothing more than reliable historical documents for Justin and were by no means considered on a par with scripture.[186] It is, I think, incontestable that Justin's predominant use of the canonical Gospels in his apologetic writings is as historical documents which record faithfully the teaching of Jesus Christ, and the events which for Justin demonstrate the fulfilment of OT prophecy in Jesus Christ. But, first of all, one cannot assume a complete identity between Justin's circumscribed 'use' of the memoirs in his apologetic writings and the extent of his own esteem for them and use of them in a cultic context. It should now be plain how skewed this approach is. Second, although he uses the Gospels primarily as historical records in his extant treatises, even here Justin has none the less allowed us other ways to see that for him and for the Church in his day, these writings were far more than mere historical records, but were considered the equivalent or virtually the equivalent of Holy Scripture.

One way to see this is by referring again to Justin's notice that the memoirs of the apostles and the writings of the prophets were alike expounded in services of Christian worship (*1Apol.* 67. 3–5).

---

[185] Cosgrove, 'Justin Martyr and the Emerging Christian Canon', 209, even thinks that Justin 'represents a reversal of the trend of the church in the second century toward regarding apostolic writings as canon'. When Cosgrove does not find in Justin's *Dialogue* a full disclosure of its author's views on the emerging New Testament writings, he concludes that Justin opposed the growing authority of these writings and accepted the words of Jesus only.

[186] Koester, *Introduction*, 342; *ACG* 41–2. As one proof Koester argues, 'While he regularly quotes the law and the prophets with the formula "it is written" (γέγραπται), he uses this term only rarely for the gospels. In the few instances where he does so, he combines this formula with other verbs. Introducing gospel quotations, the formula does not mean "it is written in Holy Scripture," but "it is recorded in a written document that Jesus said" (*Dial.* 100.1)', *ACG* 41. In point of fact, Justin uses the perfect indicative form γέγραπται, or the perfect participle form γεγραμμένος, or the perfect infinitive form γεγράφθαι in more than half of the instances in which he refers to the memoirs, in *Dial.* 100. 4; 101. 3; 103. 6 (103. 8, conj. by Thirlby; Marcovich); 104. 1; 105. 6; 106.3; 106. 4; 107.1 (in 102. 5; 106. 1 he uses the words δεδήλωται; δηλοῦται, such as he uses for Ps. 22 in 106. 1). In addition, he uses the word in *Dial.* 49. 5, where he cites Matt. 17. 13. In only one of these cases is the formula combined with another verb which could possibly compromise it as a citation formula—105. 6, 'it is written that he said' or 'it is recorded that he said'—and even that is unclear.

And on the day called Sunday, all who live in cities or in the country gather together to one place, and the memoirs of the apostles or the writings of the prophets are read, as long as time permits; then, when the reader has ceased, the president verbally instructs, and exhorts to the imitation of these good things. Then we all rise together and pray, and, as we before said, when our prayer is ended, bread and wine and water are brought...

This is a phenomenon which is never adequately explained in Koester's view. We know that the church in Corinth from time to time read not only 1 Clement, but even a recent letter from the Roman congregation, in their meetings, as Dionysius of Corinth has said (Eusebius, *HE* 4. 23. 11). This shows that not every writing read in a Christian meeting in the second century necessarily was regarded as scripture. But Justin's mention of the memoirs alongside the prophets, and even before the prophets, as inter-changeable elements in the worship service and as both the object of homi-letical instruction ('and exhorts to the imitation of these good things') indicates a parity of authority between these two groups of writings, or, as Metzger says, Justin really places the memoirs 'not merely on a level with them, but above them'.[187]

Another way to get at Justin's own conception of the apostolic writings is to examine the fairly full evidence for Justin's view of the apostolate, to which, it has been concluded, Justin believed the author of the Fourth Gospel belonged. To this let us now turn.

THE AUTHORITY OF THE APOSTLES

One might suppose that Justin would have to labour to establish, to a scep-tical teacher of Judaism, the authority of those men who are credited with being the primary means of delivering the message of Jesus. How fortunate he must have regarded himself that he did not need to do this independently, from purely Christian, and therefore debatable, sources. For Justin, the au-thority of Jesus' twelve apostles had long ago been established in the common authority of Jew and Christian alike, the OT scriptures (*1Apol.* 39. 3; 45. 5).

Again and again legitimization of the mission and the message of the apostles of Jesus to the nations is brought forth out of the prophetical writings. Texts such as Psalm 19: 2; Isaiah 2: 2–4 = Micah 4: 1–3, Psalm 110: 2 (*1Apol.* 45. 5) are scriptural commonplaces for Justin. After citing Isaiah 2: 3, 'For out of Zion shall go forth the law, and the word of the Lord from Jerusalem', Justin confidently claims he can prove that this has now come to pass. 'For from Jerusalem there went out into the world men, twelve in number, and these illiterate, of no ability in speaking: but by the power of God they proclaimed to every race of men that they were sent by Christ to teach to all the word of God' (διδάξαι πάντας τὸν τοῦ

---

[187] Metzger, *Canon*, 145.

θεοῦ λόγον)᾿ (*1Apol.* 39. 3). The twelve apostles of Jesus themselves, and their ministry, are thus the subjects of prophecy.

As to Psalm 110: 2, 'That which he says, "He shall send to thee the rod of power out of Jerusalem", is predictive of the mighty word, which his apostles, going forth from Jerusalem, preached everywhere' (*1Apol.* 45. 5). The mighty word, which could only be a word full of divine power, did not go forth simply on its own power but came through the preaching of the apostles. Psalm 19: 2–5 is expounded to the same effect: 'And hear how it was foretold concerning those who preached his doctrine and revealed his appearance, the above-mentioned prophet and king speaking thus by the Spirit of prophecy: "Day unto day uttereth speech, and night unto night showeth knowledge. There is no speech nor language where their voice is not heard. Their voice has gone out into all the earth, and their words to the ends of the world..."᾿ (*1Apol.* 40. 1). This prophecy concerns not simply the conversion of the nations, nor the advent of good news, but also the activity of the messengers themselves. Here the activity of the messengers is not described as simply repeating the powerful *verba Christi*, or as furnishing the historical records about Jesus, but as preaching Jesus' doctrine and revealing his appearance. Unknown to Justin is the modern restriction of authority to the 'words of Jesus', if this is meant to exclude the teaching of his apostles.

Foreshadowed in type by the twelve bells which belonged to Aaron's robe (Exod. 28: 33), these twelve men became the conduit for the advance of divine glory and grace in the world ('the twelve apostles, who depend on the power of Christ, the eternal Priest, through whose voice the whole earth has been filled with the glory and grace of God and his Christ', *Dial.* 42. 1), in fulfilment of Psalm 19: 4, 'Their sound has gone forth into all the earth, and their words to the ends of the world'. The prophets often spoke as if 'personating' Christ. But according to Justin, Isaiah also spoke as if personating the apostles, when he said, 'Lord, who hath believed our report? And to whom is the arm of the Lord revealed?' (*Dial.* 42. 2)

Because it is a fulfilment of several OT prophecies, the conversion of the nations through the chosen apostles of Christ functions as a 'proof from prophecy' just like prophecies about Christ's person and works and the devastation of Jerusalem: 'For with what reason should we believe', says Justin,

unless we had found testimonies concerning him preached (κεκηρυγμένα) before he came and was born as a man, and unless we saw that things had happened accordingly—the devastation of the land of the Jews, and men of every race persuaded through the doctrine from his apostles (διὰ τῆς παρὰ τῶν ἀποστόλων αὐτοῦ διδαχῆς πεισθέντας), and rejecting their old habits... (*1Apol.* 53. 3)

Again, it is not just the conversion of the nations, but their conversion 'through the doctrine from his apostles' that was predicted and fulfilled in a way which Justin thinks ought to impress the sceptic. It appears that the apostles held an indispensable position in mediating the message of salvation.

The work of the twelve apostles as predicted by the prophets is foundational to the Christian faith, so much so that Justin includes it at the end of
a creed-like list of things predicted by the OT prophets:

In these books of the prophets then we found Jesus our Christ proclaimed before-
hand (προκηρυσσόμενον) as coming, born through a virgin, and coming to manhood, and healing every sickness and every disease and raising the dead, and being
hated and unrecognized and crucified, and dying and rising again and going up
into heaven, and being and being called Son of God; and certain men as sent by
him unto every race of men, preaching these things (καὶ τινας πεμπομένους ὑπ'
αὐτοῦ εἰς πᾶν γένος ἀνθρώπων κηρύξοντας ταῦτα), and men out of the nations
rather [than out of the Jews] believing in him.[188] (*1Apol.* 31. 7; cf. 42. 4)

Though fully authorized by the OT, the apostles of Jesus also spoke, of
course, with the authority of their master by virtue of his commission to
them, and their authority may also be said to derive from his. 'And when
they had seen Him ascending into heaven, and had believed and had
received power sent thence by Him upon them, and went to every race of
men, they taught these things and were called apostles' (*1Apol.* 50. 12; cf.
1Apol. 37. 7; 42). Not only do they speak with Christ's authority, but Justin
attests that Christ has spoken 'through' them (*1Apol.* 42. 1; *Dial.* 114. 4; cf.
119. 6, where it is God who speaks through them) in just the same way that
he says God, Christ, or the Spirit spoke through the prophets.[189] The words
of Jesus, we are told, are the sharp knives of stone by which the Gentiles
have had the foreskins of their hearts circumcised. Yet these words of Jesus
are nothing other than, 'the words through (διά) the apostles of the corner-
stone cut without hands' (*Dial.* 114. 4). Even the words of Jesus, words
which elsewhere (*Dial.* 8. 2) he says 'possess a terrible power in themselves',
have been mediated through these chosen vessels, as we also know from his
many references to 'the memoirs of his apostles'.

It is also clear that for Justin the present-day source for the Christian
faith is the apostolic teaching. The gospel which went forth from Jerusalem
went forth 'through the apostles of Jesus, and it is from "the law" and "the
word" which has gone out through them that Christians have learned the
true worship of God' (*Dial.* 110. 2). Even the OT scriptures themselves,
came to the Gentiles through the gift of the apostles: 'But the Gentiles, who
had never heard anything about Christ, until the apostles set out from
Jerusalem and preached concerning Him, and gave (παρέδωκαν) them
the prophecies, were filled with joy and faith, and cast away their idols'
(*1Apol.* 49. 5). The apostles are the vehicle, after Christ they are the source,
of the Christian faith in the world. After speaking of the virginal conception

---

[188] My translation.
[189] As in *1Apol.* 31. 1; 32. 2, 8; 35. 5; 41. 1; 44. 1, 2; 48. 3; 49. 1; 53. 6, 10; 54. 5; 55. 5; 58. 1;
59. 1; 59. 8; 61. 13; 62. 1; 63. 1; *Dial.* 21. 2; 22. 1; 25. 1; 28. 5, 6; 43. 4; 52. 1; 55. 2; 58. 4; 62. 1;
62. 4; 66. 1; 78. 8; 82. 3; 85. 7, 8; 91. 1, 4; 97. 1; 102. 5; 113. 6; 114. 2; 121. 1; 124. 2; 126. 1 (nine
times), 2; 133. 2.

in words from Luke 1: 35 and Matthew 1: 21 Justin notes, 'as they who have recorded all that concerns our Saviour Jesus Christ have taught, whom we believed' (*1Apol.* 33. 5). This also shows that it is not only the apostles' oral preaching, but their writings (and the writings of their followers who recorded their preaching) which partake of this authority, for Justin personally never heard an apostle say these things, or any other things.[190]

Justin's view of the salvation-historically unique role of the apostles, their delegated authority to teach, and Christ's speaking through them, reinforces the conclusion that whatever genuinely apostolic materials he believed he had would naturally have functioned for him as scripture. This conclusion would hold whether he ever cited all his 'apostolic' writings or not. At least the 'memoirs of the apostles', including the Fourth Gospel, as well as the Apocalypse of John, because attributed to apostles, had for him the authority of Christ. And this befits the notice that the apostolic memoirs were read and expounded in worship services in Justin's day.

Some have thought, however, that Justin's possible use (or even composition) of harmonized Gospel materials in one or another form, and his occasional, possible use of apocryphal oral or written sources, show that Justin could not have entertained such lofty views of the 'apostolic memoirs' or any Christian writings. There is, I think, good evidence that Justin at times relies on such harmonistic or catechetical, extract material, rather than on the Gospels directly, as he composes his writings. But to conclude that he therefore could only have had little regard for the base documents is to ignore a very large amount of material from his writings. Whether or not Justin used harmonies or catechetical *vademecums*, it is not on these secondary, derivative documents, if they existed, that he ultimately relies for his authority. The derivative materials were evidently composed as aids to memory and writing. Bellinzoni emphasizes their limited function.

Justin and his pupils apparently used the synoptic gospels as their primary source and composed church catechisms and *vade mecums* by hamonizing material from the synoptic gospels as described above . . . It must, however, be emphasized that there is absolutely no evidence that Justin ever composed a complete harmony of the synoptic gospels; his harmonies were of a limited scope and were apparently composed for didactic purposes.[191]

---

[190] No meaningful distinction in authority can be made between what the apostles 'preached' orally and what they wrote. Justin speaks of the apostles as he speaks of the prophets 'preaching', even though he has only the prophets' written record of that preaching, and that record is scripture.

[191] Bellinzoni, *Sayings*, 141. This contradicts the opinion of Koester, *ACG* 378, etc., who thinks Justin and his school 'endeavored to produce an even more comprehensive new gospel text'. Nor can Justin's use of these secondary materials carry the weight imputed to it by Gamble, *Canon*, 29 when he concludes, 'Evidently Justin did not invest any exclusive authority in the Gospels which ultimately became canonical'. Gamble's summary, 29 n. 19, of the conclusions of Bellinzoni, is misleading. As the citation above shows, Bellinzoni did not say that Justin relied only on harmonies apart from the Synoptic Gospels.

By contrast, the public and accessible nature of the Christian writings to which he ultimately appealed is clear in Justin's work. Trypho, before he had ever met Justin (according to Justin's depiction), had thoroughly familiarized himself with the precepts of Jesus by reading what was known to him as 'the Gospel' (*Dial.* 10. 2), probably either the Gospel of Matthew or a collection of three or more Gospels in codex form,[192] but certainly not a local, Roman school production made of excerpts and harmonizations. Justin refers Trypho back to this same 'Gospel' and then, significantly, cites from Matthew 11: 27 or Luke 10: 22. It is surely no private, school document to which he commends the emperor (*1Apol.* 28. 1; 38. 7) for learning the truth about Christian doctrine and the fulfilment of the prophecies of Christ's suffering. He can also censure the philosopher Crescens for not even taking the trouble to *read* the teachings of Christ before condemning Christians (*2Apol.* 3. 3, εἴτε γὰρ μὴ ἐντυχὼν τοῖς τοῦ Χριστοῦ διδάγμασι ... ἢ εἰ ἐντυχών ...). This certainly assumes a readily available, authoritative source for these teachings of Jesus, which is unlikely to have been some school document recently put together by Justin himself or one of his pupils. It is certainly not such 'school documents' that were read and exposited in Christian worship services along with the books of the prophets. As illuminating as it may be to compare the exact wording of Justin's quotations, paraphrases, and epitomies with our present Gospel texts, when considering theories like those of Cosgrove and Koester it is necessary to keep in mind that Justin in his *Dialogue* and *Apologies* was publishing not a revised Gospel text, but a *Dialogue* and *Apologies*. Therefore Koester's assertion that Justin yearned for and sought to produce a single, harmonized and 'updated'[193] Gospel to take the place of the four, is shown to neglect what Justin actually says about his (apostolic) sources. One might as well claim that Justin longed to replace the OT scriptures with the testimonia collections[194] culled from the prophets, which he presumably used in his apologetic writings.

On the contrary, when one considers Justin's casual references to publicly accessible records of Christ's life and teachings, it becomes clear that in Rome at least by 150, if not earlier, 'standard' editions of certain 'Gospels' must have been readily available. And these apparently were the Gospels of Matthew, Mark, Luke, and John. Justin's ability to commend 'our writings' and 'the acts which took place under Pontius Pilate' to the emperors, and to upbraid Crescens for his failure to read the teachings of Christ, Trypho's acquisition of 'the Gospel' some years earlier and Justin's ability to refer him back to this work for the precepts of Jesus, are all signs which point to the public availability of the accepted Christian Gospels in Rome and else-

---

[192] This is reminiscent of Celsus' criticism of the 'threefold, and fourfold, and many-fold' form of the Gospel in *C. Cels.* 2. 27.

[193] Koester, *ACG* 401–2.

[194] Ibid. 378, attests that Justin used these.

where (the debate with Trypho is set in Ephesus) before the middle of the second century. This, indeed, is quite in line with the information given by Papias and Aristides some thirty to thirty-five or more years earlier, as we shall see.

<h2 style="text-align:center">CONCLUSIONS</h2>

It can no longer be claimed that Justin was ignorant of, avoided, or rejected the Gospel of John. Because there is little or no evidence that any Valentinians had used the Fourth Gospel before Justin, it is hardly likely that he avoided it due to its use by them or by anyone else. It would be inconsistent with his purpose to lay too much emphasis on his Christian sources and openly claim divine authority for them in dialogue with those who do not accept them as such. In these circumstances, a little can count for a lot. And what Justin allows to seep through his self-imposed grid is more than enough to justify the conclusion not only that he indeed knew and used John's Gospel, but that this Gospel furnished him with several statements, particularly regarding Christology and soteriology, which became foundational for him and for his contemporaries. We can also be confident that Justin attributed this Gospel to an apostle of Jesus, just as he did John's Apocalypse, and that he regarded it as possessing high religious authority as one of the memoirs or Gospels of the apostles.

Justin's position as a well-known teacher in Rome could imply that his approach to these Gospels was common among Christians there, and his one explicit comment about the use of the 'memoirs' in Christian services of worship confirms this in a striking way. Such a conclusion is also consistent with the fact that when Valentinian use of John becomes visible, it presupposes a previous reception of this Gospel by the orthodox. It also lays a foundation for the Roman witness of Tatian, Hegesippus, and the episcopal correspondence with Gaul and Asia Minor in the ensuing decades.

<h2 style="text-align:center">The Later Polycarp</h2>

<h3 style="text-align:center">THE WITNESS OF IRENAEUS</h3>

Polycarp of Smyrna was martyred most probably in 155 or 156,[195] forming the dramatic climax to a long and illustrious career as leader of the church in Smyrna. Though Irenaeus tells us that Polycarp wrote many letters, to

---

[195] A consensus seems to be forming on this date, after a great deal of debate. See Lightfoot, *AF* ii. 1. 646–722; Schoedel, *ApF* 48; Barnes, *Acta*, 512; Mursurillo, *Acts*, p. xiii; Birley, *Marcus Aurelius*, 112, 261; R. M. Grant, *Eusebius as Church Historian* (Oxford, 1980), 115; Bisbee, *Pre-Decian Acts*, 120–1; G. Buschmann, *Das Martyrium des Polykarp übersetzt und erklärt*, Kommentar zu den Apostolischen Vätern, 6 (Göttingen, 1998), 39–45, which see for a full bibliography.

churches and to individuals (Eusebius, *HE* 5. 20. 8), only one survives under his name, and this from very early in his career, his *Epistle to the Philippians*. We can hardly hope to obtain a realistic representation of this man's life's work from a single epistle written probably some forty to fifty years before his death. From the later period of his life we appear to have only the *Martyrdom of Polycarp* and some traces of Irenaeus' memories about his revered teacher as acknowledged sources for his life and teaching, and the worth of the latter is often questioned. Be that as it may, there can be no real doubt that Irenaeus presents Polycarp as a crucial witness to the Asian tradition and a personal and direct link to the author of the Johannine Gospel, Letters, and Apocalypse, and to other aspects of the Johannine legacy. I turn first then to Irenaeus to look for Polcarp's witness to the reception of the Johannine corpus.

It is often thought that Irenaeus' knowledge of Polycarp must have been limited to a few brief and impersonal encounters when Irenaeus was a child.[196] One might get this impression from his statement in *AH* 3. 3. 4 that he 'saw' Polycarp 'in our early age' (ἐν τῇ πρώτῃ ἡμῶν ἡλικίᾳ; *in prima nostra aetate*). In the letter to Florinus, moreover, he calls himself a παῖς when speaking about his contact with Polycarp (*HE* 5. 20. 5, 6).[197] It is the description which he gives of what he remembered from that time which tells us more about his age and maturity when he knew Polycarp. When we pay close attention to this we find that there is more to gain from the reminiscences of Irenaeus than one might think at first.

Polycarp is mentioned by name in *Against Heresies* only in 3. 4. 4, where Irenaeus is establishing the apostolic credentials of certain churches, namely the ones in Rome, in Smyrna, and in Ephesus. It is here that we learn that Polycarp 'was not only instructed by apostles and conversed (συναναστραφείς) with many who had seen Christ, but was also, by apostles in Asia, appointed bishop of the Church in Smyrna, whom I also saw in my early youth'. No doubt John is meant to be included in the mention of apostles here. Here we also learn the story of John and Cerinthus at the Ephesian bath-house told by Polycarp, and the similar story of Polycarp's encounter with Marcion. Polycarp is said to have followed apostolic practice in 'not holding even verbal communication with any corrupters of the truth'. At the end of the paragraph we learn that the church in Ephesus had the honour of not only an apostolic foundation by Paul, but an abiding apostolic presence in the person of John, up until the time of Trajan. Though this is the only chapter in the *Against Heresies* which mentions Polycarp by name, his influence, and even his teaching, will turn up elsewhere, as we shall soon see.

Thanks to Eusebius, we have more tradition about Polycarp and his Johannine connections excerpted from two letter-treatises by Irenaeus. We

[196] M. W. Holmes, LHH, 202, says simply that Irenaeus 'met Polycarp as a child'.
[197] Robert A. Lipsius, 'Irenaeus', *DCB* iii (London, 1888), 253–79 at 254.

learn from a letter to Bishop Victor of Rome in the 190s that along with the apostle Philip, John used to observe with Polycarp and all of Asia the quartodeciman Easter (*HE* 5. 24. 16, backed up by Polycrates). This comes out in Irenaeus' report of Polycarp's visit to Rome, probably in 154 or 155, when the bishop is said to have appealed directly to John's quartodeciman practice and his own personal knowledge of it. We have another excerpt from a letter written to Florinus in Rome after his theology had taken a Marcionite turn. Shocked at the opinions Florinus had broached, Irenaeus writes,[198]

These opinions the presbyters before us, those who accompanied the apostles, did not hand down to you. For while still a boy I observed you in lower Asia with Polycarp, when you were faring splendidly in the royal court and trying to find favour with him. For I remember the events of those days more clearly than those which happened recently (for the things learned from childhood grow up with the soul, becoming one with it), so that I am able to speak even of the place in which the blessed Polycarp, sitting down, used to discourse (διελέγετο), his goings and comings and character of life, and the appearance of his body, and the discourses (διαλέξεις) which he used to make (ἐποιεῖτο) to the crowds, and how he used to report (ἀπήγγελλεν) his intercourse with John and with the rest of those who had seen the Lord (ἑορακότων, cf. 1 Jn. 1. 1–2), and how he would recount their words from memory (ἀπεμνημόνευεν),[199] and certain things concerning the Lord which he had heard from them, even concerning his[200] miracles and teaching, how, having received (them) from the eyewitnesses of the Word of Life (cf. Jn. 1. 1, 4, 14; 1 Jn. 1. 1–2), Polycarp, used to report (ἀπήγγελλεν) all things in conformity with the Scriptures. To these things even at that time, through the mercy of God which came to me, I used to listen eagerly (σπουδαίως ἤκουον), making notes of them not on paper but in my heart; and ever through the grace of God do I truly ruminate on them. And I can bear witness before God that if that blessed and apostolic presbyter had heard any such thing, after crying out and shutting his ears and saying, according to his custom, 'O good God, to what time have you pre-served me that I should endure these things?', he would have fled even from the place where he was sitting or standing when he heard such words. And from his letters which he sent either to the neighbouring churches, strengthening them, or to certain of the brethren, exhorting them and warning them, this can be made clear. (*HE* 5. 20. 4–8)

The predominance of imperfect verbs here, the differentiation of elements in his memories of Polycarp (and of Florinus), his familiarity with Polycarp's mannerisms—extending to an ability to anticipate how the elder would react, based upon customary sayings and actions—require that Irenaeus' encounters with Polycarp were not few. That he gained such intimate knowledge, and that he used to listen eagerly to and could memorize many of the things he heard Polycarp say, things on which he had meditated

---

[198] I give my own translation here. Lake, LCL, translates the imperfects as if they were aorists.
[199] Not simply 'remembered'.
[200] Lake translates 'their', but the text printed in the LCL ed. clearly has αὐτοῦ.

throughout his lifetime, require that during the period in question Irenaeus had capacities exceeding those of a small boy. Either he was unusually precocious, or we should conceive of Irenaeus' experiences with Polycarp as enduring at least into his teenage years and most probably longer. This does not, of course, guarantee the accuracy of all he remembered from and about Polycarp, but I believe it does mean that doubts concerning his testimony should not be based on Irenaeus' supposed tender age or fleeting contact with the elder. This fairly lengthy report demands further attention.

We notice the Johannine associations of his language here. Having just mentioned John and 'the others who had seen (ἑορακότων) the Lord', Irenaeus speaks of Polycarp receiving traditions from these persons, 'the eyewitnesses of the Word of Life (παρὰ τῶν αὐτοπτῶν τῆς ζωῆς τοῦ λόγου)'. This is surely meant to be an allusion at least to 1 John 1: 1–2, where the author speaks τοῦ λόγου τῆς ζωῆς as that which ἑωράκαμεν, and ostensibly serves to identify this John as the author of 1 John. It may well also be meant to identify some of Polycarp's apostolic companions with the 'eyewitnesses and ministers of the word' whom Luke mentions as his sources in Luke 1: 2. But 1 John 1: 1–2 is indebted to John 1: 14, 'And the Word became flesh and dwelt among us, full of grace and truth; we have beheld his glory...' Since it is a statement of what Polycarp himself taught, and is not merely Irenaeus' conclusion, that Polycarp had received these things from the eyewitnesses of the Word of Life, it probably implies that he himself used and alluded to 1 John, something we can confirm from as far back as his letter to the Philippians written during the reign of Trajan.

Not only did Polycarp's references to those who had been eyewitnesses of the Word of Life allude to the author of 1 John, but Irenaeus tells Florinus that he could remember stories Polycarp used to tell of John and others who saw the Lord (Eusebius, *HE* 5. 20. 6; cf. 5. 24. 16). Surely we have come across some of these already: John would naturally be intended as one of the apostles who had a part in ordaining Polycarp to the episcopacy (3. 3. 4); John also kept the quartodeciman Easter with Polycarp and others in Asia (*HE* 5. 24. 16). And among these stories which Polycarp would tell about John was surely one which Irenaeus says was heard by others as well, some of whom no doubt were in his own congregations in Gaul, the story of John's fleeing the Ephesian bath-house to avoid Cerinthus. 'There are also those who heard from him that John, the disciple of the Lord, going to bathe at Ephesus, and perceiving Cerinthus within, rushed out of the bath-house without bathing, exclaiming, "Let us fly, lest even the bath-house fall down, because Cerinthus, the enemy of the truth, is within"' (*AH* 3. 3. 4). What is usually missed is that this incident functions in the context as an illustration from John's life of his words in 2 John 10–11, 'If any one come to you and does not bring this doctrine, do not receive him into the house or give him any greeting; for he who greets him shares his wicked work'.

2 John 11, and Titus 3: 10, 'A man that is an heretic, after the first and second admonition, reject; knowing that he that is such is subverted, and sinneth, being condemned of himself'. These texts were seen by Irenaeus as inculcating an apostolic practice which was observed by their disciples, and by faithful believers in his own day (*AH* 3. 3. 4; 3. 4. 2). He had cited these two apostolic texts together in *AH* 1. 16. 3. Here in 3. 3. 4, Titus 3: 10 is cited but 2 John 11 is not. It is clear that the story of John and Cerinthus (supplemented by the story of Polycarp and Marcion) is simply substituted for the citation of 2 John 10–11. After relating the two stories Irenaeus concluded, 'Such was the horror which the apostles and their disciples had against holding even verbal communication with any corrupters of the truth; as Paul also says, "A man that is an heretic, after the first and second admonition, reject; knowing that the that is such is subverted, and sinneth, being condemned of himself"'. Irenaeus later adds that even illiterate Christians converted among the barbarians have also been trained to react to false teaching in this way (4. 4. 2). It is interesting that, in his letter to Florinus, Irenaeus brings up this very topic again, the topic of the avoidance of heresy, in connection with Polycarp. He avows to Florinus that if Polycarp had heard the sorts of things Florinus was now advocating, he would have cried out, stopped his ears, and fled the scene! This is exactly the message which comes through in the story of John and Cerinthus, the story of Polycarp and Marcion, and the example of the Christians converted from the barbarians in *AH* 3. 4. 2. This interconnection of apostolic words (from 2 John) and the exemplary apostolic deeds serves to reinforce that this John was the apostle and author of 2 John. When Polycarp told the story would he not have done the same? It is not hard to imagine that Polycarp might have used this story as an object lesson to illustrate the words of one of the 'eyewitnesses of the Word of Life' in 2 John 10–11.

But the mention of Cerinthus in *AH* 3. 3. 4 touches other areas of Irenaeus' knowledge as well. How much more of Irenaeus' tradition about Cerinthus, or about John and Cerinthus, may have come from Polycarp? Irenaeus gives a synopsis of Cerinthus' teaching in 1. 26. 1, and refers to it occasionally throughout the five books, particularly in book 3. He also asserts that John wrote the Gospel (and hints that he wrote the First Epistle) against Cerinthus and his poison (*AH* 3. 11. 1; 16. 5). Was Polycarp the source for these things too?

As I have shown elsewhere, there is good reason to think that Irenaeus' description of Cerinthus' teaching in 1. 26. 1 has come from Polycarp.[201] The mode of organizing heresies in the catalogue of 1. 23–7, that is, in terms of their doctrines of creation, is also attributed to a saintly presbyter whose anti-Marcionite teaching Irenaeus invokes in 4. 27–32. In 4. 32.

[201] C. E. Hill, 'Cerinthus, Gnostic or Chiliast?', 155–8. A fuller study of these passages and their implications for our knowledge of Polycarp is being prepared.

1 Irenaeus cites this 'presbyter, a disciple of the Apostles', who declared 'that both [testaments] are indeed from one and the same God; and that there is no other God, besides him who made and formed us, nor any strength in their argument, who say that this world of ours was made either by Angels, or by a kind of Power, or by some other God' (*aut per angelos aut per quamlibet virtutem aut ab alio Deo factum esse hunc mundum*). This not only mirrors the arrangement of the heresies in 1. 23–7, but its singular description of some heresy, as teaching that the world was made 'by a certain Power', replicates the description of Cerinthus' teaching—and his alone— in 1. 26. 1. This suggests either that this presbyter knew the same source that Irenaeus used in book 1. 23–7, or, more likely, that he was himself one of Irenaeus' sources for this material, and specifically for the information on Cerinthus. As to the identity of this presbyter, there is only one person known to us who fits this man's description, a former teacher of Irenaeus' who was old enough to have known apostles and yet lived to counter the rise of Marcion, whose teaching Irenaeus had learnt by heart. That person is Polycarp.

In his letter to Florinus Irenaeus insisted that there was a good deal of Polycarp's oral teaching which he could remember accurately, having noted it down in his heart when he heard it and having ever ruminated upon it (Eusebius, *HE* 5. 20. 6–7).[202] This means that some of that well-remembered, Polycarpan teaching is evidently to be found in chapters 27– 32 of book 4 of *Against Heresies*, where Irenaeus intermittently cites the oral, anti-Marcionite teaching of a venerated elder.

A study of these chapters can add significantly to our knowledge of Poly-carp's thought, particularly his approach to Marcionism. Here I focus only on a portion which seems to invoke the elder's knowledge of the Fourth Gospel. In *AH* 4. 31. 1, in defending the ancients of the Old Testament against Marcionite slurs, the elder is cited as having taught that we should 'give thanks to God in their behalf, inasmuch as their sins have been for-given them through the advent of our Lord; for He said that they gave thanks [for us] and gloried in our salvation'. Lightfoot determined that this was an allusion to John 8: 56, 'Your father Abraham rejoiced to see my day, and he saw it and was glad'.[203] On first sight, the resemblance is not overwhelming, but if we go back and follow Irenaeus' argument from chap-ter 5 of book 4, we are bound to conclude that Lightfoot was right. We find in fact that Irenaeus' citation of the presbyter in 4. 31. 1 assumes much of the exegesis of John 8: 56, John 5: 46 ('If you believed Moses, you would believe me, for he wrote of me'), and Matthew 13: 17 ('Truly, I say to you, many prophets and righteous men longed to see what you see, and did not

---

[202] In addition, Irenaeus says he can illustrate certain points of Polycarp's teaching from Poly-carp's letters, copies of which he must have had by then (*HE* 5. 20. 8).

[203] Lightfoot, *Biblical Essays*, 61.

see it, and to hear what you hear, and did not hear it') which Irenaeus has been giving in bits and pieces throughout several chapters of the preceding argument. This must mean that Irenaeus has been making use of Polycarp's anti-Marcionite exegesis throughout much of book 4 before he cites the elder specifically in 4. 27–32. The import for us is that it confirms Polycarp's use of the Fourth Gospel.

One more instance of a probable reference to Polycarp's use of John is found in *AH* 4. 41. 2. Here Irenaeus is reflecting on the way scripture terms 'those who remain in a state of apostasy "sons of the devil" and "angels of the wicked one" '. The first of these phrases would seem ostensibly to have John 8: 44 in mind, as well as perhaps Acts 13:10; and 1 John 3: 8, 10. Here Irenaeus refers again to the teaching of one of his predecessors to explain the sense, 'For [the word] "son," as one before me has observed, has a twofold meaning: one [is a son] in the order of nature, because he was born a son; the other, in that he was made so, is reputed a son, although there be a difference between being born so and being made so'.

Since we know that John's opposition to Cerinthus, and some connection of both these men to Ephesus, was part of the tradition passed on from Polycarp, since it is apparent that Irenaeus must have received some of his knowledge of Cerinthus' system (*AH* 1. 26. 1) from Polycarp, one must also wonder if Irenaeus' assertion that John wrote the Gospel (while in Ephesus, according to Irenaeus, *AH* 3. 1. 1)[204] to thwart the teaching of Cerinthus may also have come from Polycarp.

These teachings go back to the time when Irenaeus used to listen to Polycarp's teaching, as he tells us in his letter to Florinus (*EpFlor.* Eus. *HE* 5. 20. 6). We do not know just when this was, but it is unlikely to have come from before *c.*140 and could not have been later than *c.*155. Irenaeus appears to have been in Rome when Polycarp was martyred in Smyrna,[205] and his knowledge of details of Polycarp's visit there in 154 or 155 suggests that he may have moved to the capital city by that time.[206] This means Irenaeus' contact with Polycarp was broken some months or years before the latter's death. This contact took place then probably during a period of years right around the midpoint of the century. Irenaeus' testimonies about the later period of Polycarp's life show both that Polycarp was in the habit of communicating traditions and teachings which he had received, allegedly from John and other apostles, and that he used the Fourth Gospel, and certainly the First and Second Epistles, in his own teaching.

---

[204] 'Asia' as his residence is mentioned also in 2. 22. 5.

[205] According to the scribal notations at the end of the Moscow MS of the *Mart. Polyc.* This is said to have been contained in one of Irenaeus' writings, perhaps the letter to Florinus in which he has so much to say about Polycarp.

[206] M. H. Shepherd, 'The Letter of Polycarp, Bishop of Smyrna, to the Philippians', in C. Richardson, *et al.* (eds.), *Early Christian Fathers*, LCC 1 (Philadelphia, 1953), 121–30, at 123 n. 1.

MARTYRDOM OF POLYCARP

In the words of Polycarp reported in the *Martyrdom* there are a few apparent
Johannine allusions, and the author of the work, a Christian named
Marcion, or Marcianus (20. 1),[207] also seems to be familiar with the Fourth
Gospel. From the beginning he makes plain that the martyrdom of Polycarp was 'a martyrdom in accordance with the Gospel' (1. 1; 19. 1).[208] This
is manifest, he says, first of all in that Polycarp 'waited to be betrayed as
also the Lord had done', instead of putting himself forward, as a Phrygian
named Quintus had done (4. 1); for 'the Gospel does not give this teaching'.
But it is evident from parallels drawn later with the trial and death of Jesus
that the author saw more elements of conformity with the Lord's experience
and thus more conformity with the Gospel. The police captain who arrested
Polycarp 'had been allotted the very name, being called Herod' (6. 2).
Those who betrayed Polycarp underwent 'the same punishment as Judas'
(6. 2). The police and cavalry went out armed after Polycarp, 'as against a
robber' (7. 1; cf. Matt. 26: 55). And 'the hour came [cf. John 17: 1] for
departure, and they set him on an ass [cf. John 12: 14, etc.], and led him
into the city on a "great Sabbath day"' (cf. John 19: 31)[209] (8. 1; cf. 21. 1).
When the police captain and his father tried to persuade Polycarp to offer
sacrifice, 'he at first did not answer them' (8. 2; cf. Mark 14: 61; John 9: 9–
10). A martyrdom 'according to the Gospel' meant a martyrdom that
reminded the Christian of Jesus' own, as recorded in the synoptic Gospels
and in the Fourth Gospel.[210]

Polycarp's prayer of chapter 14 apparently signifies his knowledge of both
the Gospel and the Revelation of John. He addresses God, 'O Lord God
Almighty' (14. 1),[211] repeating the title which in the NT only appears in
Revelation, and there no less than six times (4. 8; 11. 17; 15. 13; 16. 7; 19.
6; 21. 22). Particularly relevant is Revelation 15: 13, where this form of
address comes from 'those who had conquered the beast and its image and
the number of its name, standing beside the sea of glass' in heaven. In the
prayer Polycarp also mentions his expectation concerning 'the resurrection
of eternal life' (εἰς ἀνάστασιν ζωῆς αἰωνίου, 14. 2). This reflects the terminology of John 5: 29, εἰς ἀνάστασιν ζωῆς, with the characteristic

---

[207] Buschmann, *Martyrium*, 356–7.

[208] Though some have thought this was a secondary motif, added by an editor (perhaps Pionius)
long afterward, it is now generally regarded as an authentic and central motif of the original work.
It is connected to the original situation by the bad example of Quintus (ch. 4). See Buschmann,
Martyrium, 49–58, who sees perhaps too strictly an anti-Montanist focus here.

[209] On ὄντος σαββάτου μεγάλου see Buschmann, *Martyrium*, 167–9. Cf. 14. 2 in Polycarp's
prayer his reference to 'this day and this hour'.

[210] Buschmann, *Martyrium*, 143, would also include 3. 2; 6. 1, which refer to the captors 'searching' for Polycarp as comparable to the seeking of Jesus in John 18: 4, 7–8.

[211] Echoed, but not exactly, by the author in 19. 2, 'glorifying God and the Almighty Father'.
'Lord Almighty' is common in the LXX but the threefold title is found in the LXX apparently only
in Amos, though 'Lord Almighty, God of Israel' is found in 2 Sam. 7: 25, 27.

Johannine adjective αἰώνιος added.[212] Because Polycarp speaks of having a 'part' (μέρος) in the number of the martyrs for (εἰς) this resurrection, it is also possibly influenced by Revelation 20: 6, μακάριος καὶ ἅγιος ὁ ἔχων μέρος ἐν τῇ ἀναστάσει τῇ πρώτῃ.[213]

Finally, in 20. 2 the author speaks of Jesus as 'the only-begotten' (μονογενής). Though by this time the Christological term μονογενής may have made its way into the general Christian theological vocabulary, it was apparently so coined by the author of the Johannine Prologue, who in any case used it so distinctively (1: 14, 18; 3: 16, 18; cf. 1 John 4: 9). It is palpably more likely that the influence has come directly from the Fourth Gospel (or 1 John 4: 9).

Marcianus does not mention Polycarp's personal relationship to John or any other apostle by name. But this relationship is probably embedded and implied in his description of Polycarp as 'an apostolic...teacher' (16. 2). It foreshadows the later practice of Irenaeus, who in his letter to Florinus calls Polycarp 'that blessed and apostolic presbyter' (*HE* 5. 20. 7), and calls the presbyter of *AH* 4. 27–32 (i.e. Polycarp) 'the presbyter, the disciple of the apostles' (4. 32. 1). Irenaeus in the 180s said that 'all the Asiatic Churches testify' to Polycarp's personal connections with apostles, 'as do also those men who have succeeded Polycarp down to the present time' (*AH* 3. 3. 4).

The combined witness of the *Martyrdom* and Irenaeus forms a stable portrait of Polycarp's role in the Johannine legacy in the later years of his life. The public nature of Polycarp's role in passing on Johannine traditions (e.g. in telling the story of John and Cerinthus at the bath-house, which many heard from him; stories of Polycarp's own interaction with John; Polycarp's Johannine exegesis) and the examples of both Irenaeus and the Smyrnaean Marcianus, author of the *Martyrdom*, illustrate that the larger Smyrnaean community participated jointly in that Johannine legacy. There is a natural coherence and consistency between Irenaeus' testimony in this matter—spread throughout at least three works written by him over a span of ten to fifteen years—the words of Polycarp recorded in the *Martyrdom*, and the usage of Marcianus himself in the *Martyrdom* that belies the common attempts to impugn the statements of Irenaeus. Taken together, they not only establish Polycarp's role in the tradition leading up to and forming the basis for Irenaeus, they contribute to the picture of a more widespread recognition of the Fourth Gospel among the 'Great Church' in Asia from at least the middle of the second century on.

---

[212] The phrases ζωὴ αἰώνιος or αἰώνιος ζωή occur 43 times in the NT, 17 of these are in John and 6 in 1 John (John 3: 15, 16, 36; 4: 14, 36; 5: 24, 39; 6: 27, 40, 47, 54, 68; 10: 28; 12: 25, 50; 17: 2, 3; 1 John 1: 2; 2: 18; 3: 15; 5: 11, 13, 20). In all 17 occurrences of the adjective αἰώνιος in John, and in all 6 in 1 John, it describes ζωή.

[213] Buschmann, *Martyrium*, 283 n. 185, notes in Polycarp's language here 'a Johannine turn': Joh 5,29; Apc 20,6: ὁ ἔχων μέρος ἐν τῷ πρώτῃ'.

7

John among the Orthodox, before *c*.150

The period before the midpoint of the second century is, of course, of critical interest for our study. It is the period of silence for the Fourth Gospel in the Great Church. 'One of the remarkable items in the history of the traditions about John', writes Culpepper, is 'the nearly complete silence of the record during the crucial decades of the early second century'.[1] According to the dominant paradigm of scholarship, in the period before *c*.150 the Fourth Gospel was predominantly known and used by 'gnostic' or heterodox groups. To the extent it was known among the orthodox it was used with caution or suspicion, or else rejected altogether.

There are several documents from this period which might seem to support the paradigm. Convincing signs of the use of the Fourth Gospel have been held to be absent from *1 Clement*, the *Didache*, the *Ps. Barnabas*, and *2 Clement*. They are often denied as well for Ignatius' epistles, Polycarp's *Epistle to the Philippians*, and the *Shepherd* of Hermas, not to mention Papias of Hierapolis. For some of these works the silence, or near silence in any case, is puzzling and perhaps telling, in some way. But for others one will have to admit at the outset that the significance is minimal at best. Most scholars regard *1 Clement* as closely contemporary with or as predating the Fourth Gospel. It does contain some parallels to the Fourth Gospel but these are not very close or numerous. The Fourth Gospel appears to be unknown to the author of the Didache, but this work too may well be as early as or earlier than the Fourth Gospel. Some would place the *Shepherd* of Hermas in this category of early works, though I am not convinced of this and will examine the matter below. Nor, in my view, is *Ps. Barnabas* quite this early, though it may well be from about the time of Ignatius' letters and may still be unfamiliar with the recently published Gospel according to John. There is a possible trace of the Fourth Gospel's influence in this work, in its use of an Old Testament symbol which is used also by the Fourth Gospel.[2] But this is admittedly tenuous. Perhaps more significant is the epistle known as *2 Clement*, which is surely later than the Fourth Gospel and which contains no very probable influence from the Fourth Gospel, while it does contain many citations or paraphrases of Jesus' word from Synoptic sources, and from some apocryphal source(s). It remains to be seen, then, whether *2*

---

[1] R. A. Culpepper, *John, the Son of Zebedee* (Columbia, SC, 1994), 131.

[2] F.-M. Braun, *Jean le Théologien* (Paris, 1959), 81–6; R. Kieffer, 'Les Premiers Indices d'une réception de l'évangile de saint Jean', in F. Van Segbroeck *et al.* (eds.), *The Four Gospels 1992* (Leuven, 1992), 2227.

Clement is representative for large segments of the Church in this regard, or whether it is more the exception which proves the rule. If we were to find more signs of the knowledge of the Fourth Gospel in this period, then Hengel's remark may become relevant: 'The *argumentum e silentio*, which is so often misused, is no proof that an author did not know a particular text. It only shows that he did not use it explicitly. Unequivocal quotations of any of the Gospels in the Apostolic Fathers are very rare.'[3]

The Ad Diognetum

The so-called *Epistle to Diognetus* is not really an epistle, but reads more like a treatise or, in my opinion, the transcript of an oral address. Sometimes included in collections of the Apostolic Fathers, it has been acknowledged as having more in common with the early apologists. Its date and provenance have remained unsettled, though most scholars place it in the second century. Many have placed the work in the years between *c.*125 and 150,[4] though Robert M. Grant has argued for a date of *c.*177,[5] and H. I. Marrou for *c.*190–200.[6] A complicating factor is that many have judged that the final chapters, 11 and 12, are in fact from another work. The scribe of the only manuscript of the *Ad Diognetum* known signified that in his exemplar there was a gap separating these chapters from what preceded. Leslie Barnard has argued that both works are products of the same author,[7] others assign them to unrelated individuals. The evidence for the unity of the work has, in my view, been underestimated in recent years, and the gap is best seen as representing the absence of a page (or more) which was lost

---

[3] M. Hengel, *The Johannine Question*, (London, 1989), 14.

[4] Dom P. Andriessen, 'The Authorship of the Epistula ad Diognetum', *VC* 1 (1947), 129–36, who assumed the unity of the work and argued it was by Quadratus, the early Christian apologist; E. R. Fairweather, 'The So-called Letter to Diognetus. Introduction and Books', in C. C. Richardson *et al.*, *Early Christian Fathers*, LCC 1 (Philadelphia, 1953), 205–12, at 210, places chs. 1–10 before Irenaeus and probably *c.*129, acquiescing to Andriessen's theory that it was written by Quadratus. L. W. Barnard 'The Enigma of the Epistle to Diognetus', in *Studies in the Apostolic Fathers and their Backgrounds* (Oxford, 1966), 165–73, at 173, 'I should...date Chs. i-x of this Epistle not later than *c.*A.D. 130'. He refers to the Christology, the lack of reference to the Holy Spirit, 'the absence of asceticism and sacerdotalism', among other things, as supporting this. C. M. Nielsen, 'The Epistle to Diognetus: Its Date and Relationship to Marcion', *Anglican Theological Review*, 52 (1970), 77–91, argues for a date before the outbreak of Marcionism. W. H. C. Frend, *The Rise of Christianity* (Philadelphia, 1984), 261 n. 24 says, 'The use of Hellenistic–Jewish apologetic models, the absence of the Euhermerist argument against the pagan gods employed by the later Apologists, and parallels with Aristides, suggest a relatively early date, not later than A.D. 150'.

[5] Grant, *Greek Apologists*, 178, thinks the main body must be from after 176, when the attack at Lyons took place, for its reference to persecution presupposes that searches have taken place. But we do not know that this never happened before 176.

[6] H. I. Marrou, *A Diognète*, 2nd edn., SC 33 bis (Paris, 1997 repr. of the 1965 2nd edn.), 241–68, who suggested Pantaenus as author. Braun, *Jean le théologien*, accepted Marrou's positions on date and provenance (Alexandria).

[7] Barnard, 'Enigma', 173, would place chs. 1–10 before *c.* AD 130 and chs. 11–12 *c.*140.

earlier in the transmission of the text. I am also persuaded that the work best fits a situation *c.*140–50, partly because of the evidence cited by the scholars mentioned above, partly because of certain notable links with the time and situation of Polycarp, particularly in the *Martyrdom of Polycarp*. The demonstration of both of these points will have to be presented in another place. For now I simply side with those scholars who have concluded in favour of the unity of the document,[8] and with those mentioned above who have argued for date prior to *c.*150.

A number of scholars have been impressed by similarities with Asian authors such as Melito of Sardis and Irenaeus.[9] Fairweather thinks the use of the Johannine corpus, and the influence of Ephesians and 1 Peter also favour Asia Minor as a place of origin.[10] In 12. 9 the author mentions 'the Passover of the Lord'. If this is a sign, as some think, of quartodecimanism, this also would favour Asia Minor, though it would not be conclusive.

J. N. Sanders denied that this author was dependent upon the Fourth Gospel.[11] His judgement has been accepted by many advocates of the OJP,[12] though it does not agree with the statements made by most actual students of the work.[13] Barnard summarized this writer's indebtedness to the Fourth Gospel and 1 John, stating that, 'Both Chs. i–x and xi–xii of ad Diognetum are indebted directly or indirectly to the Johannine theology'.[14] After citing several examples, Barnard continues, 'although the degree of literary dependence is not clear there is little doubt that the writer was familiar with the theological ideas of both the Fourth Gospel and I John'.[15]

---

[8] E. B. Birks, 'Epistle to Diognetus', in *Dictionary of Christian Biography*, ii. 162–7, at 162; Andriessen, 'Authorship'; H. G. Meecham, *The Epistle to Diognetus: The Greek Text with Introduction, Translation and Notes* (Manchester, 1949); J. A. Kleist, *The Didache, the Epistle of Barnabas, The Epistles and the Martyrdom of St. Polycarp, The Fragments of Papias, The Epistle to Diognetus*, ACW 6 (Westminster, Md., 1948), 129–31; Marrou, *A Diognète*; S. Zincone, 'Diognetus, To', *EEChurch*, i. 237; Marco Rizzi, *La questione dell'unità dell'Ad Diognetum*, Studia patristica Mediolanensia (Milan, 1989), but see also the critical review by W. Kinzig, *JTS* NS 42 (1991), 330–4.

[9] Fairweather, 'Diognetus', 209, favours a theory which assigns chs. 1–10 to a predecessor of Irenaeus and chs. 11–12 to one of his successors.

[10] Ibid. 208–9.

[11] J. N. Sanders, *The Fourth Gospel in the Early Church* (Cambridge, 1943), 17–19. Sanders said at one point, 'the possibility of actual dependence on the Gospel or Epistle cannot be wholly excluded', but then wrote, 'chapters I–ix may safely be taken as evidence for the existence of a type of theology akin to that of the Fourth Gospel and I John, though one cannot say whether these chapters actually quote either work' (19).

[12] Hillmer did not even consider it, judging that Sander's treatment of the Apostolic Fathers was definitive. It suffers the same fate in the studies of Bauer, Haenchen, Poffet, Culpepper, and Sloyan, and even of Hengel. It was treated, with vastly different results, by Braun, *Jean le Théologien*, 71–9; Kieffer, 'Les Premiers Indices', 2231–2.

[13] Even Rudolf Brändle, *Die Ethik der 'Schrift an Diognetus'. Eine Wiederaufnahme paulinischer und johanneischer Theologie am Ausgang des zweiten Jahrhunderts*, Abhandlungen zur Theologie des alten und neuen Testaments, 64 (Zürich, 1975), 217–21, while he is very much aware of the judgements of Bauer and Sanders on the alleged difficulties which the Church of the 2nd cent. had with the Johannine writings (217–28), finds it necessary to conclude that the author of this work (Brändle considers only chs. 1–10) knew the Johannine writings firsthand.

[14] Barnard, 'Enigma', 170.

[15] Ibid. See also Kieffer, 'Les Premiers Indices', 2231–2.

Fairweather wrote that 'The Pauline influence is often perceptible, while the Johannine outlook dominates the work'.[16] As a work of apologetic addressed to a non-Christian audience, the author tends to refrain from textual citations of authorities not shared with his audience, until the final chapter, when he begins to contemplate Diognetus' conversion. But he certainly appears to be indebted to the Fourth Gospel in his view of the relation of the Christian to the world. 'Christians', he says, 'dwell in the world, but are not of the world (ἐν κόσμῳ οἰκοῦσιν οὐκ εἰσὶ δὲ ἐκ τοῦ κόσμου)' (*Diogn.* 6. 3); in John 17, Jesus says, 'but they are in the world (ἐν τῷ κόσμῳ εἰσίν)' (17: 11); 17: 14, 'and the world has hated them because they are not of the world (οὐκ εἰσὶν ἐκ τοῦ κόσμου)'. The apologist for Christianity in *Diogn.* 6. 5 says, 'The flesh hates the soul and wages war against it... also the world hates the Christians'; Jesus in John 15: 18–19 says, 'If the world hates you, know that it has hated me before it hated you. If you were of the world, the world would love its own; but because you are not of the world, but I chose you out of the world, therefore the world hates you.' In his appropriation of the 'typiquement johannique'[17] theme of the hatred of the world for Christians (see also 2. 6; 5. 11, 17) this author foreshadows the *Epistle of Vienne and Lyons* (*HE* 5. 1. 16).

The author of *Ad Diognetum* speaks of God sending his Son, and 'when he sent him, he did so as one loving, not judging (ἔπεμψεν ὡς ἀγαπῶν, οὐ κρίνων)' (7. 5), and later says, 'For God loved (ἠγάπησε) men... to them he sent his one and only Son (πρὸς οὓς ἀπέστειλε τὸν υἱὸν αὐτοῦ τὸν μονογενῆ)' (10. 2). The conception and the language seem to be indebted to John 3: 16–17, 'For God so loved (ἠγάπησεν) the world that he gave his only Son (τὸν υἱὸν τὸν μονογενῆ)... For God sent (ἀπέστειλεν) the Son into the world, not to condemn (οὐ... ἵνα κρίνῃ) the world, but that the world might be saved through him' (cf. John 12: 47; 1 John 4: 9). In *Ad Diognetum* 8. 5 the speaker declares, 'No one has either seen or recognized him (ἀνθρώπων δὲ οὐδεὶς οὔτε [εἶδεν][18] οὔτε ἐγνώρισεν), but he has revealed himself'; in John 1: 18 the Johannine author declares, 'No one has ever seen God (θεὸν οὐδεὶς ἑώρακεν πώποτε); the only Son, who is in the bosom of the Father, he has made him known', and John 8: 55; 5: 37 testify that Jesus' opponents have not heard God's voice, seen his form, or known him. When the author of *Ad Diognetum* 9. 1 says that Christians have been shown (φανερώσαντες) that they are unable 'to enter the kingdom of God (εἰσελθεῖν εἰς τὴν Βασιλείαν τοῦ θεοῦ) on our own' but also that they are now 'enabled to do so by God's power (τῇ δυνάμει τοῦ θεοῦ)', one has to wonder whether the demonstration he has in mind is not found in the announcement of Jesus in John 3: 5, 'Truly, truly, I say to you, unless one is

---

[16] Fairweather, 'Diognetus', 207–8.
[17] Braun, *Jean le Théologien*, 76.
[18] Emendation for ειπεν in MS.

born of water and the Spirit [John 3: 3, unless one is born anew], he cannot enter the kingdom of God (οὐ δύναται εἰσελθεῖν τὴν βασιλείαν τοῦ θεοῦ)'.[19] The author uses the term Logos for Christ, and while this may not in itself signify a familiarity with the Fourth Gospel, the author does, in connection with his use of this title in 7. 2, expound on the Word's role as 'the very artificer and Creator (τὸ τεχνίγην καὶ δημιουργόν) of the universe himself', which may well be based upon John 1: 2–3. And in 11. 2, 3, 7, in a section which includes several other Johannine echoes,[20] he explains, 'This is why he sent the Word, namely, that he might appear to the world; though dishonored by the chosen people [cf. John 1: 9]...This is he who was from the beginning [cf. 1 John 1: 1; John 1: 1, 2], who appeared as new yet proved to be old [cf. John 1: 15, 30]' (*Diogn.* 11. 3–4).

1 John was mentioned above in reference to *Diogn.* 10. 2; 11. 4, and there are other signs of the author's familiarity with it. There is at least one and possibly two allusions to 1 John in 10. 3 where he asks, 'And when you have acquired this knowledge, with what joy do you think you will be filled (πληρωθήσεσθαι χαρᾶς [cf. 1 John 1: 4; John 15: 11; 2 John 12]), or how will you love him who so loved you first?' (cf. 1 John 4: 19). The addition of the adverb οὕτως in the last clause probably is due to the author's know-ledge of John 3: 16 which, as we have seen, is visible elsewhere.

Not only does it appear beyond reasonable doubt that this author (both authors if chapters 11–12 are to be separated from the rest) knew the Fourth Gospel and the First Epistle, we would be justified in saying that these books have exercised a considerable influence on his theology and worldview.[21] That Sanders could not affirm a literary dependence on these Johannine works is due in no small part to his standard of proof, for he wanted to require actual quotations. But like several other Christian writers of the first half of the second century, this one seldom gives what we could call quotations, but mingles the words of his scriptural authorities, including those of the Fourth Gospel and 1 John, with his own words. In the case of the *Ad Diognetum* the intermingled Johannine words and ideas are no less important for their lack of introductory formulas and exact verbal corres-pondence. This author in his address to unbelievers did not quote Matthew, Mark, or Luke, and the Johannine material is more abundant by any measure than the Synoptic.

It is not out of place to speak of New Testament scripture with regard to this author, who also, in passing, gives us a summary of the component categories of scripture in 11. 6, 'Then is the fear of the Law sung, and the grace of the Prophets known, the faith of the Gospels is established,

[19] The 'inability' is stressed in John 3: 3–5 twice by Jesus and once by Nicodemus.
[20] On which more will be said below.
[21] See Brändle, *Ethik*, 219–21.

and the tradition of apostles is guarded, and the grace of the Church exults'. He knows multiple Gospels, and, to judge from his language and conceptions, these must certainly include John and Matthew.[22] He knows Paul as 'the apostle' (12. 5), in fact his only New Testament quotation is from 1 Corinthians 8: 1, and he knows other apostles as well (11. 3). He calls himself a disciple of apostles, 11. 1. The appearance of 'Gospels' and 'apostles' alongside the Law and the Prophets suggests a high estimation of the works which constitute his Christian scripture.

As I have observed, it is not the author's usual style in this work to cite his sources formally. But I wish to reproduce one more passage, 11. 2–3, in which an impressive number of Johannine reminiscences and allusions devolve in such a way as to suggest that the author's view of the Johannine author might be inferred from them.

2. Indeed, does anyone who has been rightly taught and has come to love the Word not seek to learn exactly the things openly made known by the Word to disciples? To them the Word appeared and revealed these things (ἐφανέρωσεν ὁ λόγος φανείς), speaking quite plainly (παρρησίᾳ λαλῶν) as he did so; though not understood by unbelievers, he explained (διηγούμενος) them to disciples who, being regarded as faithful by him learned the mysteries of the Father. 3. This is why he sent the Word, namely, that he might appear to the world (ἵνα κόσμῳ φανῇ); though dishonored by the chosen people, he was preached by apostles and believed in by Gentiles. 4. This is he who was from the beginning (οὗτος ὁ ἀπ' ἀρχῆς), who appeared as new yet proved to be old...

The appropriation of the Johannine conception of Jesus as the Logos, who revealed himself and the Father to his disciples, along with some of its distinctive vocabulary,[23] suggest that he has the author of the Fourth Gospel particularly in mind, who is his model for the 'disciples' in these sentences. First of all we have Christ called the Word, and the author's preference for 'disciples' in this passage instead of apostles, as also in the Fourth Gospel. The one rightly taught and who loves the Word will seek to learn those things made known by the Word to (his) disciples. That the Word revealed himself (ἐφανέρωσεν ὁ λόγος) to his disciples reflects the language of John 2: 11 (καὶ ἐφανέρωσεν τὴν δόξαν αὐτοῦ, καὶ ἐπίστευσαν εἰς αὐτὸν οἱ μαθηταὶ αὐτοῦ); 21:1(μετὰ ταῦτα ἐφανέρωσεν ἑαυτὸν πάλιν ὁ Ἰησοῦς τοῖς μαθηταῖς) and cf. 1 John 1: 2 (καὶ ἡ ζωὴ ἐφανερώθη, καὶ ἑωράκαμεν...). That the Word is said to have spoken boldly or openly (παρρησίᾳ λαλῶν) seems to be an allusion to John 16: 25, 29, where Jesus

[22] Cf. Matt. 5: 44 in 6. 6; Matt. 6: 25–31 in 9. 6; Matt. 3: 17 in 11. 5.

[23] It is ironic that Sanders, *Fourth Gospel*, 19, cited this section of *Diogn.* along with the condition that its use of the word Logos as a title for Christ would only be conclusive evidence of literary dependence if 'found in conjunction with other evidence for the use of the Fourth Gospel', which he went on to say was 'not quite obvious' in this passage. 'Here there is nothing inconsistent with the teaching of the Fourth Gospel, and equally nothing certainly dependent on it'. I suggest here that he missed a good deal.

announces that no longer in figures λαλήσω ὑμῖν, ἀλλὰ παρρησίᾳ, and then his μαθηταί respond, 'Ah, now ἐν παρρησίᾳ λαλεῖς, not in any figure'. When the author says that the Word 'explained' (διηγούμενος) hidden things to his disciples, he uses a word, διηγέομαι, which is not used in the New Testament. But a close cognate, ἐξηγέομι, is used for the Word's unique activity of explaining the unseen God once in the New Testament, in John 1: 18 (ἐκεῖνος ἐξηγήσατο). God's sending of the Word ἵνα κόσμῳ φανῇ seems like an expansion of the Baptist's self-testimony, that he came baptizing ἵνα φανερωθῇ τῷ Ἰσραήλ (John 1: 31). As I observed earlier, the author's mention of the people's dishonouring of the Word recalls John 1: 9, and his depiction of this Word as ὁ ἀπ' ἀρχῆς, seems a transparent allusion to 1 John 1: 1, ὁ ἦν ἀπ' ἀρχῆς (somewhat less likely, John 1: 1, ἐν ἀρχῇ ἦν ὁ λόγος), whose author attests to eye-, ear-, and hand-witness knowledge of Jesus. This chain of references to the Word's revealing activity among his disciples seems then to be modelled on the example of the author of John and 1 John. This implies that the author of the *Ad Diognetum* accepts the Johannine author's self-testimony as presented in these books and that he regards him as one of those to whom the Word revealed himself and his Father, that is, as one of Jesus' personal disciples. While this is not an explicit identification, it is evidence of an awareness of 'John's' authority as a disciple of Jesus which conforms to more definite identifications we see elsewhere. It is not unlike the implicit hints Justin gives to the careful reader of his apologetic works.

Ad Diognetum 11 belongs to the final two chapters which many believe are not part of the original work. If they are correct, the document's witness to the Johannine corpus will have to be divided, and two orthodox writings and possibly two distinct writers from roughly the same time will have to be acknowledged as showing the influence of the Fourth Gospel and First Epistle instead of one. More plausibly, I believe, based on the unity of the work, we may speak of a single work of a talented Christian orator who was quite substantially influenced by these Johannine works at some time probably just before the middle of the second century.

The Epistula Apostolorum

Its date and provenance

The work known as *Epistula Apostolorum*, preserved in a fourth- or fifth-century Coptic version and a longer Ethiopic version, and in a small Latin fragment, is an important source for our knowledge of the influence of the Fourth Gospel in the first half of the second century. In an earlier study devoted to its date and provenance I concluded, along with others, that it was written by an orthodox writer in Asia Minor, perhaps Smyrna, and that this person wrote during the ministry of Polycarp.[24] Within the range of about 115 to 150 there are two sets of dates which appear most likely, based on the correspondence with persecutions and earthquakes in the region: the years just preceding 120, and sometime in the 140s. Here it will be treated as if it belongs in the latter period. This work fictionally presents itself as a letter from the apostles given them by Christ after the resurrection and before the ascension. It represents the situation of a Christian group which perceives itself as besieged by the authorities of the world and by false Christians in their community. Against the latter it emphasizes the reality of Christ's flesh, both before and after the resurrection. Its purpose is evidently to encourage believers with an 'apostolic' reassurance of their orthodox Christological beliefs in the face of docetic challenge and to strengthen them in the face of abuse from without.

ITS KNOWLEDGE AND USE OF THE JOHANNINE CORPUS

The potential importance of this work for our purposes is foreshadowed in Schmidt's well-drawn conclusion, 'in none of the writings of the second century left to us is such a heavy use of the Gospel of John prominent as in the present work'.[25] The predominance of Johannine influence is usually recognized by students of the work, though neglected by proponents of the OJP. This author's knowledge of the first Epistle of John and the Revelation is also well attested. I shall not try to catalogue all his allusions to these works but will try to give a sense of the extent of his knowledge and the value he attributes to these works.

Use of John

For this author, just as for Justin Martyr, the Prologue of the Fourth Gospel was a crucial datum in forming his understanding of the incarnation of the Word of God. As observed above, like Justin, he uses a Christological application of John 1: 13, and relies more than once on the Johannine phrase from John 1: 14, 'the Word became flesh' (3. 2; 14. 5; 39. 16, cf. 21. 2). He refers to Jesus' turning the water into wine at the wedding in Cana (5. 1–3; John 2: 1–11). He shows a propensity similar to that of Justin, the *Gospel of Peter*, the Egerton Gospel, and Tatian's *Diatessaron*, of assimilating details from several Gospel accounts, and certain other sources, and conflating them into a single account (e.g. 3. 2 combining John 1: 14, John 1: 13, Luke 2: 7; then the chain of Gospel events in chapter 5). He knows the

---

[24] Hill, '*Epistula Apostolorum*', *JECS* 7 (1999), 1–53. See also A. Stewart-Sykes, 'The Asian Context of the New Prophecy and of *Epistula Apostolorum*', *VC* 51 (1997), 416–38. An Asian provenance was the conclusion also of C. Schmidt, *Gespräche Jesu mit seinem Jüngern nach der Auferstehung*, TU 43 (Leipzig, 1919, repr. 1927).

[25] Schmidt, *Gespräche Jesu*, 224–5. As a rough indicator, the *NTA*[2] notes give fifty-three separate references to John, five to 1 John.

Johannine designation of the Spirit as the Paraclete (5. 17).[26] Like Justin, he knows the Johannine post-resurrection appearance of Jesus in which he invites his disciples (*Ep. Apost.* includes Peter and Andrew along with Thomas) to inspect his crucifixion wounds (11. 9; 23. 1; cf. John 20: 27). He knows the Johannine logion that Jesus is 'in the Father and my Father is in me' (17. 4; 25. 3; 39. 15, cf. John 10: 38; 14: 10, 11, 20; 17: 21, 23) and the complementary promise that the disciples should be 'in' Jesus and be the dwelling place of the Father (19. 18; 36. 12; cf. John 14: 20, 23; 15: 4–7; 17: 21). He knows Jesus' 'new commandment; love one another' from John 13: 14 (18. 5). The Johannine charge to 'keep my commandments', John 14: 15; 15: 10; is repeatedly echoed in 24. 6; 36. 4; 39. 15; with overt indictments of those who confess his name but who do not keep them (27. 2, 4; 29.1; 44. 1; 46. 1; 50. 1). The author knows the Johannine commission to the apostles and that many will believe in Jesus through their message (19. 7; 23. 1; 35. 5; 41. 6; cf. John 17: 20). When the disciples express wonderment at what they have seen and heard, they are told, 'Much more blessed are they who have not seen and (yet) have believed' (29. 6 Copt.), an obvious recasting of John 20: 29. But in contrast to the *Apocryphon of James*, the author of the *Epistula Apostolorum* adapts this saying in a positive way. The disciples ask the risen Lord a question which is surely based on the conversation between Jesus and his disciples in John 16: 10, 16–19, 28, 'O Lord, in what way will one be able to believe that you will go and leave us, as you said to us, "A day will come and an hour when I shall go up to my Father"?' (29. 7 Copt.). Their later question, 'when will you go to your Father and to our God and Lord?' (33. 1 Eth.) recalls John 20: 17, 'I am returning to my Father and your Father, to my God and your God'. Other words and phrases which most likely came from the Fourth Gospel, such as 'believe in him who sent me' (28. 5, from John 5: 21; 12: 44), are sprinkled throughout the text.

It is not only the sheer number of allusions to the Fourth Gospel which reveals the author's high regard for that Gospel. Unlike several of the gnostic texts examined above, he uses that Gospel in a wholly positive way. Despite the apocryphal and pseudonymous nature of this document, it does not seek to supplant or supersede the Church's accepted Gospels. Its setting is fictitious but its polemic is serious, and it is aimed particularly at those who do not countenance the notion of incarnation derived from the words of the Fourth Gospel.

This adherence to the Fourth Gospel is reinforced in another striking way by the author. In a list of the apostles in the first chapter the author places John the son of Zebedee at the head, something which does not occur in any source previous to this time.[27] This placing of John at the head of the list of the apostles certainly indicates an esteem for this disciple.

---

[26] Though M. Hornschuh, *Studien zur Epistula Apostolorum*, PTS 5 (Berlin, 1965), 106, says this word is absent from three of the five Ethiopic MSS.

[27] See C. E. Hill, 'The Identity of John's Nathanael', *JSNT* 67 (1997), 45–61.

Is it mere coincidence that this occurs in a work which relies on the Fourth Gospel to an extent unprecedented among early Christian sources to this time?[28] The apostle list itself seems to make the connection for us, for not only does it place John at the head, but gives prominence to disciples who have prominence only in John's Gospel, and even includes Nathanael, whose name is mentioned only in that Gospel. In other words the preference for the Fourth Gospel is seen in the apostle list itself, and this list is headed by John the son of Zebedee. Hengel is certainly justified in taking this to be a clear indication that this author attributed his favourite Gospel to John. It signifies both his esteem for the Fourth Gospel and for the man he believes wrote that Gospel.[29] This attribution, incidentally, as it comes at the latest in the 140s, has to be earlier than any attribution we have from Heracleon, Ptolemy, or even Valentinus.

What is more, the esteem for the Gospel according to John, even the implication that it bore this title and was ascribed to the apostle, coupled with its opposition to Cerinthus form a perfect fit with the situation in Asia Minor from the middle years of Polycarp's life, as we may reconstruct it from Irenaeus. The antagonism between John and Cerinthus established by Polycarp is adorned in the *Epistula*, where it seems to be connected not only to John the man but to his Gospel.

Use of the Johannine Letters

The statement in chapter 2 that the apostles 'heard and felt him after he had risen from the dead' probably alludes to 1 John 1: 1; John 20: 27. 1 John 1: 1–4 is probably reflected as well in 6. 1. The relationship between acknowledging Jesus' name and doing his commandments in 27. 2 is probably based on 1 John 2: 4–5. The phrase 'walk in truth' in chapter 38 is probably borrowed from 2 John 4 or 3 John 3–4. There is no sense in which it could be argued that this author uses 1 John or its distinctive teachings to 'rehabilitate' the Fourth Gospel.

Use of Revelation

Hornschuh denied any points of contact between the *Ep. Apost.* and Revelation,[30] but the edition in NTA[2] lists nine probable references or allusions to Revelation, and there are certainly more.[31] There are some impressive parallels with the letter to the Smyrnaeans from Revelation 2, in particular regarding the social situations of the two communities, so much so as to add

---

[28] M. R. Hillmer, 'The Gospel of John in the Second Century' (Th.D. diss., Harvard University, Apr. 1966), 49, refused to make the connection: 'It is sufficient to note here the prominence given both to the Gospel of John and to John as a disciple in the Ep. Ap., and also to observe that nothing in the Ep. Ap. makes any connection between the two'.

[29] Hengel, *Question*, 12, 20, 74.

[30] Hornshcuh, *Studien*, 102.

[31] See chs. 21, 37–9.

to the suspicion that the author of *Ep. Apost.* saw his own community addressed in this letter.[32] This Asian work of the first half of the second century then knows virtually the entire Johannine corpus.

THE AUTHOR'S 'CANON' AND HIS VIEW OF APOSTOLIC WRITINGS

Although its chosen fictional setting would prevent its author from citing New Testament documents as such,[33] it occasionally betrays an assumption of the existence of authoritative, written NT documents. Not only does it incorporate hosts of words, phrases, and concepts derived from at least three of the four Gospels, predominantly the Fourth Gospel, but also at least Matthew and Luke, at times the author allows his agenda to erupt through the shallow veneer of his pseudepigraphy. At the beginning of the document (preserved only in Ethiopic) the purpose of the 'epistle' is given, 'that you may be established and not waver, not be shaken and not turn away from the word of the Gospel that you have heard. As we have heard (it), kept (it), and have written (it) for the whole world, so we entrust (it) to you, our sons and daughters' (1. 1–2). The subject is apparently still 'the Gospel', and here is thus a reference to 'the council of the apostles, the disciples of Jesus Christ' taking responsibility for the writing of the Gospel. They continue, 'we have written [*or*, write] to the churches of the East and West, towards North and South, recounting and proclaiming to you concerning our Lord Jesus Christ, as we have written; and we have heard and felt him after he had risen from the dead' (2. 1). What is meant by what they 'have written' here is evidently not the present 'epistle', but, again, the contents of the Gospel, specifically highlighting the hearing and touching of the Lord after his resurrection, in terms which recall both 1 John 1: 1 and the incident recorded in John 20: 26–9. This, it is said, was written for the whole world. There is also a significant reference by Jesus later in the book to written accounts of his words by the apostles, 'And every word which I have spoken to you and which you have written concerning me, that I am the word of the Father and the Father is in me, so you must become also to that man [i.e. Paul], as it befits you' (ch. 31 Eth.). This too apparently refers not to the present 'epistle' but to Gospels, particularly John's Gospel, wherein it is written both that Jesus is 'the Word of the Father' (John 1: 1, 14), and that 'the Father is in me' (10: 38; 14: 20). And it refers to these Gospels as 'written' by the apostles! This is another subtle indication that the author presupposes the authorship of the Fourth Gospel by the apostle John. The anachronism of this Gospel or any of the Gospels being written

---

[32] See Hill, '*Epistula Apostolorum*', 37–9.

[33] This is one reason why Koester's quotation standard, *Introduction*, 237, 'The gospels of the NT are freely used, but not quoted as canonical Scripture . . . allusions to passages from the Pauline letters occur several times, though these letters are never cited as authoritative words of the apostle', is a red herring.

so soon after Jesus' resurrection is obvious to us, but perhaps not to many of his first readers, the same assumption seems to be made in the *Apocryphon of James* (2, ll. 7–19).[34]

The *Epistula* leans heavily on the book of Acts; it knows 1 Peter (chapters 19, 27), 1 John, and Revelation, and contains a lengthy apologetic for the apostle Paul which amounts to an 'apostolic' endorsement of Paul, upon whom 'will come the completion of the testimony to me' (ch. 31 Eth.). In the second-century context this can only be understood as a defence of Paul's writings. Thus the writer knows several written texts which he considers apostolic, and he virtually identifies at least the Gospel according to John and a Pauline corpus. The 'completion of the testimony' to Jesus by Paul is interesting and seems to indicate an awareness that that approved testimony to Jesus has, by the author's time, been completed (cf. the similar sentiment in the *MF*, ll. 78–80). Paul is 'the last of the last' (31. 7).

That is, the *Epistula* seems to be advertising the notion that the authoritative sources are fixed and now closed. This appears to be the case despite other aspects of the work which would seem to the modern reader to belie this principle. We notice, for instance, that the author repeats a version of the story of the child Jesus and the teachers which is not contained in any of the four Gospels but is contained in the *Infancy Gospel of Thomas* and some later apocrypha, and which is referred by Irenaeus (*AH* 1. 20. 1) to the Marcosian Valentinians. This may have come to the author from oral or textual sources, but it has be be observed that he uses this legend, in any case, to serve the cause of the orthodox confession.[35]

And there is another, quite basic problem: if he regards these written sources so highly, how can this author presume to be so bold as to write his own fictional account of a meeting between Jesus and his apostles in which he takes so many liberties with those treasured words and adds so considerably to them? This seems to us like a complete and utter contradiction. While we can only speculate as to his motives, his attitude and endeavour must remind us, however, of the Asian presbyter who wrote the *Acts of Paul*, who, Tertullian, *De baptismo* 17, says, wrote his Pauline apocryphon 'out of love for Paul'. It may well be that the urgency of the situation has motivated the author of the *Epistula* to take up the pen against forces which had

---

[34] 'Now the twelve disciples [used to] sit all together at the [same time], remembering what the Saviour had said to each one of them, whether secretly or openly, and setting it down in books. I was writing what went in [my book]—suddenly, the Saviour appeared …'

[35] Hill, '*Epistula Apostolorum*', 25 n. 93, 'The *Ep. Apost.*'s use of this story does not at all, however, necessarily signal an unorthodox or docetic Christology. Epiphanius tells us in fact why the orthodox might be interested in such traditions about the childhood of Jesus: "For he ought to have childhood miracles too, to deprive the other sects of an excuse for saying that '[the] Christ', meaning the dove, 'came to him after [his baptism in] the Jordan'…" (*Panar.* 51. 20. 3). That is, such stories offered a way of confirming the orthodox Christology of the union of the divine and human natures of Jesus Christ before the baptism in the Jordan. This would make sense in a work such as *Ep. Apost.*, written explicitly to counteract the influences of Cerinthus.'

done damage (in his view) through their own fictional compositions. As Vielhauer put it, the *Epistula* represents 'evidently a conscious taking over of one of the most typical gnostic forms for substantiating authoritative teaching; it is thus a case of an attempt to combat the gnostic opponents with their own weapons'.[36] He may have envisioned his work as a way to reach those who might fall or who had fallen prey to a composition like the *Apocryphon of James*. Thus, though he would appear to undermine his views by the very composition he was undertaking, and though the Church which he tried so valiantly to defend would ultimately not approve of the means he and the author of the *Acts of Paul* chose to use, none the less, he has an unmistakable conception of what he regards as authentic and authoritative apostolic works.

THE VALUE OF THE EPISTULA APOSTOLORUM

As we have seen, most adherents of the consensus view of orthodox Johannophobia are themselves silent about the *Epistula Apostolorum* in their reviews of the 'silence' of the first half of the second century. For those who do consider it, its value as a witness for the orthodox use of John has usually been compromised by the perception that it is also indebted to gnostic ideas,[37] as if to suggest that the same channels of gnostic influence may also have carried in the Johannine. But, as we have seen, the extent of relevant 'gnostic' influence in the document is negligible.[38] And in any case the Johannine influence cannot be seen as analogous with the gnostic, at least with the docetic, for it is often precisely the Johannine elements—particularly the emphasis on the Word becoming flesh, and on the apostles' first-hand knowledge of the Lord's true and physical resurrection—which are used to combat the docetism which the document so thoroughly discountenances.

The value of this work to our study can also only be properly appreciated by gaining as clear a picture as possible of its date and provenance. Hengel

---

[36] Vielhauer, *Geschichte*, 687, translation from W. Schneemelcher's article, 'Dialogues of the Redeemer', in *NTA*[2] i. 228–31, at 229.

[37] Hillmer's statement, 'Second Century', 171, that the work is 'strongly influenced by gnosticism' certainly overreaches. As noted earlier, Hillmer's assessment of the mixed character of the *Epistula* is followed by Culpepper, *John*, 119.

[38] Hillmer, 'Second Century', 34, thinks that 'the whole presentation' of the Logos appearing to Mary in the form of the angel Gabriel (ch. 14) and the account of his passing through the seven heavens in his descent to earth (ch. 13) 'is related to the gnostic view of the descent of the redeemer from heaven to earth'. But the descent of Jesus from the seventh heaven, taking on the guise of the inhabitants of each heaven as he descended, as 'uncanonical' as it may be, was not necessarily considered problematic by orthodox writers in the 2nd cent. Witness Irenaeus himself (*Dem.* 9. 84; see Hill, '*Epistula Apostolorum*', 24). Somewhat oddly, Hillmer, 'Second Century', 43, also suggested that the *Ep. Apost.* 'may well be making a conscious defense against' the supposedly less apocalyptic eschatology of the Fourth Gospel. How the *Epistula*'s apocalypticism fits with its 'strong' gnostic influence is not detailed.

and Bauckham see its witness for the use of John and its identification of
the author as the son of Zebedee as pertaining to Egypt near the middle of
the century.[39] Unfortunately, the Egyptian theory has very little to support
it while there is on the other hand overwhelming evidence for tracing its
origin to Asia Minor, as I have detailed elsewhere. It is also clear that the
work must be dated before the middle of the second century. The *Epistula*
has the dubious distinction of being the first on record to set a date for the
return of Christ: according to the Ethiopic text of chapter 17, after 150
years ('when the hundred and fiftieth year is completed'), according to the
Coptic, after 120 ('when the hundredth part and the twentieth part is
completed'). Hengel agrees with Lietzmann, Gry, and Hornschuh on the
originality of the latter figure. Whereas Gry and Hornschuh have suggested
the birth of Jesus as starting point for the 120 years, and consequently date
the work to a time before 120,[40] Hengel takes the starting point to be the
resurrection, or the time when the fictional encounter took place between
Jesus and his disciples. Allowing that the author would have left the world a
few years when he wrote, we would thus safely have a period between 130
and 150 for the time of composition.[41] A date between about 117 and 148
is also supported by other internal factors, including the occurrence of
earthquakes, famines, and plagues in Asia Minor throughout the period.[42]

As a conscientiously orthodox, Asian work which predates the middle of
the second century, the value of the *Ep. Apost.* for an assessment of the
influence of the Fourth Gospel, and for the First Epistle and the Apocalypse
of John, is hard to overstate. It uses the Johannine literature extensively
against a docetic Christology. It shows a clear presupposition of the tradition of apostolic authorship, and this ties in not only with the later explicit
identifications but also adds credence to our findings regarding Justin, who
seems to presuppose that the Fourth Gospel is the testimony of one of Jesus'
apostles, and the *Ad Diognetum*, which seems to presuppose the same thing
for the Gospel and the First Epistle. We shall gain a better idea of the basis
for this common presupposition when we examine the evidence surrounding Papias of Hierapolis and his sources. Finally, the *Epistula Apostolorum*, by
showing the influence of the Gospel, the First Epistle, and the Apocalypse
of John, adds to the suspicion that authors of this period already knew of
the existence of a Johannine corpus.

Whether written before 120 or sometime in the 140s, the *Epistula* is many
years earlier than Ptolemy or Heracleon. It is earlier than anything which

---

[39] M. Hengel, *Die Johannesche Frage* (Tübingen, 1993), 59. Though in *Question*, 11, he had Asia
Minor in parentheses as a possibility, in *Frage* he simply accepts the position of Hornschuh, *Studien*,
99–115; Bauckham, 'Origin', 66.

[40] L. Gry, 'La Date de la parousie d'après l'Epistula Apostolorum', *RB* 40 (1940), 86–97;
Hornschuh, *Studien*.

[41] Hengel, *Frage*, 60.

[42] See Hill, '*Epistula Apostolorum*'.

can be securely attributed to Valentinus and at any rate appeared in Asia Minor before any of Valentinus' distinctive ideas could have made many inroads there. Indeed, it shows no awareness of the Valentinian phenomenon; the docetism it attacks is in fact of a different variety. Its provenance in Asia Minor links it to Irenaeus, Polycarp, the early Christian experience of Justin, Papias, and with the Johannine literature itself. Its knowledge of historical tradition (whether accurate or not) about Johannine details is seen in its apparent identification of Nathanael with James the son of Alphaeus. The *Epistula Apostolorum*, then, is an important witness to the Johannine tradition in Asia Minor and to the reception of a Johannine corpus among the Great Church there in the first half of the second century.

The *Shepherd* of Hermas

The *Shepherd* of Hermas is one of the early Christian texts whose silence on the Fourth Gospel has been cited as significant by proponents of the OJP.[43] But at the outset, it is obvious that the issue of dating is critical. Many scholars, including most recently J. Christian Wilson, have argued for a late first-century date for the *Shepherd*.[44] If this early dating is correct, any lack of reference to the Fourth Gospel on the part of the *Shepherd* is explained by chronology and cannot therefore be used as a prop for the OJP. On the other hand, from at least the time of the *Muratorian Fragment* on, the book has been regarded as a production of the late first half of the second century published during the episcopacy of Pius of Rome (usually dated 140–54). Let us see if we can sort out the relevant factors in determining the date of this early Roman work.

Carol Osiek speaks of 'the three "historical" references' which concern the dating of the *Shepherd* of Hermas: 'the Hermas of Rom 16: 14, identified by Origen as the author of the book; the mention of Clement in *Vis.* 2. 4. 3, usually thought to be Clement of Rome; and the date of the *Muratorian Canon*, by which the author was the brother of Pius, a prominent Roman churchman of the middle of the second century, according to Eusebius'.[45]

---

[43] See W. Bauer, *Orthodoxy and Heresy in Earliest Christianity* (Philadelphia, 1971), 209; E. Haenchen, *John 1* (Philadelphia, 1984), 9, who places the work in Rome in *c*.140.

[44] J. Christian Wilson, *Toward a Reassessment of the Shepherd of Hermas: Its Date and its Pneumatology*, Mellen Biblical Press, 18 (Lewiston, NY, 1993), 9–61; argues that it was written by a single author in the last two decades of the 1st cent. For similar dating, see also Harry O. Maier, *The Social Setting of the Ministry as Reflected in the Writings of Hermas, Clement, and Ignatius*, Canadian Corporation for Studies in Religion, Dissertations SR, 1 (Waterloo, Ontario, 1991), 58; James S. Jeffers, *Conflict at Rome: Social Order and Hierarchy in Early Christianity* (Minneapolis, 1991), 106–12. A. C. Sundberg, 'Canon Muratori', *HTR* 66 (1973), 1–41, and G. M. Hahneman, *Muratorian Fragment* (Oxford, 1992), also argue for an early date. The recent redating of a papyrus fragment of the *Mandates*, PIand I 4, to the early 2nd cent. would obviously make a decisive difference here, but caution has been expressed about this dating by others (see Metzger, *Canon*, 63 n. 36; A. Carlini, 'Testimone e testo: Il problema della datazione di PIand I 4 del *Pastore* di Erma', *SCO* 42 (1992), 17–30.

As Osiek observes, these references have led to a number of theories of multiple authorship and therefore of composite date.[46] For myself, I am reluctant to dismiss altogether the early, and according to its self-testimony, nearly contemporary statement in the *Muratorian Fragment* (on which see above),[47] despite its obvious fallibility in matters surrounding the origins of the New Testament writings,[48] particularly in the light of the preponderance of evidence which would indicate a Roman provenance for both works. Either the author's mention of Clement, or the association of his name, Hermas, with Paul's associate, or both of these, may be indications of a pseudonymous, fictional setting, and at any rate one or both may have been recognized as such by the *Muratorian Fragment*, Tertullian, and the councils he mentions (*De Pudicitia* 10. 20), which determined that the writing was 'false'. The *Muratorian Fragment* could well be correct about the author of the work being related to Pius, but wrong about when he wrote it, or could have been familiar with a final edition which did not see the light of day until the 140s. Many scholars now believe the work was written (and perhaps published), in parts, over a long period of time. Osiek's conclusions may be cited:

If the person known as Clement of Rome was a young secretary in the Roman church at the end of the first century, and Hermas was a young man at the time of the first visions, it is quite possible that he and a brother named Pius could still be alive but elderly toward the middle of the second century. The text could have been composed over a long period of years as interaction with audiences and expanded parts were added.[49]

---

[45] Carol Osiek, *The Shepherd of Hermas: A Commentary* (Minneapolis, 1999), 8–9.

[46] Ibid. 9; Wilson, *Reassessment*, 14–22. Critics have proposed from one to six authors! Wilson says 'The idea of the composition of the Shepherd of Hermas as a compilation of sources and redaction is much more appealing than any hypothesis of multiple authorship' (ibid. 23).

[47] Eusebius' ignorance of the attribution by the *MF*, *pace* Osiek (*The Shepherd*, 19), is not a very good argument for the lateness of the *MF*; there were many documents of 2nd- and 3rd-cent. Rome to which Eusebius did not have access.

[48] B. H. Streeter, *The Primitive Church: Studied with Special Reference to the Origins of the Christian Ministry* (London, 1929), 205, 'The *Muratorianum* is contemporary evidence as to the views on the Canon of the New Testament in the Roman Church about A.D. 200—or perhaps a little earlier. For that it is an authority of the first importance. It is a very poor authority on everything else. Its account, for example, of the origin of the Fourth Gospel can only be styled "a cock and bull story"'. Streeter mentions also its statement about Paul visiting Spain and its 'astonishing affirmation that all the epistles of Paul were written subsequently to the Apocalypse'. This may be overcritical, however. T. Zahn and G. Edmundson had previously theorized that Pius had a brother named Hermas (Edmundson named him Pastor, based on the *Liber Pontificalis*) which the author of the *Muratorianum* had confused with our Hermas (see Wilson, *Reassessment*, 26–8). Streeter wanted to say that the confusion was deliberate, in an attempt to 'impugn [*The Shepherd*'s] apostolicity and thereby reject its canonicity' (Wilson, *Reassessment*, 28) in the light of Montanist claims to continuing prophetic inspiration. But Wilson (29) says that 'an anti-Montanist bias cannot be demonstrated from the Muratorian fragment by itself'.

[49] Osiek, *The Shepherd*, 19.

She surmises, 'The best assignment of date is an expanded duration of time beginning perhaps from the very last years of the first century, but stretching through most of the first half of the second century.'[50]

It may be, then, that a first stage of writing of the *Shepherd* took place, or even that a first edition of was published, chronologically prior to or only shortly after the Gospel according to John was published, presumably sometime near AD 95–100. We cannot be sure of this, however, and it is possible that the book did not appear at all until the 140s. But in any case, it should be said that the judgement of Haenchen and others about Hermas' ignorance of the Fourth Gospel is not the unanimous opinion of responsible critics and should not be accepted at face value. Others have seen in the *Shepherd* what they regard as clear or suggestive signs of a knowledge of John.[51]

Sometimes cited is Visions 3. 6. 2, in which, speaking of some of the stones which had been brought near the tower, the woman tells Hermas, 'As for the others that you saw lying around in great numbers and not going into the building, the ones that are damaged are those who have known the truth but did not abide in it (οἱ ἐγνωκότες τὴν ἀλήθειαν, μὴ ἐπιμείναντες δὲ ἐν αὐτῇ), nor do they associate with the saints.' The notion of abiding in the truth may have roots in John 8: 31–2, 'Jesus then said to the Jews who had believed in him, "If you continue in my word, you are truly my disciples, and you will know the truth, and the truth will make you free"', echoed in 2 John 9, 'Any one who goes ahead and does not abide in the doctrine of Christ does not have God; he who abides in the doctrine has both the Father and the Son'.

More probably reflecting influence from John are the several occurrences of the phrase 'enter into the Kingdom of God' in Similitudes 9. 12. 5; 15. 2; 16. 2, 3, 4,[52] which may go back to John 3: 5. On the surface it may seem just as likely that the phrase has come from Matthew 19: 24 = Mark 10: 24 = Luke 18: 24; or Mark 9: 47, or even more likely that it simply derives from common Christian language. But what tells in favour of John is the concentration of several occurrences of the phrase in the short compass of Similitude 9. 12–16, combined with the presence there of several more apparent echoes of the language and theology of that Gospel. The ninth Similitude revisits the scene and imagery introduced in the third Vision, in

---

[50] Osiek, *The Shepherd*, 20. Also, 'the text arose over the course of some years, with several editions, in a milieu and from a mind in which oral communication was the norm' (21).

[51] For an extended argument that the *Shepherd* does indeed know all four canonical Gospels, see the provocative study of C. Taylor, *The Witness of Hermas to the Four Gospels* (London, 1892), on the Fourth Gospel, pp. 71–148, often singled out for its novelty, or its naïveté (Bauer, *Orthodoxy and Heresy*, 209; Wilson, *Reassessment*, 56 n. 155). For a more positive, critical analysis of Taylor's argument, see J. Drummond, 'Shepherd of Hermas', *The New Testament in the Apostolic Fathers* (Oxford, 1905), 105–23, at 118.

[52] According to Osiek, *The Shepherd*, 234 n. 10, the phrase 'kingdom of God' occurs in *The Shepherd* only in the ninth *Similitude*, and for the first time here in *Sim.* 9. 12. 3.

which Hermas sees stones being brought and built into a great tower (a figure for the Church). Similitude 9. 12. 1 begins the explanatory section of the new vision. Here Hermas is told that the ancient, massive rock foundation he saw and the newly chiselled door carved in it, both symbolize the Son of God, who, like the rock, is old, but like the door, is new. He is told, 'The Son of God is far older than all his creation, with the result that he was the Father's counselor in his creation' (9. 12. 2).[53] This surely has texts like Proverbs 8: 22–31; Wisdom 9: 9, and Sirach 24: 10 behind it, but also very possibly John 1: 2–3, 'He was in the beginning with God, all things were made through him, and without him was not anything made'. This is because we soon see other allusions to or direct citations of John 1: 3 in connection with the Logos' role in creation (Justin, *2Apol.* 6. 3, 4–5; Tatian, *Or.* 19. 4; Ptolemy, *Flor.* (*Panar.*) 33. 3. 6; Athanagoras, *Plea* 10. 2; Irenaeus, *AH* 3. 11. 1, 2; 3. 21. 10; *Dem.* 43; Clement of Alexandria, *Strom.* 6. 16).[54]

Stones were brought from the deep and taken through the door to be built into the tower; Hermas is told this symbolizes entering the kingdom of God by entering through the door, the Son of God (9. 12. 3, 4, 8). One may only enter the tower through the door, and 'so too a man cannot enter the kingdom of God except by the name of his Son, who was loved by him' (9. 12. 5, εἰς τὴν βασιλείαν τοῦ θεοῦ ἄλλως εἰσελθεῖν οὐ δύναται ἄνθρωπος εἰ μὴ διὰ τοῦ ὀνόματος τοῦ υἱοῦ αὐτοῦ τοῦ ἠγαπημένου ὑπ αὐτοῦ); 'But the door (ἡ ... πύλη) is the Son of God; there is only this one entrance to the Lord. No one, therefore, will enter into him in any other way than through his Son' (9. 12. 6, ἡ δὲ πύλη ὁ υἱὸς τοῦ θεοῦ ἐστιν. Αὕτη μία εἴσοδός ἐστι πρὸς τὸ κύριον. Ἄλλως οὖν οὐδεὶς εἰσελεύσεται πρὸς αὐτὸν εἰ μὴ διὰ τοῦ υἱοῦ αὐτοῦ). These statements seem to depend upon two Johannine sayings of Jesus, John 10: 7, ἀμὴν ἀμὴν λέγω ὑμῖν ὅτι ἐγώ εἰμι ἡ θύρα τῶν προβάτων, and John 14: 6, ἐγώ εἰμι ἡ ὁδὸς καὶ ἡ ζωή. Οὐδεὶς ἔρχεται πρὸς τὸν πατέρα εἰ μὴ δι' ἐμοῦ.[55] Though the idea of Jesus as the door or gate is found elsewhere in early Christian literature (particularly Ignatius, *IPhil.* 9. 1, on which see below), the exclusivity of Jesus as the only way to the Father is nowhere stressed in language so similar to John 14: 6. And the two thoughts side by side seem to echo these two sayings of Jesus found in John, even though Hermas has chosen the word ἡ πύλη for his image instead of ἡ θύρα as in John. Thus while it may not be strictly accurate to call this a 'literary allusion', he seems to know the Fourth Gospel at the level of ideas. And as for the fact that the stones had to be raised from the deep to be placed into the tower, Hermas is told,

[53] Text and translation are taken from LHH.
[54] All of these texts are treated to some extent above.
[55] Braun, *Jean le théologien*, 164–5 sees literary dependence.

it was necessary...for them to come up through the water in order to be made alive, for otherwise they could not enter the kingdom of God, unless they laid aside the deadness of their former life...For before a man...bears the name of the Son of God, he is dead, but when he receives the seal, he lays aside his deadness and receives life. The seal, therefore, is the water; so they go down into the water dead and they come up alive...(9. 16. 2–4).

This, in particular, shows why John 3: 5, 'Jesus answered, "Truly, truly, I say to you, unless one is born of water and the Spirit, he cannot enter the kingdom of God"', is the probable, ultimate source for the idea of 'entering the kingdom of God'—a phrase which occurs in the *Shepherd* only in Similitude 9. Entering the tower is entering the kingdom of God, and to do so one must not only enter through the gate (the Son of God), one must come through the water and bear the name of the Son of God.

Again, there is no literal citation here. It is Johannine concepts which Hermas adapts and incorporates freely (in 9. 16. 2–4 combined with a Pauline view of sin as death) into images that are all his own. If 'direct dependence' is not demonstrable[56] it is because it is not a question of Hermas copying from a text in front of him. But this is not the key issue. The occurrence of so many evocations of Johannine themes in Similitudes 9. 12–16 makes a strong case for his knowledge of the Fourth Gospel, at least at the time he wrote the ninth Similitude.

The evidence from such a long document as the *Shepherd* for the author's knowledge of the Fourth Gospel, may not be too impressive, but it certainly precludes us from saying with any assurance that Hermas did not know it. And the evidence being what it is, even the lack of formal citation of the Fourth Gospel cannot support a theory of orthodox avoidance of John. This is because the quality of evidence pertaining to John is virtually the same as the quality of evidence pertaining to the other three Gospels, Acts, Paul, and the rest of the NT. 'There are no explicit allusions or quotations from Synoptic or Pauline writings', says Osiek.[57] No NT text is ever

---

[56] Osiek, *The Shepherd*, 233 n. 2. H. Koester, *Introduction to the New Testament* (Berlin, 1982), ii. 258 also observes that 'the first part, the five *Visions*, though no doubt written by a Christian author, never uses the name of Jesus Christ!'. His conclusion, from this and other data, that *The Shepherd* overlays Christian interpretations onto what was originally a Jewish substratum (cf. G. Schlaeger, 'Der Hirt des Hermas eine ursprünglich jüdische Schrift', *Nieuw Theologisch Tijdschrift*, 16 (1927), 327–42), is unnecessary. A Jewish background for the author seems plain, and the Jewish features of the text do not require the supposition of a literary incursion and takeover. His failure to post explicit Christian signs in portions of his work seems to be more a matter of his style, and perhaps points also to assumptions he made about his intended audience.

[57] Osiek, *The Shepherd*, 26. Graydon F. Snyder, *The Apostolic Fathers: A New Translation and Commentary*, vi. *The Shepherd of Hermas* (London, 1968), 15, 'though Hermas surely knew the Gospels, there is no evidence that he used them'. Wilson, *Reassessment*, 56, thinks, 'Whether he knew any one of the four canonical gospels in written form is doubtful. More likely he knew an oral form of the gospel tradition'. And yet, the evaluation of Drummond, 'Shepherd of Hermas', 106, should serve as a caution, 'It is the way of Hermas not to quote, but to take suggestions, and alter to suit his own purposes'; 119, 'It is the custom of Hermas to transform ideas of which he avails himself, and adapt them to his own composition'.

'quoted' by Hermas. But, as Koester says, 'that does not mean that the author did not know them because he also does not quote the Old Testament, although there can be no doubt that he knew it well'.[58] Perhaps the strongest relationship the *Shepherd* has to any NT document[59] is the one it has to the Epistle of James, but Hermas never cites it, and Osiek can say that most scholars think the parallels 'are insufficient to prove literary dependence'.[60] The reminiscences of John 3: 5; 10: 7; 14: 6 in Similitude 9. 12–16 are among the clearest recollections of NT passages in the book. However one judges the value of Hermas for attesting or not attesting to the reception of the Johannine literature, that same judgement will have to be applied not only to this literature but to all Christian scriptures, with the possible exception of James.

A prime reason for Hermas' approach to his biblical sources is no doubt to be found in the presentation of the *Shepherd* as a series of revelations. Though the 'apocalyptic genre', to which in some sense the *Shepherd* belongs, does not rule out appeal to written authorities, it is by its nature self-referential and at least lends itself to free and independent development. This is certainly the case with the *Shepherd*, which, though 'deeply influenced by both biblical traditions and some strands of Hellenistic Jewish teaching', does not demonstrate this by citation or exposition of scripture.[61]

And it may not be an accident that the clearest Johannine elements are in the ninth Similitude. Most of those who have argued for multiple authorship have assigned this similitude to one of the later authors, and associated it with the *Muratorian Fragment*'s testimony about the author being Bishop Pius' brother.[62] And many of those, including Brox and Osiek, who argue for single authorship but several redactions, place Similitude 9, particularly because it seems to be a reworking of Visions 3, in the latest redaction.[63]

We also must note in passing that there are certain signs of the author's acquaintance with both 1 John and Revelation. *Mandates* 3. 1, 'and the

---

[58] Koester, *Introduction*, ii. 258. The only text 'cited' is from the mysterious *Eldad and Modat* in *Vis.* 2. 3. 4!

[59] Wilson, *Reassessment*, 57, thinks the author knew Hebrews because in *Mand.* 4. 3. 1–6 he says 'I have heard from certain teachers that there is no other repentance except that one when we went down into water and received forgiveness of our former sins'.

[60] Osiek, *The Shepherd*, 26. The Oxford Committee which published *The New Testament in the Apostolic Fathers* (Oxford, 1905), rated it only a 'C' (on a descending scale of probability from 'A' to 'D', 'A' denoting certainty) in likelihood that the author used James. But see O. J. F. Seitz, 'Relationship of the Shepherd to the Epistle of James', *JBL* 63 (1944), 131–40.

[61] To restrict someone like the author of *The Shepherd*, who is obviously literate and who ostensibly functions as a scribe (*Vis.* 2. 1. 3–4), to a knowledge of only oral Christian tradition is hardly reasonable.

[62] Adolph Hilgenfeld, *Hermae Pastor Graece* (Leipzig, 1866), pp. xxi–xxix; Martin Dibelius, *Der Hirt des Hermas*, HNT: Die Apostolischen Väter, 4 (Tübingen, 1923), 420–1; Stanislas Giet, 'Les Trois Auteurs du Pasteur d'Hermas', in E. A. Livingstone (ed.), *Studia Patristica*, 8 = TU 93 (1966), ii. 10–23; all cited by Osiek, *The Shepherd*, 9. Also M. W. Holmes, in LHH 331.

[63] N. Brox, *Der Hirt des Hermas*, Kommentar zu den Apostolischen Vätern, 7 (Göttingen, 1991), 26–8; Osiek, *The Shepherd*, 10.

Lord who dwells in you shall thus be glorified, for the Lord is true in every word and with him there is no lie', is reminiscent of three verses, 1 John 1: 5, 'that God is light and in him is no darkness at all'; 1 John 1: 8, 'If we say we have no sin, we deceive ourselves, and the truth is not in us'; 1 John 2: 4, 'He who says "I know him" but disobeys his commandments is a liar, and the truth is not in him'. Wilson writes, 'Hermas possibly knew Revelation. The visions display an apocalyptic form similar to that of Revelation. Both use the figure of the beast as a designation for the Roman Empire', though he is quick to point out that both of these features could have been obtained 'from contemporary Roman Christians' (58).[64] But we also have in Vis. 3. 2 the notion of being inscribed in the books of life with the saints, which echoes a major image of the Johannine Apocalypse (cf. *GTr.* 19. 34– 21. 3).

It appears likely, then, that the author did know the Fourth Gospel, at least by the time he wrote Similitude 9, and this would probably be no later than the 140s. It may have been from one to four decades earlier. It is possible that he knew 1 John and the book of Revelation, but we cannot say this with even the same amount of confidence. Certainly the prophets and the apostles were authorities recognized by Hermas and his first readers (Vis. 3. 5. 1; Sim. 9. 15. 4; 16. 5; 9. 25. 1–2). This suggests that he did have Christian textual authorities which were associated with Paul and no doubt other Christian apostles. But Hermas was obviously not interested in specifying his Christian textual authorities, far less in defending them, so such authorities as he had remain for the most part far beneath the surface. The value of the *Shepherd* for supporting the OJP is neutralized, if not by its early date, then by its general evasiveness about its textual authorities, even ones which we must assume that its author held in some sense. Thus whereas the *Shepherd* may hold only limited weight as evidence for the reception of the Fourth Gospel in the second century, it can hardly function as evidence that the orthodox avoided or rejected that Gospel.

The *Odes of Solomon*

The *Odes of Solomon* must be mentioned at some point, and so I will look at them here, though with a good deal of hesitation due to so many uncertainties about them. This work has been said to embody pre-Synoptic and pre-Johannine materials and its composition has been placed relatively early, even before the end of the first century, and on the other hand it has been dated to the third century. Its relation to gnosticism has been much debated. In terms of our subject here, we note that the 'accommodating' *Odes* have been called upon to support quite contrasting positions. First, their

---

[64] Wilson, *Reassessment*, 58.

'gnostic' quality could be emphasized (von Loewenich called them 'synkre-tistische-gnostisch')[65] and their parallels with John seen as evidence for the gnostic reception of John. On the other hand, they could be from an idiosyncratic writer of the mainstream Church, probably in Syria, and the ambiguity of the parallels seen as due not to direct knowledge but to a common milieu with John, and therefore the *Odes* might support, if any-thing, the obscurity of John in the first half of the second century.[66] Or, conceivably, their fairly numerous but always inexact parallels could still be interpreted as real evidence of literary dependence and counted as evidence of the widespread knowledge of John in the second century. It can be said that, after many initial comparisons with gnosticism, the tendency among scholarship of recent decades has been away from the perception of the *Odes* as very closely aligned with emergent gnosticism.[67] The 'Jewish' elem-ents have received much attention as well in the light of the Qumran hymns.[68] The nature of the Johannine parallels has still proved elusive, but here too a near consensus is expressed by Charlesworth: 'As we have seen, the Odes share with the Gospel of John many striking and significant parallels, but specialists on the Odes have cautioned against assuming that the Odes are dependent on John and have urged consideration of a shared community.'[69] But Hengel objects to this sort of presentation as misleading, saying that 'The Syriac Odes are at least two generations later than the Fourth Gospel. It is because of their poetic form that they do not "quote" John directly. The Johannine parallels show a clear further development in them.'[70] Nagel has given the question a thorough study and concludes that one thesis does not rule out the other but that they can and probably

---

[65] Loewenich, *Das Johannes-Verständnis*, 115.

[66] This is apparently how Barrett, *John* (1978), 113, saw it: 'the (Syriac) Odes do not prove the existence of John as a Greek document'.

[67] See J. T. Sanders, 'Nag Hammadi', in J. E. Goehring *et al.*, *Gnosticism and Early Christian World* (Sonoma, Cal.f., 1990), 51–66. 'The Odes of Solomon and the *Trimorphic Protennoia* are kindred documents in that they help to show what sort of speculative thinking existed in the intellectual milieu out of which the prologue arose. All three documents imply non-rabbinic speculative Juda-ism of the Roman period—probably of the Diaspora ... as their common matrix' (59). He agrees with Charlesworth in positing an early 2nd-cent. date for the *Odes*.

[68] In particular, the work of Charlesworth, 'Les Odes de Salomon et les manuscrites de la Mer Morte', *RB* 77 (1970), 522–49; idem, 'Qumran, John and the Odes of Solomon', in J. H. Charles-worth (ed.), *John and Qumran* (London, 1972).

[69] J. H. Charlesworth, 'Odes of Solomon (Late First to Early Second Century A.D.): A New Translation and Introduction', in *OTP* ii, 725–34, at 732. Charlesworth cites the article he and Culpepper wrote in 1973 for this point, J. H. Charlesworth and R. A. Culpepper, 'The Odes of Solomon and the Gospel of John, *CBQ* 35 (1973), 298–322. This was Barrett's view in 1978, who spoke of 'coincidences or parallelisms in language ... the evidence is hardly sufficient to justify direct dependence' (*St John*, 112).

[70] Hengel, *Question*, 143 n. 26 (citing the *CBQ* article mentioned in the previous note). See also Braun, *Jean le Théologien*, 224–51, 288–9, 291, 295; Kieffer, 'Les Premiers Indices', 2230. For the date of the *Odes* Hengel refers to Louise Abramowski, 'Sprache und Abfassungszeit der Oden Salomos', *Oriens Christianus* 68 (1984), 80–90. In the context of Syrian writings Hengel also mentions the early 3rd-cent. *Didaskalia* as also presupposing the Fourth Gospel 'as a matter of course'.

should complement one another. He joins other scholars[71] who propose that 'The common background of *Odes of Solomon* and the Gospel of John lies not *before*, but *in* the Johannine school-tradition'.[72] And yet, in what sense we can legitimately speak of the *Odes* belonging to a historical 'Johannine school-tradition', presumably in Syria, is not immediately clear. Brownson has even proposed that the *Odes* come from the group of seceders mentioned in 1 John.[73]

It is probably unwise to be dogmatic about the *Odes of Solomon* at this stage in their interpretation. I am inclined to recognize some common modes of thought, and the use of some similar words and phrases, which are independent of the Fourth Gospel. But this does not mean we can so easily dismiss Hengel's view that the odist was familiar with the Fourth Gospel. The evidence seems patient of an approach which recognizes that the odist was familiar with many NT texts, but did not set out to give an 'interpretation' of any of them, and certainly did not compose his hymns with these books open before him.[74] The evidence is indeed perplexing. No matter how we judge it, however, what must be acknowledged is the illegitimacy of drawing conclusions about the obscurity of the Fourth Gospel, even if we are convinced that there is no literary dependence here. This is, first of all, because the evidence for John is about the same as the evidence for Matthew, Mark, Luke, and Paul. Charlesworth himself says,

Since the discovery of the Odes of Solomon, numerous attempts have been made to prove that the Odist is dependent on one or more of the books in the New Testament. The arguments have persuaded few; they are not persuasive because of the ambiguity of the parallels, and because the *oral* tradition continued to be influential even until Tatian compiled his so-called Diatessaron around the year A.D. 175. To be sure, the Odes share many of the traditions that have been recorded in the New Testament, but that by no means suggests that they are to be linked with one or more of the canonical records of these traditions.[75]

---

[71] H. Jordan, *Geschichte der altchristlichen Literatur* (Leipzig, 1911), 458; Charlesworth and Culpepper, 'Odes', 320–1.

[72] Nagel, *Rezeption*, 190.

[73] J. Brownson, 'The Odes of Solomon and the Johannine Tradition', *Journal for the Study of the Pseudepigrapha*, 2 (1988), 49–69.

[74] Sanders, 'Nag Hammadi', links the *Odes* to the *Trimorphic Protennoia*, to the Johannine Prologue, to Col. 1. 15–20, and to 1 Pet. 1. 20; 3. 18–20 as hymnic creations but literarily independent of one another. He sees them all as 'parallel developments demonstrating several close similarities' (65). 'One could hardly conclude that the author(s) of the Odes had dismantled 1 Pet 3:18–20 and scattered so many of the statements from that fragment around in the Odes of Solomon in often different contexts' (64). He speaks similarly about the parallels with the Johannine Prologue in the *Odes* and in the *Trimorphic Protennoia*. But why must we necessarily think in terms of conscious 'dismantling'? It is possible that both the *Odes* and the *TP* are independent of all NT documents; on the other hand, literary influence does not always manifest itself in terms of strict, verbally and contextually faithful reproduction.

[75] Charlesworth, 'Odes of Solomon', 731–2.

In other words the Fourth Gospel does not fare any worse than do the other books of the New Testament, and so if the *Odes* are viewed as evidence for the unfamiliarity of John, they will have to have much the same import for Matthew and Paul, among others.

Second, most scholars who deny influence from the Fourth Gospel tend to date the *Odes* quite early, to the early second century,[76] or perhaps earlier. If the *Odes* are this early it is not very surprising that they should not contain any clearer signs of literary indebtedness to the Fourth Gospel. In the end, the *Odes of Solomon* probably do not advance anyone's agenda about the Fourth Gospel very far.

Papias of Hierapolis

DATING PAPIAS' WRITING AND HIS SOURCES

What is left of the tradition recorded by Papias is quite important for the assessment of the fortunes of the Fourth Gospel in the early Church. I have alluded several times to Papias as providing early tradition about the origin of the Fourth Gospel. It is crucial then to get as good an idea as we can of the date of his writing. Some have dated Papias' work quite early, by 110 or even before. This would place his accession of the tradition in all likelihood well before the year 100, and some have suggested twenty or so years earlier.[77] On the other hand, some have dated Papias quite certainly too late, around 140 or later. How can the parameters be set?

Vernon Bartlet pointed out that Eusebius mentions Papias' books

immediately after his account of Clement, whose death he has recorded shortly before (iii, 34) as falling in the third year of Trajan, i.e. *c.*A.D. 100. Only half a page, too, before passing thus straight from Clement to Papias as a writer (iii, 39), Eusebius had intimated that needs of space forced him to confine himself, as regards men of the revered sub-Apostolic generation, to those alone 'whose tradition of the Apostolic doctrine is still current in written memoire.' He then refers back to his chapter on Ignatius, takes up Clement of Rome, and proceeds at once to Papias; and with him he ends his third book, *which nowhere goes beyond the age of Trajan.* Nay more, he opens his next book with the twelfth year of Trajan (*c.* 110), and goes on to events in his last year (116–117), before referring to the age of his successor Hadrian... It is manifest, then, that Eusebius, who was a good judge in such matters, saw no reason—though his bias here lay that way—to infer from internal evidence that Papias wrote after rather than before A.D. 110, though he is

---

[76] Ibid. 726–7; Sanders, 'Nag Hammadi', 61.

[77] V. Bartlet, 'Papias's "Exposition": Its Date and Contents', in H. G. Wood (ed.), *Amicitiae Corolla: A Volume of Essays Presented to James Rendel Harris, D. Litt. on the Occasion of his Eightieth Birthday* (London, 1933), 15–44, at 20–2, places it *c.* 110; also R. W. Yarbrough, 'The Date of Papias: A Reassessment', *JETS* 26 (1983), 181–91; U. H. J. Körtner, *Papias von Hierapolis: Ein Beitrag zur Geschichte des frühen Christentums*, FRLANT 133 (Göttingen, 1983), 225–6.

at pains to refute Irenaeus's statement that Papias was actually 'a hearer and eye-witness of the sacred Apostles.'[78]

Irenaeus, some time in the 180s, speaks of Papias as an 'ancient man' (ἀρχαῖος ἀνήρ), places him in the generation of Polycarp, and assumes that he could have been a hearer of John the apostle. We may surely conclude that Papias must have been in age closer to Polycarp than to Irenaeus. But Papias' placing of himself in the line of succession of tradition is, strictly speaking, more parallel to that of Irenaeus, than to Polycarp. That is, Papias' need to rely not merely on the 'presbyters', the followers of the apostles, but also on men of the next generation ('if ever anyone came who had followed the presbyters', *HE* 3. 39. 4) would seem to forbid putting his writing quite this early. Papias in fact seems to imply that the apostles, including Andrew, Philip, and John, were no longer alive—or at least no longer accessible—not only when he wrote, but when he was 'learning well' his 'interpretations'. Though the report is debated, Irenaeus attests that John lived until the reign of Trajan. This would mean Papias was not collecting his interpretations until after 98, or at any rate, not long before this. Also, it seems from his language in 3. 39. 4 (ἀνέκρινον) that John the Elder and Aristion, alive when Papias was collecting the teachings of the elders (λέγουσιν; Eusebius attests that Papias had heard Aristion and Elder John in person), were dead by the time he wrote. Hengel alludes to a fragment from Philip of Side's *Church History* (Lightfoot/Harmer, fr. 5), which says that Papias spoke of some of those Christ raised from the dead surviving until Hadrian's time. This would mean that we could not date Papias' writing before *c.* 118 and most probably a bit later.[79] And while it seems implausible that anyone raised or healed by Jesus would have survived to the time of Hadrian, there may have been something in Papias' book which mentioned Hadrian. With due caution, the parameters provided by these factors seem to fit together reasonably well. We may conclude that Papias was 'learning well' his interpretations and traditions in the very early years of the second century, and that he wrote his books probably in the 120s or possibly as late as the early 130s.[80]

[78] Bartlet, 'Papias's "Exposition"', 21–2.

[79] It is true that Philip's information is not repeated anywhere else, and it is possible he confused for Papias what Eusebius recorded from the writing of the early apologist Quadratus. In a work addressed to Hadrian Quadratus claimed that 'those who were cured, those who rose from the dead, who not merely appeared as cured and risen, but were constantly present, not only while the Saviour was living, but even for some time after he had gone, so that some of them survived even till our own time' (Eusebius, *HE* 4. 3. 3). Quadratus does not say that they survived to the time of Hadrian but 'even till our own time', which most likely means not to the present but to the early part of Quadratus' own life. Also, Philip claims to have read this in Papias' second book, and he preserves in the same context a couple more details which are not contained in Eusebius' account (e.g. Eusebius says that Papias 'relates the resurrection of a corpse in his time', and Philip speaks of 'Manaim's mother, who was raised from the dead').

[80] Hengel, *Frage*, 77, places Papias' writing between 120 and 135. Campenhausen, *Formation*, 129, says between 110 and 130.

PAPIAS AND THE FOURTH GOSPEL

Much has been said over the years about Eusebius' failure to record any-thing Papias said about the Third and Fourth Gospels in the place where he quotes Papias on the First and Second Gospels. Particularly with respect to the Fourth Gospel this silence has been pregnant with meaning for many scholars because of Papias' residence in Asia and his proximity, according to Irenaeus, to the aged apostle John himself. Did Papias know the Fourth Gospel? Did he know it and avoid it because it had heretical tendencies or associations?[81] Did he say something about it which Eusebius did not like and so suppressed?[82] In 1998 I published findings which, I believe, demon-strate that Papias indeed wrote about the origins of the Fourth Gospel and that Eusebius indeed recorded this information but without direct attribu-tion of his source. But before I review those findings it needs to be observed that Papias' knowledge of the Fourth Gospel, even from a time before he wrote his books, is verified by three other references to his work outside of the passage or passages used in Eusebius, *HE* 3. 24.

First, there are Armenian fragments published by F. Siegert in 1981.[83] In one of these fragments a thirteenth-century writer, Vardan Vardapet, com-menting on the aloe brought by Nicodemus to embalm the body of Jesus in John 19: 39, refers to a report of Papias that 'there are fifteen kinds of aloe in India'.[84] This is not very enlightening on the whole, but is still a prima-facie indication that Papias recorded some kind of tradition on the burial of Jesus which used John, the only Gospel to mention the aloe.

Then there is the exegetical tradition of certain 'elders, the disciples of the apostles' cited by Irenaeus which referred to John 14: 2, 'In my Father's house are many mansions' (*AH* 5. 34. 2). Irenaeus is undoubtedly citing from some book which purported to give the teachings of some elders, disciples of the apostles. If this is not Papias' book, it 'yields additional and independent testimony to the same date and character as that of Papias'.[85] But from the character of Irenaeus' other references to 'the elders' there should in fact be very little doubt that it is from Papias' book.[86] This is not

---

[81] Bauer, *Orthodoxy and Heresy*, 187, for instance, wrote, 'For Papias, the contents of the Fourth Gospel apparently belonged to the long-winded prattle in which the great masses took pleasure, to the "foreign commandments," but not to the truth as it was given by the Lord to the believers and is contained in the uniform tradition of the church and which is rooted in the circle of the twelve (EH 3. 39. 3–4)'; 'the other two gospels are at least suspect to him... the Fourth Gospel, no doubt, because of its content, origin, and the friends it had made. After all, the preference of the Montan-ists and Valentinians for the Fourth Gospel shows us that ecclesiastical circles were not the first in which it was recognized as a canonical expression of a particular religious persuasion'. See also ibid. 204.

[82] Hengel, *Frage*, 88; Bauckham, 'Origin', 45–53.

[83] F. Siegert, 'Unbeachtete Papiaszitate bei armenischen Schriftstellern', *NTS* 27 (1981), 605–14.

[84] Lightfoot, Harmer-Holmes, Papian fragment no. 25. See Siegert, 'Papiaszitate', 608–9. Also cf. the testimonies of LHH, nos. 19, 20, 23, which contain, however, some questionable material.

[85] J. B. Lightfoot, *Essays on the Work Entitled Supernatural Religion* (London, 1893), 197.

[86] Ibid. 197.

only an indication that Papias knew the Fourth Gospel but also that teachers in the generation before him were using this Gospel and using its quotations of Jesus' words as genuine. I shall have more to say about them at another point.

Third, scholars from J. B. Lightfoot to Robert M. Grant have also seen a Johannine influence in the order and identities of the disciples named by Papias in an introductory section of his book cited by Eusebius in *HE* 3. 39. 4: 'but if ever anyone came who had followed the presbyters, I inquired into the words of the presbyters, what Andrew or Peter or Philip or Thomas or James or John or Matthew, or any other of the Lord's disciples had said...' Andrew, Philip, and Thomas are disciples whose roles attain prominence only in the Fourth Gospel and the sequence in which they appear here is very reminiscent of their appearance in John 1: 40 and 21: 2 and contrary to any Synoptic list.[87]

These small fragments at least make it clear that Papias used the Fourth Gospel in the first quarter of the second century. Now we come to a notice which has been overlooked because of Eusebius' failure to record explicitly its source. The Papian material in question is contained, I believe, in *HE* 3. 24. 5–13, where Eusebius gives us tradition concerning both Matthew and John.

5. Yet nevertheless of all the disciples of the Lord, only Matthew and John have left us their recollections (ὑπομνήματα). A record preserves (κατέχει λόγος) that they took to writing out of necessity (ἐπάναγκες). 6. Matthew having first preached to Hebrews, and when he was on the point of going to others, supplied to those from whom he was sent through his writing the lack of his presence by handing down the Gospel according to himself, written in his native tongue. 7. And after Mark and Luke had already made the publication of the Gospels according to them, John, it is said (φασί), used all the time a proclamation (κηρύγματι) which was not written down, and at last came to writing for the following cause. After the three Gospels which had been previously written had already been distributed to all, and even to himself, they say that he welcomed (ἀποδέξασθαι) them and testified to their truth (ἀλήθειαν αὐτοῖς ἐπιμαρτυρήσαντα),[88] but that there was therefore only lacking to the Scripture (or writing) the account (διήγησιν) concerning things which had been done by Christ at first and at the beginning of the proclamation (κηρύγματος). 8. The record (ὁ λόγος) is certainly true. It is at least possible to see that the three evangelists had written down (συγγεγραφότας) only the things done by the Saviour during one year after John the Baptist had been put in prison and that they stated this at the beginning of their narratives. [He goes on to produce the testimonies of Matt. 4: 12; Mark 1: 14; Luke 3: 19–20.] 11. Now they say (φασι) that on account of these things, the apostle John was exhorted (παρακληθέντα) to hand down (παραδοῦναι) in the Gospel according to himself the time passed over in silence by the first evangelists and the things which had been done by the

[87] Lightfoot *Supernatural*, 194–8; Hengel, *Question*, 17–21; Culpepper, *John*, 111–12; R. M. Grant, *Irenaeus of Lyons* (London, 1997), 35.
[88] Note the Johannine language employed in the depiction of John's action.

Saviour at this time (that is, things before the imprisonment of the Baptist), and that he signified this when saying 'this beginning of marvels did Jesus' [John 2: 11], and then by calling to mind (μνημονεύσαντα) the Baptist in the midst of the acts of Jesus as still then baptizing at Aenon near Salem, plainly indicating this when he says 'for John was not yet cast into prison' [John 3: 24]. 12. Thus John in the Scripture (or writing) of the Gospel according to him hands down (παραδίδωσιν) the things done (πραχθέντα) by Christ when the Baptist had not yet been cast into prison, but the other three evangelists record (μνημονεύουσιν) the things after the Baptist had been shut up in prison. 13. If this be understood, no longer do the Gospels seem to disagree with one another, because that according to John contains the first things of the acts of Christ, but the rest of the narrative of what happened to him at the end of the period. And fittingly John passed over the genealogy of our Saviour according to the flesh, because it had been already written out by Matthew and Luke, and began with the description of his divinity since this had been reserved for him by the Divine Spirit as for one greater than they.[89]

Though this account in Eusebius is well known, it is not usually recognized that Eusebius is here paraphrasing a written account.[90] Hugh Lawlor has demonstrated that Eusebius' use of κατέχει λόγος, which Eusebius uses at the beginning of this account, normally signifies a written source.[91] In a footnote Lawlor suggested that the information on Matthew's Gospel from 3. 24. 5–6 has come more or less intact from the Papian account, of which Eusebius gives only the last lines in the better known passage in 3. 39. 16, where Eusebius mentions Papias by name.[92] Unfortunately, Lawlor failed to recognize[93] that Eusebius' words demand that the information he reproduces

---

[89] My translation.

[90] H. Merkel, 'Frühchristliche Autoren Über Johannes und die Synoptiker', in A. Denaux (ed.), *John and the Synoptics*, BETL (Leuven, 1992), 403–8, at 406, thinks Eusebius, if he was not the originator of this tradition, was the first to write it down.

[91] 'In the majority of cases where Eusebius introduces a narrative with the words λόγος (κατ)έχει, the document on which he relies is either indicated in the immediate context, or may be discovered by a search through the passages from previous writers scattered over his pages. Only a few instances of the phrase remain, in which it does not seem possible to name the document referred to, and in none of these is the use of documentary evidence excluded, or improbable', H. J. Lawlor, *Eusebiana* (Amsterdam, 1973), 22. See also the previous comments by F. J. A. Hort, *Judaistic Christianity* (Grand Rapids, Mich., 1980 repr. of 1894 orig.), 170–4; J. B. Lightfoot, *AF* ii 1. 58, 'the expression is not confined to oral tradition but may include contemporary written authorities, and . . . it implies authentic and trustworthy information'. This significance of the phrase is accepted also by P. Sellew, 'Eusebius and the Gospels', in H. W. Attridge and G. Hata (eds.), *Eusebius, Christianity, and Judaism* (Leiden, 1992), 110–38, at 119, though at 120 he seems to regard its occurrence in 3. 24. 5 as pertaining only to a record stating that Matthew wrote originally in Hebrew (for which Eusebius could claim Irenaeus and Origen as authorities). But what is claimed for the λόγος is that Matthew and John took to writing out of some necessity, and the stories which follow naturally relate the substance of that λόγος.

[92] 'His assertion about St. Matthew is scarcely more than a fair inference from extracts which he gives elsewhere from Papias (iii. 39. 16), Irenaeus (v. 8. 2), and Origen (vi. 25. 4). That it was made by Papias in so many words, in the passage of which no more than the two concluding sentences are now preserved (iii. 39. 16), is far from incredible', Lawlor, *Eusebiana*, 22.

[93] Lawlor points to the use of φασί, 'they say' (used in 3. 24. 7, 11), as evidence that this part of the tradition is oral. But this hardly is valid. See e.g. 2. 15. 1 where φασί is used when the written sources, Clement of Alexandria and Papias, are actually named in the context, and cf. Lawlor's own

on John's Gospel in 3. 24 has come from the same source.[94] It must be acknowledged that Eusebius attributes to this same written record both his Matthean and his Johannine traditions: 'A record preserves that they [Matthew and John] took to writing out of necessity'.[95] And indeed the stories which follow bear out this claim, that both Matthew and John took to writing through some pressing need. Both accounts also stress the respective apostles' work of preaching (κηρύξας of Matthew; κηρύγματι and κηρύγματος of John) before they wrote. What is more, after introducing the accounts of both Gospels with κατέχει λόγος, Eusebius follows the first excerpt about John with the words, καὶ ἀληθής γε ὁ λόγος ('and the record is surely true'), the λόγος here naturally referring to the preceding one. Eusebius is definitely presenting this account of the origins of Matthew and John as from a single written source, and, though he does not name that source, there is no credible alternative to regarding it as Papias of Hierapolis.[96]

Confirmation that Eusebius' source is Papias comes from two other factors. The first consists of the several parallels which link this source with the accounts of the origins of Mark and Matthew in *HE* 2. 15. 1–2 and 3. 39. 15–16 which Eusebius explicitly attributes to Papias. The second consists of the parallels which link this source with later authors who are known or suspected to have used Papias' account of the origins of the Gospels, including Irenaeus, Clement of Alexandria, the *Muratorian Fragment*, Origen, and Victorinus of Pettau. I shall mention these here in abbreviated form and refer the reader to my 1998 article for a fuller treatment.

Parallels with Papias' accounts of the other Gospels

There are several links between the accounts of Mark and Matthew in *HE* 2. 15. 1–2; 3. 39. 15–16 and the accounts of Matthew, John, and Luke in 3. 24. 3–15 which point to a common source. Though the circumstances

---

note 2 on p. 36, which identifies at least 1. 12, 1, 3, (cf. 13. 11); 2. 2. 2 as using φασί when there is a written work as the source, and 7. 12 where Eusebius uses it as equivalent to κατέχει λόγος. Lawlor may be right in saying that 'φασί is a favourite word of Eusebius for unwritten report' (36), but it is not so used exclusively. Sellew at any rate is unjustified in contrasting it too sharply with κατέχει λόγος, regarding it as signifying 'oral legends' or written sources of questionable reputation ('Eusebius on the Gospels', 117–18, 121). From 2. 2. 4 it becomes clear that the source for φασί in 2. 2. 2 is Tertullian's *Apology* 5.

[94] Bartlet, 'Papias's "Exposition"', 15–44, is the only writer I have seen who has suggested Papias as this source, though he employed relatively few arguments to support it. Bartlet perceptively, in my opinion, recognized that Eusebius is reporting from Papias in 3. 24, 'probably paraphrasing his wording but slightly' (260).

[95] Sellew, 'Eusebius and the Gospels', 121, also assumes that they are connected, and regards the tradition concerning John as a legend. It may of course be a legend, but this is not necessarily signified by Eusebius' use of φασί, and it will have been legend already by the time of Eusebius' source. Bauckham, 'Origin', 52, regards *HE* 3. 24. 5–16, as reflecting only Eusebius' own understanding of the relations between the four Gospels.

[96] See Hill, 'What Papias Said about John'.

related in the stories of each Gospel are quite different, their presentations show common elements and concerns.

1. *Authorial humility.* We find a common concern to maintain that the Evangelists did not take it upon themselves to initiate the writing but were responding to the requests of their hearers (Matthew, *HE* 3. 24.5, 6; Mark, *HE* 2. 15. 1, partially 3. 39. 15; John, *HE* 3. 24. 5, 11; with Luke a 'cause' is found in the desire to correct the doubtful propositions of others, *HE* 3. 24. 15).[97]

2. *Distillation of apostolic preaching.* The written Gospels of Matthew and John in our fragment (3. 24. 6, 7), and of Mark in 3. 39. 15, are presented as the setting down in writing of what was previously preached or taught by an apostle (for Luke, more than one apostle, 3. 24. 15).

3. *Apostolic 'memoirs'.* We find a prevalent use of the term 'recollections' (and its cognates) to associate the Gospels with the firsthand experience of the Lord's words and ministry by the apostles. In 3. 24. 5 Eusebius introduces the witness of his written source by saying that 'only Matthew and John have left us their recollections (ὑπομνήματα).[98] In 2. 15. 1 Eusebius also relates the story of the origin of the Gospel of Mark, and calls Mark a recollection (ὑπόμνημα)[99] of Peter's teaching, saying that his sources for the story were Clement of Alexandria and Papias (cf. the participle μεμνημένον in 6. 14. 6). In the account of Mark's Gospel in 3. 39. 15, the Gospel is said to be an accurate account of all that he (probably Peter, not Mark) remembered (ἐμνημόνευσεν) of the things said or done by the Lord, and a record of what Peter had recounted (ἀπεμνημόνευσεν).

4. *Order.* The accounts have a common concern for the 'order' of events in the Gospels, particularly in the attempt to correlate one Gospel to another (3. 24. 7–13; 3. 39. 15, 16). An emphasis on the supplemental nature of John's Gospel in our fragment[100] fits with the concern for the proper

---

[97] These were true 'aetiologies'. We find in fact for Mark and Luke the word αἰτία (Mark, 2. 15. 1; 3. 24. 14; Luke, 3. 24. 15) and for Matthew and John the word ἐπάναγκες (3. 24. 5). For Matthew and John this is explicitly attributed to Eusebius' source, and it should be evident that for Mark and Luke it reflected an interest in accounting for the circumstances surrounding the genesis of each Gospel.

[98] As I have observed above, this is probably a precursor of Justin's characteristic use of the term ἀπομνημονεύματα for the Gospels.

[99] This word can have a fairly wide range of meanings. Lampe, *PGL*, lists: '1. memorial, reminder; 2. record; a. minutes; b. account; c. copy; d. petition; 3. commentary; 4. division, section, "book" of treatise'. See also van den Hoek, 'Techniques of Quotation in Clement of Alexandria', 225, who records the meaning 'note' or 'notebook, as well as a more literary 'memoranda'. Hegesippus gave this name to his book, on which see N. Hyldahl, 'Hegesipps Hypomnemata', *Studia Theologica*, 14 (1960), 70–113. According to M. Durst, 'Hegesipp's "Hypomnemata": (Titel oder Gattungsbezeichnung?', *Römische Quartalschrift*, 84 (1989), 299–330, Hypomnemata, or Reminiscences, was not the title of Hegesippus' work but was a descriptive word used by Eusebius, something like, notices, records, writings, or books. The full title of Clement of Alexandria's *Stromateis* is *Miscellanies of Notes* (ὑπομνήματα) *of Revealed Knowledge in Accordance with the True Philosophy*, in which the word ὑπομνήματα may revert to philosophical usage of Arrian in his 'reminiscences' of the Stoic Epictetus (J. Ferguson, *Clement of Alexandria. Stromateis. Books One to Three*, 11).

[100] The view of John's Gospel as supplementary to the other three became a commonplace among later patristic theologians. See Wiles, *Spiritual Gospel*, 11, 13–21.

'order' of the events in Mark's Gospel felt in the report of Papias' elder in 3. 39. 15. Mark wrote accurately 'all that he remembered, not, indeed, in order, of the things said or done by the Lord'; in this he was simply following Peter's style, who taught according to need, 'not making, as it were, an arrangement of the Lord's oracles'. John, on the other hand, it is implied in our fragment, gave the proper order, even naming the first of the Lord's signs (John 2: 11) (3. 24. 11).

5. *Canonical ratification.* We also note the attempt to find some kind of endorsement for each Gospel, or Gospel writer, from another accepted (apostolic), textual authority: of Mark by Peter (*HE* 2. 15. 2); of Luke[101] by Paul (*HE* 3. 4. 7); of John by John (in his indications of chronology in John 2: 11 (3. 24. 8–10) and probably in testimony cited from 1 John (3. 39. 17).[102] For Matthew we cannot point to a textual affirmation that has survived, though his Gospel is vouched for by John in the story told about John's Gospel in 3. 24. 7.

These common elements and concerns point to a common source. From a comparison with the other Papian fragments on the Gospels in Eusebius, then, there is fairly conclusive support for regarding Eusebius' source in 3. 24. 5–13 as being Papias' tradition about the Fourth Gospel. Besides these common elements, there are a few stylistic features which link the Papian material together which I shall examine at another point. The identity of this source may be established further by pointing to parallels with those writers whom we know were dependent upon Papias in their accounts of Matthew and Mark.

Parallels with other authors who knew Papias' work

Irenaeus, Clement of Alexandria, the author of the *Muratorian Fragment*, Origen, and Victorinus, all writing before Eusebius, seem to have known Papias' traditions about Matthew and Mark. This fact suggests that they would also have been familiar with whatever Papias said about John and Luke, and hence a likely place to find remnants of that witness. Here I quote specifically what each says about the origins of the Fourth Gospel.

Afterwards, John, the disciple of the Lord, who also had leaned upon his breast, did himself publish a Gospel during his residence at Ephesus in Asia. (Irenaeus, *AH* 3. 1. 1)

John, the disciple of the Lord, preaches this faith, and seeks, by the proclamation of the Gospel, to remove that error which by Cerinthus had been disseminated among men, and a long time previously by those termed Nicolaitans ... The disciple of the Lord therefore desiring to put an end to all such doctrines, and to establish the rule

---

[101] For this, see the appendix to Hill, 'What Papias Said about John'.

[102] Lightfoot, *Supernatural*, 206; Bauckham, 'Origin', 47, 55; and possibly by Andrew and others, according to the *MF*.

of truth in the Church...thus commenced his teaching in the Gospel...(Irenaeus, *AH* 3. 11. 1)

But that John, last of all, conscious that the outward facts had been set forth in the Gospels, was urged on (προτραπέντα) by his disciples (γνωρίμων), and, divinely moved by the Spirit, composed a spiritual Gospel. (Clement, *Hypotyposeis* in Eusebius, *HE* 6. 14. 7)

The fourth [book] of the Gospels is that of John [one] of the disciples. When his fellow-disciples and bishops urged (*cohortantibus*) [him], he said: 'Fast together with me today for three days and, what shall be revealed to each, let us tell [it] to each other'. On the same night it was revealed to Andrew, [one] of the Apostles, that, with all of them reviewing [it], John should describe all things in his own name. And so, although different beginnings (*varia...principia*) might be taught in the separate books of the Gospels, nevertheless it makes no difference to the faith of believers, since all things in all [of them] are declared by the one sovereign Spirit—concerning his nativity, concerning [His] passion, concerning [His] resurrection, concerning [His] walk with His disciples, and concerning His double advent: the first in humility when He was despised, which has been; the second in royal power, glorious, which is to be. What marvel, then, if John so constantly brings forward particular [matters] (*singula*) also in his Epistles, saying of himself: 'What we have seen with our eyes and have heard with [our] ears and our hands have handled, these things we have written to you.' For thus he declares that he was not only an eyewitness and hearer, but also a writer of all the wonderful things (*mirabilium*) of the Lord in order (*per ordinem*). (*Muratorian Fragment*, ll. 9–34)

There is a report noted down in writing that John collected the written Gospels in his own lifetime[103] in the reign of Nero, and approved of and recognized those of which the deceit of the devil had not taken possession; but refused and rejected those which he perceived were not truthful. (Origen, *Hom. Luke* 1, fr. 9)[104]

For when Valentinus [*sic*], Cerinthus and Ebion and the others of the school of Satan were spread over the world, all the bishops came together to him (*convenerunt ad illum*) from the most distant provinces and compelled him to write a testimony. (Victorinus, *CA* 11. 1)[105]

---

[103] ἔτι περιόντα βίω. An emphasis on John being still alive, expressed in similar terms, is found also in Eusebius, *HE* 3. 18. 1 (ἔτι τῷ βίῳ ἐνδιατρίβοντα) and 3. 23. 1 (ἔτι τῷ βίῳ περιλειπόμενος).

[104] Translation from *NTA*[2] i. 46. Greek text from M. Rauer, *Origenes Werke*, ix, 2nd edn., *GCS* 49 (Berlin, 1959): Λόγος ἐστὶ παραγραπτέος Ἰωάννην ἔτι περιόντα βίῳ ἐπὶ Νέρωνος τὰ συγγεγραμμένα εὐαγγέλια συναγαγεῖν καὶ τὰ μὲν ἐγκρῖναι καὶ ἀποδέξασθαι, ὧν οὐδὲν ἡ τοῦ διαβόλου ἐπιβουλὴ καθήψατο, τὰ δὲ ἀπολέξασθαι καὶ καταργῆσαι, ὅσα μὴ τῆς ἀληθείας ἐχόμενα συνέγνω. It is possible here that the word παραγραπτέος, translated 'noted down in writing' above, should actually be 'in a margin'.

[105] Bauckham, 'Origin', 63–5, is probably correct in thinking that the words of Jerome in *De vir. illust.* 9 and the Monarchian Prologue to John are not beholden directly to Papias, but only to Irenaeus and some other source, the Prologue probably being dependent upon Jerome. See Bauckham for translations.

The following is a list of some of the parallels between one or more of these writers and the source paraphrased by Eusebius in *HE* 3. 24.

1. *Writing by request.* In *HE* 3. 24. 11 Eusebius' source says that John was urged on (παρακληθέντα) to write his Gospel, that he 'took to writing out of necessity (ἐπάναγκες)' (3. 24. 5) and did not simply take it upon himself. We find the same idea in Clement (προτραπέντα, *HE* 6. 14. 7), the *MF* (*cohortantibus*), and later in Victorinus. The identities of the requesters (Clement: disciples; *MF*: fellow disciples, including Andrew, and bishops; Victorinus: bishops) and the circumstances surrounding the request fluctuate in the accounts dependent upon Papias. Eusebius does not give the identities of those who requested John to write. The *MF*'s more elaborate account, containing details unparalleled in any other writer who knew Papias, perhaps represents significant expansions on Papias' simpler account.

2. *Order in the Gospels.* From these sources Richard Bauckham had deduced that Papias must have said something about John's 'order'.[106] It turns out that he was right, as confirmed by our fragment. All accounts (including the source in *HE* 3. 24) are aware of differences between John's and the other three Gospels, and the question of 'order' is present here in 3. 24 as it is in Papias' account of Mark (3. 39. 15) and in the *MF*'s account of John, the latter of which states that 'he was not only an eyewitness and hearer, but also a writer of all the wonderful things of the Lord in order (*per ordinem*)'. Another uncanny parallel between our fragment and the *MF*, in the substitution of a word for 'marvels' (τῶν παραδόξων; *mirabilium*) for 'signs' (τῶν σημείων) in reference to John 2: 11,[107] seems to require a relationship between these two works.[108]

The author of the *MF* makes a point that Luke 'began his story from the birth of John' and is well aware that the four Gospels teach 'different beginnings' (*varia...principia*), though, he says, this makes no difference to the faith of believers. The fragment used by Eusebius in 3. 24 also focuses

---

[106] Bauckham's suspicion that Papias might have upbraided the other Gospels on this basis, however, turns out to be unsupported. The source explicitly says that John 'welcomed them and testified to their truth', finding fault only in their omission of some important events at the beginning of Jesus' ministry. That all the writers dependent upon Papias also regard the last Gospel as only complementary to the first three therefore appears as no surprise.

[107] All Greek MSS of John 2: 11 have σημείων, and in Eusebius' two other citations of the verse he preserves the correct reading.

[108] Another striking point of contact should be recognized between the *MF* and the excerpt from Papias' elder on Mark in *HE* 3. 39. 15. The elder remarks that Mark should not be criticized for 'writing down single points (ἔνια) as he remembered them', but he 'had not heard the Lord, nor had he followed him', but only set out to give a complete and faithful account of what he remembered of Peter's teaching. The author of the *MF* says it is not to be wondered at that John 'so constantly brings forward particular matters (*singula*)' in his Gospel and Epistles, for he *was* an eyewitness and hearer and a writer of all the marvelous things of the Lord in order. There is here not only a striking coincidence in vocabulary (ἔνια; *singula*), but also in the justification given for each author: Mark writing from memory cannot be faulted for writing particular points as he remembered them, for he had not heard the Lord (but was following Peter's *ad hoc* preaching); John naturally brings forth particular points in the right order, for he did see and hear the Lord.

on the different beginnings of the Gospels,[109] evincing some concern about the question of why John did not record the Lord's genealogy (cf. the role of the genealogies in Clement's account in *HE* 6. 14. 5–6) like Matthew and Luke did, but instead 'began (ἀπάρξασθαι) with the description of his divinity' (3. 24. 13).[110]

3. *The evangelists as 'publishers'.* The fragment cited in 3. 24 uses the word ἔκδοσις for the 'publication' of the Gospels of Mark and Luke. The verb ἐκδίδωμι is used in the sense of 'publish' by Irenaeus in *AH* 3. 1. 1, where he is recounting the various origins of the Gospels, in the very place where his knowledge of Papias' notes on Matthew and Mark is most evident. He uses the term here specifically of John: 'Then John, the disciple of the Lord, who had even rested on his breast, himself also gave forth (ἐξέδωκεν) the Gospel, while he was living at Ephesus in Asia'.[111] The words ἔκδοσις and ἐκδίδωμι are not commonly used in this sense by Eusebius, occuring elsewhere only in a citation from Origen, where, interestingly enough, that writer relates what he had learned 'from tradition' about the four Gospels (*C. Matt.* 1). Of Matthew, he says that he 'published (ἐκδεδωκότα) it for those who from Judaism came to believe, composed as it was in the Hebrew language' (*HE* 6. 25. 4). This account too shows signs of familiarity both with the excerpt from Papias in *HE* 3. 39. 15 and with Eusebius' source in 3. 24. 5.

4. *The number and order of the Gospels.* Both the fragment in *HE* 3. 24. 7 and all the writers dependent upon Papias who specify any order place John last of the four Gospels.[112] (In fact, I do not know of any ancient source which deviates from this.) All also have Matthew (at least an assumed Hebrew or Aramaic original) chronologically first and all, with the possible exception of Clement of Alexandria,[113] have Mark and Luke in the present canonical order.

A Greek fragment of a work of Origen's, thought to be from his *Homilies on Luke*,[114] also shows important similarities with our fragment. Here Origen

---

[109] The connection noticed by Bartlet, 'Papias's "Exposition"', 27.

[110] For a discussion of the 'order' of events in the Gospels visible in this fragment in 3. 24. 7–13 in relation to Irenaeus' statement about the age of Jesus for which he claims support from the Asian elders in *AH* 2. 22. 5, see Hill, 'What Papias Said about John'.

[111] The Greek here is preserved in Eusebius, *HE* 5. 8. 4.

[112] Irenaeus in *AH* 3. 1. 1; the *MF*; Clement in his *Hypot.* (*HE* 6. 14. 7); Origen in his *C. Matt.* (*HE* 6. 25. 6); Victorinus in his *CA* 11. 1 (not stated but presupposed), and of course Eusebius, who, before introducing his selection from Papias on Matthew and John says, 'it was reasonable for the ancients to reckon it in the fourth place after the other three' (3. 24. 2).

[113] On Clement's deviation, see Hill, 'What Papias Said about John', 603–5.

[114] So listed in *NTA*². M. Rauer, *Origenes Werke*, ix. *Die Homilien zu Lukas in der Übersetzung des Hieronymus und die griechischen Reste der Homilien und des Lukas-kommentars*, GCS 49 (Berlin, 1959), 230, suggested that this fragment is instead from his commentary on John. Rauer also called attention to the parallel with our section in Eusebius, *HE* 3. 24. 7. H. Merkel, *La Pluralité des Evangiles comme problème théologique et exégétique dans l'Eglise ancienne*, tr. J.-L. Maier (Berne, 1978), p. x n. 31, questions whether it is Origen's, though his grounds are unclear. The authorship of the fragment, however, is not critical; the report it cites is.

refers to 'a report noted down in writing that John collected the written Gospels in his own lifetime in the reign of Nero, and approved of and recognized those of which the deceit of the devil had not taken possession; but refused and rejected those which he perceived were not truthful'. We know of no other written source from the period before Origen which mentions that John knew and approved of the previous three Gospels, Origen and Eusebius' source even sharing the word ἀποδέξασθαι for 'recognized' (*HE* 3. 24. 7).[115] Though stated a bit differently, Eusebius' source and Origen also agree that John's evaluation of the previous canonical Gospels involved a testimony to their truthfulness: Eusebius, 'he welcomed them and testified to their truth'; Origen, 'but refused and rejected those which he perceived were not truthful'. It is likely then that this written report, wherever Origen found it, is either the portion of Papias' work from which Eusebius' excerpt was taken,[116] or was based on it. If not, then we have to reckon with two early and independent witnesses to John's 'canonizing' activity with respect to the Gospels.

I think this is sufficient for us to conclude that source which Eusebius paraphrases in *HE* 3. 24. 5–17 is Papias of Hierapolis. As to the contents of the fragment, it relates that, after all three former Gospels had been published, John still used his unwritten proclamation; that he approved of these three Gospels; that he noted their omission of events from the earlier part of Jesus' ministry; that he was exhorted (παρακληθέντα, 3. 24. 11) by some to supply that lack by handing down in writing what was previously unwritten. This it gives as the motivation for his writing.

USE OF THE REST OF THE JOHANNINE CORPUS

Besides this, we also know that Papias used at least 1 John and Revelation. Eusebius says plainly that Papias used testimonies from 1 John (*HE* 3. 39. 17). He does not say what these testimonies were, but it is very likely that they included a citation of 1 John 1: 1–4 as ratifying John's Gospel. A use of Revelation is demonstrated if the reference by Irenaeus to some of the 'men who saw John face to face', who attested to the correctness of the number 666 in Revelation 13. 7 (*AH* 5. 30. 1), is rightly attributed to the books of Papias. In any case it is demonstrated by the testimony of Andrew of Caesarea (in Cappadocia), who cites Papias' exegesis of Revelation 12: 9 (*On the Apocalypse* 34. 12, LHH, no. 11) and indicates that the latter bore some kind of witness to

---

[115] In the light of this, it will seem possible that this is the Greek word lying behind the *MF*'s report that Andrew and the others should 'recognize' (*recognoscentibus*) John's Gospel.

[116] We should not overlook the possibility that Origen had obtained a copy of Papias' *Exposition of the Lord's Logia* by the time he lived in Caesarea, and that this copy remained in the library Origen founded there, where it was found and used later by Eusebius. H. Crouzel, F. Fourier, and P. Périchon, *Origène, Homélies sur S. Luc: Texte latin et fragments grecs: introduction et notes*, SC 87 (Paris, 1962), 81, place the homilies on Luke in Caesarea in 233–4. Origen's *Commentary on John* was completed at Caesarea.

the trustworthiness (τὸ ἀξιόπιστον)[117] of the Apocalypse of John (*Preface to the Apocalypse*, LHH no. 10). This is information which Andrew could not have got from Eusebius and by all appearances has been gained from his own reading of Papias' work in the fifth century.

CONCLUSION

Even apart from the 'new' fragment of Papias' writing now identified, there exists ample evidence that Papias had used the Fourth Gospel and that he and others of his generation used it as an authoritative source for their knowledge of Jesus. But with this fragment added, not only is this evidence richly augmented, but it seems to provide a sort of skeleton key to much of the rest of the second century. We have seen above that the apostolic authorship of the Fourth Gospel is either mentioned explicitly (Ptolemy, Irenaeus, the *Muratorian Fragment*, Theodotus, Clement of Alexandria, Tertullian, etc.) or is assumed (*Epistle of Vienne and Lyons*, Hegesippus, *Epistula Apostolorum*, the *Ad Diognetum*, Justin, Theophilus, etc.), and an authority consistent with such an attribution is assumed by others (Athenagoras, Melito, Tatian) throughout the remainder of the second century and seems to require a much earlier recognition. We are now able to see that such recognition was published in a book somewhere between *c.* 120 and 135 by Papias of Hierapolis. It probably occurred originally in a section not far removed from that which also recorded the tradition of the presbyter concerning Matthew, Mark, and Luke. It tells us that by this time these four Gospels were regarded as important enough that the circumstances of their origins were topics of vital interest to Church leaders. Restoring these fragments to Papias' work also strengthens the link between these four Gospels and the Dominical 'Logia' which it was the purpose of Papias' books to exposit.[118]

By the time Papias wrote—and no doubt many years earlier, for Papias has this as a tradition from an earlier elder (Elder John)—the Gospel according to John was accepted as among the four which obviously held a special status among the churches where he expected his book to be read. This Gospel was attributed even at that time to John the apostle of Jesus. If his use of 1 John included, as Lightfoot, Bauckham and we have suggested, testimony for the

---

[117] Most probably this indicates Papias' attribution of the Apocalypse to John the apostle. Also, less directly, Eusebius, in mentioning Papias' belief in a thousand-year kingdom of Christ on earth, says that he supposed Papias had misread 'the apostolic accounts', not recognizing their mystic and symbolic language. One of these 'apostolic accounts' would surely have been Revelation. (See Lightfoot, *Supernatural*, 214–15 n. 4.)

[118] See Lawlor, 'Eusebius on Papias', *Hermathena*, 19 (1922), 167–222, esp. 197–8, 'The conclusion to be drawn from the foregoing investigation seems to be that the title which Papias prefixed to his treatise means interpretations (or translations) of written documents relating to our Lord, which were of sufficient authority in the Church of Asia to be placed on a par, or nearly on a par, with the Jewish Scriptures, and which may have contained incidents as well as sayings—probably a Gospel or Gospels' (cf. 204).

purpose of ratifying the Fourth Gospel (as he evidently used 1 Peter to 'ratify' Mark's Gospel) we may well imagine that he, like the author of the *Muratorian Fragment*, did so on the assumption that 1 John was written by the same person who wrote the Gospel according to John. Andrew of Caesarea's citation of one instance of Papias' interpretation of a portion of the Apocalypse, and his statement that Papias attested to the trustworthiness of that book assures us that Papias and his generation in Asia Minor valued it. While this does not guarantee that Papias ascribed the Apocalypse to the same John, the apostle, it does beg for comparison with Justin, who in narrating a debate which allegedly took place in Asia Minor some time after 135 (the end of the Bar Kochba revolt) did so ascribe it. We are not far away from being able to affirm that Papias, some time probably in the years 120–35 not only possessed at least these three of the five known Johannine works, but also knew them as a 'corpus' of writings attributed to the same man.

Another point should be made here. It has often been stressed, particularly by Hillmer, that the commentary written by Heracleon (and the exegesis of Ptolemy) shows a respect for the text of the Fourth Gospel which is consistent with scriptural status. That this first occurred with a Valentinian has been a pillar for the orthodox Johannophobia theory. We have seen that the work of Heracleon implies the existence of a scriptural status on the part of the orthodox, which can in fact be documented. It ought to be observed that the writing of commentaries is not the only test for the presence of a conception of scripture. What we see with Papias is also consistent with such a conception. He is evidently furnishing 'introductions' to the four Gospels as they are the basis, or at least the chief basis, for his collection of expositions of the Lord's Logia.

The evidence from Papias, then, is of tremendous importance. But again I emphasize that the addition of this long-neglected testimony injects no egregious or incongruous element but simply fills in the gaps and helps to make sense of the later second-century data. I shall say more about this later, but it already appears that a large part of the foundation which underlay the use of the Fourth Gospel in the second half of the second century has begun to be uncovered.

The *Apology* of Aristides of Athens[119]

In the years immediately preceding 125 Christians, particularly in Asia Minor, had suffered intense persecution.[120] After his arrival in Athens in

---

[119] See B. Pouderon, M.-J. Pierre, and B. Outtier, 'A propos de l'Apologie d'Aristide: Recherches sur un prototype commun aux versions syriaque et arménienne', *Revue des Sciences Religieuses*, 74 (2000), 173–93, at 175 for the texts. Pouderon, Pierre, and Outtier are preparing a new edn. for *Sources chrétiennes*.

[120] See Hill, '*Epistula Apostolorum*'.

that year during his great imperial tour, the Emperor Hadrian himself was initiated into the Eleusinian mysteries. These events did not portend well for the treatment of Christians throughout the empire. Perhaps this is why, while still in Athens, the emperor was presented with two 'apologies' by Christian rhetors, Quadratus and Aristides.[121] The *Apology* of Quadratus is now lost entirely, except for a tiny fragment given by Eusebius. The *Apology* of Aristides, however, has been recovered, though not in quite its original form. It survives entire in a fourth- or fifth-century Syriac translation, and in part in a fifth-century Armenian version (chapters 1–2), two fourth-century Greek fragments (5. 3–6; 15. 6–16. 1) found at Oxyrhynchus, and a very valuable Greek paraphrase of almost the entire work incorporated in the tenth-century into the *Life of Barlaam and Joasaph* 26–7 by one Euthymius in Bithynia.[122] The occasion for the work as given by Eusebius is borne out by the title in the Syriac version, and the address of the Armenian.[123] We may safely conclude that Eusebius is correct as to date. According to Eusebius the work had been 'preserved by many' in his day (*HE* 4. 3. 2). A faithful Greek text was extant at least into the late tenth century when it was incorporated into the romance of *Barlaam and Ioasaph*.

By far the bulk of the text of this early apology is given to the description and refutation of the religious practices of polytheists, the Barbarians, the Greeks, and the Egyptians (chapters 3–13). Aristides gives one chapter (14)

---

[121] Eusebius, *HE* 4. 3. 3, 'Aristides too, a man of faith and devoted to our religion, has, like Quadratus, left behind a defence of the faith addressed to Hadrian. His writing too is preserved by many'. From his *Chronicon* we have the following, 'Codratus, a pupil of the Apostles, and Aristides of Athens, a philosopher of our faith, gave to Hadrian apologetic entreaties at his command. He had, however, also received from Serennius, that glorious judge, a writing concerning the Christians, that it was certainly wrong to kill them on the basis of rumor alone without trial or any accusation. He wrote to Armonius Fundanus, proconsul of Asia, that he should not condemn them without formal condemnation and trial; and a copy of this edict survives to this day' (translation of R. L. Wolff, 'The Apology of Aristides: A Re-examination', *HTR* 30 (1937), 233–47, at 239).

[122] See Wolff, 'Apology'. On the relative accuracy of the Syriac and the Greek of *Barlaam*, the Greek fragments of an ancient recension discovered at Oxyrhynchus have provided a trustworthy guide. After a close comparison with the first of these fragments, Grenfell and Hunt (*Oxyrhynchus Papyri* 15, no. 1778) said, 'Though open to criticism especially for its verbosity, to which much of its comparative length is due, the Syriac has at any rate some of the advantages claimed for it by Dr Rendel Harris, in places reproducing the original more faithfully than BJ [i.e. *Barlaam and Joasaph*] and retaining words and phrases which the Greek redactor discarded. The latter often preserves the language of Aristides with much fidelity but... makes such short cuts and readjustments as seemed suitable for his purpose.' To put it simply, the Syriac tends to expand, *Barlaam* to contract, but each is essentially faithful to the original. H. J. M. Milne, 'A New Fragment of the *Apology* of Aristides', *JTS* 25 (1924), 73–7, affirmed this conclusion after studying the second fragment, finding eight amplifications and two omissions in the Syriac. 'On the whole, however, the Syriac gives a tolerably close rendering, although it does not appear to reproduce the terseness and austerity of the Greek' (75).

[123] The address in the Syriac, however, goes on puzzlingly to mention Antoninus Pius (138–61). Grant, *Greek Apologists*, 38–9, suggested that the original apology written for Hadrian was reworked and presented again to Antoninus Pius. This theory is countered, however, by Pouderon *et al*, 'A propos', *181–2*. They show that the Armenian and the Syriac go back to a common Eastern redaction, and therefore, since the Armenian is consistent in referrring to Hadrian in both the title and the address, attribute the reference to Antoninus to confusion on the part of a Syrian scribe.

to the religion of the Jews. His description of the faith of the Christians, begun in chapter 2, is taken up again in the last three chapters, where it is followed by his plea for fair and reasonable treatment of them. Like Justin and the apologists generally, Aristides' apologetic method involves a sparing and indirect use of his Christian authorities. It would be a mistake, however, to conclude from the absence of direct quotation or attribution that Aristides did not have any such authorities. Several NT works can be recognized in his diction and theology,[124] and perhaps more important than this, he informs the emperor of his debt to Christian 'writings' and, providing a lead which Justin would later follow (*1Apol.* 28. 1), exhorts the emperor himself to read them.[125]

GREEK	SYRIAC
15.1 And if you would read, O King, you may judge the glory of his presence from the holy gospel writing,[126] as it is called among themselves.	2.4 This is taught in the gospel, as it is called, which a short time ago was preached among them; and you also if you will read therein, may perceive the power which belongs to it.

The Syriac and Greek of *Barlaam* agree in using some form of the word 'gospel' here. The gospel is something which is said to have been proclaimed, but it is also stated that the king could read about the life of Jesus in it.[127] This rather strikingly confirms what we know of the usage of the word gospel at this time, when its primary meaning was still the preached good news of Jesus Christ, but when it had also come to be used of certain writings which contain this gospel. The significant thing here is that Aristides refers to 'the gospel' in a written source or sources. As we know even from later usage, the singular can also be used when plural Gospels are in view.[128] And indeed, as I shall later suggest, the content ascribed to 'the

---

[124] J. A. Robinson, 'Appendix: The Remains of the Original Greek of the Apology of Aristides', in *Texts and Studies* (Cambridge, 1891), 65–118 at 82. Robinson identified traces from 2 Macc. 7: 28; Col. 1: 17; and several passages from Romans, from 1 Thess. 2: 13; probably 1 Tim. 1: 8; Heb. 11: 8–9; and Acts 13: 17; and though not paralleled in the Syriac, the Greek fragments also show a borrowing from Matt. 13: 17, 37. Robinson also believed that Aristides used the *Preaching of Peter*, a work evidently considered genuine by Clement of Alexandria. Schneemelcher is more cautious, saying that 'at least considerable connection between his Apology and the KP can be pointed out' (Schneemelcher, *NTA*² 34). Grant, *Greek Apologists*, 39, says, 'It is hard to tell whether "Peter" influenced Aristides or vice versa, but there must be some relation'.

[125] Translations are those of D. M. Kay in *ANF* x.

[126] Ἐκ τῆς παρ' αὐτοῖς καλουμένης εὐαγγελικῆς ἁγίας γραφῆς. The word ἁγίας, as it is not attested in the Syriac or Armenian, is probably not original (Pouderon *et al.*, 'A propos', 176).

[127] Robinson, *TS* 82, 'On two occasions the Emperor is referred to Christian writings. In the first case a written Gospel is distinctly implied, as the matter in hand is the outline of our Lord's Life'.

[128] See *Dial.* 10. 2; 100. 1; Irenaeus, *AH* 3. 5. 1; 3. 11. 7. On the use of the singular 'Gospel' in *Dial* 10. 1; 100. 1, Barnard, *Justin Martyr*, 57, says, 'This seems to refer to a *collection* of written memoirs as is the case with Irenaeus and many subsequent writers'.

gospel' in this section would seem to encompass information from more than one of our present Gospels. This 'gospel' in written form is publicly accessible, presumed to be known generally to Christians, and something it is assumed the emperor could obtain without great trouble. The Syriac makes the 'power', said to be perceived in the reading of the Gospel, to be the power of the gospel itself (rather than being the power or 'glory of his presence' in the Greek of *Barlaam*). This is consistent with a later reference in chapter 16 where Aristides again commends these writings to Hadrian and (according to the Syriac) confesses that he himself had felt the effects of such power:

GREEK	SYRIAC
And that you may know, O King, that in saying these things I do not speak at my own instance, if you deign to look into the writings of the Christians, you will find that I state nothing beyond the truth.	Take, then, their writings, and read therein, and lo! you will find that I have not put forth these things on my own authority, nor spoken thus as their advocate; but since I read in their writings I was fully assured of these things as also of things which are to come.

This text too, like the first, challenges the emperor to read the Christian writings or scriptures (the Greek of *Barl.* has ταῖς γραφαῖς). It is clear that these writings at least include, if they are not limited to, specifically Christian writings and not only the Old Testament because of the information about Christ which he says, particularly in chapter 2, that they contain. The contents of these writings are alluded to three more times in the surviving Syriac, in this relatively short section on the superiority of the Christian 'race'.

But the Christians, O King, while they went about and made search, have found the truth; and as we learned from their writings, they have come nearer to truth and genuine knowledge than the rest of the nations. (15. 1 Syriac)

And as for their words and precepts, O King, and their glorying in their worship, and the hope of earning according to the work of each one of them their recompense which they look for in another world,—you may learn about these from their writings. (16 Syriac)

Thus far, O King, I have spoken; for concerning that which remains...there are found in their other writings things which are hard to utter and difficult for one to narrate,—which are not only spoken in words but also wrought out in deeds. (17 Syriac)

Aristides attests that he could determine from these writings that the Christians have come closer to truth and genuine knowledge than the rest of the nations; the nature of their words, precepts, their glorying in their worship, and much about their future hope and recompense; and in their 'other writings' were contained things 'hard to utter and difficult for one the narrate', which pertain to deeds and not just to words. While there is no way to know for certain what these writings were, it would seem from their contents as reported in the second passage that they are not confined to Gospels.[129] And it would be a reasonable guess that the reference to 'other writings' in the last passage might be a reference to Christian, non-Gospel, literature. Though the contents are alluded to in the most general terms, there are certainly shades of some of the epistolary material (2 Pet. 3: 15–16 in reference to Paul's letters; Jas. 1: 22–5) here. We know then that Aristides had come to know specific writings identified very closely with the Christian movement; that one or more of these was known by the term 'Gospel'; that they in all likelihood included non-Gospel writings; that these writings played a significant part in his conversion; that he now commends these writings to the emperor. For our purposes here we must ask whether there is there any good reason to think these writings, at least one or more of which was known by the term 'Gospel', may have included what we now call the Gospel according to John?

In the brief catalogue of biographical facts about Jesus repeated by Aristides is the statement that 'he himself was pierced by the Jews, and he died and was buried' (2. 5 Syr.).[130] As the editors say, this necessarily evokes John 19: 37.[131] Such a comment is justified, and is solid, prima-facie evidence of Aristides' knowledge of the Fourth Gospel, because John's is the only account of the crucifixion known up to this time to record the piercing (John 19: 34).[132] Of course, it is possible that this detail could have come from tradition outside that Gospel. But, apart possibly from the allusion in Revelation 1: 7, the piercing is evidently only attested in works which are much later than and dependent on the Fourth Gospel: *Sibylline Oracles* 8. 296; Apollinarius of Hierapolis; Irenaeus, *AH* 3. 22. 2; 4. 33. 2; 4. 35. 3; *Acts of John* 97; Clement (Theodotus), *Excerpts of Theodotus* 61. 3.[133] Further,

---

[129] Thus Hengel's statement, 'He recommends to Caesar only generally the reading of scripture, which for him is identical with "the Gospel"' (*Frage*, 66) is not strictly accurate.

[130] The agreement of the Syriac and Armenian shows ἐκκεντέω must have been in the original, though the Greek of *Barlaam* has simply 'through the cross' (15. 1). Pouderon *et al.*, 'A propos', 191, conclude that the author who adapted the apology to his new context in *Barl.* ignored the verb ἐκκεντέω because 'the word was unknown in the formulas of faith in usage in the 10th century' when he worked.

[131] Pouderon *et al.*, 'A propos', 191.

[132] It is true that the piercing here is explicitly assigned to the Jews, whereas in John's account it is done, of course, by one of the Roman soldiers. Yet this extension is effectively made by the Fourth Gospel itself (John 19: 37) as well as by Revelation 1: 7. It might be objected that the reference is not to the piercing of Jesus' side, but to the crucifixion itself. Yet similar references to the 'piercing' of Jesus in 2nd-cent literature do not pertain to the crucifixion generally, but to the piercing specifically: *Sib. Or.* 8. 296. Apollinarius of Hierapolis; Irenaeus, *AH* 3. 22. 2; 4. 33. 2; 4. 35. 3; the *AJ* 97; Clement (Theodotus), *Theod.* 61. 3).

[133] Cf. Justin, who several times cites Zechariah 12: 10, the text which the author of the Fourth Gospel says was fulfilled by this event (John 19: 37, ὄψονται εἰς ὃν ἐξεκέντησαν). The verb used in the most common LXX tradition does not mean 'pierced' but 'treated despitefully' (not

it is of critical importance that this reference to a detail recorded only in John occurs in chapter 2[134] of the apology, in precisely the context in which Aristides states that his information about Jesus the Messiah comes from 'the gospel, as it is called', which he enjoins the emperor to read![135] There is thus every reason to believe that here Aristides is repeating a distinctive aspect of the crucifixion of Jesus which he had read in the Fourth Gospel, a Gospel which conceivably would be available in Athens for the emperor to peruse if he so chose.[136]

A familiarity with the Fourth Gospel seems to be indicated in another portion of chapter 2. Nagel also observes that Aristides speaks of Jesus Christ as 'having come down from heaven' (ἀπ' οὐρανοῦ καταβάς), which parallels two Johannine passages, John 3: 13, ὁ ἐκ τοῦ οὐρανοῦ καταβάς, and John 6: 38, ὅτι καταβέβηκα ἀπὸ τοῦ οὐρανοῦ.[137] Aristides' mention in the same context of Jesus' 'taking flesh' (σάρκα ἀνέλαβε)[138] also echoes John 1: 14. This too comes in the section in which Aristides encourages the emperor to 'read' about these things in 'the Gospel'.

There is attested in the work of Aristides the Athenian philosopher an emphasis on the textual authorities of Christianity which is quite remarkable for the time and the newly flourishing apologetic 'genre'. Only for the Christians, and not for the other 'races' of men, not even for the Jews, does he appeal to written sources for the validation of his information. Already

---

ἐκκεντέω but κατορχέομαι). See R. E. Brown, *The Gospel according to John (xiii–xxi)* (Garden City, NY, 1970), 938. Either Justin has a Greek text with ἐκκεντέω in it, or he is translating from the Hebrew. In the latter case his citation has almost certainly been influenced by the Gospel of John.

[134] The editor who incorporated the apology into *Barlaam* transferred this section to a later part of his dialogue, now numbered ch. 15. The Sryiac and Armenian have the original placement.

[135] The information he gives cannot all have come from only one of our Gospels (canonical or, as far as we know, early non-canonical). He mentions that Jesus was confessed as Son of God Most High (*Barl.* ὁ υἱὸς τοῦ θεοῦ τοῦ ὑψίστου), a title found only in Mark 5: 7 and Luke 1: 32; 8: 28; not in Matthew or John. He then mentions Jesus' descent from heaven and birth through a Hebrew virgin. The descent might be inferred from any Gospel, but is explicit only in John. The virgin birth is recounted only by Matthew and Luke. Then comes the mention of the piercing, the burial (not in *Barl.*), the resurrection after three days, and the ascension to heaven. The 'piercing' must come from John and the ascension could come from any but Mark (even from Mark if he had the long ending, 16: 19). At minimum this seems to require at least Luke and John, but it is hard to rule out Matthew. All this Aristides refers to 'the gospel', which he alleges the emperor can read. This must at least raise the question whether a collection of multiple Gospels, known as 'the Gospel', may have been in circulation at this time.

[136] The Greek of *Barlaam* has in ch. 15 the statement that God made all things 'through the only-begotten Son and the Holy Spirit' (ἐν υἱῷ μονογενεῖ). This surely is based in part on John 1: 1–14, but it is absent from the Syriac (the Armenian is not extant at this point). This Greek version also contains a reference to Jesus' voluntary death on the cross (διὰ σταυροῦ θανάτου ἐγεύσατο ἑκουσίᾳ βουλῇ), which probably is based on John 10: 17, 18. Neither of these is found in the Syriac, though there are points at which the Greek of *Barlaam* preserves the original better, as compared with the Oxyrhynchus fragments.

[137] Nagel, *Rezeption*, 118–19.

[138] In the Syriac, 'And it is said that God came down from heaven, and from a Hebrew virgin assumed and clothed himself with flesh'. Pouderon *et al.* 'A propos', 189, indicate that the Armenian has 'took flesh' (*marmin arnul*).

by 125, at just about the time Papias wrote, but in an environment separated from him by stretches of land and sea, Christianity was in the mind of one of its apologists very much a 'textual' and perhaps we should say a 'scriptural' religion. We may not be able to tell whether his references to Christian γραφαί are references to Christian 'scriptures' or simple references to Christian 'writings'. But Aristides in any case refers the Roman emperor to them as authoritative sources for the morals of the Christians and for their teaching about their Saviour. This means he must have specific writings in mind which could have been supplied to the emperor, and these included probably two or more known as Gospels. From Aristides' preservation of incarnational language and of a detail of Jesus' crucifixion known from only one Christian Gospel, we may safely conclude that one of these Gospels—the one that his contemporary, Papias of Hierapolis, ascribed to John the apostle—was among them.

The Long Ending to Mark

In *The Johannine Question* Martin Hengel observed that the long ending of Mark, Mark 16: 9–20, may be the first 'secondary "mélange"' of texts from John and the Synoptics which represents a tradition seen elsewhere and more extensively in works such as the Secret Gospel of Mark, *Egerton Papyrus 2*, and the *Gospel of Peter*.[139]

Mark 16. 9 reproduces in the briefest form the appearance of Jesus to Mary Magdalene. Subsequent verses give a harmonizing summary of the reports of John 20, Luke 24 and Matt. 28 and expand them with apocryphal material which has connections with Papias...It is the first attempt at a partial 'gospel harmony', but is still much freer in form than that of Tatian fifty or sixty years later.[140]

Hengel's insight about the significance of the longer ending of Mark is now supported by a full-scale investigation of that added passage by James Kelhoffer.[141]

---

[139] Hengel, *Question*, 11 (*Frage*, 57–8). See also his 'The Titles of the Gospels and the Gospel of Mark', in Hengel, *Studies in the Gospel of Mark*, J. Bowden (London, 1985), 167–8 n. 47.
[140] Hengel, *Question*, 11.
[141] J. A. Kelhoffer, *Miracle and Mission: The Authentication of Missionaries and their Message in the Longer Ending of Mark*, WUNT 2 112 (Tübingen, 2000). Kelhoffer's study is comprehensive. J. Hug, *La Finale de l'évangile de Marc. Mc 16, 9–20*, Études Bibliques (Paris, 1978), had earlier concluded that the longer ending was independent of the canonical Gospels and Acts, and Hug's view had enjoyed the approval of many other scholars (see Kelhoffer, *Miracle*, 131). But Kelhoffer demonstrates that Hug's case 'rests upon faulty methodological assumptions concerning gospel traditions in the second century. In particular, Hug posits that an unreasonably rigid standard of demonstrating one author's copying nearly *verbatim* and *at length* from another writing is necessary for recognizing the dependence of the LE on any NT text. Such a narrow approach to possible literary dependence allows no room for the author of Mark 16: 9–20 to adapt or even condense traditional, written materials for his own purposes' (37). The mere improbability that an author in the 2nd cent. would be using a source which independently combined elements found in the four Gospels, without either

Mark 16: 1–8 tells how Mary Magdalene and Mary the mother of James came to the tomb of Jesus on the day after the Sabbath. The addition (the LE) begins in verse 9 by recapping the story of Mary Magdalene coming alone to the tomb (as in John 20). It then reports her informing those who had been with him, and their initial unbelief. Then, in verse 12, it gives a concise summary, apparently based on Luke 24: 13–35, of Jesus' appearance to two of them as they were walking in the country, and the incredulous response from the rest. It then relates an appearance to the eleven as they sat at table, Jesus' upbraiding of their unbelief, and his commission to them to preach the gospel, accompanied by certain miraculous signs (14–18). It ends with a report of Jesus' ascension and a statement of the disciples' preaching, accompanied by the signs, in a way which seems dependent upon the stories of the book of Acts.

Kelhoffer carefully observes the marks of the author's knowledge of the four Gospels and probably Acts.[142] We shall only be concerned here with the Johannine parallels, of which he cites ten which support the case for the author's literary dependence on this Gospel:

1) the similar interest in miracles which the believer will perform; 2) analogous sayings concerning the alternative between salvation and condemnation; 3) the LE's Johannine definition of faith; 4) the title ὁ... κύριος; 5) the appearance to Mary Magdalene; 6) the reference to Mary as ἐκείνη; 7) use of the verb ἀπαγγέλλω referring to Mary; 8) the transitions μὲν οὖν and 9) μετὰ δὲ ταῦτα; 10) the use of the verb ἐφανερώθη.[143]

Like John, this author uses the term σημεῖα for the miraculous works which will accompany believers and will attest the disciples' message (Mark 16: 17, 20). His seven uses of πιστεύω and its cognates is reminiscent of the role played by belief in the Fourth Gospel.[144] Particularly significant for literary dependence is number 5, Mary's visit alone to the tomb, which is mentioned only by John (John 20: 11–18; cf. 20: 1), and the verbal correspondences 6, 7, 8, 9, and 10. Kelhoffer observes that 'a particularly distinctive feature John and the LE share is how they use the pronoun ἐκείνη absolutely to denote "that woman,"' that is, Mary Magdalene; 'Such a use of ἐκείνη most probably stems from a deep familiarity with this Johannine passage'.[145] Numbers 8 (μὲν οὖν... δέ in Mark 16: 19–20; John 20: 30–1) and 9 (μετὰ δὲ ταῦτα in Mark 16: 12a; John 21: 1) 'may suggest that the LE's author sought to imitate even the most minute details of John's

---

the source or the 2nd-cent. author knowing these four Gospels, is by itself virtually fatal to Hug's theory. See Kelhoffer's thorough and devastating exposé of Hug's methods, *Miracle*, 130–7. Hug's approach is like that of H. Koester, whose principles for determining literary dependence in ancient writings are also poignantly criticized by Kelhoffer, *Miracle*, 124–30.

[142] Kelhoffer, *Miracle*, 137–50; see his chart on pp. 138–9.
[143] Ibid. 148; cf. Hengel, *Frage* 58.
[144] Kelhoffer, *Miracle*, 479.
[145] Ibid. 149.

narrative'.[146] The connection with John 21 is strengthened by the epitom-
ist's (if we may call him that) 'use of the verb φανερόω in connection with a
post-resurrection appearance' which is 'extremely rare for any first- or
second-century Christian author.[147] Moreover, the aorist passive form
(ἐφανερώθη) is identical in Mark 16: 12, 16: 14, and John 21: 14. As is
the case with the distinctive use of ἐκείνη, reliance upon the text of John
would explain the identical forms and uncommon use of this term'.[148] This
is significant for showing that chapter 21 was part of this author's Gospel
according to John. Both the long ending of Mark and the *Gospel of Peter*
from probably a bit later, know the Gospel with this ending.

Now, what else can we know about this writing and its author? Kelhoffer
puts Mark 16: 9–20 in the category of forgery, along with such works as the
apocryphal epistle of Paul to the Laodiceans, and possibly *5 Ezra*, both of
which, like the LE, reworked passages from an existing corpus to which it
sought to be attached. He believes the author, besides using traditional
motifs, also added 'ideas not prominently reflected in the sources he used—
for example, baptism as a requirement for salvation, ordinary believers as
miracle-workers, picking up snakes and drinking a deadly substance'.[149] Yet
'the majority of Mark 16: 9–20 should be regarded not as a novel composition but rather as an attempt to *imitate* traditional formulations, of which
the majority find their closest analogies toward the ends of Matthew, Luke
and John'.[150] In fact the LE 'offers an important, early witness to the
emerging four-Gospel canon in the second century'.[151]

How old is this addendum, and where is it most likely to have originated?
The longer ending is not preserved in the 'Alexandrian' MSS ℵ or B, nor is
it apparently known to Clement, Origen, or Eusebius,[152] but is preserved in
A C D L W Θ Ψ and the majority of later MSS. It is generally regarded as
a Western interpolation. We know that it existed in MSS of Mark's Gospel
at least by 180 or so, for, writing in the third book of *Against Heresies* (3. 10.
5), Irenaeus cites from Mark 16: 19 and attributes it to Mark writing 'towards the conclusion of his Gospel'. By all appearances its placement in the
text of Mark could not have been brand new when Irenaeus referred to it.
This is confirmed by its use by Tatian in composing the *Diatessaron*, and by
Justin (cf. Mark 16: 20 and Justin, *1Apol.* 45. 5; Mark 16: 9 and *1Apol.* 67. 8;
Dial. 138. 1; Mark 16: 17–18 and *Dial.* 76. 6),[153] and possibly to the author

---

[146] Kelhoffer, *Miracle and Mission*, 149.
[147] Kelhoffer (ibid.) knows of only John 21: 14 and Barn. 15: 9 outside of Mark 16: 12, 14.
[148] Kelhoffer, *Miracle*, 149.
[149] Ibid. 151.
[150] Ibid. 473.
[151] Ibid. 474.
[152] This is one reason why Kelhoffer's statement, 'Thus one can wonder whether the Gospel of
Mark would ultimately have been included in the NT canon without the addition(s) of the Longer
Ending (and elsewhere, the Shorter Ending)' (*Miracle*, 480), is overdone.
[153] Ibid. 172–5.

of the *Gospel of Peter.* Kelhoffer concludes that 'With confidence one may thus date the LE to ca. 120–150 CE',[154] and at a later point specifies 'possibly to the earlier part of this range'.[155] He thinks it would be possible to lower the *terminus ante quem* to *c.*140 or earlier, if the *Acts of Pilate* referred to by Justin is the same work as the document now known to us by that name, which definitely cites from Mark's long ending. But as we have seen above, Justin was not referring to any literary work by the title of *Acts of Pilate* but was in fact referring to 'acts' or deeds of Jesus performed under Pilate's governorship and recorded in the 'memoirs of the Apostles'. Still, there may be earlier evidence of a knowledge of the longer ending than Kelhoffer allows. Kelhoffer denies that the parallels to the *Epistula Apostolorum* are sufficient to establish dependence,[156] though, in my opinion, this is still quite possible.[157] If so, then the longer ending and its use of John and the three Synoptics together must have preceded the 140s, and perhaps by many years, as the *Epistula Apostolorum* appears to have been written no later than the 140s and may be as early as the second decade of the second century. Besides this, Hengel has noted connections with Papias, *HE* 3. 39. 9. Here Papias is said to have related a story about Justus Barsabas (cf. Acts 1: 23–4), who 'drank poison but by the Lord's grace suffered no harm'.[158] Hengel does not claim that this means Papias, or his source, knew the longer ending. Perhaps this story about Justus Barsabas made the rounds in early second-century Asia Minor and was known to the author of the long ending. This could be one reason why this author says that certain signs would accompany 'believers' and not

[154] Ibid. 175.

[155] Ibid. 475. On p. 243 he proposes that the longer ending's author 'wrote after the collection of the NT Gospels (probably not before ca. 110–120 CE)'.

[156] Ibid. 171 n. 49, saying that the parallels 'cannot establish a literary relationship between the *Epistula* and the LE', though at 186 n. 91 he writes that 'both the *Epistula Apostolorum* and the *Gospel of Peter* are arguably later than, and influenced in part by, the LE'.

[157] See Hill, '*Epistula Apostolorum*', 9–10, 14, 21–2; Hengel, *Frage*, 57, who also cites Schmidt, *Gespräche Jesu*, 220–1, 224, and C. D. G. Müller in *NTA*[5] (German) i. 208 n. 8; 210 nn. 31, 40; 222 n. 129). Reference in Mark 16: 10 to the disciples 'mourning and weeping' after the crucifixion may be the source for the same depiction in *Ep. Apost.* 9, 10, though this also occurs in *GP* 7 (27); 14 (58–9) (cf. *Ap. Jas.* 10. 6b–14 which refers to the disciples at a later time). The *GP*, Kelhoffer, *Miracle* 58, thinks, knows Mark and its long ending. It is very unlikely that the *Ep. Apost.* is dependent upon the *GP*, or that the LE is dependent upon the *Ep. Apost.* If there is any literary dependence here it is most likely that both *GP* and *Ep. Apost.* are each dependent upon the LE. Cf. also *Ep. Apost.* 11, the report of the women and the unbelief of the disciples after the resurrection, with Mark 16: 9–11, 13.

[158] Kelhoffer, *Miracle*, 433–42, argues very plausibly that Philip of Side in his *Church History* has preserved the original version of Papias' account when he says that what Justus ingested was 'viper's venom' (ἰὸν ἐχίδνης πιών) instead of Eusebius' 'harmful drug' (δηλητήριον φάρμακον ἐμπιόντος). Kelhoffer shows that many in antiquity knew that snake venom was only harmful if it was injected into the bloodstream through a bite, but that if imbibed into the stomach it was harmless, and sometimes beneficial. Eusebius, Kelhoffer thinks, knew this and so reworded the account to preserve the miraculous nature of the reported event. On the other hand, the accuracy of Philip of Side is not something one can assume implicitly. If he knew the long ending of Mark, it is not unlikely that Philip may have seen the wonder of Justus' act in terms of Mark 16: 18a–b, 'they will pick up serpents, and if they drink any deadly thing, it will not hurt them', and that the mention here of serpents right alongside the drinking of something deadly affected his report of what happened to Justus.

simply apostles, for Justus Barsabas, as is well known from the book of Acts,[159] was explicitly not chosen as Judas' replacement among the apostles.[160] Hengel at any rate is probably not far wrong in placing the composition of the longer ending between 110 and 125.[161]

The longer ending of Mark, then, takes its place among the witnesses to an authoritative use of the Fourth Gospel, and a four-Gospel collection, among mainstream Christians[162] of the first half of the second century. Tatian's *Diatessaron* was a more-or-less strict attempt to combine or amalgamate the accounts of Matthew, Mark, Luke, and John. Other works, such as the *Gospel of Peter*, the Egerton Papyrus 2, and the *Secret Gospel of Mark*, as mentioned by Hengel, might be called 'retellings' of Jesus' life which incorporated materials from these and perhaps other Gospels, and which expanded, condensed, or rearranged them according to *ad hoc* principles.[163] The longer ending of Mark, though restricted in its scope and containing very little expansive material, is comparable to these other works in strategy. Kelhoffer comments that 'Those who had already come to esteem Gospels like Matthew, Luke and John would probably have regarded such an addition including post-resurrection appearances and a commissioning as a (more) satisfactory culmination than ἐφοβοῦντο γάρ at the end of Mark'.[164] May we not also detect at least similar concerns behind the elder's observation in *HE* 3. 39. 15 that Mark made no effort to write things down 'in order (τάξει)' or to 'make an ordered arrangement (σύνταξιν . . . ποιούμενος)', and the attempt to add to Mark's 'un-ordered' account a more suitable ending by conflating elements from Matthew, Luke, and John? Could the longer ending represent an 'editorial' paragraph added in an early edition of the four Gospels, produced in Asia Minor? One might observe that the three actions of (*a*) binding the four Gospels together into a codex, (*b*) adding Mark 16: 9–20 to the end of the Gospel, and (*c*) teaching about the origins and mutual relations of the Gospels, as Papias' elder did, all seem to radiate from a conviction that these four Gospels belong in a special way together.

---

[159] The connection with the Acts passage appears in Eusebius, *HE* 3. 39. 9–10. Probably it was mentioned by Papias too, as it appears in the summaries of both Eusebius and of Philip of Side in his *Church History*. See Kelhoffer, *Miracle*, 435.

[160] Kelhoffer, *Miracle*, 478, points out that there are no extant narratives of apostles drinking harmful substances and surviving before the 4th cent. or later. He also notes the 'general paucity of interest of subsequent Christian writers in the LE's third and fourth sign's' (i.e. picking up snakes and drinking deadly liquids).

[161] Hengel, *Frage*, 58 (in *Question*, 11, he had said 110–30).

[162] This author show no signs of 'gnostic' or heretical proclivities, but is very concerned with conformity to the four Gospels and with the Church's outward mission.

[163] Providing a special analogy is the *Gospel of Peter*, which, after a sort of conclusion which follows Mark 16: 8, adds information about the disciples weeping and mourning, which seems to be based on the LE, and then appends an account apparently based on John 21, about the disciples going fishing.

[164] Kelhoffer, *Miracle*, 474.

The Elder John and the Other Elders Cited by Papias

It should be beyond dispute that non-gnostic Christian teachers in the early years of the second century were making use of the Fourth Gospel as a source of Jesus' authentic teaching. This much we have from Irenaeus' report of 'the elders' teaching about the many mansions in the Father's house (John 14: 1), which in all probability came from Papias. From this same period, and perhaps from the same 'elders' comes evidence from Irenaeus of some reference to the number 666 in Revelation 13: 8. It is evident from Papias' witness to the four Gospels that his tradition goes back to a source (with reasonable probability John the Elder) and a time long since past when he wrote, probably sometime between 120 and 135. All this brings us down to the period contemporary with Polycarp's early *Letter to the Philippians* and the letters of Ignatius, that is, most likely in the first or perhaps in the second decade of the second century—nearly contemporary with the publication of the Johannine corpus itself. It is time to examine each of these more closely to see what they may tell us about the use of the Johannine works at this very critical time.

The many mansions of the Father's house

And as the presbyters say, 'Then those who are deemed worthy of an abode in heaven shall go there, others shall enjoy the delights of paradise, and others shall possess the splendour of the city; for everywhere the Saviour shall be seen according as they who see him shall be worthy'. 2. [They say, moreover], that there is this distinction between the habitation of those who produce an hundred-fold, and of those who produce sixty-fold, and that of those who produce thirty-fold: for the first will be taken up into the heavens, the second will dwell in paradise, the last will inhabit the city; and that it was on this account the Lord declared, 'In My Father's house are many mansions.' For all things belong to God, who supplies all with a suitable dwelling-place; even as His Word says, that a share is allotted to all by the Father, according as each person is or shall be worthy. And this is the couch on which the guests shall recline, having been invited to the wedding. The presbyters, the disciples of the apostles, affirm that this is the gradation and arrangement of those who are being saved, and that they advance through steps of this nature; also that they ascend through the Spirit to the Son, and through the Son to the Father... (*AH* 5. 36. 1)

The presbyters in question may or may not be the same ones who testified to the age of the Lord in *AH* 2. 22. 5, who are said there to have been conversant with John in Asia. They may or may not be 'the elders who saw John, the disciple of the Lord' who related a dominical saying about the abundant plant and animal life in the kingdom, as through the disciple John (5. 33. 3, 4). But that they represent a presbyterial tradition recorded in Papias' book may be regarded as virtually certain.[165] If not, then what Irenaeus repeats here is roughly contemporary tradition in any case. The presbyterial 'exegesis' of three eschatological sayings of Jesus, one from the parable of the sower in Matthew 13: 8, 23 or Mark 4: 8, 20,[166] one from John 14: 2, one from the parable of the marriage feast in Matthew 22: 14 or Luke 14: 15–24,[167] also conforms to what we know were the kind of traditions which drew Papias' interest.

This passage again would confirm that the Fourth Gospel was regarded, in the generation previous to Papias' writing, as an authentic source for Jesus' sayings, such that it would draw the exegetical comments of 'the elders' Papias knew in his younger days. What we have here is a kind of midrashic exegesis, interpreting one text by means of another, and then another. While this may not be the same thing as writing a commentary, the main difference is simply that this kind of exegetical teaching is oral and not written. It cannot be held that this mode of scriptural exegesis, evidently carried over from Jewish practices, necessarily shows any less respect for the authority or the sanctity of the texts involved than does the commentary of Heracleon written several decades later.

The Jewish–Christian nature of this exegesis invites further comment. Not only is the 'style' midrashic, but the content is closely paralleled in non-Christian Jewish sources. The elders' exegesis in *AH* 5. 36. 1 is apparently given to support a three-tiered stratification of the coming world, the city, paradise, and heaven, corresponding to the inheritance of the thirty-fold, sixty-fold, and hundred-fold blessing. This finds a parallel (its only real parallel, as far as I can see) in *Testament of Dan* 5. 12–13.[168] What is more, the conception of paradise apparent, not so much here, but in *AH* 5. 5, where Irenaeus also cites 'the elders' as his source,[169] is the same as we find in a prominent strand of Jewish eschatology represented by *4 Ezra* 4. 7–8; 6. 26; 7. 36; 14. 7–9; *2 Baruch* 13. 3; 25. 1; 46. 7; 48. 30; 76. 2, and *Pseudo-Philo* 48. 1.[170]

---

[165] Lightfoot, *Supernatural*, 198–202; B. W. Bacon, 'Date and Habitat of the Elders of Papias', *ZNW* 12 (1911), 176–87, at 176, 182–6. Körtner, *Papias*, 36–43, prefers to think that Irenaeus' 'elders' are not connected to Papias. In the light particularly of 5. 33. 3, 4, where the connection is explicitly made for at least some group of 'the elders who saw John, the disciple of the Lord', it should probably be assumed that similar references to such elders will have come from Papias, more especially when the traditional material is eschatological in nature.
[166] The descending order, 100, 60, 30, probably indicates Matthew's version, for Mark has them in ascending order.
[167] The mention of the 'worthiness' of the guests in the elders' exegesis probably indicates that the underlying source is Matthew (22: 8) instead of Luke.
[168] 'And the saints shall refresh themselves in Eden; the righteous shall rejoice in the New Jerusalem... The Holy One of Israel will rule over them in humility and poverty, and he who trusts in him shall reign in truth in the heavens' (tr. of H. C. Kee, *OTP* i).
[169] *AH* 5. 5. 1, 'Wherefore also the elders who were disciples of the apostles tell us that those who were translated were transferred to that place (for paradise has been prepared for righteous men, such as have the Spirit; in which place also Paul the apostle, when he was caught up, heard words which are unspeakable as regards us in our present condition), and that there shall they who have been translated remain until the consummation [of all things], as a prelude to immortality.'
[170] See Hill, *Regnum Caelorum*[2], 47–50, 65–7

The same presbyterial source responsible at least for the paradise teaching in *AH* 5. 5, if not also for the teaching in 5. 36. 1, was almost certainly responsible for the famous chiliastic saying recorded by Papias and repeated by Irenaeus in *AH* 5. 33. 3–4 which parallels so closely the description of the Messiah's kingdom in *2 Baruch* 23.[171] All this is pointed out because of the discrepancy it creates with the dominant theory about the early use of John, which says that it was dominated by 'gnostic' elements. This source on the other hand demonstrates that it was used very early on by a Christian exegete, or by an exegetical tradition, with a background in Jewish exegesis and quite possibly a chiliastic eschatology borrowed from popular Judaism. In these references to presbyterial teachings inherited by Papias we can see a tradition which valued at least the Gospel according to Matthew, the Gospel according to John, the letters of Paul, and the Revelation.

A PRESBYTERIAL EXEGESIS OF REVELATION 13: 7?

Such, then, being the state of the case, and this number being found in all the most approved and ancient copies [of the Apocalypse], and those men who saw John face to face bearing their testimony [to it]…I do not know how it is that some have erred following the ordinary mode of speech, and have vitiated the middle number in the name, deducting the amount of fifty from it, so that instead of six decads they will have it that there is but one. (*AH* 5. 30. 1)

We cannot say whether, in the presentation of Papias (if this is the ultimate source),[172] 'the men who saw John face to face' saw John the son of Zebedee or John the Elder. Irenaeus surely has the former in mind, but given his apparent mistaking of some of Papias' attributions, it is possible that the men he speaks of—even possibly Papias himself—are men who had known the elder. But we can say that whichever John they saw, Irenaeus' reference to them assumes that someone in Papias' day or earlier either quoted or commented upon the text of Revelation 13: 7.

THE ELDER JOHN

I return now to the tradition about Gospel origins examined above under the name of Papias. As I mentioned, while only the material on Mark and

---

[171] *AH* 5. 33. 3–4. 'as the elders who saw John, the disciple of the Lord, related that they had heard from him how the Lord used to teach in regard to these times, and say: The days will come in which vines shall grown, each having ten thousand branches…And these things are borne witness to in writing by Papias, the hearer of John, and a companion of Polycarp, in his fourth book; for there were five books compiled by him.'

[172] The mention of 'those men who saw John face to face' recalls his later description in 5. 33. 3–4, where Irenaeus will refer to 'the elders who saw John', and explicitly tells us he got the information in question from Papias' book.

Matthew is explicitly attributed to 'the Elder' in the citation by Eusebius in *HE* 3. 39. 15–16, there are links with the other Papian material in *HE* 3. 24. 5–13 which show the likelihood that the bulk of Papias's tradition on the origins of all four Gospels has come from the same source. Here I cite some of that evidence. The periphrastic use of ποιεῖν in the middle voice with an accompanying noun, used three times in the short space of 3. 39. 15,[173] is a distinctive stylistic feature of this fragment, at least ostensibly attributable to the 'elder' he is citing. It also occurs in 3. 24. 7 where Eusebius is paraphrasing a written account of the circumstances which led to John's writing: 'But Mark and Luke having already made the edition (τὴν ἔκδοσιν πεποιημένων)[174] of the Gospels according to them ...'

The elder quoted by Papias in 3. 39. 15 also has a distinctive way of speaking about the contents of the Gospels. A great deal of attention has been given to his mention of the Lord's λόγια, which he says Mark and Matthew contained. This has sometimes obscured the fact that this presbyter also speaks of the Gospel of Mark as recording 'the things said or done by the Lord' (τὰ ὑπὸ τοῦ κυρίου ἢ λεχθέντα ἢ πραχθέντα), using here the aorist passive participle.[175] The source preserved by Eusebius in 3. 24 uses the same notation. The passive participle, aorist or perfect, of πράσσω for the deeds of Jesus in the Gospels occurs no less than four times in Eusebius' paraphrase and summary of this source (πραχθέντα in 3. 24. 12; πεπραγμένα or πεπραγμένων in 3. 24. 7, 8, 11).[176] Related to this is a rather peculiar way of referring to the contents of the Gospels as 'the acts of Jesus' or 'the acts of Christ' (3. 24. 10, τῶν τοῦ Ἰησοῦ πράξεων; 11, τῶν Ἰησοῦ πράξεων; 13, τῶν τοῦ Χριστοῦ πράξεων). In all the writings of Eusebius, 'acts of Jesus' turns up only two more times; 'acts of Christ' never, 'acts and teachings of the Saviour' once. In *Demonstratio evangelica* 3. 5. 67, we read, 'And note what a remarkable thing it is that they all agreed in every point in their account of the acts of Jesus'. And later in *Dem. evang.* 3. 5. 89 where he is alluding to tradition, 'Mark, being his friend and companion, is said to have recorded the accounts of Peter about the acts of Jesus'. As we know, the earliest authority for this tradition about Mark is Papias'

---

[173] Ἐποιεῖτο τὰς διδασκαλίας; σύνταξιν ... ποιούμενος; ἐποιήσατο πρόνοιαν. This feature occurs twenty-one times in the NT, mostly in Luke and Paul, and only once in the Johannine literature (John 14: 23).

[174] This phrase at least is not typical of Eusebius' own speech. The word ἔκδοσις, edition or publication, occurs four times in the *Historia ecclesiastica* and sixty-two times in all of Eusebius' works. In no other instance is it found as the object of ποιεῖν.

[175] This fact is often ignored by those who wish to see in this fragment a reference merely to a 'sayings collection' without plot or narrative.

[176] Also, in describing the work of the other evangelists Eusebius reports in 3. 24. 10 what Luke recorded 'before beginning the Acts of Jesus' (τῶν τοῦ Ἰησοῦ πράξεων) in Luke 3: 19, 20. In ending his reflections on the information provided by this source, Eusebius says, 'If this be understood the Gospels no longer appear to disagree, because that according to John contains the first of the acts of Christ (τῶν τοῦ Χριστοῦ πράξεων) and the others the narrative of what he did at the end of the period' (3. 24. 13).

elder, whom Eusebius quoted in *HE* 3. 39. 15. But it is only in *HE* 3. 24. 10, 11 that Eusebius speaks of the 'acts of Jesus'. I suspect that the words of the elder had already been brought to Eusebius' mind, for in the previous chapter (*Dem. evang.* 3. 4. 49) Eusebius had used a distinctive phrase in reference to the Gospels which we can with certitude ascribe to the elder, τὰ λεχθέντα καὶ πραχθέντα—the only occurrence of these two participles apart from *HE* 3. 39. 15 in Eusebius' works. I observed above in the examination of Justin that he is evidently familiar with this terminology, for the Gospels ('the acts which took place under Pontius Pilate', *1Apol.* 35. 9; cf. 48. 3), which he could not have got from Eusebius but which he could well have got from Papias' book.

We know from explicit attribution that Papias' material on the origin of Mark's Gospel came from 'the elder', and the context in Eusebius all but requires that this be the notorious John the Elder. The way Eusebius introduces the short saying about Matthew, not 'Papias said' but 'it was said' (εἴρηται) may suggest that Papias is citing a source here as well. From here we must observe strong similarities in vocabulary and expression between 3. 39. 15–16 and 3. 24. 3–15, features which are not Eusebius' style. This may signify that Papias is citing a single source for his information on the four Gospels. But even if the idiom is Papias', the substance has come from a certain elder of an earlier generation. Thus, much of what we concluded from Papias' fragments above also pertains rightfully to this earlier generation.

This means that the Elder John, then, or one of his contemporaries, passed on traditions about the origins of the four Gospels, two written by apostles, two by the disciples of apostles. Among these was the Gospel according to John, written by the apostle some time after the first three. Putting together what we find in the Papian fragments, including the newly identified Papian fragment in *HE* 3. 24. 3–15, we obtain a very early and very valuable picture of Christian thought concerning its foundational documents. We find that attempts were being made in the years before Papias wrote to offer a rationale for the number and identities of the Gospels acknowledged by the Church.

1. There is a concern to make clear that the Evangelists did not take it upon themselves to initiate the writing but were responding to the requests of their hearers (Matthew, *HE* 3. 24. 5, 6; Mark, *HE* 2. 15. 1, partially 3. 39. 15; John, *HE* 3. 24. 5, 11), or in the case of Luke, that he rightly wrote to correct the doubtful propositions of others, *HE* 3. 24. 15. We do not know to what extent this concern for the modesty of the Evangelists stemmed from apologetic or polemic issues, or whether it was simply a fairly standard aspect of the Church's catechesis (cf. Heb. 5. 4–5). Just prior to relating his Papian material in 3. 24 Eusebius cites the example of Paul, who, though a powerful thinker and arguer, 'committed to writing no more

than short epistles'. And of all who had been with the Lord, he continues, 'only Matthew and John have left us their recollections'. 'A record preserves (κατέχει λόγος) that they took to writing out of necessity (ἐπάναγκες)' (3. 24. 5). It was maintained from this early time that John's Gospel handed down tradition about the period passed over in silence by the former Evangelists (3. 24. 11).

2. There are references to each Gospel being essentially a written record of what was preached or taught by one (or in Luke's case, more than one) of the apostles (3. 24. 6, 7, 15; 39. 15). The fact that the two authors were said to be Mark and Luke, two non-apostles, apparently did not affect the assessment of their apostolic witness, for Mark was considered Peter's interpreter/translator,[177] and Luke 'was long a companion of Paul, and had careful conversation with the other apostles' (3. 4. 6).

3. The term 'recollections' (*HE* 2. 15. 1 (cf. 6. 14. 6); 3. 24. 5; 3. 39. 15) is used to associate the Gospels with the firsthand experience of the Lord's words and ministry by the apostles. As we have seen, this tradition was probably the basis for Justin's practice of calling the four Gospels the apostolic 'memoirs', and this traditional designation was even known to the author of the *Apocryphon of James*. What I have not commented on up until now is that this way of conceiving of the apostolic Gospels may well have had its source in the Gospel according to John. Jesus promises his disciples in John 14: 26, 'But the Counselor, the Holy Spirit, whom the Father will send in my name, he will teach you all things, and bring to your remembrance (ὑπομνήσει) all that I have said to you'; and later echoes, 'When the Spirit of truth comes, he will guide you into all the truth; for he will not speak on his own authority, but whatever he hears he will speak, and he will declare to you the things that are to come. He will glorify me, for he will take what is mine and declare it to you' (John 16: 13–14). This promise to the disciples by Jesus could have been an exegetical starting point for the presbyterial tradition we are considering. In 3. 24. 5 Eusebius introduces the witness of his written source by saying that 'only Matthew and John have left us their recollections' (ὑπομνήματα). In 2. 15. 1 Eusebius also relates the story of the origin of the Gospel of Mark, and calls Mark a recollection (ὑπόμνημα) of Peter's teaching, saying that his sources for the story were Clement of Alexandria and Papias. Thus John 14: 26 could be taken as a justification not only for John, but for Matthew, Mark (being a record of Peter's recollections), and Luke, and possibly for a collection. It is interesting to recall that the *Apocryphon of James* stands against the notion of the continuation of prophecy even among the apostles (6. 21–31); it uses the name Paraclete but does not apply it to the Holy Spirit. (See more under no. 8 below.)

---

[177] See A. D. Baum, 'Der Presbyter des Papias über einen "Hermeneuten" des Petrus', *TZ* 56 (2000), 21–35.

4. The term 'acts' is used to describe the Gospels. This has been examined above, where we saw the preponderance of 'acts' of Jesus in Eusebius' language when he is using or referring to this source, and twice in the writings of Justin Martyr. This is potentially significant because of the title given to the second volume of Luke's work, the Acts of the Apostles. The language preserved in Eusebius' paraphrase of Papias' tradition of the elder seems to bring us into the environment in which Luke's second volume gained its present title.

5. There is a recognition of some of the discrepancies between John and the Synoptic Gospels, manifested in a concern for the 'order' of events in the Gospels, both in Mark and in John (3. 24. 7–13; 3. 39. 15, 16). We have here, of course, nothing so elaborate as the detailed harmonizing attempted by Epiphanius (see above). But this shows that the differences between the Gospels were acknowledged and attempts were made to explain them very soon after the Gospel was published. And despite the fact that John's appeared later and differed from the Synoptics more than they differed from each other, it is not apparent that this was *ipso facto* determined to be the more problematic for John than for the others. In fact, 3. 39. 15 seems to suggest that it was Mark's 'order' which had to be 'defended'. The tradition recorded by the elder, that John wrote down what happened 'at the beginning' of Jesus' preaching, while it cannot begin to solve all the problems that would eventually surface, is, as far as it goes, quite helpful. It offers a plausible accounting for John's references to the first and second signs which Jesus performed after coming from Judea into Galilee (2: 11; 4: 54) and for his reference to the Baptist not yet being cast into prison (3: 24).

6. There is the chronological ordering of the four Gospels themselves, with an evident accompanying interest in explaining the reasons for a new Gospel by John so much later than the others (the justification being that the others had left out the beginnings of Jesus' ministry and that it was reserved for John to relate more vividly and plainly the divinity of the Lord). This is not the same as the motive given by Irenaeus, but it is not unrelated to it. The vivid and plain revelation of the divinity of the Lord has a connection with the heresy of Cerinthus, though it is virtually certain that this specific motivation was not found in what Papias recorded, but likely came to Irenaeus from Polycarp.

7. The attempt is made to find some kind of endorsement for each Gospel, or Gospel writer, from another accepted (apostolic), and textual authority. The Gospel according to Mark is validated by Peter in 1 Peter 5: 13, where Peter mentions Mark and calls him 'my son' (*HE* 2. 15. 2; cf. Origen in *HE* 6. 25. 5).[178] The Gospel according to

---

[178] It is hard to tell in *HE* 2. 15. 2 whether this is to be attributed to Papias or to Clement of Alexandria. It comes immediately after Eusebius introduces Papias and is most naturally seen as the

Luke[179] is attested by Paul, for through the 'we' passages in the book of Acts we know that he was a companion of Paul's (*HE* 3. 4. 6), and Paul used to say 'According to my Gospel' (Rom. 2: 16; 2 Tim. 2: 8), referring to Luke (*HE* 3. 4. 7; 3. 24. 15; cf. Origen in *HE* 6. 25. 6).[180] The Gospel according to John is attested in relation to the other three by John himself in his indications of chronology in John 2: 11 (3. 24. 8–10) and probably in testimony cited by Papias from 1 John (3. 39. 17), in much the same manner as we see in the *MF*.[181] For Matthew's Gospel as of yet we cannot point to a textual affirmation that has survived in the fragments. Yet his Gospel is still vouched for by John in the story told about John's Gospel in 3. 24. 7. This leads also to the observation of the next quality.

8. John has a role in ratifying the first three Gospels. In 3. 24. 7 we have the report that John welcomed (ἀποδέξασθαι) the three previous Gospels, which had been distributed to all, including himself, and 'testified to their truth' (ἀλήθειαν αὐτοῖς ἐπιμαρτυρήσαντα), his only qualification being that they lacked 'the account of what was done by Christ at first and at the beginning of the preaching'. Such a 'ratifying', or 'canonizing', activity on the part of John is confirmed by Origen, who in commenting on the prologue to Luke reports from an old writing that 'John collected (συναγαγεῖν) the written Gospels in his own lifetime in the reign of Nero, and approved of and recognized (ἐγκρῖναι καὶ ἀποδέξασθαι) those of which the deceit of the devil had not taken possession; but refused and rejected those which he perceived were not truthful' (Origen, *Hom. Lk.* 1, fr. 9). We cannot be sure that Origen got this from Papias, but it was certainly from an old written source, and very likely this source at least was based on Papias' report. Origen's source put this activity of John in the reign of Nero, though it may be possible that there is a scribal error here for Nerva. This means probably that by the very early years of the second century it was said in Asia Minor that John himself had ratified or canonized[182] the three previous Gospels, Matthew, Mark, and Luke.

These almost formalized qualities in Papias' presentation imply already a surprisingly high degree of reflection, and no doubt even research.[183] And

content of what Papias said in support of what Clement says. Eusebius' use of the word φασίν, 'they say', could refer to both Clement and Papias, or if it refers to only one of them it fits the Papian context better, where Papias is himself repeating traditional material.

[179] For this, see the appendix to Hill, 'What Papias Said about John', 625–9.

[180] Hengel, *Studies in the Gospel of Mark*, 69, has written that 'the best explanation of the fact that [Marcion] chose the Gospel of Luke seems to me to be that its title and tradition already attributed it to a disciple of Paul'.

[181] Lightfoot, *Supernatural*, 206; Bauckham, 'Origin', 47, 55. In the *MF* there is also the implicit ratification by Andrew and possibly others.

[182] There was evidently no word for 'canonize' in use at this time. Eusebius did use the word κυρῶσαι in 2. 15. 2, to ratify or confirm, for what Peter is said by Clement to have done for the Gospel which Mark wrote. The words used by Eusebius in 3. 24. 7 are ἀποδέξασθαι and ἀλήθειαν αὐτοῖς ἐπιμαρτυρήσαντα.

[183] I have not yet commented on the historical quality of the traditions themselves. As critics from at least the time of Eusebius down to the present have noted, there is much in the remaining

while we are not in a position to say categorically that all of this material came from the Elder John or another presbyter and not from Papias, we are certainly justified in thinking that the great bulk of it did. These qualities tell us that the subject of the Church's Gospels, their authorities, and how they came to be, was a topic of interest in early second-century Asia. They also apparently tell us that a special recognition, probably implying a collection, of these four Gospels should be assigned to a time well before Papias published his books. At that time the attempt was already made to place the recognition or reception (ἀποδέξασθαι) of the first three Gospels well within the lifetime of the apostle John. If the fragment from Origen goes back to this same source, it might have specified that John received them in the reign of Nero (possibly Nerva?), though this might have been added to the tradition sometime between Papias and Origen. The same kind of recognition is obviously implied for John's Gospel as well, at a time remarkably close to that assumed by most for the publication of the Fourth Gospel.

I observe also that in the fragmentary presbyterial traditions conveyed by Papias reference is made or presupposed to the four Gospels, the Acts, 1 Peter, 1 John, the Letters of Paul and the Revelation of John as religious authorities. All of these books except Revelation are invoked in some way in the elder's traditions about the origins of the four Gospels.[184] This kind of 'cross-referencing' depicts an interest in linking together a collection of authoritative writings and interpreting them in light of each other—one mark of a 'canonical' consciousness. It is the kind of exegetical activity one might expect to accompany or follow the publication of an 'edition' of the New Testament which included at least these books.[185] In any case, as corroborated by the longer ending of Mark, the elder's tradition in Papias

traditions collected by Papias which does not inspire confidence. On the other hand, it is a fallacious method which would require that all of Papias' traditions be placed on the same level in this regard. Papias' sources were, as he and Eusebius tell us, diverse, and each report he gives cannot be presumed to be of the same quality. Nor do the presence of presumably legendary details in the Gospel traditions themselves necessarily rule out any historical basis. For our purposes here, at any rate, we do not have to pass a final judgement on the historical credentials of the details of these Gospel traditions. We merely have to acknowledge their existence, and their transfer to Papias in the first or, at the latest, the second decade of the 2nd cent.

[184] Even the Letters of Paul, if indeed the notes on Luke's Gospel in either *HE* 3. 4. 7 or 3. 24. 15 are based on Papias, as they seem to be. See Hill, 'What Papias Said about John', 625–9.

[185] Here note the theory of David Trobisch, *Die Endredaktion des Neuen Testaments: Eine Untersuchung zur Entstehung der christlichen Bibel*, Novum Testamentum et Orbis Antiquus, 13 (Göttingen, 1996); ET, *The First Edition of the New Testament* (Oxford, 2000). Trobisch proposes that there was a final 'redaction' and a 'first edition' of the New Testament in virtually its present form in about the middle of the 2nd cent. While there are many details of his work that I cannot endorse, his argument, based on the use of the codex form, the universal and relatively consistent practice of abbreviating the *nomina sacra*, the regular grouping of books (Gospels, Acts and Catholic Epistles, Pauline Corpus, and Revelation), the sequencing of the books within the groups, and the consistency of their titles in the manuscripts, is impressive. Evidence for a standard collection of Pauline epistles in existence in Antioch and throughout Asia Minor, probably in Rome as well, by the end of the first decade of the 2nd cent. may be drawn from 2 Peter 3 and the Ignatian correspondence (see C. E. Hill, 'Ignatius and the Apostolate: The Witness of Ignatius to the Emergence of Christian Scripture', in

shows a very early recognition of the Fourth Gospel as part of an authoritative collection of 'Gospels' believed to be authentic records of Jesus' life
written by his apostles and by their associates.

Polycarp's Letter to the Philippians

Despite its erstwhile popularity, P. N. Harrison's view that chapters 13 and
14 of Polycarp's *Letter to the Philippians* were from an epistle written shortly
after Ignatius' departure, and chapters 1–12 were written much later,
c.135[186] is on the wane and is regarded by many as unnecessary.[187] There
is no good reason to doubt that Polycarp's entire *Letter to the Philippians* was
written shortly after Ignatius' stay in Smyrna somewhere around 110.

It would not be illegitimate to expect that Polycarp, if he had known or
been in any sense a disciple of the author of the Fourth Gospel, as Irenaeus
says he was, should reflect something of this author's thought and language.
And yet we find that the marks of John's Gospel on Polycarp's *Letter to the
Philippians* are minimal at best, many would say non-existent. 'While it is
likely that Polycarp knew the Gospels of Matthew and Luke,' writes Koester,
'it is certain that he did not know the Gospel of John'.[188] The same scholar
writes that 'for Polycarp there is no apostolic authority other than Paul'.[189]
But even if we should find Polycarp's letter devoid of any trace of the
Fourth Gospel whatsoever, it seems precarious to assume that in this single,
short epistle, directed toward a particular problem in a particular church,
we must possess the sum total of all the man knew or believed at the time.
According to Irenaeus, Polycarp wrote many letters 'either to the neighbouring churches, strengthening them, or to some of the brethren,
exhorting and warning them' (Eusebius, *HE* 5. 20. 8)—as bishop in one of
the chief cities in Asia Minor it could not have been otherwise—and we
have but one. It is hard, then, to hold Polycarp responsible for publishing a

---

M. F. Wiles and E. J. Yarnold (eds.), *Studia Patristica*, 36 (Leuven, 2001), 226–48). Evidence for such
a Gospels canon may be hinted at in Ignatius, but comes into the clear in the fragmentary Papian
remains.

[186] P. N. Harrison, *Polycarp's Two Epistles to the Philippians* (Oxford, 1936).

[187] See e.g. Metzger, *Canon*, 59–60; J.-B. Bauer, *Die Polykarpbriefe*, KAV 5 (Göttingen, 1995), and
the review of his edn. by H. Maier, *JTS* NS 47 (1996), 642–5. Koester, *Introduction*, 306–8, still
accepts Harrison's theory at face value.

[188] Koester, 'Ephesos', 135. It is possible that Polycarp did not know the Fourth Gospel because
it had not yet been published or distributed. But by 107 or later this is doubtful, more especially if
the Fourth Gospel was published at Ephesus, and if, as I argue below, Ignatius knew this Gospel.
An absence of influence here from the Fourth Gospel is a difficulty for any theory that has it written
in Asia Minor before this time. This is why Koester believes he can claim it as support for his
theory that the Fourth Gospel originated in Syria. Also citing Polycarp's failure to use the Fourth
Gospel is Bauer, *Orthodoxy and Heresy*, 209; Haenchen, *John 1*, 8–9.

[189] Koester, *Introduction*, 307.

full index of everything he knows, or even all the authorities he accepts, in a single letter.[190]

As for the extraordinary statement that 'for Polycarp there is no apostolic authority other than Paul',[191] this too outruns the evidence. Did Polycarp think there was only one apostle, or was it this apostle alone who had authority? Paul himself did not believe any such thing (Gal. 2: 2), and, apart from perhaps Marcion, we do not know of anyone who did. It is refuted by Polycarp's reference to plural 'apostles' in 6. 3 and 9. 2.

It is true that Polycarp mentions Paul by name, but not John. His reference to Paul, however, is quite tailored to its context.[192] Polycarp is writing to a Pauline church in Philippi which had, as far as we know, no Johannine foundation or presence. Writing at their invitation (3. 1), he mentions Paul specifically because of his personal ministry in the Philippian church (3. 2; 11. 3; already alluded to in 2. 2, a faith 'which was famous in past years'). Polycarp does not mention John, but nor does he mention Matthew, Luke, Mark, or Peter, all of whom were certainly known to himself and to the Philippians. Polycarp surely has the Gospels of Matthew and Luke (2. 3; 7. 2, etc.)[193] but never mentions their authors. He uses the words and thoughts of 1 Peter numerous times in chapter 2 and throughout the epistle; few would try to deny that he was well acquainted with 1 Peter, yet he never mentions its author by name. It is his explicit mention of Paul, then, not his non-mention of John, which is unusual.

But what about the muted or non-existent influence of the Fourth Gospel in his letter to the Philippians? As several have observed, it is likely that the Fourth Gospel did not figure prominently in this letter simply because it offered less paraenetic material for the letter's particular purpose. It was noted above when examining Tertullian's early works, that his moral treatises (a much greater corpus of words than Polycarp's single epistle) contain scarcely any references to the Fourth Gospel, though he knew and valued it as an apostolic writing at the time he wrote. Polycarp's special concern in this letter was to address the problem of avarice and the fallout from the recent deposition of a Philippian presbyter for this sin. The speeches of Jesus in the Fourth Gospel are generally of a different nature. We may well wonder whether allusions to the Fourth Gospel would have been so sparse if the problems in Philippi had had to do with Christology. As we shall see in a moment, when the subject of heresy surfaces briefly in chapter 7, the bishop will quite effortlessly call upon Johannine sources, and possibly on the Fourth Gospel itself. The anti-heretical use of the Johannine writings

---

[190] It is sometimes said that Ignatius shows more signs of Johannine influence than does Polycarp, the alleged disciple of John. This is true, but the Ignatian corpus is more than four times longer than the letter to the Philippians.

[191] Koester, *Introduction*, 307.

[192] Hengel, *Frage*, 72.

[193] Koester, *Introduction*, 306.

evident in *Ad Phil.* 7. 1 is entirely consistent with the depiction of Polycarp in Irenaeus' letter to Florinus (Eusebius, *HE* 5. 20. 6), where he speaks of Polycarp's appeal to John in fighting heresy. In fact, we have learnt in an earlier section that Polycarp's habit of fleeing heresy was based partly upon 2 John 10 and, according to Irenaeus, the personal example of John the apostle (*AH* 1. 16. 3; 3. 3. 4; 4. 2). At the critical point in his epistle, then, Polycarp selected the Johannine material most appropriate to the need. It so happened that this material shows the most resemblance[194] to expressions in 1 and 2 John and not in the Gospel. Robert Grant's assessment, so different from Koester's, reflects Polycarp's situation much more realistically: 'Such an echo of the Epistle suggests that he knew the Gospel as well, even though there is no trace of it in his letter.'[195]

But is there in fact no trace of it in his letter? Some have seen the trace of the love commandment of John 13. 34 in the phrase 'loving the brotherhood' in *Ad Phil.* 10. 1. Haenchen is of course technically correct in saying that 'The phrase *fraternitatis amatores* ("lovers of the brotherhood") in Pol. *Phil.* 10. 1 does not constitute proof that he made use of the Fourth Gospel'.[196] Anyone who has spent much time with Polycarp's epistle must know that most of its biblical allusions (including NT allusions) are given in short phrases, so the terseness of this two-word phrase is not a necessary barrier to its being regarded as an allusion. What is more important, however, is that the phrase has more in common with 1 Peter 2: 17, τὴν ἀδελφότητα ἀγαπᾶτε. And Polycarp has numerous borrowings from this book. But this passage, I think, does not present the strongest case for Johannine influence.

A stronger case can be made from 7. 1, where Polycarp shows a more than passing acquaintance with the first two Johannine epistles, and quite possibly one or more passages from the Fourth Gospel.[197]

7. 1 'For everyone who does not confess that Jesus Christ has come in the flesh is an anti-Christ'; and whosoever does not confess the testimony of the Cross is of the devil: and whosoever perverts the oracles of the Lord for his own lusts, and says that there is neither resurrection nor judgment,—this man is the first-born of Satan. 2. Wherefore, leaving the foolishness of the crowd, and their false teaching, let us turn back to the word which was delivered to us in the beginning...[198]

[194] Though see below.
[195] Grant, *Irenaeus of Lyons*, 37. Note the concession, significant because of the identity of its author, of J. N. Sanders, *St John*, 35, speaking of Papias' and Polycarp's use of 1 John, 'it is often argued that this must mean that they also knew the FG. Though this argument is not conclusive, it is quite probable'.
[196] Haenchen, *John 1*, 8.
[197] A tendency to overstate his case is on display again when Koester claims that 'one looks in vain for any trace of knowledge of the Johannine writings in Polycarp's own letter' ('The Story of the Johannine Tradition', *Sewanee Theological Review*, 36 (1992), 17–32, at 18).
[198] The translation of K. Lake, LCL.

Though the problem of heresy is not said to be present in Philippi, it was present in Asia Minor, even evidently in Smryna, as we also know from the letters of Ignatius, copies of which Polycarp was sending to the Philippians along with his own letter (13. 2). Let us notice the probable Johannine allusions. First, as is fairly widely admitted, Polycarp's statement of the first confessional problem involves a direct conflation of 1 John 4: 2–3 and 2 John 7,[199] whether this was intentional or not. It is interesting to note that, like Polycarp, Irenaeus uses 2 John 7 and 1 John 4: 2–3 together, citing them formally in *AH* 3. 16. 8. Second, in the next clause, confessing the testimony of the cross, in this anti-docetic context, may go back to 1 John 5: 6–8, which speak of a testimony of the water and the blood. But this is itself dependent upon the account in John 19: 34–5, which speaks of a testimony in relation to the cross, 'But one of the soldiers pierced his side with a spear, and at once there came out blood and water. He who saw it has borne witness—his testimony is true, and he knows that he tells the truth—that you may believe.' That this text lies behind Polycarp's phrase is made more likely by a passage in Irenaeus. Irenaeus specifically points to John 19: 34–5 when dealing with the docetic heresy of Marcion in *AH* 4. 33. 2, 'And how, again, supposing that He was not flesh, but was a man merely in appearance, could He have been crucified, and could blood and water have issued from His pierced side?' Significantly, this comes immediately following his extended section on the anti-Marcionite arguments he learnt from the apostolic presbyter, who we have seen was none other than Polycarp. Third, the phrase 'of the devil' in 7. 1, as many have pointed out, may be dependent upon 1 John 3: 8, 'He who commits sin is of the devil'.[200] But both it and the final clause, 'this man is the first-born of Satan', may on the other hand be dependent upon Jesus' words to his opponents in John 8: 44, 'You are of your father the devil, and your will is to do your father's desires'. Indeed, the polemical context of the Gospel material matches the polemical character of *Ad Phil.* 7. 1—and Polycarp's reply to Marcion himself as reported by Irenaeus (*AH* 3. 3. 4)—much better than does the epistolary reference. Fourth, the next sentence in Polycarp's letter, 'let us turn back to the word which was delivered to us in the beginning' seems to reflect the wording of 1 John 2: 7, 24; 3: 11; 2 John 5. But this in turn is based on the commandment of Jesus from John 13: 34 and is set in the vocabulary coined in John 1: 1.

---

[199] 2 John 7, οἱ μὴ ὁμολογοῦντες Ἰησοῦν Χριστὸν ἐρχόμενον ἐν σαρκί. Οὗτός ἐστιν ὁ πλάνος καὶ ὁ ἀντίχριστος; 1 John. 4: 2–3, πᾶν πνεῦμα ὃς ὁμολογεῖ Ἰησοῦν Χριστὸν ἐν σαρκὶ ἐληλυθότα ἐκ τοῦ θεοῦ ἐστιν, καὶ πᾶν πνεῦμα ὃς μὴ ὁμολογεῖ τὸν Ἰησοῦν ἐκ τοῦ θεοῦ οὐκ ἐστιν; Polycarp, *Phil.* 7. 1, πᾶς γὰρ ὃς ἂν μὴ ὁμολογῇ Ἰησοῦν Χριστὸν ἐν σαρκὶ ἐληλυθέναι, ἀντιχριστός ἐστιν. The use of 1 and 2 John here is acknowledged in the edns of Lake (LCL), Shepherd (LCC; also in his introduction, 'The Letter of Polycarp', 125), LHH, and others.

[200] The reference is made in the edns. of LHH, and of Shepherd (LCC).

Thus, while it is possible that these four Johannine allusions could all be satisfied from the two Epistles alone, the second and third ones are somewhat more likely to reflect knowledge of the Fourth Gospel. And given the sort of textual interplay which exists between the Johannine Gospel and Epistles themselves, reverberations back to the Fourth Gospel are not improbable for the fourth allusion too. This is why even Grant's assessment of 7. 1, 'Such an echo of the Epistle suggests that he knew the Gospel as well',[201] does not go far enough. And in fact, the possible allusions to John 8: 44, 19: 34–5, and 13: 34 in *Ad Phil.* 7. 1 mentioned above are not the only possible traces of influence from the Fourth Gospel in his letter.[202]

When Polycarp states that Jesus 'promised us to raise us from the dead' (καθὼς ὑπέσχετο ἡμῖν ἐγεῖραι ἡμᾶς ἐκ νεκρῶν) in 5. 2, it is possible that he is simply deducing a promise from general Christian teaching. The rest of the sentence, 'and that if we walk as citizens worthy of him, "we shall also reign with him"', if we continue to believe', incorporates a promise which appears only in 2 Timothy 2: 12. But it is at least as probable that in the first part of the sentence Polycarp has in mind an assurance given verbally by Jesus himself, and the only promises from Jesus of his personal agency in raising the believer from the dead to be found in the Gospels[203] come three times in the space of fifteen verses in John 6: 40, 44, and 54, 'I will raise him up at the last day' (cf. John 5: 21; 6: 39).[204] Even though this is not a direct quotation, then, Polycarp's reference to such a promise on the part of Jesus may well reflect a knowledge of the Fourth Gospel. His familiarity with the Johannine vocabulary of the 'resurrection of life' (John 5: 29) will be seen many years later in his prayer recorded in the account of his martyrdom (14. 2), as we have already observed.

The points of contact with specific teachings of the Fourth Gospel are not many in number, but their strength is greater than is often recognized. There are no actual citations of the Fourth Gospel but there are indeed several 'traces' of it. Combined with the somewhat more obvious—but not more plentiful—traces of 1 and 2 John in *Ad Phil.* 7. 1, they give us a reasonable assurance that Polycarp indeed knew and valued the Fourth Gospel by the time he wrote his letter to the Philippians probably just before but in any case not long after AD 110.

---

[201] Grant, *Irenaeus of Lyons*, 37.

[202] Hengel, *Frage*, 72.

[203] P. V. M. Benecke wrote on behalf of 'the Oxford Committee', 'No such promise is given in the Synoptic Gospels, whereas it is put plainly in John. The reference seems certainly to be to a Johannine tradition, though it need not necessarily be to our Fourth Gospel' (*NTAF* 104). The variation of expressions in John 5 and 6 may account for the lack of a more specific reference in Polycarp.

[204] The possibility is also mentioned by Shepherd, 'The Letter of Polycarp', 125 n. 4. Though the verb ἀνίστημι is used in John 6, ἐγείρω, the verb used by Polycarp, had been used when the topic of Jesus' raising of the dead was broached in John. 5: 21, also later for his raising of Lazarus from the dead (12. 1, 9, 17).

Ignatius of Antioch

There is widespread agreement that the martyrdom of Ignatius of Antioch, and his authentic correspondence[205] composed in Asia Minor en route to Rome, occurred in the reign of Trajan, AD 98–117. Eusebius placed it in *c.*107–8, though many would place it later in that reign.[206] I shall assume here a date 'within a few years of A.D. 110, before or after'.[207]

The alleged failure of Ignatius of Antioch to use the Fourth Gospel and his failure to mention John, its reputed apostolic author, have been expressly cited as problematic for the recognition of the Fourth Gospel among the orthodox and therefore as part of the negative but validating evidence for the OJP.[208] Despite several significant studies in the twentieth century which supported the conclusion that Ignatius did know the Fourth Gospel,[209] Christine Trevett has not long ago observed, 'In recent decades there have been fewer claims for literary dependence on Ignatius's part and other explanations have been sought for the "general theological affinity" with the Gospel and the Johannine "spirit" of the Ignatian corpus'; 'though some critics (notably H. J. Bardsley) have discerned Johannine *logia* from the Gospel in its present form behind every Ignatian thought, few recent writers on Ignatius have claimed even "reminiscences" of, or allusions to, the Gospel as we have it'.[210] Charles Munier too has written of a convergence of opinion among

---

[205] Once thought to have been settled, the question of the authenticity of the Ignatian corpus has taken new life in the pages of *Zeitschrift für Antikes Christentum. Journal of Ancient Christianity*: R. Hübner, 'Thesen zur Echtheit und Datierung der sieben Briefe des Ignatius von Antiochen', *ZAC* 1 (1997), 44–72; A. Lindemann, 'Antwort auf die "Thesen zum Echtheit und Datierung der Sieben Briefe des Ignatius von Antiochen"', *ZAC* 1 (1997), 185–94; G. Schölgen, 'Die Ignatianen als pseudepigraphisches Brief-corpus. Anmerkung zu den thesen von Reinhard M. Hübner', *ZAC* 2 (1998), 16–25; M. Edwards, 'Ignatius and the Second Century. An Answer to R. Hübner', *ZAC* 2 (1998), 214–26. The authenticity of the traditional seven-letter collection (the middle recension) is here accepted.

[206] Frend, *Rise*, 124, and Christine Trevett, *A Study of Ignatius*, 3–9, are two who accept the date of *c.*107 as well-attested and plausible.

[207] Lightfoot, *AF* ii. 2. 1, 30.

[208] Haenchen, *John 1*, 7–8, 'Contacts between the Fourth Gospel and the letters of Ignatius are only apparent'; Culpepper, *John*, 108, sees Ignatius' (lack of) testimony in the context of 'the nearly complete absence of any explicit reference to the apostle or to the Gospel of John in the first half of the second century'; Barrett, *St John*, 102, also sees it as a problem for apostolic authorship.

[209] e.g., Sanday, *Criticism of the Fourth Gospel*, 104–8, who is convinced that Ignatius is thoroughly affected by Johannine thought, most probably through long acquaintance with its literature; P. Dietze, 'Die Briefe des Ignatius und das Johannesevangelium', *Theologische Studien und Kritiken*, 78 (1905), 563–603; W. R. Inge, writing for the Oxford Committee, *NTAF*, also in 1905, determined that 'Ignatius's use of the Fourth Gospel is highly probable, but falls some way short of certainty' ('Ignatius', 83); H. J. Bardsley, 'The Testimony of Ignatius and Polycarp to the Writings of St John', *JTS* 14 (1913), 207–20, 489–500, who also thought a personal relationship with the Johannine author possible; W. Burghardt, 'Did Saint Ignatius of Antioch Know the Fourth Gospel?', *Theological Studies*, 1 (1940), 1–26, 130–56; Loewenich, *Das Johannes-Verständnis*, 25–38; C. Maurer, *Ignatius von Antiochien und das Johannesevangelium*, ATANT 18 (Zurich, 1949); Braun, *Jean le Théologien*, 262–82.

[210] Trevett, *Study of Ignatius*, 21. With a similar but not quite so one-sided an assessment, William R. Schoedel, 'Polycarp of Smyrna and Ignatius of Antioch', in *ANRW* 2. 27. 1 (Berlin, 1993), 272–358, at 306–7, writes that 'the majority who comment on these matters seem to feel that the problem is still up in the air, and many incline to the opinion that literary dependence is unlikely'.

recent scholars 'tending to exclude a relation of direct dependence between Ignatius and the Fourth Gospel... but to recognize so much the more firmly that the two writings belong to the same doctrinal milieu, use the same religious language and witness to incontestable spiritual affinities'.[211] This convergence is certainly exemplified in the outstanding, major commentary on Ignatius' letters in recent decades by William Schoedel, who has judged it 'unlikely that Ignatius was acquainted with the Gospel of John'.[212]

Two prominent patristic scholars who have been willing to buck the trend, however, are Robert M. Grant and Charlesworth's predecessor in the George Collord chair at Princeton, Bruce Metzger.[213] Grant even underwent a change of mind on the subject.[214] In his early article, 'The Fourth Gospel and the Church', Grant had concluded against Ignatius' knowledge of the Fourth Gospel.[215] But twenty-one years later he would write, 'the thesis that Ignatius used the Gospel of John seems highly probable. I should be willing to admit that perhaps Ignatius knew its author instead of, or even in addition to, the book itself',[216] and, 'there is no reason to suppose that Ignatius did not know the Pauline epistles and the gospels of Matthew and John'.[217] In his 1987 book on the New Testament canon, Metzger maintained that, 'in contrast to the paucity of allusions to

---

[211] C. Munier, 'Où en est la question d'Ignace d'Antioche? Bilan d'un siècle de recherches 1970–1988', *ANRW* 2. 27. 1 (Berlin, 1993), 359–484, at 395.

[212] W. R. Schoedel, *Ignatius of Antioch*, Hermeneia (Philadelphia, 1985), 9. A major force in bringing about the present state of affairs in this regard surely has been Helmut Koester's 1957 book, *Synoptische Überlieferung bei den Apostolischen Vätern*, and his article from the same year, 'Geschichte und Kultus im Johannesevangelium und bei Ignatius von Antiochien', *Zeitschrift für Theologie und Kirche*, 54 (1957), 56–69. Though it dealt only with Synoptic parallels, the approach exemplified in *Synoptische Überlieferung*, favouring (hypothetical) pre-Synoptic, oral tradition, or (hypothetical) written documents which were sources for both the Gospel writers and the Apostolic Fathers, has been found congenial for questions of NT parallels in general. One might say that Koester has taken Bultmann's form and redactional theories about the Gospels and extrapolated from them, assuming the continued existence of some of the (hypothetical) pre-Synoptic and pre-Johannine oral traditions and written sources, on into the 2nd cent.

[213] There have of course been a few others. A. and C. Faivre, 'Genèse d'un texte et recourse aux Écritures. Ignace, *aux Éphésiens* 14, 1–16, 2', *Revue des Sciences Religieuses*, 65 (1991), 173–96, do not treat the subject at length, but judge that Ignatius probably knew John and a fourfold Gospel. The Faivres believe, however, that the Ignatian corpus is inauthentic and later than Polycarp.

[214] As noted by Pryor, 'Text of John 1: 13', 306–307 n. 35. Pryor noted a similar reversal on the part of J. N. Sanders himself. In his 1943 book, *The Fourth Gospel in the Early Church*, Sanders denied that anything in Ignatius 'proves conclusively that Ignatius knew or used the Fourth Gospel as we have it, but it seems clear that there is a fairly close affinity between his theology and language and those of the Fourth Gospel' (14). But in his commentary on John, published posthumously in 1968, Sanders wrote 'there are many resemblances in thought and language to the FG, though nothing that can be called a quotation... There are so many of these passages in Ignatius that it seems reasonable to suppose that he knew the FG' (J. N. Sanders, *St John* (London, 1968), 32).

[215] R. M. Grant, 'The Fourth Gospel and the Church', *HTR* 35 (1942), at 92.

[216] R. M. Grant, 'Scripture and Tradition in St Ignatius of Antioch', *CBQ* 25 (1963), 322–35, at 325. This was reprinted in R. M. Grant, *After the New Testament* (Philadelphia, 1967), from which Pryor takes his citations.

[217] Grant, 'Scripture and Tradition', 327. Pryor attributes these changes in Sanders and Grant partly to the books of C. Maurer and F.-M. Braun (see previous note) which appeared in the

the Synoptic Gospels, Ignatius' epistles not infrequently present echoes of the fourth Gospel'.[218] He went on to treat several passages which show, he thought 'that Ignatius was well acquainted with Johannine theology and suggest that he may have gained this familiarity from having read the Fourth Gospel'.[219] This endorsement is not exceptionally vigorous, but in the light of the current 'convergence of opinion' it is none the less exceptional. In addition, René Kieffer has gone back to the work of F.-M. Braun and has amplified Braun's conclusion that Ignatius was certainly dependent upon the Gospel according to John.[220] And now, very recently, Titus Nagel has added his voice to this opposing opinion.

The dissent of scholars like Grant, Metzger, Kieffer, and Nagel should at least sustain the impression that the case may not be as cut-and-dried as it is sometimes represented to be. But before proceeding to examine the relevant evidence, a few preliminary observations about the argument are in order.

First, it is worth noting that many of those writers who do not see direct influence from the Johannine Gospel on Ignatius, and therefore would count this against the reception of John, also recognize no direct influence from the written Gospels of Matthew or Luke, let alone Mark.[221] If the judgement of these scholars about Ignatius' ignorance of John is correct, the Fourth Gospel would fare no worse than the Second and Third, and perhaps no worse than the First. In this case the absence of clear and direct dependence upon John is not so remarkable at all, and the evidence for orthodox Johannophobia will be about the same as for orthodox Marcophobia, Lukophobia, and Mattheophobia. If it is objected that the Fourth Gospel should be expected to be more visible because Ignatius is writing from Asia Minor, in later tradition the home of the Fourth Gospel, it should also be said, (*a*) that the Synoptic Gospels (at least Matthew) appear to be known in Asia Minor from the book of Revelation and from Polycarp's contemporary letter to the Philippians, and (*b*) that it may be more reasonable to hold the bishop of Antioch responsible for representing Syrian traditions[222] than Asian ones.

---

intervals. Grant actually mentions Maurer ('Scripture and Tradition', 325). On the other hand, the reversals of Sanders and Grant also came after the appearance of Helmut Koester's *Synoptische Überlieferung*, published in 1957. For Grant's overall analysis of Koester's methods, see 'Scripture and Tradition', 325–8.

[218] Metzger, *Canon*, 46; see pp. 46–8. Note also C. P. Hammond-Bammel, 'Ignatian Problems', *JTS* NS 33 (1982), 62–97.

[219] Metzger, *Canon*, 47–8.

[220] Kieffer, 'Les Premiers Indices', 2234–8.

[221] This would include Koester and Schoedel, who acknowledge only an indirect influence from Matthew. Many, on the other hand, believe Ignatius did know Matthew's Gospel, but that the question of his knowledge of the Gospels of Mark and Luke cannot be decided from his writings. See Metzger, *Canon*, 45–6.

[222] We cannot pass this by without observing that Ignatius' 'silence' about the Johannine literature surely poses much greater problems for the view that this literature originated in Syria, unless one adopts an unlikely date for the Fourth Gospel after the martyrdom of Ignatius.

The second observation concerns a flaw in reasoning. Ignatius' strong affinities with the Fourth Gospel are universally recognized (even, on the part of some, extending to an affirmation that Ignatius and the Fourth Gospel are greatly indebted to (the same) gnostic or gnosticizing forms of thought).[223] But how are these affinities to be accounted for? Do they signify that Ignatius actually knew and used the Fourth Gospel as a literary source, or are they satisfied by the assumption of a common theological and spiritual milieu, or common access to pre-Johannine tradition? We cannot now know, of course, to what extent Jesus tradition now contained in the Fourth Gospel, even what we might call distinctively Johannine material, might have circulated before the publication of the Gospel. Inge, still keeping the apostle in view, suggested about the Johannine logia, 'if they formed part of the Apostle's oral teaching, they must have been familiar to his disciples, and may have been collected and written down long before our Gospel was composed'.[224] Koester and Schoedel, keeping the apostle out of view, speak of anonymous tradition which was used by Ignatius and the Fourth Gospel in common.[225] These studies then decide against literary dependence and for a common milieu of some kind. But if it is true that 'nothing in these passages proves conclusively that Ignatius knew or used the Fourth Gospel as we have it', that 'one cannot say with any certainty that Ignatius knew our Fourth Gospel',[226] then it is hard to see how Ignatius can be used to illustrate 'the reluctance shown by the early Church to accept the Fourth Gospel as Scripture'.[227] One can hardly 'accept' what one does not know exists. For Ignatius' alleged silence to advance the argument of the OJP we ought to be able to conclude that he knew the Fourth Gospel but ignored or rejected it (preferably due to some gnostic affinities he did not like). But no one has been able to demonstrate this. Some have explicitly stated their belief that the Fourth Gospel was written after Ignatius' letters. Others leave the matter ambiguous. But whether it is because he wrote first or simply because he wrote in ignorance, Ignatius' 'silence' with regard to the Fourth Gospel or its alleged author is in fact of no service in establishing an orthodox reticence or antagonism towards it. And, more problematically, if we accept the hypothesis that Ignatius' affinities with the Fourth Gospel are due to a common spiritual milieu, and include his access to pre-Johannine, Jesus tradition, we must tend to think that this common milieu and Ignatius' eager acceptance of the said pre-Johannine Jesus tradition make it extremely unlikely that he would have found any serious fault with the written Gospel—even with

[223] e.g. H. Schlier, *Religionsgeschichtliche Untersuchungen zu den Ignatiusbriefen*, BZNW 8 (Giessen, 1929); H. W. Bartsch, *Gnostisches Gut und Gemeindertradition bei Ignatius von Antiochien* (Gütersloh, 1940).
[224] Inge, 'Ignatius', *NTAF* 83.
[225] e.g. Schoedel, *Ignatius*, 10, suggesting that at least in *IEph*. 14. 2 Ignatius and John are dependent upon a common source.
[226] Sanders, *Fourth Gospel*, 14.
[227] Ibid. 85.

the allegedly gnostically tinged aspects of that Gospel—had he lived to see its publication. In this case, the appeal to Ignatius' 'silence' as testimony against the Gospel itself, or as evidence of the orthodox avoidance of that Gospel, is obviously illegitimate.

A third observation concerns the standards of precision required by some scholars for a literary parallel to be assessed as instancing literary knowledge. Authors often speak of the lack of 'clear evidence of literary dependence on John'.[228] But what would such evidence look like if it existed?[229] Bauer opined that, 'the oft-cited "reminiscences" are ambiguous and do not lead to a firm conviction of dependence; on the contrary, they make the absence of any actual quotations appear to be all the more curious'.[230] The ambiguity of most of the 'reminiscences' is not to be denied, but on what basis can we assume that if he knew a particular writing, any writing, Ignatius must have provided us with 'actual quotations'? It is well known that Ignatius' method of 'literary borrowing', is far from exact, even for the Old Testament[231] and for 1 Corinthians, the one New Testament book about which there seems to be agreement among scholars.[232] Why should it be thought so curious, then, that he does not *change* his method and supply us with more precise citations from a proposed Johannine source? Should each point of difference, no matter how minute, between an Ignatian expression and a suggested NT source, or each disparity from the context of the suggested source, be counted as evidence that Ignatius does not know the source in question, but is indebted to some other form of tradition, or to some known or unknown proverbial or rhetorical commonplace? It is writers like Bauer, Sanders, Koester, and Paulsen[233] who tend to be the

---

[228] Shoedel, *Ignatius*, 185.

[229] 'Conclusive proof' that Ignatius 'knew or used the Fourth Gospel as we have it' was sought by Sanders in 1943. Haenchen in 1980 asked for 'really conclusive proof': 'But none of the three passages [i.e. *IPhilad.* 7. 1 (John 3: 18; 8: 14); *IPhilad.* 9. 1 (John 10: 7, 9); *IRom.* 7. 3 (John 6: 33)] offers really conclusive proof for the dependence of Ignatius on the Fourth Gospel' (*John 1*, 7). One may certainly despair of such proof ever being found, but why does the OJP position demand that proof for a counter position be 'conclusive' or 'really conclusive'? Do its defenders mean to assert that they have 'conclusive proof' that Ignatius did not know or use the Fourth Gospel more or less as we have it? Or do they believe that the absence of 'conclusive proof' of one assertion constitutes 'conclusive proof' of its converse?

[230] Bauer, *Orthodoxy and Heresy*, 209. Studies such as H. Rathke's *Ignatius und die Paulusbriefe*, TU 99 (Berlin, 1967), at 39–40, tend to rest the question of authority upon factors such as the use of citation formulas and exact, literal citation (despite his acknowledgement that Ignatius probably did not have his copy of Paul's letters at hand when writing). Such an approach is not uncommon.

[231] Though he honours the OT as scripture, Ignatius does not cite it with literal precision, and only twice (*IEph.* 5. 3; *IMagn.* 12) with an introductory formula. The rest of the time, as in his use of Ps. 1: 3 in *IMagn.* 13. 1; of Isa. 52: 5 in *ITrall.* 8. 2 (cf. Rom. 2: 24; 2 Clem. 13: 2), of Isa. 5: 26; 11. 12, in *ISmyrn.* 1. 2; of Ps. 33: 9 in *IEph.* 15. 1, he weaves the words from scripture into his own sentences, much as he does with words apparently taken from NT sources (cf. Grant, 'Scripture and Tradition', 323).

[232] Schoedel, *Ignatius*, 9; reiterated in his 'Polycarp of Smyrna and Ignatius of Antioch', 307.

[233] H. Paulsen, *Studien zur Theologie des Ignatius von Antiochien*, Forschungen zur Kirchen- und Dogmengeschichte, 29 (Göttingen, 1978).

literalists here, proceeding as if a source—at least a NT source—can only have been known if the secondary author quotes it precisely and with reasonable contextual fidelity. But both common sense and the examples of many of his contemporaries[234] show us that it is quite illegitimate to impose such a standard.

Almost unnoticed amid the convergence of recent opinion have been the voices of other writers who have pointed in the direction of a different, I shall venture to say more realistic, approach to the problem. In simple but starkly contrasting words, Metzger observes that, 'It agrees with the style of Ignatius, and particularly with the circumstances under which the epistles were composed, that quotations are few in number, brief in extent, and made evidently from memory'.[235] Christine Trevett, too, has come to the realization that, 'apparent deviation from a Gospel norm' on Ignatius' part 'may be due to deliberate modification on his part, for reasons of dogma or anti-heretical polemic. It might even reflect, simply, his general lack of concern for careful quotation or contextual accuracy.'[236] And Robert Grant's words about Ignatius' use of Paul, though forty years old, are still well worth repeating:

This is to say that he can take Pauline expressions and use them in contexts of his own. Such usage is hardly surprising. Ignatius, in fact, could not have used Pauline expressions in Pauline contexts.

Now what does this use of 1 Cor show? It shows that Ignatius used the letter in several different ways and that sometimes he quoted, sometimes alluded, sometimes he allusively quoted and sometimes he quotingly alluded. Any idea of exactness in analyzing his usage must be read in by the analyst. It does not exist in Ignatius' own writings.[237]

Yet, even since Grant wrote, the analysts have continued to read in the idea of exactness in a big way. And even if we could be justified (and of course we cannot) in supposing that Ignatius' unwavering aim was precise citation and documentation of his sources, we should still have to consider it unlikely that his captors allowed him to cart all his books along with him on the journey from Antioch to Rome. Cyril Richardson wrote as early as 1935,

Journeying to his martyrdom in Rome he could hardly have been provided with a large library nor have been anxious to cite with the exactitude of a scholar those quotations of which he made use. It is just in the unique and original way, in which he takes Pauline ideas and phrases and makes them his very own,

---

[234] See, again, Whittaker, 'Indirect Tradition' and my discussion above.
[235] Metzger, *Canon*, 44.
[236] C. Trevett, 'Approaching Matthew from the Second Century: The Under-Used Ignatian Correspondence', *JSNT* 20 (1984), 59–67, at 64–5.
[237] Grant, 'Scripture and Tradition', 324

that Ignatius is most interesting as a personality and most baffling as a literary problem.[238]

It is surprising how routinely scholars assume that Ignatius, if he knew any NT books, had to have them in front of him as he wrote and must have held to the ideal of precise literal transcription, or perhaps that he had to have memorized each book he knew, word for word, and felt compelled to reproduce exactly each source for his thoughts. Conceiving of Ignatius' plight as being compounded by the want of an author's normal 'writing library', however, would by itself seem to shed considerable light on his 'allusive quotes' and 'quoting allusions'. We may find, under these circumstances, that there has been a tendency to impose anachronistic and circumstantially unrealistic standards on Ignatius in the attempt to adjudge the question of 'literary dependence' on, or even knowledge of, New Testament materials. This may mean that calculating the likelihood of an indebtedness to a particular literary source will not be a straightforward task achievable by adherence to pre-established canons, but it also means that factors other than the exactness of verbal or contextual correspondence in any case will have to be considered.

IGNATIUS AND THE APOSTLES

Elsewhere I have argued that any valid attempt to examine the question of Ignatius' knowledge of NT materials (particularly the epistolary materials) must take his views of the apostolate into account as a necessary part of his literary environment.[239] Possible 'echoes' and 'reminiscences' of NT sources can be and often are presented as isolated from any environment they might have in Ignatius' views regarding religious authority, and the NT sources themselves are often presented as, in principle, on a par with sayings from a wide array of sources. Seen discretely, and compared in minute detail with the possible NT prototypes for precision of correspondence, there may seem little to distinguish a given NT background from a pagan proverb or a (later) gnostic commonplace. But if, let us say, it should have to be recognized that Ignatius has a very high opinion of the apostles of Jesus, and that they play an important part in his overall approach to ecclesiastical authority, this fact will serve to remedy the seeming isolation of particular 'reminiscences', providing for them a context in an established feature of Ignatius' religious outlook.

---

[238] C. C. Richardson, *The Christianity of Ignatius of Antioch* (New York, 1935), 66. Grant, too, in 1963 asked in passing, 'Was he using books at the time he wrote his letters?' ('Scripture and Tradition', 326). Cf. Metzger, *Canon*, 44. Trevett, *Study of Ignatius*, 16, observes that Ignatius' external conditions, let alone his internal complexities, did not make for 'carefully structured letter-writing, for systematic theology or rigorously reasoned argument'. I should add, 'or for exact reproductions of all his literary borrowings'.

[239] Hill, 'Ignatius and the Apostolate', from which much in the following sections is reworked.

If this holds any promise for the question of Ignatius' knowledge of the Fourth Gospel, it will only be to the extent that it is likely that he would have regarded this Gospel, if he knew it, as the immediate or perhaps the mediate product of an apostle's teaching. This, it hardly needs to be said, most scholars of recent decades have been unable to assume. And indeed it ought not to be assumed—but there is solid reason to believe that the Fourth Gospel was considered an apostolic production at about this time. The common assumption is that the attribution to John the apostle was not original to the Gospel at its first publication but came many years after-wards, under circumstances which are now obscure at best. But in this study we have, I believe, come to see that the Fourth Gospel was con-sidered the product of John at just about this time by at least one Christian teacher in Asia, and that his teaching on this subject seems to imply a rather wider circulation among others. From the scant remains of Papias' work it has emerged that by at about this time in Asia Minor, Jesus' apostle Matthew was credited with an arrangement of the λόγια, that Peter was seen as the ultimate source for another (Eusebius, *HE* 3. 39. 15–16), and that John was considered the author of the Fourth Gospel (*HE* 3. 24. 3–13). This view cannot simply be assumed without question to have been held by the visiting bishop of Antioch, but its existence in Asia Minor at this time does mean that it cannot be ignored and must be considered as a possible context for Ignatius' Johannine 'reminiscences'. (I observe here that the Gospel which is now almost universally regarded as coming from Syria, the Gospel according to Matthew, fares little better with Ignatius than does the Gospel according to John. There is but one probable 'citation' (along with several other 'echoes'), and that one is disputed by many scholars.)

I proceed then to a brief review of Ignatius' view of the apostolate. His attitude towards the apostles is introduced in the letter to the Magnesians 6. 1.[240] 'Be zealous to do all things in harmony with God, with the bishop presiding in the place of God and the presbyters in the place of the council of the apostles (εἰς τόπον συνεδρίου τῶν ἀποστόλων), and the deacons, who are most dear to me, entrusted with the service of Jesus Christ...' The bishop 'presides' (προκαθημένου) in the place (εἰς τόπον)[241] of God, the deacons in the place of Christ, and the presbyters preside (the same verb is assumed) in the place of the council of the apostles. This places the council of the apostles in the heavenly hierarchy along with the Father and the Son. In a way reminiscent of the twenty-four elders of the book of Revelation,[242] the apostles are presented by Ignatius as occupying such an

---

[240] Translations of Ignatius in this section will be my own.

[241] Though Lightfoot, *AF* ii/2. 119, preferred τύπον, reading with the Syriac, Arabic and apparently the Armenian versions, Lake LCL, i. 201, and Schoedel, *Ignatius*, 112, follow the Greek and Latin MSS of the middle recension and the long recension in reading τόπον.

[242] Schoedel, *Ignatius*, 113, makes this comparison but ultimately retreats from it. See Hill, 'Ignatius and the Apostolate', 233–6.

exalted position that they can function in a comparison alongside the Father and Christ as permanent and heavenly archetypes of authority to which the temporal authority of the Church below can always, and can only, be compared.

It is particularly in the letter to the Trallians, like the letter to the Magnesians written from Smyrna, that Ignatius' view of the apostolate comes to the surface. In a double reference, the apostles are seen as both a sanhedrin of God, their title from *IMagn.* 6.1, and an apostolic 'band': 'Likewise, let all respect the deacons as Jesus Christ, as (they respect) also the bishop, who is a type of the Father, and the presbyters as the council (συνέδριον) of God and the band (σύνδεσμον) of the apostles' (*ITrall.* 3. 1; cf. also 2. 2). It is not a historical relation they might have had as a council to Jesus Christ in his earthly ministry that is in view; nor is it merely a territorial jurisdiction during their historical ministries after the resurrection of Christ.[243] It is rather their transcendent relation, even now, as a council or sanhedrin to God.[244] And this too, of course, like *IMagn.* 6. 1, would be very reminiscent of the twenty-four presbyters in John's Apocalypse,[245] written in and circulated throughout Asia Minor some ten to twenty years earlier.[246]

Later he will tell the Trallians, 'it is right that each of you, and especially the presbyters, should refresh the bishop, to the honour of the Father of Jesus Christ, and of the apostles' (*ITrall.* 12. 2).[247] For the Trallian presbyters to refresh their bishop will bring honour to God, who is represented by the bishop, and honour to the apostolate, which is represented by them, the presbytery. This again assumes the same typological patterns observed above.[248]

---

[243] As in *Ep. Apost.* 1.

[244] As the sanhedrin of God he pictures them, as Lightfoot says, 'as it were, on thrones encircling the Eternal Throne. The terrestrial hierarchy is thus a copy of the celestial' (Lightfoot, *AF* ii/2. 158).

[245] While these twenty-four elders are not identified as apostles—though early Christian interpretation often said that the twelve apostles were represented by them, along with the twelve patriarchs or tribes—Revelation does have a transcendent concept of the twelve apostles in 21: 14. For Clement of Alexandria's development of these themes see *Strom.* 6. 13. 105. 1; 106. 21–108. 1; 7. 10. 56. 5–6; and cf. Hill, *Regnum Caelorum*², 174–5.

[246] Cf. also Matt. 19: 28; Luke 22: 28–30.

[247] There is a textual question here. The translation above follows the Greek and Latin texts of the middle recension, but the long recension inserts καὶ εἰς τιμὴ before Ἰησοῦ Χριστοῦ, thus making a triplet rather than a doublet. The Armenian, Coptic, and Arabic also reflect the extra καί. In this case the placement of the apostles here as sharing honour with the Father and Jesus Christ would be even more striking. The special mention of the presbyters, however, makes the traditional text more plausible. The Father and the apostles are probably singled out because of Ignatius' special exhortation to the presbyters of Tralles (who had not accompanied their bishop, Polybius, to visit Ignatius).

[248] See H. Chadwick, 'The Silence of Bishops in Ignatius', *HTR* 43 (1950), 169–72, at 170. Schoedel, *Ignatius*, 160 n., says, 'There is little reason... to regard the reference to the apostles in [*ITrall.*] 12. 2 as going beyond Ignatius' usual treatment of them as venerable figures of the past who subordinated themselves to God or Christ as the elders subordinate themselves to the bishop (see on *Mag.* 6. 1)'. In other words, they function simply as historical exemplars, though venerable

In his last letter to a church, *ISmyrn.* 8. 1, he exhorts the congregation,
'Let all of you follow the bishop, as Jesus Christ (followed) the Father, and
(follow) the presbytery as if it were the apostles. And reverence the deacons
as the command of God'. The last two of these three exhortations, 'Follow
the presbytery as if it were the apostles. And reverence the deacons as the
command of God', do not set the apostles or the command of God as
examples to follow, but rather as authorities to be obeyed or agreed to. The
Smyrnaeans should follow the presbytery as if it were the very council of
the apostles themselves. Once again, though the authority of the presbytery
on earth is ratified in no uncertain terms, it is the analogue which has the
higher, heavenly authority, in company with the Father himself, and the
command of God. The place of the apostles in the divine hierarchy speaks
clearly of transcendent authority.

These texts reveal a surprisingly well-developed conception of the
apostles which views their significance as moving well beyond their historical relationship to Jesus, beyond their historical roles in the early preaching
of the gospel, and beyond what is merely exemplary for the Christian. The
apostles are a definite and closed group which participate in the transcendent, heavenly hierarchy, along with Jesus Christ and the Father, on which
the earthly hierarchy is modelled. Such exalted and quasi-divine notions
of the apostolate and of apostolic authority are at least commensurate
with those which accompanied the emergence of a new set of Christian,
'apostolic' scriptures, and are entirely consonant with the attitudes we have
discovered in Papias and in his elder. If Ignatius was aware of a body of
apostolic teaching, whether oral or written, we can be assured that he held
it up as embodying divine authority.

All of this, it might be said, is well and good, but it is also a fact that Ignatius
never mentions the apostle John or anything written, or orally taught, by him.
Even in his epistle to the Ephesians he does not mention John, though he does
mention Paul.[249] This is true, though his mention of Paul to the Ephesians
seems to be closely connected to his awareness of repeating the apostle's
'journey to death' in Rome.[250] Nor does he mention Peter in the epistle, or
Matthew, or the author of Revelation, who he must have known had been
associated with Ephesus. And yet in *IEph.* 11. 2 Ignatius compliments the
Christians of Ephesus by claiming that they 'were always of one mind with[251]
the apostles in the power of Jesus Christ'. Ignatius is operating under the

and ancient, of Godly subordination. But neither their historical role in Jesus' earthly ministry nor
their exemplary function is in view here. Their function as members of the heavenly hierarchy is
the fulcrum for the exhortation.

[249] Hengel, *Frage*, 69
[250] Haenchen, *John 1*, 8.
[251] Συνήνεσαν, from συναινέω, to agree with, be in accord with, is the reading of the Greek
and Latin MSS of the middle recension; the Greek of the long recension, the Armenian, and the
Arabic read συνήσαν, from σύνειμι, to be with.

impression that there has been a long-standing, congenial relationship between the Ephesian church and 'the apostles', implying at least one more
apostle besides Paul.[252] The fourth-century redactor of the long recension of
Ignatius' letters understood him as referring to the apostles 'Paul, and John,
and most faithful Timothy'. Indeed, Ignatius' casual reference here foreshadows what Irenaeus will recount in *AH* 3. 3. 4, about Ephesus' double
apostolic foundations in both Paul and John. Is it a coincidence that a tradition would soon emerge which associates Ephesus in a special way with the
ministry of John? Justin, portraying himself as in Ephesus at the time, already
identifies the Asian prophet and author of Revelation as John the apostle
(*Dial.* 81). Irenaeus will explicitly speak of John's residence in Ephesus or in
Asia (*AH* 2. 22. 5; 3. 1. 1), will have a story from Polycarp about John at the
Ephesian bath-house (3. 3. 4), and will state repeatedly that Polycarp had
known John (and other apostles) in Asia Minor (3. 3. 4; *Ep. Flor.* Eusebius, *HE*
5. 20. 6; *Ep. Vict.* Eusebius, *HE* 5. 24. 16). John's residence and burial in
Ephesus will be noted by Polycrates, bishop of Ephesus (Eusebius, *HE* 5. 24.
3); the *Acts of John* will assume a ministry of John's in Ephesus; as will Clement
of Alexandria (*Qds* 42), who will link it with a story he had learnt from tradition. And from there a nearly universal tradition follows.

Ignatius' doctrine of the apostolate is part of the essential setting for examining the question of his possible borrowings from any writings which had any
claim to being apostolic in his day. It shows us that the matter of apostolic
authority is not only viable in his thought, it is of tremendous importance. It
cannot confirm as certain any particular parallel, but it does show the greater
likelihood that Ignatius would be attentive and solicitous about any body of
apostolic teaching, whether it had to do directly with the life of Christ or with
moral or theological instruction. Judging from his views on the apostles and
their authority, we can at least say that if he regarded any written Gospel or
Gospels as the work of an apostle, or perhaps as approved by an apostle, he
would have regarded them as bearing divine authority, regardless of whether
we can find verifiable examples of his use of those Gospels in his writings. If he
too, like Papias' Elder, believed this to pertain to the Fourth Gospel, the one
according to John, we can scarcely doubt that he held it in this high regard.
The question whether Ignatius did know of any written Gospel or Gospels
which he might have regarded in this way will be addressed in due course.
Now let us turn to the question of Ignatius' 'echoes' or 'reminiscences' of the
Fourth Gospel.

IGNATIUS AND THE FOURTH GOSPEL

If Ignatius has an exalted view of the apostles, their authority, and their
teaching, and if it appears that he has certain written Gospels on which he

---

[252] See Lightfoot, *AF* ii/2. 62.

relies for knowledge about Jesus Christ, and which are closely connected to apostles, do we have enough evidence to say whether or not the Fourth Gospel was among them? For some, the answer seems to rest solely on the question of whether we have in Ignatius indisputable cases of literal citation of the Gospel[253] (preferably with attribution), or cases when no other alternative theory is possible. But I have charged that this prejudices the case and is methodologically unsound. Metzger, as we have seen above, thinks the echoes of John are far more abundant than echoes of the Synoptic Gospels.[254] Some of the strongest of these will now be examined.

IRom. 7. 2–3 (John 4: 10, 14; 6: 33, etc.)

2. My lust has been crucified, and there is no fire of material love in me; but water living [and speaking][255] in me, speaking to me from within, 'Come to the Father'. 3. I take no pleasure in the food of corruption, nor in pleasures of this life. I desire the bread of God (ἄρτον θεοῦ), that is, the flesh (σάρξ) of Christ who is of the seed of David; for drink I desire his blood, which is incorruptible love.

'Living water' in 7. 2 inevitably reminds us of Jesus' phrase in John 4: 10 (11); 7: 38, a cipher for the Holy Spirit. On the other hand, 'living water' is 'a common Greek metaphor, found also in Did. 7 and *Odes. Sol.* 6. 17, etc.',[256] and many other places. 'Speaking water' also could refer in Hellenism to water which was supposed to imbue the one who drank it with prophetic powers. But as Schoedel says, 'it must be recognized that if Ignatius borrowed the theme from Hellenism, he gave the prophetic waters a purely symbolic significance. For he could scarcely have been thinking of water that was actually drunk.'[257] That Ignatius is speaking of spiritual water here certainly moves us closer to John 4: 10; 7: 38. But it is not this figure alone which points to John. The text at this point has been corrupted by a number of variants. Instead of 'water living and speaking (λαλοῦν)', the author of the long recension wrote ἀλλόμενον, welling up, which would be a rather more clear indication of indebtedness to John 4 (4: 14). Lightfoot regarded this as the most probable reading, noting the corruption of the text and suggesting that the alternative reading, λαλοῦν, 'might very easily suggest itself to a scribe from the following λέγον'.[258] And what the inner voice told Ignatius, 'Come to the Father' (Δεῦρο πρὸς τὸν πατέρα),

[253] Paulsen, *Studien*, 36–7.

[254] Metzger, *Canon*, 46. Metzger goes on to cite *IMagn.* 7. 2 (cf. John 1: 1; 8: 28–9); *IPhilad.* 7. 1 (cf. John 3: 8); several phrases from *IRom.* 8: 2 echoing words from John 12: 31; 14: 30; 16; 11; 4: 10; 7: 38; 6: 33; 7: 42; *IPhilad.* 9. 1 (cf. John 10: 7, 9; 14: 6; 8: 30–59; 17: 20–3). Culpepper, *John*, 109, says the closest 'echoes' are in *IRom.* 7. 2; *IMagn.* 8. 2; *IPhilad.* 7. 1 and 9. 1.

[255] Or 'welling up'. See below.

[256] Richardson, *Ignatius*, 73–4. Also Loewenich, *Das Johannes-Verständnis*, 35–6.

[257] Schoedel, *Ignatius*, 185.

[258] Lightfoot, *AF* ii/2. 225. He points to the popularity of the motif of the 'living waters welling up', from John 4: 14, later in the 2nd cent among Naassenes, Sethians, and in Justin the Gnostic, as referred to in Hippolytus, *Ref.* 5. 9, 19, 27. None of this is noted by Schoedel.

also has quite plausible links to John, where several times there is reference
to Jesus going πρὸς τὸν πατέρα (14: 12, 28; 16: 17; 20: 17), and once
there is his unique claim that 'no one comes to the Father except through
me' (οὐδεὶς ἔρχεται πρὸς τὸν πατέρα εἰ μὴ δι᾽ ἐμοῦ, 14: 6). Kieffer
remarks, 'If one receives from Jesus the living water which he has promised
in John 4: 10 and 7: 38, one may follow him to the Father'.[259]

'The seed of David' in 7. 3 may simply be by now a traditional title, or it
may have come from Romans 1: 3 or Titus 2: 8, but the phrase does occur
in John 7: 42 as well, these three being the only occurrences in the NT. But
the reference in 7. 3 to 'the bread of God, that is, the flesh (σάρξ) of Christ
who is of the seed of David', and the mention of 'the bread of God' in *IEph.*
5. 2, also seem to hark back to Johannine expressions. John 6: 33 contains
the only occurrence of the term ἄρτος θεοῦ in the NT,[260] and John 6: 51,
53, 54, 55, 56 repeatedly identify this bread with the σάρξ of Jesus—not
with his σῶμα, as in the Synoptic accounts of the Last Supper and in Paul.
Schoedel allows that 'the link between the bread of God and Christ's flesh
and between the drink and Christ's blood is reminiscent of John 6: 26–59.
But there is no clear evidence of literary dependence on John here or
elsewhere.'[261] Again, it ought to be asked, what would such evidence look
like if it existed? Would it be confined to the appearance of one or more
instances of precise quotation, or this combined with the citation of an
author's name (for even a word-for-word correspondence may mean no
more than that John and Ignatius were dependent on the same pre-
Johannine source)? We are not told, but it is plain that, for Schoedel, such
evidence would be something quite different than it was for Lightfoot, who
wrote,

Here again is an expression taken from S. John's Gospel, vi. 33. Indeed the whole
context is suggested by this portion of the Evangelist's narrative.[262] The contrast of
perishable and imperishable food—the bread and the cup as representing the flesh
and blood of Christ—the mystical power emanating therefrom—are all ideas contained in the context (vi. 48–59). The later interpolator has seen the source of
Ignatius' inspiration, and has introduced expressions freely from the Gospel; 'the
heavenly bread' (vi. 31, 32, 50, 58), 'the bread of life' (vi. 48), 'eternal life'

[259] Kieffer, 'Les Premiers Indices', 2236.
[260] Nor does it occur, according to Kieffer, ibid. 2236, in the LXX. Kieffer finds it remarkable
too that in *IRom.* 7. 3 ἄρτος θεοῦ uses this rare phrase without the two articles.
[261] Schoedel, *Ignatius*, 185. By citing Paulsen, *Studien*, 36–7, here it seems that Schoedel must
mean that there are no instances of literal citation ('kein einziges wörtliches Zitat') which can be
confirmed.
[262] Inge, 'Ignatius', *NTAF* 81, felt compelled to say that Lightfoot's assertion here 'seems
to be justified, especially in view of John 4[23] καὶ γὰρ ὁ πατὴρ τοιούτους ζητεῖ τοὺς
προσκυνοῦντας αὐτόν'. After reviewing other possibilities Inge concluded, 'on the whole direct
literary dependence seems much the most probable hypothesis' (82). See also Metzger, *Canon*, 47.
A. and C. Faivre, 'Genèse d'un texte', 191, agree that in *IRom* 7. 2–3 Ignatius unites several
allusions to John. These writers evidently do not restrict themselves solely to the question of literal
citation and/or attribution.

(ζωὴ αἰώνιος, vi. 27, 40, 54). For ἄρτος θεοῦ compare also *Ephes.* 5 with the note.[263]

Can we absolutely rule out the possibility that Ignatius had some unknown written or unwritten source(s)[264] other than John which contained all of this information about Jesus? Perhaps not. Can we pronounce it absolutely impossible that Ignatius and John came up with these details independently of one another? More likely we can, but still perhaps not. But is either of these explanations nearly as well-suited to the evidence as that which attributes these parallels to his familiarity with the Fourth Gospel, since (*a*) we know from other sources that this Gospel as a self-contained literary work was known by about this time in Asia Minor (and possibly elsewhere), and was known as the work of an apostle, (*b*) since Ignatius would have been very interested in the teaching of an apostle, and (*c*) since we know of no other source for the life of Jesus which comes close to showing the same correspondences?

IMagn. 7. 1 (John 5: 19; 8: 28)

'Just as then the Lord did nothing without the Father (ὁ κύριος ἄνευ τοῦ πατρὸς οὐδὲν ἐποίησεν), being united with Him (ἡνωμένος ὤν), whether through himself or through the apostles, so you do nothing without the bishop and the presbyters.' That the Lord did nothing without the Father is the teaching of Jesus himself as recorded in the Fourth Gospel, 5: 19, 'Truly, truly I say to you, the Son can do nothing of his own accord (οὐ δύναται ὁ υἱὸς ποιεῖν ἀφ᾽ ἑαυτοῦ οὐδέν), but only what he sees the Father doing; for whatever he does, that the Son does likewise'; 8: 28, 'When you have lifted up the Son of man, then you will know that I am he, and that I do nothing on my own authority (ἀπ᾽ ἐμαυτοῦ ποιῶ οὐδέν) but speak thus as the Father taught me' (cf. 5: 30; 10: 37). Sanders rejected the idea of literary dependence, because Ignatius' statement, 'is in no sense a quotation of either passage'. None the less, Ignatius seems to be alluding to a well-known aspect of the historical life of Jesus, and extending that history into the ministries of the apostles, who were his instruments on earth after his resurrection. That Jesus always acted in concert with the Father is something which appears explicitly, so far as we know, only in the Fourth Gospel, where it indeed appears as a recurring theme. Ignatius' statement, while not a quotation, does reproduce John's

---

[263] Lightfoot, *AF* ii/2. 226. The reference to *IEph.* 5 is to Ignatius' mention there of 'the bread [of God]' ('of God' is not supported by all the MSS), as a possible Christological reference, which would also seem to point to John 6: 33.

[264] Sanders, *Fourth Gospel*, 13, 'The only exact verbal parallels are ὕδωρ ζῶν and ἄρτος θεοῦ, precisely the kind of phrases which would survive unchanged in an oral tradition'. True enough, perhaps, but also precisely the kind of phrases which would survive in the memory of one familiar with the Fourth Gospel but who did not have a copy in front of him at the time of writing. Here again, though other 'echoes' are acknowledged by Sanders, the determination is based solely on the number and extent of 'exact verbal parallels'.

characteristic words ποιέω, οὐδέν, and Πατήρ (he might have used θέος). Ignatius' parenthetical comment, that Jesus was 'united with him', seems to be based on another statement of the Johannine theme in John 10: 30, 'I and my Father are one'. Ignatius assumes that the unity of the Son with the Father, as a feature of Jesus' earthly life, is known to the Magnesians in Asia Minor, for it is the basis of his charge to them to act in unity with their bishop and presbyters.[265] Related to this, in *IEph.* 5. 1 he appeals for the same purpose to the present (as opposed to the earthly) unity of Jesus with the Father (cf. *ISmyrn.* 8. 1). Grant easily concluded that, 'such a picture is clearly Johannine (Jn 17, 23, etc.)'.[266]

It is possible, again, that Ignatius shared with the Johannine author a common, oral tradition of the Lord's unity with the Father, both 'ontologically' and in his actions on earth; it is possible that this common tradition was so common he could assume it would be familiar to readers in various churches of Asia Minor. On the other hand, would it not be easier to attribute the wide geographic extension of such ideas to the circulation of a written source or sources in which they are spelt out? We now know that there was circulating in Asia Minor at about this time a written account of the life of Christ, even one attributed to an apostle, in which the unity of Jesus Christ with the Father, in being and in action, was a prominent and distinguishing theme.

IMagn. 8. 2 (*John* 1: 1; 8: 28–9)

'On this account they [i.e. the prophets] were persecuted, being inspired by his grace, to persuade the disobedient that God is one, who manifested himself through Jesus Christ his Son, who is his Word (λόγος) proceeding from silence (ἀπὸ σιγῆς), who in all respects pleased the one who sent him.' Here Jesus Christ, the Son of God, is called the Father's Λόγος, as in John 1: 1, 14 (Rev. 19: 13), and he is said to have pleased the one who sent him in all respects, a seeming allusion to John 8: 29. What has attracted more attention, however, is that Ignatius says this Word has proceeded from silence, that is, from σιγή, and this is irresistibly reminiscent of the gnostic mythology of Valentinus (as described by Irenaeus, *AH* 1. 11. 1), who gave the name of Sige to the aeonic consort of Arrhetos, one of whose offspring was called Logos! J. N. Sanders said that Ignatius, and the author of the Johannine Epistles,

both represent a stage in the development of the type of theology which they share with the Gospel—and indeed with such Gnostics as Valentinus—before it became differentiated into the two opposing forms of the 'orthodox' represented by the author of the Fourth Gospel and the 'heretical' represented by the predecessors of

---

[265] On the comparisons, between Christ, the Father, and the apostles on the one side and the Magnesians, their bishop and their presbyters, see Schoedel, *Ignatius*, 116, and for the possible connections with Acts 1: 1–2, see Hill, 'Ignatius and the Apostolate', 232.

[266] Grant, 'Scripture and Tradition', 329, which see for more.

Valentinus. It at least goes to show that Ignatius did not borrow the term *Logos* from the Fourth Gospel.[267]

But does it indeed show that? It is certain that Ignatius could not have had Valentinus' scheme in mind, and as far as we know these names (particularly Sige) and this 'genealogy' were not used by any gnostics previous to Valentinus; Irenaeus' reports indicate otherwise.[268] More to the point, Sanders' reading, which would place Ignatius midway in a trajectory from the Fourth Gospel to Valentinus, would mean that Ignatius was holding to some sort of hypostatization of Sige, as a mediating deity, which would look quite out of place, to say the least, in a sentence in which he is stressing the oneness of God. Some have instead thought to identify Sige as a name for God the Father, based on *IMagn.* 7. 2, where Christ is said to have proceeded (προελθόντα) from the one Father. But if this is so—and it has to be considered doubtful—we are not very far along on the supposed trajectory. Writers since Sanders have had the Nag Hammadi corpus to aid in the search for more gnostic parallels.[269] But Schoedel has shown that these connections too are dubious. A simpler and more innocent explanation is also more probable. Lightfoot observed, 'σιγὴ and λόγος are correlative terms, λόγος implying a previous σιγή'.[270] Schoedel discusses the gnostic materials and decides for a similar explanation: 'If we look at the passage from the point of view of a tradition in which Christ had become known as the Word (cf. John 1: 1), a desire to complete the image by referring to "silence" as well as to "speech" is comprehensible.'[271] Schoedel points out that 'Ignatius is still very close to the purely metaphorical use of language' and that 'he does not appear to exploit the possible mythological or metaphysical implications of his terminology'.[272]

Most probably, then, the reference to silence is Ignatius' own idea, an extension from an earlier starting point, the conception of Jesus Christ as the Logos of God. Was this conception too original to Ignatius? This is not so likely. Here we do not have to postulate the existence of sources for ideas not known until some forty to fifty years later, for this early identification of

---

[267] Sanders, *Fourth Gospel*, 12.

[268] Besides, in Valentinus' system, Logos is not the child but the grandchild of Sige. Since exactitude is a virtue in the matter of determining dependence, Ignatius ought to have said that Jesus Christ was God's Logos proceeding from Aletheia. But even this would have been wrong, for in the Valentinian pleroma Logos is not at all identified with the person of Jesus Christ (Irenaeus, *AH* 1. 9. 2). And while we are on the subject, another sign of Ignatius' indebtedness to Valentinianism could be reckoned from his reference here to the prophets being inspired by Charis (see 'Ptolemy' in Irenaeus, *AH* 1. 8. 5). What all this goes to show is that anyone who, like Ignatius, has a penchant for using abstract religious terms, particularly terms which also occur in John, is bound to produce some of the names of the Valentinian aeons at some point.

[269] See the list of passages which may show affinities in Schoedel, *Ignatius*, 120.

[270] Lightfoot, *AF* ii/2. 127. See his extended comments.

[271] Schoedel, *Ignatius*, 121.

[272] Ibid. Kieffer, 'Les Premiers Indices', 2237, points to Wisdom 18: 14–15, where the word comes from silence. Cf. Denzley, 'Genesis Traditions', who reveals other possible parallels.

Jesus Christ as the Logos of the Father by Ignatius (cf. also *ISmyrn. praescr.*) has John 1: 1, 14 and Revelation 19: 13, and only them, for known, literary precedents. It is, moreover, possible that, besides his conception of Christ as the pre-existent Logos of the Father, other aspects of Ignatius' understanding of Christ as divine 'in the fullest sense'[273] are indebted to the Fourth Gospel (*IMagn.* 6. 1, Jesus Christ 'was from eternity with the Father (πρὸ αἰώνων παρὰ πατρὶ ἦν)', cf. John 1: 1, 2; 17: 5; *IRom. praescr.*, 'Jesus Christ his only (μόνου) Son', cf. μονογενής in John 1: 18; 3: 16).[274]

One more apparent sign of familiarity with the Fourth Gospel meets us in the concluding phrase of *IMagn.* 8. 2, 'who in all respects pleased the one who sent him' (ὃς κατὰ πάντα εὐηρέστησεν τῷ πέμψαντι αὐτον). This is very close to John 8: 29, 'And he who sent (ὁ πεμψας) me is with me; he has not left me alone, for I always do what is pleasing to him (ἐγὼ τὰ ἀρεστὰ αὐτῷ ποιῶ πάντοτε)'. This too is not a literal 'citation'; it is, again, doubtful that Ignatius had books at hand from which he or a scribe could check any citations for full, literal precision (if indeed he had such an ideal). But the agreements in vocabulary are none the less so close in the words, 'always', 'pleasing', and 'the one who sent him', that one cannot but suspect John 8: 29 as the ultimate source. We recall that in just the previous chapter Ignatius' words seemed to borrow from John 8: 28, 'that I do nothing on my own authority but speak thus as the Father taught me'.[275]

IPhilad. 7. 1 (*John 3: 6, 8; 8: 14*)

'For even if some wished to deceive me according to the flesh, nevertheless the Spirit, being from God, is not deceived. For it "knows whence it comes and whither it goes", and it proves the secret things' (*IPhilad.* 7. 1). On the surface this looks like a clear allusion to Jesus' words in John 3: 8,[276] 'The wind (πνεῦμα) blows where it wills, and you hear the sound of it, but you do not know whence it comes or whither it goes; so it is with every one who is born of the Spirit' (cf. also 8: 14).[277] Not only does Ignatius take a distinctive and memorable phrase known only, so far as we know, from its appearance in the Fourth Gospel, but he also relates it to the Spirit, as does that Gospel. Maurer regarded this as certain evidence that Ignatius was

---

[273] Schoedel, *Ignatius*, 20.

[274] In his Christology 'dominated by the idea of incarnation...Ignatius is most nearly approached in the NT by John, but he has also moved significantly beyond the evangelist', Schoedel, *Ignatius*, 20.

[275] Noticed also by Sanders, *Fourth Gospel*, 12. Between these two references, in *IMagn.* 7. 1, there is another probable Johanninne allusion which I shall not consider separately. Ignatius refers to Jesus Christ 'who came forth from the one Father, and is with the one (εἰς ἕνα ὄντα), and departed (to the one)'. This recalls John 16: 28, 'I came from the Father and have come into the world; again, I am leaving the world and going to the Father' (cf. 13: 3; 14: 12, 28, etc.) and John 1: 18 'the only Son, who is (ὁ ὢν) in the bosom of the Father'. This cluster of Johannine-sounding material is not unlike *IRom.* 7. 2–3 treated above.

[276] Metzger, *Canon*, 47.

[277] Inge, 'Ignatius', *NTAF* 82, 'Both passages may have been floating in his mind'.

acquainted with the Fourth Gospel.[278] Von Loewenich thought this was the clearest sign of dependence in all of Ignatius' letters.[279] Even Schoedel has acknowledged that 'Here we have the strongest possibility in Ignatius of a dependence directly on the Fourth Gospel'. But Schoedel is quick to add, 'Yet in the absence of other positive evidence of such dependence the question must be left open'.[280] If it is merely a lack of 'positive evidence' which prevents us affirming such dependence, we may well think we have already encountered much that looks like 'positive evidence', and may well wonder how much it will take to register on the scale. But it must be said that not all scholars are willing to come even so close as Schoedel on this matter. It has been maintained that this material which seems to be common to Ignatius and John is from a gnostic source,[281] or from an unwritten—and otherwise unknown—saying of Jesus,[282] or from a hypothetically 'traditional theological maxim...perhaps deriving from a liturgical context'.[283] In the abstract, none of these options could be ruled out (depending on one's definition of 'gnostic'). But why any of these postulations of a common dependence upon hypothetical sources is thought to be more likely than Ignatius' dependence upon a known literary source is not clear. If the author of the Fourth Gospel got this from a traditional maxim, whether attributed to Jesus in the tradition or not, he has shown spectacular artistry in the way he has woven the extraneous matter into the complex fabric of his Gospel (or, the Gospel he took over and rewrote, perhaps before it was further rewritten by another redactor). It is a variation on a theme which runs through the Fourth Gospel, the question of 'whence Jesus is' and 'whither he is going', which belongs to the peculiar narrative purpose of the Gospel. When combined with the 'positive evidence' we have seen so far, then, this reference to the spirit from God knowing whence it comes and whither it goes is best seen as reflecting a knowledge of a distinctive expression of a distinctive theme of the Fourth Gospel.

IPhilad. *9. 1–2 (John 10: 7, 9; 14: 6; 8: 30–59; 17: 20–23)*

The priests also are good; but the High Priest is better, who is entrusted with the Holy of Holies, who alone is entrusted with the hidden things of God, he being the door of the Father, through which enter Abraham and Isaac and Jacob, and the

---

[278] Maurer, *Ignatius*, 25–7.

[279] Loewenich, *Das Johannes-Verständnis*, 36. He pronounces Schlier's gnostic parallels unconvincing.

[280] Schoedel, *Ignatius*, 206, again referring to Paulsen, *Studien*, 36–7, where the question rests on the lack of clear, literal citation.

[281] G. P. Wetter, 'Eine gnostische Formel im vierten Evangelium', *ZNW* 18 (1917/18), 49–63.

[282] Von der Goltz, as mentioned by Richardson, *Ignatius*, 74; Sanders, *Fourth Gospel*, 13, 'the most natural explanation of this passage is that both Ignatius and the author of the Fourth Gospel used in their own ways a saying of Jesus about the Spirit which they found in their common tradition'. Why is this the most natural? Evidently because despite the 'certain features in common', there are 'noticeable differences'.

[283] Koester, *ACG* 258.

prophets and the apostles and the Church. All these things are in the unity of God. 2. But the Gospel has something distinctive, the coming of the Saviour, our Lord Jesus Christ, his passion and resurrection. For the beloved prophets announced their message pointing to him, but the Gospel is the completion of incorruption.

Lightfoot thought Ignatius' mention of the door was 'doubtless an allusion to John x. 9',[284] 'I am the door; if any one enters by me, he will be saved'. Besides the common use of θύρα as a figure for Jesus, Inge observed a further correspondence, Ignatius's εἰσέρχονται and σωτῆρος and John's εἰσέλθη and σωθήσεται.[285] Others have also seen a hint of John 14: 6 here, in the restriction of God's trust to Jesus alone, here presented in the role of the High Priest.[286] According to Sanders, 'This does indeed emphasise two doctrines taught in the Fourth Gospel—the pre-existence of the Christ and the impossibility of salvation otherwise than through him, but these doctrines were very commonly held, and cannot be said to have been originated by the Fourth Gospel'.[287] At the very least, then, this is one more indication of the close agreement in Christology, down to the common use of a metaphor for Jesus, between Ignatius and the Fourth Gospel. The doctrine might have been commonly held, but not necessarily expressed with common vocabulary and a common metaphor. The other close parallel is offered by Hermas, Shepherd Sim. 9. 12, where Hermas too uses the metaphor (though substituting πύλη for θύρα), but this he places in his own peculiar allegory which at any rate shows other marks of dependence upon the Fourth Gospel. The mention of Abraham may also recall the announcement of Jesus in John 8: 56, 58,[288] and as for the prophets, Moses 'wrote of me', said Jesus in John 5: 46, and Isaiah 'said this because he saw his glory and spoke of him', said the author of John 12: 41. We know that the passage in which Jesus declares that 'Abraham rejoiced that he was to see my day; he saw it and was glad' (John 8: 56) was later used by orthodox theologians to show the salvation of the OT saints, in the face of Marcionite attacks.[289]

The contrasts in *IPhilad.* 9. 1–2 ('but the high Priest is better'; 'but the Gospel has something distinctive'; 'but the Gospel is the completion of incorruption') indicate that Ignatius here is really following up on the controversy reported in the previous chapter, which took place when he visited Philadelphia. This controversy had something to do with the 'archives' and the gospel. It is an interesting coincidence that Ignatius should show so many parallels to the Fourth Gospel and its distinctive witness to Jesus in a section in which the authority and legitimacy of 'the gospel' is under review.

[284] Lightfoot, *AF* ii/2. 275.
[285] Inge, 'Ignatius', *NTAF* 83.
[286] e.g. Loewenich, *Das Johannes-Verständnis*, 35.
[287] Sanders, *Fourth Gospel*, 13.
[288] Inge, 'Ignatius', *NTAF* 83.
[289] Irenaeus, *AH* 4. 5; 4. 31. 1, and see my discussion above.

ISmyrn. praescr.; 1. 1, 2

...to the church which is in Smyrna in Asia, abundant greeting in a blameless spirit and in the Word of God. I glorify Jesus Christ, the God who has made you so wise. For I perceived that established in immovable faith, as if nailed (καθηλωμένος) on the cross of the Lord Jesus Christ both in flesh and in spirit... fully persuaded as to our Lord that he was

> truly as being from the family of David according to the flesh,
> Son of God according to the will and power of God,
> truly born of a virgin,
> baptized by John, in order that all righteousness might be fulfilled by him,
> 2. truly nailed up (καθηλωμένον) for us in flesh under Pontius Pilate and Herod the Tetrarch,
> from the fruit of which are we, from the divinely blessed passion,
> that he might raise an ensign for ever through the resurrection unto his saints and faithful ones, whether among the Jews or among the Gentiles,
> in the one body of his Church.

Here at the beginning of his letter to the Smyrnaean Christians Ignatius presents a 'collection of semi-credal statements dominated by the anti-docetic "truly"'.[290] Among the elements *ISmyrn.* 1. 1–2 also refers to Christ being nailed up (καθηλωμένος) for us, and in the previous paragraph had commended his former hosts for being established in faith 'as if nailed to the cross of the Lord Jesus Christ'. As observed above in the treatment of Justin, John's is the only Gospel (besides the *Gospel of Peter* 6. 21) to make clear that nails were used in the crucifixion of Jesus (John 20: 25). This fact is indeed known later to *Ps. Barn.* 5. 14, who finds in it a fulfilment of Ps. 119. 120, as Justin also found in it a fulfilment of Ps. 22: 16. And it is something which could have been a commonplace among Christians without knowledge of the Fourth Gospel. But Ignatius' use of it in a credal context, where it occurs amid other details attested in the Gospels, make it likely, though not certain, that this element too had a written authority behind it. It functions here as part of the historical bedrock of the gospel.

There is also a possible sign of his familiarity with the language of John 1: 13 when he refers to Jesus as 'Son of God according to the will and power of God, truly born of a virgin'. This too is far from certain; it may be a reflection on Romans 1: 3–4 and Luke 1: 35 alone.[291] I only cite it here because Ignatius is showing the kind of argument derived from John 1: 13 that we find in Justin and Irenaeus, an argument based not (yet) on a textual variant, perhaps, but based on the language of John 1: 13, written about believers but applied by Christian exegetes to Christ.

All of this, I would maintain, indicates that Ignatius was quite familiar with the Fourth Gospel, despite the lack of any full or exact quotations.

[290] Schoedel, *Ignatius*, 220.
[291] Pryor, 'Text of John 1: 13', 307–8.

Again I mention the probability that Ignatius, the prisoner in transition, did not write his letters with any of his books before him. And yet we have seen a number of passages which correspond to thoughts and distinctive phrases unique, up to this point, to the Fourth Gospel, even down to the preservation of some of the same precise vocabulary. One ought to agree not only with the later Sanders, 'There are so many of these passages in Ignatius that it seems reasonable to suppose that he knew the FG',[292] but also with Kieffer, that 'We have therefore in Ignatius a supplementary proof of the fact that the Gospel of John was known in Asia Minor before the gnostics got hold of it', and this by *c.*110.[293] And yet the level of familiarity hardly seems explicable from recent contact he might have had with this Gospel in Asia Minor; it suggests that Ignatius may have known this Gospel in Syria as well. This would mean that the Johannine Gospel was familiar to Christian communities in these two parts of the empire at the time of Ignatius' journey in *c.*107–10.

IGNATIUS AND THE REST OF THE JOHANNINE LITERATURE

As to Ignatius' assertion about the agreement of the Ephesian church with the apostles in *IEph.* 11. 2, it is interesting to note that the dictated letter from Christ to the Ephesians in Revelation specifically tells the Ephesians, 'I know...how you cannot bear evil men but have tested those who call themselves apostles but are not, and found them to be false' (2: 2; cf. 2 John 4). And his stress on the Ephesian church's faithfulness in the face of heresy and heretics had been stressed in 6. 2, 'Indeed Onesimus himself highly praises your good order in God, that all live according to truth, and that no heresy dwells among you. On the contrary, you do not even listen to anyone unless he speaks concerning Jesus Christ in truth'; and then again in 9. 1, 'But I have learned that some from elsewhere have passed through, who have evil teaching, whom you did not allow to sow among you, having stopped your ears (βύσαντες τὰ ὦτα) so that you might not receive what they sow'. This reference in 9. 1 may be based on something Onesimus had told them. But it too, along with 6. 2, seems to echo Revelation 2: 2, and both are curiously close to statements made in 2 John (arguably written to the Ephesian church), 'I rejoiced greatly to find some of your children following the truth' (v. 4); 'If any one comes to you and does not bring this doctrine (ταύτην τὴν διδαχήν), do not receive him into the house or give him any greeting' (v. 10). It is very likely that these Johannine references are among the sources of Ignatius' information which he mentions in *IEph.* 9. 1.

[292] Sanders, *St John*, 33.
[293] Kieffer, 'Les Premiers Indices', 2238.

It is also very interesting that Ignatius' approach to heresy as he describes
it here conforms to the practice which Irenaeus credits to Polycarp, as we
have observed it above, even to the extent of paralleling Polycarp's custom
of stopping his ears against the intrusion of heresy: 'he would have cried
out, and shut his ears (ἐμφράξας τὰ ὦτα), and said according to his
custom, "O good God, to what time hast thou preserved me that I should
endure this?" He would have fled even from the place in which he was
seated or standing when he heard such words' (*HE* 5. 20. 7)! Irenaeus
speaks of this stopping of one's ears and fleeing as far off as possible elsewhere as 'that ancient tradition of the apostles' (*AH* 3. 4. 2) and relates one
famous instance of John's putting it into practice (3. 3. 4). Elsewhere he
founds the policy on John's written instructions in 2 John 10 (1. 16. 3).
That Ignatius would congratulate the Ephesians for their avoidance of
heresy and write of stopping their ears against it in a letter written from
Smyrna (he had never visited Ephesus) points to the Johannine–Polycarpan
nexus. Once again, this relates closely to the use made of the Johannine
traditions in Polycarp's letter to the Philippians, and attested in Irenaeus'
traditions about John through Polycarp.

We have seen possible traces of 2 John and of Revelation, though there
may be no instance of the use of 1 John in the letters of Ignatius.[294] In none
of these cases can we be as definite as we can about the Gospel. What we
have is certainly consistent with the supposition that he knew 2 John and
the Apocalypse, but does not require it.

Conclusion

Ignatius' knowledge of John can be taken as proved. Though Ignatius does
not provide us with any conclusive evidence of the existence of a Johannine
corpus at this time, we must also remember that Ignatius' letters are fragments of what he could have revealed to us. Because of the contemporaneous writing of Polycarp's letter to the Philippians, and because Polycarp
apparently sent along to the Philippians copies of at least some of Ignatius'
letters, it is not out of order to consider them together for a moment. (This
is, after all, how the Philippians received them.) Naturally, we cannot
assume that the two Christian leaders agreed on everything, or that they
shared an acquaintance with all the same literature. But we may say that in
a certain way Ignatius confirms and completes the witness of Polycarp to
the Fourth Gospel and that Polycarp confirms and completes the witness of
Ignatius to the Johannine Epistles, at least to 1 and possibly 2 John. We can

---

[294] S. E. Johnson, 'Parallels between the Letters of Ignatius and the Johannine Epistles', in E. W.
Conrad and E. G. Newing (eds.), *Perspectives on Language and Text: Essays and Poems in Honor of Francis I.
Andersen's Sixtieth Birthday July 28, 1985* (Winona Lake, Ind., 1987), 327–38, agues that the Johannine
Epistles are later than Ignatius, and more sectarian.

accept their common witness to the existence and in some sense to the authority of these works in the second and perhaps in the first decade of the second century.

The First Users of the Fourth Gospel

Who indeed used and claimed the authority of the Fourth Gospel first? It was neither the Valentinians, nor the Ophites, nor the Basilideans, nor the unnamed gnostic myth-makers behind *AH* 1. 29. The first good documentary evidence of the knowledge of the Gospel of John[295] is in fact none other than 1 John (possibly also 2 John, and 3 John).[296] Of course these all, or at least the Gospel and First Epistle, may have come from the same author. If common authorship is denied, as it has often been, particularly since the publication of an article by C. H. Dodd in 1937, it would seem that we should have to take seriously this great advocate of the diversity of authorship when he says, 'I conceive the First Epistle of John, then, to have been written by an author who was quite possibly a disciple of the Fourth Evangelist, and certainly a diligent student of his work. He has soaked himself in the Gospel, assimilating its ideas and forming his style upon its model.'[297]

Brown believed that the secessionists of 1 John 2: 19; 4: 1 also claimed the Fourth Gospel as their own and that they too should therefore be regarded as partisans of the Fourth Gospel, who simply interpreted it differently from the party represented by the author of 1 John.[298] But such a theory, despite its popularity, is not only conjectural, being supported by no documentary evidence, there now is much to be said against it. Brown cannot identify this group, more than to say that they may have started off on the road that led to Cerinthus and some of the later heretical teachers. But Cerinthus' antagonism to Johannine Christianity is already evident from the story of John and Cerinthus at the bath-house. And not only have we found that the usual idea that the Fourth Gospel was popular first

---

[295] I leave out of account here the hypothetical last redactor of the Fourth Gospel who allegedly tacked on ch. 21 at a very early stage, and who, according to H.-M. Schenke, 'The Function and Background of the Beloved Disciple in the Gospel of John', in C. W. Hedrick and R. Hodgson, jun. (eds.), *Nag Hammadi, Gnosticism, and Early Christianity* (Peabody, Mass., 1986), 111–25, at 116, 'blatantly and recklessly identified the Beloved Disciple as the author of the Gospel'. If the existence of such a redactor could be thought probable, which in my view it cannot, we would have to reckon him/her to be the first user we know of and to attribute to him/her the notion of the apostolic authorship of the first twenty chapters of the Fourth Gospel.

[296] Most still hold that these were written after the Fourth Gospel, but even if they are thought to have preceded its publication, it can hardly be argued that they were unfamiliar with the Johannine Gospel in some form. They might thus still be used as the first attestation of that Gospel, if not in written, in oral form.

[297] C. H. Dodd, 'The First Epistle of John and the Fourth Gospel', *BJRL* 21 (1937), 129–56, at 156.

[298] Brown, *Community*, 24, 149–50.

among fringe or heterodox groups and was avoided by the orthodox or Great Church is not true. We have also found a substantial tradition among heterodox documents which used the Fourth Gospel of a polemical relationship with that Gospel. This includes the *Ap. Jas.*, the opposition in *Ep. Apost.*, and the group mentioned by Irenaeus in *AH* 3. 11. 9, all of whom seem to have affinities with the Cerinthian legacy. This is also consonant with Irenaeus' contention that John wrote to dispel the ideas of Cerinthus. John was indeed known throughout this period by gnostics and by other groups which competed with the mainstream Church, but there is abundantly more evidence that it was also known, and used as a positive authority, by the orthodox, beginning with 1, 2, and 3 John.

Summary and Conclusions

One of the three major planks of the OJP has been the silence of the early writers of the Church with regard to the Fourth Gospel. While we cannot say that this Gospel was known to all of the Apostolic Fathers and early writers of the mainstream Church, we are able to confirm a surprisingly strong presence among them, and thus to affirm that there is no 'silence' which needs to be accounted for. On the contrary, instead of a silence one might better speak of a din, a relative tumult, an increasing uproar. John's comparatively late origin means that some early texts, *1 Clement* and *Didache*[299] in particular, probably originated before the publication or wide distribution of the Fourth Gospel. But beginning perhaps as early as the first decade of the second century with the letters of Ignatius we have excellent evidence that the Syrian bishop was quite familiar with the Fourth Gospel when he wrote to churches in Asia Minor on his way to Rome. As we have seen, the number and specificity of his parallels with unique Johannine material, despite the lack of direct citation, cannot realistically be assigned to common oral tradition from a variety of unknown quarters and seems to require a literary knowledge. Literal citation cannot be considered the only sign of literary knowledge, and is itself not a sure sign of scriptural 'reception'. There are traces of the Gospel in the letter of the young Polycarp to the Philippian church, traces which must be seen as reinforced by the more evident use of the Gospel in the contemporary Ignatian correspondence.

Very close in time to the writing of these two bishops we have the oral tradition of certain Asian elders as recorded by Papias. Not only do these elders demonstrate the use of this Gospel and its words of Jesus, but one of them, with near certainty the enigmatic Elder John himself, passes on information about the circumstances of composition of the four Gospels, includ-

---

[299] For a comparison with John, see Braun, *Jean le Théologien*, 251–62.

ing the Gospel according to John. In this tradition, preserved at points almost word for word by Eusebius, but also presupposed by a number of second-and third-century authors, the Gospel is explicitly attributed to John, one of the personal disciples of Jesus who is coupled with Matthew. This source provides justification for a four-Gospel canon and possibly a four-Gospel codex. Still in the 120s we have in Syriac and partly in Greek the *Apology* of the Christian teacher Aristides in Athens, who also, like Papias' elder, knows a plurality of authoritative Christian Gospels and shows strong evidence that one of these was the Gospel according to John. At about this time, a Christian scribe added to a copy of the Gospel of Mark an ending he thought suitable, which incorporated elements from Matthew, Luke, and John.

Perhaps around 130 or so, but possibly as early as 120 or before, we have the attestation of Papias himself, who gave his own comments or preserved earlier ones on portions of at least the Fourth Gospel and the book of Revelation, and used 1 John as well. At least parts of the Shepherd by Hermas, written some time in this period and at any rate no later than the 140s, give clear evidence that the author, in Rome, knew the Fourth Gospel. The *Epistula Apostolorum* might be as early as the second decade of the second century, but whether it is this early or from the 140s, it shows a high degree of orthodox admiration in Asia Minor towards the Fourth Gospel and its author, regarded as John the son of Zebedee. The address to Diognetus is likely also no later than 150, and it too shows the clear influence of the Fourth Gospel and the First Letter, and appears to presuppose that the author of these works had been a personal disciple of Jesus.

Nor is it to be forgotten that we have only a fraction of the Christian literature which was produced in this period. We know, then, that there were no fewer instances of the use of the Fourth Gospel by the orthodox than which now exist in the record; but there may well have been more. All of this is before the first use of the Fourth Gospel by a known, heterodox teacher can be verified. The consensus theory of orthodox Johannophobia not only claims a shortage of orthodox use of the Fourth Gospel in the first half or even three-quarters of the second century but also prescribes at least one motive for it, and that motive is conscious avoidance based on the conviction either that the Fourth Gospel was itself heterodox, dangerous, or 'on the fringes' in significant ways, or that it was at least the gnostics' 'special gospel' or was 'much the preserve of heretics'. But not only have we been unable to find any reliable evidence for the use of the Fourth Gospel by the Basilideans, Saturnilians, Carpocratians, and various other sects before about the middle of the second century, what evidence we have about the Cerinthians and others, including some of the early Valentinians, is that they too used the Fourth Gospel but in an essentially predatory and adversarial way. This attitude is at any rate demonstrable in several of the earliest, second-century gnostic and Valentinian/'Sethian' texts, such as the *Trimorphic Protennoia, Second Apocalypse of James, Apocryphon of James, Acts of John, Gospel of Truth,* and *Gospel of Thomas.*

III

The 'Johannine Corpus' in the Second Century

8

The Evidence for a Johannine Corpus

It would present a very incomplete picture of the setting for ecclesiastical use of the Gospel according to John in the second century if I spoke only of it separately, as independent from its most prominent literary associations. It had from very early on, of course, close associations with other 'gospel' literature, particularly with the Gospels according to Matthew, Mark, and Luke. But for at least a great number of authors, surely representing the popular mind, it was viewed not only as a Gospel among other Gospels but also as a Gospel among other works attributed to John the apostle. Many writers who knew one member of what we now call the Johannine corpus knew two or more of them, and without exception at least up until the beginning of the third century, all who give them an attribution attribute them to the same person. This also helps explain and justify the observation that the authority imputed to any one member of the corpus seems to have been imputed to each. There is indeed sufficient reason to speak of ecclesiastical awareness of a Johannine literary corpus from early in the second century. At least with Papias himself, between 120 and 135, we see clear knowledge of the Gospel, the First Epistle, and the Revelation of John, and most probably the elder he cites made some connection between the Gospel and the First Epistle. From that point on we see intermittent signs of a recognition and reception not just of the Gospel, but of the Apocalypse and 1 John, and in a few authors 2 John and, in Irenaeus and the *MF*, 3 John. Here I want to explore further this awareness of a Johannine literary corpus, and even the possibility of there being an edition of this corpus available in the second century, before exploring the implications for the study of the history of the NT canon.

Evidence from Common Use

I begin with a simple review of the probable use of the members of the Johannine corpus on the part of the authors studied. The list in Table 1 cannot of course be considered definitive; there are some whose knowledge of one or more of these books is at least not certain, and, on the other hand, it is also true that a given author may know and receive more books than are now visible in their sometimes quite fragmentary works which remain. I have included in Table 1 those attestations which have some

Table 1.   *Use of the Johannine writings in the second century*

	Gospel	Apocalypse	1 John	2 John	3 John
Ignatius	x				
Polycarp	x		x	x	
Long ending of Mark	x				
Papias' Elders	x	x	x		
Aristides	x				
Papias	x	x	x		
Odes of Sol.	x				
Hermas	x	?	?		
Ep. Apost.	x	x	x		
Ad Diognetum	x		x		
Justin	x	x			
Mart. C, P, A	x				
Celsus	x				
Gosp. Peter	x				
P. Egerton	x				
Tatian	x				
Cl. Apollinarius	x				
Melito	x	x			
Ap. Jn.	x				
Tr. Protennoia	x				
2 Apoc. Jas.	x				
Ap. Jas.	x		x		
Gosp. Truth	x	x	x		
Acts of John	x	?			
Gosp. Thomas	x				
Basilideans	x				
Ptolemy	x				
Heracleon	x				
Theodotus	x				
Theophilus	x	x			
Athenagoras	x				
Ep. of Vienne and Lyons	x	x	x		
Hegesippus	x	x			
Sib. Or. 1, 8	x	x			
Irenaeus	x	x	x	x	x
Polycrates	x				
Clement Al.	x	x	x	x	
Murat. Fragm.	x	x	x	x	x
Asian source	x				
Apollonius	x		x		
Tertullian	x	x	x		
Pass. Perpetua and Felicitas	x	x			
Montanists	x	x			

literary basis (not just a probability based on circumstantial evidence) and which I consider to be at least probable.

This table, like the rest of this study above, is limited to those authors who appear to have known the Fourth Gospel. There are, to be sure, some authors who seem to know the Apocalypse who show no firm signs of knowledge of the Gospel. These would include *5 Ezra*[1] and probably the *Ascension of Isaiah*.[2] The work known as the *Apocalypse of Peter* has associations with both the Gospel and the Apocalypse which are not certain but, in the case at least of the latter, probable.[3] There are many in the table who show a knowledge or reception of another member of the Johannine corpus outside of the Fourth Gospel. This is the case with at least twenty-three of the forty-four. The totals are markedly different if we separate out the eleven in the table known as heterodox, only two of which seem to know another member of the Johannine corpus besides the Gospel. Twenty-one of the remaining thirty-three orthodox sources show knowledge of at least two members, thirteen of them know at least three. But it must be kept in mind that often the data are quite fragmentary and haphazardly preserved. The real proportion of orthodox and heterodox writers who knew multiple members of the Johannine corpus is no doubt even higher for both groups. The point is that we can see a tendency to use not just the Fourth Gospel but other members of the Johannine corpus throughout the second century.

Evidence from Intertextual Use

The evidence for the reception of a Johannine corpus goes beyond the mere tendency for two or more members of the corpus to show up in the writings of the second century. Whenever we see an attribution of common author-ship regarding two or more works to the apostle John, there is of course evidence of an awareness of a Johannine literary corpus. This would include at least, in all probability both Papias and the elder he quotes, implicitly the *Ep. Apost.*, explicitly Justin, Hegesippus, Irenaeus, Clement, the *MF*, Tertul-lian. But the perception of the unity between the members of the Johannine corpus is seen most conspicuously in the intertextual exegesis of a passage in one Johannine work by means of another passage in another Johannine work, sometimes explicitly referring to the common author. Here I note a few examples.

---

[1] Probably of Roman provenance from around the mid-second century; see Hill, *Regnum Cae-lorum*[2], 120–23.

[2] Probably from the early decades of the second century. J. Knight, *Disciples of the Beloved One: The Christology, Social Setting and Theological Context of the Ascension of Isaiah*, JSP Supplement Series 18 (Sheffield, 1996), believes the Fourth Gospel was known to the author of the Ascension of Isaiah (295–96), but is less sure about Revelation. I tend to see it as the other way around; see Hill, *Regnum Caelorum*[2] (Grand Rapids, Mich., 2001), 109–16.

[3] See Hill, *Regnum Caelorum*, 116–20.

The practice is seen several times in Irenaeus. In *AH* 3. 16. 5 Irenaeus uses
1 John 2: 18 to expand upon John 20: 31, linking them by reference to
John as their common author. In a short space in 3. 16. 8 he links together
2 John 7–8; 1 John 4: 1–2; John 1: 14; and 1 John 5: 1 on the subject of the
unity of the person Jesus Christ. As observed above, the unity of the Johannine works in Irenaeus' mind is strikingly demonstrated in 4. 20. 11, where
he exegetes John's experience in the Apocalypse by referring to his previous
experience recorded in the Gospel. Referring to John's vision of the risen
Jesus Christ in Revelation 1: 12–17, Irenaeus says,

> But when John could not endure the sight (for he says, 'I fell at his feet as dead;'
> that what was written might come to pass: 'No man sees God, and shall live' [Exod.
> 33: 20]), and the Word reviving him, and reminding him that it was He upon
> whose bosom he had leaned at supper, when he put the question as to who should
> betray Him, declared: 'I am the first and the last, and He who liveth, and was dead,
> and behold I am alive for evermore, and have the keys of death and of hell' [Rev.
> 1: 18].

CLEMENT OF ALEXANDRIA

In exegetical notes which probably were published in his *Hypotyposeis*, Clement wrote, 'Following the Gospel according to John, and in accordance with
it, this Epistle [i.e. the First Epistle] also contains the spiritual principle' (*Fr.
Cass.* 3). To Clement the common authorship was supported by the style
and the 'spiritual principle' both works shared. This would anticipate the
comments of Dionysius of Alexandria, who on the basis of style concluded
that the Gospel and all three Epistles had been written by the apostle,
though he also concluded that Revelation should be assigned to some other
John (*HE* 7. 25). Clement's words, 'Following the Gospel according to John'
indicate his view of the chronology of these Johannine writings; they could
also be indirect evidence for a published edition in which 1 John followed
the Gospel. But I shall say more on this below.

THE *MURATORIAN FRAGMENT*

Also observed above is the interesting way in which the author of the *MF*
uses the first verses of 1 John to 'ratify' not only the Fourth Gospel, but its
'singular' method.

> The fourth [book] of the Gospels is that of John [one] of the disciples...And so,
> although different beginnings might be taught in the separate books of the Gospels,
> nevertheless it makes no difference to the faith of believers, since all things in all [of
> them] are declared by the one sovereign Spirit...What marvel, then, if John so
> constantly brings forward particular [matters] also in his Epistles, saying of himself:

'What we have seen with our eyes and have heard with [our] ears and our hands have handled, these things we have written to you.' For thus he declares that he was not only an eyewitness and hearer, but also a writer of all the wonderful things of the Lord in order.

He perceives John in the first verses of 1 John to be talking not about the letter he was writing at the time, but about what he had already 'written' in the Gospel! The practice of 'ratifying' the four Gospels from some other writing now in the New Testament, we have seen, was already being done by Papias' elder at a time nearly contemporary with the publication of the Gospel itself. This accentuates the perceived appropriateness of reading the Fourth Gospel and the Epistles (at least 1 John) together in the second-century Church, and of recognizing in them a common authority.

The Manuscript Evidence

For an understanding of the rise of the Johannine corpus there is also something to be gained by a discussion of the original or early forms under which the Johannine writings were copied and distributed. The coherence of the second-century evidence has prompted the question whether this literary corpus ever existed as a physical entity. Presumably the Apocalypse was originally sent out to the seven Asian churches addressed in chapters 2–3, and was sent out as an independent writing. So too for 2 and 3 John. Whether or not copies were made early for other churches or individuals, the Gaius of 3 John and the 'Elect Lady' of 2 John probably received these letters alone, unattached to other writings. It may or may not have been the same for the Gospel and for 1 John; some in fact have thought that the latter was a sort of 'cover letter' for the former.

It has been recently argued that the codex form—which as far as our physical evidence provides was the nearly exclusive form of production in the second century for the texts which make up our New Testament—was first adopted for Christian writings to be used in accommodating the four Gospels.[4] We have seen that the place of John alongside the Synoptics in the consciousness of at least some Asian churches is datable at least from the time of Papias' presbyterial source in the first or second decade of the second century. This sense of Gospel unity may already imply a codicological expression, or at least that such an edition was 'in the works', for we do not yet have proof that codices existed in the elder's day which could accommodate this much material. But it is also quite possible that a four-Gospel codex was not the first multiple-work codex in use among Christians.

---

[4] T. C. Skeat, 'Irenaeus and the Four-Gospel Canon', *NovT* 34 (1992), 194–9; idem, 'The Oldest Manuscript of the Four Gospels?', *NTS* 43 (1997), 31; J. K. Elliott, 'Manuscripts, the Codex and the Canon', *JSNT* 63 (1996), 105–23, at 107.

It may be that single-codex collections of the three Synoptic Gospels[5] or of the Pauline writings,[6] or both, might have already existed by the time the Fourth Gospel was circulated. It is quite imaginable under these circumstances that all the Johannine works (or several of them) might have been gathered into a codex and published under one cover to send to churches, more or less concurrently with the practice of publishing the Fourth Gospel by itself or bound with the other three. We do not need to speculate further about which edition might have been first. It is conceivable that all three forms of publication of the Johannine Gospel (alone, with other Gospels, with other Johannine works) coexisted for a time in the second century, before collections of the four Gospels together became standard.

There is no sufficient codicological proof for an early publication of the Johannine corpus as a unit, though at least two recovered manuscripts, and one or more literary references, support that possibility. The fifth-century (or late fourth-century) bilingual Codex Bezae is perhaps the single most-studied NT manuscript. But despite the deserved attention which has been paid to its many distinctive readings, relatively little has been written about its original form as a codex. In its present state Bezae contains the four Gospels, then several pages are missing, after which is preserved only the Latin version of 3 John 11–15 (the Greek would have been on the left-hand, facing page, which is missing), followed by the book of Acts. What preceded 3 John in the original? The gap is not large enough to have accommodated the Pauline corpus or the rest of the Catholic Epistles.[7] Nearly a century ago John Chapman made a good case that the missing pages held the Apocalypse and 1–2 John,[8] a case which remains, in the words of D. C. Parker, 'the most scientifically argued and acceptable that we have'.[9] The original contents of Bezae on Chapman's reckoning would have been: Matthew, John, Luke, Mark, Revelation, 1–3 John, Acts. This would be an instance of all the Johannine works occurring together, though with the addition of the three Gospels and Acts. Such an arrangement

---

[5] This might help us to understand why Justin, writing *c*.150, seems to quote the three Gospels in very close conjunction, often conflating elements from more than one of them, while his allusions to the Fourth Gospel tend to be separated from these. Was he using a harmony of the Synoptic Gospels based on an earlier edition of these Gospels in codex form, a form in which they perhaps existed already prior to the publication of John?

[6] H. Y. Gamble, 'The Pauline Corpus and the Early Christian Book', in William S. Babcock (ed.), *Paul and the Legacies of Paul* (Dallas, 1990), 265–80, argues that the codex was first adopted to accommodate an edn. of the *corpus Paulinum*, 'near the beginning of the second century at the latest' (see pp. 277–8). He rightly mentions 2 Pet. 3. 15–16, *1 Clement*, Ignatius, and Polycarp as evidence. His statement that at this time 'there simply were no other Christian texts for which there existed either the materials or the motives for collection and for presentation as a corpus' (277), however, overlooks the possibility of the three Gospels or even Luke–Acts.

[7] The missing material ended with 3 John. From at least the 3rd cent on, the seven-letter Catholic Epistle collection ended with Jude. Also, the usual order by this time was Acts, Catholic Epistles.

[8] J. Chapman, 'The Original Contents of Codex Bezae', *The Expositor*, 6th ser. 12 (1905), 46–53.

[9] D. C. Parker, *Codex Bezae: An Early Christian Manuscript and its Text* (Cambridge, 1992), 9.

would be unique,[10] as far as we know, but then Bezae itself is unique in so many ways. Certainly by the time Bezae was produced in the late fourth or the fifth century the whole New Testament (even the whole Bible) was being accommodated in multiple-quire codices. Is it not possible that the choice of these books was partly dictated by the use by the scribe of Bezae (or more likely, by one of his predecessors) of an exemplar which contained all the Johannine literature together, to which was added the remaining Gospels and Acts? Certain aspects of the recension of John in Bezae seem to support its distinctive character as compared with the recensions of the other Gospels in the same codex.[11] I note that the order of appearance here would be Gospel, Apocalypse, 1, 2, 3 John.

Second, there is the early uncial manuscript 0232 (P. Antinoopolis 12), probably from the late third century or early fourth century, containing 2 John 1–9 on both sides of a single codex leaf.[12] The top of the page has numbers, 164 and 165, in a second hand. Roberts says that 160 previous pages, on the one hand, would not be filled by the other catholic epistles, even with the addition of the pastorals, and on the other hand that 160 pages are inadequate for the Pauline corpus. But 'If we were to assume that the codex held a corpus of the Johannine writings, with the Gospel, Revelation, and I John all preceding II John, the number of pages required would be only a little short of 160, and the surplus pages might have been accounted for by titles, etc.'[13] It is possible, of course, that 2 John could have been inserted in a disparate collection made for individual, personal use (as 1 and 2 Peter and Jude were placed in the idiosyncratic $\mathfrak{P}^{72}$). But the well-trained hand of the writing and the use of parchment tend to suggest a community book rather than one produced for personal use. Thus this does

---

[10] Metzger, *Canon*, 295–6. See Kurt Aland and Barbara Aland, *The Text of the New Testament: An Introduction to the Critical Editions and to the Theory and Practice of Modern Textual Criticism*, 2nd edn., tr. E. R. Rhodes (Grand Rapids, Mich., 1981), 78–9, for a list of the various combinations in extant MSS.

[11] It is well known that Bezae's greatest 'divergences' from the textual tradition are found in Luke and Acts, F. Kenyon, *The Text of the Greek Bible: A Student's Handbook* (London, 1953 repr. of 1949 orig.), 90. B. Weiss, *Textkritik*, 225 (as cited by M. W. Holmes, 'Codex Bezae as a Recension of the Gospels', in D. C. Parker and C.-B. Amphoux, *Codex Bezae: Studies from the Lunel Colloquium June 1994* (Leiden, 1996), 123–60, at 124 n. 2), 'identified some 4300 *Sonderlesarten* in D: while the largest number are found in Luke (ca. 1700), Mark—about 500 verses shorter—has some 1150; Matthew has 775 and John only 655'. Holmes points to other studies which have reinforced the differing characters of the recensions of the Gospels in Bezae: he credits J. Delobel with discovering that the degree of harmonization is, in Holmes's words, 'scanty in Matthew, more extensive in Mark, very strong in Luke, and almost absent in John' ('Colex Bezae', 124); he cites J. D. Yoder, 'The Language of the Greek Variants of Codex Bezae', *NovT* 3 (1959), 241–8, at 246, to the effect that Matthew and John 'differ sharply' from the other texts in Bezae in terms of the style of expressions in the variants.

[12] Originally dated by Roberts to the middle of the 3rd cent., C. H. Roberts, J. W. B. Barns, and H. Zilliacus, *The Antinoopolis Papyri* (London, 1950–67), i. 24–6. J. Van Haelst, *Catalogue des papyrus lifferaries juifs et chrétiens* (Paris, 1976), 195 concurred with this, though Aland later said the 5th or 6th cent. Comfort and Barrett, *CT* 648, would place it *c.*300.

[13] Roberts, *AP* i. 24–5; van Haelst, *Catalogue*, 557 no. 555; cf. Comfort and Barrett, *CT* 648.

Figure 11. 0232 (P. Antinoopolis 12). Parchment MS containing 2 John 1–9. C. H. Roberts dated it to the third century and suggested it is from a codex of the Johannine writings. Courtesy of the Egypt Exploration Society.

create a prima-facie likelihood that 0232 was indeed once part of an edition of the Johannine corpus. And I note that, like the hypothetical reconstruction of Codex Bezae, this reconstruction would have both the Gospel and the Apocalypse before the Epistles.

Thus the codicological evidence does not prove but does suggest the existence of separate codices of the Johannine corpus. I mention again Clement of Alexandria's words, 'Following the Gospel according to John, and in accordance with it, this Epistle [i.e. the First Epistle] also contains the spiritual principle' (*Fr. Cass.* 3), which could indicate that the First Epistle 'followed' the Gospel in a codex used by him. But there is literary evidence of at least one Johannine codex used in the third century which provides a more definite witness. The author of the treatise *Contra Noetum* 15, usually said to be Hippolytus, in the early third century[14] not only assumes that the same John wrote the Gospel and the Apocalypse, he offhandedly indicates that he possesses these two documents in the same codex: 'For while thus presenting this Word [i.e. in John 1] that was from

---

[14] Caroline P. Bammel, 'The State of Play with regard to Hippolytus and the *Contra Noetum*', *Heythrop Journal*, 31 (1990), 195–211, at 197, says that 'the *Contra Noetum* has generally been thought to be earlier than the *Elenchos* (the heresy attacked is less developed than that ascribed by Hippolytus himself to Callistus and by Tertullian to Praxeas)', though she notes that 'Nautin dated it later'. The *Elenchos*, or *Refutation of All Heresies*, is probably from sometime not too long after the episcopacy of Callistus, which ended in 222.

the beginning, and has now been sent forth, he said below (ὑποβάς) in the Apocalypse, "And I saw heaven opened, and behold a white horse; and He that sat upon him (was) Faithful and True... and His name is called the Word of God"'. Ὑποβαίνω does not mean 'later' in time but refers to a later section in the same book![15] That this is the meaning of the term is confirmed by the author's earlier use of it in chapter 12,[16] as well as by contemporary examples.[17] This author then was using a codex which contained both the Fourth Gospel and the Apocalypse, in that order. Not only this, but he seems to assume that his readers would understand a reference to John the Evangelist writing in the Apocalypse 'below'. Perhaps the codex used by this author and assumed for his readers contained all the Johannine corpus, as Roberts conjectures was the case for 0232 (P. Antinoopolis 12). Whether other Johannine books, or any other books for that matter, were also contained in the codex is an open question, but as far as we know, a codex containing the Fourth Gospel and the Apocalypse would already have been a large one by current standards of book-making and it is certain that it could not have contained a great deal more material, certainly not the author's entire New Testament.

Unfortunately, we know little for certain about the author of the *Contra Noetum*, as is reflected in the current dispute among scholars about the Hippolytan corpus. Is he the same man who wrote the *Commentary on Daniel* and the treatise *On Christ and Antichrist*, who at one point apostrophizes to John the Seer, 'Tell me, blessed John, apostle and disciple of the Lord,[18] what didst thou see and hear concerning Babylon? Arise, and speak; for it sent thee also into banishment' (*Antichr.* 36)?[19] Or is he the author of the *Refutation of All Heresies*, writing in Rome, who staunchly opposed several groups who misused John's Gospel to support their heresies?[20] Is he the author of the work *Matters concerning the Gospel and Apocalypse according to John*

---

[15] LSJ, citing Strabo (1st cent. BC/1st cent. AD), *Geographus*, Parthenius (1st cent. BC), and Hermogenes (2nd cent.) *Inv.* 'a little below (in the book)'.

[16] In this case, referring to John 1: 10–11 after John 1: 1–3.

[17] This usage also checks out in Hippolytus' near contemporary in Alexandria, Clement, *Protr.* 4. 44 (LCL; 4. 50. 3 *TLG*) where he cites *Sib. Or.* 5. 483–4 then cites as 'lower down' 5. 486–7; 7. 63 Loeb; 7. 74. 5 *TLG*, citing Orpheus, *Frag.* 5; 8. 68 Loeb, 8. 79. 4 *TLG* on Isa. 45. 19–20 then as 'lower down' verses 21–3; *Paed.* 2. 1. 10 on Rom. 14: 3, then verse 6; presumably also in *Strom.* 2. 4. 18 on Plato, though no references are given; *Strom.* 4. 12. 82 from Basilides' 23rd book of the *Exegetics*, and from the same in 4. 12. 83; *Strom.* 5. 1. 2 citing Rom. 1: 11–12 then v. 17; *Strom.* 5. 1. 11 citing Timon of Phlius (no reference), 'Then a little below he adds'; *Strom.* 5. 10. 63 citing *Barnabas* 6. 5 then 8–10; *Strom.* 5. 10. 66 citing 1 Cor. 2: 6–7 then 3: 1–3; *Strom.* 5. 14. 96 citing Plato in the *Lysis*?; [*Strom.* 6.16. 148 the noun ὑπόβασις used, καθ' ὑπόβασιν]; *Strom.* 6. 18. 165 citing Paul in 2 Cor. 10: 15–16, then in 2 Cor. 11: 6.

[18] 'Apostle and disciple of the Lord' is the traditional designation of the author of the Fourth Gospel.

[19] V. Loi, 'L'identità letteraria di Ippolito di Roma', 86; M. Simonetti, 'A modo di conclusione: una ipotesi di lavoro', 151–6; both from Loi *et al.* (eds.), *Recherche su Ippolito*, Studia Ephemeridis 'Augustinianum', 13 (Rome, 1977).

[20] J. Frickel, *Das Dunkel um Hippolyt von Rom. Ein Lösungsversuch: Die Schriften Elenchos und Contra Noetum*, Grazer Theologische Studien, 13 (Graz, 1988).

mentioned on the famous statue?[21] Are two or more of these the same?[22] Or is the author of the *Contra Noetum* identical with none of these?[23] Some have proposed that the author of the *Contra Noetum* was from Asia Minor (Noetus himself was from Smyrna).[24] Did this 'Hippolytus' then have had access to an old, Asian form of the text of these Johannine works? In any case, we can be confident that this author, probably in the early or middle third century, had a codex of the Gospel of John which also contained the Apocalypse of John, and he ascribed both works to the same John.[25]

The existence of (at least) two early forms of binding and distribution of the Fourth Gospel, one together with the three other Gospels and one with other Johannine works, perhaps an entire Johannine corpus, would have a parallel, and perhaps a precedent, in Christian publication. The Gospel according to Luke and its sequel, the Acts of the Apostles, could have been bound together in the same volume, yet from a very early time the two volumes of Luke's work were separated, and volume one was bound instead with other Gospels. This was an editorial decision motivated by a literary concern, the concern to have all the authoritative Gospels together. But the concern was not merely literary, for these were documents of some religious authority, and the binding of Luke together with other works of the same genre has to be related to some conception of a Christian canon of New Covenant scriptures. As we have seen, this may have been happening (the conceptual justification existed) well before the time when Papias wrote,

---

[21] Is he the 'Hippolytus' who according to Dionysius bar Salibi wrote in opposition to 'the heretic Gaius' in defence of the Gospel and Apocalypse? See the discussion above.

[22] On the other hand, some experts, 'regarding the Trinitarian theology as suspiciously far advanced' (Bammel, 'State of Play', 197) for the Monarchian controversies of the early 3rd cent, are convinced that the *Contra Noetum* has been redacted (or, according to one scholar, even written) in the 4th cent, in the wake of the Apollinarian and Marcellan disputes. Most of the objections pertain to material in chs. 17 and 18 and do not involve the instances of ὑποβαίνω in chs. 12 and 15—though, theoretically, they too could be the work of a later interpolater. See R. M. Hübner, 'Melito von Sardes und Noet von Smyrna', in *Oecumenica et Patristica: Festschrift für Wilhelm Schneemelcher* (Chambésy, 1989), 220–3; J. Frickel, 'Hippolyts Schrift Contra Noetum: Ein Pseudo-Hippolyt', in H. C. Brennecke, E. L. Grasmück, and C. Markschies (eds.), *Logos: Festschrift für Louise Abramowski zum 8. July 1993* (Berlin, 1993), 87–123, who raises some questions regarding 15. 1–7. On the other hand, Loi, 'L'identità', 86 n. 48, draws attention to correspondences in Trinitarian theology and in Christology between *Noet.* and the Hippolytan exegetical treatises, *In Canticum*, *On the Blessings of Moses*, and *On the Blessings of Jacob*, as also does Brent, *Hippolytus*, 223–58, citing also passages from *Anichr.* and *CDan.* These appear sufficient to demonstrate the 3rd-cent character of the *Contra Noetum*. The uses of ὑποβαίνω in chs. 12 and 15 should thus be regarded as genuine.

[23] Brent's view (*Hippolytus*) is that *Noet.* was written by Hippolytus, but that Hippolytus was the successor of the author of the *Refutatio*.

[24] Loi, 'L'identità'; Simonetti, 'Ipotesi di lavoro'.

[25] This makes me wonder, when Irenaeus in the 180s spoke of 'all good and ancient copies' of the Apocalypse as containing the reading 666 instead of 616 (at Rev. 13: 8), in what form these 'good and ancient copies' existed? Also, we may deduce from some of Justin's comments that he attributed the Gospel according to John to an apostle (see above). When Justin mentions John's Revelation, he is quite confident that its author John is one of the twelve apostles of Jesus. Was his confidence supported by the existence of an edn. of John's works, a *corpus Johanneanum* like there was a *corpus Paulinum*?

and the comments about the Gospels and their origin which we read in the tradition he received sound like the kind of notations that would accompany or soon follow an edition of the four Gospels.

The Johannine Writings, in Corpus and Canon

The tendency of scholarship has been not only to consider the fortunes of each member of the Johannine corpus individually but to regard each as having quite distinct paths towards acceptance as part of a NT canon, or even towards recognition as apostolic writings.[26] If we are thinking of their paths all the way to the fourth century (and even beyond), this might certainly be appropriate. But it is a mistake to assume that the Johannine writing began their life in the Church as essentially disparate documents and took paths which eventually converged only in the fourth century when they were finally received into the Church's canon. Almost exactly the opposite appears to have been the case. There is in fact much more confusion and misunderstanding in the fourth century than in the second.

Besides the excellent possibility that there were collections, codices, containing all or several of the Johannine works together in the second century, there is, as we have seen throughout this study, quite abundant evidence from the way the Johannine writings were used in that century that at least the Gospel, the Apocalypse, and the First Letter of John were commonly viewed as a 'corpus'. Not only were these three viewed as works of the same author, each held a surprisingly firm place among the religious documents which functioned in various ways as scripture among the Christian churches. And with regard to the two shorter Johannine epistles, we cannot simply base our judgement of the matter upon the frequency of their use or the depth of their influence among remaining literary sources. Not only would such a judgement hardly acknowledge the vast difference in size between the works, or the relative suitability of each work to the particular secondary writer's needs, it would take no account of the likely form in which these works were known and preserved. The almost complete absence of influence from 3 John in particular on Christian writers of the second century does not necessarily mean that it was only received at some point much later than the other Johannine writings. In fact, when related to the range of developments in the second and third centuries, this might

---

[26] R. A. Culpepper, *John, the Son of Zebedee* (Columbia, SC, 1994), 92, 'Each of the Epistles followed a different path toward its ultimate reception as an apostolic writing'. J.-D. Kaestli, 'Remarques sur le rapport du quatrième Evangile avec la gnose', in Kaestli *et al.* (eds.), *La Communanté johannique* (Paris, 1990), 355, thinks that 'The corpus formed by the Gospel and the three Epistles had therefore not been accepted universally as early as the second century'. He says that the fact that 3 John was translated into Latin independently from 2 John indicates that in the West the three epistles achieved canonical status one after the other (355 n. 10).

even be seen as another factor favouring the existence of a Johannine corpus from very early on. For we might ask how an *anonymous* letter so short as 3 John, one which is almost invisible in the literary corpus of the second century (we cannot speak definitively about early preaching or private reading), could ever have ended up in collections of the 'Catholic Epistles' in the third century if it had not always existed bound together with 1 and 2 John, and possibly with other Johannine works? It is much less likely that it was discovered or rehabilitated sometime in the third century and inserted into a collection of seven letters, than that it had always existed among the churches and was transmitted, though seldom cited, in a corpus where it enjoyed some measure of security in the company of other writings, at least 1 and 2 John. The way Dionysius of Alexandria casually refers to 'the second or third extant epistles of John' (*HE* 7. 25. 11) shows that in the mid-third century the three customarily circulated together in codices in which the 'second' and 'third' epistles followed 'the Catholic Epistle' in their present canonical order (also Origen, in Eusebius, *HE* 6. 25. 10). In a case such as this one, in which the documented assumption was unity of authorship with 1 John,[27] and that authorship was assumed to be apostolic, copious citation of 3 John is not at all necessary to justify the probability that it was accepted along with the documents with which it was bound.

Thus the existence of a Johannine corpus helps explain how both 2 and 3 John survived to find their place in an authoritative collection of 'Epistles called Catholic' (Eusebius, *HE* 2. 23. 25), separate collections of which, as far as we know, began only in the third century. If 2 and 3 John circulated originally, or from an early time, bound with 1 John and the Gospel, or with these plus the Apocalypse, they would have been preserved in at least one form in all the churches which received an early copy. But as we know, if this form of publication existed, it never became dominant. Very soon the preferred mode of transmission of the Fourth Gospel was either by itself or alongside the three other Gospels in single codices. Once churches or individuals possessed a four-Gospel codex, it would be natural that copies of the three Johannine Epistles would be commissioned to be produced not in an edition alongside another copy of the Fourth Gospel, but either along with the Apocalypse of John, or, according to genre, with other epistles which held authority in the Church. As the Pauline Epistles (with or without Hebrews) were already a cohesive entity and a perceived authorial unit, they would naturally be bound together, as they probably had been for some time previously. The most common practice, evidently, was to bind the Johannine Epistles with the Petrine Epistles, James, and Jude (*HE* 2. 23.

---

[27] Irenaeus, the *MF*, Clement, Origen, and Dionysius, though Origen (*C. Matt.* 5; cited in Eusebius, *HE* 6. 25. 10) already notes doubts about 2 and 3 John. I shall follow the fortunes of these epistles below.

24–5),[28] and then, though we do not know just when this began, to append these seven to the book of the Acts of the Apostles.[29] This, however, left the Apocalypse without any natural partners among the NT writings, and it indeed tends to be transmitted separately or in irregular combinations in the manuscript tradition. This then became the standard way the Johannine corpus was reproduced, even after the technology of the codex was able to comprehend larger units of text, even the entire NT corpus.

From the several lines of evidence cited here we may feel no hesitation in saying that the Johannine works were indeed a 'corpus' throughout most of the second century. This corpus may well at one time have been expressed in physical form, as we have seen some evidence of this. But in any case, these books existed as a definite conceptual corpus, for writers use them as if they belong together and emanated from a single, authoritative source.

It was apparently not until the third century that things began to change. It may be, in fact, that the breakup of a physical Johannine corpus contributed to the breakup of the literary corpus, making it easier to question the origins and scriptural status of individual books. Starting with questions either raised directly or prompted by the words of Gaius of Rome and others near the beginning of the century, the Apocalypse was apparently the first whose traditional authorship and standing in the Church came under question (*HE* 7. 25. 1–3). The impetus and presenting cause for this scrutiny, from Gaius, to Dionysius, to Eusebius, was the doctrinal problem of chiliasm. While Dionysius dismissed out of hand the suggestion of Cerinthian authorship (*HE* 7. 25. 2) and demonstrated to the satisfaction of his opponents that Revelation could not be understood after the literal sense (7. 24. 9), it was these issues of authorship and proper hermeneutics which stimulated Dionysius' critical examination. Based on various dissimilarities of style, vocabulary, and teaching, Dionysius concluded that the Revelation could not be attributed to the apostle John, who wrote the Gospel, the Catholic Epistle, and the 'the second or third extant epistles of John' (7. 25. 11).[30] The 'holy and inspired' prophet (7. 25. 6–7) who wrote the Revela-

---

[28] Commonly in the present canonical order, but see Metzger, *Canon*, 299–300, for the full variety of sequences.

[29] Aland and Aland, *Text*, 78, say that 'the Apostolos (i.e., Acts and the Catholic letters) is found alone in 18 papyri (12 fragmentary), 29 uncials (27 fragmentary), and 40 minuscules (5 fragmentary)'.

[30] Dionysius' conclusions about the Apocalypse have sometimes led to efforts to find antecedents in Origen, but these have been less than convincing. R. M. Grant, 'Ancient and Modern Questions about Authenticity', in B. H. McLean (ed.), *Origins and Method* (Sheffield, 1993), 297, in fact has stated that Origen came to doubt the apostolic origin of Revelation in his later years. For this Grant refers to Guéraud and Nautin's edn. of *On Passover* (O. Guéraud and P. Nautin (eds.), *Origène. Sur le Pâque. Traité inédit publié d'après un papyrus de Toura*, Christianisme antique, 2 (Paris, 1979), 119 n. 23, 172, ll. 16–17), which concerns a restoration of a lacuna in Origen's text in a reference to John's Apocalypse: ἐν γὰρ [τῇ φερομέν]ῃ Ἰωάννου Ἀπ[οκαλύψει]. Guéraud and Nautin say that the restored word φερομένη here indicates that the authorship given for the Apocalypse was not admitted by all. But this appears to be simply mistaken. First, Origen does not even mention here John's apostolic identity, and since the Apocalypse itself claims to have been written by someone

tion, he now suggested, might have been another John in Ephesus. 'But I think (οἶμαι) that there was a certain other [John] among those that were in Asia, since it is said (φασίν) both that there were two tombs at Ephesus, and that each of the two is said to be John's' (Eusebius, *HE* 7. 25. 16). Though Dionysius continued to treat the work as inspired and refused to lower its esteem in the eyes of the brethren (7. 25. 4), he effectively helped to loosen it from its place in a conceptual Johannine corpus and opened the door for its rejection by some.

For Eusebius' strange equivocation on the book—it is either 'confessed' or it is spurious—is no doubt based upon the report and the researches of Dionysius. Eusebius gave no more credit to the Cerinthus hypothesis than did Dionysius. But now faced with Dionysius' display of the stylistic differences between the Apocalypse and the other works attributed to the apostle, and with the same writer's proposal that another John lay buried in Ephesus, and beset by lingering doubts about the book's relation to chiliasm, Eusebius was unable to adjudicate in a definitive way the matters of authorship and canonicity. For Eusebius, if the Apocalypse was apostolic, it was canonical; if not apostolic, its place among the homologoumena was in jeopardy (*HE* 3. 25. 2, 4)—a concern evidently felt more acutely by him than by Dionysius— and if it was not genuine, it was a forgery and therefore ἐν τοῖς νόθοις.

Eusebius' *Ecclesiastical History* was very well read in antiquity. The critical work of Dionysius on authorship which Eusebius preserved, and his own halting endorsement, certainly contributed to more widespread doubts, at least in the East. While it is contained in the canon lists in Codex Claromontanus, in the so-called Cheltenham Canon (Mommson's, *c*.360), in Athanasius' Festal Letter of 367, and the Synods of Hippo Regius (393) and of Carthage (397), the Apocalypse is absent from some other Eastern canon lists: Cyril of Jerusalem, *Catech. Lects.* 4. 5 (*c*.350); the disputed Canon 60 of the Laodicean Synod of 363; the 'Apostolic Canons' (*c*.380); the canon of Gregory of Nazianzus. The canon of Amphilochius of Iconium (after 394) leaves the matter in doubt: 'the Revelation of John, some approve, but the

---

named John it is hardly likely that Origen would have expressed any doubts about that bare fact. Also, the term φερομένη, as applied to documents, is best translated 'extant' or 'current among us', and as such is a neutral term, though often used with a positive, not a negative, connotation. In *C. John* 1. 4 Origen mentions 'the Scriptures which are current (τῶν τοίνυν φερομένων γραφῶν) and are believed to be divine in all the churches'. Origen goes on to speak of 'men who are wise in Christ, who have profited by those epistles which are current (ἐν ταῖς φερομέναις ἐπιστολαῖς)', who are convinced that 'the apostolic writings are to be pronounced wise and worthy of belief'. Cf. also Dionysius in *HE* 7. 25. 11 on the second and third 'extant epistles of John', and Eusebius in *HE* 1. 12. 1; 2. 15. 1, etc. Guéraud and Nautin also refer to the *Hom. Jos.* 7. 1 (from *c*.240) where Origen gives a list of the writings of the apostles, from which list the Apocalypse is missing, but only from some of the Latin manuscripts (see Metzger, *Canon*, 139–40). Yet this is slim evidence for positing a rejection on the part of Origen of a work which he for decades had used, and would continue to use (*C. Cels.* 6. 6, 23; 8. 17), as possessing the highest authority. It is just as probable that Revelation was omitted in transmission, due to later doubts about it (see below). It appears that Origen either did not know the criticism of Revelation reported by Dionysius or that he considered it unworthy of mention.

most say it is spurious'.[31] The 'most' here must have included the East Syrian churches.[32] According to Kurt and Barbara Aland there are in the textual tradition two uncial and 147 minuscule manuscripts which contain the entire NT with the sole exception of Revelation.[33] Clearly, in the latter half of the fourth century the position of John's Apocalypse among the churches was much less certain than it appears to have been, so far as we can tell, at any time in the second.

The fortunes of the Second and Third Epistles are comparable. Origen in about AD 230 already notes that these epistles were not considered genuine by some (οὐ πάντες φασὶν γνησίους εἶναι ταύτας, *C. John* 5 (Eusebius, *HE* 6. 25. 10)). Unlike the case concerning the Apocalypse, however, here we have no indication of the reasons for the suspicions. Very likely these objectors again were or at least included Syrian Christians, among whom the seven Catholic Epistles, or the four shortest of them, struggled to find a place (Origen also mentions here that 2 Peter was disputed). Dionysius reveals no doubts about the two shorter Johannine Epistles. The coincidence between the two tombs he had mentioned and the two Johns mentioned by Papias, however, was perceived by Eusebius late in the third century or early in the fourth. The church historian saw this as a possibility (but only as a possibility) for explaining the now apparent divergences from Johannine style in the Apocalypse, proposing that Papias' second John, 'unless anyone prefer the first, saw the revelation which passes under the name of John' (*HE* 3. 39. 6). In an earlier section of his book Eusebius had also hinted about the possibility that 2 and 3 John might have been authored by some other John (3. 25. 3).

Though with respect to 2 and 3 John Eusebius did not explicitly raise the suggestion of Papias' elder, others did. By about 392, when Jerome wrote *De viris illustribus*, the coincidence of the title 'Elder' used both of Papias' second John and by the author of the second and third Johannine epistles had been fully recognized, and had even been connected with Dionysius' report of the two Ephesian tombs. Jerome wrote that 2 and 3 John 'are said to be the work of John the presbyter to the memory of whom another sepulchre is shown at Ephesus to the present day, though some think that there are two memorials of this same John the evangelist' (*De vir. illust.* 9). In his chapter on Papias he related again that many had opined 'that the two later epistles of John are not (the work) of the Apostle, but of the Elder' (*De vir. illust.* 18). A later writer, Philip of Side (according to an epitomizer), would say that this connection was made to explain why the ancients had accepted only the First Epistle.[34] Jerome did not identify any who held to

---

[31] See Metzger, *Canon*, 310–15.
[32] Ibid. 218–23.
[33] Aland and Aland, *Text*, 78.
[34] Philip of Side, *Christian History* (AD 434–9). Text from the Bodleian Codex Baroccianus 142, printed in LHH 570–3, as no. 6.

this view, and he evidently did not hold it himself.[35] It is interesting that Jerome did not even mention Eusebius' idea, which he certainly knew, that this John may have been responsible not for the two Epistles but for the Apocalypse.[36]

This disagreement about the authorship of the two smaller Johannine epistles is surely related to their fluctuating fortunes in the canonical lists of the fourth century.[37] Apostolic authorship and full canonicity were usually maintained. All three epistles are included by Cyril of Jerusalem, *Catech. Lects.* 4. 36 (350); the disputed Canon 60 of the Laodicean Synod of 363; Athanasius' 39th festal letter of 367; the list inserted into Codex Claromontanus; Gregory of Nazianzus; the author of the *Apostolic Canons* (*c.*380); the third Synod of Carthage in 397, which approved the acts of an earlier synod at Hippo Regius in North Africa in 393 ('of John, apostle, three'). But Amphilocius of Iconium, writing around the same time as Jerome, stated in his NT list that some receive three Epistles of John and others only one as canonical. Contained in the so-called Cheltenham Canon (Mommsen's), after listing 'three Epistles of John, 350 lines', are the words, 'one only'. It is interesting to note that even the acceptance of the alternative authorship, however, did not necessarily mean the exclusion of 2 and 3 John from the canon. A portion of the late fifth-or early sixth-century *Decretum Gelasianum* which may go back to Pope Damasus I and a Roman synod in 382, in its list of 'the order of the Scriptures of the New Testament' accepted and venerated by 'the holy and catholic Roman church', specifies 'of the apostle John—one epistle; of the other John, the elder—two epistles'.

Throughout the third and fourth centuries, as the Apocalypse and the two shorter Johannine Epistles suffered from doubts either about authorship or about canonicity, or both, the Fourth Gospel and the First Epistle remained the gold standard for genuineness. The stability of the Gospel, the more significant in the light of modern scholarship, is seen in the remarkably consistent tradition of orthodox ecclesiastical use from the time of Papias' elders on through the fourth-century canon lists, none of which omits or casts doubt on it. If the alleged rejection of John by Gaius is to any degree historical, it was extremely isolated and apparently fated to an immediate obsolescence.

---

[35] See *Ep.* 53. 9, written in 394, where he lists only the apostle John as author of the Johannine epistles.

[36] Philip of Side mentions it, and says those who take this view have been led astray.

[37] On these lists, see Metzger, *Canon*, 310–15.

Conclusion

The Myth of Orthodox Johannophobia

THE BROKEN SILENCE OF THE EARLIEST SOURCES

None of the three planks of the orthodox Johannophobia paradigm identified at the beginning of this study appears solid anymore; even together they cannot hold the weight they have been forced to bear. It is not that the earliest sources are silent, so much as that we have been hard of hearing, a condition aggravated by routine misconceptions about the standards of literary borrowing in the period.[1] While there are some early Christian sources which attest no clear signs of John's influence, these are not in the end very consequential in the light of the predominantly early date of these sources and the growing recognition that echoes of the Fourth Gospel can indeed be heard through an impressive number of other early witnesses. After the Johannine Epistles, the influence of this Gospel is evident in the writings or oral teachings of Ignatius, Polycarp, (John) the Elder, Aristides, Papias, the longer ending of Mark, the later portions of the *Shepherd* of Hermas, the *Epistula Apostolorum*, the *Ad Diognetum*, all before about 150. These represent the Great Church in at least Syria, Asia Minor, Greece, and Italy. The witness of Papias and his sources is of particular magnitude, as it seems to represent a substratum of tradition about the four Gospels which became widely diffused. This witness is consistent with the eminence of the four Gospels which is assumed by the longer ending of Mark, well before the comments made by Irenaeus in the 180s. The availability and even apparent popularity of the Fourth Gospel is certainly suggested by its strong representation among the surviving papyrus fragments of early Christian writings. It is also seen in the pointed suggestions by both Aristides in the 120s and Justin in the 150s that the reigning emperor read the Christian Gospels, a category of writings which evidently included the Gospel according to John. By the middle of the century, when Justin Martyr, Tatian, Valentinus, Ptolemy, and Hegesippus were in Rome, this Gospel must have been quite a well-known and prominent Christian authority. Justin's notice that the apostolic memoirs were read in Christian services of worship in Rome must have encompassed John as well, suggesting, again, not only that it was no newcomer to the scene but that it also

---

[1] See also the summary section in Ch. 7, above.

played a leading role in the life of the Church. Such a leading role at this time would be the fitting antecedent to the wall and ceiling frescos, shepherd lamps, and eucharistic cups, inspired by the Fourth Gospel, half a century later.

A problem created by the orthodox Johannophobia paradigm was that it left the obvious and widespread acceptance of the Fourth Gospel as scripture from about the time of Irenaeus without any credible, historical precedent. One result of this study, then, is that it provides a more historically satisfying and plausible picture of how the fortunes of the Fourth Gospel and the entire Johannine corpus in the first and second halves of the century are connected. We may now see that the powerful influence of this Gospel in the second half of the second century is indeed commensurate with foundations visible in the first half. I shall say more about the influence of the Gospel throughout the second century momentarily. Here I only observe that, at whatever point Valentinus and his followers took up the Fourth Gospel and used it for their cause, they did so knowing they could count on members of Great Church churches being familiar with it and ready to hear it as an authority, an apostolic authority.

THE MYTH OF GNOSTIC JOHANNOPHILIA

Surely one of the most striking results of this investigation, but not of this only, for other studies have been at least tending towards the same conclusion, is that the major use of the Fourth Gospel among heterodox or gnostic groups up until the Valentinians Ptolemy, Heracleon, and Theodotus, is best described as critical or adversarial.[2] This exposes and should correct the tendency of earlier scholarship to assume that any Johannine borrowings or allusions in gnostic literature are evidence of gnostic/Johannine affinity, or of a common family history. The underlying animosity is perhaps seen most clearly in the *Acts of John* and the *Apocryphon of James*, but is also unmistakable in *Trimorphic Protennoia*, the *Second Apocalypse of James*, and the *Gospel of Thomas*. In other words, not only does the Fourth Gospel not appear to have been prized by any known heterodox group (the Valentinians being a special case), it was perceived by most of them as a threat. This is to say that Johannophobia is apparent in this period not from the orthodox but only from the heterodox side. The offence of this Gospel among heterodox writers seems to have centred upon two facets of the Gospel (and of the First Epistle): (a) first and foremost on its Christology, including its presentation of the full incarnation of the Logos of God, his true human nature and true physical suffering and death on the cross, and his bodily resurrection, and (b) its assumption of a special and permanent authority joined to the witness of those who were Jesus' original disciples.

---

[2] See also the summary section in Ch. 5, above.

These concerns are seen both from the orthodox side, in the use of Johannine ideas and terminology by 1 and 2 John, Polycarp, the *Epistula Apostolorum*, and Irenaeus against their opponents, and in the heterodox productions mentioned above.

The Valentinians developed distinctive approaches to this Gospel and even a certain keenness for John's Prologue, and Heracleon wrote a commentary on the Gospel (the reasons for which have been explored above). Despite the monumental importance which has been attached to these phenomena, they really do not prove what they have customarily been taken to prove. First, it is obvious that the Valentinians developed similar approaches to the other three Gospels, Acts, Paul, and other NT writings, treating them all with a characteristic 'freedom', but a freedom still quite constrained by their peculiar theological system. The penchant for plundering John's Prologue has more to do with its use of dynamic, abstract nouns than with any underlying unity in the structure of their respective cosmologies. Second, by the time of the Valentinian adoption, the Fourth Gospel was firmly received as an apostolic Gospel among the Great Churches and had thus become fair game for any rival Christian factions to use as they saw fit. From the apologetic work of Justin in the 150s and even from the earlier work of the apologist Aristides in the 120s we perceive that the Christian Gospels, evidently including John, were already well-known, representative writings of the Christian faith and must have been fairly easily accessible, even to outsiders. Trypho claims to be familiar with the written 'Gospel', and though this may or may not signal an awareness of the Gospel κατὰ Ἰωάννην, we can be sure that this Gospel was among the Christian Gospels known to Celsus the opponent of Christianity in the 160s or 170s. All of this points to a common reception of this Gospel in the mainstream, Great Church, well-before its appropriation by Valentinians, indeed, before Valentinus himself formed his movement. Third, as we have seen, the Ptolemaic exegesis of the Johannine Prologue could only have been persuasive to those who already had accepted his system of pleromic aeons. If the Fourth Gospel proved susceptible to the 'spiritual' or 'allegorical' exegesis of the Valentinians, it proved no less susceptible to the 'spiritual' or 'allegorical' exegesis of orthodox writers such as Origen. And as to specifically docetic exegesis of the Fourth Gospel, this, we find, was astonishingly rare, if it can even be said to have existed at all. On the contrary, it is evident from both heterodox and orthodox sources that John remained a stubborn obstacle to docetism, often requiring textual manipulation or calling forth radical reinterpretation on the part of Valentinian and gnostic exegetes. This, again, supports Irenaeus' statements about the authorial intention of the Fourth Gospel and is directly contrary to the prevailing view of the last century or so of scholarship. It is also true that not all Valentinian exegesis of John's Gospel required as much imagination, and we have good evidence that the later Valentinian exegetes showed what

would today be considered more 'respect' for the text—probably in response to orthodox criticism.[3] In sum, a tendency to exaggerate Valentinian
fondness for the Fourth Gospel and to misjudge its nature stands in acute
need of correction. This correction should be made in future studies.

THE PLACE OF THE FOURTH GOSPEL IN THE CHURCH

The third plank of the orthodox Johannophobia consensus is the contention
that 'many pre-Nicene critics' within the Great Church, and particularly in
Rome, 'did not consider it reliable and authentic',[4] that they held significant reservations towards, and sometimes categorically rejected, the Fourth
Gospel. It is often said that this Gospel 'struggled' to gain admittance into
the Church's canon and came quite close to being permanently discarded,
due to its gnostic associations. But, quite to the contrary, there is no good
evidence that any of the writers of the Great Church opposed or rejected
the Gospel according to John in the second century, least of all for being
gnostic or docetic, and not even for being inauthentic. The concerns which
did surface had mostly to do with John's narrative departures from the
Synoptic Gospels, concerns which were already receiving harmonizing
answers from at least the time of Papias and his elder. The only criticism of
John's distinctive theological assertions one encounters in documentary
sources come from the heterodox, docetic writers themselves. Despite the
common assumption, the Johannophobes mentioned by Irenaeus in *AH* 3.
11. 9 were certainly not considered by him to be among the orthodox.
Their characteristics much more resemble those of the author of the *Apocryphon of James*, and the Cerinthian legacy in the second century. If Gaius of
Rome early in the third century did criticize and reject this Gospel, which
now has to be considered doubtful, he found no known followers, though
he may indeed have inspired others who criticized and rejected the Apocalypse. The Alogi introduced to us in Epiphanius' *Panarion* are either his
cipher for Gaius or, more probably, his consolidation of various criticisms
of the Fourth Gospel and the Apocalypse which he knew from disparate
quarters, into a single, identifiable group.

Not only are the sources ignorant of the kind of suspicion, neglect, and
antagonism on the part of catholic writers which the consensus of scholarship would lead us to expect, the overwhelming impression gained from
orthodox sources throughout most of the second century is that of an unmistakable and seemingly instinctive respect for this Gospel. From the
writings of Ignatius, Polycarp, Papias, Aristides, and Hermas, we are already assured that John's Gospel must have been well-known among
Church leaders in Syria, Asia Minor, Athens, and Rome in the early

---

[3] M. F. Wiles, *The Spiritual Gospel* (Cambridge, 1960), 97, which see for some examples.
[4] J. H. Charlesworth, *The Beloved Disciple* (Valley Forge, Pa., 1995), 407.

decades of the second century. That fact in itself is indicative of something more than a common notoriety. There may be hints of something greater in Ignatius, merely judging from his general reverence for apostolic teaching, though this is little more than an inference. Aristides' references to 'Gospels' as definite textual authorities, however, juxtaposed with his knowledge of details from John's Gospel point to a certain eminence for this Gospel. The 'citation' and midrashic use of John 14: 2 by 'the elders' quoted by Irenaeus, almost certainly from Papias (*AH* 5. 36. 1), indicates a scripture-like function for this saying of Jesus from the Fourth Gospel—and all indications are that this comes from a Jewish-Christian source. It is hard to overstate the importance of the presbyter's tradition about the origins of the four Gospels recorded by Papias (Eusebius, *HE* 3. 24; 3. 39. 15–16), showing that by the first or second decade of the second century John had found a place alongside Matthew, Mark, and Luke and was considered the Gospel of an apostle. This tradition, traces of which show up in a number of later authors, including Justin, Irenaeus, and the *MF*, demonstrates a considerable interest in linking and interpreting these texts together, in reconciling their differences, and in finding apostolic ratification for each one. This too is consistent with a scriptural authority already recognized among Christian congregations in Asia Minor. Also, the use of John along with Matthew and Luke by the author of the long ending of Mark shows where this author thought he must go for materials to construct a suitable, 'improved' conclusion to a Christian Gospel.

But the popularity of this Gospel among Christians is seen in many ways, and attempts to judge it can no longer be restricted to the literary sources of the period. One must take account of the unusually strong representation of the Fourth Gospel in the papyrus finds of the second and third centuries, attending as well to the signs of sacred use of those manuscripts in the forms of scribal subdivisions of the text and in the practice of binding John together with one or more of the Synoptic Gospels. The early catacomb paintings in Rome, even if they cannot be dated earlier than about AD 200, also testify to the popularity of the Johannine presentation of the events of Jesus' life and even to the official endorsement of this presentation. Among the very earliest surviving examples of Christian art are depictions of Jesus as the good shepherd of John 10, the encounter of Jesus with the Samaritan woman from John 4, the healing of the paralytic from John 5, and the raising of Lazarus from John 11. 'Good shepherd' chalices were in use in churches in the early third century. As the years went on, these and other Johannine images (the wedding at Cana, the healing of the man born blind) continued to be represented in Christian art, such as in the murals in the Christian baptistery at Dura Europos, in Christian sarcophagi beginning from the mid-third century, in glass and ceramic art, and in mosaics.

Such effects of the Johannine Gospel in material culture from the end of the second century onward indicate without a doubt that the Fourth Gospel was no newcomer to orthodox Christian churches at that time, but rather that it had been widely known and officially sanctioned from a much earlier date. This must naturally be combined with the evidence cited above for judging that the Fourth Gospel also belonged in Justin's category of 'apostolic memoirs' along with the Synoptic Gospels (*1Apol.* 66. 3). These 'memoirs', he tells his pagan readers, were read and preached on in Christian services of worship in Rome at around the midpoint of the century.

A particularly poignant result of our investigation has to do with Rome itself. Far from being Walter Bauer's bastion of orthodox, Johannophobic sentiment, the church of the capital city shows nothing but signs of approval of this source, beginning with the later portions of the *Shepherd* of Hermas, extending to Justin's *Apologies* and his report of a sacral use of the apostolic memoirs, to the inferences reasonably drawn from Valentinian use and probably from Celsus' researches, to Hegesippus' identification of John the Patmos Seer with the Evangelist, to Rome's correspondence with the churches in Vienne and Lyons, with Polycrates, and with Irenaeus, to the official-sounding pronouncements of the *Muratorian Fragment*, to the catacomb paintings, and to Tertullian's report of John's surviving a boiling cauldron in Rome. Once again I must state that, if Gaius of Rome did reject the Fourth Gospel for its discrepancies with the Synoptic Gospels (certainly not because 'he sensed in the gospel of John a spirit of heresy with which his Roman-ecclesiastical attitude could not be reconciled'),[5] he was quite isolated and cut off from the main ecclesiastical parties in Rome at the time, or ever after.

The Consciousness of a Johannine Corpus

It is important, however, not to isolate the Fourth Gospel from its literary milieu in the second century. Another prime concern of this study has been to seek to reflect more accurately the relationship of the Fourth Gospel to the rest of the Johannine corpus and indeed to gain an idea of the conception of the Johannine writings in the second century. From various vantage points we see that there was a strong conception of these books as belonging to an authorial corpus. Not only do we find a relatively high instance of common use of two or three or more of the Johannine books in second-century authors, we also find several striking instances of intertextual use, in which one Johannine book is used to interpret another, as if the author's thought or situation could be illuminated from the one as from the other. This study has also considered evidence pointing to the existence of codices containing the Johannine works—a physical Johannine corpus—in the second and third centuries. These data join with the several explicit and

---

[5] W. Bauer, *Orthodoxy and Heresy in Earliest Christianity* (Philadalphia, 1971), 207–8.

implicit attributions of these books to the same author, John the apostle and disciple of the Lord, to demonstrate that the Fourth Gospel was commonly considered not simply as one of four Gospels functioning with special authority in the Church, but as one of a group of writings which emanated from a common, authoritative source. The existence of the idea of a Johannine corpus in the second century has at least two apparent implications, each bolstered by the evidence for a physical Johannine corpus. First, it helps explain how 2 and 3 John, which seem to have been of little import in the second century, judging from the level of their use in surviving literary sources, both survived to be included in an authoritative collection of Catholic Epistles at least by the late third century, and why, earlier, Irenaeus in Gaul, Tertullian in North Africa, the *Muratorian Fragment* in Rome, and Clement, Origen, and Dionysius in Alexandria all assumed the attribution to John. Second, the conception of a Johannine corpus implies that those who held it will have viewed all five Johannine books as mediating the same kind of religious authority (not, of course, that they were equally popular). The force of this implication needs to be invoked only for 3 John and perhaps to some extent for 2 John, for from the allusions and citations we possess, we can easily confirm that an equivalent authority was recognized for the Gospel, the Apocalypse, and the First Epistle.

Johannine Origins and History

It was noted at the beginning of this study how scholars have regularly used the second-century evidence as a foundation for their overall theories of the history of the Johannine community and for the compositional origins of the Johannine books. Beginning with the historical question of the place of the Fourth Gospel in the second half of the second century, it is often said that Irenaeus had to 'defend' this Gospel, and that it was his demonstration of how this 'tainted' work could actually be used against the heretics which eventually secured for it a position in the Church's canon.[6] But while Irenaeus certainly 'exposed' what he saw as the faulty exegesis of Valentinian heretics (particularly of the Prologue), this does not amount to a 'defence' of the book itself. There is no sense in which his use of John could be taken as revolutionary or controversial among the orthodox and no indication that he was trying to effect a takeover of an alien or disputed text. On the

---

[6] J. N. Sanders, *The Fourth Gospel in the Early Church* (Cambridge, 1943), 66, 84; M. R. Hillmer, 'The Gospel of John in the Second Century' (Th.D. diss., Harvard University, Apr. 1966), 172; D. M. Smith, 'The Problem of John and the Synoptics', in A. Denaux (ed.), *John and the Synoptics* (Leuven, 1992), 157; J. D. G. Dunn, 'John and the Synoptics as a Theological Question', in R. A. Culpepper and C. C. Black (eds.), *Exploring the Gospel of John* (Louisville, Ky., 1996), 308; idem, 'Pseudepigraphy', in R. P. Martin and P. H. Davids (eds.), *Dictionary of the Later New Testament and its Developments* (Downers Grove, Ill., 1997), 981.

contrary, his casual indications of previous orthodox use of this Gospel, we have seen, are quite abundantly confirmed by the earlier records of the second century.

Likewise, the prevailing paradigm sees an important role for the First Epistle in its construction of Johannine history, a role which foreshadowed the work of Irenaeus. According to Brown, 1 John showed 'that there was an orthodox way to read the Gospel, and the Epistle's campaign against the secessionists ultimately encouraged writers like Irenaeus to employ the Gospel in a war against Gnostics who were spiritual descendants of the secessionists. Thus the ultimate contribution of the author of I John to Johannine history may have been that of saving the Fourth Gospel for the church.'[7] That Irenaeus, and indeed others before him, like the author of the *Epistula Apostolorum*, employed both 1 John and the Gospel against the heterodox is of course obvious; what is far from obvious is that they or any others had to 'save' the Fourth Gospel for the Church. 'The secessionists' mentioned in 1 John 2: 18–19, Brown wrote, 'probably moved rapidly in the second century toward docetism, gnosticism, Cerinthianism, and Montanism. This explains why the Fourth Gospel, which they brought with them, is cited earlier and more frequently by heterodox writers than by orthodox writers.'[8] But now that the 'earlier and more frequent' citation by heterodox writers is shown not to be factual, it therefore stands in no need of an 'explanation'. If they brought the Fourth Gospel with them, the secessionists probably took it along as a text which they were determined to counteract and refute. It is more likely, given the evidence of the second century, that it was some event like the publication of the Fourth Gospel which exposed the presence and the true sentiments of the group which eventually 'seceded' and which led to their secession. Heterodox groups tended to adopt the same critical approach to the Fourth Gospel as they did to the First Epistle. They were as vexed by the eyewitness accounts of the reality of Jesus' 'flesh' in John 1: 14; 19: 34–7, as they were by the eyewitness testimony of 1 John 1: 1–4; 4: 2–3; 5: 6.

Turning now to the origins of the Fourth Gospel itself, the complementary phenomena of gnostic Johannophilia and orthodox Johannophobia have also been thought to require that this Gospel was produced either in a gnostic intellectual/religious milieu or else in an obscure corner of the Christian world, in any case not in an urban centre like Ephesus and not by a genuine apostle of Jesus or even by a famous and influential school in Christian Asia Minor. The evidence, as we have it, provides quite a different picture. In the light of what we must term a surprisingly wide influence of the Fourth Gospel throughout the second century, even in the first half of the century, a location such as Ephesus would have to be considered a very

---

[7] R. E. Brown, *The Community of the Beloved Disciple* (New York, 1979), 149–50.
[8] Ibid. 24.

fitting place from which the Johannine Gospel might have originated, or from which it saw its first significant circulation. The tradition of Ephesus may not be recoverable before the time of Hegesippus and Irenaeus, but other factors support an origin in Christian Asia Minor if not specifically the city of Ephesus. The influence of the Fourth Gospel on Ignatius, as he passed through Asia Minor, on Polycarp writing in Smyrna, on Papias and his elders in or around Hierapolis, and very profoundly on the *Epistula Apostolorum* in Asia Minor, and on the Asian émigrés in Vienne and Lyons, argues for this, as does the fictional, geographical placement of the adventures of John in the *Acts of John*. The explicit Asian setting of the Johannine Apocalypse and the corroboration by Justin in Ephesus also constitutes evidence, to the extent that this work's author was identified with the author of the Fourth Gospel.

The question of authorship is in itself complex and involves more attention to the text of the Gospel and to redactional and community issues than I am able to give in this volume. But the objection which rises either against apostolic authorship or against production by a well-known school, based on the early 'non-use' of the Gospel in the first half of the second century,[9] has to be regarded as neutralized. At least we can say that the emergence of the tradition of apostolic authorship does not have the trappings of a ploy calculated to gain acceptance for an otherwise dubious Gospel. Alternatively, some have supposed that the attribution was first made by gnostic writers and only later picked up by the orthodox. But, as we have seen, the gnostics did not find John particularly to their liking, and so no obvious motivation for their fabrication of an apostolic source exists. While Ignatius and the early Polycarp do not identify the source of their Johannine reminiscences and borrowings, we have in the presbyterial tradition about Gospel origins now attributable to the first or second decade of the second century a clear identification with John the disciple of Jesus. What is more, this tradition is never contradicted but only augmented (sometimes quite fancifully) by later writers, both orthodox and heterodox, until the controverted reports which surface at a much later time about Gaius and the Alogi. Throughout the remainder of the second century we find the apostolic authorship of the Fourth Gospel mentioned explicitly (Ptolemy, Irenaeus, Polycrates, the *Muratorian Fragment*, Theodotus, Clement of Alexandria, Tertullian, etc.), or assumed (*Epistula Apostolorum*, the *Acts of John*, the *Ad Diognetum*, Justin, Hegesippus, Theophilus, *Epistle of Vienne and Lyons*, etc.), or we sense an authority consistent with such an attribution (Aristides, the long ending of Mark, Athenagoras, Melito, Tatian), in writers so dispersed as to seem to require a much earlier recognition in the Church. The testimony preserved in Papias' book provides an indication of such a recognition in Asia. We have also seen that at least many of the second-century sects (in

---

[9] e.g., Culpepper, *John*, 131.

fact, Marcion seems to be the exception) evidently thought there was little to be gained by disputing either the apostolic authorship of John's Gospel or the traditional attributions of any other of the Church's scriptures. Energy was instead typically channelled into efforts to interpret these functionally authoritative texts in ways congenial to sectarian interests, while also employing the argument that each sect possessed a superior revelation. While some tried to compete with the Great Church, compiling their own versions of apostolic succession, some also sought to overpower it with a claim of apostolic *supersession*.

The notion of gnostic Johannophilia of course works its way even into theories of the compositional history of the Fourth Gospel. An orthodox redactor is sometimes posited as the earliest 'saviour' of this Gospel, predating the efforts of both Irenaeus and the author of 1 John. The alleged signs of redactional activity and compositional stages, pre-eminently the 'aporias' in the text,[10] are certainly not strictly of a theological nature, but are also sociological and literary. But to the extent that redactional theories rely on historical judgements about gnostic affinity with and for the Fourth Gospel in its early history of reception, to such an extent these theories are in need of fundamental rethinking. The 'incarnational' teachings of John, which the second-century docetists found so hard to negotiate, could conceivably be credited to an isolatable stage in the composition history, in order to reveal a gnostic substratum of the Gospel. The point to be pressed here is that there is no sufficient historical basis for choosing these 'problem' verses as likely instances of redactional activity by a member of the 'authorship team', however understood.

Thus the second-century evidence points neither to a gnostic or obscure origin for this Gospel, nor to the need for anyone in the Church, whether it be Irenaeus, the author of 1 John, or a hypothetical redactor of the Gospel, to rescue this Gospel from gnostic hands and invent or endorse for it a fictional authorship. This is not to say, of course, that the evidence of the second century can finally decide for us who produced any of the Johannine literature. But it does tell us much about those who first read these books, and their beliefs about these books and the circumstances under which they were written. The surprisingly wide and authoritative use of the Fourth Gospel in particular, and of the Apocalypse and the First Epistle secondarily,

---

[10] Fernando F. Segovia has recently written, 'by and large I find that the proposed aporias can be readily explained in other—and, I would add, simpler—ways' ('The Tradition History of the Fourth Gospel', in R. A. Culpepper and C. C Black (eds.), *Exploring the Gospel of John* (Louisville, Ky., 1996), 179–89, at 186). Segovia's own pilgrimage (as he himself speaks of it) signals a shift in much of Johannine scholarship from the effort to find traditional layers in the text (thought to represent stages of Johannine history), to an emphasis on the unity of the text and what the finished text reveals of the strategies for writing and reading, to an emphasis on the cultural place of the reader. Yet the traditional criticism model is still employed by many scholars—even practitioners of newer waves of criticism acknowledge it—and it continues to exercise a controlling influence in more historically oriented studies.

and their habitual attribution to a common apostolic origin, point to a very early and seemingly instinctive recognition of authority which befits some authoritative source.

All this, and the entire foregoing study, indicates that the long-prevalent understanding of the rise of the Johannine corpus in the Church must be abandoned and replaced with something more historically accurate. Both in its peculiar narrative of the life and sayings of Jesus and in its distinctive Christological expressions, the Fourth Gospel had a profound influence in the mainstream Church of the second century such as the bulk of modern scholarship has left us entirely unprepared to appreciate. The first half of the second century can no longer be called a silent period in the witness to the Fourth Gospel. This Gospel's Christology apparently never was perceived as 'gnostic' or heterodox, and was not a detriment but an advantage to the book's wide reception. And the vaunted gnostic affection for John, in preference to other Gospels, simply does not materialize in the sources remaining to us. In the present circumstances, the issue most to be reckoned with is surely the sometimes shocking, adversarial nature of many of the earliest gnostic appropriations of John (and of 1 John). Nor did this Gospel snake its independent way through the period as a maverick and unaccompanied force. Not only was it quickly associated with three other authoritative Gospels, but it belonged from apparently quite an early time (almost certainly from prior to Papias' writing, perhaps from the time of its original circulation) to a literary corpus attributed to an apostle of Jesus. Assessments of the 'Johannine school' and its history, and treatments of the rise of a New Testament canon, should recognize what looks like a mostly shared history of the use and reception of the books of the Johannine corpus in the second century, despite the fragmentation of that history in the succeeding centuries.

CHRONOLOGY

All dates are approximate. Numbers in parentheses refer to Figure 12.

107	Ignatius in Asia Minor (1)
107	Polycarp in Smyrna (2)
110–20	Papias' Elders in Asia Minor (3)
110–30	Longer Ending of Mark, place unknown
120–32	Papias' Exegesis of the Lord's Oracles in Hierapolis (5)
135–45	Odes of Solomon in Syria (6)
140–5	Latest portions of Shepherd of Hermas in Rome (7)
140–55	Apocryphon of James place unknown
140–50	Epistula Apostolorum in Asia Minor (8)
140–50	Ad Diognetum in Asia Minor (9)
145–55	Acts of John place unknown
145–80	Gospel of Truth place unknown
150–80	Second Apocalypse of James place unknown
151–60	Justin in Rome (previously Asia Minor) (10)
160–70	Gospel of Peter in Syria (or Asia Minor) (11)
160–80	Papyrus Egerton place unknown
160–80	Celsus, A True Discourse in Rome (or Alexandria) (12)
160–200	Basilideans cited by Hippolytus, in Egypt (13)
161–9	Martyrdom of Carpus, etc. in Pergamum (14)
161–80	Sibylline Oracles 1, 8, in Asia Minor (15)
160–4	Melito's Peri Pascha in Sardis (16)
162–75	Tatian in Rome (17)
164–6	Claudius Apollinarius of Hierapolis (18)
165–80	Apocryphon of John place unknown
170–80	Ptolemy in Rome (19)
170–95	Trimorphic Protennoia place unknown
175–7	Theophilus in Antioch (20)
175–80	Hegesippus in Rome (21)
175–200	Gospel of Thomas in Syria (22)
176–7	Athenagoras in Athens (23)
177	Epistle of Vienne and Lyons in Gaul (24)
180–200	Heracleon's commentary, in Rome (25)
180–8	Irenaeus, Against Heresies (26)
185–210	Muratorian Fragment (27)
188–210	Clement in Alexandria (28)
190–5	Polycrates in Ephesus (29)
190–210	Epiphanius' Asian Source in Asia (30)
197–203	Early works of Tertullian in Carthage (31)
200	Apollonius in Ephesus (32)
200–3	Proclus and Gaius in Rome (33)
202–3	Passion of Perpetua and Felicitas in Carthage (34)

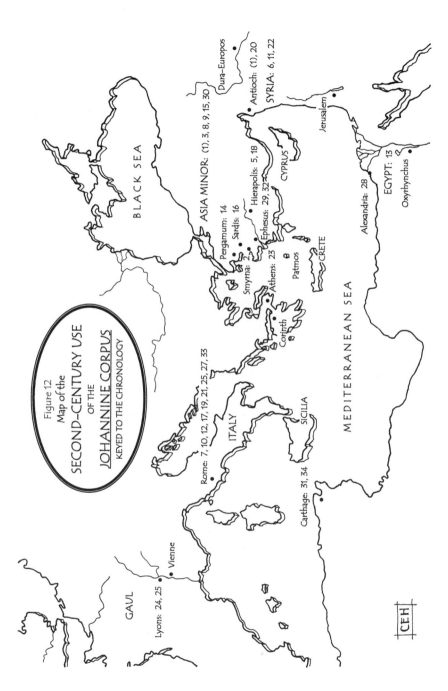

Figure 12. Map of the second-century use of the Johannine corpus keyed to the chronology.

BIBLIOGRAPHY

Editions and Translations (including Introductions)

Attridge, Harold W., and George W. MacRae, 'NHC I, 3: The Gospel of Truth', *Nag Hammadi Codex I (The Jung Codex): Notes*, Nag Hammadi Studies, 23 (Leiden, 1985), 39–135, at 88–9.

Barnard, Leslie W., *St. Justin Martyr: The First and Second Apologies*, ACW 56 (New York, 1997).

Bauer, J.-B., *Die Polykarpbriefe*, Kommentar zu den Apostolischen Vätern, 5 (Göttingen, 1995).

Bell, H. I., and T. C. Skeat, *Fragments of an Unknown Gospel and Other Early Christian Papyri* (London, 1935).

—— and —— *The New Gospel Fragments* (London, 1935).

Bethge, Hans-Gebhard, 'The Letter of Peter to Philip', *NTA²* i. 32–47.

Blatz, Beate, 'The Coptic Gospel of Thomas', *NTA²* i. 110–16.

Borret, Marcel, *Origène Contra Celse: Introduction, texte critique, traduction et notes*, 5 vols., SC 132, 136, 147, 150, 227 (Paris, 1967–76).

Buschmann, Gerd, *Das Martyrium des Polykarp übersetzt und erklärt*, Kommentar zu den Apostolischen Vätern, 6 (Göttingen, 1998).

Butterworth, G. W. (tr.), *Clement of Alexandria*, LCL (Cambridge, Mass., 1982).

Casey, Robert P., *The Excerpta ex Theodoto of Clement of Alexandria* (London, 1934).

Chadwick, Henry, *Origen:* Contra Celsum (Cambridge, 1965).

Charlesworth, James H. (ed.), *The Old Testament Pseudepigrapha*, 2 vols. (New York, 1983, 1985).

—— 'Odes of Solomon (Late First to Early Second Century A.D.): A New Translation and Introduction', *OTP* ii. 725–34.

Collins, J. J., 'Sibylline Oracles (Second Century B.C.–Seventh Century A.D.): A New Translation and Introduction', *OTP* i. 317–472.

Comfort, Philip W., and David P. Barrett, *The Complete Text of the Earliest New Testament Manuscripts* (Grand Rapids, Mich., 1999).

—— *The Text of the Earliest New Testament Greek Manuscripts: A Corrected, Enlarged Edition of* The Complete Text of the Earliest New Testament Manuscripts (Wheaton, Ill., 2001).

Cramer, J. A., *Anecdota Graeca e codd. manuscriptis Bibliotheca Regiae Parisiensis* (Oxford, 1839), ii. 88.

Crouzel, Henri, F. Fourier, P. Périchon, *Origène, Homélies sur S. Luc: Texte latin et fragments grecs: Introduction et notes*, SC 87 (Paris, 1962).

de Boor, C., 'Neue Fragmente des Papias, Hegesippus und Pierius in bisher unbekannten Excerpten aus der Kirchengeschichte des Philippus Sidetes', TU 5/2 (1888), 165–84.

De Bruyne, L., 'La "Capella greca" di Priscilla', *Rivista di archeologia cristiana*, 46 (1970), 291–330.

Drijvers, Hans J. W., 'The Acts of Thomas', *NTA²* 324–5.

Dulaey, M., *Victorin de Poetovio, Sur l'apocalypse, suivi du* Fragment chronologique *et de* La construction du monde: *Introduction, texte critique, traduction, commentaire et index* (Paris, 1997).

Elliott, J. K., *The Apocryphal New Testament: A Collection of Apocryphal Christian Literature in an English Translation* (Oxford, 1993).

Fairweather, E. R., 'The So-called Letter to Diognetus: Introduction and Books', in Cyril C. Richardson, *et al.*, *Early Christian Fathers*, LCC 1 (Philadelphia, 1953), 205–12.

Ferguson, John (tr.), *Clement of Alexandria*. Stromateis. *Books One to Three*, The Fathers of the Church (Washington, DC, 1991).

Geffcken, J., *Die Oracula Sibyllina*, GCS 8 (Leipzig, 1902).

Grant, Robert M., *Gnosticism: An Anthology* (London, 1961).

—— *Irenaeus of Lyons* (London, 1997).

Grenfell, Bernard P., and Arthur S. Hunt, *et al.* (eds.), *The Oxyrhynchus Papyri*, 66 vols. to date (London, 1898–).

Gronewald, M., in *Kölner Papyri (PKöln)*, vi = Abh. RWA, Sonderreihe Papyrologica Coloniensia, 7 (Cologne, 1987).

Guérard, O., and P. Nautin (eds.), *Origène. Sur le Pâque. Traité inédit publié d'après un papyrus de Toura*, Christianisme antique, 2 (Paris, 1979).

Gwynn, John, 'Hippolytus and his "Heads against Caius"', *Hermathena*, 6 (1888), 397–418.

Hall, Stuart G., *Melito of Sardis: On Pascha and Fragments* (Oxford, 1979).

Hartel, Guilelmus, *S. Thasci Caecili Cypriani Opera Omnia*, CSEL 3 (Vienna, 1871).

Harvey, W. Wigan, *Sancti Irenaei Episcopi Lugdunensis Libros Quinque Adversus Haereses*, 2 vols. (Cambridge, 1862).

Heine, Ronald, E., *The Montanist Oracles and Testimonia* (Macon, Ga., 1989).

Hoffmann, R. Joseph, *Celsus*. On the True Doctrine. *A Discourse Against the Christians* (Oxford, 1987).

Holl, Karl (ed.), *Epiphanius. Ancoratus und Pararion Haer.*, GCS, 3 vols. (Leipzig, 1915–33).

Holmes, Michael W. (ed. and reviser), *The Apostolic Fathers: Greek Texts and English Translations*, updated edn. of *The Apostolic Fathers: Greek Texts and English Translations of their Writings*, 2nd edn., ed. and tr. J. B. Lightfoot and J. R. Harmer; ed. and revised by Michael W. Holmes (Grand Rapids, Mich., 1999).

Isenberg, W. W., 'The Gospel of Philip (II*3*)', in *NHLE*[3] 139–41.

Jeremias, Joachim, and Wilhelm Schneemelcher, 'Papyrus Egerton 2', in *NTA*[2] i. 96–99.

Junod, Eric, and Jean-Daniel Kaestli, *Acta Iohannis*, i. *Praefatio—Textus*; ii. *Textus alli—Commentarius, Indices*, Corpus Christianorum Series Apocryphorum, 1–2 (Turnhout, 1983).

Kirchner, Dankwart, 'The Apocryphon of James', in *NTA*[2] i. 285–91.

Kleist, J. A., *The Didache, the Epistle of Barnabas, The Epistles and the Martyrdom of St. Polycarp, The Fragments of Papias, The Epistle to Diognetus*, ACW 6 (Westminster, Md., 1948).

Koester, H., 'The Gospel of Thomas (II,2)' in *NHLE*[3] 124–6.

Lake, Kirsopp, J. E. L. Oulton, and H. J. Lawlor, *Eusebius. The Ecclesiastical History*, 2 vols., LCL; i, ed. and tr. Kirsopp Lake (Cambridge, Mass., and London, 1925);

ii. ed. and tr. L. E. L. Oulton, taken from the edn. published in conjunction with H. J. Lawlor (Cambridge, Mass., and London, 1930).

Lawlor, Hugh Jackson, and John Ernest Leonard Oulton, *Eusebius, Bishop of Caesarea: The* Ecclesiastical History *and the* Martyrs of Palestine, *Translated with Introduction and Notes*, 2 vols. (London, 1954 repr. of 1927 edn.).

Lightfoot, Joseph Barber, *The Apostolic Fathers: Clement, Ignatius, and Polycarp. Revised Texts with Introductions, Notes, Dissertations, and Translations*, 2nd edn., 2 parts in 5 vols. (Grand Rapids, Mich., 1981 repr. of the 1889–90 edn.).

MacRae, George W., 'The Thunder: Perfect Mind (VI, 2)', *NHLE*³ 295.

Mara, M. G., *Évangile de Pierre*, SC 201 (Paris, 1973).

Marcovich, Miroslav (ed.), *Hippolytus*. Refutatio Omnium Haeresium, PTS 25 (Berlin, 1986).

—— *Tatiani. Oratio ad Graecos* (Berlin, 1995).

—— *Iustini Martyris. Dialogue cum Tryphone*, PTS 47 (Berlin, 1997).

Marrou, H. I., *A Diognète*, 2nd edn., SC 33bis (Paris, 1997 repr. of the 1965 2nd edn.).

Meecham, H. G., *The Epistle to Diognetus: The Greek Text with Introduction, Translation and Notes* (Manchester, 1949).

Mènarde, J.-E., *L'Évangile selon Philippe: Introduction, Texte-Traduction, Commentarie* (Paris, 1967).

Meyer, Marvin, 'The Letter of Peter to Philip (VIII, 2)', *NHLE*³ 431–3.

Musurillo, Herbert, *The Acts of the Christian Martyrs: Introductions, Texts, and Translations* (Oxford, 1972).

Rauer, Max, *Origenes Werke*, ix. *Die Homilien zu Lukas in der Übersetzung des Hieronymus und die griechischen Reste der Homilien und des Lukas-kommentars*, GCS 49 (Berlin, 1959).

Rhenanus, B., *Opera Q. S. Fl. Tertulliani* (Basle, 1521; 3rd edn. 1539).

Richardson, Cyril C., *et al.* (eds.), *Early Christian Fathers*, LCC 1 (Philadelphia, 1953).

Roberts, Alexander, and James Donaldson (eds.), *The Ante-Nicene Fathers*, 10 vols., revised by A. Cleveland Coxe (Grand Rapids, Mich., 1978 reprint).

Roberts, C. H., J. W. B. Barns, and H. Zilliacus, *The Antinoopolis Papyri* (London, 1950–67).

Robinson, J. A., 'Appendix: The Remains of the Original Greek of the Apology of Aristides', in *Texts and Studies* (Cambridge, 1891), 65–118.

Rousseau, Adelin, and Louis Doutreleau, *Irénée de Lyon: Contre les Hérésies Livre III*, i: *Introduction, notes justificatives et tables*, SC 210 (Paris, 1974).

—— and —— *Irénée de Lyon: Contre les Hérésies Livre III*, ii. *Texte et traduction*, SC 211 (Paris, 1974).

—— and —— *Irénée de Lyon: Contre les Hérésies Livre I*, i. *Introduction, notes justificatives et tables*, SC 263 (Paris, 1979).

—— and —— *Irénée de Lyon: Contre les Hérésies Livre I*, ii. *Texte et traduction*, SC 264 (Paris, 1979).

—— and —— *Irénée de Lyon: Contre les Hérésies Livre II*, i. *Introduction, notes justificatives et tables*, SC 293 (Paris, 1982).

—— and —— *Irénée de Lyon: Contre les Hérésies Livre II*, ii. *Introduction, notes justificatives et tables*, SC 294 (Paris, 1982).

—— B. Hemmerdinger, C. Mercier, and L. Doutreleau, *Irénée de Lyon: Contre les Hérésies Livre IV*, 2 vols., SC 100 (Paris, 1965).

Rousseau, Adelin, Louis Doutreleau, and Charles Mercier, *Irénée de Lyon: Contre les Hérésies Livre V*, i. *Introduction, notes justificatives et tables*, SC 152 (Paris, 1969).

————and———, *Irénée de Lyon: Contre les Hérésies Livre V*, ii. *Texte et traduction*, SC 153 (Paris, 1969).

Sagnard, François, *Clément d'Alexandrie. Extraits de Théodote. Texte grec, introduction, traduction et notes*, SC 23 (Paris, 1948; repr. 1970).

Schäferdiek, Knut, 'The Acts of John', in *NTA*[2] ii. 152–71.

Schenke, H.-M., 'The Gospel of Philip', *NTA*[2], i. 179–87.

Schneemelcher, Wilhelm, 'The Gospel of Peter: Introduction', in *NTA*[2] i. 216–22.

——— 'Dialogues of the Redeemer', in *NTA*[2] i. 228–31.

Schoedel, William R., *Athenagoras*. Legatio *and* De Resurrectione, OECT (Oxford, 1972).

Sedlacek, I., *Dionysius bar Salibi in Apocalypsim, Actus et Epistulas catholicas*, CSCO, Scriptores syri, 2, CI (1909, text; 1910, Latin version).

Shepherd, Massey H., 'The Letter of Polycarp, Bishop of Smyrna, to the Philippians', in C. Richardson *et al.* (eds.), *Early Christian Fathers*, LCC 1 (Philadelphia, 1953), 121–130.

Siegert, F., 'Unbeachtete Papiaszitate bei armenischen Schriftstellern', *NTS* 27 (1981), 605–14.

Smith, J. P., *St Irenaeus: Proof of the Apostolic Preaching*, ACW 16 (New York, 1952).

Snyder, Graydon F., *The Apostolic Fathers: A New Translation and Commentary*, vi. *The Shepherd of Hermas* (London, 1968).

Swanson, Reuben (ed.), *New Testament Greek Manuscripts: Variant Readings Arranged in Horizontal Lines Against Codex Vaticanus. John* (Sheffield, 1995).

Turner, John D., 'Trimorphic Protennoia (XIII, *1*)', in *NHLE*[3] 511–13.

Unger, Dominic J. (tr.), *St Irenaeus of Lyons*: Against the Heresies, ACW 55, rev. John J. Dillon (New York, 1992).

Völker, Walter, *Quellen zur Geschichte der christlichen Gnosis* (Tübingen, 1932).

Waldstein, Michael, and Frederik Wisse, *The Apocryphon of John. Synopsis of Nag Hammadi Codices II, 1; II, 1 and IV, 1 with BG 8502, 2*, Nag Hammadi Studies, 33 (Leiden, 1995).

Wartelle, André, *Saint Justin. Apologies. Introduction, texte critique, traduction, commentarie et index*, Études Augustiniennes (Paris, 1987).

Waszink, J. H., *Tertullian. The Treatise* Against Hermogenes, ACW 24 (New York, 1956).

Whittaker, Molly, *Tatian*, Oratio ad Graecos *and Fragments* (Oxford, 1982).

Williams, Frank, *The Panarion of Epiphanius of Salamis, Books II and III* (Leiden, 1994).

Williams, Francis, E., 'The Apocryphon of James: I, 2: 1. 1–16. 30' in H. W. Attridge (ed.), *Nag Hammadi Codex I (The Jung Codex): Introductions, Texts, Translations, Indices*, Nag Hammadi Studies, 22 (Leiden, 1985), 13–53.

——— 'NHC I, 2: The Apocryphon of James', in H. W. Attridge (ed.), *Nag Hammadi Codex I (The Jung Codex): Notes*, Nag Hammadi Studies, 23 (Leiden, 1985), 7–37.

——— 'The Apocryphon of James (I, 2)', in J. M. Robinson (gen. ed.), *The Nag Hammadi Library in English*, 3rd, completely revised edn. (San Francisco, 1988).

Wilson, R. McL., *The Gospel of Philip: Translated from the Coptic Text, with an Introduction and Commentary* (London, 1962).

Wood, Simon, *Clement of Alexandria. Christ the Educator*, The Fathers of the Church (New York, 1954).

Wordsworth, John, and Henry Julian White, *Novum Testamentum Latine: Secundum editionem sancti Hieronymi ad codicum manuscriptorum fidem recensuerunt* (Oxford, 1911).

Secondary Sources

Abrahamowski, Louise, 'Ein gnostischer Logostheologe: Umfang und Redaktor des gnostischen Sonderguts in Hippolyts "Widerlegung aller Häresien"', in *Drei christologische Untersuchungen*, BZNW 45 (Berlin, 1981).

—— 'Die "Erinnerungen der Apostel" bei Justin', in P. Stuhlmacher (ed.), *Das Evangelium und die Evangelien*, WUNT 28 (Tübingen, 1983), 341–53.

—— 'Sprache und Abfassungszeit der Oden Salomos', *Oriens Christianus*, 68 (1984), 80–90.

Aland, Kurt, 'Der Text des Johannesevangeliums im 2. Jahrhundert', in W. Schrage (ed.), *Studien zum Text und zur Ethik des Neuen Testaments: Festscrift zum 80. Geburtstag von Heinrich Greeven*, BZNW 47 (Berlin, 1986), 1–10.

—— and Barbara Aland, *The Text of the New Testament: An Introduction to the Critical Editions and to the Theory and Practice of Modern Textual Criticism*, 2nd edn., tr. E. R. Rhodes (Grand Rapids, 1981).

Andriessen, P., 'The Authorship of the Epistula ad Diognetum', *VC* 1 (1947), 129–36.

Ashton, John, *Understanding the Fourth Gospel* (Oxford, 1990).

Attridge, Harold W., 'The Gospel of Truth as an Exoteric Text', in C. W. Hedrick and R. Hodgson, Jun., *Nag Hammadi, Gnosticism, and Early Christianity* (Peabody, Mass., 1986), 239–55.

Bacon, Benjamin W., 'Date and Habitat of the Elders of Papias', *ZNW* 12 (1911), 176–87.

—— 'Marcion, Papias, and "the Elders"', *JTS* 23 (1922), 134–60.

Bammel (Hammond-Bammel), Caroline P., 'Ignatian Problems', *JTS* NS 33 (1982), 62–97.

—— 'Herakleon', *Theologische Realenzyklopädie*, xv (Berlin, 1986), 54–7.

—— 'The State of Play with Regard to Hippolytus and the *Contra Noetum*', *Heythrop Journal*, 31 (1990), 195–211.

Bardsley, H. J., 'The Testimony of Ignatius and Polycarp to the Writings of St. John', *JTS* 14 (1913), 207–20, 489–500.

Barnard, Leslie W., *Studies in the Apostolic Fathers and their Backgrounds* (Oxford, 1966).

—— *Justin Martyr* (Cambridge, 1967).

Barrett, C. K., *The Gospel according to John: An Introduction with Commentary and Notes on the Greek Text* (London, 1955).

—— *The Gospel according to John: An Introduction with Commentary and Notes on the Greek Text*, 2nd edn. (Philadelphia, 1978).

—— *Essays in John* (London, 1982).

Barnes, Timothy D., 'Pre-Decian *Acta Martyrum*', *JTS* 19 (1968), 509–31.

—— 'The Embassy of Athenagoras', *JTS* NS 26 (1975), 111–14.

—— 'Eusebius and the Date of the Martyrdoms', in *Les Martyrs de Lyon* (1978), 137–41.

—— *Tertullian: A Historical and Literary Study* (Oxford, 1971; with corrections and a postscript, 1985).

Barth, Carola, *Die Interpretation des Neuen Testaments in der valentinianischen Gnosis*, TU 37/3 (Leipzig, 1911).

Bartlet, Vernon, 'Papias's "Exposition": Its Date and Contents', in H. G. Wood (ed.), *Amicitiae Corolla: A Volume of Essays Presented to James Rendel Harris, D.Litt. on the Occasion of his Eightieth Birthday* (London, 1933), 15–44.

Bartsch, H. W., *Gnostisches Gut und Gemeindertradition bei Ignatius von Antiochien*, (Gütersloh, 1940).

Bauckham, Richard J., 'Papias and Polycrates on the Origin of the Fourth Gospel', *JTS* NS 44 (1993), 24–69.

—— *God Crucified: Monotheism and Christology in the New Testament* (Grand Rapids, 1998).

Bauer, Walter, *Johannes*, Handbuch zum Neuen Testament, 2, Die Evangelien, 2 (Tübingen, 1912).

—— *Rechtgläubigkeit und Ketzerei im ältesten Christentum* (Tübingen, 1934), ET, *Orthodoxy and Heresy in Earliest Christianity* (Philadelphia, 1971).

Baum, Armin D., 'Der Presbyter des Papias über einen "Hermeneuten" des Petrus', *TZ* 56 (2000), 21–35.

Beasley-Murray, George R., *John*, Word Biblical Commentary, 36 (Milton Keynes, 1987).

Bell, H. I., *Recent Discoveries of Biblical Papyri: An Inaugural Lecture Delivered before the University of Oxford on 18 November 1936* (Oxford, 1937).

Bellinzoni, Arthur J., *The Sayings of Jesus in the Writings of Justin Martyr, Nov. T.* Suppl. 17 (Leiden, 1967).

Birks, Edward Bickersteth, 'Epistle to Diognetus', *Dictionary of Christian Biography*, ii (London, 1880), 162–7.

Birley, Anthony R., *Marcus Aurelius: A Biography*, rev. edn. (London, 1987).

Bisbee, Gary A., *Pre-Decian Acts of Martyrs and Commentarii*, Harvard Dissertations in Religion, 22 (Philadelphia, 1988).

Bolgiani, F., 'Tatian', *Encyclopedia of the Early Church* (New York, 1992), ii. 815.

Brändle, Rudolf, *Die Ethik der "Schrift an Diognetus": Eine Wiederaufnahme paulinischer und johanneischer Theologie am Ausgang des zweiten Jahrhunderts*, Abhandlungen zur Theologie des alten und neuen Testaments, 64 (Zürich, 1975).

Braun, F.-M., *Jean le Théologien et son Évangile dans l'église ancienne* (Paris, 1959).

Brent, Allen, *Hippolytus and the Roman Church in the Third Century: Communities in Tension before the Emergence of a Monarch-Bishop*, VC Suppl. 31 (Leiden, 1995).

Broshi, M., *The Dead Sea Scrolls* (Tokyo, 1979).

Brown, Raymond E., 'The Gospel of Thomas and St John's Gospel', *NTS* 9 (1962–3), 155–77.

—— *The Gospel according to John (i–xii)*, AB 29 (Garden City, NY, 1966).

—— *The Gospel according to John (xiii–xxi)*, AB 29A (Garden City, NY, 1970).

—— 'The Relation of "The Secret Gospel of Mark" to the Fourth Gospel', *CBQ* 36 (1974), 466–85.

—— *The Community of the Beloved Disciple* (New York, 1979).

—— *The Epistles of John*, AB 30 (New York, 1982).

—— 'The Gospel of Peter and Canonical Gospel Priority', *NTS* 33 (1987), 321–43.

—— *An Introduction to the New Testament* (New York, 1997).

Brownson, J., 'The Odes of Solomon and the Johannine Tradition', *Journal for the Study of the Pseudepigrapha*, 2 (1988), 49–69.

Brox, Norbert, *Der Hirt des Hermas*, Kommentar zu den Apostolischen Vätern, 7 (Göttingen, 1991).

Bruce, F. F., *The Gospel of John: Introduction, Exposition and Notes* (Grand Rapids, Mich., 1983).

—— *The Canon of Scripture* (Downers Grove, Ill., 1988).

Burge, Gary, 'John, Letters of', in R. P. Martin and P. H. Davids (eds.), *Dictionary of the Later New Testament and its Developments* (Downers Grove, Ill., 1997), 587–99.

Burghardt, Walter J., 'Did Saint Ignatius of Antioch Know the Fourth Gospel?', *Theological Studies*, 1 (1940), 1–26, 130–56.

Burke, Gary T., 'Walter Bauer and Celsus: The Shape of Late Second-Century Christianity', *The Second Century*, 4 (1984), 1–7.

Cameron, Ronald D., *Sayings Traditions in the* Apocryphon of James, HTS 34 (Philadelphia, 1984).

Campenhausen, H. von, *The Formation of the Christian Bible*, tr. J. A. Baker (Philadelphia, 1972; German orig., 1968).

Carlini, Antonio, 'Testimone e testo: Il problema della datazione di PIand I 4 del *Pastore* di Erma', *SCO* 42 (1992), 17–30.

Chadwick, Henry, 'The Silence of Bishops in Ignatius', *HTR* 43 (1950), 169–72.

—— *Early Christian Thought and the Classical Tradition: Studies in Justin, Clement, and Origen* (Oxford, 1966).

Chapman, J., 'The Original Contents of Codex Bezae', *The Expositor*, 6th ser. 12 (1905), 46–53.

—— *John the Presbyter and the Fourth Gospel* (Oxford, 1911).

Charlesworth, James H., 'Les Odes de Salomon et les manuscrites de la Mer Morte', *RB* 77 (1970), 522–49.

—— 'Qumran, John and the Odes of Solomon', in J. H. Charlesworth (ed.), *John and Qumran* (London, 1972).

—— 'Tatian's Dependence upon Apocryphal Traditions', *Heythrop Journal*, 15 (1974), 5–17.

—— *The Beloved Disciple: Whose Witness Validates the Gospel of John?* (Valley Forge, Pa., 1995).

—— 'The Dead Sea Scrolls and the Gospel according to John', in R. A. Culpepper and C. C. Black (eds.), *Exploring the Gospel of John* (Louisville, Ky., 1996), 65–97.

—— and R. Alan Culpepper, 'The Odes of Solomon and the Gospel of John', *CBQ* 35 (1973), 298–322.

—— and C. E. Evans, 'Jesus in the Agrapha and Apocryphal Gospels', in B. Chilton and C. E. Evans (eds.), *Studying the Historical Jesus Evaluations of the State of Current Research*, NTTS 19 (Leiden, 1994), 479–533.

Charteris, A. H., *Canonicity: A Collection of Early Testimonies to the Canonical Books of the New Testament* (Edinburgh, 1880).

Chestnutt, Randall D., 'Review of Martin Hengel, *The Johannine Question*', *Restoration Quarterly*, 34 (1992), 121.

Cosgrove, Charles H., 'Justin Martyr and the Emerging Christian Canon: Observations on the Purpose and Destination of the Dialogue with Trypho', *Vigiliae Christianae*, 36 (1982), 209–32.

Crossan, J. D., *The Cross that Spoke: The Origins of the Passion Narrative* (San Francisco, 1988).

Culpepper, R. Alan, *John, the Son of Zebedee: The Life of a Legend* (Columbia, SC, 1994).

Culpepper, R. Alan, and C. Clifton Black (eds.), *Exploring the Gospel of John: In Honor of D. Moody Smith* (Louisville, Ky., 1996).

Davey, D. M., 'Justin Martyr and the Fourth Gospel', *Scripture*, 17 (1965), 117–22.

Davies, Stevan L., *The Gospel of Thomas and Christian Wisdom* (New York, 1983).

—— 'The Christology and Protology of the Gospel of Thomas', *JBL* 111 (1992), 663–82.

Dechow, Jon F., *Dogma and Mysticism in Early Christianity: Epiphanius of Cyprus and the Legacy of Origen*, Patristic Monograph Series, 13 (Macon, Ga., 1988).

De Conick, A., *Seek to See Him: Ascent and Vision Mysticism in the Gospel of Thomas*, VC Suppl. 33 (Leiden, 1996).

—— ' "Blessed are Those Who have Not Seen" (Jn 20: 29): Johannine Dramatization of an Early Christian Discourse', in John D. Turner and Anne McGuire (eds.), *The Nag Hammadi Library after Fifty Years: Proceedings of the 1995 Society of Biblical Literature Commemoration*, Nag Hammadi and Manichaean Studies, 44 (Leiden, 1997), 381–98.

Denaux, A. (ed.), *John and the Synoptics*, BETL 101 (Leuven, 1992).

den Boeft, J., and J. Bremmer, 'Notiunculae Martyrologicae II', *VC* 36 (1982), 383–402.

Denker, J., *Die theologiegeschichtliche Stellung des Petrusevangeliums: Ein Beitrag zur Frühgeschichte des Doketismus*, Europäische Hochschulschriften, 23, Theology, 36 (Berne and Frankfurt, 1975).

Denzey, Nicola F., 'Genesis Traditions in Conflict? The Use of Some Exegetical Traditions in the *Trimorphic Protennoia* and the Johannine Prologue', *VC* 55 (2001), 20–44.

Dibelius, Otto, 'Studien zur Geschichte der Valentinianer', *ZNW* 9 (1908), 230–47.

Dietze, P., 'Die Briefe des Ignatius und das Johannesevangelium', *Theologische Studien und Kritiken*, 78 (1905), 563–603.

Dodd, C. H., *A New Gospel* (Manchester, 1936; repr. from *BJRL* 20 (1936)).

—— 'The First Epistle of John and the Fourth Gospel', *BJRL* 21 (1937), 129–56.

—— *The Interpretation of the Fourth Gospel* (Cambridge, 1953).

Donovan, Mary Ann, *One Right Reading? A Guide to Irenaeus* (Collegeville, Minn., 1997).

Drijvers, Hans J. W., 'Facts and Problems in Early Syriac-Speaking Christianity', *The Second Century*, 2 (1982), 157–75.

—— 'East of Antioch: Forces and Structures in the Development of Early Syriac Theology', in Hans J. W. Drijvers, *East of Antioch: Studies in Early Syriac Christianity* (London, 1984), 1–27.

—— 'Marcionism in Syria: Principles, Problems, Polemics', *The Second Century*, 6 (1987–8), 153–72.

Drummond, J., 'Shepherd of Hermas', in *The New Testament in the Apostolic Fathers* (Oxford, 1905), 105–23.

Dunderberg, Ismo, '*Thomas*' I-sayings and the Gospel of John', in Risto Uro (ed.), *Thomas at the Crossroads: Essays on the* Gospel of Thomas (Edinburgh, 1998), 33–64.

—— '*Thomas* and the Beloved Disciple', in Risto Uro (ed.), *Thomas at the Crossroads: Essays on the* Gospel of Thomas (Edinburgh, 1998), 65–88.

Dunn, J. D. G., 'John and the Synoptics as a Theological Question', in R. Alan Culpepper and C. Clifton Black (eds.), *Exploring the Gospel of John: In Honor of D. Moody Smith* (Louisville, Ky., 1996), 301–13.

—— 'Pseudepigraphy', in R. P. Martin and P. H. Davids (eds.), *Dictionary of the Later New Testament and its Developments* (Downers Grove, Ill., 1997), 977–84.

Durst, Michael, 'Hegesipp's "Hypomnemata": Titel oder Gattungsbezeichnung?', *Römische Quartalschrift*, 84 (1989), 299–330.

Edwards, M. J., 'Gnostics and Valentinians in the Church Fathers', *JTS* ns 40 (1989), 26–47.

—— 'Ignatius and the Second Century: An Answer to R. Hübner', *ZAC* 2 (1998), 214–26.

Edwards, Ruth B., *The Expository Times*, 102 (1990), 88.

Ehrman, Bart, *The Orthodox Corruption of Scripture: The Effect of Early Christological Controversies on the Text of the New Testament* (New York, 1993).

Elliott, J. K., 'Manuscripts, the Codex and the Canon', *JSNT* 63 (1996), 105–23.

Epp, J. Eldon, 'Issues in the Interrelation of New Testament Textual Criticism and Canon', in L. M. McDonald and J. A. Sanders (eds.), *The Canon Debate* (Peabody, Mass., 2002), 485–515.

Evans, C. A., 'On the Prologue of John and the *Trimorphic Protennoia*', *NTS* 27 (1981), 395–401.

Faivre, A. and C., 'Genèse d'un texte et recourse aux Écritures: Ignace, *aux Éphésiens* 14,1–16,2', in *Revue des Sciences Religieuses*, 65 (1991), 173–96.

Fasola, Umberto, 'Cemetery', in *Encyclopedia of the Early Church* (New York, 1992), i. 155–8.

Fee, Gordon, 'The Myth of Early Textual Recension in Alexandria', in E. J. Epp and G. D. Fee, *Studies in the Theory and Method of New Testament Textual Criticism* (Grand Rapids, Mich., 1993), 247–73 at 249 (orig. publ. in R. N. Longenecker and M. C. Tenney, *New Dimensions in New Testament Study* (Grand Rapids, Mich., 1974)).

Fenton, J. C., *The Gospel according to John in the Revised Standard Version with Introduction and Commentary* (Oxford, 1970).

Ferguson, Everett, 'Canon Muratori: Date and Provenance', *Studia Patristica*, 17/2 (Oxford, 1982), 677–83.

—— 'Review of Geoffrey Mark Hahneman, *The Muratorian Fragment and the Development of the Canon*', *JTS* ns 44 (1993), 696.

Filoramo, G., *A History of Gnosticism*, tr. A. Alcock (Oxford, 1990)

Finney, Paul Corby, 'Art', *Encyclopedia of Early Christianity*, 2nd edn., ed. E. Ferguson (New York, 1990), 97–103.

—— 'Catacombs', *Encyclopedia of Early Christianity*, 2nd edn., ed. E. Ferguson (New York, 1990), 182–4.

—— *The Invisible God: The Earliest Christians on Art* (New York, 1994).

Fiocchi Nicolai, Vincenzo, 'Painting', *Encyclopedia of the Early Church* (New York, 1992), ii. 629–32.

Flusser, David, *The Spiritual History of the Dead Sea Sect* (Tel Aviv, 1989).

Forbes, Clarence A., 'Books for the Burning', *Transactions and Proceedings of the American Philological Association*, 67 (1936), 114–25.

Franzmann, M. and M. Lattke, 'Gnostic Jesuses and the Gnostic Jesus of John, Part II', in H. Preißler and H. Seiwert (eds.), *Gnosisforschung und Religionsgeschichte: Festschrift für Kurt Rudolph zum 65. Geburtstag* (Marburg, 1994), 143–54.

Frend, W. H. C., *Martyrdom and Persecution in the Early Church: A Study of a Conflict from the Maccabees to Donatus* (Oxford, 1965; repr. Grand Rapids, 1981).

—— *The Rise of Christianity* (Philadelphia, 1984).

Frickel, Josef, *Hellenistische Erlösung in christlicher Deutung: Die gnostische Naassenerschrift. Quellenkritische Studien—Strukturanalyse—Schichtenscheidung—Rekonstruction der Anthropos-Lehrschrift*, Nag Hammadi Studies, 19 (Leiden, 1984).

—— *Das Dunkel um Hippolyt von Rom: Ein Lösungsversuch. Die Schriften Elenchos und Contra Noetum*, Grazer Theologische Studien, 13 (Graz, 1988).

—— 'Hippolyts Schrift Contra Noetum: Ein Pseudo-Hippolyt', in H. C. Brennecke, E. L. Grasmück, and C. Markschies (eds.), *Logos: Festschrift für Louise Abramowski zum 8. July 1993* (Berlin, 1993), 87–123.

Funk, Robert W., Roy Hoover, and the Jesus Seminar, *The Five Gospels: The Search for the Authentic Words of Jesus. New Translation and Commentary* (Toronto, 1993).

Gamble, Harry Y., *The New Testament Canon* (Philadelphia, 1985).

—— 'The Pauline Corpus and the Early Christian Book', in William S. Babcock (ed.), *Paul and the Legacies of Paul* (Dallas, 1990), 265–80.

—— 'Canonical Formulation of the New Testament', in C. A. Evans and S. E. Porter (eds.), *Dictionary of New Testament Background* (Downers Grove, Ill., 2000), 183–95.

—— 'The New Testament Canon: Recent Research and the Status Quaestionis', in Lee Martin McDonald and James A. Sanders (eds.), *The Canon Debate* (Peabody, Mass., 2002), 267–94.

Geffcken, J., *Komposition und Entstehungszeit der Oracula Sibylla*, TU, NF 8/1 (Leipzig, 1902).

Giuntella, Anna Maria, 'Shepherd, The Good: II. Iconography', *Encyclopedia of the Early Church* (New York, 1992), ii. 776–8.

Grant, Robert M., 'The Fourth Gospel and the Church', *HTR* 35 (1942), 95–116.

—— 'The Origin of the Fourth Gospel', *JBL* 69 (1950), 304–22.

—— 'Scripture and Tradition in St. Ignatius of Antioch', *CBQ* 25 (1963), 322–35.

—— *After the New Testament* (Philadelphia, 1967).

—— *Eusebius as Church Historian* (Oxford, 1980).

—— *Greek Apologists of the Second Century* (Philadelphia, 1988).

—— 'Ancient and Modern Questions about Authenticity', in B. H. McLean (ed.), *Origins and Method: Towards a New Understanding of Judaism and Christianity. Essays in Honour of John C. Hurd*, JSNT Sup. 86 (Sheffield, 1993), 295–301.

Gry, Leon, 'La Date de la parousie d'après l'Epistula Apostolorum', *RB* 40 (1940), 86–97.

Gunther, J. J., 'Early Identifications of Authorship of the Johannine Writings', *JEH* 31 (1980), 407–27.

Haenchen, Ernst, *John 1: A Commentary on the Gospel of John Chapters 1–6*, tr. R. W. Funk, Hermeneia (Philadelphia, 1984).

Hahneman, Geoffrey M., *The Muratorian Fragment and the Development of the Canon*, Oxford Theological Monographs (Oxford, 1992).

—— 'The Muratorian Fragment and the Origins of the New Testament Canon', in Lee Martin McDonald and James A. Sanders (eds.), *The Canon Debate* (Peabody, Mass., 2002), 405–15.

Haines-Eitzen, Kim, *Guardians of Letters: Literacy, Power, and the Transmitters of Early Christian Literature* (Oxford, 2000).

Hall, Stuart G., 'The Origins of Easter', in E. A. Livingstone (ed.), *Studia Patristica*, 15/1 (Leuven, 1984), 554–67.

Harnack, Adolf von, *Das Neue Testament um das Jahr 200* (Freiburg, 1889).

—— 'Tertullians Bibliothek christlicher Schriften', *Sitzungsberg. d. kön. Preuss. Akad. d. Wiss. zu Berlin* (1914), 303–34.

Harris, J. Rendel, *Hermas in Arcadia and Other Essays* (Cambridge, 1896).

Harrison, P. N., *Polycarp's Two Epistles to the Philippians* (Oxford, 1936).

Head, Peter M., 'On the Christology of the Gospel of Peter', *VC* 46 (1992), 209–24.

Heard, R. G., 'The Απομνημονεύματα in Papias, Justin and Irenaeus', *NTS* 1 (1954–5), 122–9.

Henne, P., 'La Datation du *canon de Muratori*', *RB* 100 (1993), 54–75.

Heine, Ronald E., 'The Role of the Gospel of John in the Montanist Controversy', *The Second Century*, 6/1 (1987–8), 1–19.

Heinrici, G., *Die Valentinianische Gnosis und die Heilige Schrift: Eine Studie* (Berlin, 1971).

Helderman, J., ' "In ihren Zelten … " Bemerkungen bei Codex XIII Nag Hammadi p. 47: 14–18, im Hinblick auf Joh i 14', in T. Baarda, A. F. J. Klijn, and W. C. van Unnik (eds.), *Miscellanea Neotestamentica* (Leiden, 1978), i. 181–211.

—— 'Anapausis in the Epistula Jacobi Apocrypha', in R. McL. Wilson (ed.), *Nag Hammadi and Gnosis*, Nag Hammadi Studies, 14 (Leiden, 1978), 36–7.

Hengel, Martin, *Studies in the Gospel of Mark*, tr. J. Bowden (London, 1985).

—— *The Johannine Question* (London, 1989).

—— *Die johanneische Frage: Ein Lösungsversuch*, with a contribution on the Apocalpyse by Jörg Frey, WUNT 67 (Tübingen, 1993).

Hill, Charles E., 'Hades of Hippolytus or Tartarus of Tertullian: The Authorship of the Fragment *De universo*', *VC* 43 (1989), 105–26.

—— 'The Debate over the Muratorian Fragment and the Development of the Canon', *WTJ* 57 (1995), 437–52.

—— 'The Identity of John's Nathanael', *JSNT* 67 (1997), 45–61.

—— 'Justin and the New Testament Writings', in E. A. Livingstone (ed.), *Studia Patristica*, 30 (Leuven, 1997), 42–8.

—— 'What Papias Said about John (and Luke): A "New" Papian Fragment', *JTS* ns 49 (1998), 582–629.

—— 'The *Epistula Apostolorum*: An Asian Tract from the Time of Polycarp', *JECS* 7 (1999), 1–53.

—— 'Cerinthus, Gnostic or Chiliast? A New Solution to an Old Problem', *JECS* 8 (2000), 135–72

—— *Regnum Caelorum: Patterns of Millennial Thought in Early Christianity*, 2nd edn. (Grand Rapids, Mich., 2001).

—— 'Ignatius and the Apostolate: The Witness of Ignatius to the Emergence of Christian Scripture', in M. F. Wiles and E. J. Yarnold (eds.), *Studia Patristica*, 36 (Leuven, 2001), 226–48.

Hillmer, Melvyn Raymond, 'The Gospel of John in the Second Century' (Th.D. dissertation, Harvard University, Apr. 1966).

Holmes, Michael W., 'Codex Bezae as a Recension of the Gospels', in D. C. Parker and C.-B. Amphoux (eds.), *Codex Bezae: Studies from the Lunel Colloquium June 1994* (Leiden, 1996), 123–60.

Hopkins, Clark, *The Discovery of Dura-Europos*, ed. Bernard Goldman (New Haven, 1979).

Horbury, William, 'The Wisdom of Solomon in the Muratorian Fragment', *JTS* ns 45 (1994), 149–59.

Hornschuh, Manfred, *Studien zur Epistula Apostolorum*, PTS 5 (Berlin, 1965).

Hort, Fenton J. A., *Judaistic Christianity* (Grand Rapids, Mich., 1980, repr. of 1894 orig.).

Hübner, Reinhard M., 'Melito von Sardes und Noet von Smyrna', in *Oecumenica et Patristica: Festschrift für Wilhelm Schneemelcher* (Chambésy-Genf, 1989), 220–3.

——'Thesen zur Echtheit und Datierung der sieben Briefe des Ignatius von Antiochen', *ZAC* 1 (1997), 44–72.

Hug, J., *La Finale de l'évangile de Marc: Mc 16, 9–20*, Études Bibliques (Paris, 1978).

Hurtado, Larry, 'The Origin of the *Nomina Sacra*: A Proposal', *JBL* 117 (1998), 655–73.

Hyldahl, Niels, 'Hegesipps Hypomnemata', *Studia Theologica*, 14 (1960), 70–113.

Inge, W. R., 'Ignatius', in *The New Testament in the Apostolic Fathers*, by a Committee of the Oxford Society of Historical Theology (Oxford, 1905), 63–83.

Janssens, Yvonne, 'Le Codex XIII de Nag Hammadi', *Le Muséon*, 87 (1974), 341–413.

——'Traits de la Passion dans l'*Epistula Iacobi Apocrypha*', *Le Muséon*, 88 (1975), 97–101.

——'Une source gnostique du Prologue', in M. de Jonge (ed.), *L'Evangile de Jean: Sources, redaction, théologie*, BETL 44 (Gembloux, 1977), 355–8.

——*La Protennoia trimorphe (NH, XIII,1)*, BCNH 4 (Quebec, 1978).

——'The Trimorphic Protennoia and the Fourth Gospel', in A. H. B. Logan and A. J. Wedderburn (eds.), *The New Testament and Gnosis: Essays in Honor of Robert McL. Wilson* (Edinburgh, 1983), 229–43.

Jeffers, James S., *Conflict at Rome: Social Order and Hierarchy in Early Christianity* (Minneapolis, 1991).

Jensen, Robin Margaret, *Understanding Early Christian Art* (London, 2000).

Johnson, S. E., 'Parallels between the Letters of Ignatius and the Johannine Epistles', in E. W. Conrad and E. G. Newing (eds.), *Perspectives on Language and Text: Essays and Poems in Honor of Francis I. Andersen's Sixtieth Birthday July 28, 1985* (Winona Lake, Ind., 1987), 327–38.

Jordan, H., *Geschichte der altchristlichen Literatur* (Leipzig, 1911).

Junod, Eric, and Jean-Daniel Kaestli, *L'Histoire des Actes apocryphes des apôtres du IIIe au IXe siècle: Le Cas des Actes de Jean*, Cahiers de la Revue de Théologie et de Philosophie, 7 (Geneva, 1982).

Kaestli, Jean-Daniel, 'L'Exégèse valentinienne du quatrième évangile', in J.-D. Kaestli, J.-M. Poffet, and J. Zumstein (eds.), *La Communauté johannique et son histoire: La Trajectoire de l'évangile de Jean aux deux premiers siècles* (Paris, 1990), 323–50.

——'Remarques sur le rapport du quatrième évangile avec la gnose et sa réception au IIe siècle', in J.-D. Kaestli, J.-M. Poffet, and J. Zumstein (eds.), *La Communauté johannique et son histoire: La Trajectoire de l'évangile de Jean aux deux premiers siècles* (Paris, 1990), 351–6.

Käsemann, Ernst, *The Testament of Jesus: A Study of the Gospel of John in the Light of Chapter 17* (ET: Philadelphia, 1968).

Katz, P., 'The Johannine Epistles in the Muratorian Canon', *JTS* ns 8 (1957), 273–4.

Kelhoffer, James A., *Miracle and Mission: The Authentication of Missionaries and their Message in the Longer Ending of Mark*, WUNT 2/112 (Tübingen, 2000).

Kenyon, Frederic, *The Text of the Greek Bible: A Student's Handbook* (London, 1953; repr. of 1949 orig.).

Kieffer, René, 'Les Premiers Indices d'une réception de l'évangile de saint Jean', in F. Van Segbroeck, C. M. Tuckett, G. Van Belle, and J. Verheyden (eds.), *The Four Gospels 1992: Festschrift Franz Neirynck*, BETL 100 (Leuven, 1992), iii. 2225–38.

Kinzig, Wolfram, 'Review of Marco Rizzi, *La questione dell'unità dell' Ad Diognetum*', *JTS* ns 42 (1991), 330–4.

Knapp, Henry M., 'Melito's Use of Scripture in *Peri Pascha*: Second-Century Typology', *VC* 54 (2000), 343–74.

Knight, Johnathan, *Disciples of the Beloved One: The Christology, Social Setting and Theological Context of the Ascension of Isaiah*, JSP Supplement Series, 18 (Sheffield, 1996).

Körtner, Ulrich H. J., *Papias von Hierapolis: Ein Beitrag zur Geschichte des frühren Christentums*, FRLANT 133 (Göttingen, 1983).

Koschorke, K., 'Eine gnostische Paraphrase des johanneische Prologs', *VC* 33 (1979), 383–92.

Koester, Helmut, *Synoptische Überlieferung bei den apostolischen Vätern*, TU 65 (Berlin, 1957).

——'Geschichte und Kultus im Johannesevangelium und bei Ignatius von Antiochien', *Zeitschrift für Theologie und Kirche*, 54 (1957), 56–69.

——'Apocryphal and Canonical Gospels', *HTR* 73 (1980), 105–30.

——*Introduction to the New Testament*, ii. *History and Literature of Early Christianity* (Berlin, 1982).

——'Introduction', to 'Tractate 2. The Gospel according to Thomas', in B. Layton (ed.), *Nag Hammadi Codex II, 2–7 together with XIII, 2**, Brit. Lib. Or. 4926(1), and P. Oxy. 1, 645, 655, Nag Hammadi Studies, 20 (Leiden, 1989), 38–49.

——*Ancient Christian Gospels: Their History and Development* (Philadelphia, 1990), 245–6.

——'The Story of the Johannine Tradition', *Sewanee Theological Review*, 36 (1992), 17–32.

——'Ephesos in Early Christian Literature', in Helmut Koester (ed.), *Ephesos: Metropolis of Asia Minor*, HTS (Valley Forge, Pa., 1995), 119–40.

Kuntzmann, Raymond, and Michèle Morgen, 'Un exemple de réception de la tradition johannique: 1 Jn 1, 1–5 et Évangile de Vérité NHI, p. 30, 16–31, 35', in Alain Marchadour (ed.), *Origine et postérité de l'Évangile de Jean: XIIIe Congrès de l'ACFEB Toulouse (1989)* (Paris, 1990), 265–76.

Kurfess, 'Oracula Sibyllina I/II', *ZNW* 40 (1941), 151–65.

Kysar, Robert, 'The Contribution of D. Moody Smith to Johannine Scholarship', in R. Alan Culpepper and C. Clifton Black (eds.), *Exploring the Gospel of John: In Honor of D. Moody Smith* (Louisville, Ky., 1996), 3–17.

Ladeuze, P., *Caius de Rome, le seul Aloge connu*, in *Mèlanges Godefroid Kurth* (Liege, 1908).

Lalleman, P. J., *The Acts of John: A Two-Stage Initiation into Johannine Gnosticism*, Studies on the Apocryphal Acts of the Apostles, 4 (Leuven, 1998).

Lancellotti, Maria Grazia, *The Naassenes: A Gnostic Identity Among Judaism, Christianity, Classical and Ancient Near Eastern Traditions*, Forschungen zur Anthropologie und Religionsgeschichte, 35 (Münster, 2000).

Lawlor, Hugh, J., *Eusebiana: Essays on* The Ecclesiastical History *of Eusebius Pamphili, ca 264–349 A.D. Bishop of Caesarea* (Oxford, 1912; repr. Amsterdam, 1973).

——'Eusebius on Papias', *Hermathena*, 19 (1922), 167–222.

Lightfoot, Joseph Barber, *Essays on the Work Entitled* Supernatural Religion *Reprinted from* The Contemporary Review, 2nd edn. (London, 1893).

Lindars, Barnabas, *The Gospel of John*, New Century Bible (London, 1972).

Lindemann, A., 'Antwort auf die "Thesen zum Echtheit und Datierung der Sieben Briefe des Ignatius von Antiochen" ', *ZAC* 1 (1997), 185–94.

Lipsius, Robert A., 'Irenaeus', *DCB* iii (London, 1888), 253–79.

Llewelyn, S. R., 'A Fragment of the Gospel of John', in S. R. Llewelyn and R. A. Kearsly, *New Documents Illustrating Early Christianity*, vii. A Review of the Greek Inscriptions and Papyri Published in 1982–83, The Ancient History Documentary Research Centre Macquarie University (Sydney, 1994), 242–8.

Loewenich, Walther von, *Das Johannes-Verständnis im zweiten Jahrhundert* (Giessen, 1932).

Logan, A. H. B., 'John and the Gnostics: The Significance of the Apocryphon of John for the Debate about the Origins of the Johannine Literature', *JSNT* 43 (1991), 41–69.

—— *Gnostic Truth and Christian Heresy* (Edinburgh, 1996).

Löhr, Winrich A., 'Gnostic Determinism Reconsidered', *VC* 46 (1992), 381–90.

—— *Basilides unde seine Schule: Eine Studie zur Theologie-und Kirchengeschichte des Zweiten Jahrhunderts*, WUNT 83 (Tübingen, 1996).

—— 'Ptolemäus, *Gnostiker*', *TRE* ii. 27 (Berlin, 1997), 699–702.

Loi, Vincenzo, 'L'identità letteraria di Ippolito di Roma', in V. Loi *et al.* (eds.), *Ricerche su Ippolito*, Studia Ephemeridis 'Augustinianum', 13 (Rome, 1977), 67–88.

—— 'Quartodeciman', *Encyclopedia of the Early Church* (New York, 1992), ii. 728.

Lüdemann, Gerd, 'Zur Geschichte des ältesten Christentums in Rom. I. Valentin und Marcion II. Ptolemäus und Justin', *ZNW* 70 (1979), 86–114.

Lührmann, Dieter, 'POx 2949: EvPt 3–5 in einer Handschrift des 2/3. Jahrhunderts', *ZNW* 72 (1981), 216–26.

—— 'Das neue Fragment de PEgerton 2 (PKöln 255)', in F. Van Segbroek, C. M. Tuckett, G. Van Belle, and J. Verheyden (eds.), *The Four Gospels 1992: Festschrift Frans Neirynck*, BETL 100 (Leuven, 1992), iii. 2239–55.

Luttikhuizen, G. P., 'The Letter of Peter to Philip and the New Testament', in R. McL. Wilson (ed.), *Nag Hammadi and Gnosis* (Leiden, 1978), 96–102.

—— 'The Thought Pattern of Gnostic Mythologizers and their Use of Biblical Traditions', in J. D. Turner and A. McGuire (eds.), *The Nag Hammadi Library after Fifty Years. Proceedings of the 1995 Society of Biblical Literature Commemoration*, Nag Hammadi and Manichaean Studies, 44 (Leiden, 1997), 89–101.

McDonald, Lee Martin, *The Formation of the Christian Biblical Canon* (Peabody, Mass., 1995).

—— and Stanley E. Porter, *Early Christianity and its Sacred Literature* (Peabody, Mass., 2000).

—— and James A. Sanders (eds.), *The Canon Debate* (Peabody, Mass., 2002).

McGehee, M., 'Why Tatian Never "Apologized" to the Greeks', *JECS* 1 (1993), 143–58.

MacRae, George W., 'Gnosticism and the Church of John's Gospel', in C. W. Hedrick and R. Hodgson, jun. (eds.), *Nag Hammadi, Gnosticism, and Early Christianity* (Peabody, Mass., 1986), 89–96.

Maier, Harry O., *The Social Setting of the Ministry as Reflected in the Writings of Hermas, Clement, and Ignatius*, Canadian Corporation for Studies in Religion, Dissertations Studies in Religion, 1 (Waterloo, Ontario, 1991).

—— 'Review of J.-B. Bauer, *Die Polykarpbriefe*', *JTS* ns 47 (1996), 642–5.

Marinone, Mariangela, 'Paralytic, Healing of the: Iconography', *Encyclopedia of the Early Church* (New York, 1992), ii. 650.

Markschies, Christoph, *Valentinus Gnosticus? Untersuchungen zur valentinianischen Gnosis mit einem Kommentar zu den Fragmenten Valentins*, WUNT 65 (Tübingen, 1992).
——'Das Problem des historischen Valentin—Neue Forschungen zu Valentinus Gnosticus', in E. A. Livingstone (ed.), *Studia Patristica*, 24 (Leuven, 1993), 382–9.
——'Valentinian Gnosticism: Toward the Anatomy of a School', in J. D. Turner and A. McGuire, *The Nag Hammadi Library after Fifty Years: Proceedings of the 1995 Society of Biblical Literature Commemoration*, Nag Hammadi and Manichaean Studies, 44 (Leiden, 1997), 401–38.
——'New Research on Ptolemaeus Gnosticus', *ZAC* 4 (2000), 225–54.
Martimort, A. G., 'L'Iconographie des catacombes et la catéchèse romain', *Rivista di archeologia cristiana*, 25 (1949), 105–14.
Massaux, *Influence de l'Évangile de s. Matthieu sur la littérature chrétienne avant s. Irénée* (Louvain, 1950).
Maurer, *Ignatius von Antiochien und das Johannesevangelium*, ATANT 18 (Zurich, 1949).
May, Gerhard, *Schöpfung aus dem Nichts: Die Entstehung der Lehre von der creatio ex nihilo*, Archiv für Kulturgeschichte, 48 (Berlin, 1978).
Mayeda, Goro, *Das Leben-Jesu-Fragment Papyrus Egerton 2 und seine Stellung in der urchristlichen Literaturgeschichte* (Berne, 1946).
Merkel, H., *La Pluralité des Evangiles comme problème théologique et exégétique dans l'Eglise ancienne*, tr. J.-L. Maier (Berne, 1978).
——'Frühchristliche Autoren Über Johannes und die Synoptiker', in A. Denaux (ed.), *John and the Synoptics*, BETL (Leuven, 1992), 403–8.
Metzger, Bruce M., *The Canon of the New Testament: Its Origin, Development, and Significance* (Oxford, 1987).
Milne, H. J. M., 'A New Fragment of the *Apology* of Aristides', *JTS* 25 (1924), 73–7.
Nagel, Titus, *Die Rezeption des Johannesevangeliums im 2. Jahrhundert: Studien zur vorirenäischen Auslegung des vierten Evangeliums in christlicher und christlich-gnostischer Literatur*, Arbeiten zur Bibel und ihrer Geschichte, 2 (Leipzig, 2000).
Nautin, Pierre, *Hippolyte et Josipe* (Paris, 1947).
——*Lettres et éscrivains chrétiens des IIe et IIIe siècles*, Patristica, 2 (Paris, 1961).
——'Hippolytus', *Encyclopedia of the Early Church* (New York, 1992), i. 383–5.
——'Theophilus', *Encyclopedia of the Early Church* (New York, 1992), ii. 831–2.
Neirynck, F., 'Papyrus Egerton 2 and the Healing of the Leper', *ETL* 61 (1985), 153–60.
——'The Apocryphal Gospels and the Gospel of Mark', in J.-M. Sevrin (ed.), *The New Testament in Early Christianity: La Réception des écrits néotestamentaires dans le christianisme primitif*, BETL 86 (1989), 123–75.
Nelson, William, 'The Interpretation of the Gospel of John in the Gnostic "Gospel of Truth": A Study in the Development of Early Christian Theology' (dissertation, Princeton University, 1963).
Nielsen, Charles M., 'The Epistle to Diognetus: Its Date and Relationship to Marcion', *Anglican Theological Review*, 52 (1970), 77–91.
Osborn, Eric F., *Justin Martyr*, BHTh. 47 (Tübingen, 1973).
Osiek, Carol, *The Shepherd of Hermas: A Commentary* (Minneapolis, 1999).
Pagels, Elaine, *The Johannine Gospel in Gnostic Exegesis: Heracleon's Commentary on John* (Nashville, Tenn., 1973).
——'Exegesis of Genesis 1 in the Gospels of Thomas and John', *JBL* 118 (1999), 477–96.

Parker, D. C., *Codex Bezae: An Early Christian Manuscript and its Text* (Cambridge, 1992).

Paulsen, Henning, *Studien zur Theologie des Ignatius von Antiochien*, Forschungen zur Kirchen- und Dogmengeschichte, 29 (Göttingen, 1978).

Pearse, Roger, 'Early Editions 1450–1850' [of Tertullian's works] at www.tertullian. org/editions/editions.htm.

Pearson, Birger A., 'Pre-Valentinian Gnosticism in Alexandria', in Birger A. Pearson (ed.), *The Future of Early Christianity: Essays in Honor of Helmut Koester* (Minneapolis, 1991), 455–66.

Perkins, Pheme, 'Johannine Traditions in *Ap. Jas.* (NHC I, 2)', *JBL* 101 (1982), 403–14.

—— *Gnosticism and the New Testament* (Minneapolis, 1993).

Perrin, Nicholas, *Thomas and Tatian: The Relationship between the* Gospel of Thomas *and the* Diatessaron (Atlanta, Ga., 2002).

Peterson, William, L., 'Tatian's Diatessaron', in H. Koester, *Ancient Christian Gospels: Their History and Development* (Philadelphia, 1990), 403–29.

—— *Tatian's Diatessaron: Its Creation, Dissemination, Significance, and History in Scholarship*, *VC* Suppl. 25 (Leiden, 1994).

Pervo, Richard, 'Johannine Trajectories in the Acts of John', *Apocrypha*, 3 (1992), 47–68.

Pickering, S. R., 'The Significance of Non-Continuous New Testament Textual Materials in Papyri', in D. G. K. Taylor (ed.), *Studies in the Early Texts of the Gospels and Acts* (Birmingham, 1999), 121–41.

Plümmacher, E., 'Apostolische Missionsreise und statthalterliche Assisetour', *ZNW* 85 (1994), 259–78.

Poffet, J.-M., 'Indices de réception de l'Évangile de Jean au IIe siècle, avant Irénée', in J.-D. Kaestli, J.-M. Poffet, and J. Zumstein (eds.), *La Communauté johannique et son histoire: La Trajectoire de l'évangile de Jean aux deux premiers siècles* (Paris, 1990), 305–21.

Pollard, T. E., *Johannine Christology and the Early Church* (Cambridge, 1970).

—— 'John the Evangelist, Gospel of', *Encyclopedia of the Early Church*, (New York, 1992), i. 448–9.

Pouderon, B., M.-J. Pierre, and B. Outtier, 'A propos de l'Apologie d'Aristide: Recherches sur un prototype commun aux versions syriaque et arménienne', *Revue des Sciences Religieuses*, 74 (2000), 173–93.

Prigent, Pierre, 'Hippolyte, Commentateur de l'Apocalypse', *TZ* 28 (1972), 391–412.

—— 'Les Fragments du De Apocalypse d'Hippolyte', *TZ* 29 (1973), 313–33.

—— and R. Stehly, 'Citations d'Hippolyte trouvée dans le ms. Bodl. Syr 140', *TZ* 30 (1974), 82–5.

Procter, Everett, *Christian Controversy in Alexandria: Clement's Polemic against the Basilideans and Valentinians*, American University Studies, 7, Theology and Religion, 172 (New York, 1995).

Pryor, John, 'Of the Virgin Birth or the Birth of Christians? The Text of John 1: 13 Once More', *Nov T* 27 (1985), 296–318.

—— 'Justin Martyr and the Fourth Gospel', *The Second Century*, 9 (1992), 153–69

Quasten, Johannes, *Patrology*, 3 vols. (Westminster, Ma., 1984; repr. of 1950 orig.).

Quispel, Giles, 'The Gospel of Thomas and the New Testament', *VC* 11 (1957), 189–207.

Rankin David, *Tertullian and the Church* (Cambridge, 1995).

Rathke, Heinrich, *Ignatius und die Paulusbriefe*, TU 99 (Berlin, 1967).

Reekmans, Louis, 'La Chronologie de la peinture paléochrétienne: Notes et réflections', *Rivista di archeologia cristiana*, 49 (1973), 271–91.

Richardson, Cyril C., *The Christianity of Ignatius of Antioch* (New York, 1935).

Riley, G. J., *Resurrection Reconsidered: Thomas and John in Controversy* (Minneapolis, 1995).

—— 'The Gospel of Thomas in Recent Scholarship', *Currents in Research*, 2 (1994), 227–52.

Riley, Mark T., 'Q. S. Fl. Tertulliani Adversus Valentinanos: Text, Translation, and Commentary' (Ph.D. dissertation, Stanford University, 1971).

Rizzi, Marco, *La questione dell'unità dell'Ad Diognetum*, Studia patristica Mediolanensia, 16 (Milan, 1989).

Roberts, C. H., *Manuscript, Society and Belief in Early Christian Egypt* (Oxford, 1979).

Robinson, Gesine (Schenke), ' "Die dreigestaltige Protennoia", Eine gnostische Offenbarungsrede in koptischer Sprache aus dem Fund von Nag Hammadi', *TLZ* 99 (1974), 731–46.

—— 'The Trimorphic Protennoia and the Prologue of the Fourth Gospel', in J. E. Goehring. (ed.), *Gnosticism and the Early Christian World: In Honor of James M. Robinson* (Sonoma, Calif., 1990), 37–49.

Robinson, James M., 'Foreword', in E. Haenchen, *John 1: A Commentary on the Gospel of John Chapters 1–6*, tr. R. W. Funk, Hermeneia (Philadelphia, 1984), pp. ix–xiii.

—— 'Sethians and Johannine Thought: The *Trimorphic Protennoia* and the Prologue of the Gospel of John', in B. Layton (ed.), *The Rediscovery of Gnosticism*, ii (Leiden, 1981), 642–70.

Robinson, Theodore H., 'The Authorship of the Muratorian Canon', *The Expositor*, 7/1 (1906), 481–95.

Röhl, Wolfgang G., *Die Rezeption des Johannesevangeliums in christich-gnostischen Schriften aus Nag Hammadi*, Europäische Hochschulschriften, Publications Universitaires Européennes, 23, Theologie, 428 (Frankfurt am Main, 1991).

Romanides, J. S., 'Justin Martyr and the Fourth Gospel', *Greek Orthodox Theological Review*, 4 (1958–9), 115–34.

Rostovtzeff, Mikhail, *Dura-Europos and its Art* (Oxford, 1938).

Rouleau, D., *L'Épitre apocryphe de Jacques (NH I, 2)*, Bibliothèque Copte de Nag Hammadi, Section 'Textes', 18 (Quebec, 1987).

Rowland, Christopher, 'The Parting of the Ways: The Evidence of Jewish and Christian Apocalyptic and Mystical Material', in J. D. G. Dunn (ed.), *Jews and Christians: The Parting of the Ways A.D. 70 to 135* (Grand Rapids, 1999, repr. of 1992 orig.), 2213–38.

Salmon, G., 'The Commentary of Hippolytus on Daniel', *Hermathena*, 8 (1893), 161–90.

—— 'Heracleon', *DCB* ii. 897–901.

—— 'Ophites', *DCB* iv. 86.

Sanday, William, *The Criticism of the Fourth Gospel* (Oxford, 1905).

Sanders, Jack T., 'Nag Hammadi, *Odes of Solomon* and NT Christological Hymns', in James E. Goehring (ed.), *Gnosticism and the Early Christian World: In Honor of James M. Robinson* (Sonoma, Calif., 1990), 51–66.

Sanders, Joseph N., *The Fourth Gospel in the Early Church: Its Origin and Influence on Christian Theology up to Irenaeus* (Cambridge, 1943).

—— *The Foundations of the Christian Faith: A Study of the Teaching of the New Testament in the Light of Historical Criticism* (London, 1951).

—— 'John, Gospel of', in *Interpreters Dictionary of the Bible* (Nashville, Tenn., 1962), ii. 932–46.

—— *A Commentary on the Gospel According to St. John*, ed. and completed by B. A. Mastin (New York, 1968).

Santagata, Giuliana, 'Lazarus: Iconography', *Encyclopedia of the Early Church* (New York, 1992), i. 477.

Satomayer, Manuel, 'Sacrophagi, Early Christian', *Encyclopedia of the Early Church* (New York, 1992), ii. 755–6.

Saxer, V., 'Martyr: III. Acts, Passions, Legends', *Encyclopedia of the Early Church* (New York, 1992), i. 533–4.

Schenke, H.-M., 'The Function and Background of the Beloved Disciple in the Gospel of John', in C. W. Hedrick and R. Hodgson, Jun. (eds.), *Nag Hammadi, Gnosticsim, and Early Christianity* (Peabody, Mass., 1986), 111–25.

Schlaeger, G., 'Der Hirt des Hermas eine ursprünglich jüdische Schrift', *Nieuw Theologisch Tijdschrift*, 16 (1927), 327–42.

Schlier, Heinrich, *Religionsgeschichtliche Untersuchungen zu den Ignatiusbriefen*, BZNW 8 (Giessen, 1929).

Schmidt, Carl, *Gespräche Jesu mit seinem Jüngern nach der Auferstehung*, TU 43 (Leipzig, 1919, repr. 1927).

Schnackenburg, Rudolf, *Das Johannesevangelium*, Herders Theologischer Kommentar zum Neuen Testament, 1 (Freiburg, 1965); tr. Kevin Smyth, *The Gospel According to St John*, i (London, 1968).

Schnelle, Udo, *Antidocetic Christology in the Gospel of John: An Investigation of the Place of the Fourth Gospel in the Johannine School*, tr. L. M. Maloney (ET: Minneapolis, 1992).

Schoedel, William R., *Ignatius of Antioch*, Hermeneia (Philadelphia, 1985).

—— 'Polycarp of Smyrna and Ignatius of Antioch', *ANRW* 2. 27. 1 (Berlin, 1993), 272–358.

Schölgen, Georg, 'Die Ignatianen als pseudepigraphisches Brief-corpus: Anmerkung zu den thesen von Reinhard M. Hübner', *ZAC* 2 (1998), 16–25.

Schottroff, Louise, *Der Glaubende und die feindliche Welt*, WMANT 37 (1970).

Schrage, W., *Das Verhältnis des Thomas-Evangeliums zur synoptischen Tradition und zu den koptischen Evangelienübersetzungen*, BZNW 29 (Berlin, 1964).

Schwartz, E., 'Über den Tod der Söhne Zebedaei: Ein Beitrag zur Geschichte des Johannesevangelium', *Abhandlungen der Kgl. Gesellschaft der Wissensch. zu Göttingen*, 7/5 (1904); repr. in K. H. Rengstorf (ed.), *Johannes und sein Evangelium* (Darmstadt, 1973), 202–73.

Scott, A. B., 'Churches or Books? Sethian Social Organization', *JECS* 3 (1995), 109–22.

Seitz, O. J. F., 'Relationship of the Shepherd to the Epistle of James', *JBL* 63 (1944), 131–40.

Sell, Jesse, 'Johannine Traditions in Logion 61 of the Gospel of Thomas', *Perspectives in Religious Studies*, 7 (1980), 23–37.

Sellew, Philip, 'Eusebius and the Gospels', in H. W. Attridge and G. Hata (eds.), *Eusebius, Christianity, and Judaism* (Leiden, 1992), 110–38.

Sevrin, J.-M., 'Le Quatrième Évangile et le gnosticisme: Questions de méthode', in J.-D. Kaestli, J.-M. Poffet, and J. Zumstein (eds.), *La Communauté johannique et son histoire: La Trajectoire de l'évangile de Jean aux deux premiers siècles* (Paris, 1990), 251–68.

Simonetti, Manlio, 'A modo di conclusione: Una ipotesi di lavoro', in V. Loi (ed.), *Recherche su Ippolito*, Studia Ephemeridis 'Augustinianum', 13 (Rome, 1977), 151–6.

——'Un falso Ippolito nella polemica monotelita', *Vetera Christianorum*, 24 (1987), 113–46.

Skeat, T. C., 'Irenaeus and the Four-Gospel Canon', *Nov. T.* 34 (1992), 194–9.

——'The Origin of the Christian Codex', *Zeitschrift für Papyrologie und Epigraphik*, 102 (1994), 263–8.

——'The Oldest Manuscript of the Four Gospels?', *NTS* 43 (1997), 1–34.

Sloyan, Gerard S., *John*, Interpretation: A Bible Commentary for Teaching and Preaching (Atlanta, Ga., 1988).

——*What are they Saying about John?* (New York, 1991).

——'The Gnostic Adoption of John's Gospel and its Canonization by the Church Catholic', *Biblical Theology Bulletin*, 26 (1996), 125–32.

Smith, D. Moody, *Johannine Christianity: Essays on its Setting, Sources, and Theology* (Columbia, SC, 1984).

——*John Among the Gospels: The Relationship in Twentieth-Century Research* (Minneapolis, 1992).

——'The Problem of John and the Synoptics in Light of the Relation between Apocryphal and Canonical Gospels', in A. Denaux (ed.), *John and the Synoptics*, BETL 101 (Leuven, 1992), 147–62.

Smith, J. D., jun., 'Gaius and the Controversy over the Johannine Literature' (Ph.D. dissertation, Yale University, 1979).

Smith, Morton, *Clement of Alexandria and a Secret Gospel of Mark* (Cambridge, Mass., 1973).

——*The Secret Gospel: The Discovery and Interpretation of the Secret Gospel According to Mark* (New York, 1973).

——'Clement of Alexandria and Secret Mark: The Score at the End of the First Decade', *HTR* 75 (1982), 449–61.

Snyder, Graydon F., *Ante Pacem: Archaeological Evidence of Church Life before Constantine* (Macon, Ga., 1985).

Stanton, Graham N., 'The Fourfold Gospel', *NTS* 43 (1997), 317–46.

Stewart-Sykes, Alistair, 'The Asian Context of the New Prophecy and of *Epistula Apostolorum*', *VC* 51 (1997), 416–38.

Streeter, B. H., *The Four Gospels* (London, 1926).

——*The Primitive Church: Studied with Special Reference to the Origins of the Christian Ministry* (London, 1929).

Sundberg, Albert C., 'Towards a Revised History of the New Testament Canon', *Studia Evangelica*, 4/1 (1968), 452–61.

——'Canon Muratori: A Fourth-Century List', *HTR* 66 (1973), 1–41.

Tabernee, William, 'Noiseless Books and Pilfered Manuscripts: Early Christian "Desk-Top" Publishing in Carthage', at http://divinity.lib.vanderbilt.edu/burns/chroma/reading/tabberneebks.html.

Tardieu, M., *Écrits gnostiques: Codex de Berlin*, Sources gnostiques et manichéennes, 1 (Paris, 1984).

Taylor, C., *The Witness of Hermas to the Four Gospels* (London, 1892).

Tregelles, Samuel P., *Canon Muratorianus* (Oxford, 1867).

Trevett, Christine, 'Approaching Matthew from the Second Century: The Under-Used Ignatian Correspondence', *JSNT* 20 (1984), 59–67.

——*A Study of Ignatius of Antioch in Syria and Asia*, Studies in the Bible and Early Christianity, 29 (Lewiston, NY, 1992).

Trobisch, David, *Die Endredaktion des Neuen Testaments: Eine Untersuchung zur Entstehung der christlichen Bibel*, Novum Testamentum et Orbis Antiquus, 13 (Göttingen, 1996); ET, *The First Edition of the New Testament* (Oxford, 2000).

Tuckett, Christopher M., *Nag Hammadi and the Gospel Tradition: Synoptic Tradition in the Nag Hammadi Library* (Edinburgh, 1986).

Turner, Eric G., *The Typology of the Early Codex* (Philadelphia, 1977).

van den Hoek, Annewies, 'Techniques of Quotation in Clement of Alexandria: A View of Ancient Literary Working Methods', *VC* 50 (1996), 223–43.

VanderKam, J. C., *The Dead Sea Scrolls Today* (Grand Rapids, Mich., 1994).

van der Vliet, J., 'Spirit and Prophecy in the Epistula Iacobi Apocrypha (NHC I, 2)', *VC* 44 (1990) 25–53.

van Haelst, J., *Catalogue des papyrus littéraires juifs et chrétiens* (Paris, 1976).

van Unnik, 'The "Gospel of Truth" and the New Testament', in F. L. Cross (ed.), *The Jung Codex* (London, 1955), 79–129.

——'The Origin of the Recently Discovered "Apocryphon Jacobi"', *VC* 10 (1956) 146–56.

Vielhauer, Philip, *Geschichte der urchristlichen Literatur* (Berlin, 1975).

Vouga, Francois, 'The Johannine School: A Gnostic Tradition in Primitive Christianity?', *Biblica*, 69 (1988), 371–85.

——'Jean et la gnose', in A. Marchadour (ed.), *Origine et postérité de l'évangile de Jean: XIIIe congrès de l'ACFEB Toulouse (1989)* (Paris, 1990), 107–25.

Walls, A. F., 'The Montanist "Catholic Epistle" and its New Testament Prototype', in F. L. Cross (ed.), *Studia Evangelica*, iii/2. *The New Testament Message* (Berlin, 1964), 437–46.

Westcott, Brooke Foss, 'Clement of Alexandria', *Dictionary of Christian Biography*, i (London, 1877), 551–67.

——*A Survey of the History of the Canon of the New Testament*, 6th edn. (Grand Rapids, Mich., 1980, repr. of 1889 edn.).

Wetter, G. P., 'Eine gnostische Formel im vierten Evangelium', *ZNW* 18 (1917/18), 49–63.

Whittaker, John, 'The Value of Indirect Tradition in the Establishment of Greek Philosophical Texts or the Art of Misquotation', in John N. Grant (ed.), *Editing Greek and Latin Texts: Papers given at the Twenty-Third Annual Conference on Editorial Problems, University of Toronto 6–7 November 1987* (New York, 1989), 63–95.

Wiles, Maurice F., *The Spiritual Gospel: The Interpretation of the Fourth Gospel in the Early Church* (Cambridge, 1960).

Williams, Jacquelin A., *Biblical Interpretation in the Gnostic Gospel of Truth from Nag Hammadi*, SBL Dissertation Series, 79 (Atlanta, Ga., 1988).

Williams, Michael Allen, *Rethinking 'Gnosticism': An Argument for Dismantling a Dubious Category* (Princeton, 1996).

Wilpert, G., *Le pitture delle Catacombe Romane* (Rome, 1903).

Wilson, J. Christian, *Toward a Reassessment of the Shepherd of Hermas: Its Date and its Pneumatology*, Mellen Biblical Press, 18 (Lewiston, NY, 1993).

Wolff, R. L., 'The Apology of Aristides: A Re-examination', *HTR* 30 (1937), 233–47.

Wright, David F., 'Papyrus Egerton 2 (The Unknown Gospel): Part of the Gospel of Peter?', *The Second Century*, 5 (1985–6), 129–50.

Wright, N. T., *What St Paul Really Said: Was Paul of Tarsus the Real Founder of Christianity?* (Grand Rapids 1997).

Yamauchi, Edwin, M., 'Jewish Gnosticism? The Prologue of John, Mandaean Parallels and the Trimorphic Protennoia', in R. van den Broek and M. J. Vermaseren (eds.), *Studies in Gnosticism and Hellenistic Religions Presented to Gilles Quispel on the Occasion of his 65th Birthday* (Leiden, 1981), 467–97, at 480–4.

—— 'The Issue of Pre-Christian Gnosticism Reviewed in the light of the Nag Hammadi Texts', in J. D. Turner and A. McGuire (eds.), *The Nag Hammadi Library after Fifty Years: Proceedings of the 1995 Society of Biblical Literature Commemoration* (Leiden, 1997), 72–88.

Yarbrough, Robert W., 'The Date of Papias: A Reassessment', *JETS* 26 (1983), 181–91.

Yoder, J. D., 'The Language of the Greek Variants of Codex Bezae', *Nov. T.* 3 (1959), 241–8.

Zahn, Theodore, 'Aloger', *RE*³ (1896), i. 386–8.

—— 'Die Wanderungen des Apostels Johannes', *Neue Kirchliche Zeitschrift*, 10 (1899), 191–218.

Zincone, S., 'Diognetus, To', *Encyclopedia of the Early Church* (New York, 1992), i. 237.

Zumstein, J., 'La Communauté johannique et son histoire', in J.-D. Kaestli, J.-M. Poffet, and J. Zumstein (eds.), *La Communauté johannique et son histoire: La Trajectoire de l'évangile de Jean aux deux premiers siècles* (Paris, 1990), 359–74.

—— 'La Rédaction finale de l'évangile selon Jean (à l'exemple du chapitre 21)', in J.-D. Kaestli, J.-M. Poffet, and J. Zumstein (eds.), *La communauté johannique et son histoire: La Trajectoire de l'évangile de Jean aux deux premiers siècles* (Paris, 1990), 207–30.

—— 'Zur Geschichte de johanneischen Christentums', *TLZ* 122 (1997), cols. 417–28.

INDEX OF ANCIENT TEXTS

Bold numbers denote references to illustrations.

INDEX OF MODERN AUTHORS

Bold numbers denote references to illustrations.

SUBJECT INDEX

Bold numbers denote references to illustrations.

Acts of the Apostles 371, 413
Acts of John 20, 54, 94, 258–63, 279, 446, 466
Acts of Paul 371–2
Acts of Pilate 332, 405
Adonis 233
adoptionism 99, 102, 191, 227, 292, 308
Against Heresies 58, 63, 86, 96, 168
Against the Heresy of Artemon 178, 196–7
Agape 219
Agathonice 311
Aion 285
Akhmim Fragment 306
Alcinous 68
Aletheia 219, 283
Alexandria 16–17, 18, 42, 53, 60, 122, 126, 128,
    211, 214
allegorical exegesis 467
aloe 385
Alogi 14, 16, 22, 28, 42, 52, 53, 63, 66, 165,
    166, 172–3, 175–82, 185, 187, 190, 191,
    194, 200, 203, 204, 468
Amphilochius of Iconium 462, 464
Anacreon 233
Andrew 134, 135, 384, 386
Andrew of Caesarea 396
Anicetus 227
anti-Semitism, in Gospel of John 62
antichrists 143, 176
Antinoöpolis 152
Antioch 423
Antoninus Pius 224
Apocalypse of John 86, 127, 142, 173, 174–5,
    177, 179, 461–3
  Apollonius on 139
  authorship 90
  and Cerinthus 179–80, 182, 192, 229–30
  Christology 291
  dualism in 286
  Epiphanius on 138
  use by *Epistula Apostolorum* 369–70
  and Gospel of John 66
  Hermas on 379–80
  Ignatius on 441–2
  as independent writing 453
  Irenaeus on 99–101

  and Justin 314, 342–4, 349
  manuscripts of 154–5
  and Montanists 147
  in *Muratorian Fragment* 136
  use by Papias 111, 394–5
  Tertullian on 140–1, 146
  use by Theophilus 80–1
Apocalypse of Peter 136, 451
apocalyptic genre 379
apocrypha 130
Apocryphon of James 25, 45, 55, 115–17, 204,
    250–8, 261, 268, 368, 372, 412, 444, 446,
    466, 468
Apocryphon of John 47, 51, 239–41, 244, 248, 249,
    277
Apollinarian dispute 458 n. 22
Apollinarius of Hierapolis 294, 296–8
Apollonius of Ephesus 138–9, 208
apologetics 315–16
apologists 16, 19, 26, 54
Apology to Autolycus 75
apostolic authority 117, 254–5, 346–51, 431
apostolic authorship 373, 395, 472–4
Apostolic Canons 462, 464
Apostolic Fathers 15, 19, 21, 22 n. 43, 24–5, 38,
    41
apostolic memoirs 337–42, 389, 412, 465, 470
apostolic teaching 144–5, 389, 469
Appolinarius of Hierapolis 40, 54, 215, 312
Arche 208
Aristides 396–402, 445, 465, 467, 468, 469
Arrhetos 219, 435
Arsinoe 152
Ascension of Isaiah 451
Asia 87, 90, 473
Asia Minor 1, 39, 46, 61, 75, 94, 113, 169, 362,
    366, 369, 396, 419, 423, 444, 468, 473
Athanasius 464
Athenagoras 16, 24, 25, 81–3, 87, 128, 208
Athens 468
Athropos 219
Attis 233
authorship, of Johannine corpus 137, 395–6, 428
Autogenes 240
autosoterism 267

John 134, 135, 257–8, 368–9, 384, 386
  authority as disciple 366
  Beloved Disciple 30 n. 87, 32 n. 100, 49, 119, 120, 144, 146, 168, 271, 443 n. 295
  and Cerinthus 352, 355, 443
  as inspired 79, 80–1
  leaned on Lord's breast 110
  as prisoner 145–6
  son of Zebedee 30 n. 87, 32 n. 100, 46, 89, 96 n., 257, 260, 368–9, 373, 409, 445
John the Baptist 115–16, 141–2, 186
Judas Thomas 271, 273
Justin 5, 14, 15 n. 8, 19, 22, 24, 25, 36, 37–8, 39, 41, 42, 47, 53, 66, 312–13, 367, 373, 465, 467, 470
  and Apocalypse 314, 342–4, 349
  apologetics 315–16
  on apostolic authority 346–51
  on apostolic memoirs 253, 337–42, 345–6, 412
  on Epistles of John 344
  Johannophobia of 314
  knowledge of Gospel of John 70
  on Logos 83, 316–17
  martyrdom 312
  use of Gospel of John 16, 313–14, 316–17, 351
  on Valentinians 221
Justin the Gnostic 432 n. 258
Justus Barsabas 405–6

Kingdom of God 376–8

Labyrinth 178, 196–7, 198
Lactantius 91
lamps 161–2
Laodicea 259 n. 214, 297
Laodicean Synod 462, 464
Last Supper 433
Lazarus, raising of 155, 156–7, **158**, 164, 469
Letter of Peter to Philip 45, 237
Letter to Flora 212–15, 221
light imagery 269, 274 n. 279
literary customs, of antiquity 67–71
literary dependence 425–7, 437, 440–1
Logos 14 n. 5, 21 n. 38, 82–3, 217–18, 219, 247, 285, 316–17, 364, 372 n. 38, 435–7, 466
Luke 94, 99, 106, 412, 414, 458
  Marcion on 107, 115
Lukophobia 423
Lyons 83–4, 470

Manichaeans:
  determinism 280
  docetism 288

Marcellan dispute 458 n.22
Marcellina 227
Marcianus 358–9
Marcion 14, 18, 19, 78, 107, 115, 117, 263 n. 232, 279, 352, 355–6
Marcionites 6, 15, 40, 99, 113, 115, 133 n. 158, 143, 174, 206 n. 4, 356
Marcophobia 423
Marcosians 99, 108, 371
Marcus Aurelius 79, 81, 91
Mark 107, 115, 117, 227–8, 253–4, 339, 410, 412, 413
  longer ending 402–6, 415
Martyrdom of Polycarp 5, 41, 352, 358–9, 362
martyrs, martyrdom 85–6, 87, 147, 311, 358
Mary (mother of Jesus) 94, 403
Mary Magdalene 403
Mattheophobia 215–16, 423
Matthew 213, 215–16, 280, 386, 414
  use by Ebionites 107, 114
  Valentinians on 106
Maximilla 177 n. 11
Melito of Sardis 17, 22, 40, 46 n. 183, 54, 76, 78, 122, 156, 208, 215, 294–6, 297–8, 312, 362
'memoirs of the apostles' 253–4, 322 n. 122, 325, 329, 335, 345, 349
Menander 224
miracles 403, 405 n. 158
Monarchian controversies 458 n. 22
monergism 281
Monogenes 219, 283, 284
Montanists, Montanism 15, 22, 29, 34, 39, 41, 76, 113, 116, 131, 135, 147–8, 192, 194, 472
Montanus 29, 138
Muratorian Fragment 5, 30 n. 88, 43–4, 51, 102, 128–38, 167, 168, 170, 172, 194, 199–200, 204, 208, 374–5, 379, 392, 452–3, 469, 470, 471

Naassenes 23, 39, 50, 54, 230, 232–4, 275 n. 283, 286, 432 n. 258
Nag Hammadi 20, 21, 25, 30, 33, 35, 39, 45, 54, 55, 61, 115, 235–8, 242–3, 249, 276, 277
Natalius 131
Nathanael 369
Nepos 175
Nero 124 n. 131, 145 n. 194, 414–15
Nerva 89, 414–15
new birth 325–6, 336
New Prophecy 112, 147
New Testament canon 1, 458, 475